A FIELD GUIDE TO THE
MAMMALS OF
SOUTH-EAST
ASIA

A FIELD GUIDE TO THE
MAMMALS OF
SOUTH-EAST
ASIA

CHARLES M. FRANCIS

Illustrated by Priscilla Barrett, Robin Budden,
John Cox, Sandra Doyle, Brin Edwards, Ray Hutchings,
William Oliver, Guy Troughton and Lyn Wells

NEW
HOLLAND

First published in 2008 by New Holland Publishers (UK) Ltd
This impression published in 2008 by New Holland Publishers (UK) Ltd
London, Cape Town, Sydney, Auckland

www.newhollandpublishers.com

Garfield House, 86-88 Edgware Road, London W2 2EA, United Kingdom
80 McKenzie Street, Cape Town 8001, South Africa
Unit 1, 66 Gibbes Street, Chatswood, New South Wales, Australia 2067
218 Lake Road, Northcote, Auckland, New Zealand

10 9 8 7 6 5 4 3 2 1

ISBN 978 1 84537 735 9

Senior Editor: Krystyna Mayer
Designer: Alan Marshall
Production: Melanie Dowland
Editorial Consultant: James Parry
Editorial Direction: Rosemary Wilkinson
Indexer: David McAllister

Reproduction by Modern Age Repro Co. Ltd, Hong Kong
Printed and bound in Singapore by Tien Wah Press (Pte) Ltd

Figure Credits

The line drawings in the text were derived from a variety of sources. Some were prepared by digitally tracing over photographs of museum material. Others were reproduced from published materials or from original drawings prepared by other artists, with permission of the original publisher or artist as listed below. For figures previously used in published sources, the original publication is listed in the form of author and year, and refers to entries in the Bibliography. Note that in many cases these drawings were rearranged or resized and in a few cases edited slightly from their original form.

American Museum of Natural History, by Jennifer Perrott Emry from Musser (1973): 72; by Patricia J. Wynne from Musser et al. (2006): 73

Charles M. Francis: 6, 8 (with R. Budden), 14, 16, 21, 26 (d,f,g), 27, 30 (b,c), 33, 38, 40, 41, 42, 43, 44, 45, 46, 49, 63, 66, 68, 69, 70, 71, 74

Sergei Kruskop, from Borissenko and Kruskop (2003): 9,10,11, 30a, 31c, 31d, 36, 39

Alex Borisenko: 7, 37

Mammal Society of Japan, by Patricia J. Wynne from Lunde et al. (2003): 17, 18, 19; by Patricia J. Wynne from Lunde et al. (2004): 22

New Holland Publishers (UK) Ltd: 1, 4

The Sabah Society and Karen Phillipps, from Payne, Francis and Phillipps (1985): 2, 3, 12, 20, 23, 24, 25, 26 (a,b,c,e), 28, 29, 31 (a,b), 32, 34, 35, 47, 54, 56, 57, 61, 65

Nico Van Strien, from Strien (1983): 13, 15, 48, 50, 51, 52, 55, 58, 59, 60, 62, 64, 67

CONTENTS

PREFACE AND ACKNOWLEDGEMENTS

This book is intended to help both general naturalists and scientists to identify wild mammals that may be encountered in South-East Asia, as well as to increase public understanding of the diversity of mammals that occur in the region, thus encouraging efforts to conserve them.

This is the first comprehensive field guide to mammals of this region, but it would not have been possible without the pioneering efforts of many previous mammalogists working in the region and publishing their work. I have drawn particularly heavily on *A Field Guide to the Mammals of Borneo* by Junaidi Payne and myself, with illustrations by Karen Phillipps. I am grateful to Junaidi, Karen and the Sabah Society for allowing me to use parts of that book as a starting point for this one. I also made extensive use of Corbet and Hill (1992) as a starting point for developing the species lists and basic taxonomic information, for checking distribution maps, for references and for tables of identification characters, although the species lists have since been updated to reflect Wilson and Reeder (2005) and other recent published scientific papers. Many other books on mammals of the world and of the region were also useful in preparing this book, as well as many original papers in the scientific literature. A list of some of the most important references is included in the bibliography.

I have been fortunate to have been able to work in the field in the region for many years, particularly on bats. Much of the information in this book on bats, as well as some other groups of mammals, is based on field data I collected myself, often with various colleagues. I am very grateful to all those who have supported my field work in South-East Asia. D.R. Wells and D. Melville provided my first introduction to the fascinating fauna of this region during a season of field work in Peninsular Malaysia and Sarawak in 1979. Ken Scriven has provided ongoing

support over the years. The Sabah Wildlife Department (originally part of the Sabah Forest Department), and the Canadian volunteer organization CUSO, supported me during several years of field work in Sabah, providing logistical support and funding. I am particularly grateful to Mahedi Andau, Director of the Sabah Wildlife Department, for allowing me to work on mammals as well as birds during my stay in Sabah, and to the many of his staff who accompanied and assisted me during field work there. I greatly appreciated working with Junaidi Payne and Karen Phillipps during field work while preparing *Mammals of Borneo*. The Malaysian Economic Planning Unit and the National Parks and Wildlife Department (PERHILITAN) allowed me to carry out field work from 1991 to 1996 in Peninsular Malaysia. The Wildlife Conservation Society (WCS) generously supported my research in Peninsular Malaysia, as well as subsequent field work in Laos from 1995 to1998. I thank the WCS Lao staff for assistance during field work in Laos, particularly Bill Bleisch, William Robichaud, Rob Tizard, Will Duckworth, Chanhthavy Vongkhamheng, Khamkhoune Khounboline and Khoonmy. Nik Aspey and Antonio Guillén-Servent also assisted me on surveys there. More recently, Sara Bumrungsri has given me the opportunity to work with him in Thailand. The Senckenberg Museum, through Joerg Habersetzer, provided equipment for recording bat echolocation calls. Michael Bradstreet allowed me to take time off my duties at Bird Studies Canada to survey mammals in the region, while Trevor Swerdfager allowed me to use some in-kind support for this project from the Canadian Wildlife Service of Environment Canada.

I am grateful to the staff of several museums for allowing me to use their facilities and collections. These include Judith Eger at the Royal Ontario Museum; Paula Jenkins, Daphne Hills and the late John E. Hill at the

Natural History Museum, London (formerly known as the British Museum (Natural History)); Paul Bates at the Harrison Museum; the late Karl Koopman at the American Museum of Natural History; and Richard D. Thorington at the National Museum of Natural History at the Smithsonian. I am particularly grateful to John E. Hill for teaching me the basics of mammal taxonomy.

During preparation of this book, many people generously answered numerous questions about individual species, provided myself or the artists with reprints or manuscripts of their work, unpublished information and photographs, or helped in other ways. These include Alexei Abramov, Bruce Banwell, Paul Bates, Isabel Beasley, Bill Bleisch, Alex Borisenko, John Burton, Polly Campbell, Michael Carleton, Gabor Csorba, Jennifer Daltry, Yoan Dinata, Will Duckworth, K. Fletcher, Angela Frost, Neil Furey, Thomas Geissmann, Lon Grassman, Colin Groves, Antonio Guillén-Servent, Simon Hedges, Kristofer Helgen, Jeremy Holden, Tigga Kingston, Andrew Kitchener, Sergei Kruskop, Darrin Lunde, Tony Lynam, Debbie Martyr, Masaharu Motokawa, Susan Murray, Phil Myers, Tilo Nadler, W.F. Perrin, Le Khac Quyet, Alan Rabinowitz, Scott Roberton, Roland and Julia Seitre, Andrew T. Smith, Carly Starr, Ulrike Streicher, Steven Swann, Rob Timmins, Joe Walston, Roland Wirth, Fahong Yu and many others.

The distribution maps in this book, as well as some of the ecological information, were derived from the Southeast Asian Mammal Databank (SAMD), a project of the Instituto Ecologia Applicata in Italy with funding support from the World Conservation Union (IUCN) and many different partners. I thank them for permission to use the maps in this book. Laine Shaw and Andrew Couturier helped to prepare the maps in suitable format for publication.

I am also very grateful to the artists Brin Edwards, Sandra Doyle, John Cox, Guy Troughton, Robin Budden, Lyn Wells, Priscilla Barrett, William Oliver, Ray Hutchins and John Buerling for contributing their time and skills towards producing the colour plates. Karen Phillipps, Alex Borisenko, Sergei Kruskop, and Nico van Strien kindly allowed me to use some of their line drawings in the text, while the American Museum of Natural History, the Sabah Society and the Mammalogical Society of Japan gave permission to reproduce a selection of line drawings from their publications. I am also grateful to the editorial staff at New Holland publishers for helping to see this book through to fruition, including Jo Hemmings, Sarah Whittley, James Parry, Krystyna Mayer, Charlotte Judet and Liz Dittner.

Finally, I would like to thank my wife, Cecilia Fung, and my daughter, Fiona Francis, for accompanying me in the field when possible, for tolerating my absences for field trips and museum work when they could not join me, and for putting up with my preoccupation during many weekends and evenings while completing this book.

Disclaimer Although this book contains much scientific information, it is not intended as a primary source of new scientific data on mammals in the region. In keeping with the usual format for field guides, the text does not include references to sources. Information in this guide has been drawn from a wide variety of sources, including primary and secondary publications, as well as unpublished data from my own field work and that of colleagues. Whenever possible, I have attempted to verify information from multiple sources, to minimize the risk of errors. Nevertheless, independent information was not always available, and I may inadvertently have replicated published mistakes or introduced new ones. As a result, readers interested in citing technical details should not consider this guide as a primary source, but instead should seek out original sources of information. This is particularly true for measurements, which are provided as guides to approximate sizes of animals, and are not necessarily indicative of actual specimens.

INTRODUCTION

The primary aim of this field guide is to provide a convenient means for both the general public and professional scientists to identify all of the mammals currently known to occur in mainland Asia, including Myanmar (also known as Burma), Thailand, Lao People's Democratic Republic (generally referred to as Laos in this book), Vietnam, Cambodia, Peninsular Malaysia and Singapore. The hope is that people using this book will be able to identify any mammal that they observe well in this region by looking through the colour plates and reading the corresponding text descriptions. In most cases, it should be possible to identify animals to species, but for some mammals it may only be possible to narrow this down to a group of closely related species, unless the animal has been collected and prepared as a museum specimen. Some species are difficult to identify, even for experts, and users should not expect to identify every mammal they find, especially those that are only glimpsed in the field.

This book describes every species of wild mammal presently known to occur in the region, including smaller offshore islands. It describes approximately 470 species of land mammal from South-East Asia. Sea mammals, including the cetaceans (whales, dolphins and porpoises) and the Dugong, are also included. Because of the nomadic or migratory nature of many marine mammals, the book includes not only species that have been confirmed as occurring in the region, but also those that have been recorded nearby and are likely to show up in South-East Asian waters.

New knowledge is being gained every year on mammals in this region by researchers working both in the field and in the museum. Ongoing field surveys in new areas, or using new techniques such as camera traps for large mammals, harp traps and clap nets for bats, and various trapping methods for small mammals, are providing new information on the distribution and ecology of species, and even discovering new species. New study techniques, particularly those that incorporate genetic studies combined with re-examination of morphological characters, are leading to further new discoveries, as well as better understanding of species limits in many groups. Much uncertainty about species limits remains, not only in small mammals such as insectivores, rodents and bats, but also in some groups of large mammals such as muntjacs and some primates.

As a result, a book like this must be considered a work in progress. No doubt I have overlooked some published works with information on mammals in the region, created errors through my mistakes in interpreting the literature or perpetuated previously published errors. I would be most grateful to hear from anybody who finds errors in this book, or who has new information on mammals in the region, so that I can incorporate this information into future editions or reprints. I can be contacted at:

National Wildlife Research Centre
Environment Canada
Ottawa, Ontario, Canada, K1A 0H3
E-mail: charles.francis@ec.gc.ca

WHAT IS A MAMMAL?

Mammals are distinguished from other animals by several features. Nearly all species, except a few egg-laying mammals in Australia and New Guinea, give birth to live young, and all species feed their young on milk. Most mammals have fur or hair, although in some sea mammals, such as whales and dolphins, the hairs are scattered and inconspicuous. All species are warm-blooded and share many features of internal anatomy. Most have four limbs: two hind legs and two front legs, wings or arms. A few mammals somewhat resemble, and could be confused with, other types of animal. Bats

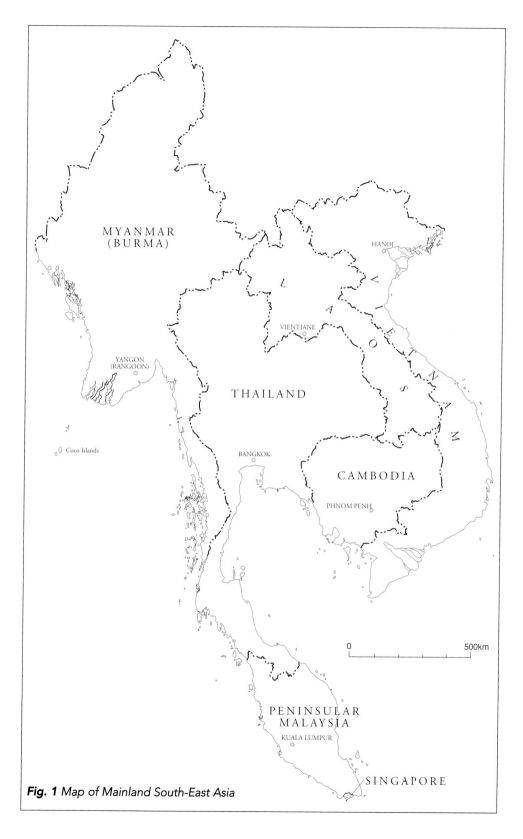

Fig. 1 Map of Mainland South-East Asia

MYANMAR
(BURMA)

HANOI

L
A
O
S

V
I
E
T
N
A
M

VIENTIANE

YANGON
(RANGOON)

THAILAND

Coco Islands

BANGKOK

CAMBODIA

PHNOM PENH

0   500km

PENINSULAR
MALAYSIA

KUALA LUMPUR

SINGAPORE

are sometimes confused with birds because they can fly, but they are structurally very different, with wings formed of skin stretched between long fingers, fur rather than feathers and teeth instead of beaks. They also give birth to live young. Whales, dolphins and porpoises are often confused with fish, but they are actually mammals that have lost most of their hair and their hind legs and replaced their front legs with flippers. They still breathe air, and give birth to live young and feed them on milk. The pangolin somewhat resembles a reptile because of its scales, lack of teeth and long tongue, but the scales are actually formed from packed hairs, and it has all the remaining features of a mammal.

CLASSIFICATION AND NAMING

To help keep track of the large number of animals in the world and to indicate their relationships, animals are classified at different levels. Individuals that can freely interbreed and produce fertile offspring are considered to belong to one species. Closely related species are put in the same genus. Genera (plural of genus) that share many features are grouped in families which, in turn, are grouped into orders, which are grouped into classes. All mammals are grouped in the class Mammalia. Mammals, along with other vertebrates such as birds (class Aves) reptiles (class Reptilia) and fish (class Pisces) are grouped in the phylum Chordata.

Every species of animal known to science has been designated a scientific name. These names are usually based on Latin or Greek, and are used by scientists all over the world regardless of their own language. Scientific names are always written in italics to distinguish them. The name is composed of two parts, indicating the genus and the species. If populations of a species in different geographical areas can be consistently distinguished from one another by measurements or colour, then they are given subspecies names. For example, *Callosciurus* is the genus name for several species of similar medium-sized squirrels in South-East Asia. *Callosciurus finlaysoni* refers specifically to the Variable Squirrel. *Callosciurus finlaysoni sinistralis*, sometimes abbreviated *C. f. sinistralis*, is the form of Variable Squirrel found in north-west Thailand, while *C. f. boonsongi* is the form found in north-east Thailand. These subspecies differ in colour, but are thought likely to interbreed in areas where their range overlaps other subspecies. In this book, subspecies are generally mentioned only if their colour patterns are very distinctive, to the extent that they might complicate identification, or where there is some doubt as to whether they really should be considered full species, rather than subspecies.

Unfortunately, although there are official rules for selecting scientific names, the names can change for a number of reasons. The relationships between many animals are still not well understood, and as a result not everyone agrees on the taxonomy. A common problem is determining relationships between populations of closely related animals from different geographical areas. Some people may consider them to be all the same species and use the same name for all of them, while others consider each a separate species, using a different name for each. At the genus level, some authors may consider two species to be in the same genus, while others may consider the differences between them so large that they should be in separate genera. New research sometimes shows that animals living together in the same area, and formerly considered all one species, differ in subtle ways that had not previously been noticed, and are actually more than one species. This sometimes leads to problems when deciding to which species the original name should be applied. New genetic research is helping to clarify many of the relationships but is unlikely to solve all of the problems. Depending on the authors' viewpoint, or when a work was written, books may differ in the name used for a particular animal.

The classification and scientific names

used in this field guide usually follow those given in Wilson and Reeder (2005), except where more recent research (published or otherwise), provides new information (including a few newly described species). In some cases, where the names in Wilson and Reeder (2005) do not match the names used in Corbet and Hill (1992), and where there is still substantial disagreement in the literature, I have used the older names because these may be more familiar to people using other reference books. In these cases, the alternative name is usually mentioned as well under "Taxonomic notes".

The arrangement of species in this book, like most other similar books, is based on grouping closely related species together. Traditionally, orders are arranged starting with those believed to have diverged earliest from the remainder of the mammal lineages, and families are arranged within orders on a similar basis. This is sometimes thought to be a ranking from most "primitive" to most "advanced", but this is misleading – all mammals alive today are equally "advanced" in that all are descended from the same primitive ancestor over the same time period. In this respect, the sequence of orders is rather arbitrary and it becomes, as much as anything, a matter of convenience as long as closely related species are presented near one another. Ongoing research is leading to many changes in our understanding of taxonomic relationships among mammals, which has led some authors to change the sequence. However, as much of this research is still ongoing, I have chosen to retain the sequence followed by Corbet and Hill (1992) for orders, families and usually genera, as this is similar to the arrangement used in many published works from the region. Within each genus, I have attempted to arrange species that are most similar to one another close together. In some cases, the sequence on the colour plates has been altered, either to present superficially similar species together (e.g. the Dugong is presented with the cetaceans), or for convenience to fit species on plates.

English names are a particular challenge, because many larger mammals have multiple names in the literature, while most of the smaller mammals (bats, rodents) do not have widely used English names, largely because the scientists who study them use only the scientific name. As a result, it has been necessary to invent many of the names used in this book. Duckworth and Pine (2003) proposed a set of rules for developing English names, and gave examples of names for many mammals in the Indochinese region. I have followed most of the principles they advocate in choosing names, but have not always adopted the names they recommended, particularly if an alternative name is already well established. Because many of the English names in this book are not widely known, the scientific name is presented along with the English name whenever a species is mentioned in the text.

HOW TO IDENTIFY MAMMALS

The first step in identifying a mammal is to determine to which group or family it belongs. This usually involves initially determining the order (e.g. primate, rodent or carnivore), then the family or subfamily (e.g. within primates, is it a langur, a macaque or a gibbon?). The easiest way to do this is to look through the colour plates until you find animals that look generally similar in shape to your animal. In many cases, this will be straightforward (for example, gibbons are fairly easily distinguished from other primates by long arms and the absence of a tail), but in some cases it may be necessary to check more closely. For example, treeshrews look superficially similar to squirrels, even though they are not at all closely related. In these cases, it may be useful to check the descriptions of each order or family in the text, to find a description of the main diagnostic differences. Some of these differences may be hard to observe in the field (for example, treeshrews and squirrels have very different teeth), but often there are other characters, such as the shape of the body or head, that can help. With practice, most animals can fairly readily be identified at least to family, based on their overall shape and behaviour, and the search reduced.

Once the family has been determined, the colour plates for that family should be examined closely to find the most similar looking illustration. If you are not completely sure of the family, then check similar species in each family. Always read the captions opposite the plates. These highlight the key identification features and make sure that you are looking at the most reliable characters. For some species colour patterns may be very important (for example, squirrels), while for others, colour may be unreliable and shape may be more important (for example, some horseshoe bats). The captions also indicate if there is more variation than is apparent in the plates. For example, in the Variable Squirrel, it was possible to illustrate only some of the many variations of this species – in some areas, this species may have colour patterns that are different from any of those shown. Size is also important for distinguishing many mammals. For each species, one key measurement for the group is given on the caption page. Additional measurements are provided in the text. Measurements are based on standard techniques for measuring museum specimens (see page 26). However, the apparent size of a live animal may vary depending on its posture. If it hunches its back, the body may seem shorter and the tail proportionately longer.

Once you have found a likely candidate for the species, check the range maps to determine whether it is likely to occur in your region. For some small mammals and bats, if you are working in a region that has been poorly studied, you may find animals in new areas outside the range shown, but this is less likely for larger mammals.

As a final check on a species, you should consult the main species account in the text, double checking the description, and also the "Similar species" section, which highlights species with which it might be confused. For groups that contain many different species (such as bats and rodents) you should also read the section describing the genus. Some very diverse genera, such as *Rhinolophus*, are further divided into groups of species that share certain features. These characters are often somewhat more technical (e.g. dentition or shape of the noseleaf) but should be checked to ensure that the identification is correct.

Many of the larger mammals can be identified from a distance, but fieldworkers who have received the appropriate specialist training will usually capture smaller species for close examination. Rodents caught in cage traps can usually be identified without handling them. If they need to be held, heavy gloves can be useful to avoid being bitten.

For some of the smaller species, such as bats, shrews and some rodents, the teeth need to be examined to confirm the identity. These can usually be seen in a live bat, for example, by gently prying open the mouth with a toothpick or similar tool. A magnifying lens is generally necessary to see the smallest teeth.

The number and arrangement of teeth is given in many of the genus and family accounts as a "Dental formula". This is a shorthand way of indicating the number of teeth in one side of the upper and lower jaws. The teeth are always given in the order: incisors, canines, premolars and molars (see Fig. 7). For example, the dental formula for most *Myotis* bats is: 2/3 1/1 3/3 3/3, indicating 2 incisors, 1 canine, 3 premolars and 3 molars on each side of the upper jaw; and 3 incisors, 1 canine, 3 premolars and 3 molars on each side of the lower jaw, for a total of 38 teeth.

Some teeth are very small, and could be easily overlooked. Occasionally teeth are missing or have fallen out. Usually, if this happens, there is a gap where the tooth used to be, or the two sides of the jaw are not symmetrical, but sometimes the result can be confusing. To show the patterns of the teeth and their relative sizes, diagrams are provided of the tooth rows for many species.

With present knowledge, some species can be positively identified only after museum preparation of the skull. For the benefit of scientists using this book, some of the diagnostic characters of the skulls of these species are included. In the future, when more field studies have been done, other distinctive features may be found to identify these species in life.

Details of skulls are also useful for identifying dead mammals or their remains. Experts can often determine the identity of a mammal using only its skull. A comprehensive guide to skulls is beyond the scope of this book, but diagrams of some of the main skull types are included in the text, so that readers can determine the group to which a skull belongs. For confirmation, the specimen can be sent to a reputable museum for comparison with skulls of known species.

Young mammals can present a challenge for identification, as they often differ in size and colour from adults. The young of larger mammals are often seen with adults, but in smaller species, such as rodents or bats, the young may be trapped alone. This is a particular problem in the case of rats, because fur colour is important for identification. Young can often be recognized by having fluffier and darker fur than adults, and by having fresh, unworn teeth that have not fully erupted from the gums. Young bats can usually be recognized by their greyer fur and incompletely formed wing bones – if held to the light the joints of the wings appear to have pale bands where the cartilage has not yet turned to bone. In some cases it may not be possible to identify young mammals with certainty.

COLOUR PLATES

Nearly every mammal included in this book is illustrated in the 72 colour plates, with the exception of a few that so closely resemble another species as to be indistinguishable in external appearance, as well as a few for which no adequate specimens or descriptions were available. For some species, multiple illustrations have been provided, either to illustrate differences between sexes or ages, or to illustrate geographic variation if this is particularly striking. Young animals are illustrated in only a few cases, mainly for some of the larger animals in which they have very different patterns from adults, or in cases where their colour pattern can help to identify the adults.

In the majority of cases, the artists had to base their illustrations on a combination of museum specimens, to determine colour patterns, and photographs to determine shape. Only a few had seen their subjects in life. While it would have been desirable to work with more live animals, this was logistically not possible. This presented a challenge for illustrating many species, especially the smaller ones, because of a lack of photographs. Many species have never been photographed, while for others the available photographs were not taken at the appropriate angle or in suitable lighting conditions to show the key identification characters. In many cases, it was necessary to base the shape of an animal on another, closely related species. Basing the colour on museum specimens also has some limitations, because the colour of bare skin is not preserved, and fur colours may change over time.

While an effort was made to check these illustrations with experts who had seen the animals in the field, it is quite likely that some illustrations have not perfectly captured some of the subtle variations among species in shape or colour. Of course, no matter how accurate the illustration, animals in the field are likely to be observed from angles or in poses and lighting that differ from the illustrations. This should always be taken into account when using this guide. It is the reason why it is always important to check the species accounts as well as the plates, in order to determine which characters are most important and reliable for identification purposes.

SPECIES ACCOUNTS

Measurements

The account for each species starts with a series of standard measurements. These measurements have been taken from a wide variety of both primary and secondary sources, including field measurements, museum specimens and published ranges in various books. They are intended mainly as an aid to readers to determine the approximate size of each species in relation to other similar species. The measurements are given as a range intended to capture the normal variation in reproductively mature adults of each species, but not necessarily the extremes. However, for measurements taken from published sources, it has not always been possible to verify their accuracy, and in a few cases, where measurements were not available, I have estimated them from those of similar species. Thus, these measurements, especially external body measurements, should be used only as a general guide to the expected size of each species.

When observing mammals in the field, it is important to recognize that most measurements are taken on captured animals that have been straightened out (but not stretched) before taking the measurement.

The head and body length, in particular, may appear rather different in a live animal in a natural posture. Skull measurements are also given for some species, particularly if these can be helpful for identification. Although it is sometimes possible to measure the teeth on a live mammal, most skull measurements can only be taken on museum specimens.

Depending on the type of mammal, and the availability of information, several different measurements are provided for each mammal. The measurements used in this book are as follows.

BODY MEASUREMENTS (Figs 2–4)

Head-and-body length (HB) Measured from the anus to the front of the nose when the animal is stretched out.

Tail (T) Measured from the anus to the tip of the fleshy or bony part of the tail *excluding* hairs that project beyond the end.

Hind foot (HF) From the heel to the end of the longest toe, excluding the claws.

Ear length (E) From the bottom of the external opening of the ear to the tip.

Forearm (FA) (in bats) From the outside of the elbow to the outside of the wrist in the bent wing.

Total length (TL) (in whales and dolphins)

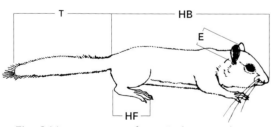

Fig. 2 Measurements of a typical mammal.

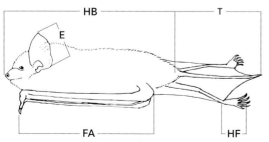

Fig. 3 Measurements of a bat.

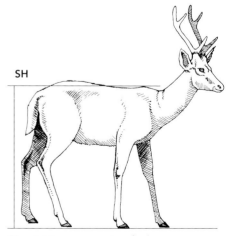

Fig. 4 Measurements of a large mammal.

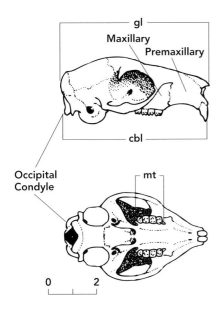

Fig. 5 *Skull measurements of a rodent.*

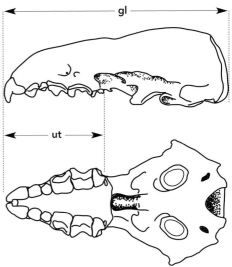

Fig. 6 *Skull measurements of a shrew* (Anourosorex squamipes).

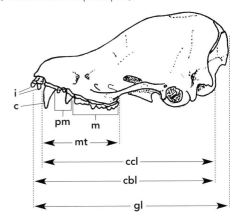

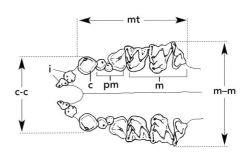

Fig. 7 *Skull measurements and dentition of a bat* (Myotis horsfieldi).

from the front of the head to the notch in the tail flukes.

Shoulder height (SH) Height from the ground to the top of the shoulder when animal is standing.

SKULL MEASUREMENTS (Figs 5–7)

Greatest length (gl) The longest distance from the back of the skull to the front of the skull.

Condylobasal length (cbl) From the back of the occipital condyles to the front of the premaxillae.

Condylocanine length (ccl) From the back of the occipital condyles to the front of the canines.

Maxillary toothrow (mt) The length of the upper toothrow from the back of the molars to the front of the canines (excluding the incisors); usually this is measured to the base of the canine, but for bats this extends to the front of the curve of the canine; for rodents, which have no canines, this includes only the molars and premolars (3 teeth in rats, 4 in squirrels – the tiny premolar at the front is excluded).

Upper toothrow (ut) For shrews the relationships of the teeth are unclear, and the whole toothrow is measured.

Molar width (m–m) The width across the outside of the widest upper molars (at the bases).

Canine width (c–c) the width across the outside of the base of the upper canines.

All measurements are in millimetres (mm) unless explicitly stated as (m) for metres. Weights are in grams (g), except where specified as kilograms (kg).

Identification

Following the measurements, a concise description is given of the species, including the overall coloration and emphasizing the most important identification characters. The text concentrates on identification characters visible on the live animal. Where necessary, this includes dental characters that can often be seen in a live animal, if it has been captured. However, more technical characters such as skull shape or baculum shape are also mentioned, if these are important for identification, for the benefit of people working in museums or who have found a dead specimen.

The colour description is intended to complement the colour plates, rather than to duplicate them. In particular, the text highlights the range of variation in colour, while the plates show the pattern of colours. These should be considered together.

Taxonomic notes are included only for those species for which there are known issues related to taxonomy, for example if the scientific name differs from that used in Wilson and Reeder (2005), or if recent research suggests that more than one species may be represented within a group.

Voice A description is provided only if information on vocalizations is available and may be helpful for identification, for example with primates. Calls can be difficult to describe in words, but it is hoped that the brief descriptions provided will help to differentiate among species and also help to remember sounds once they have been learned.

Echolocation This is only applicable to bats. All insectivorous bats emit distinctive, high-frequency echolocation calls. These usually cannot be heard by the human ear (most are in the frequency range 20–200kHz), but with the aid of a bat detector (see page 21 under finding and studying mammals) it is possible to measure some of the main characteristics of these calls. For most bats, echolocation calls vary in frequency over time and change with the behaviour of the bat, so that it is hard to define simple diagnostic characters. However, for both horseshoe bats (Rhinolophidae) and roundleaf bats (Hipposideridae) the calls have a distinctive constant-frequency component that is very consistent within a population, although it may vary geographically. It can reliably be measured even for bats that are in the hand, and can often help to differentiate species that are very similar in appearance. This information is given in this section, if available, along with information on where it was recorded.

Similar species This section highlights distinctions from other mammals with which the species might be confused. The list is not exhaustive but concentrates on the most similar species, including species that may look different in the illustrations but sometimes look similar in life. In most cases, for some of the larger groups such as bats or rodents, this section only describes similar species within a genus or smaller group. It is always important to check the genus accounts to make sure the correct genus has been selected.

Ecology and habitat

Basic habitat preferences, as well as a summary of the general ecology, are given for each species, where known. This section includes mainly information that might be helpful in finding or identifying a mammal or learning more about its ecology. For many species, especially bats, shrews and rodents, very little is known, and the only information available is the capture site of the few specimens that have been collected. For large mammals, which are often much better known, only a summary of the available information has been included.

The habitat is described in fairly general terms. Many mammals in the region are found only in forests, but little information is available on the range of forest types that they can use. The descriptions provided are generally based on habitats where the species has been found, but these are not necessarily the preferred habitats. For example, forest species have been caught or seen in highly disturbed areas such as recently logged forest or secondary growth, and are reported as using such habitats, but little information is available on whether they are breeding successfully in those areas, or whether they are still dependent on remaining patches of mature forest. When describing habitats, the term "gardens" includes land with fruit trees, shrubs and patches of secondary forest, while "plantations" refers to cocoa, oil palm and rubber tree plantings unless otherwise stated.

Distribution and status

This section first describes the known distribution of the species within mainland South-East Asia. For widespread species, this is generally just a list of countries, but more detail may be given for species with a more restricted range. This description is supplemented by range maps that are presented for most species on the caption pages opposite the colour plates. Distributional information was derived from a range of primary and secondary published sources, as well as information provided by participants in the Southeast Asia Mammal Database project (SAMD 2006). The range maps were generated from the maps produced during that project, but some were adjusted to enhance visibility of small ranges or to correct errors.

It is important to note that the range maps indicate the regions where a species is expected to occur in suitable habitat based on known observations. Because much of the original habitat in many areas has been heavily disturbed or altered, the actual sites where a species is found may be much more restricted. On the other hand, many species, especially of smaller animals, are still relatively poorly known, and the distribution of known records reflects as much the distribu-

tion of research projects as that of the mammals themselves. There is some variation in the maps, as to whether the distribution shows only known localities, or is extrapolated to a broader area. For a few species, dotted lines enclose the historical range.

If a species occurs outside mainland South-East Asia, this range is described next, starting with the word "Also".

After the range is listed, the status is indicated in general terms. In most cases, this is based on the assessment prepared for the IUCN Red List, as part of the SAMD (2006) project, although in a few cases I adjusted the assignments if they did not seem to be consistent with other similar species. Quantitative definitions of the classifications can be found in the IUCN (2001) booklet (available on the IUCN website), but these can be qualitatively summarized as follows.

Status uncertain This usually corresponds to the Data Deficient category of IUCN, although any additional information that might contribute to understanding its status is also indicated.

Not currently at risk This usually corresponds to the Least Concern category of IUCN and implies that current threats to the species are not sufficiently serious that it is an immediate conservation concern, although this may change in the future.

Near Threatened This implies that the species has undergone moderate to substantial population declines, but not yet sufficiently severe to meet the higher criteria.

Vulnerable This usually indicates that the species has undergone substantial population declines in the recent past, and is still under threat. Unless the threats are reduced or removed, the species is likely to become Endangered in the near future.

Endangered This implies that the species population is relatively low, has been declining and continues to experience threats that could lead to its extinction unless the problems are reversed.

Critically Endangered This implies that only a very small population remains of the species, that the population is still threatened and that immediate action is required to prevent extinction in the very near future.

Extinct A few species that occurred until recently in the region are presumed to now be Extinct, but are nevertheless described in this book in the hope that they may still persist.

FINDING AND STUDYING MAMMALS

Although mammals are generally more difficult to observe than birds, there are many different ways to see and study them. The best approach depends on the types of mammal and their preferred habitats.

Observing mammals in the field

Many species of mammal can be observed by walking quietly through a forest or other suitable habitat and watching carefully. During the day, monkeys, apes, and many squirrels are active in trees, treeshrews and some squirrels are found in low bushes, while larger mammals such as pigs, deer, mongooses, bears and otters are active on the ground or in the water.

Many of the larger mammals are quite shy and difficult to approach closely. They need to be stalked very quietly. Luck is required to see some of the wary or less common species. Some animals, such as monkeys, can be gradually accustomed to a human observer, but time and patience are required. This is especially difficult in areas where mammals are actively hunted. Binoculars are very useful for watching many of the tree-dwelling animals and are often essential to see the diagnostic features of some of the smaller squirrels.

Most other mammals are active mainly at night, including the flying squirrels, civets, rats, mice and bats. Large terrestrial mammals such as pigs and elephants can be active at any time of day. Many mammals are less wary at night than during the day, making them easier to observe. A good way to locate them is by using a headlamp or spotlight. The eyes of most nocturnal animals reflect a red or yellowish glow in the light. One way to survey mammals is to walk through the forest using a headlamp to find eyeshine, and a brighter light to see the animals better once they are found, especially if they are high in the trees. This is easiest on a well-marked, relatively clear trail, where one can walk quietly with minimal risk of tripping or falling. A 30- or 50-watt spotlight can be especially useful for observing animals in the tops of tall rainforest (especially if used with binoculars), but it may be too bright for mammals that are close. A red lamp (easily constructed by placing red cellophane over a spotlight) may be less likely to scare away the animals, so they can be observed over a longer period of time.

Mammals are most easily found in relatively open areas. Good places to search are along rivers, in small open clearings, along wide paths or on disused logging roads. Many mammals can be located by the noise of their movements – crashing of branches or rustling of leaves. Some species have distinctive calls, including many primates, some squirrels and muntjacs. With practice many of these mammals can be identified based only on the call. Gibbons can be heard and identified from great distances, even when they cannot be seen. Unfortunately very little is known about the calls of many of the nocturnal animals, such as the flying squirrels.

Sea mammals, such as whales and dolphins, can be found most readily by travelling out to sea in boats. One option is to accompany local fishermen when they make offshore trips. The fishermen themselves may be able to provide valuable information on the numbers of animals they meet, and the best locations to find them, to help with planning such a trip. Unfortunately, many records of cetaceans have come from animals becoming trapped in fishing nets, or washing up on shore.

Tracks

Many large mammals are detected most readily by tracks or signs. Animal tracks can be useful for carrying out surveys, especially of many of the larger mammals. Carefully counting and measuring tracks of some of the larger ungulates can give information on population numbers and age structure.

Some species, such as elephants, tapirs, rhinos and bears, can usually be identified fairly easily to species from their footprints. Others, such as large cats, deer and pigs, can sometimes be identified to species, but at other times only to one of a group of closely related species, depending on the number of species occurring in the area. The main characters for identifying tracks are shape and size, although other factors, such as the distance between footprints and habitat, can be helpful clues. Some care is required in identifying species, as shape varies depending on the hardness of the ground, and size varies not only with the size of the animal, but also with the soil. In wet mud, tracks may become smaller if the sides collapse inwards, while in some soils heavy rain may enlarge tracks. Sketches of footprints of selected species are included in the text, mostly of the hind foot as it would look on moderately firm ground. A few examples are provided of animals on soft ground, where the toes or hoofs are often more spread out and, in the case of pigs, deer and cattle, the dew toes may be visible. Illustrations show typical-sized adults, but tracks will vary in size for larger or smaller individuals; young animals can have substantially smaller tracks, although they may be accompanied by tracks of an adult.

Other signs, such as broken branches, claw marks and faeces, can also be useful for identifying some species, but are not discussed in detail in this book.

Camera traps

In recent years, a very successful method for surveying mammals has been developed using cameras along with an infrared or motion detector. The camera is placed in the forest, usually tied to a tree trunk, in an area where mammals might be expected, for example along a trail or next to a stream. The camera can be left in place for a few days to a few weeks, depending on the amount of activity expected. If possible, cameras should be used that provide a date/time stamp for each photograph, as this gives valuable information on animal activity levels. When the camera is checked, the film can be developed (or the pictures downloaded in the case of a digital camera) and the camera can be reset or moved to a new location. Care should be taken to put cameras in areas where they are not likely to be damaged by animals or removed by other people using the area.

Bat detectors

Bats (except most of the fruit bats, Pteropodidae), have a sophisticated form of sonar or echolocation to find their way in the dark. They emit short pulses of sound through their mouths or nostrils, and listen for the echo to learn about obstacles or food in front of them. Each species of bat has a distinctive frequency and pattern of its echolocation calls. Many species can potentially be identified from their echolocation calls even without capturing them.

However, although a few species have some components of their calls that we can hear, most of the calls are very high frequency and inaudible to human ears. Bat detectors are special high-frequency microphones combined with electronic devices that transform these high-frequency sounds to forms that we can understand. There are several different types of bat detector. The most flexible and accurate (and most expensive) are those that digitize and capture the whole signal, which can then be analysed on a computer, or played back more slowly at a frequency we can hear (time expansion). Another type (frequency division) transforms the sound by dropping it to a constant fraction of the original sound (e.g. one-tenth or one-sixteenth). This loses some information (e.g. harmonics) but can still allow identifica-

Fig. 8 *A small mammal cage trap set on a vine to catch arboreal rats or squirrels.*

tion of many species. The results are usually recorded for later analysis on a computer. The third main type (heterodyne) can be tuned to various frequencies, allowing quick measurements of the main frequency components of the call in the field. This is suitable for some types of survey, but the frequency measurements are less precise than those analysed on computers, and they are not suitable for automatic monitoring of many different species.

In this book, echolocation call frequency information is provided only for the horseshoe (Rhinolophidae) and roundleaf (Hipposideridae) bats, because their calls involve a constant-frequency component that is very specific to each species and can even be recorded in the hand. As a result, considerable reference data are available. For other species, the call structure varies with behaviour and must be recorded from free-flying bats to obtain reliable information. A number of researchers are now working on obtaining this information, using methods such as recording bats immediately after releasing them. However, most species have not yet been recorded and more information is required before a sufficiently comprehensive library is available to determine the range of variation in each species and the best characteristics for identifying each species by its calls.

Capturing mammals

Many of the smaller animals, such as insectivores, rodents and bats, need to be captured for positive identification. Trapping and handling mammals must be done carefully to avoid accidental injuries and ensure

the animals can be released in good health. It is a job for professionals working in the field, who have the appropriate experience and qualifications. Before setting traps for mammals, it is also important to have appropriate permits, especially for work in a protected area such as a park or reserve. Research permits may be required, as well as permits to trap any protected species.

Many of the most commonly used traps for small mammals such as rats, mice, squirrels and treeshrews involve some sort of box or cage with a trap door that closes when the animal enters (e.g. Fig. 8). Cage traps made of wire mesh are available locally in many areas, while others such as folding sheet metal box traps (e.g. Sherman or Longworth traps) may need to be imported. These can be set on the ground or tied to fallen trees, tree branches or lianas. Many different foods are suitable for bait, including oil palm fruit, salt fish and fruits such as small ripe bananas. A larger version baited with raw meat or fish and set on the ground by a stream or a path can be used to catch some mustelids and viverrids.

The smallest mammals, such as shrews and ground-dwelling mice, can be caught in pit-fall traps. These consist of any smooth-sided container dug into the ground so that the edges are level with the ground. They must be deep enough that the animals cannot jump out and escape. Small fences made of branches or wire mesh can be useful to guide animals into the traps. Drainage holes should be placed in the bottom so that trapped animals do not drown in heavy rain, and the traps should be checked frequently. Food can be placed in the bottom, both as bait and so that the animals have something to eat when caught.

For bats, one of the most effective cap-

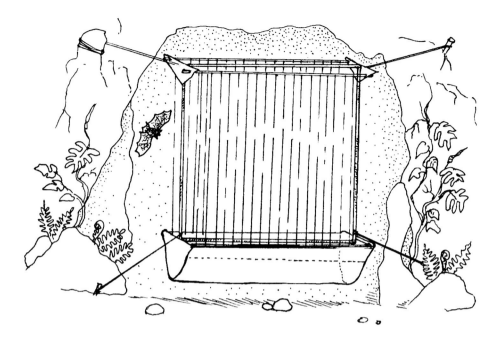

Fig. 9 A 3-bank harp trap suspended in front of a cave entrance. These traps can also be positioned on legs.

ture methods, and safest for the bats, is a harp trap. This consists of a metal frame, typically 1.5–2.0m square, that supports two to four banks of tightly strung, narrow (0.2 mm diameter) vertical fishing line (Fig. 9). Bats usually have enough momentum to fly through one or two rows of fishing line before sliding down in between the rows and into a holding bag with funnel-like plastic sides. These traps should be placed across narrow paths or small streams, so the bats are channelled through the traps. The traps should be checked at least once per hour, and should not be set in areas with very large numbers of bats, for example near the entrance to a large colony, unless they are being watched closely.

Fine nets, called mist nets, are also used to catch bats and are particularly effective with frugivorous species which have no echolocation. They have the disadvantage that insectivorous bats can often detect them with echolocation and avoid them, and those that do hit the net may escape by chewing holes in the net. For insectivorous bats, mist nets are most effective if they have very find threads (including monofilament) and if they are placed across streams, near cave entrances or other areas where bats concentrate (Fig. 10). Fruit bats can be captured most effectively by placing nets near fruiting or flowering trees. In tall lowland rainforest, many fruit bats are most abundant in the canopy of the forest, and it can be very effective to hang nets from tree tops. This can be done by restringing them to be tall and narrow and suspending them from a single rope suspended over a branch, or by using multiple ropes or a series of stacked tall poles. Occasionally small flying squirrels or nocturnal birds may be caught in mist nets as well.

For insectivorous bats, nets should be watched continuously, so that the bats do not chew holes in them and escape. Fruit bat teeth have less effective cutting edges and the bats are thus less likely to escape, so for them it may be possible to check the nets less frequently (e.g. every half-hour), depending on bat activity. Bats can become quite tangled in a net, and proper training is required to learn how to remove bats and other animals without injury to either the animals or the surveyor.

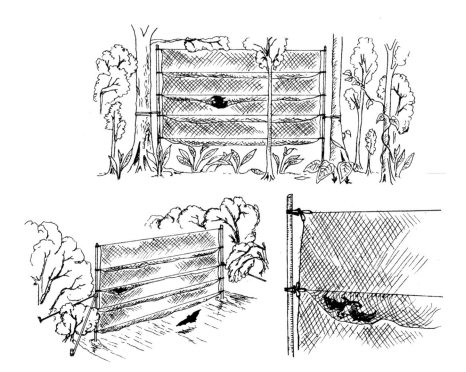

Fig. 10 *Mist nets set across a stream and between trees in the forest, with an inset showing how bats get caught.*

Another capture method involves a mobile "flap net". This is made from a small, lightweight fishing net about 2.5 x 3.0m made from thread 0.1–0.15mm in diameter with mesh about 14–18mm on each side. This is tied with stronger supporting cords to the ends of two long (4–5m) lightweight poles (carbon fibre collapsible fishing poles are suitable) into a trapezoidal shape. The two poles are held by the surveyor, who uses a headlight to watch for bats (potentially recording them at the same time, using a bat detector) and swings the net to scoop up any bats that are encountered (Fig. 11). This requires an area wide enough to swing the net, but it can be very effective on wide paths or narrow roads through forest, over ponds or streams, or near a roost entrance. Of course, care must be taken when walking at night with long poles not to trip or fall, and to avoid power cables and other potential dangers.

Bats can also be found at roost by searching inside caves, hollow trees or other suitable roosting sites. Sometimes bats can be captured directly by hand, or with an insect net on a long pole. This has the added advantage that it provides useful information on roosting sites for each species, which can help with conservation planning – some bat species may be limited in their habitat use by availability of suitable roost sites.

Regardless of the capture technique, care should be taken to minimize handling time and to release the animal in a suitable habitat and at a suitable time of day. For example, if possible, bats should be released at night in or near their capture or roost sites, so that they can continue feeding or find their roost in safety. If an animal needs to be held for a little while, it should be provided with food and water and kept from overheating. Fruit bats can be given a solution of sugar and water before release.

Surveys of mammal remains

In some areas, an effective survey technique is to search for the remains of animals, particularly skulls or skull bones. Searching inside caves often leads to discovery of the remains of many bats that have died inside

Fig. 11 Using a flap net to catch bats over a stream.

the cave and occasionally other species as well. A particularly effective technique is to find the roosting site of an owl, and collect the pellets that accumulate under the roost. Owls usually swallow their prey whole and then later regurgitate the fur and bones from their prey as a pellet. Some researchers collecting owl pellets in Thailand and Laos have found the remains of large numbers of shrews that had rarely been captured in any other way – owls are very effective small mammal collectors! One species of shrew (*Crocidura hilliana*) was first described on the basis of skulls found in owl pellets.

Identification of skulls, especially partial skulls (which are often all that remain in an owl pellet) goes beyond the scope of this book, although some diagrams of skulls and toothrows are provided. Confirmation will generally require comparison of the remains with reference material in museums.

Collecting scientific specimens

In some cases, such as when carrying out surveys of small mammals in new areas, or when a potential new species has been captured, it may be necessary to collect a mammal and prepare it as a museum specimen. As with capturing mammals, it is important to ensure that appropriate permits have been obtained before collecting any animals, and that the specimen can be properly preserved and stored in an appropriate museum.

Scientific specimens are particular important for confirmation of the identity of new geographic records or for describing a new species. It may also be desirable to collect one or two specimens of each species in ecological studies to allow for later confirmation of the identity, although this can sometimes now be done genetically (see below). If specimens are collected, in order for them to be useful, appropriate documentation must be recorded on a label attached to the specimen giving the exact location (preferably from a GPS) and date it was captured. It must also be properly stored and maintained, preferably in a national museum with appropriate storage areas and trained curatorial staff.

Before preparing any specimen, it is important first to record external measurements, as described above, including, if possible, the body weight, and write those on the label that will be attached to the specimen. Colour photographs should also be taken, preferably with the numbered label in the photograph (so the photos can later be matched to the specimen) as well as a colour reference strip in case the colours of the animal change over time. This is especially easy with a digital camera; as museums improve the electronic catalogues of their collections, they may be able to store the photographs with the catalogues.

Specimens may be prepared as dry skins and skeletons or preserved in alcohol. Skins are particularly difficult to prepare and maintain in hot humid climates like those in much of South-East Asia. They must be quickly dried in the field and then stored in a cool, dry area in a bug-proof cabinet. Otherwise, they will deteriorate rapidly or be eaten by insects. Dry skins tend to be better for studying fur colour and texture, but the shape of the animal is lost. Instructions for preparing scientific study skins are available in a number of museum reference manuals and should be consulted before collecting mammals. Alternatively, if possible, try to find an opportunity to work with an experienced mammal collector.

Specimens to be stored in alcohol should first be fixed for a few days, either in a 10 per cent solution of formalin (equivalent to 4 per cent formaldehyde) or else in 75 per cent ethanol. Formalin is much less pleasant to humans and must be handled carefully, but it fixes the animal more thoroughly. If possible, it should be buffered to reduce its acidity and minimize damage to teeth and bones, which can otherwise be eroded. A mixture of 6g dibasic and 4g monobasic sodium phosphate per litre of 10 per cent formalin is recommended, but calcium carbonate can be used for short-term storage. It is important to ensure that the insides of the animal are thoroughly fixed, either by injecting some of the solution into the body cavity, or by slitting open the body cavity to allow the liquid to penetrate. Once the animal has been fixed (which takes only a day or two in formalin), it should be transferred to a fresh solution of 70–80 per cent ethanol for long-term storage. If the animal was fixed in formalin, it should first be thoroughly rinsed in water to remove as much as possible of the formalin. All specimens should be stored in a dark area, to minimize the amount of fading that takes place. The containers should be checked periodically to ensure that the alcohol has not evaporated.

Regardless of the preparation technique, it is very important first to collect some tissue samples that can be used for later genetic analyses. To maximize the preservation of genetic material, these should be collected as soon as possible after death (and before contact with formalin) and stored in 95–99 per cent ethanol. Suitable tissues from a freshly dead animal include liver or other internal organs that are particularly rich in DNA. However, if the animal has been dead for several hours or days, muscle or skin tissue may be more appropriate, as there are fewer enzymes to break down the DNA. Tissue samples stored in ethanol will keep for several years, especially at low temperatures, but for long-term storage it is recommended to transfer them to a museum facility with ultracold freezers. Ideally, tissue samples from each specimen should be stored in more than one institution, to guard against loss in case of freezer failure or other equipment problems. The tissue samples must be carefully labelled with a specimen number that can be matched back to the museum voucher. This can be written on the vial with an alcohol-resistant pen or scratched into the vial to ensure that it does not rub off.

Genetic approaches to identification

A new initiative to identify animals using genetic techniques has recently been developed, called DNA barcoding. This involves sequencing part of the mitochondrial genome called the Cytochrome c Oxidase subunit I (COI) gene. The sequences of this gene are different for nearly every species of animal. An international library of animal barcodes is being developed and maintained on an Internet database (www.barcodinglife.ca). A recent study on South-East Asian bats has shown that about 98 per cent of currently recognized species can be separated based on the DNA barcodes. Sequencing of other genes may allow further refinements of identification. A researcher can collect a small piece of skin, or even a tuft of fur, extract the DNA and sequence it in a lab, and then determine whether it matches a known species in the database. This can be particularly useful to confirm species identity in ecological studies of small mammals where the objective is to study live animals with minimum disturbance. However, it does not completely eliminate the need for museum specimens, because it is essential that the reference sequences in the library be matched to known vouchers, so they can be linked to traditional taxonomy. Also, if the DNA sequence does not match a known form, specimens are required to determine whether it may represent a new species. Differences in DNA alone do not necessarily indicate a new species, as there is some variation within species, but large differences from known sequences may indicate something new.

WHERE TO FIND MAMMALS

The area covered by this book spans nearly 28 degrees of latitude, from tropical lowland rainforest near the equator in Peninsular Malaysia, to upper montane habitats 5,000 metres above sea level at the edge of the Himalayas in North Myanmar. This diversity in habitats leads to a high diversity in mammals.

The Isthmus of Kra, at about 8°N in peninsular Thailand, represents a significant biogeographical barrier, with many species reaching their northern or southern limits there. To the south is the Sunda sub-region, including Peninsular Malaysia as well as Sumatra, Java and Borneo and adjacent small islands. Many species are shared among these large islands as the seas between them are relatively shallow and the whole Sunda sub-region was connected at various times in the past when sea levels were much lower. The majority of mammal species in this region are adapted to lowland evergreen rainforest, which is perhaps the richest and most diverse forest in the region. The dominant tree species are dipterocarps, but with a very high diversity of other tree species – over 800 different species of tree and shrub have been recorded from a single 50-hectare study plot in Malaysia. In its natural state, the main canopy is 30–40m tall with multiple layers of understorey trees and shrubs, and some tall emergent trees reaching up to 60m or more.

Some of the mammals in this region are restricted to higher elevations in hill or montane forest, where the trees are lower, often moss covered, with different species composition. Other important habitats include swamp forest, with similar species to the lowland rainforest but generally lower diversity, and coastal mangroves with a number of specialists, some of which have more recently moved into gardens and disturbed areas. Only a few mammal species are specialized for open habitats such as rice fields or grasslands; some of these mammals are recent invaders from other regions. Of course, these include some of the most familiar mammals, such as the rats and mice that invade human houses.

In the Indochinese sub-region north of the peninsula, the highest diversity of mammals is still in forested areas, but there is a greater diversity of forest types. Deciduous forests, which shed their leaves during the dry season, occur in many areas, although they were formerly much more extensive. These range from mixed deciduous and broadleaf evergreen forests with a relatively dense understorey of shrubs and bamboos, to sparse dry dipterocarp forest with limited tree diversity and an understorey mainly of grasses. Natural grasslands also occur. Some mammals, such as elephants, wild cattle, a few deer species and some carnivores, may be most abundant in grasslands or savannahs consisting of a mixture of grassy areas and trees. This region also has a higher diversity of species adapted for open areas, including many species of rodent, some of which have expanded with increasing agriculture. Areas with increased rainfall support broadleaved evergreen forests with an increased diversity of fruiting trees, thus supporting many species of mammal. Montane forests are dominated by different tree species with many more oaks and beeches and fewer dipterocarps, supporting a different suite of mammal species. A surprisingly rich area of diversity, with many endemic species (found nowhere else in the world), is in the Annamite Mountains that separate Laos and Vietnam. Many bats, as well as a number of rodent species, including the newly discovered Kha-nyou, *Laonastes aenigmamus*, and several species of langur, are found only around forest-covered limestone outcrops, which usually contain large numbers of caves. Wetlands, including coastal mangrove forests as well as swamps and marshes along large rivers and lakes, are a very important habitat for many species, including some specialized mammals such as otters.

Northern Myanmar extends into the Himalayan sub-region, with many Himalayan and Chinese species reaching their southern limits there. Many of these species are montane specialists, found in alpine rhododendron forests and scrub, or grassy meadows and rock piles above the tree line. Others are adapted for drier country, such as that found in India, and reach their eastern limits in Myanmar.

In most countries in the region, mammals are most readily found in many of the protected areas such as national parks and wildlife sanctuaries, both because these often contain some of the best remaining habitats, and also because the animals are more likely to be protected from hunting, so are less shy and occur in greater numbers. A variety of parks and wildlife sanctuaries has been established in each country, covering most of the major habitat types, although the facilities and access vary considerably.

Local travel guides should be consulted for further details.

CONSERVATION OF MAMMALS IN SOUTH-EAST ASIA

Originally, nearly all the region was covered in forest of one type or another. At an escalating rate over the past century, much of this forest has been cleared for agriculture or urban development. Much of what remains has been selectively logged or otherwise degraded.

The greatest single threat to most mammals and other wildlife in the region has been the loss or conversion of their natural habitats, especially forest. Most of the terrestrial mammals in the region are adapted for forest cover and cannot survive in agricultural or cleared areas. Some species appear to be able to survive in disturbed forests such as selectively logged or otherwise degraded areas, though possibly in reduced numbers, and the long-term viability of their populations is still unknown. Others are rarely found outside relatively intact tall forests; even selective logging can result in loss of roosting sites or shelter, as well as changes in the food supply through loss of fruiting trees and reduced diversity of insects.

As a result, most forest species have undoubtedly experienced a decline in their overall population size over the past few decades, the losses being most severe in species that cannot tolerate disturbance. Loss of habitat results in a direct loss of populations – if two-thirds of a forest is gone, the remaining forest cannot support more than one-third of the original population size of the species. The clearing of forest results in permanent loss of all the mammals that used to occur there – they cannot simply move somewhere else. In addition, much remaining forest may be fragmented into small patches. The smallest fragments of forest may be too small to support viable populations of many mammals, particularly the larger species. If the fragments are isolated patches, animals may not be able to move among areas, or recolonize if a population becomes locally extinct.

An additional threat to many larger mammals, both large and small, is hunting and trapping both for food and for the so-called medicinal trade. Formerly, when human densities were much lower and when mammal populations were higher with more extensive intact habitat, hunting and trapping of some species may have been sustainable. However, with increasing human populations, with increased availability of firearms, with reduced areas of suitable habitat, with easier access to formerly remote areas by road, and particularly with an increased demand for wildlife for internal and international trade, excessive hunting and trapping is now threatening many animals with extinction. At least two species of mammal, Schomburgk's Deer and Kouprey, have apparently already been hunted to extinction. Both species of rhinoceros are critically endangered, with limited chances of survival in the region, largely due to illegal hunting. Pangolins, which until recently were relatively common, have undergone a dramatic population decline of 90 per cent or more in the past 10 to 20 years, owing to trapping and trading of their skins for alleged medicinal values. Large carnivores such as tigers and bears, as well as several primates, are threatened by a combination of habitat loss and hunting. Even smaller mammals such as bats have been locally wiped out from some cave colonies by excessive trapping. Marine mammals such as dolphins and dugongs are also threatened by a combination of factors, including deliberate hunting, accidental drowning in fishing nets, reduction of food supplies as a result of overfishing, and degradation of water conditions from pollution.

The net result is that an unfortunately high number of mammal species in the region is now listed as Endangered or Critically Endangered, as indicated in the status section of the respective species accounts, with many further species listed as Near Threatened or Vulnerable.

In order to protect the tremendous diversity of mammals in the region, several measures are required, of which the most important are protecting large areas of suitable habitat, and reducing the amount of hunting, trapping and wildlife trade. Adequately large areas of all the major habitat types need to be set aside in the form of gazetted parks and reserves, to protect not only mammals but also all other aspects of wildlife diversity. Although many areas have been designated in each country in the region, these are not always large enough, and enforcement and management are generally lagging behind. Greater efforts, and resources, are required to ensure protection of reserves once they are designated.

In addition, suitable management practices are required outside reserves. Areas being managed for forestry should be managed to preserve as much as possible of the natural tree diversity. Forestry practices are required that minimize damage to the forest during selective logging. Degraded areas should be allowed to regenerate or, if necessary, replanted with natural species. Priority should be given to restoring areas near existing reserves to expand their area and carrying capacity, as well as the provision of corridors to connect different reserves, thus increasing the viability of populations within them.

The other major requirement is to halt, as far as possible, trade in wildlife, nearly all of which is now unsustainable. This includes strengthening national and international laws to limit wildlife trade, and enhancing enforcement capacity and penalties for violating these laws.

Education is also a vital component of any conservation programme. People will protect only those things that they understand and value. In this respect, I hope that this book will play a role in enhancing understanding of the diversity of mammals in the region, and the need for immediate conservation actions to protect them. While these mammal species still exist, there is still a chance to protect this tremendous level of biodiversity so that future generations can observe and enjoy the mammals of South-East Asia.

Plate 1. GYMNURES AND MOLES

1. MOONRAT
Echinosorex gymnurus, p. 176
HB 320–400. Large; elongate muzzle; long shaggy fur; white on head and variable amounts on front half of body.

2. SHORT-TAILED GYMNURE
Hylomys suillus, p. 176
HB 120–140. Elongate muzzle; conspicuous rounded ears; short, nearly hairless tail; short spines in fur. Fur dark reddish-brown (2a) to grey-brown (2b).

3. CHINESE GYMNURE
Hylomys sinensis, p. 176
HB 110–125. Like *H. suillus*, but has longer, thin tail; one less premolar in lower jaw. *H. megalotis* (not illustrated) from C Laos has longer, thicker tail.

4. SLENDER SHREW-MOLE
Uropsilus gracilis, p. 177
HB 65–90. Elongate snout; small eyes hidden in fur; small but visible ears; long scaly tail; front feet only slightly enlarged.

5. KLOSS'S MOLE
Euroscaptor klossi, p. 178
HB 125–135. No visible eyes or ears; enlarged, rounded front feet, large claws; short club-shaped tail. See text for differences from *E. longirostris*, *E. parvidens* and *Parascaptor leucura* (not illustrated).

6. LARGE CHINESE MOLE
Euroscaptor grandis, p. 178
HB 150. Similar to *E. klossi*, but of a larger size.

7. LONG-TAILED MOLE
Scaptonyx fuscicauda, p. 179
HB 65–90. No visible eyes or ears; somewhat enlarged, elongate front feet; moderate-length scaly tail.

Plate 2. BROWN-TOOTHED SHREWS AND MOLE-SHREW

1. INDOCHINESE SHORT-TAILED SHREW
Blarinella griselda, p. 181
HB ~80. Small; moderately short tail; five unicuspid teeth, last one small and hard to see. *B. wardi* from N Myanmar (not illustrated) is similar, but slightly smaller; relatively smaller third upper unicuspid.

2. HODGSON'S BROWN-TOOTHED SHREW
Episoriculus caudatus, p. 181
HB 50–75. Small; moderately long tail; four unicuspids, last one small and hard to see. *E. baileyi* (not illustrated) is similar, but slightly larger; has bigger upper incisors.

3. LONG-TAILED BROWN-TOOTHED SHREW
Episoriculus macrurus, p. 182
HB 59–66. Similar to *E. caudatus*, but greyer, tail much longer than body, dark above, usually paler below.

4. LOWE'S BROWN-TOOTHED SHREW
Chodsigoa parca, p. 182
HB 65–85. Small; orange-brown tips to teeth; only three unicuspids; tail longer than HB with tuft of longer hairs at tip; feet pale; footpads separated.

5. VAN SUNG'S SHREW
Chodsigoa caovansunga, p. 183
HB 58–64. Similar to *C. parca*, but tail shorter without tuft of hairs at tip; feet brown; footpads touching.

6. LESSER STRIPE-BACKED SHREW
Sorex bedfordiae, p. 180
HB 50–70. Small; moderately long tail; dark stripe on back; five unicuspid teeth all similar in size.

7. MOLE-SHREW
Anourosorex squamipes, p. 183
HB 85–110. Tiny eyes; no visible ears; very short, scaly tail; front feet not especially enlarged.

Note All species on this plate except *Anourosorex* have reddish-brown or orange tips to incisors and some unicuspids.

32

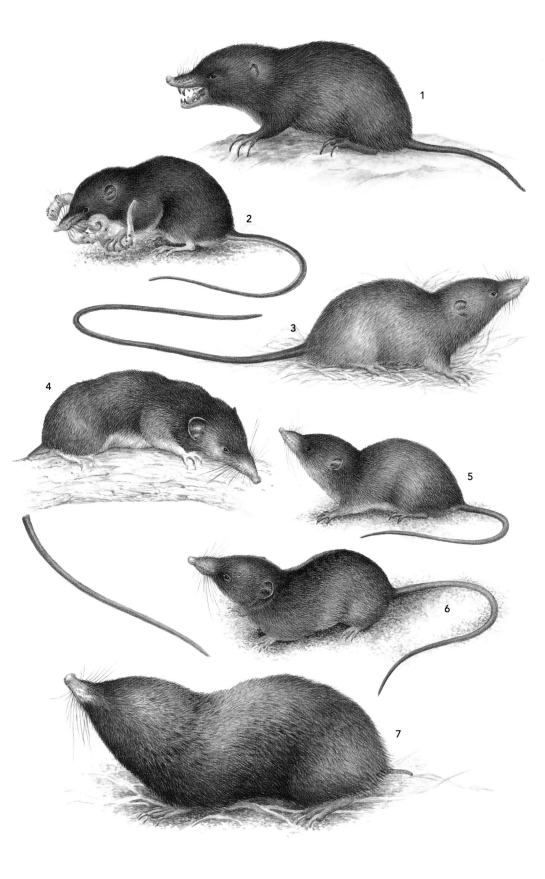

Plate 3. WHITE-TOOTHED SHREWS

1. HIMALAYAN WATER SHREW
Chimarrogale himalayica, p. 183
HB 110–130. Long silvery guard hairs on back; only slightly paler below than above; tail usually all dark; feet fringed with short stiff hairs. *C. hantu* from Peninsular Malaysia (not illustrated) is very similar, but with cusp on upper incisor.

2. STYAN'S WATER SHREW
Chimarrogale styani, p. 184
HB 80–110. Like *C. himalayica*, but underparts silvery grey, sharply contrasting with upperparts; tail dark above, pale below.

3. WEB-FOOTED WATER SHREW
Nectogale elegans, p. 184
HB 90–130. Silvery-white underparts contrast with dark upperparts; rows of white hairs along dark tail.

4. HOUSE SHREW
Suncus murinus, p. 185
HB 90–145. Relatively large; moderate-length thick tail; four upper unicuspids. Often found around houses.

5. PYGMY WHITE-TOOTHED SHREW
Suncus etruscus, p. 184
HB 50–56. Very small; four upper unicuspids.

6. VORACIOUS SHREW
Crocidura vorax, p. 188
HB 54–90. Small to medium-sized; sharply bicoloured tail. *C. rapax* (not illustrated) is similar, but smaller with an indistinctly bicoloured tail.

7. KE GO SHREW
Crocidura kegoensis, p. 187
HB 48. Very small; dark mark on muzzle and ears; relatively flat skull.

8. INDOCHINESE SHREW
Crocidura indochinensis, p. 187
HB 65–70. Medium-small; medium-length tail with long bristles at base; flat skull. The similar *C. wuchihensis* (not illustrated) is smaller.

9. SUNDA SHREW
Crocidura monticola, p. 186
HB 53–65. Very small; uniformly dull grey-brown; tail with bristles on basal half.

10. SOUTH-EAST ASIAN SHREW
Crocidura fuliginosa, p. 185
HB 70–100. Medium-large; sparsely haired tail; see text for distinctions from *C. malayana*, *C. negligens*, *C. hilliana* and *C. attenuata* (not illustrated).

Note Species on this page have white tips to all teeth. *Crocidura* have only three unicuspid teeth, while *Suncus* have an extra, very small posterior unicuspid, although it can be hard to see.

Plate 4. TREESHREWS

1. FEATHER-TAILED TREESHREW
Ptilocercus lowii, p. 189
HB 135–150. Grey to grey-brown; long tail with feather-like tip; largely nocturnal.

4. NORTHERN TREESHREW
Tupaia belangeri, p. 190
HB 160–230. Pointed muzzle; long tail; pale mark on shoulder; greyish fur.

2. NORTHERN SLENDER-TAILED TREESHREW
Dendrogale murina, p. 190
HB 115–135. Pointed muzzle; very thin, lightly haired tail; stripes on face.

5. COMMON TREESHREW
Tupaia glis, p. 190
HB 135–205. Pointed muzzle; long tail; pale mark on shoulder; reddish fur.

3. LESSER TREESHREW
Tupaia minor, p. 190
HB 110–140. Small; pointed muzzle; pale mark on shoulder; relatively long, thin tail.

Plate 5. FLYING-FOXES AND TAILLESS FRUIT BATS

1. LARGE FLYING-FOX
Pteropus vampyrus, p. 195
FA 185–200. Largest bat in region; dark back; orange collar; underparts usually dark. Roosts in large colonies in open trees.

2. INDIAN FLYING-FOX
Pteropus giganteus, p. 196
FA 140–180. Similar to *P. vampyrus* but slightly smaller; collar paler; underparts usually pale.

3. LYLE'S FLYING-FOX
Pteropus lylei, p. 196
FA 145–160. Similar to *P. vampyrus* but much smaller; underparts pale or dark; pointed ears.

4. ISLAND FLYING-FOX
Pteropus hypomelanus, p. 196
FA 120–145. Relatively small; underside varies from dark brown to pale brown; rounded ears.

5. SUNDA TAILLESS FRUIT BAT
Megaerops ecaudatus, p. 199
FA 51–58. Brownish fur with paler, grey bases; dark rims to ears; only one pair of lower incisors; upturned rostrum; protruding nostrils.

6. NORTHERN TAILLESS FRUIT BAT
Megaerops niphanae, p. 199
FA 53–61. Like *M. ecaudatus*, but rostrum more sloping; nostrils smaller.

7. WHITE-COLLARED FRUIT BAT
Megaerops wetmorei, p. 199
FA 45–51. Small; short rostrum; dark rims to ears; white tufts on sides of neck in adult male.

Note Heads of flying-foxes are drawn at a smaller scale than heads of *Megaerops*.

Plate 6. SMALL AND MEDIUM FRUIT BATS

1. GREY FRUIT BAT

Aethalops alecto, p. 201
FA 42–46. Small; uniformly dark grey-brown to reddish-brown; thick fluffy fur; no tail; one pair of lower incisors.

2. DUSKY FRUIT BAT

Penthetor lucasi, p. 198
FA 57–62. Medium-sized; short grey to grey-brown fur; dark edges to ears; one pair of lower incisors.

3. BLACK-CAPPED FRUIT BAT

Chironax melanocephalus, p. 200
FA 43–46. Small; contrasting dark head; yellow tufts on sides of neck in adults; two pairs of lower incisors.

4. SPOTTED-WINGED FRUIT BAT

Balionycteris maculata, p. 200
FA 40–45. Small; dark fur; pale pinkish-white spots on face and wing joints; one pair of lower incisors.

5. HILL FRUIT BAT

Sphaerius blanfordi, p. 201
FA 52–60. No tail; interfemoral membrane thickly covered with hair; fur grey or brown with grey bases; pale rims to ears; pale wing bones; two pairs of lower incisors.

6. GREATER SHORT-NOSED FRUIT BAT

Cynopterus sphinx, p. 198
FA 65–76. Pale rims to ears; pale wing bones; collar orange to yellow-orange in adult males (6a), paler yellow in adult females (6b) and young; two pairs of upper and lower incisors.

7. HORSFIELD'S FRUIT BAT

Cynopterus horsfieldi, p. 198
FA 68–76. Like *C. sphinx* but averages heavier; cheek teeth large and rectangular with extra cusps in middle.

8. FOREST SHORT-NOSED FRUIT BAT

Cynopterus cf. *brachyotis* "Forest", p. 197
FA 56–63. Smallest *Cynopterus* in region; muzzle short; collar of adult male dark orange.

9. SUNDA SHORT-NOSED FRUIT BAT

Cynopterus cf. *brachyotis* "Sunda", p. 197
FA 59–70. Averages smaller than *C. sphinx* with shorter ears; muzzle relatively long; collar of adult male yellowish-orange.

Plate 7. *DYACOPTERUS*, ROUSETTES AND NECTAR BATS

1. DAYAK FRUIT BAT
Dyacopterus spadiceus, p. 200
FA 77–81. Large; short greyish-brown fur; heavy muzzle with large rectangular cheek teeth; only three upper cheek teeth.

4. CAVE NECTAR BAT
Eonycteris spelaea, p. 202
FA 62–70. Elongate muzzle; small teeth; no claw on second digit.

2. GEOFFROY'S ROUSETTE
Rousettus amplexicaudatus, p. 194
FA 78–87. Large; elongate muzzle; claw on second digit; lower molars relatively circular.

5. GREATER LONG-TONGUED NECTAR BAT
Macroglossus sobrinus, p. 202
FA 44–50. Elongate muzzle; long tongue; very small teeth; no grooves on upper lip or around nostrils (5b).
Frequently feeds on banana flowers (5c).

3. LESCHENAULT'S ROUSETTE
Rousettus leschenaultii, p. 194
FA 75–85. Large; elongate muzzle; claw on second digit; last lower molar elongate.

6. LESSER LONG-TONGUED NECTAR BAT
Macroglossus minimus, p. 202
FA 39–44. Like *M. sobrinus*, but slightly smaller; distinct grooves below each nostril and in middle of upper lip (6b).

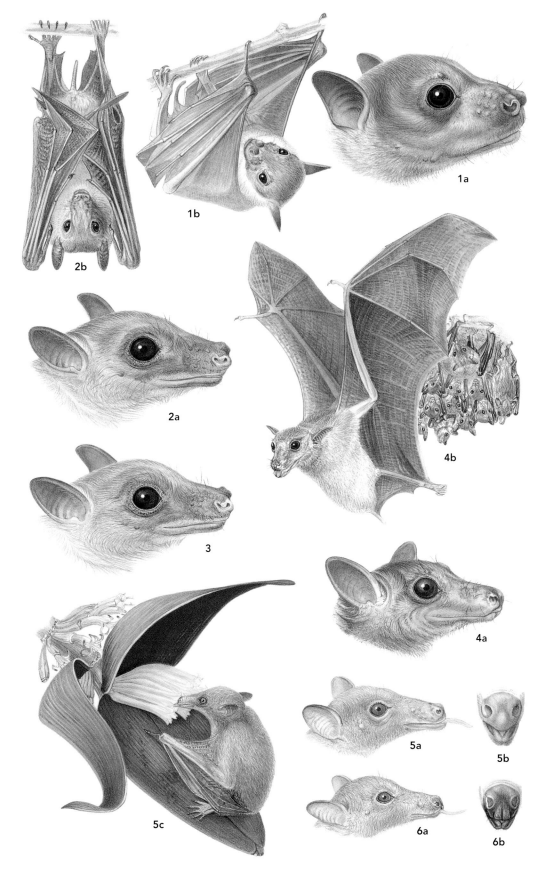

Plate 8. *RHINOPOMA, CRASEONYCTERIS* AND SHEATH-TAILED AND TOMB BATS

1. LESSER MOUSE-TAILED BAT

Rhinopoma hardwickii, p. 203
FA 53–64. Long, protruding mouse-like tail; short grey-brown fur; distinct ridge of skin on tip of muzzle. See text for distinctions from *R. microphyllum* (**not illustrated**).

2. KITTI'S HOG-NOSED BAT

Craseonycteris thonglongyai, p. 207
FA 22–26. Very small; no bony tail; pig-like nose with slight ridge of skin on tip.

3. LESSER SHEATH-TAILED BAT

Emballonura monticola, p. 204
FA 43–45. Small; dark brown fur; short tail protrudes from middle of interfemoral membrane; alert posture.

4. LONG-WINGED TOMB BAT

Taphozous longimanus, p. 205
FA 54–63. Medium-sized; chin naked; gular pouch in male (4c), lacking in female (4d); extensive fur on interfemoral membrane and base of wing; small wing pouch; colour varies from brown to blackish.

5. POUCHED TOMB BAT

Saccolaimus saccolaimus, p. 206
FA 71–78. Relatively large; tail protrudes from middle of interfemoral membrane; dark back with white speckles; underside usually white, sometimes dark brown; translucent wings; no wing pouch; glandular pouch under chin.

6. THEOBALD'S TOMB BAT

Taphozous theobaldi, p. 205
FA 70–76. Relatively large; chin furred without throat pouch, sometimes with dark "beard" in male (6c); well-developed wing pouch (similar to 7e); no fur on interfemoral membrane or legs.

7. NAKED-RUMPED TOMB BAT

Taphozous nudiventris, p. 206
FA 71–80. Relatively large; no fur on lower back or upper side of flight membranes; chin naked, with distinct gular pouch in male (7c) but not female (7d); well-developed wing pouch (7e).

8. BLACK-BEARDED TOMB BAT

Taphozous melanopogon, p. 205
FA 60–63. Medium-sized; chin furred without pouch, often with black "beard" in male (8c); well-developed wing pouch (8d); colour varies from grey-brown to buffy.

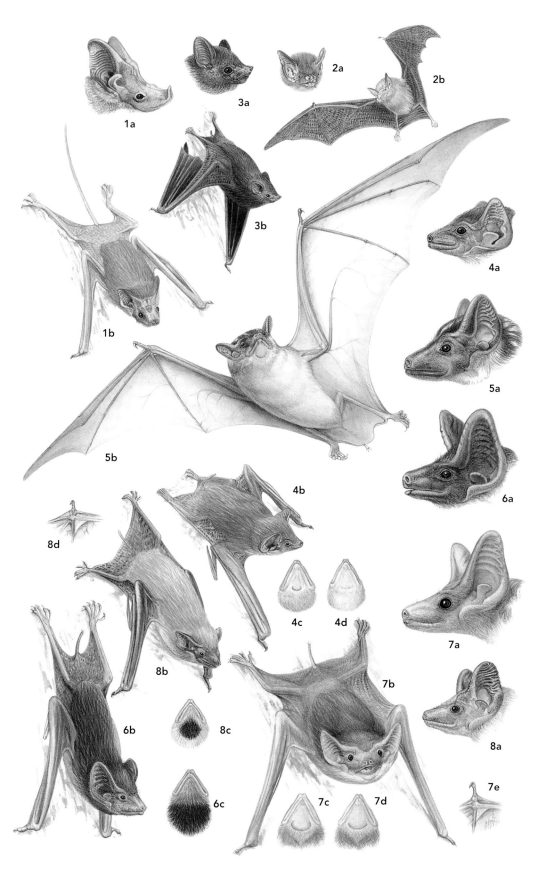

Plate 9. FALSE-VAMPIRES, HOLLOW-FACED BAT AND HORSESHOE BATS

1. LESSER FALSE-VAMPIRE
Megaderma spasma, p. 208
FA 56–63. No tail; large ears are joined on top of head; posterior noseleaf convex on sides, rounded at top; intermediate noseleaf heart-shaped and broad.

5. BIG-EARED HORSESHOE BAT
Rhinolophus macrotis, p. 211
FA 42–47. Large ears; tall rounded lancet; long broad sella narrowing to rounded tip with cup-shaped base; tall connecting process rounded at tip, forming notch.

2. GREATER FALSE-VAMPIRE
Megaderma lyra, p. 207
FA 65–72. Large; no tail; large ears joined on top of head; posterior noseleaf with straight sides and square top; intermediate noseleaf narrow; chin protruding.

6. MARSHALL'S HORSESHOE BAT
Rhinolophus marshalli, p. 212
FA 41–48. Very large ears; short rounded lancet; long sella with broad base; narrow connecting process.

3. MALAYAN SLIT-FACED BAT
Nycteris tragata, p. 207
FA 46–55. Very long tail with T-shaped tip; large separate ears; deep hollow slit in middle of face fringed with flaps of skin like a noseleaf.

7. BOURRET'S HORSESHOE BAT
Rhinolophus paradoxolophus, p. 211
FA 53–57. Enormous ears; short rounded lancet; long, very broad sella expanded into cup-shaped base; narrow connecting process.

4. SIAMESE HORSESHOE BAT
Rhinolophus siamensis, p. 211
FA 38–42. Like *R. macrotis*, but smaller with higher frequency echolocation calls.

Note Diagrams beside each *Rhinolophus* face show profile of noseleaf. See also diagrams of sella in Fig. 33.

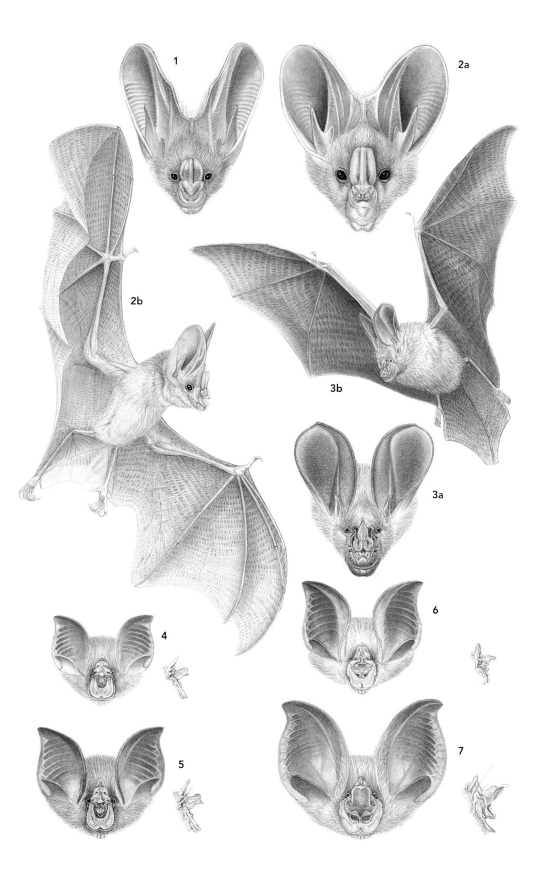

Plate 10. HORSESHOE BATS

1. CONVEX HORSESHOE BAT
Rhinolophus convexus, p. 214
FA 42–43. Small; tall, pointed connecting process; rounded lancet.

2. ACUMINATE HORSESHOE BAT
Rhinolophus acuminatus, p. 213
FA 44–50. Relatively large; triangular, pointed connecting process; short lancet; short fur uniformly dark grey (2a,2b) or orange (2c).

3. LEAST HORSESHOE BAT
Rhinolophus pusillus, p. 213
FA 33–40. Very small; pointed connecting process; broadly pointed lancet; fur colour variable. Refer to text for distinctions from *R. subbadius* and *R. shortridgei* (not illustrated).

4. BLYTH'S HORSESHOE BAT
Rhinolophus lepidus, p. 213
FA 39–43. Small; pointed connecting process, sometimes curved forwards; tall, bluntly pointed lancet; fur varies from grey to orange.

5. CROSLET HORSESHOE BAT
Rhinolophus coelophyllus, p. 212
FA 41–45. Short lancet; thickened lobes enclosing base of connecting process, thickly covered with long hairs; broadly arched connecting process.

6. SHAMEL'S HORSESHOE BAT
Rhinolophus shameli, p. 212
FA 44–49. Similar to *R. coelophyllus*, but larger with lower frequency echolocation call.

7. LESSER WOOLLY HORSESHOE BAT
Rhinolophus sedulus, p. 210
FA 38–45. Lateral lappets at base of sella; long, woolly blackish fur; dark noseleaf; relatively small.

8. GREAT WOOLLY HORSESHOE BAT
Rhinolophus luctus, p. 210
FA 62–76. Largest *Rhinolophus*; lateral lappets at base of sella; long, woolly dark grey fur; dark noseleaf.

9. TREFOIL HORSESHOE BAT
Rhinolophus trifoliatus, p. 210
FA 45–56. Lateral lappets at base of sella; long, woolly pale greyish fur; yellowish noseleaf; pale brown wing membranes with yellow elbows and knees.

Note Diagrams beside each *Rhinolophus* face show profile of noseleaf. See also diagrams of sella in Fig. 33.

48

Plate 11. HORSESHOE BATS

1. INTERMEDIATE HORSESHOE BAT
Rhinolophus affinis, p. 214
FA 48–54. Large; rounded connecting process; sella concave in middle; underparts slightly paler than upperparts.

2. THOMAS'S HORSESHOE BAT
Rhinolophus thomasi, p. 216
FA 42–46. Rounded connecting process; lancet short, stubby and with narrow point in middle; underparts only slightly paler than upperparts; canines only slightly longer than largest premolars.

3. RUFOUS HORSESHOE BAT
Rhinolophus rouxii, p. 216
FA 44–52. Like *R. thomasi*, but averages larger; canines more than 30% longer than upper premolar; wing relatively short and rounded.

4. CHINESE HORSESHOE BAT
Rhinolophus sinicus, p. 216
FA 44–55. Like *R. thomasi*, but averages larger; canines twice as long as upper premolar; wing relatively long and pointed.

5. PENINSULAR HORSESHOE BAT
Rhinolophus robinsoni, p. 217
FA 43–46. Medium-small; rounded connecting process; sella broad at base, narrowing abruptly in middle.

6. INDOCHINESE HORSESHOE BAT
Rhinolophus chaseni, p. 216
FA 43–46. Rounded connecting process; tall, triangular lancet; sella broad at base, narrowing slightly in middle, rounded at tip; underparts only slightly paler than upperparts.

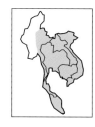

7. LESSER BROWN HORSESHOE BAT
Rhinolophus stheno, p. 215
FA 42–48. Rounded connecting process; tall, triangular lancet; sella narrow, pointed at top; underparts distinctly paler than upperparts.

8. MALAYAN HORSESHOE BAT
Rhinolophus malayanus, p. 215
FA 38–44. Rounded connecting process; tall, triangular lancet; sella broad, squared at top; underparts distinctly paler than upperparts.

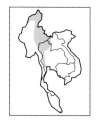

9. DOBSON'S HORSESHOE BAT
Rhinolophus yunanensis, p. 218
FA 51–64. Large; long woolly fur; broadly rounded connecting process; sella broad at base, narrowing abruptly in middle.

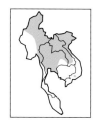

10. PEARSON'S HORSESHOE BAT
Rhinolophus pearsonii, p. 217
FA 49–55. Medium-sized; long woolly fur; broadly rounded connecting process; sella broad at base, narrowing abruptly in middle.

Note Diagrams beside each *Rhinolophus* face show profile of noseleaf. See also diagrams of sella in Fig. 33.

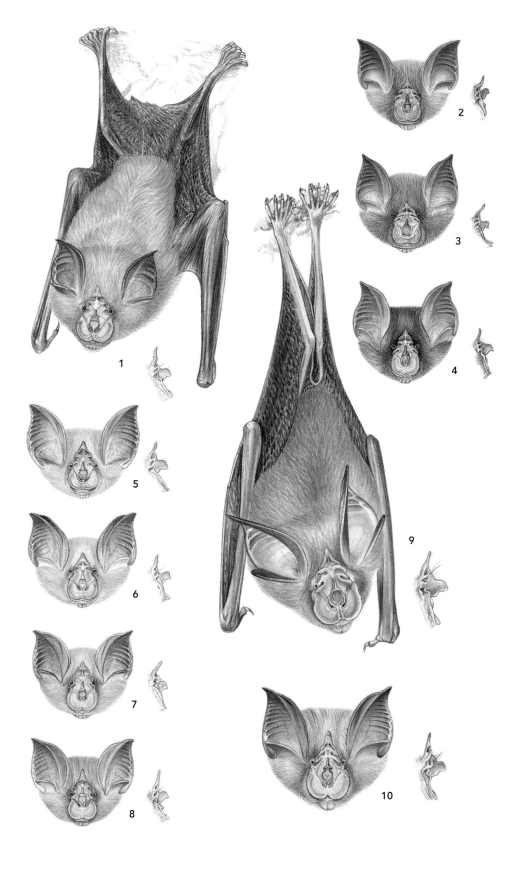

Plate 12. LARGE ROUNDLEAF BATS

1. SHIELD-FACED ROUNDLEAF BAT
Hipposideros lylei, p. 224
FA 73–84. Large; two lateral leaflets; greatly enlarged "shield" behind noseleaf in male (1a); small ridges in female (similar to 3b); posterior noseleaf connected to anterior leaf at sides.

2. SHIELD-NOSED ROUNDLEAF BAT
Hipposideros scutinares, p. 224
FA 78–83. Similar to *H. lylei*, but noseleaf slightly broader; "shield" of male smaller (2a); female with very small shield (2b); lower frequency echolocation calls.

3. PRATT'S ROUNDLEAF BAT
Hipposideros pratti, p. 225
FA 81–89. Similar to *H. lylei*, but averages larger; "shield" of male averages smaller (3a); female with small ridges instead of shield (3b); posterior noseleaf not joined to anterior leaf at sides.

4. GREAT ROUNDLEAF BAT
Hipposideros armiger, p. 224
FA 85–103. Very large; relatively small anterior noseleaf; narrow posterior noseleaf; four lateral leaflets, outer one very narrow; adult males have swollen area behind noseleaf (4a); smaller or lacking in females (4b).

5. PENDLEBURY'S ROUNDLEAF BAT
Hipposideros turpis, p. 224
FA 75–81. Similar to *H. armiger*, but smaller; only three lateral leaflets; males with swollen area behind posterior noseleaf.

6. INTERMEDIATE ROUNDLEAF BAT
Hipposideros larvatus, p. 222
FA 51–67. Medium-sized; three lateral leaflets; posterior noseleaf broader than anterior noseleaf. Includes several superficially similar species – see text.

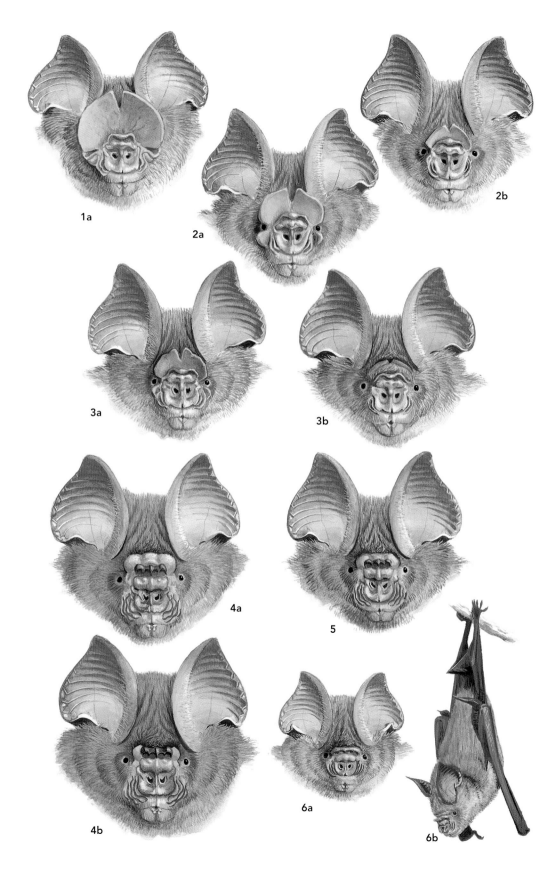

1a   2a   2b

3a   3b

4a   5

4b   6a   6b

Plate 13. LARGE AND MEDIUM ROUNDLEAF BATS

1. BOONSONG'S ROUNDLEAF BAT
Hipposideros lekaguli, p. 223
FA 71–79. Large; three lateral leaflets; posterior noseleaf formed into three backward-facing pockets; intermediate noseleaf with raised triangular ridge in middle.

2. DIADEM ROUNDLEAF BAT
Hipposideros diadema, p. 223
FA 76–87. Large; dark fur with pale patches on shoulders and edges of wings; three or four lateral leaflets; females usually more orange and buff (2b) than males (2a).

3. RIDLEY'S ROUNDLEAF BAT
Hipposideros ridleyi, p. 221
FA 47–51. Large ears; dark fur; very large, dark noseleaf that covers muzzle; enlarged disc on internarial septum that hides nostrils; no lateral leaflets.

4. SMALL-DISC ROUNDLEAF BAT
Hipposideros orbiculus, p. 221
FA 46–49. Similar to *H. ridleyi*, but slightly smaller ears and noseleaf; internarial disc smaller, not completely covering nostrils.

5. ANNAMITE ROUNDLEAF BAT
Hipposideros rotalis, p. 221
FA 45–49. Very large ears; enlarged, partly unpigmented noseleaf that covers muzzle; internarial septum forms large disc that hides nostrils; deep notch in anterior noseleaf; one pair of lateral leaflets.

6. KHAOKHOUAY ROUNDLEAF BAT
Hipposideros khaokhouayensis, p. 222
FA 46–49. Similar to *H. rotalis*, but internarial disc smaller, does not cover nostrils; lacks lateral leaflets.

7. FAWN ROUNDLEAF BAT
Hipposideros cervinus, p. 222
FA 44–52. Two lateral leaflets; intermediate noseleaf narrower than posterior noseleaf; ears relatively narrow and triangular; tail relatively short.

8. CANTOR'S ROUNDLEAF BAT
Hipposideros galeritus, p. 222
FA 45–50. Two lateral leaflets; intermediate noseleaf wider than posterior noseleaf; ears very broad; tail relatively long.

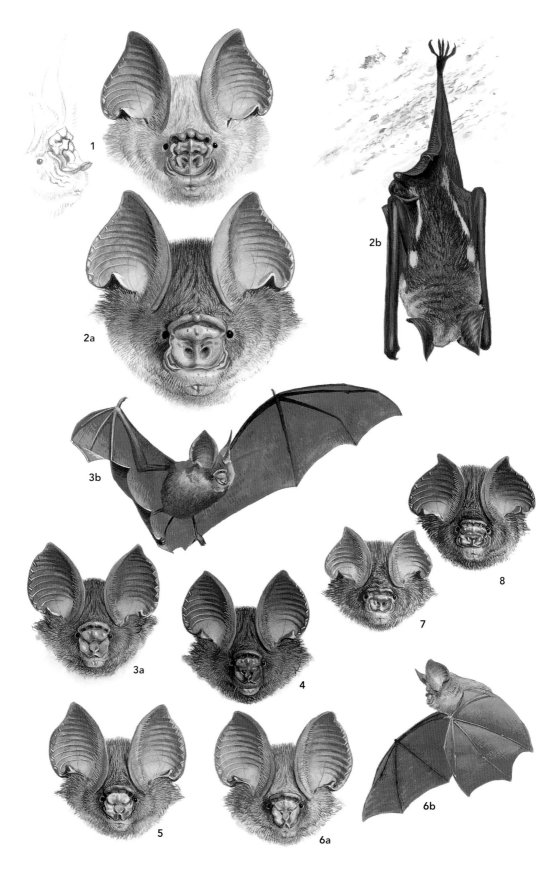

Plate 14. SMALL ROUNDLEAF BATS

1. BICOLOURED ROUNDLEAF BAT
Hipposideros bicolor, p. 218
a) 131-kHz species, b) 142-kHz species
FA 41–48. Fairly large ears; no lateral leaflets; relatively straight-sided internarial septum. 131-kHz species has lower echolocation call; averages longer forearm; paler, less curled noseleaf. See text for distinctions from *H. nequam* (not illustrated).

2. LARGE-EARED ROUNDLEAF BAT
Hipposideros pomona, p. 219
FA 38–43. Similar to *H. bicolor*, but slightly smaller with larger ears. Fur colour varies from brown and white (2a) to all orange (2b). Note that other species are also sometimes orange.

3. DAYAK ROUNDLEAF BAT
Hipposideros dyacorum, p. 220
FA 38–43. No lateral leaflets; dark noseleaf; ears relatively short and triangular; fur on underparts dark.

4. ASHY ROUNDLEAF BAT
Hipposideros cineraceus, p. 220
a) widespread species; b) Malaysian species
FA 33–42. Small; short ears; no lateral leaflets. Widespread species has internarial septum swollen in middle, higher frequency echolocation call. Malaysian species has septum swollen only at base.

5. THAI ROUNDLEAF BAT
Hipposideros halophyllus, p. 220
FA 35–38. Small; no lateral leaflets; internarial septum with two kidney-shaped lobes in centre that are usually darker than rest of noseleaf.

6. LEAST ROUNDLEAF BAT
Hipposideros doriae, p. 221
FA 34–37. Small; dark fur; no lateral leaflets; posterior noseleaf lacks supporting septa.

7. TRIDENT ROUNDLEAF BAT
Aselliscus stoliczkanus, p. 226
FA 39–45. Small; posterior noseleaf raised into three points; triangular pad in middle of noseleaf; two lateral leaflets.

8. ASIAN TAILLESS ROUNDLEAF BAT
Coelops frithii, p. 225
FA 34–44. No tail; ears small and rounded, lacking ridges; anterior noseleaf divided into two lobes; lappets protruding from beneath noseleaf long and narrow. See text for *Paracoelops megalotis* (not illustrated).

9. MALAYSIAN TAILLESS ROUNDLEAF BAT
Coelops robinsoni, p. 225
FA 34–37. Like *C. frithii*, but averages smaller; lappets under noseleaf are broad and rounded.

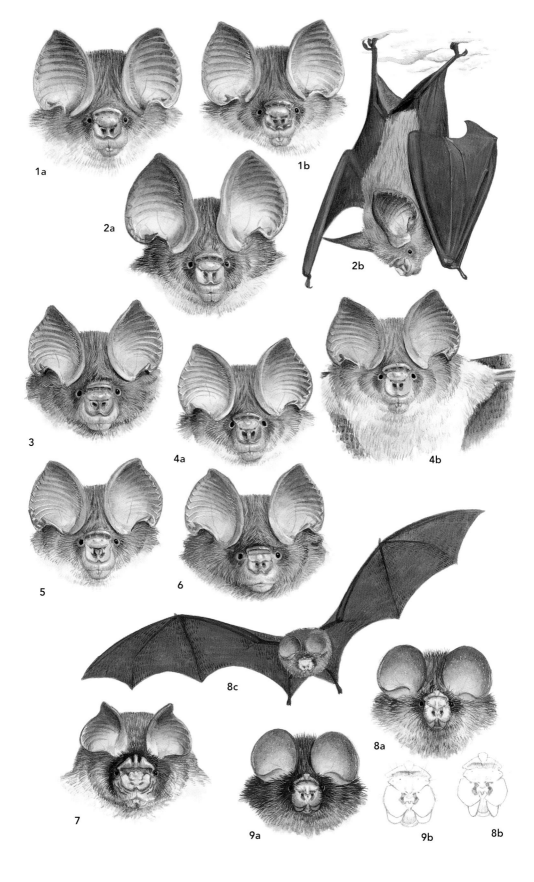

1a 1b 2a 2b 3 4a 4b 5 6 8c 8a 7 9a 9b 8b

Plate 15. MYOTIS

1. HAIRY-FACED MYOTIS
Myotis annectans, p. 232
FA 45–49. Medium-large; feet not enlarged; fur with dark bases and pale tips; often has orange patch on belly; middle upper premolars usually missing.

2. LARGE BROWN MYOTIS
Myotis montivagus, p. 232
FA 41–45. Medium-large; relatively small feet; dark brown fur; middle upper premolars present, but small and intruded in toothrow.

3. ASIAN WHISKERED MYOTIS
Myotis muricola, p. 231
FA 33–37. Medium-small; feet small; wing membrane inserted at bases of toes (3b); middle upper premolar slightly intruded in toothrow; underparts with buffy to pale brown tips to fur.

4. EURASIAN WHISKERED MYOTIS
Myotis mystacinus, p. 231
FA 34–37. Like *M. muricola*, but paler with whitish tips to fur on underparts.

5. PETERS'S MYOTIS
Myotis ater, p. 232
FA 34–39. Like *M. muricola*, but averages larger; fur darker; middle upper premolar smaller, largely intruded in toothrow.

6. THICK-THUMBED MYOTIS
Myotis rosseti, p. 232
FA 29–31. Small; greyish-brown; thickened pad at base of thumb (6b); only two upper and lower premolars.

7. RIDLEY'S MYOTIS
Myotis ridleyi, p. 233
FA 27–32. Small; heavy body; dark grey-brown fur; only two upper and lower premolars.

8. BLACK-AND-ORANGE MYOTIS
Myotis formosus, p. 230
FA 45–52. Moderately large; orange fur; black and orange wings; black rims to ears. See text for distinctions from *M. hermani* (not illustrated).

Note *Myotis* can be distinguished from other bats by ear and tragus shape, with narrow tragus angled slightly forwards and tapering to tip. Most species have three upper and lower premolars on each side.

Plate 16. MYOTIS

1. RICKETT'S MYOTIS
Myotis ricketti, p. 234
FA 53–56. Large; greatly enlarged feet with large claws; wing membrane inserted at ankle; short fur.

5. HORSFIELD'S MYOTIS
Myotis horsfieldii, p. 233
FA 35–38. Feet enlarged; wing membrane inserted on side of foot (5b); middle upper premolars only slightly displaced inwards; long canines; low forehead.

2. INDOCHINESE MYOTIS
Myotis laniger, p. 235
FA 31–36. Small; feet slightly enlarged with membrane inserted on side of foot (2b); long narrow ears; high forehead; moderately small canines. Refer to text for distinctions from *M. annamiticus* (not illustrated).

6. CHINESE MYOTIS
Myotis chinensis, p. 230
FA 65–69. Largest *Myotis*; large ears; well-developed middle premolar.

3. SMALL-TOOTHED MYOTIS
Myotis siligorensis, p. 234
FA 30–35. Small; light brown fur; feet slightly enlarged; high forehead; middle upper premolar not reduced; small canines.

7. SZECHUAN MYOTIS
Myotis altarium, p. 230
FA 43–46. Moderately large; long ears; foot quite long; wing membrane inserted at base of toe; middle premolars small but within toothrow.

4. HASSELT'S MYOTIS
Myotis hasseltii, p. 234
FA 38–43. Feet enlarged; wing membrane inserted at base of foot (4b); middle premolars small, intruded inwards.

Note *Myotis* can be distinguished from other bats by ear and tragus shape, with narrow tragus angled slightly forwards and tapering to tip. Most species have three upper and lower premolars on each side.

Plate 17. PIPISTRELLES

1. JAVAN PIPISTRELLE
Pipistrellus javanicus, p. 237
FA 30–36. Dark brown fur with darker bases; tragus narrow with rounded tip; anterior upper premolar slightly displaced inwards; forehead slightly domed; canine with small secondary cusp; male with medium-length penis.

2. JAPANESE PIPISTRELLE
Pipistrellus abramus, p. 238
FA 29–33. Similar to *P. javanicus*, but fur greyish-brown, male with very long penis.

3. KELAART'S PIPISTRELLE
Pipistrellus ceylonicus, p. 239
FA 33–42. Relatively large; fur varies from grey-brown to red-brown; forehead sloping or slightly domed.

4. NARROW-WINGED BROWN BAT
Philetor brachypterus, p. 241
FA 30–36. Dark brown fur; fifth finger very short; head flattened; ears large and broadly triangular; short tragus; only one upper premolar; complex genitalia.

5. NARROW-WINGED PIPISTRELLE
Pipistrellus stenopterus, p. 239
FA 37–42. Relatively large; fur short, reddish-brown to dark brown; fifth finger short; forehead sloping or domed.

6. COROMANDEL PIPISTRELLE
Pipistrellus coromandra, p. 238
FA 26–34. Fur dark brown to reddish-brown; forehead sloping evenly; canine with distinct secondary cusp.

7. LEAST PIPISTRELLE
Pipistrellus tenuis, p. 238
FA 25–31. Small; fur mid-brown to dark brown; ear relatively short; tragus narrow; skull with narrow rostrum, evenly sloping profile.

8. MOUNT POPA PIPISTRELLE
Pipistrellus paterculus, p. 238
FA 27–34. Fur uniform brown above, sandy brown tips below; tragus relatively short; male with extremely long penis.

9. BIG-EARED PIPISTRELLE
Hypsugo macrotis, p. 241
FA 33–34. Large ears; reddish-brown fur; partially translucent whitish wings; anterior upper premolar very small, displaced inwards; forehead sloping.

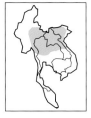

10. CHINESE PIPISTRELLE
Hypsugo pulveratus, p. 241
FA 32–37. Dark fur with pale tips; short narrow tragus; anterior upper premolar moderate size, displaced inwards; forehead swollen.

11. CADORNA'S PIPISTRELLE
Hypsugo cadornae, p. 242
FA 33–37. Reddish-brown fur; broad ears; short broad tragus; anterior upper premolar very small. See text for descriptions of *H. lophurus*, *H. joffrei* and *H. anthonyi* (not illustrated).

12. CHOCOLATE PIPISTRELLE
Falsistrellus affinis, p. 243
FA 36–38. Long, soft dark fur with frosted tips; pale underparts; broad rounded ears; tragus broad, pointed in front; narrow muzzle.

Plate 18. MIXED VESPERTILIONID BATS

1. THICK-THUMBED PIPISTRELLE
Glischropus tylopus, p. 240
FA 29–35. Slightly shaggy fur; pink pad on sole of foot (1b); triangular, pink thickened pad at base of thumb (1c); second upper incisor displaced outwards.

2. GREATER BAMBOO BAT
Tylonycteris robustula, p. 249
FA 26–30. Very flat skull; flattened broad body; rounded grey or pinkish pads on foot (2b) and base of thumb (2c); fur sleek and smooth, dark brown with frosted pale tips; thickened skin at base of ear.

3. LESSER BAMBOO BAT
Tylonycteris pachypus, p. 249
FA 24–28. Like *T. robustula*, but smaller; fur shorter and fluffier, usually more reddish; skin at base of ear thinner.

4. LEAST FALSE-SEROTINE
Hesperoptenus blanfordi, p. 247
FA 24–29. Short forearm, but heavy body; smooth, glossy dark brown fur; thickened dark pad at base of thumb; sloping skull profile making head pointed; second upper incisor displaced inwards.

5. DORIA'S FALSE-SEROTINE
Hesperoptenus doriae, p. 246
FA 38–41. Blackish-brown fur; rounded profile; only one upper premolar; first upper incisor large and conical, second very small, but not displaced inwards.

6. TICKELL'S FALSE-SEROTINE
Hesperoptenus tickelli, p. 247
FA 49–56. Light yellowish-brown fur and wing bones; dark membranes; first upper incisor large and conical; second incisor small, displaced inwards.

7. TOMES'S FALSE-SEROTINE
Hesperoptenus tomesi, p. 247
FA 50–53. Large; dark blackish-brown fur; rounded forehead; first upper incisor large and conical, second incisor small, displaced inwards.

8. DISC-FOOTED BAT
Eudiscopus denticulus, p. 235
FA 35–38. *Myotis*-shaped ears; pale fur; flattened skull; enlarged disc-like pads on hind feet.

9. GREAT EVENING BAT
Ia io, p. 246
FA 71–79. Very large; broad, triangular ears; two upper premolars, anterior very small.

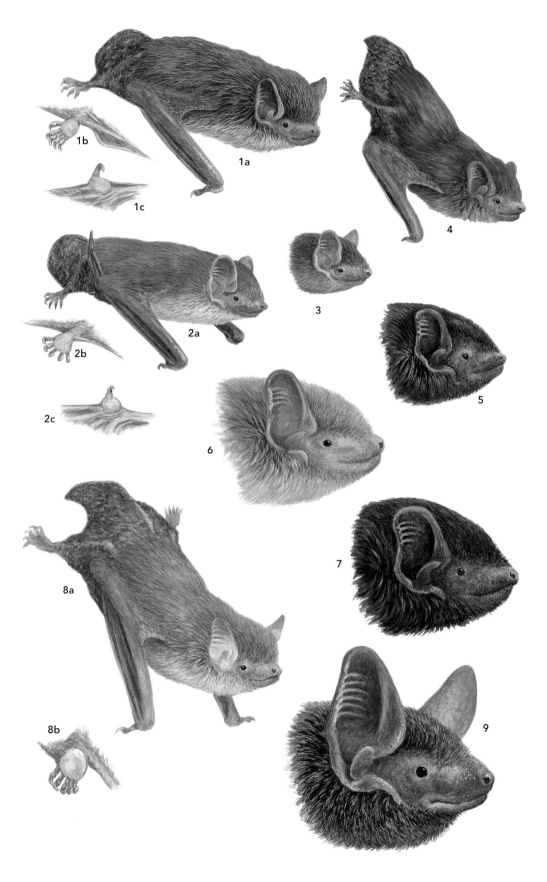

Plate 19. MIXED VESPERTILIONID BATS

1. HARLEQUIN BAT
Scotomanes ornatus, p. 248
FA 54–61. Orange fur with prominent white marks on top of head, shoulders and middle of back; only one upper incisor on each side.

2. EASTERN BARBASTELLE
Barbastella leucomelas, p. 236
FA 38–43. Ears broad, facing forwards, joined at base over forehead.

3. GOLDEN-COLLARED BAT
Thainycteris aureocollaris, p. 244
FA 47–51. Fur with black bases, buff to orange tips; yellowish fur forms collar under chin.

4. BENOM GILDED PIPISTRELLE
Arielulus societatis, p. 244
FA 35–38. Fur black with reddish-orange tips on the back, golden yellow tips on underparts and head; pale rims to ears and tragus; posterior upper molar small.

5. BLACK GILDED PIPISTRELLE
Arielulus circumdatus, p. 244
FA 40–44. Like *A. societatis*, but larger; posterior upper molar larger with distinct second cusp.

6. EURASIAN SEROTINE
Eptesicus serotinus, p. 245
FA 53–57. Large; broad muzzle with sloping profile; ears narrow, somewhat triangular at top; narrow tragus; two upper incisors, but only one upper premolar on each side.

7. EURASIAN NOCTULE
Nyctalus noctula, p. 240
FA 49–58. Uniform brown to dark brown fur; broad ears; short tragus; narrow wings with short fifth finger; two upper incisors on each side.

8. LESSER ASIAN HOUSE BAT
Scotophilus kuhlii, p. 248
FA 45–52. Short, yellowish-brown fur; long narrow tragus bent forwards; only one upper incisor and one upper premolar on each side.

9. GREATER ASIAN HOUSE BAT
Scotophilus heathii, p. 248
FA 57–69. Like *S. kuhli*, but larger with longer forearm; fur varies from yellow-brown to dark orange-brown.

Note See text for identification of *Eptesicus pachyotis* and *E. dimissus* from Myanmar and Thailand.

Plate 20. TUBE-NOSED BATS

1. HUTTON'S TUBE-NOSED BAT

Murina huttoni, p. 251
FA 35–37. Fur orange-brown with dark bases; long ears; both premolars large; upper molars without indentation; lower molars with well-developed posterior section.
M. harrisoni (not illustrated) is similar but with fur uniformly reddish-brown, wing membrane attaches to base of toe instead of end of toe.

2. SCULLY'S TUBE-NOSED BAT

Murina tubinaris, p. 253
FA 28–33. Upperparts greyish-brown, single hairs with four alternating dark-light bands; underparts greyish-white with dark bases; anterior upper premolar small.

3. LESSER TUBE-NOSED BAT

Murina suilla, p. 252
FA 27–32. Upperparts brown to orange-brown with grey bases; underparts greyish-white with darker bases; anterior upper premolar small; canine relatively short.

4. ROUND-EARED TUBE-NOSED BAT

Murina cyclotis, p. 250
Back fur orange to reddish-brown; both premolars large; upper molars with indentation on outer edge; lower molars with reduced posterior section. Malaysian form *M. c. peninsularis* (4b) distinctly larger (FA 34–41) than mainland forms (4a; FA 29–34).

5. BRONZED TUBE-NOSED BAT

Murina aenea, p. 251
FA 34–38. Fur with dark brown bases, tips shiny golden or bronze on upperparts, buff on underparts; dentition similar to that of *M. cyclotis*.

6. ROZENDAAL'S TUBE-NOSED BAT

Murina rozendaali, p. 252
FA 28–32. Upperparts with dark bases, shiny golden tips; underparts white to base; both upper premolars similar in size; canine long.

7. GOLDEN TUBE-NOSED BAT

Murina aurata, p. 253
FA 28–30. Hair of upperparts alternating dark-pale bands with golden tips; underparts with long black bases, white tips; anterior upper premolar small; canines short.

8. GREATER TUBE-NOSED BAT

Murina leucogaster, p. 252
FA ~42. Large; upperparts reddish-brown with dark bases; underparts yellowish-white; anterior upper premolar small, about half height of posterior premolar.

Note Tube-nosed bats and the Hairy-winged Bat (see Pl. 21) are distinguished from other bats by enlarged, tubular nostrils, and somewhat rounded ears with a long, pointed tragus. See text for diagrams of teeth.

Plate 21. BENT-WINGED AND HAIRY-WINGED BATS

1. LARGE BENT-WINGED BAT
Miniopterus magnater, p. 258
FA 47–53. Third finger of
wing with last bone about
three times longer than
second last; short broad
ear with short tragus; fur
typically dark brown to blackish, but sometimes
with reddish patches or all reddish.

2. SMALL BENT-WINGED BAT
Miniopterus pusillus, p. 259
FA 40–43. Like *M. magnater*,
but much smaller; relatively
short, narrow skull.

3. COMMON BENT-WINGED BAT
Miniopterus schreibersii, p. 258
FA 42–46. Like *M. magnater*,
but somewhat smaller.

4. MEDIUM BENT-WINGED BAT
Miniopterus medius, p. 258
FA 38–44. Intermediate in size
between *M. schreibersii* and
M. pusillus, especially skull
measurements.

5. HAIRY-WINGED BAT
Harpiocephalus harpia, p. 253
FA 45–51. Similar to *Murina* but
larger with greatly reduced
third upper molar; fur varies
from bright orange with dark
bases to reddish-brown with
grey bases; extensive hairs on tail membrane
and bases of wings.

Plate 22. KERIVOULA AND PHONISCUS

1. CLEAR-WINGED WOOLLY BAT
Kerivoula pellucida, p. 256
FA 29–32. Light grey-brown to orange-brown fur with paler bases; long narrow ears; translucent pale wings; very high, domed forehead.

2. PAINTED WOOLLY BAT
Kerivoula picta, p. 256
FA 32–39. Light orange fur; wings with distinctive black and orange pattern.

3. KRAU WOOLLY BAT
Kerivoula krauensis, p. 255
FA 29–33. Small; dark blackish-brown fur with narrow, shiny golden tips on back, pale tips below.

4. HARDWICKE'S WOOLLY BAT
Kerivoula hardwickii, p. 255
FA 29–34. Grey-brown to brown fur; fairly large ears; may represent a complex of species (see text). *K. titania* (not illustrated) is similar, but slightly larger.

5. PAPILLOSE WOOLLY BAT
Kerivoula papillosa, p. 254
FA 39–49. Large; domed forehead; orange-brown fur. *K. lenis* (not illustrated) is similar but smaller; *K. kachinensis* (not illustrated) has a much flatter skull (see text).

6. WHITEHEAD'S WOOLLY BAT
Kerivoula whiteheadi, p. 257
FA 28–29. Fur of upperparts light brown with dark bases; underparts whitish; elongate premolars.

7. LEAST WOOLLY BAT
Kerivoula minuta, p. 256
FA 25–29. Very small; long fluffy fur orange-brown with dark bases; small ears; rounded premolars.

8. SMALL WOOLLY BAT
Kerivoula intermedia, p. 256
FA 26–31. Very similar to *K. minuta*, but slightly larger, especially skull and body mass.

9. LESSER GROOVE-TOOTHED BAT
Phoniscus atrox, p. 257
FA 31–35. Fur with four bands of colour ending with golden tips; tragus white; canine long with groove on outside; middle upper premolar rounded.

10. GREATER GROOVE-TOOTHED BAT
Phoniscus jagorii, p. 257
FA 35–42. Similar to *P. atrox*, but larger; middle upper premolar elongate.

Note *Kerivoula* and *Phoniscus* are distinguished from other bats by funnel-shaped ears, long, narrow tragus and three well-developed upper and lower premolars on each side.

1

2a

2b

3

4

5

6

7

8

9

10

Plate 23. FREE-TAILED BATS

1. LA TOUCHE'S FREE-TAILED BAT
Tadarida latouchei, p. 259
FA 53–55. Moderately large; short dense fur; thick protruding tail; ears joined by narrow fold of skin at base.

2. SUNDA FREE-TAILED BAT
Mops mops, p. 260
FA 41–46. Medium-sized; thick dark fur above and below; ears joined by narrow band of skin (2b); only one upper premolar.

3. JOHORE WRINKLE-LIPPED BAT
Chaerephon johorensis, p. 260
FA 44–49. Medium-sized; ears joined by broad band of skin that extends backwards on top of head to form a pocket (3b); underside pale; two upper premolars.

4. ASIAN WRINKLE-LIPPED BAT
Chaerephon plicatus, p. 259
FA 40–50. Moderately small; ears joined on top of head by narrow band of skin at base (4b); underside pale; two upper premolars.

5. WROUGHTON'S FREE-TAILED BAT
Otomops wroughtoni, p. 261
FA 63–67. Large; pale marks on back of neck; ears long, joined for much of length by fold of skin.

6. NAKED BAT
Cheiromeles torquatus, p. 261
FA 74–86. The world's heaviest insectivorous bat; body largely lacking fur; dark grey body skin; thick, protruding tail; ears large, well separated.

Note All free-tailed bats have thick tails that protrude beyond the tail membranes, and narrow wings.

74

Plate 24. PANGOLINS, COLUGOS AND LORISES

1. SUNDA PANGOLIN
Manis javanica, p. 174
HB 400–650. Scaly; front claws 50% longer than hind claws; long tail with 30 or more scales along side; small ears.

4. SUNDA SLOW LORIS
Nycticebus coucang, p. 262
HB 260–300. Large eyes; no tail; colour varies from grey-brown to orange-brown; dark stripe on back branches to connect to ears and eyes.

2. CHINESE PANGOLIN
Manis pentadactyla, p. 174
HB 400–580. Scaly; front claws twice as long as hind claws; conspicuous ear lobes; short tail with <20 scales along side.

5. ASIAN SLOW LORIS
Nycticebus bengalensis, p. 262
HB 300–380. Grey-brown to orange-brown; dark stripe on back ends on back of nape.

3. SUNDA COLUGO
Galeopterus variegatus, p. 191
HB 330–420. Grey (3a) or reddish (3b) with complex pattern of pale and dark marks; extensive gliding membrane encloses tail.

6. PYGMY LORIS
Nycticebus pygmaeus, p. 263
HB 210–290. Small; relatively large ears; usually orange-brown; dorsal stripe varies from narrow and inconspicuous to broad.

Plate 25. PRESBYTIS AND TRACHYPITHECUS LANGURS

1. WHITE-THIGHED LANGUR
Presbytis siamensis, p. 264
HB 430–690. Upperparts
vary from greyish to brown;
tail, feet and hands dark;
pale below; whitish patch
on outer thigh. Infants with
"cruciform" pattern – pale except for dark
stripe up back and across arms.

2. BANDED LANGUR
Presbytis femoralis, p. 263
HB 460–590. Upperparts dark
brown to blackish; underside
pale. Infants "cruciform".
P. f. femoralis (2a) very dark
above, sometimes with
reddish tone; sharply demarcated white areas
on underparts. *P. f. robinsoni* (2b) dark brown to
blackish above; indistinctly greyish below with
white insides of thighs.

3. SUNDAIC SILVERED LANGUR
Trachypithecus cristatus, p. 265
HB 415–540. Fur long, dark
grey above and below with
silvery tips; dark face. Infants
with bright orange fur.

4. ANNAMESE SILVERED LANGUR
Trachypithecus margarita, p. 265
HB 500–600. Fur medium to
dark grey with pale frosting;
contrasting darker feet and
arms; paler underparts;
dark face except for pinkish rings around eyes.
Infants orange.

5. INDOCHINESE SILVERED LANGUR
Trachypithecus germaini, p. 265
HB 490–570. Dark grey above
and below; long pale hairs
around face; dark face. Infants
orange.

Plate 26. TRACHYPITHECUS LANGURS

1. CAPPED LANGUR
Trachypithecus pileatus, p. 268
HB 500–700. Distinct black cap on top of head; dark face; grey above; underparts and facial hairs contrasting pale yellowish (1a) or orange (1b).

2. SHORTRIDGE'S LANGUR
Trachypithecus shortridgei, p. 268
HB 600–750. Silvery grey above and below; dark feet and end of tail; dark face; pale orange-yellow eyes.

3. PHAYRE'S LANGUR
Trachypithecus phayrei, p. 266
HB 520–620. Upperparts uniformly brown to grey, often frosted; underparts vary from same as back to contrastingly paler; face dark with pale skin on lips and around eyes. *T. p. shanicus* (3a) has limited white marks around eyes; *T. p. crepusculus* (3b) usually has complete pale rings.

4. TENASSERIM LANGUR
Trachypithecus barbei, p. 266
HB 500–700. Fur dark greyish-black without pale frosting; grey tail; dark face with pale mouth, pale rings around eyes.

5. DUSKY LANGUR
Trachypithecus obscurus, p. 265
HB 500–700. Body dark grey or greyish-brown with paler crown, legs and tail; dark face with contrasting pale marks around mouth; pale rings around eyes, often incomplete.

Note Infants of all *Trachypithecus* spp. are yellowish to orange, as in Dusky Langur.

1a

1b

3a

3b

2

4

5

Plate 27. FRANCOIS'S LANGUR AND RELATIVES

1. FRANCOIS'S LANGUR
Trachypithecus francoisi, p. 266
HB 470–630. Largely black; white stripe from side of mouth to edges of ears. Infants pale orange; immatures may be black with pale orange head.

2. CAT BA LANGUR
Trachypithecus poliocephalus, p. 267
HB 490–590. Dark brownish-black body; pale yellowish to orange head and shoulders; pale area on rump.

3. INDOCHINESE BLACK LANGUR
Trachypithecus ebenus, p. 268
HB 600–700. All glossy black above and below.

4. DELACOUR'S LANGUR
Trachypithecus delacouri, p. 267
HB 570–730. Largely black body; indistinct white stripe on face; large white patch on thigh and rump.

5. HATINH LANGUR
Trachypithecus hatinhensis, p. 267
HB 500–660. Similar to *T. francoisi*, but white facial stripes continue behind ear to back of head; immatures may have pale forehead, similar to *T. laotum*.

6. LAO LANGUR
Trachypithecus laotum, p. 267
HB 460–530. Like *T. francoisi*, but white forehead.

Note In all species, infants are orange; as they change into adult patterns, the head may have more extensive pale areas than an adult's, and may resemble that of other species.

Plate 28. SNUB-NOSED MONKEY AND DOUCS

1. TONKIN SNUB-NOSED MONKEY
Rhinopithecus avunculus, p. 269
HB 510–620. Flattened face with pale eye-rings, thick pinkish lips; black back; white to brownish-white head and underparts; long, white-tipped tail.

2. GREY-SHANKED DOUC
Pygathrix cinerea, p. 269
HB 610–760. Arms pale grey; legs medium to dark grey; yellow-brown face skin; white on sides of face.

3. RED-SHANKED DOUC
Pygathrix nemaeus, p. 268
HB 610–760. Reddish lower legs; black shoulders, white lower arms; yellow-brown face skin; white on sides of face.

4. BLACK-SHANKED DOUC
Pygathrix nigripes, p. 269
HB 610–760. Black legs; blue-grey facial skin; black on sides of face.

Note All doucs distinguished by white rump and very long white tail with tassel at end. Hybrids have sometimes been reported and may show intermediate features.

Plate 29. MACAQUES

1. RHESUS MACAQUE
Macaca mulatta, p. 272
HB 470–585. Medium build; medium-length tail; rump and upper thigh reddish; hairs on crown directed backwards.

2. LONG-TAILED MACAQUE
Macaca fascicularis, p. 271
HB 450–550. Medium build; long tail; upperparts uniformly grey-brown or reddish-brown; limited overlap in range with *M. mulatta*.

3. ASSAMESE MACAQUE
Macaca assamensis, p. 271
HB 510–735. Thickset, heavy build; medium-length tail; greyish hindquarters; hairs on crown parted in middle.

4. NORTHERN PIG-TAILED MACAQUE
Macaca leonina, p. 270
HB 470–585. Short tail, often held curved back; narrow diagonal red lines on face; brown to golden-brown back; whitish face.

5. SOUTHERN PIG-TAILED MACAQUE
Macaca nemestrina, p. 270
HB 470–585. Short tail, often curled forwards; back and crown are usually dark brown or blackish; body varies from grey-brown to orange-brown.

6. STUMP-TAILED MACAQUE
Macaca arctoides, p. 271
HB 485–635. Very heavy build; very short tail usually held down and not visible; long shaggy fur; facial skin dark pink to bright red.

Note In all macaques, adult males are distinctly larger and heavier than females.

Plate 30. HYLOBATES GIBBONS AND SIAMANG

1. WHITE-HANDED GIBBON
Hylobates lar, p. 273
HB 450–600. Fur of both sexes varies from brown (1a) to blonde (1b) to black (1c); hands and feet contrasting white; white ring around face.

3. PILEATED GIBBON
Hylobates pileatus, p. 274
HB 470–600. Adult male (3b) black with white hands and face; female (3a) greyish-white with black on belly and top of head; young all greyish-white.

2. AGILE GIBBON
Hylobates agilis, p. 274
HB 450–650. Hands same colour as feet; white on forehead does not form complete ring around face. Usually black (2b), but occasionally blonde (2a).

4. SIAMANG, p. 273
Symphalangus syndactylus
HB 750–900. Much larger than other gibbons; all black; both sexes with throat pouch that inflates when calling; very loud, distinctive call.

1a

1b

1c

2a

3a

3b

2b

4

Plate 31. HOOLOCK AND CRESTED GIBBONS

1. BUFF-CHEEKED GIBBON
Nomascus gabriellae, p. 275
HB ~500. Male (1b) largely black with short buff to reddish patches on cheeks that do not reach ears; brownish patch on chest. Female (1a) largely buffy brown to orange-brown; black only on crown; no white on face.

2. SOUTHERN WHITE-CHEEKED GIBBON
Nomascus siki, p. 276
HB ~500. Both sexes similar to *N. leucogenys*, but male (shown) has white cheek patches extending only to lower edges of ears, but touching mouth at bottom; relatively short hair.

3. NORTHERN WHITE-CHEEKED GIBBON
Nomascus leucogenys, p. 276
HB ~500. Male (3b) all black with white patches on cheeks that extend to tops of ears, but do not touch corner of mouth. Female (3a) buffy with black crown, white ring on face.

4. BLACK CRESTED GIBBON
Nomascus concolor, p. 275
HB ~500. Male (4b) all black; female (4a) buffy with black crown, extensive black on underside. Hainan Crested Gibbon, *N. hainanus* (not illustrated), very similar but female lacks black on underparts.

5. HOOLOCK GIBBON
Hoolock hoolock, p. 275
HB 450–650. Male (5b) largely black; white eyebrows separated (as shown) or joined; white whiskers on chin. Female (5a) varies from buffy to brown; darker brown on underparts and cheeks; white eyebrows and thin white line around eyes and face.

Note All crested gibbons (*Nomascus* spp.) have longer hairs in the middle of the head that form a distinct crest.

Plate 32. WILD DOGS

1. GOLDEN JACKAL
Canis aureus, p. 277
HB 600–800. Golden-brown to greyish-brown; dark hairs on back form saddle; pointed ears; tail with dark tip.

3. RACCOON DOG
Nyctereutes procyonoides, p. 278
HB 500–680. Yellowish-brown to grey-brown with extensive black hairs; black mask on face; relatively short tail.

2. RED FOX
Vulpes vulpes, p. 278
HB 550–700. Slender body; pointed face; pointed ears; usually reddish-brown, but sometimes dark brown; tail bushy.

4. DHOLE
Cuon alpinus, p. 279
HB 800–1,050. Large; reddish-brown with pale areas below; long bushy tail mostly or all black; rounded ears with white centres.

Plate 33. BEARS AND RED PANDA

1. RED PANDA
Ailurus fulgens, p. 281
HB 510–630. Reddish fur; white and dark markings on face; long, bushy banded tail.

3. SUN BEAR
Helarctos malayanus, p. 279
HB 1,100–1,400. Short fur; small rounded ears; buffy U- or V-shaped mark on chest; pale muzzle; holds head low.

2. ASIAN BLACK BEAR
Ursus thibetanus, p. 280
HB 1,200–1,500. Large; long shaggy hair; large erect ears; white V on chest; muzzle largely dark.

Plate 34. MARTENS AND BADGERS

1. YELLOW-THROATED MARTEN
Martes flavigula, p. 282
HB 450–650. Long slender body with long dark tail; dark stripe on side of neck bordering yellowish chin, throat and chest. Considerable geographic variation in colour: back varies from pale yellowish-brown with darker head (as shown) to uniformly rich reddish-brown.

2. STONE MARTEN
Martes foina, p. 281
HB 400–540. Brown with reddish, yellowish or grey tinge; throat white or yellowish with variable dark patches; tail relatively short.

3. SMALL-TOOTHED FERRET-BADGER
Melogale moschata, p. 285
HB 330–380. Black and white head pattern; body fur varies from light brown to greyish; medium-length tail with only tip white; white stripe on top of head does not extend down back; small teeth.

4. LARGE-TOOTHED FERRET-BADGER
Melogale personata, p. 284
HB 330–390. Similar to *M. moschata*, but white stripe usually extends down back; tail averages longer with more extensive white tip; typically less black on face; larger teeth.

5. HOG BADGER
Arctonyx collaris, p. 285
HB 550–700. Large; long pig-like snout; dark stripes on face variable in extent, black or dark brown; short tail; body colour varies from greyish to brown.

1

2

3

4

5

Plate 35. WEASELS

1. LEAST WEASEL
Mustela nivalis, p. 283
HB ~200. Small; relatively short tail; brown fur with white underparts.

4. YELLOW-BELLIED WEASEL
Mustela kathiah, p. 284
HB 200–290. Dark brown upperparts; contrasting yellowish or light orange underparts; tail coloured as back; no mask.

2. MALAY WEASEL
Mustela nudipes, p. 283
HB 300–360. Body golden-brown to bright orange; head and tip of tail white; long bushy tail.

5. STRIPE-BACKED WEASEL
Mustela strigidorsa, p. 284
HB 275–325. White stripe down middle of back; body colour dark brown to reddish-brown; pale on throat and centre of belly; bushy tail.

3. SIBERIAN WEASEL
Mustela sibirica, p. 283
HB 250–390. Dark mask on face; body colour highly variable, ranging from golden-brown to reddish to dark brown; underparts similar except for pale chin.

Plate 36. OTTERS

1. EURASIAN OTTER
Lutra lutra, p. 285
HB 550–720. Fur dense with longer, paler guard hairs giving grizzled effect; W-shaped border between hair on face and bare skin on tip of nose; tip of tail rounded in cross-section.

3. HAIRY-NOSED OTTER
Lutra sumatrana, p. 286
HB 500–800. Upperparts including sides of neck dark brown; irregular white patches on chin and throat; tail rounded in cross-section; tip of nose covered with hair.

2. ORIENTAL SMALL-CLAWED OTTER
Aonyx cinerea, p. 287
HB 360–550. Small; dark brown to greyish-brown with pale throat and sides of neck; small claws.

4. SMOOTH OTTER
Lutrogale perspicillata, p. 286
HB 650–750. Pale throat and sides of neck; smooth shiny fur; tail somewhat flattened in cross-section; straight border between bare skin on nose and fur on face.

Plate 37. CIVETS

1. SMALL INDIAN CIVET
Viverricula indica, p. 289
HB 530–640. Relatively slender with short legs; numerous dark spots forming rows along back and sides; tail with 6–9 discrete dark bands, pale tip.

2. MALAY CIVET
Viverra tangalunga, p. 289
HB 610–670. Black stripe down back; tail with about 15 black bands joined on top; black and white markings on throat; many small spots on sides.

3. LARGE-SPOTTED CIVET
Viverra megaspila, p. 288
HB 720–850. Black stripe down back; irregular pattern of large dark spots on sides; tail largely black with incomplete white bands at base; bold black and white throat pattern.

4. LARGE INDIAN CIVET
Viverra zibetha, p. 287
HB 750–850. Black stripe down back does not continue on tail; sides irregularly mottled grey and black; tail with five or six broad black bands separated by complete white bands; bold black and white throat pattern.

Plate 38. PALM CIVETS AND LINSANGS

1. MASKED PALM CIVET
Paguma larvata, p. 290
HB 510–760. Colour highly variable from light brown to dark brown or reddish; no dark spots or stripes; dark mask on face; white cheeks; broad white stripe from forehead to neck in most of region (1a); narrow white stripe in Malaysia (1b) and some northern populations.

2. COMMON PALM CIVET
Paradoxurus hermaphroditus, p. 290
HB 420–500. Colour varies from olive-brown to grey-brown or sometimes reddish; three distinct black stripes on back with extensive black spots on sides sometimes forming additional stripes; dark mask on face with white behind eyes.

3. SMALL-TOOTHED PALM CIVET
Arctogalidia trivirgata, p. 291
HB 440–530. Colour varies from olive-brown to greyish-brown; three dark stripes on back; no spots on sides; long tail; face blackish, usually with thin white stripe on forehead.

4. SPOTTED LINSANG
Prionodon pardicolor, p. 289
HB 350–370. Long and slender with long tail; irregular pattern of black splotches on body that usually do not form dark bands except on neck; tail with eight or nine complete dark bands.

5. BANDED LINSANG
Prionodon linsang, p. 289
HB 350–450. Like *P. pardicolor*, but black splotches form dark bands across back; tail usually with seven complete dark bands.

1a

1b

2

3

4

5

Plate 39. BINTURONG, BANDED CIVETS AND OTTER CIVET

1. BINTURONG
Arctictis binturong, p. 291
HB 650–950. Fur long and shaggy, blackish with pale grey tips especially on head; tail long with thick fur at base; ears round with long tufts of hair at tips.

3. BANDED CIVET
Hemigalus derbyanus, p. 292
HB 450–560. Usually buffy-brown, but sometimes light grey or dark orange; dark brown or black bands across back; no spots on legs; tail banded at base, all dark on distal half.

2. OWSTON'S CIVET
Chrotogale owstoni, p. 292
HB 510–630. Greyish-white to buffy-brown; dark bands across back; small black spots on legs; tail banded at base, all dark on distal half.

4. OTTER CIVET
Cynogale bennettii, p. 292
HB 575–680. Broad muzzle with white lips, very long white whiskers, white spot above eye; short tail; brown to grey-brown body.

Plate 40. MONGOOSES

1. SMALL ASIAN MONGOOSE

Herpestes javanicus, p. 293
HB 320–420. Relatively small, but males much larger than females; fur finely speckled buff and dark brown, often with strong reddish cast, especially on head; long tail.

2. INDIAN GREY MONGOOSE

Herpestes edwardsii, p. 293
HB 370–480. Grizzled grey; long tail; no white stripe on shoulder.

3. SHORT-TAILED MONGOOSE

Herpestes brachyurus, p. 293
HB 380–445. Dark blackish-brown with fine buff or orange speckling; relatively short, tapered tail.

4. CRAB-EATING MONGOOSE

Herpestes urva, p. 294
HB 440–480. Large; long, shaggy brownish to greyish grizzled fur; conspicuous pale stripe on sides of neck; pale chin; relatively short but bushy tail.

Plate 41. LARGE CATS

1. CLOUDED LEOPARD
Neofelis nebulosa, p. 296
HB 650–950. Irregular cloud-like dark splotches on pale coat; long thick tail; largely arboreal.

3. TIGER
Panthera tigris, p. 294
HB 1,700–2,300. Very large; variable pattern of black stripes on orange coat; relatively shorter tail.

2. LEOPARD
Panthera pardus, p. 295
HB 1,050–1,300. Long tail; two colour phases: spotted form (2a) has black rosettes with brown centres on pale coat; black form (2b) is all black with indistinct patterns of black rosettes.

1

2b

2a

3

Plate 42. SMALLER CATS

1. MARBLED CAT
Pardofelis marmorata, p. 296
HB 450–530. Complex marbled pattern of dark splotches and black lines on back; spots on legs; stripes on head; long tail.

2. LEOPARD CAT
Prionailurus bengalensis, p. 297
HB 400–550. Orange to yellowish coat; black spots vary from small (as shown) to large and round to large and irregular; medium-length tail.

3. FLAT-HEADED CAT
Prionailurus planiceps, p. 297
HB 445–505. Greyish-brown body with fine black speckling; often some orange on head; relatively short, unmarked tail; short rounded ears; flat sloping forehead.

4. FISHING CAT
Prionailurus viverrinus, p. 297
HB 720–780. Large; light grey-brown coat; black stripes on head and neck; small spots tend to form rows on flanks and back; relatively short tail.

5. JUNGLE CAT
Felis chaus, p. 297
HB 500–650. Back fur varies from ashy grey to yellowish-brown; a few black marks on legs; tail with dark rings at tip; pointed ears with short tufts.

6. ASIAN GOLDEN CAT
Catopuma temminckii, p. 296
HB 760–840. Back fur usually unmarked, varies from golden to tawny to greyish, rarely all black; narrow black and white stripes on head; rounded ears; relatively short tail with white underside. In N Myanmar, marbled form may occur – see text.

Plate 43. KILLER WHALES, PILOT WHALE, MELON-HEADED WHALE AND RISSO'S DOLPHIN

1. PYGMY KILLER WHALE
Feresa attenuata, p. 299
TL 2.2–2.6m. Dark grey-brown to black back, paler sides; white patches on lips and belly; tall dorsal fin; rounded head; flippers smoothly rounded in front.

2. KILLER WHALE
Orcinus orca, p. 300
TL 6.0–9.5m. Largest dolphin; tall, triangular dorsal fin in male, smaller and more curved in female; black with white mark behind eye, pale saddle on back; rounded flippers.

3. SHORT-FINNED PILOT WHALE
Globicephala macrorhynchus, p. 300
TL 3.0–5.5m. Generally black; bulbous forehead with no beak; low dorsal fin; pale patch on back; curved flippers.

4. FALSE KILLER WHALE
Pseudorca crassidens, p. 300
TL 3.2–4.0m. Conical rounded head; slender body; conspicuous dorsal fin; largely black; flippers with hump on leading edge.

5. RISSO'S DOLPHIN
Grampus griseus, p. 301
TL 3.6–4.0m. Domed forehead with crease in middle; no beak; very prominent dorsal fin; grey body.

6. MELON-HEADED WHALE
Peponocephala electra, p. 299
TL 2.2–2.7m. Relatively small; dark grey to black; domed forehead with no beak; tall, curved dorsal fin; pointed flippers.

Plate 44. STRIPED DOLPHINS

1. FRASER'S DOLPHIN
Lagenodelphis hosei, p. 301
TL 2.3–2.7m. Short beak; dark grey above; broad black stripe on side; dorsal fin slightly curved; relatively small flippers.

2. SPINNER DOLPHIN
Stenella longirostris, p. 302
TL 1.3–2.3m. Long narrow beak; low forehead; tall, triangular dorsal fin; black back forming relatively straight border with grey sides.

3. STRIPED DOLPHIN
Stenella coeruleoalba, p. 302
TL 1.8–2.7m. Long distinct beak; tall, curved dorsal fin; black back; pale grey stripe from eye to below dorsal fin, and along sides; narrow black lines behind eye.

4. PANTROPICAL SPOTTED DOLPHIN
Stenella attenuata, p. 302
TL 2.0–2.5m. Long narrow beak; dark cape, broadest below dorsal fin; thin black line from flippers to mouth; varies from heavily spotted (as shown) to nearly unspotted.

5. LONG-BEAKED COMMON DOLPHIN
Delphinus capensis, p. 301
TL 1.8–2.5m. Long beak; black back forming V below dorsal fin; pale yellow or buff patch in front, grey patch at back forming hourglass pattern.

Plate 45. DUGONG, PORPOISE AND DOLPHINS

1. DUGONG
Dugong dugon, p. 310
TL 2.5–3.5m. Broad rounded head; thick lips; paddle-like flippers; no dorsal fin; generally moves slowly.

2. IRRAWADDY DOLPHIN
Orcaella brevirostris, p. 304
TL 2.0–2.5m. Rounded forehead; no beak; large flippers; small dorsal fin low on back; plain colour varies from light grey to dark blue-grey.

3. FINLESS PORPOISE
Neophocaena phocaenoides, p. 305
TL 1.5–2.0m. Small; rounded forehead; no dorsal fin; small flippers; colour varies from light grey (as shown) to very dark grey.

4. ROUGH-TOOTHED DOLPHIN
Steno bredanensis, p. 303
TL 1.8–2.8m. Forehead slopes into slender beak; dark grey above with pale underparts and lips; irregular white spots on sides; relatively tall dorsal fin.

5. INDO-PACIFIC HUMPBACKED DOLPHIN
Sousa chinensis, p. 303
TL 2.4–2.8m. Long beak; domed forehead; usually has hump on back with short dorsal fin; relatively plain colour varies from dark grey to whitish or pink.

6. INDO-PACIFIC BOTTLENOSE DOLPHIN
Tursiops aduncus, p. 304
TL 2.0–2.6m. Moderate length, thick beak; somewhat bulbous forehead; large dorsal fin; large flippers; relatively plain grey colour. See text for distinctions from Common Bottlenose Dolphin, *T. truncatus* (not illustrated).

Plate 46. BEAKED WHALES AND SMALL SPERM WHALES

1. CUVIER'S BEAKED WHALE
Ziphius cavirostris, p. 306
TL 5.5–7.5m. Sloping forehead; jaw not arched; colour varies from pale brown to dark reddish-brown to slate-grey; small dorsal fin.

2. BLAINVILLE'S BEAKED WHALE
Mesoplodon densirostris, p. 306
TL 4.5–6.0m. Low forehead with distinct beak; arched lower jaw with prominent tooth in adult male; back dark grey with extensive scarring and blotching.

3. GINKGO-TOOTHED BEAKED WHALE
Mesoplodon ginkgodens, p. 307
TL 4.7–5.2m. Prominent beak; arched lower jaw with small lobed tooth in male.

4. PYGMY SPERM WHALE
Kogia breviceps, p. 305
TL 2.7–3.4m. Large blunt forehead; low jaw; crescent gill-like mark behind eye; small dorsal fin behind middle of back; swims sluggishly when on surface.

5. DWARF SPERM WHALE
Kogia sima, p. 306
TL 2.1–2.7m. Similar to *K. breviceps* but averages smaller; forehead more pointed; dorsal fin taller, usually slightly further forwards.

1

2

3

4

5

Plate 47. LARGE WHALES

1. GREAT SPERM WHALE
Physeter macrocephalus, p. 305
TL 8–12m. Large head, square forehead; wrinkled back with low, stepped dorsal fin; broad square-ended tail raised on dive, dark underneath; blow angled forwards and to left.

2. HUMPBACK WHALE
Megaptera novaeangliae, p. 309
TL 11–13m. Large flippers with white and black markings; low, stepped dorsal fin; broad notched tail visible when dives, largely white below.

3. SEI WHALE *Balaenoptera borealis*, p. 308
TL 12–14m. Dark grey with white scar marks; dorsal fin visible at same time as blow; one ridge on top of head.

4. BRYDE'S WHALE *Balaenoptera edeni*, p. 308
TL 10–12m. Dark grey with white scar marks; dorsal fin visible at same time as blow; three prominent ridges on top of head.

5. FIN WHALE *Balaenoptera physalus*, p. 308
TL 18–20m. Very large; dark grey to blackish back; fin visible shortly after blow; lower lip and baleen white on right side of head, dark on left.

6. BLUE WHALE *Balaenoptera musculus*, p. 307
TL 22–24m. Largest whale; mottled bluish-grey back pattern; broad rounded head; small fin rarely visible until whale dives.

7. MINKE WHALE *Balaenoptera acutorostrata*, p. 309
TL 7–8m. Smallest rorqual; narrow pointed head; white marks on flippers; blow is relatively inconspicuous.

Plate 48. ELEPHANT AND RHINOCEROSES

1. ASIAN ELEPHANT
Elephas maximus, p. 311
SH 1,500–3,000. Very large;
distinctive shape with long
trunk; moderately large ears;
adult males with large tusks.

3. LESSER ONE-HORNED RHINOCEROS
Rhinoceros sondaicus, p. 313
SH 1,600–1,800. Large; three
folds of skin across back;
horizontal fold of skin below
rump; only one horn, which is
moderate size in male, small in female.

2. ASIAN TWO-HORNED RHINOCEROS
Dicerorhinus sumatrensis,
p. 313
SH 1,200–1,300. Large; only
one fold of skin crosses back;
two horns, but rear horn is
small and often inconspicuous.

Plate 49. TAPIR AND PIGS

1. ASIAN TAPIR
Tapirus indicus, p. 312
SH 900–1,050. Elongate nose; short tail. Adult with distinctive black and white body pattern (1a). Young initially with dark body and horizontal white stripes; gradually acquires adult pattern as young grow older (1b).

2. BEARDED PIG
Sus barbatus, p. 315
SH 700–900. Elongate snout with flat tip; prominent bristles on top of snout, under chin and on cheeks, longer and more conspicuous in male (2a) than female (2b). Averages larger than *S. scrofa*; colour varies from blackish to reddish-brown to grey, depending in part on mud wallow. Babies with brown and beige stripes (2c).

3. EURASIAN WILD PIG
Sus scrofa, p. 314
SH 600–800. Elongate snout with flat tip; colour varies from blackish to reddish – may be affected by mud colour; lacks large bristles on snout.
Widespread form (3a) has well-developed mane. *S. s. vittatus* from Peninsular Malaysia (3b) tends to have shorter mane; sparser, whitish fur; white band of fur on muzzle. Babies have brown and beige stripes (3c).

1a
1b
2a
2b
2c
3a
3b
3c

Plate 50. MOUSEDEER AND SMALL MUNTJACS

1. LESSER MOUSEDEER
Tragulus kanchil, p. 315
SH 200–230. Very small; fur relatively uniformly coloured, reddish-brown finely speckled with black; brown and white markings on throat appear as one white line in profile.

2. SILVER-BACKED MOUSEDEER
Tragulus versicolor, p. 317
SH ~250. Small; back and flanks silvery grey speckled with dark; head and shoulders orange-brown; throat markings usually show one white line in profile.

3. GREATER MOUSEDEER
Tragulus napu, p. 316
SH 300–350. Larger; back fur mottled orange, greyish and blackish; dark brown and white throat markings usually show two white lines in profile.

4. LEAF MUNTJAC
Muntiacus putaoensis, p. 322
SH ~400. Small; reddish; male with tiny antlers on short pedicels, often hidden by fur.

5. ANNAMITE MUNTJAC
Muntiacus truongsonensis, p. 321
SH ~400. Small; dark fur with black legs; head with yellowish and black markings; male with tiny antlers on short pedicels, often hidden by fur. Distinctions from Roosevelt's Muntjac, *M. rooseveltorum*, and Puhoat Muntjac, *M. puhoatensis* (not illustrated) uncertain; range map includes all three.

6. GONGSHAN MUNTJAC
Muntiacus gongshanensis, p. 322
SH 500–550. Medium-sized; body mid- to dark brown; legs, belly, top of tail black; contrasting white undertail and insides of legs; head pale brown with dark marks on pedicels; antlers relatively short.

7. FEA'S MUNTJAC
Muntiacus feae, p. 322
SH 500–550. Medium-sized; dark brown sides, speckled with yellow; belly usually similar colour to back or paler, but may appear dark in shadow; legs and top of tail dark; yellowish top of head with black stripes on pedicels.

8. RED MUNTJAC
Muntiacus muntjak, p. 320
SH 500–550. Medium-sized; fur varies from reddish-brown to reddish-yellow; tail coloured as back; male (8a) with long pedicels, short antlers; head colour as back, with dark stripes on pedicels and forehead. Female (8b) lacks pedicels and antlers (as in other muntjacs). Fawn (8c) lightly spotted.

Note Only male muntjacs have pedicels and antlers.

Plate 51. LARGE-ANTLERED MUNTAC, TUFTED DEER, MUSK-DEER AND HOG DEER

1. LARGE-ANTLERED MUNTJAC

Muntiacus vuquangensis, p. 322
SH 650–700. Larger than other muntjacs; fur colour yellowish-brown to grey-brown; dark lines on forehead; male (1a) with large antlers distinctly forked, stout, moderately long pedicels; female (1b) lacks antlers or pedicels.

2. TUFTED DEER

Elaphodus cephalophus, p. 320
SH 500–700. Coarse, slightly shaggy fur, dark brown on body, greyer on neck; black legs; tuft of hair on top of head; male with small antlers often hidden by tuft; white marks at base of ear.

3. BLACK MUSK-DEER

Moschus fuscus, p. 318
SH ~600. No antlers; male with long protruding upper canines; long hind legs make rump higher than shoulders; fur dark brown to blackish above and below; ears dark.

4. FOREST MUSK-DEER

Moschus berezovskii, p. 317
SH 500–600. Similar to *M. fuscus*, but fur speckled brown with underside paler than back; long white stripes in middle and sides of throat; ears brown at bases, white in middle, black at tip.

5. HOG DEER

Axis porcinus, p. 320
SH 650–720. Male (5a) like small version of Sambar, *Rusa cervicolor*; fur light brown to greyish-brown; tail same colour as back above, white below; antlers slender with three tines; adult female (5b) often retains some spots; young (5c) extensively spotted.

Plate 52. LARGE DEER

1. SIKA
Cervus nippon, p. 319
SH 650–1,100. Antlers of male with five tines (1a); female lacks antlers (1b); coat varies from very dark in winter (1a) to pale brown in summer (1b); belly usually paler; young (1c) heavily spotted; adults retain some to many white spots; small white patch on rump around base of tail.

2. SCHOMBURGK'S DEER
Rucervus schomburgki, p. 319
SH 1,050. Uniformly brown fur, slightly redder legs; antlers of male (2a) with numerous long tines; female (2b) uniformly brown. Possibly Extinct.

3. ELD'S DEER
Rucervus eldii, p. 319
SH 1,200–1,300. Brown above, white belly; antlers of male (3a) with prominent brow tine that forms continuous curve with main branch, several small tines at tip of main branch; tail brown above; female (3b) paler than *Rusa unicolor*.

4. SAMBAR
Rusa unicolor, p. 318
SH 1,400–1,600. Large; dark brown or greyish-brown above, dark below; tail black above, white below; antlers of adult male (4a) usually with only three tines; female (4b) usually darker than females of other deer; young (4c) may be lightly spotted.

1a

1b

1c

2b

2a

3b

3a

4a

4b

4c

Plate 53. WILD CATTLE AND BUFFALO

1. GAUR
Bos frontalis, p. 324
SH 1,700–1,850. Adult male (1b) very muscular; high ridge of muscles on back; hollow area on forehead between horns; body black; lower legs greyish-white or yellowish. Adult female (1b) smaller and less muscular; often browner. Newborn calf (1c) yellowish in some populations, brown in others.

2. BANTENG
Bos javanicus, p. 323
SH 1,500–1,700. Adult male (2a) black with white legs and white rump; narrow curved horns. Adult female (2b) brown with white legs and white rump; horns closer together, more upright.

3. KOUPREY
Bos sauveli, p. 325
SH 1,700–1,900. Adult male (3a) with very large dewlap; horns curved, tips often split; dark area between horns; rump dark. Adult female (3b) grey; horns lyre-shaped. Possibly Extinct.

4. WATER BUFFALO
Bubalus bubalis, p. 325
SH 1,600–1,900. Adult (4a) with long horns sticking out to sides, slightly larger in male than female; uniformly grey; pale marks on neck. Calf (4b) grey. Wild animals more muscular and much more wary than domestic ones.

Plate 54. TAKIN, SHEEP AND SAOLA

1. TAKIN
Budorcas taxicolor, p. 325
SH 700–1,400. Distinctive head
shape; thick legs. Adult male
(1a) with thick short horns
curved backwards; fur thick
and woolly; colour varies from
greyish-black to dark brown to yellowish-brown.
Adult female (1b) usually greyer; horns smaller
and straighter. Young (1c) greyish, often with
dark line down back.

3. SAOLA
Pseudoryx nghetinhensis, p. 325
SH 800–900. Slender; long,
smooth curved horns in adults
(short and straighter in young);
black and white marks on face,
feet and rump.

2. BLUE SHEEP
Pseudois nayaur, p. 326
SH 800–900. Light bluish-grey,
sometimes with browner tinge.
Male (2a) with large curved
horns; black marks on belly and
flanks. Female (2b) with shorter,
straighter horns; fewer black marks.

1a

1c

1b

2b

2a

3

Plate 55. SEROWS AND GORALS

1. SOUTHERN SEROW
Capricornis sumatraensis, p. 326
SH 850–940. Short body; long legs; body mainly black with black legs; adults with long mane on back of neck, varies from all reddish to dirty white to all black.

2. CHINESE SEROW
Capricornis milneedwardsi, p. 326
SH 850–940. Similar to *C. sumatraensis* but fur with extensive white bases, giving overall greyish colour; lower legs usually contrasting reddish or whitish; mane dirty white (2a) or dark (2b).

3. RED SEROW
Capricornis rubidus, p. 327
SH 850–950. Similar shape to other *Capricornis*; fur reddish with white on chin and belly; short reddish mane; black line down back.

4. CHINESE GORAL
Naemorhedus griseus, p. 327
SH 500–700. Smaller and more slender than *Capricornis*; no mane; short greyish-brown to brown fur; short curved horns; thin dark line on back.

5. RED GORAL
Naemorhedus baileyi, p. 327
SH 550–600. Similar to *N. griseus*, but body and legs reddish-brown; thin dark line on back.

Plate 56. GIANT AND *CALLOSCIURUS* SQUIRRELS

1. BLACK GIANT SQUIRREL
Ratufa bicolor, p. 330
HB 370–405. Very large with long tail; upperparts and tail black or very dark brown; underparts vary from buff to light orange; cheeks white with thin black moustache.

2. CREAM-COLOURED GIANT SQUIRREL
Ratufa affinis, p. 330
HB 310–380. Very large; long tail; fur varies from uniformly light buff to orange-brown above with paler underparts.

3. PREVOST'S SQUIRREL
Callosciurus prevostii, p. 331
HB 200–270. Medium to large; distinctive pattern of black upperparts, white sides, orange underparts.

4. PLANTAIN SQUIRREL
Callosciurus notatus, p. 331
HB 175–225. Brownish agouti above; orange belly; black and buff stripes on sides; usually has reddish tip to tail.

5. SUNDA BLACK-BANDED SQUIRREL
Callosciurus nigrovittatus, p. 331
HB 170–240. Brownish agouti above; grey belly; black and buff stripes on sides; tail grey with no red tip; sides of head and chin both orange-brown.

6. IRRAWADDY SQUIRREL
Callosciurus pygerythrus, p. 331
HB 170–200. Upperparts agouti with grey or brown tinge; often has pale patch on legs, as shown; no black or buff bands on flanks; underparts vary from orange to buff to grey (see text).

7. PHAYRE'S SQUIRREL
Callosciurus phayrei, p. 332
HB 210–250. Upperparts greyish to brownish agouti; tip of tail black; underparts buff to orange; black stripe on flank.

Plate 57. *CALLOSCIURUS* SQUIRRELS

1. GREY-BELLIED SQUIRREL
Callosciurus caniceps, p. 334
HB 210–240. Geographic and seasonal variation in colour; legs and feet always greyish; belly usually grey though sometimes with reddish sides.

a, b) *C. c. caniceps* (mainland part of range). Back yellowish-brown to bright red-brown in dry season; grey in wet season; tail tip black.
c) *C. c. bimaculatus* (peninsular Myanmar and Thailand N of 7°N). Upperparts mostly grey with some red patches; flanks reddish; tail tip black.
d) *C. c. concolor* (Peninsular Malaysia). Back greyish agouti with golden tinge; grey flanks and belly; tail tip not black.

2. INORNATE SQUIRREL
Callosciurus inornatus, p. 334
HB 220–230. Upperparts grey and brown agouti; underside grey; tail relatively plain with little or no banding, tip usually not dark. Does not overlap in range with *C. caniceps*.

3. PALLAS'S SQUIRREL
Callosciurus erythraeus, p. 332
HB 200–260. Varies in colour; most forms have upperparts agouti with grey or brown tinge; reddish on underparts. Some major variations:

a, b) *C. e. sladeni* (C Myanmar). Highly variable population, with some individuals largely rufous; some very pale grey with yellowish feet and underparts; some closely resembling typical *C. e. erythraeus*.
c) *C. e. atrodorsalis* (W Thailand and S Myanmar). Lower back with broad black stripe.
d) *C. e. erythraeus* group (most of range). Upperparts, feet and tail agouti, variably tinged with reddish; belly reddish except for agouti stripe up middle.
e) *C. e. flavimanus* (S Vietnam, S Laos and Cambodia). Upperparts greyish agouti; feet pale, usually yellow-orange; underparts vary from cream to bright red-brown.

4. STRIPE-BELLIED SQUIRREL
Callosciurus quinquestriatus, p. 334
HB 210–240. Upperparts agouti; belly white with three black stripes, one on each side and one up middle.

Plate 58. VARIABLE SQUIRREL

1. VARIABLE SQUIRREL
Callosciurus finlaysonii, p. 333
HB 210–220. Extreme
geographic variation in colour
pattern; no single character
defining species. In some areas
more than one colour phase
exists. Colours may also vary seasonally. Some of
the major colour variations are illustrated here, but
additional combinations exist, with intermediates
where populations meet (see text).

a) *C. f. sinistralis* (NW Thailand). Greyish upperparts, often with reddish tinge; reddish underparts
and sides of head; red tail with white base.

b, c) *C. f. menamicus* (N Thailand and N Laos).
Dark phase: dark reddish-brown; slightly paler
below; slightly darker at base of tail. Pale phase:
reddish-orange back, belly and tail; greyish agouti
on sides and legs.

d) *C. f. finlaysoni* (Si Chang Island and Thailand).
Largely white with yellow or grey tinge.

e, f) *C. f. bocourti* (E and C Thailand). Dark phase:
dark grey to black above, including tail; white
below with white head. Pale phase: grey agouti
above; white head, underparts and tail.

g) *C. f. floweri* (SC Thailand). Brown-grey agouti
above; white below; often has reddish around
head and tail; white marks around eye.

h) *C. f. cinnamomeus* (SE Thailand and SW
Cambodia). Largely orange-brown, darker in
middle of back; often with small patches of
greyish agouti on legs and face.

i) *C. f. subssp* (C Laos). Glossy black with large
patches of dark red.

j) *C. f. folletti* (Phai Island and Thailand). Greyish-
white to beige; pale buffy underparts; tail pale,
often with black tip.

k) *C. f. boonsongi* (NE Thailand). Black fur with
white rims to ears.

l) *C. f. harmandi* (Phu Quoc and Vietnam).
Upperparts vary from dark reddish-brown to pale
grey-brown; pale orange below; grey tail.

Plate 59. STRIPED AND *SUNDASCIURUS* SQUIRRELS

1. WESTERN STRIPED SQUIRREL
Tamiops mcclellandii, p. 335
HB 110–125. Small; white tufts on tips of ears; dark stripe down middle of back with two pale stripes and two dark stripes on each side; outer pale stripe typically wider and paler than inner stripe, contiguous with cheek stripe; outer dark stripes vary from black to brown.

2. CAMBODIAN STRIPED SQUIRREL
Tamiops rodolphii, p. 335
HB 105–125. Similar to *T. mcclellandii*, but all four pale stripes typically similar in width; inner pair often tinged yellow-orange; central black stripe with thin brown line up middle.

3. SWINHOE'S STRIPED SQUIRREL
Tamiops swinhoei, p. 335
HB 120–155. Similar to *T. mcclellandii* but inner pale stripes dull, similar in colour to head; dark stripes vary from black to dark brown; outer pale stripes do not connect to face stripes; belly hairs grey.

4. EASTERN STRIPED SQUIRREL
Tamiops maritimus, p. 336
HB 100–145. Similar to *T. swinhoei*, but dark stripes generally less conspicuous; belly hairs grey with whiter tips.

5. INDOCHINESE GROUND SQUIRREL
Menetes berdmorei, p. 338
HB 180–210. Medium-sized with moderate-length tail; buff and dark stripes on sides; typically pale stripe above and below broad dark stripe; sometimes additional dark stripe above; lower pale stripe may be indistinct.

6. LOW'S SQUIRREL
Sundasciurus lowii, p. 336
HB 130–150. Dark brown to reddish-brown upperparts; pale eye-ring; relatively short bushy tail; belly fur uniformly white or buff.

7. SLENDER SQUIRREL
Sundasciurus tenuis, p. 336
HB 115–155. Olive-brown upperparts; buff marks around eye and on nose; long slender tail; belly fur white or buff with grey bases.

8. HORSE-TAILED SQUIRREL
Sundasciurus hippurus, p. 336
HB 210–290. Bushy black tail; reddish-brown upperparts; contrasting grey head and thighs; reddish-orange underparts.

Plate 60. LONG-NOSED AND GROUND SQUIRRELS

1. ORANGE-BELLIED SQUIRREL
Dremomys lokriah, p. 338
HB 170–200. Upperparts greyish to brownish agouti; underparts mixture of orange, orange-buff and grey; buff spot behind ear; some populations have dark line down middle of back; muzzle often less pointed than that of *D. pernyi*.

2. PERNY'S LONG-NOSED SQUIRREL
Dremomys pernyi, p. 338
HB 180–210. Upperparts brownish agouti; orange spot behind ear; greyish underparts; elongate muzzle; often reddish around base of tail.

3. RED-CHEEKED SQUIRREL
Dremomys rufigenis, p. 337
HB 170–210. Reddish cheeks, face and underside of tail; brownish agouti above; belly fur with grey bases, white tips.

4. RED-THROATED SQUIRREL
Dremomys gularis, p. 337
HB ~220. Like *D. rufigenis*, but throat also red; underparts darker greyish.

5. RED-HIPPED SQUIRREL
Dremomys pyrrhomerus, p. 337
HB ~215. Like *D. rufigenis*, but hips and thighs reddish-orange; muzzle averages slightly more elongate.

6. THREE-STRIPED GROUND SQUIRREL
Lariscus insignis, p. 338
HB 170–230. Upperparts dark brown to reddish-brown; three black stripes on back; underparts white, sometimes with buff tinge.

7. SHREW-FACED GROUND SQUIRREL
Rhinosciurus laticaudatus, p. 339
HB 180–210. Elongate muzzle; upperparts dark reddish agouti with no stripes; tail relatively short, often grizzled grey; underparts buffy white.

Plate 61. GIANT FLYING SQUIRRELS

1. RED GIANT FLYING SQUIRREL

Petaurista petaurista, p. 340
HB 400–520. All forms have distinct black tip to tail.
a) *P. p. taylori* (S Myanmar, W Thailand). Dark reddish-brown with light speckles on head and back.
b) *P. p. melanotus* (Malaysia). Bright orange-brown body; black feet and eye-ring. c) *P. p. candidula* (N Thailand, Myanmar). Reddish or orange-brown with extensive white or grey frosting on back and head; greyish tail.

2. INDIAN GIANT FLYING SQUIRREL

Petaurista philippensis, p. 341
HB 400–490. Variable in colour; tail usually all dark.
a) *P. p. annamensis* (Vietnam). Dark brown to dark red with extensive pale frosting; tail brownish-black to glossy black. b) *P. p. lylei* (Thailand, E Myanmar). Upperparts dark grey-brown with extensive grey frosting; tail dark brown; underside buff. c) *P. p. cineraceus* (W Myanmar). Upperparts and tail dark grey with extensive frosting; tail sometimes has a darker tip; underside is greyish-white.

3. YUNNAN GIANT FLYING SQUIRREL

Petaurista yunanensis, p. 341
HB 400–500. Upperparts dull reddish-brown; back hairs lightly frosted with extensive dull grey tips; tail dark brown to black.

4. CHINDWIN GIANT FLYING SQUIRREL

Petaurista sybilla, p. 341
HB 350–400. Smaller than other *Petaurista*. Largely orange-brown, mottled with dark grey and buff on back; feet and tail without black.

Plate 62. LARGE AND MEDIUM FLYING SQUIRRELS

1. LESSER GIANT FLYING SQUIRREL
Petaurista elegans, p. 341
HB 338–365. a) *P. e. punctata*
(Malay Peninsula). Upperparts
reddish mixed with black;
extensive large white spots on
back; tail black; underside buff. b) *P. e. marica*
(rest of mainland range).

2. BLACK FLYING SQUIRREL
Aeromys tephromelas, p. 342
HB 355–426. Large; upperparts
and head dark brownish-black;
underparts sparsely haired
dark grey-brown.

3. SMOKY FLYING SQUIRREL
Pteromyscus pulverulentus,
p. 342
HB 220–290. Medium-large;
upperparts smoky brownish-
grey with fine white frosting;
white below with grey tinge;
pale grey on cheeks; tail narrow, flattened.

4. HAIRY-FOOTED FLYING SQUIRREL
Belomys pearsonii, p. 342
HB 190–200. Medium;
upperparts with dark bases,
mottled grey and red tips;
underparts creamy-white; tail
reddish-brown, rounded above, flattened below;
tufts of hair behind ear.

5. HORSFIELD'S FLYING SQUIRREL
Iomys horsfieldi, p. 343
HB 165–230. Medium;
upperparts grey-brown to
red-brown with pale tips;
orange edge to gliding
membrane; tail rounded, orange-brown;
underside white, sometimes with orange tinge.

Plate 63. SMALL FLYING SQUIRRELS

1. PHAYRE'S FLYING SQUIRREL
Hylopetes phayrei, p. 345
HB 145–195. Back dark with grey-brown to buffy-brown tips; tail varies from buffy-brown to dark brown, rounded on top, flat below; underparts creamy-white; face greyish-white.

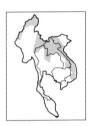

2. PARTICOLOURED FLYING SQUIRREL
Hylopetes alboniger, p. 345
HB 175–225. Similar to *H. phayrei*, but larger; colour varies from extensively white-frosted (as shown) to darker, like *H. phayrei* illustration.

3. GREY-CHEEKED FLYING SQUIRREL
Hylopetes platyurus, p. 344
HB 115–135. Medium-small; upperparts black with red tips; tail flat with narrow base, has white patch at base; underparts and cheeks greyish-white.

4. RED-CHEEKED FLYING SQUIRREL
Hylopetes spadiceus, p. 344
HB 155–185. Upperparts black with red tips; tail flat with narrow base, has orange patch at base; underparts and cheeks buffy white with reddish tinge.

5. WHISKERED FLYING SQUIRREL
Petinomys genibarbis, p. 343
HB 160–180. Back dark grey with red-brown tips; lower back contrasting pinkish-brown; tuft of whiskers on cheek behind eye.

6. TEMMINCK'S FLYING SQUIRREL
Petinomys setosus, p. 343
HB 105–125. Small; upperparts black with whitish tips to hairs; underparts white with grey bases; dark ring around eye; tail relatively flat, dark with grey base; tail with white tip in northern populations.

7. VORDERMANN'S FLYING SQUIRREL
Petinomys vordermanni, p. 344
HB 95–120. Small; upperparts dark with reddish tips; reddish tail and crown; buffy underparts; buffy cheeks with dark eye-ring; tail flat below, slightly rounded above.

8. MALAYSIAN PYGMY FLYING SQUIRREL
Petaurillus kinlochii, p. 345
HB 80–90. Very small; upperparts dark grey with buff streaks; underparts white with grey bases; tail flat and feathery with white tip.

Plate 64. TYPICAL RATS

1. HOUSE RAT
Rattus rattus, p. 350
HB 105–215. Underparts
buffy-brown with grey bases,
sometimes creamy white; long
guard hairs on lower back;
large, well-striated footpads;
dark tail; climbs well.

2. MALAYSIAN WOOD RAT
Rattus tiomanicus, p. 351
HB 140–190. Underparts pure
white or creamy white; upperparts sleek with relatively short
guard hairs; well-developed
footpads for climbing; dark tail.

3. LESSER RICEFIELD RAT
Rattus losea, p. 353
HB 120–180. Medium-small;
narrow feet with small
unridged footpads; tail shorter
than HB; fur varies from grey-
brown to red-brown.

4. PACIFIC RAT
Rattus exulans, p. 352
HB 90–140. Small; coarse
spiny fur; greyish-brown above;
white with grey bases below;
all-dark tail.

5. RICEFIELD RAT
Rattus argentiventer, p. 351
HB 140–210. Speckled brown
fur; silvery grey underparts;
dark brown tail; small
unridged footpads; often has
orange tuft in front of ear.

6. OSGOOD'S RAT
Rattus osgoodi, p. 354
HB 125–170. Thick soft fur;
dark brown above; dark grey
below; dark tail; dark feet.

Note Most *Rattus* have all-dark tails (except some
R. norvegicus), fur with numerous soft spines and
elongate footpads.

Plate 65. LARGE RATS

1. NORWAY RAT
Rattus norvegicus, p. 352
HB 160–265. Large; shaggy fur; tail dark above, slightly paler below, sometimes with pale splotches; pale feet; poorly developed footpads; relatively small ears and eyes; usually around towns.

2. ANNANDALE'S RAT
Rattus annandalei, p. 354
HB 145–220. Grey-brown back; white or pale yellow below; soft shaggy fur with inconspicuous spines.

3. WHITE-FOOTED INDOCHINESE RAT
Rattus nitidus, p. 353
HB 160–180. Relatively soft fur; belly white with grey bases; feet white, narrow with well-developed ridged footpads for climbing.

4. INDOCHINESE FOREST RAT
Rattus andamanensis, p. 353
HB 155–200. Conspicuous long black guard hairs all over back; creamy white underparts, sometimes with orange patch on chest; large footpads; large ears; long tail.

5. MÜLLER'S RAT
Sundamys muelleri, p. 359
HB 210–280. Very large; long dark tail; coarse shaggy fur with long guard hairs but no conspicuous spines; white or pale grey underparts.

6. MILLARD'S GIANT RAT
Dacnomys millardi, p. 363
HB 230–290. Very large; thick short fur without spines; upperparts brown flecked with buff; underparts pale; long dark tail.

7. GREATER BANDICOOT RAT
Bandicota indica, p. 355
HB 190–330. Very large; dark above and below, including feet; long coarse fur; broad front incisors; tail shorter than HB.

8. SAVILE'S BANDICOOT RAT
Bandicota savilei, p. 355
HB 150–240. Moderately shaggy fur, varies from brownish-grey to red-brown above, grey-buff below; tail shorter than HB, sometimes with white tip. See text for distinctions from *B. bengalensis* (not illustrated).

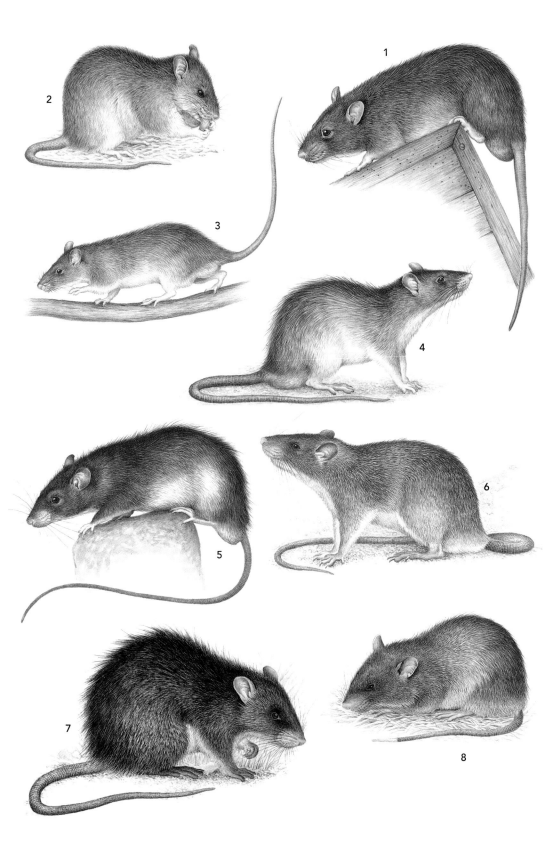

Plate 66. TREE, WHITE-TOOTHED, SOFT-FURRED AND LIMESTONE RATS

1. MANIPUR RAT
Berylmys manipulus, p. 357
HB 135–185. Smooth stiff fur, steel grey above; sharply separated pure white below; distal half to two-thirds of tail white; feet white above; front teeth broad, pale yellow or white; smaller than other *Berylmys*.

2. BERDMORE'S RAT
Berylmys berdmorei, p. 356
HB 190–260. Similar to *B. manipulus*, but slightly larger; tail shorter than HB, dark above, mottled pale below.

3. BOWERS'S RAT
Berylmys bowersi, p. 357
HB 235–300. Very large; similar colour to other *Berylmys*; tail varies geographically from all dark to dark at base, white on distal half. See text for distinctions from *B. mackenziei* (not illustrated).

4. MALAYAN WOOLLY TREE RAT
Pithecheir parvus, p. 368
HB 150–180. Long, soft reddish-brown fur with grey bases, lacking stiff spines; white underparts; short face; long smooth tail.

5. GREY TREE RAT
Lenothrix canus, p. 367
HB 165–220. Soft woolly fur; grey to grey-brown above; pale below; tail dark at base, white at tip; many separate cusps on teeth.

6. CRUMP'S SOFT-FURRED RAT
Diomys crumpi, p. 365
HB 100–135. Short silky fur; dark blackish-grey to brownish-grey above; white with grey bases below; tail sharply bicoloured, dark above, pale below; feet white.

7. POPA SOFT-FURRED RAT
Millardia kathleenae, p. 365
HB 130–165. Short soft fur; light brown to grey above; tail distinctly shorter than HB, dark above, pale below; only four footpads.

8. LAO LIMESTONE RAT
Saxatilomys paulinae, p. 358
HB 145–150. Relatively small; shiny greyish-black above; dark grey below with light frosting; long tail, dark above, indistinctly paler below; large bulbous footpads.

9. TONKIN LIMESTONE RAT
Tonkinomys daovantieni, p. 358
HB 185–215. Moderately large; shaggy, dark greyish-black above, medium-grey below; usually has white mark on forehead and chest; short tail, dark above, white below and at tip; large bulbous footpads.

Plate 67. *NIVIVENTER* AND *CHIROMYSCUS*

1. CONFUCIAN NIVIVENTER

Niviventer confucianus, p. 361
HB 125–170. Long soft fur yellowish or greyish-brown; usually lacks spines or long guard hairs; pure white below; tail dark above, pale below.

2. INDOMALAYAN NIVIVENTER

Niviventer fulvescens, p. 361
HB 130–170. Yellowish-brown to reddish-brown; extensive dark brown spines and long guard hairs; pure white or yellowish-white below; long bicoloured tail.
N. tenaster (not illustrated) is similar, but averages more yellowish-brown with longer ears.

3. CAMERON HIGHLANDS NIVIVENTER

Niviventer cameroni, p. 360
HB 130–170. Bright reddish-brown above with many spines and long guard hairs; white below; very long tail dark above, white below and at tip.

4. BRAHMAN NIVIVENTER

Niviventer brahma, p. 362
HB 135–145. Long soft fur; orange-brown to yellow-brown above; indistinct dark marks around eye and across muzzle; underparts grey with white tips; very long tail dark above, slightly paler below.

5. SMOKE-BELLIED NIVIVENTER

Niviventer eha, p. 362
HB 110–130. Orange-brown above; dark marks only around eye; fur of underparts grey with white tips; long tail dark above, slightly paler below.

6. LIMESTONE NIVIVENTER

Niviventer hinpoon, p. 362
HB 120–160. Upperparts largely grey with extensive spines; underparts buff with grey bases; tail same length as HB, dark above, pale below.

7. DARK-TAILED NIVIVENTER

Niviventer cremoriventer, p. 359
HB 130–165. Reddish-brown to orange-brown above; long guard hairs and many spines; white below; feet with large footpads; long dark tail with tuft at tip. The widespread *N. langbianis* (not illustrated) is similar, but more yellowish-grey.

8. FEA'S TREE RAT

Chiromyscus chiropus, p. 362
HB 145–160. Orange-brown above, usually brighter on sides of face; dark mark around eye; pure white below; first hind toe with nail instead of claw.

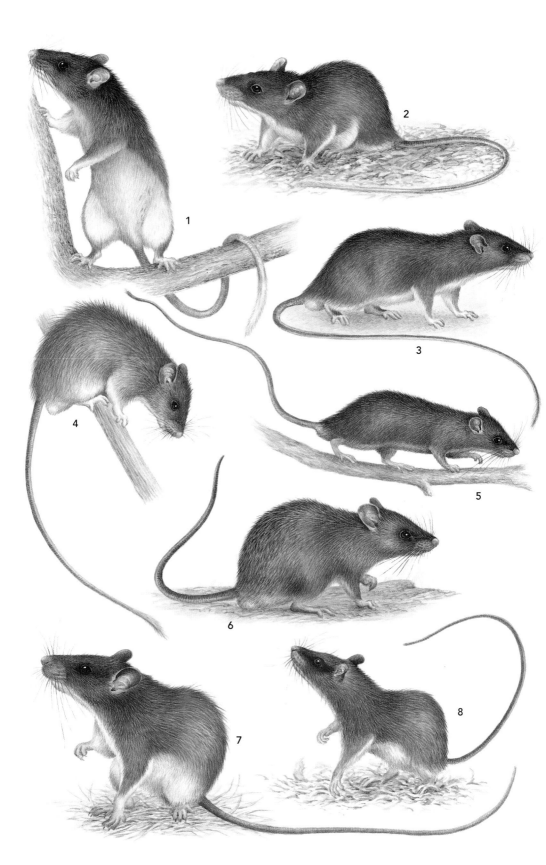

Plate 68. *LEOPOLDAMYS* AND *MAXOMYS* RATS

1. LONG-TAILED GIANT RAT
Leopoldamys sabanus, p. 363
HB 200–275. Large; smooth fur; brown on back; brighter orange on sides; creamy-white below; very long tail dark above, pale below and at tip.

2. EDWARD'S GIANT RAT
Leopoldamys edwardsi, p. 364
HB 210–280. Very large; plain brown above without orange sides; white below; long dark tail. *L. milleti* (not illustrated) is similar, but dark blackish-brown above; *L. ciliatus* (not illustrated) from Peninsular Malaysia is best distinguished by range.

3. NEILL'S RAT
Leopoldamys neilli, p. 364
HB 200–235. Similar to *L. edwardsi*, but smaller; upperparts mottled black and brown; tail dark above, white below and at tip.

4. RAJAH MAXOMYS
Maxomys rajah, p. 366
HB 165–225. Upperparts brown, sometimes tinged orange; white below often with brown streak in middle; fur with extensive spines; tail shorter than HB, dark above, pale below.

5. RED SPINY MAXOMYS
Maxomys surifer, p. 366
HB 160–210. Upperparts orange- or reddish-brown with extensive stiff spines; white below, often with orange under neck or on insides of front legs; tail dark above, white below.

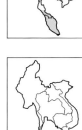

6. WHITEHEAD'S MAXOMYS
Maxomys whiteheadi, p. 366
HB 105–150. Small; dark brown to red-brown above; grey to orange-grey below; many soft spines; bicoloured tail shorter than HB.

7. MALAYAN MOUNTAIN MAXOMYS
Maxomys inas, p. 367
HB 125–160. Medium size; spiny fur; upperparts reddish-brown; underparts with grey bases, red-brown tips; bicoloured tail slightly longer than HB.

8. INDOCHINESE MAXOMYS
Maxomys moi, p. 367
HB 140–215. Bright orange upperparts; fur soft, without spines; sharply demarcated white below; bicoloured tail; only five footpads.

Plate 69. TYPICAL AND *VANDELEURIA* MICE

1. ASIAN HOUSE MOUSE
Mus musculus, p. 369
HB 65–90. Dark grey-brown above; only slightly paler below; soft fur; tail all dark, slightly longer than HB.

2. LITTLE INDIAN FIELD MOUSE
Mus booduga, p. 371
HB 60–75. Small; pointed rostrum; light brown above; white below; short bicoloured tail; incisors curved backwards.

3. COOK'S MOUSE
Mus cookii, p. 370
HB 80–105. Relatively large; brown to grey-brown above; pale grey with dark grey bases below; bicoloured tail slightly shorter than HB.

4. FAWN-COLOURED MOUSE
Mus cervicolor, p. 370
HB 70–95. Brownish-grey above; white to pale grey below; tail short, mid-grey above, paler below; pale buff incisors angled forwards.
M. fragilicauda (not illustrated) looks very similar but has longer tail with loose skin.

5. SHORTRIDGE'S MOUSE
Mus shortridgei, p. 371
HB 95–120. Fur with many stiff spines; grey-brown above; greyish-white below; tail short, dark grey above, pinkish below.

6. RICEFIELD MOUSE
Mus caroli, p. 369
HB 65–85. Small; rich brown to brownish-grey above; white or white with grey bases below; tail as long as HB, dark above, white below; incisors orange, curved forwards.

7. INDOCHINESE SHREWLIKE MOUSE
Mus pahari, p. 371
HB 75–105. Long, shrew-like nose; small eyes and ears; spiny fur; bluish-grey to brown-grey above; white with grey bases below; tail as long as HB, all grey.

8. LONG-TAILED CLIMBING MOUSE
Vandeleuria oleracea, p. 372
HB 55–85. Small; soft fur; extremely long, all-brown tail; orange- to pinkish-brown above, blending to white below; nail instead of claw on outer toe.

Note *Mus* can be distinguished from small rats by having all footpads round.

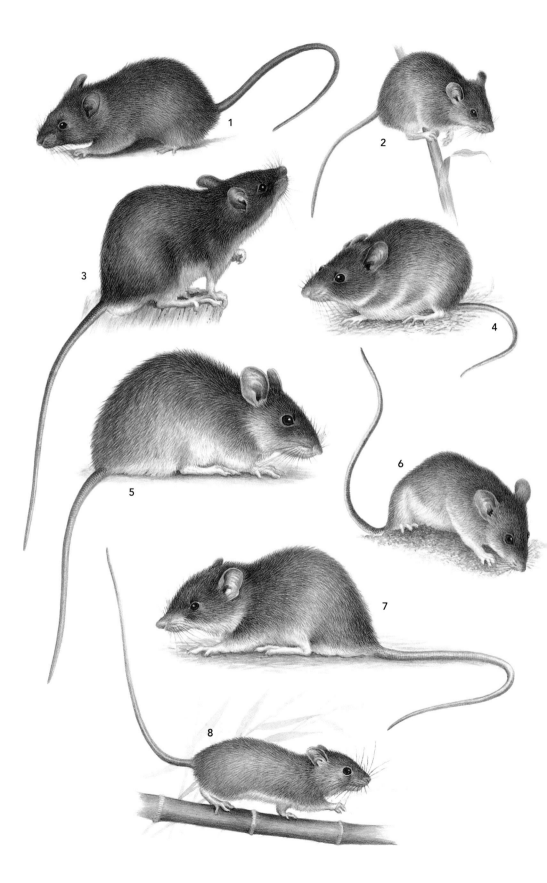

Plate 70. MARMOSET-RATS, MICE, PYGMY-DORMOUSE AND VOLES

1. GREATER MARMOSET-RAT
Hapalomys longicaudatus, p. 368
HB 150–170. Soft woolly fur; grey-brown above, orange on flanks, white below; short face; nail instead of claw on hind toe; ears with tufts of long brown hairs; long dark tail.

2. LESSER MARMOSET-RAT
Hapalomys delacouri, p. 368
HB 100–135. Similar to *H. longicaudatus*, but smaller; orange-brown above without contrasting flank colour.

3. INDOMALAYAN PENCIL-TAILED TREE-MOUSE
Chiropodomys gliroides, p. 372
HB 70–105. Small; nail on first toe; soft thick fur; red-brown to grey-brown above; white below; long tail with tuft of fur at tip.

4. VERNAY'S CLIMBING MOUSE
Vernaya fulva, p. 373
HB 60–80. Small; very long, dark tail; yellow-brown above; grey with buff tips below; all toes with claws, not nails.

5. HARVEST MOUSE
Micromys minutus, p. 371
HB 50–75. Very small with rounded head; small ears; grey-brown above, silvery below; thin tail slightly longer than HB.

6. SOUTH CHINA WOOD MOUSE
Apodemus draco, p. 373
HB 80–105. Soft fur; yellow-brown to orange-brown, grey bases above; contrasting white below; long dark tail paler below; large ears. *A. latronum* (not illustrated) is larger with a longer toothrow.

7. SOFT-FURRED PYGMY-DORMOUSE
Typhlomys cinereus, p. 374
HB 70–100. Soft fur; dark brown-grey above, buff below; long thin tail; narrow feet; cusps on molars merged into ridges.

8. FORREST'S MOUNTAIN VOLE
Neodon forresti, p. 376
HB 95–115. Short rounded ears; short bicoloured tail; very dark brown above; pale brown below.

9. CLARKE'S VOLE
Microtus clarkei, p. 375
HB 105–120. Dark brown above; slate grey with silvery tips below; tail 50% of HB, sparsely covered with short hairs.

10. PÈRE DAVID'S VOLE
Eothenomys melanogaster, p. 375
HB 90–100. Dark brown to blackish above; slate grey below, sometimes with buff tinge; tail <40% of HB.

11. KACHIN VOLE
Eothenomys cachinus, p. 375
HB 110–125. Bright tawny-brown above; grey with buff tips below; tail 40–50% of HB.

Note Voles can be distinguished from mice by their short rounded ears and the triangular cusps on their molars.

Plate 71. BAMBOO RATS AND KHA-NYOU

1. CHINESE BAMBOO RAT
Rhizomys sinensis, p. 377
HB 230–450. Medium to very large; thick soft fur; buffy brown to reddish-brown with grey bases; short tail (<25% of HB); posterior footpads separate.

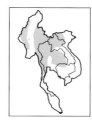

4. LESSER BAMBOO RAT
Cannomys badius, p. 376
HB 150–265. Small; soft dense fur reddish-brown with grey bases; often with white patch on forehead; ears largely hidden; short tail.

2. INDOMALAYAN BAMBOO RAT
Rhizomys sumatrensis, p. 377
HB 280–480. Medium to very large; sparse coarse hair; pale brownish-grey; medium-length tail (35–50% of HB); posterior footpads joined together.

5. KHA-NYOU
Laonastes aenigmamus, p. 378
HB 210–290. Rat-like head; bushy, squirrel-like tail; dark greyish black with variable grey frosting.

3. HOARY BAMBOO RAT
Rhizomys pruinosus, p. 377
HB 260–350. Medium-sized; dark brown to grey-brown fur frosted with white; two separate pads; medium-length tail (35–40% of HB).

Plate 72. PORCUPINES AND RABBITS

1. MALAYAN PORCUPINE
Hystrix brachyura, p. 378
HB 590–720. Largely black with white bands on quills; sometimes with slight crest on neck; tail short with rattle-like quills.

2. BRUSH-TAILED PORCUPINE
Atherurus macrourus, p. 379
HB 380–520. Greyish-brown to brown; long spines on back; medium-long scaly tail with tuft of rattle-like quills at tip.

3. LONG-TAILED PORCUPINE
Trichys fasciculata, p. 378
HB 375–435. Resembles large rat; relatively short, flattened spines; long tail with brush of flattened spines at tip.

4. BURMESE HARE
Lepus peguensis, p. 380
HB 360–500. Long ears with black tips; mottled brown above; reddish-orange patch on nape; tail black on top, grey on sides, white below; incisors with Y-shaped grooves.

5. CHINESE HARE
Lepus sinensis, p. 380
HB 350–450. Similar to *L. peguensis*, but tail brown on top; ears sometimes lack black tips; incisors with V-shaped groove.

6. ANNAMITE STRIPED RABBIT
Nesolagus timminsi, p. 381
HB 350–400. Pale brown to brownish-grey above; broad black or dark brown stripes on sides of back and across lower back; orange rump; relatively short ears.

7. MOUPIN PIKA
Ochotona thibetana, p. 379
HB 140–180. Small; rounded ears; no tail; yellow-brown to dark brown above; light grey to greyish-yellow below; pale buff patch behind ears.

O. forresti (not illustrated) is similar, but with darker underparts, grey patch behind ears.

Order **PHOLIDOTA**

Family *MANIDAE* PANGOLIN

Pangolins are readily recognized by their very distinctive scales, which cover the entire upperparts including the tail. The jaws are elongate and lack teeth (Fig. 12). The infant travels clinging to the upper side of the base of the mother's tail. When it walks, it curls its front claws inwards, producing a very distinctive footprint (Fig. 13). The two species in Asia are similar, distinguished by differences in tail length, conspicuousness of the ears and relative size of the front claws. All pangolins are threatened by illegal wildlife trade, especially because of false beliefs about the medicinal values of their scales. In some countries trade is extremely heavy, and populations have declined dramatically.

SUNDA PANGOLIN
Manis javanica PLATE 24
Measurements HB 400–650, T 350–560 (80–90% of HB), HF 61–97. Wt up to 7 kg
Identification Distinctive brownish, scaly mammal, with long claws. Head and tail long and tapered, held below level of body when animal is travelling on the ground. Tail

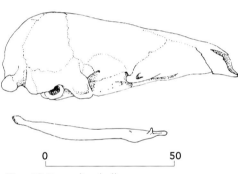

Fig. 12 *Pangolin skull.*

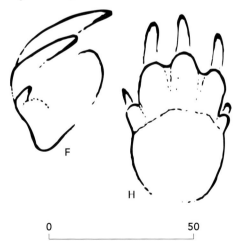

Fig. 13 *Footprints of Pangolin.*

wrapped around body when animal is disturbed, to protect the non-scaly underparts. External ear lobes inconspicuous, reduced to a small ridge; scales on top of head extend nearly to nostrils; front claws less than 50% longer than hind claws; prehensile tail relatively long, with about 30 scales along edge and a well-developed, smooth, glandular pad on underside to grip around branches.
Similar species Chinese Pangolin, *M. pentadactyla*, has relatively large, conspicuous ears, longer front claws and shorter tail with fewer than 20 scales along edge.
Ecology and habitat Usually nocturnal, sleeping during the day in underground burrows. Food consists exclusively of ants and termites taken from nests in trees, on the ground or below ground. Insect nests are opened with the strongly clawed feet and the contents licked up with the long, sticky tongue. Occurs in tall and secondary forests as well as cultivated areas, including gardens. Most often seen on roads at night, where it is slow-moving and conspicuous, although the eyes reflect very little torchlight.
Distribution and status SE Asia: S Myanmar, Thailand, S Laos, Vietnam, Cambodia and Peninsular Malaysia. Also Sumatra, Java, Borneo and adjacent small islands. Endangered. Populations have declined more than 90 per cent in some parts of range, due to illegal trapping and hunting.

CHINESE PANGOLIN
Manis pentadactyla PLATE 24
Measurements HB 400–580, T 250–380 (50–70% of HB)

Identification Upperparts, including tail, covered with large brown scales. Scales on top of head extend only partway to nostrils; front feet with very long claws, about twice as long as hind claws; external ear lobes well developed and conspicuous; tail relatively short with 16–19 scales along edge, and only small pad under tip. **Similar species** Sunda Pangolin, *M. javanica*, has smaller ears, shorter front claws and longer, more flexible tail. **Ecology and habitat** Mainly nocturnal, with similar habits to *M. javanica*. Feeds mainly on termites. Known from tall and secondary forests and cultivated areas, including gardens. In Laos, found mainly in hills and mountains, with *M. javanica* in lowlands.

Distribution and status SE Asia: N Myanmar, N Thailand, Laos and Vietnam. Also E Nepal, E Bangladesh, NE India, C and S China and Taiwan. Endangered. Populations have declined dramatically due to illegal trapping and hunting.

Order INSECTIVORA
Gymnures, shrews and moles

The Insectivora includes a mixture of small mammals with several common characters including large numbers of teeth, usually relatively undifferentiated, with rounded or pointed tops. In this respect, they differ from the rodents, which they superficially resemble: rodents have chisel-like front teeth (incisors), with a long diastema behind them, and cheek teeth with complex ridges on the surface. Most insectivores typically have a more pointed muzzle than rodents, and their front feet typically each have five long digits with sharp claws, while in rodents the inner digit on each front foot is short, with a flat nail instead of a sharp claw.

Recent research suggests that the order Insectivora is an artificial group, and the different families in this group are not necessarily one another's closest relatives. Instead, similarities may be due to retention of traits that characterized the primitive ancestors of all current mammals. Some scientists have suggested splitting them into several different orders. Among the families in the region, the family Erinaceidae is sometimes placed in the order Erinaceomorpha, while the families Talpidae and Soricidae are sometimes placed in the order Soricomorpha. However, there is not yet full agreement on how the different families should be grouped so, to avoid confusion, they are retained together in this book.

Family *ERINACEIDAE*
GYMNURES

Four species of gymnure occur in South-East Asia. The Moonrat is very distinctive, with its large size and black-and-white coloration. The three smaller gymnures bear more similarity to one another, but can be distinguished by tail length and ear size. They are distinguished from shrews by their generally larger size and larger, more conspicuous external ears. The skull has a well-developed zygomatic arch, unlike that of shrews (Fig. 14). Most species have 44 teeth (3 incisors, 1 canine, 4 premolars and 3 molars on each side of both the upper and lower jaw), although *H. sinensis* has one fewer premolar on each jaw. The cheek teeth are relatively rectangular with low cusps.

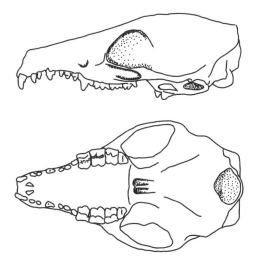

Fig. 14 *Skull of* Hylomys suillus.

MOONRAT

Echinosorex gymnurus PLATE 1

Measurements HB 320–400, T 205–290,
HF 65–75. Wt 870–1,100

Identification Large insectivore with elongate muzzle. Front part of body white to
greyish-white; remainder of body largely
black, often with extensive pale grey frosting. Fur with long, coarse guard hairs,
appearing rather shaggy; soft, woolly underfur. White variable in extent, usually including head and at least part of back, often
extending in a triangular wedge down lower
back. Usually has dark marks around eye,
which may form a dark mask. In Borneo,
most individuals are all white with scattered
black hairs, but white animals are rare on the
mainland. Tail long, scaly, with very short
hairs, dark at base, whitish or pinkish near
tip. Has a distinct, pungent odour with
strong ammonia content, different from the
musky smell of carnivores. Footprints are relatively rounded, with five distinct toes on all
feet (Fig. 15a).

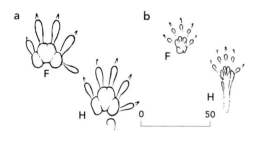

Fig. 15 *Footprints of* Echinosorex gymnurus
(a) and typical treeshrew, Tupaia *sp. (b).*

Ecology and habitat Nocturnal and terrestrial. Roosts in hollow logs, under roots of
trees, or in abandoned burrows during the
day. Does not dig its own burrows. Occurs in
lowland forest, including mature forest, as
well as some secondary forest, plantation,
mangrove. Prefers damp areas, often entering water. Feeds on earthworms, frogs, crustaceans, insects and other small animals.

Distribution and status SE Asia: peninsular
Myanmar, Thailand and Malaysia. Also
Sumatra and Borneo. Not immediately at

risk, but probably declining owing to loss of
intact forest.

SHORT-TAILED GYMNURE

Hylomys suillus PLATE 1

Measurements HB 120–140, T 19–30
(14–24% of HB), HF 20–23, E 15–20.
Wt 50–70. Skull: gl 33.5–35.6

Identification Resembles a large shrew with
an elongate muzzle, but with conspicuous
rounded ears and a distinctive short, slender,
nearly hairless tail. Upperparts dark brown to
reddish-brown, with a grey tinge from grey
bases to hairs; underparts light grey to greyish-white, the hairs with grey bases and white
tips. Fur with some flattened spines. Skull
has 4 upper and lower premolars on each
side. **Similar species** Chinese Gymnure, *H.
sinensis*, has longer tail; Large-eared
Gymnure, *H. megalotis*, has longer, thicker
tail, larger ears.

Ecology and habitat Occurs mainly in hill or
montane forest with dense undergrowth.
Mainly terrestrial, though sometimes climbs
low bushes. Active both day and night.
Feeds on arthropods and earthworms.
Shelters in nests of dead leaves made in hollows in the ground, or under rocks.

Distribution and status SE Asia: Myanmar,
Laos, Vietnam, Cambodia, Thailand and
Peninsular Malaysia. Also SW China
(Yunnan), Sumatra, Java, Borneo and some
small islands. Not currently at risk.
Populations probably stable.

CHINESE GYMNURE

Hylomys sinensis PLATE 1

Measurements HB 110–125, T 63–73
(50–63% of HB), HF 24–27, E 18–19. Skull: gl
31.1–33.6

Identification Small gymnure with thin, scaly
tail of medium length. Upperparts mottled
dark brown with a slightly reddish tinge;
underparts paler and greyish, the hairs with
grey bases and white to buffy tips. Fur with
some flattened spines. Tail pigmented
above, pale below. Skull has 3 lower and 3–4
upper premolars on each side. **Taxonomic
notes** Species sometimes placed in genus

Neotetracus. **Similar species** Other gymnures have 4 upper and lower premolars; Short-tailed Gymnure, *H. suillus*, has much shorter tail; Large-eared Gymnure, *H. megalotis*, has thicker, longer tail, larger ears.

Ecology and habitat Mainly or entirely terrestrial. Found in cool damp forests with fallen logs and rocks for cover. Usually found at higher altitudes than *H. suillus* where ranges overlap, but also in lowland forest elsewhere. Tolerant of some forest disturbance.

Distribution and status SE Asia: N Myanmar and N Vietnam. Also S China (Sichuan and Yunnan). Species not currently at risk. Populations probably stable.

LARGE-EARED GYMNURE
Hylomys megalotis   NOT ILLUSTRATED
Measurements HB 115–135, T 83–91

(65–75% of HB), HF 20–21.5, E 21–23. Skull: gl 36.4–39.2

Identification Overall colour grey to brownish grey; individual hairs long, soft, with grey bases with buff or buff and black tips; lacks spines. Nose very elongate. Ears large and rounded. Tail thick and long. Teeth relatively robust with 4 upper and lower premolars on each side. **Similar species** Other gymnures have shorter tails, smaller ears and some spines in their pelage.

Ecology and habitat Occurs in limestone karst areas.

Distribution and status SE Asia: Central Laos. Status is uncertain; it is known only from the type series of specimens from the Khammouane limestone area. Might be expected to inhabit other limestone areas near there.

Family *TALPIDAE* MOLES

Moles spend much of their time underground with adaptations for digging, including enlarged front feet. Their eyes are greatly reduced and they rely instead on their senses of smell and touch to locate food. They can sometimes be located by raised tunnels, as they often dig close to the surface. The South-East Asian species are currently separated into four genera, two of which (*Uropsilus* and *Scaptonyx*) are highly distinctive, and two of which (*Euroscaptor* and *Parascaptor*) are very similar to each other.

Genus *Uropsilus* The moles in this genus superficially resemble shrews more closely than they do moles, with front feet not especially enlarged and externally visible ear. Readily distinguished from true shrews in region by very thin, elongate snout and tiny eyes that are largely hidden in fur. Dental formula varies among species in the genus: 2/(1–2) 1/1 (3–4)/(3–4) 3/3. Up to four species currently recognized, all occurring in C and S China, but only one is known from our region. The other species can be distinguished by differences in dental formula, but these can be difficult to determine as some teeth, even when present, are very small and inconspicuous.

SLENDER SHREW-MOLE
Uropsilus gracilis   PLATE 1
Measurements HB 65–90, T 60–80 (90–100% of HB)

Identification Small, shrew-like animal with a very long, thin snout formed from two elongate tubular nostrils with a groove along the top. External ear small, but large enough to stick out beyond fur. Eyes tiny and hidden in fur. Fur soft, upperparts dark brown to greyish-brown, underparts contrasting slate-grey, sometimes with paler tips. Tail long and scaly with short, inconspicuous hairs. Lower parts of legs and arms, as well as hands and feet, nearly hairless and scaly; claws curved but short and weak. One lower incisor, 4 upper and lower premolars. **Similar species** All other genera of moles have enlarged front feet with strong claws; no shrews in region have such a long thin snout and long tail.

Ecology and habitat Found in hill forest at altitudes of 1,200–4,500m. Unlike other moles, believed to behave more like a shrew, foraging mainly in leaf litter rather than digging underground. Presumably feeds mainly on invertebrates.

Distribution and status SE Asia: N Myanmar. Also adjacent areas of China (Sichuan and W Yunnan). Status uncertain.

Genus _Euroscaptor_ These moles closely resemble the European moles, _Talpa_, and are often placed in that genus. They have greatly enlarged front feet, wider than they are long, turned sideways with long claws. The nose narrows to a small, skinny tip; eyes are tiny, completely hidden in the fur; no externally visible ears. Skull elongate with narrow zygomatic arches (Fig. 16). Dental formula varies slightly, but is usually 3/3 1/1 4/4 3/3. The anterior 3 premolars in each jaw are all small. The several species in this genus are externally all very similar, with fur colour varying within and among species, and hence not a reliable identification character. The distribution of most species is poorly known, as they are rarely trapped and difficult to identify; in some cases, the same specimens have been reported as different species in different literature sources.

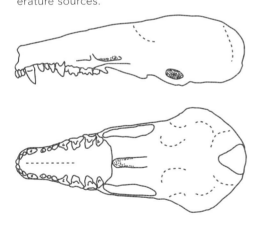

Fig. 16 *Lateral and ventral views of skull of Euroscaptor klossi.*

KLOSS'S MOLE
Euroscaptor klossi PLATE 1
Measurements HB 125–135, T 5–10. Wt 50–72g. Skull: gl 30.5 – 32.5
Identification Fur soft and dark grey to brownish-grey, slightly paler underneath. Enlarged front feet with long claws. No visible eyes or ears. Tail short and club-shaped (thicker near tip than base). Molars relatively large, 8–9mm across. **Taxonomic note** This species is sometimes considered part of *E. micrura* from the Himalayas. Animals from Peninsular Malaysia are smaller, with shorter tails than those from Thailand, and are sometimes considered a different species. Genetic studies are required to resolve this uncertainty. **Similar species** Large Chinese Mole, *E. grandis*, is larger; Long-nosed Chinese Mole, *E. longirostris*, has longer, thinner tail.

Ecology and habitat Found in forest and cultivated areas including tea plantations and vegetable gardens, especially in areas with loose sandy soils. Tunnels underground, but primarily near surface, so that tunnels are easily visible. Feeds mainly on earthworms as well as arthropods such as insects, and some small vertebrates including snakes and lizards.

Distribution and status SE Asia: montane areas of Myanmar, Thailand, Laos, Vietnam and Peninsular Malaysia. Also Nepal and India. Not currently at risk.

LARGE CHINESE MOLE
Euroscaptor grandis PLATE 1
Measurements HB 150, T 10, HF 18. Skull: gl 37
Identification Similar to Kloss's Mole *E. klossi*, differing in larger size. Tail short and club-shaped (thicker near tip than base).
Ecology and habitat Known records are from montane areas.
Distribution and status SE Asia: NE Myanmar and NW Vietnam. Also S China. Status uncertain; only a few records in region, but probably not currently at risk.

LONG-NOSED CHINESE MOLE
Euroscaptor longirostris NOT ILLUSTRATED
Measurements HB ~130, T ~15–20 (15% of HB). Skull: gl 32–33.
Identification Similar to other *Euroscaptor* moles, differing in longer tail that is tapered

and not club-shaped; narrower, more tapered rostrum.

Ecology and habitat Montane forest.

Distribution and status SE Asia: NW Vietnam. Also S China. Status uncertain; very little information from region.

SMALL-TOOTHED MOLE

Euroscaptor parvidens NOT ILLUSTRATED

Measurements HB 140, T 6 (hairs at tip of tail 10), HF 14. Skull: gl 34, palatal breadth across anterior molars 7.2, palatal length to anterior border of alveoli 13.4

Identification Externally similar in appearance to other *Euroscaptor* moles, distinguished by its short tail; very slender skull (ratio of palatal length to breadth = 0.53); small cheek teeth; last upper premolar (pm^4) with a well-developed cingulum cusp.

Ecology and habitat Type specimen was found on forest floor in red basaltic soil at 800m altitude.

Distribution and status SE Asia: Vietnam. Status uncertain; known from only two localities in Vietnam.

Genus *Parascaptor* Very similar to *Euroscaptor*, and also often included in genus *Talpa*. Main distinguishing feature is reduced dental formal (3/3 1/1 3/3 3/3), with one less small premolar and remaining 3 upper premolars relatively larger than in *Euroscaptor*. Also has distinct groove in skull behind auditory bullae.

BLYTH'S MOLE

Parascaptor leucura NOT ILLUSTRATED

Measurements HB 130–140, Tail ~10% of HB. Skull: gl 27–31

Identification Similar in appearance to *Euroscaptor* moles, distinguished by having only 3, relatively larger premolars in each

jaw; short, club-shaped tail; relatively wide molars, groove in base of skull behind auditory bullae.

Ecology and habitat Montane forest at 1,000–2,500m altitude.

Distribution and status SE Asia: N Myanmar and N Laos. Also adjacent areas of Assam and S China (Yunnan and SW Sichuan). Status uncertain; only a few records from region.

Genus *Scaptonyx* A distinctive mole with forefeet only moderately enlarged, elongate rather than rounded as in *Euroscaptor* and *Parascaptor*. Tail relatively long. Ear openings large but with no external pinnae. Eyes minute, covered with a thin layer of translucent skin.

LONG-TAILED MOLE

Scaptonyx fuscicauda PLATE 1

Measurements HB 65–90, T 30–50 (approx 50–60% of HB)

Identification A distinctive, small mole with elongate snout, moderately enlarged but still elongate front feet with long, flattened claws for digging; hind feet smaller but still with large, broad claws; hind and forefeet covered with small scales. Tail moderately long, about half length of head and body, covered with scales and sparse long hairs. Fur soft and velvety, uniform dark slate-grey.

Ecology and habitat Known from disturbed and primary hill and montane forest at 1,300–4,100m altitude. Presumably spends much of time underground, but has been found on the surface.

Distribution and status SE Asia: N Myanmar and Vietnam. Also adjacent parts of S China. Status uncertain; probably not currently at risk.

Family *SORICIDAE* SHREWS

Shrews include the smallest mammals in the world apart from some bats. They have rather short legs, a sparsely haired tail, short fur and small eyes. Many of the smaller species are difficult to identify. Even distinguishing among genera can be difficult, unless the animals have been prepared as museum specimens, as the differences among species and among genera are often based on characters such as number and size of the teeth.

All shrews have a single, enlarged incisor on each upper jaw, followed by 2 to 5 small, single-cusped (unicuspid) teeth (canine and premolars), and 4 larger, multicusped teeth (one premolar and 3 molars), though the posterior molar is usually small. The number of unicuspid teeth is important for identifying genera, but sometimes the posterior ones can be small and hard to see. The colour of the teeth can also help to distinguish genera; some groups have reddish-orange tips to some of the teeth, especially the incisors and some of the unicuspids.

Genus *Sorex* Small shrews (HB 50–80) with tail similar length to head and body. Teeth with reddish-orange tips; 5 unicuspid teeth, all fairly similar in size.

LESSER STRIPE-BACKED SHREW
Sorex bedfordiae PLATE 2
Measurements HB 50–70, T 45–70 (85–105% of HB), HF 11–15. Skull: gl 17.0–18.6, ut 7.0–7.8
Identification Small shrew with long tail. Upperparts mid-brown, hairs with grey bases that show through; dark brown stripe down middle of back; underside slate-grey with buff, light brown or white tips to hairs. Teeth with red-orange tips; 5 small unicuspid teeth.
Similar species Greater Stripe-backed Shrew, *S. cylindricauda*, which is not known from region but occurs nearby in China, is similar in appearance but larger (HB 70–77, gl 19.5–20.2) with proportionately shorter tail (80%).
Ecology and habitat Montane forest.
Distribution and status SE Asia: N Myanmar. Also S China (Yunnan). Status poorly known.

Genus *Blarinella* Small shrews with short tail, about half body-length. Anterior teeth with distinct reddish-orange tips. Large, well-developed claws. 5 unicuspid teeth, but posterior teeth small and compressed inwards, so they are not visible from the side (Fig. 17). Formerly considered to include only one species, *B. quadraticauda*, but recent work has shown that there are three distinct species, with *B. wardi* and *B. griselda* occur-

ring in the region, while *B. quadraticauda* is confined to China.

MYANMAR SHORT-TAILED SHREW
Blarinella wardi NOT ILLUSTRATED
Measurements HB 60–75, T 32–40 (about 50% of HB), HF 10–14. Skull: cbl 18.4–19.8 (mean 19.1), breadth 7.8–9.0 (8.4), ut 7.0–8.4 (8.1), m–m 4.5–5.0 (4.8)
Identification Small, stout-bodied shrew with relatively short tail, 5 unicuspid teeth (Fig. 17a); incisors and at least some unicuspids with reddish-orange tips. Body colour essentially the same above and below, dark slate-grey and brown. Relatively small, narrow skull. Third upper unicuspid relatively small, only

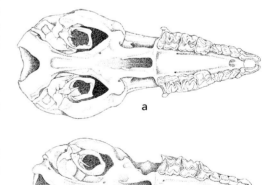

Fig. 17 *Ventral views of skulls of* Blarinella wardi *(a) and* Chodsigoa caovansunga *(b).*

about 25% longer than small 4th unicuspid. **Similar species** Indochinese Short-tailed Shrew, *B. griselda*, has larger, broader skull, third upper unicuspid relatively larger.
Ecology and habitat High montane forest.
Distribution and status SE Asia: NE Myanmar. Also adjacent parts of China (Yunnan). Appears to be relatively common in appropriate habitat.

INDOCHINESE SHORT-TAILED SHREW

Blarinella griselda PLATE 2
Measurements HB ~80, T 35, HF 13.
Skull: gl 20.7, breadth 9.4, ut 8.6, m–m 5.3
Identification Small, stout-bodied shrew similar to *B. wardi*, with uniformly dark brown fur above and below. Relatively larger, broader skull. Third upper unicuspid not particularly short, about twice height of small fourth unicuspid. **Similar species** Myanmar Short-tailed Shrew, *B. wardi*, is smaller and has a narrower skull, third upper unicuspid is relatively smaller.
Ecology and habitat Recorded from montane forest, 1,500–1,700m altitude in N Vietnam.
Distribution and status SE Asia: N Vietnam. Also China. Poorly known in region, but relatively widespread in China.

Genus *Episoriculus* Medium-small to small shrews; incisors and some other upper teeth with reddish brown tips; only 4 upper unicuspid teeth of which posterior tooth is minute, not visible from side and often hard to see at all. Posterior molar relatively well developed, more than half length of first upper molar. Relatively long tail (80–170% of head and body length). Has often been included in the genus *Soriculus*, which is now considered to include only one species, *S. nigrescens*. The latter occurs in the Himalayas and Assam in NE India, near the edge of the region, and might occur in N Myanmar. It can be distinguished by a relatively stout body (HB 80–90) with a short tail (about half HB), relatively long front claws (2.5–4 mm), and a relatively small third lower molar.

HODGSON'S BROWN-TOOTHED SHREW

Episoriculus caudatus PLATE 2
Measurements HB 50–75, T 34–66 (60–110% of HB), HF 11–14.5, E 5–9.
Skull: gl 16.7–19.1, ut 7.1–8.5
Identification Upperparts brown, individual hairs with grey bases; underparts similar but sometimes with paler tips. Incisors relatively small with small reddish-brown tips.
Taxonomic notes Considerable geographic variation in size may indicate that this is a complex of species; form in Myanmar is relatively small and dark. **Similar species** Bailey's Brown-toothed Shrew, *E. baileyi*, is larger, with relatively large upper incisor; Long-tailed Brown-toothed Shrew, *E. macrurus*, has much longer tail.
Ecology and habitat Montane forests at altitudes of 1,800–3,600m.
Distribution and status SE Asia: N Myanmar. Also S China. Not currently at risk.

BAILEY'S BROWN-TOOTHED SHREW

Episoriculus baileyi NOT ILLUSTRATED
Measurements HB 63–81, T 60–75 (85–110% of HB), HF 13–14.5, E 7–10.
Skull: gl 19–20.6, ut 8.4–9.3
Identification Fur soft and thick; upperparts grey bases with dark brown tips, appearing overall brown flecked with grey; underparts grey bases with narrow whitish to light brown tips. Incisors large and robust with extensive reddish-brown tips. **Taxonomic note** Formerly included as a subspecies of *E. leucops*, which is now recognized as occurring only in Nepal. Specimens from Vietnam are slightly larger than those from Myanmar. **Similar species** Hodgson's Brown-toothed Shrew, *E. caudatus*, has smaller skull with shorter toothrow, relatively small upper incisors; Long-tailed Brown-toothed Shrew, *E. macrurus*, has much longer tail, greyer body fur, smaller skull.
Ecology and habitat Montane broadleaved and coniferous forest.
Distribution and status SE Asia: N Myanmar and N Vietnam. Also Sikkim and Assam in India. Not currently at risk.

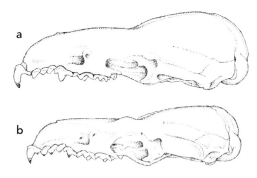

Fig. 18 Skull profiles of Chodsigoa parca *(a)*
and C. caovansunga *(b)*.

LONG-TAILED BROWN-TOOTHED SHREW

Episoriculus macrurus PLATE 2

Measurements HB 59–66, T 80–100
(130–150% of HB), HF 14–17, E 8–10.5.
Skull: gl 16.9–18.3, ut 7.2–7.7

Identification Upperparts grey, with narrow
brownish tips on some hairs, appearing grey
with brown flecks. Tail much longer than
body, dark above, pale below. **Similar
species** Other *Episoriculus* have shorter tails;
Van Sung's Shrew, *Chodsigoa caovansunga*,
has only 3 upper unicuspid teeth, shorter tail;
Lowe's Brown-toothed Shrew, *C. parca*, has
larger skull.

Ecology and habitat Terrestrial, probably
feeding among dead leaves. Has been
found among dwarf bamboo, scrub and
grasses in montane forest.

Distribution and status SE Asia: NW
Myanmar and N Vietnam. Also Nepal, NE
India, W and S China. Not currently at risk.

Genus *Chodsigoa* Similar to *Episoriculus*
shrews, but with only three unicuspids, all
well developed (Figs 17, 18). Incisors and
some unicuspids with reddish-brown tips.

LOWE'S BROWN-TOOTHED SHREW

Chodsigoa parca PLATE 2

Measurements HB 65–85, T 70–100, HF
15–20, E 6–8. Skull: gl 19.0–21.0, ut 8.1–9.2

Identification Slate-grey above with brownish tinge, slightly paler below. Feet distinctly

pale, skin white with short, sparse brown
hairs. Tail longer than head and body; dusky
brown above, slightly paler below; appears
naked, but has moderately long thin hairs,
ending in small tuft at tip of tail. Two pads in
middle of hind foot separated by approximately width of a pad (Fig. 19a). Skull large
with tall braincase (Fig. 18a). **Similar species**
Van Sung's Shrew, *C. caovansunga*, is smaller
with lower braincase, shorter hairs on tail,
pads on hind feet touching or nearly so;
Episoriculus shrews have an extra small unicuspid in upper toothrow (though this can
be hard to see), shorter hairs on tail.

Ecology and habitat Montane forest at altitudes of 1,200–2,750m. Has been reported
near streams, including under rocks or logs.

Distribution and status SE Asia: NE
Myanmar, N Thailand and N Vietnam. Also S
China. Not currently at risk.

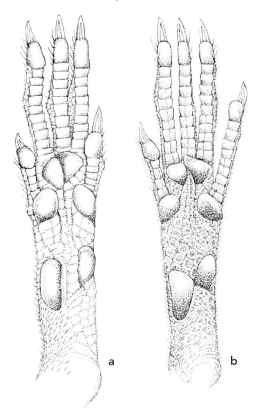

Fig. 19 Undersides of hind feet of
Chodsigoa parca *(a) and* C. caovansunga
(b).

VAN SUNG'S SHREW
Chodsigoa caovansunga PLATE 2

Measurements HB 58–64, T 51–68, HF 14–16. Skull: gl 17.3–18.4, ut 7.6–8.1.

Identification Upperparts dark slate-grey with brownish tinge formed from short brown tips on hairs; underparts similar but tips pale brown or light grey. Fore and hind feet overall brownish. Tail similar in length to body; bicoloured, dark above, pale below; appearing naked but actually covered with very short hairs; no tuft of hairs at tip of tail. Pads on hind feet very close together or touching (Fig. 19b). Skull relatively short with low braincase (Fig. 18b). **Similar species** Lowe's Brown-toothed Shrew, *C. parca*, is larger, with longer hairs on tail, pale feet, pads on feet well separated.

Ecology and habitat Terrestrial. Occurs in montane forest, including areas of bamboo, at altitudes of 1,300–2,000m.

Distribution and status SE Asia: N Vietnam. Poorly known; recorded only from type locality in N Vietnam, but likely more widespread in montane forest in N Vietnam and S China.

Genus *Anourosorex* Round-bodied shrews with very short tail, no external ear, tiny eyes, moderately long foreclaws, teeth without red-brown tips. Skull with only two unicuspids, very small posterior molar. Apparently spends much of time burrowing like a mole. Only one species in region.

MOLE-SHREW
Anourosorex squamipes PLATE 2

Measurements HB 85–110, T 10–20, HF 12–16, E 0. Skull: gl 23.3–26.3

Identification Medium-sized shrew with very short tail, no external pinnae, minute eyes. Upperparts mottled brown and grey, individual hairs with grey bases and dark brown tips; hairs on lower rump with shiny tips from a mucilaginous secretion; underparts vary from brown to light grey, hairs with grey bases. Tail short and scaly, no longer than hind feet. Claws on front feet longer than hind feet, but front feet not enlarged and hind feet slightly larger than forefeet. **Similar species** Short-tailed moles (*Euroscaptor* and *Parascaptor*) have greatly enlarged front feet with long, broad claws; Slender Shrew-mole, *Uropsilus gracilis*, also has tiny eyes with relatively small feet, but has a long tail.

Ecology and habitat Terrestrial and fossorial, burying into ground and leaf litter. Reported mainly from montane forest at altitudes of 1,500–3,100m.

Distribution and status SE Asia: N Myanmar, N Thailand, Laos and N Vietnam. Also NE India (Assam), Bhutan, China and Taiwan. Not currently at risk.

Genus *Chimarrogale* Medium-large shrews with moderately long tail; dense, dark fur with long silvery guard hairs on hindquarters; tail thickly haired; feet with fringe of short, stiff hairs. Very small pinnae. Teeth white without red or brown tips; 3 upper unicuspid teeth.

HIMALAYAN WATER SHREW
Chimarrogale himalayica PLATE 3

Measurements HB 110–130, T 90–100 (80–85% of HB), HF 19–22. Skull: gl 25–28, ut 11.1–12.5

Identification Upperparts dark grey-brown with conspicuous long, silvery guard hairs on hindquarters; underparts slightly paler greyish-brown, not sharply demarcated; tail slender but densely haired, usually dark above and below; feet fringed with short, rather stiff hairs. **Similar species** Styan's Water Shrew, *C. styani*, is slightly smaller and has sharply demarcated pale underparts.

Ecology and habitat Lives in or near small forest streams, feeding on aquatic insects and other invertebrates, but may wander through forest away from streams.

Distribution and status SE Asia: N Myanmar, N Laos and N Vietnam. Also Nepal, N India (Assam), China and Taiwan. Not currently at risk, but apparently dependent on relatively clean mountain streams, and therefore vulnerable to forest loss and pollution.

STYAN'S WATER SHREW
Chimarrogale styani PLATE 3
Measurements HB 80–110, T 90–100

Identification Upperparts dark grey-brown with conspicuous silvery guard hairs on hindquarters; underparts contrastingly silvery-grey, sharply demarcated from colour of upperparts. Tail slender but densely haired, dark above, pale below. Feet fringed with short, rather stiff hairs. **Similar species** Himalayan Water Shrew, *C. himalayica*, is larger, with underparts darker, not sharply demarcated from upperparts; Web-footed Water Shrew, *Nectogale elegans*, has distinctive pattern of rows of white hairs on a dark tail.

Ecology and habitat Lives in or near small forest streams at altitudes of 1,500–3,100m.

Distribution and status SE Asia: NE Myanmar. Also SW and SE China. Poorly known, but believed not to be currently at risk.

MALAYAN WATER SHREW
Chimarrogale hantu NOT ILLUSTRATED
Measurements HB 95–120, T 85–100 (80–100% of HB), HF 21–22. Wt 30g. Skull: cil 25–28, mt 11.4–13.4

Identification Upperparts dark grey-brown, with scattered silver guard hairs, longest and most conspicuous on hindquarters; underparts greyish-brown. Upper incisors with distinct cusp on inside edge. **Taxonomic notes** Sometimes included in *C. phaeura* from Borneo, but distinguished by deeper braincase (*C. hantu* 7.7–8.0, *C. phaeura* 7.3–7.5). **Similar species** Himalayan Water Shrew, *C. himalayica*, lacks cusps on upper incisors, does not overlap in range.

Ecology and habitat Lives in or near small forest streams in hill forest.

Distribution and status SE Asia: Peninsular Malaysia. Not currently at risk, but could be threatened by degradation of water quality from pollution or forest loss.

Genus *Nectogale* Medium-sized shrew; tail moderately long with several rows of white hairs; hind feet with fringes of short stiff hairs on edges of toes. Teeth white without red or brown tips; 3 upper unicuspid teeth. No external pinnae.

WEB-FOOTED WATER SHREW
Nectogale elegans PLATE 3
Measurements HB 90–130, T 90–110

Identification Upperparts slate-grey, with long silvery guard hairs; underparts silvery-white. Tail dark with several rows of stiff white hairs: two rows on either side start at base of tail and curve under tail to meet on underside for distal half; two further lateral rows extend along middle third; a dorsal row continues along distal third. Feet have fringes of short white hairs on edges of toes; round disc-like pads on soles of feet. Snout long and pointed. **Similar species** Styan's Water Shrew, *Chimarrogale styani*, has tail more uniformly haired, dark above and pale below.

Ecology and habitat Cold mountain streams; swims and dives to catch aquatic invertebrates and small fish. Sleeps in burrows in stream banks.

Distribution and status SE Asia: N Myanmar. Also Nepal, India (Sikkim), Bhutan and China. Not currently at risk, but susceptible to pollution or degradation of stream habitats.

Genus *Suncus* Medium-large to very small shrews; tail short to moderately long, with scattered, long erect hairs; teeth white without red or brown tips; 4 upper unicuspid teeth, though last one can be small and hard to see (Fig. 20a).

HOUSE SHREW
Suncus murinus PLATE 3
Measurements HB 90–145, T 46–86 (50–64% of HB), HF 17–23. Skull: gl 27–37, upper toothrow 12.5–16.0

Identification Relatively large, thickset shrew. Entire body and tail uniform mid-grey to brownish-grey. Tail thick, especially at base, narrower at tip. Has a musk gland, sometimes visible, on middle of each side of the body. **Taxonomic notes** Considerable variation throughout range, and may represent a complex of species. **Similar species**

Water shrews, *Chimarrogale* spp., have long slender tails, different habitat; most other shrews are smaller.

Ecology and habitat Usually found in or near houses or in disturbed habitats.

Distribution and status SE Asia: Myanmar, Thailand, Laos, Vietnam, Cambodia and Peninsular Malaysia. Also Pakistan, India, Nepal, S China, Sumatra, Java, Borneo, Sulawesi and smaller Indonesian islands and the Philippines. Widespread and abundant in disturbed areas; apparently introduced in some areas, including the Philippines.

PYGMY WHITE-TOOTHED SHREW
Suncus etruscus PLATE 3

Measurements HB 50–56, T 30–40 (60–75% of HB), HF 7.0–8.0. Wt 1.8–2.5g. Skull: cbl 14.5, upper toothrow 5.3–6.4

Identification A very small shrew; upperparts dark grey with fine whitish grizzling; underparts somewhat paler. Ears and feet dark brown. Tail slightly thickened, brownish, with dense short hairs and scattered long hairs on basal two-thirds. **Taxonomic notes** Form in peninsular Thailand and Malaysia is sometimes considered to be a separate species, *S. malayanus*, but few specimens have been critically examined to determine diagnostic characters; quite likely specimens currently referred to *S. etruscus* from throughout the range represent a complex of species. **Similar species** Sunda Shrew, *Crocidura monticola*, is slightly larger, with only 3 small upper unicuspid teeth; most other shrews are substantially larger.

Ecology and habitat Terrestrial. Has been reported from tall dipterocarp forest in Peninsular Malaysia.

Distribution and status SE Asia: Myanmar, Thailand, Laos, Vietnam and Peninsular Malaysia. Also S Europe, N Africa, Madagascar, through Middle East to India, S China and Borneo. Although rarely captured, apparently widespread and not at risk.

Genus *Crocidura* Medium to small shrews; tail moderate to very long, usually with scattered long hairs or bristles; teeth white with-

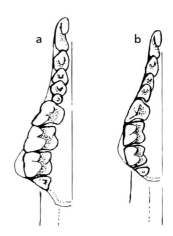

Fig. 20 *Right upper toothrows of* Suncus murinus *(a) and* Crocidura fuliginosa *(b).*

out red or brown tips; only 3 upper unicuspid teeth (Fig. 20b, 21). The genus contains over 170 currently recognized species throughout Africa, Europe and Asia, of which 11 are known from the region. Many species are represented by relatively few specimens and the taxonomy is still somewhat uncertain. Most species are similar in colour and can be difficult to distinguish without examining the skulls; range limits can help with identification, as many of the most similar species do not overlap in range. The similar species sections in the text, below, emphasize forms that overlap in geographical distribution.

SOUTH-EAST ASIAN SHREW
Crocidura fuliginosa PLATE 3

Measurements HB 70–100, T 60–90 (65–75% of HB), HF 15–19. Wt 11.5–16g. Skull: gl 21.5–25.0, upper toothrow 9.2–11.0

Identification Upperparts dark brownish-grey; underparts slightly paler. Tail brownish, with few or no long hairs. Individuals found in peninsular Thailand and Malaysia are distinctly smaller than those elsewhere. **Taxonomic notes** Formerly considered to include many forms that are now considered separate species; as a result, range listed here is much less extensive than suggested in some earlier publications; may still represent more than one species. **Similar species**

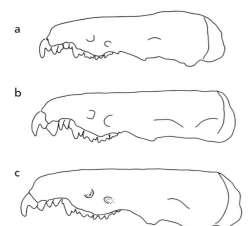

Fig. 21 *Lateral views of skulls of* Crocidura attenuata *(a)*, C. hilliana *(b) and* C. fuliginosa *(c)*.

Malayan Shrew, *C. malayana*, in area of overlap, is slightly larger and broader across teeth; Peninsular Shrew, *C. negligens*, has more rounded lingual edge to large upper premolar; Hill's Shrew, *C. hilliana,* is slightly smaller with more robust upper unicuspid teeth (Fig. 21b); other *Crocidura* in region are smaller.
Ecology and habitat Terrestrial. Found in forest, both primary and degraded, from hills to lowlands, as well as in open disturbed areas. Feeds on insects and other invertebrates.
Distribution and status SE Asia: Myanmar, Thailand, Laos, Vietnam, Cambodia and N Peninsular Malaysia. Also NE India and S China. Not currently at risk, although not usually abundant.

MALAYAN SHREW
Crocidura malayana   NOT ILLUSTRATED
Measurements HB 77–100, T 56–78, HF 13–16. Wt 10–14.5g. Skull: gsl 22.5–24.5, upper toothrow 9.2–10.8
Identification Very similar in external appearance to *C. fuliginosa*, but differs genetically and, at least within area of overlap in range, in slightly larger skull with broader rostrum and palate: width across outside of upper unicuspid teeth 2.9–3.4 v 2.4–2.7 in sympatric populations of *C. fuligi-*

nosa. Also, middle cusp (mesostyle) of second upper molar is simple or only very shallowly notched in *C. malayana*, but distinctly notched (bifid) in *C. fuliginosa*.
Ecology and habitat Terrestrial. Reported from both hill and lowland forest, in a variety of forested habitats.
Distribution and status SE Asia: peninsular Thailand and Malaysia and some small offshore islands. Not currently at risk; possibly most common *Crocidura* in Peninsular Malaysia.

PENINSULAR SHREW
Crocidura negligens   NOT ILLUSTRATED
Measurements HB 75–95, T 55–69 (67–92% of HB), HF 13.5–15.8. Wt 9.5–12.5g. Skull: gl 20.5–22.3, upper toothrow 9.2–9.9
Identification Genetically closely related to *C. malayana*, but has distinctly smaller skull with more rounded, globular braincase. Lingual (inside) edge of large upper premolar tends to be rounded. **Taxonomic notes** Has been confused in the past with *C. attenuata*, which is genetically very different, and is restricted to north of the peninsula.
Similar species Malayan Shrew, *C. malayana*, and South-East Asian Shrew, *C. fuliginosa*, are larger, with more angular lingual edge to premolar; Grey Shrew, *C. attenuata*, does not overlap in range.
Ecology and habitat Terrestrial. Reported from both primary and secondary forest, but specific habitat requirements and tolerance to habitat degradation unknown.
Distribution and status SE Asia: peninsular Thailand and Malaysia, S of the Isthmus of Kra, and a few offshore islands. Poorly known.

SUNDA SHREW
Crocidura monticola   PLATE 3
Measurements HB 53–65, T 24–37, HF 8.5–11.0. Wt 3. Skull: gl 15.0–17.5, mt 6.6–7.3
Identification Very small shrew with uniformly dull grey-brown fur. Tail paler than body, with scattered long, bristle-like hairs on basal 10mm. Braincase relatively high and somewhat domed. **Similar species** Pygmy White-toothed Shrew, *Suncus etruscus*, has an extra

small tooth, smaller skull and hind foot; other *Crocidura* within its range are larger; Kego Shrew, *C. kegoensis*, has a flatter braincase.

Ecology and habitat Terrestrial. Recorded from both lowland and hill forest.

Distribution and status SE Asia: peninsular Thailand and Malaysia. Also Java, Borneo and some smaller Indonesian islands. Not currently at risk, though relatively poorly known in region.

GREY SHREW
Crocidura attenuata NOT ILLUSTRATED
Measurements HB 65–90, T 40–60, HF 13–16. Skull: gl 19.0–22.5, upper toothrow 8.2–9.7

Identification Upperparts dark grey-brown, underparts slightly paler and greyer. Tail dark, nearly naked except for scattered long hairs (3–5mm) on basal third. Long hairs also on lower back and limbs. Lingual (inside) edge of large upper premolar rounded.

Taxonomic notes Specimens formerly referred to this species from Peninsular Malaysia have been subsequently identified as *C. negligens*, which does not apparently overlap in distribution with *C. attenuata*.

Similar species South-East Asian Shrew, *C. fuliginosa*, tends to have more angular inner edges to large upper premolar; Hill's Shrew, *C. hilliana*, has more robust teeth (Fig. 21b).

Ecology and habitat Terrestrial.

Distribution and status SE Asia: Myanmar, Thailand, Vietnam, Laos and Cambodia. Also S China. Widespread; not currently at risk.

INDOCHINESE SHREW
Crocidura indochinensis PLATE 3
Measurements HB 65–70, T 45–50 (65–70% of HB), HF 13, E 10–11. Skull: gl 17.0–17.2, mt 7.5–7.6

Identification Upperparts dark brownish-grey; underparts more greyish. Tail medium in length, nearly naked with thinly scattered short hairs and only a few longer bristles near base. Relatively flat skull. **Taxonomic notes** Formerly considered part of *C. horsfieldi*, which does not occur in region.

Similar species Wuchih Shrew, *C. wuchihensis*, is smaller; Voracious Shrew, *C. vorax*, and Chinese Shrew, *C. rapax*, have distinctly bicoloured tail covered with short fine hairs.

Ecology and habitat Terrestrial. Primary and secondary hill forest.

Distribution and status SE Asia: N Myanmar, N Thailand, Laos and Vietnam. Poorly known, as many historic records were confused with other species. Probably not currently at risk.

KE GO SHREW
Crocidura kegoensis PLATE 3
Measurements HB 48, T 27, HF 10, E 5. Skull: gl 14.9, mt 6.5

Identification Very small shrew. Upperparts dark greyish-brown, individual hairs with grey bases and brown tips; underparts slightly paler and greyer, blending on sides with upperpart colours. Dark mark on muzzle with dark ears. Front and hind feet with pale brown skin. Tail brown above, only slightly paler below, covered with very short brown hairs, mixed with scattered long bristles on basal half. Ears pale. Large upper premolar with deeply curved indentation on posterior edge, molars with deep notches on inner side (Fig. 22a). **Similar species** Wuchih Shrew, *C. wuchihensis*, has pale ears, white skin on top of feet, lacks dark mark on side of muzzle, shallower notch on

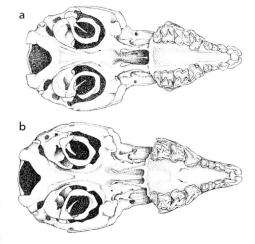

Fig. 22 *Ventral views of skull of* Crocidura kegoensis *(a) and* C. wuchihensis *(b).*

large premolar and molars (Fig. 22b); other *Crocidura* in region are larger; Pygmy White-toothed Shrew, *Suncus etruscus*, is smaller, with an extra unicuspid tooth.

Ecology and habitat Only known record is from lowland rainforest.

Distribution and status SE Asia: N Vietnam. Poorly known – only one confirmed specimen.

WUCHIH SHREW
Crocidura wuchihensis NOT ILLUSTRATED
Measurements HB 59–65, T 37–42, E 6–9. Skull: gsl 15.7–17.1, upper toothrow 6.8–7.3

Identification Moderately small shrew. Upperparts dark greyish-brown, individual hairs with grey bases and brown tips mixed with some longer silvery hairs; underparts slightly paler and greyer. Front and hind feet whitish, with pale brown hairs in middle, darker brown on sides. Tail nearly naked, very thinly covered with short brown hairs, mixed with scattered long bristles on basal half; dark brown above, paler below but not sharply demarcated. Ears pale. **Taxonomic notes** Formerly confused with *C. horsfieldi*, which is now believed not to occur in region. **Similar species** Indochinese Shrew, *C. indochinensis*, is larger; Ke Go Shrew, *C. kegoensis*, is slightly smaller, with dark mark on muzzle, dark ears, different teeth (Fig. 22). **Ecology and habitat** Recorded from montane evergreen forest at 1,300–1,500m altitude.

Distribution and status SE Asia: N Vietnam. Also Hainan, China. Poorly known; probably not currently at risk.

HILL'S SHREW
Crocidura hilliana NOT ILLUSTRATED
Measurements T 45. Skull: gl 21.0–23.5, upper toothrow 8.8–10.2

Identification Originally described from skull remains, with information on external appearance based on only one preserved specimen, described later. Medium-sized, uniformly dark grey-brown with slightly paler hands, feet, muzzle and tail. Tail with scattered long bristle hairs along 85 per cent of its length. Skull moderately large. Upper incisor large, robust,

with well-developed posterior cusp, first upper unicuspid large, nearly as high as incisor, about twice height and more than twice crown area of remaining unicuspids (Fig. 21b).

Similar species South-East Asian White-toothed Shrew, *C. fuliginosa*, averages slightly larger, first upper unicuspid relatively small, about half height of incisor and only slightly higher than remaining unicuspids; Grey Shrew, *C. attenuata*, is smaller on average, with slender upper incisor, relatively small second and third upper unicuspids (Fig. 21). Other *Crocidura* in its range are smaller.

Ecology and habitat Lowlands in a variety of habitats from forest to cultivated lands.

Distribution and status SE Asia: E Thailand, and C Laos. Poorly known; probably not currently at risk.

VORACIOUS SHREW
Crocidura vorax PLATE 3
Measurements HB 55–90, T 41–51 (~70% of HB), HF 11–14. Skull: gl 17.7–20.1, upper toothrow 7.2–8.2

Identification Medium-sized; upperparts pale greyish-brown, fur with dark grey bases, then a narrow grey band, and pale brownish tips, appearing speckled. Tail sharply bicoloured, dark above, pale below, covered with short, fine hairs that hide scales, with scattered longer bristles on basal two-thirds. Skull has low but clearly defined sagittal crest. **Similar species** *C. fuliginosa* and *C. attenuata* are larger, with darker, greyer fur and dark tail only sparsely haired with scattered longer bristles restricted to near base; Chinese Shrew, *C. rapax*, is smaller on average, with tail indistinctly bicoloured.

Ecology and habitat Terrestrial.

Distribution and status SE Asia: NE Thailand and Laos. Also India, and S and C China. Poorly known in region, but probably not currently at risk.

CHINESE SHREW
Crocidura rapax NOT ILLUSTRATED
Measurements HB 55–70, T 38–47 (~66% of HB), HF 11–13. Skull: gl 17.5–18.3, upper toothrow 7.1–8.1

Identification Small to medium-small; upperparts pale greyish-brown, fur with narrow grey bases and pale brownish tips. Tail indistinctly bicoloured, dark above, slightly paler below, covered with short, fine hairs with scattered longer bristles on basal two-thirds.
Similar species Voracious Shrew, *C. vorax*, is usually slightly larger, with a more distinctly bicoloured tail and pronounced sagittal crest on the skull; both South-East Asian Shrew, *C. fuliginosa*, and Grey Shrew, *C. attenuata*, are larger, with darker, greyer fur, and tail that is only sparsely haired except for scattered, longer bristles near base; Hill's Shrew, *C. hilliana*, is larger.
Ecology and habitat Terrestrial.
Distribution and status SE Asia: N Myan-

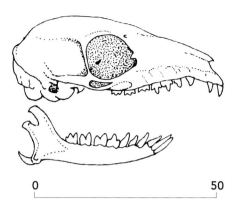

Fig. 23 *Lateral view of skull of* Tupaia *sp.*

mar. Also India and S China. Poorly known in region, but probably not currently at risk.

Order **SCANDENTIA**

Superficially, treeshrews resemble squirrels, but differ in many details of anatomy and behaviour. They have a very long muzzle with a total of 38 teeth, with pointed incisors and several premolars (Fig. 23), unlike the chisel-like incisors of rodents. All feet have five well-developed digits with claws, which tend to show well on footprints (Fig. 15b).

Treeshrews have been variously classified as primates or insectivores, but are now recognized as distinct from both and are placed in their own order, Scandentia.

Family *PTILOCERCIDAE* FEATHER-TAILED TREESHREWS

Although often placed as a subfamily within the Tupaiidae, this species differs in many morphological and genetic ways from other treeshrews and is now considered to be in its own family.

FEATHER-TAILED TREESHREW
Ptilocercus lowii PLATE 4
Measurements HB 134–150, T 160–202, HF 24–30
Identification Upperparts fluffy grey to grey-brown; underparts pale brownish-grey, the individual hairs with grey bases and buffy-white tips. Eyes and ears relatively large. Tail long and naked except for a feather-like tip of long hairs sticking out on either side, starting about halfway along the tail, the first few long hairs black, the remainder white.
Similar species No other mammal in region

has similar feathery tail with naked base.
Ecology and habitat Nocturnal. Usually arboreal, often travelling on vines. Lowland forest from sea level to about 1,000m altitude. Also reported from disturbed habitats, including secondary forest and plantation. Sometimes travels on ground. Diet mainly insects and other arthropods.
Distribution and status SE Asia: peninsular Thailand and Malaysia. Also Sumatra, Borneo and some offshore islands. Vulnerable. Relatively few records; apparently declining owing to loss of lowland rainforest habitat.

Family *TUPAIIDAE* TREESHREWS

The Slender-tailed Treeshrew, *Dendrogale*, is readily distinguished from other species by its narrow tail and distinctive face pattern. Within the genus *Tupaia*, three species occur in the region, of which the larger two are very similar to each other and are distinguished mainly by colour and range.

The Shrew-faced Ground Squirrel, *Rhinosciurus laticaudatus*, sometimes resembles a treeshrew at a distance, but can be distinguished by its shorter tail, pale underparts, lack of a pale mark on the neck, the modified digits on the front feet and the very different teeth.

COMMON TREESHREW
Tupaia glis PLATE 4
Measurements HB 135–205, T 125–195 (80–105% of HB), HF 42–49. Wt 90–190g
Identification Hairs on upperparts banded dark and pale, appearing finely speckled, with a strong reddish tint; underparts buff. Usually has a pale stripe on each shoulder. Female has 2 pairs of mammae. **Taxonomic note** The form in Borneo is now considered a distinct species, *T. longipes*. **Similar species** Northern Treeshrew, *T. belangeri*, lacks reddish tinge, and has 3 pairs of mammae in female.
Ecology and habitat Diurnal. Most often observed active around fallen trees and branches, in low woody vegetation or on the ground. Diet mainly insects and other arthropods, and sweet or oily fruits. Occurs in forests as well as in gardens and plantations near forest.
Distribution and status SE Asia: peninsular Thailand and Malaysia. Also Sumatra, Java and smaller Indonesian islands. Potentially threatened by loss of lowland forest.

NORTHERN TREESHREW
Tupaia belangeri PLATE 4
Measurements HB 160–230, T 150–200 (~100% HB), HF 38–45, E 16–17
Identification Hairs on upperparts banded dark and pale, appearing finely speckled brown. Underparts buff. Usually has a pale stripe on each shoulder. Female has 3 pairs of mammae. Moderate geographic variation, generally olive-brown in much of range, but in some northern populations there are also reddish forms similar to *T. glis*. Further studies, including use of genetics, are needed to determine whether additional species are represented. **Similar species** Common

Treeshrew, *T. glis*, is more reddish in areas where range overlaps in peninsular Thailand, and female has only 2 pairs of mammae.
Ecology and habitat Diurnal. Mainly terrestrial and in low bushes. Found in a range of forest habitats including evergreen forest, as well as deciduous forest especially near streams and rivers. Tolerant of moderate forest disturbance, and found in gardens and plantations.
Distribution and status SE Asia: Myanmar, Thailand, Laos, Vietnam and Cambodia. Also Nepal and S China. Not currently at risk.

LESSER TREESHREW
Tupaia minor PLATE 4
Measurements HB 110–140, T 140–160 (115–130% of HB), E 10–14, HF 25–29. Wt 30–70g
Identification Hairs on upperparts banded light and dark, giving an overall speckled olive-brown appearance. Underparts buffy, often with a reddish tinge towards the rear. Upper side of tail darker than body. Tail long and relatively thin. **Similar species** Other *Tupaia* treeshrews in region are larger, with bushier tails; Northern Slender-tailed Treeshrew, *Dendrogale murina*, has relatively shorter, thinner tail, and stripes on face; small tree squirrels have less pointed muzzle.
Ecology and habitat Diurnal and mainly arboreal. Often seen at 3–8m above ground, sometimes to 20m, travelling along lianas or branches of small trees. Diet includes insects and fruits. Occurs in forests, gardens and plantations.
Distribution and status SE Asia: peninsular Thailand and Malaysia. Also Sumatra and Borneo. Potentially threatened by loss of lowland forest.

NORTHERN SLENDER-TAILED TREESHREW
Dendrogale murina PLATE 4
Measurements HB 115–135, T 105–130, HF 26–30, E 10–18. Wt 35–55g
Identification Upperparts brownish-black, speckled with orange-brown. Underparts sharply contrasting pale buff to pale orange.

Muzzle pointed, with buffy-orange stripe below and above eye, contrasting with dark mask through eye and darker crown. Tail thickly covered with short dark hair. **Similar species** Lesser Treeshrew, *Tupaia minor*, has longer, slightly bushier tail, lacks stripes on face, does not overlap in range; striped squirrels, *Tamiops* spp., have more rounded heads, different face pattern and paler striped backs.

Ecology and habitat Diurnal. Primarily scan-sorial (climbing), found in trees and bushes near ground, but may sometimes be in canopy. Most records from evergreen forest, but also recorded from disturbed forest and areas of extensive bamboo.

Distribution and status SE Asia: SE Thailand, SE Laos, Vietnam and Cambodia. Appears to be patchily distributed and relatively poorly known, but apparently not currently at risk.

Order DERMOPTERA

Family *CYNOCEPHALIDAE* COLUGOS

The order Dermoptera includes only one living family, with only two known species, one confined to the southern Philippines and the other found elsewhere in South-East Asia. Colugos, also known as flying lemurs, cannot truly fly, but instead glide with the aid of a membrane between their legs. The teeth are highly specialized and unlike those of any other mammal: there are no teeth at the front of the upper jaw and the two pairs of lower front teeth look like finely toothed combs (Fig. 24).

SUNDA COLUGO

Galeopterus variegatus   PLATE 24
Measurements HB 330–420, T 180–270, HF 65–73. Wt 925–1,700g

Identification Usually grey, with extensive black and white markings, but some individuals are tinged reddish-brown, or are totally reddish-brown with light buff or orange markings. Most distinctive feature is the gliding membrane, which extends between front and hind legs and encloses tail. All four legs relatively long with long, sharp claws on toes which are connected by webs. Small young may be carried with adult, sometimes wrapped in gliding membrane. **Taxonomic note** Formerly included in genus *Cynocephalus*. **Similar species** Flying squirrels have long bushy tail completely free of any enclosing membrane and much shorter legs. **Ecology and habitat** Nocturnal, but sometimes active in the morning and late afternoon. Clings to the sides of tree trunks or glides between tall trees. May also hang under horizontal branches. Rests in tree holes or crowns of trees. Diet poorly known, but believed to feed on leaves, leaf shoots, flower buds and sap. Occurs in tall and sec-ondary forests, gardens and tree plantations.

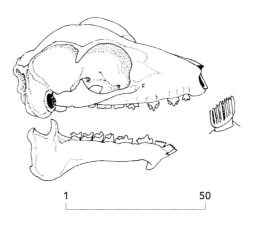

Fig. 24 *Skull of* Galeopterus variegatus, *with enlarged detail of lower incisor showing comb-like cusps.*

Distribution and Status SE Asia: S Myanmar, S Thailand, Laos, Vietnam, Cambodia and Peninsular Malaysia. Also Sumatra, Java, Borneo, Bali and many smaller Indonesian islands. Near Threatened. Populations are declining due to habitat loss and hunting.

Order CHIROPTERA
Bats

Bats are the only mammals capable of true flight. Two other groups of South-East Asian mammals, the colugos and the flying squirrels, are often said to fly, but they can only glide, and are not capable of powered flight. They have gliding membranes between their legs, allowing them to travel quite long distances between tall trees, but they cannot flap them to gain lift. Bats, in contrast, have their forelimbs modified into wings, with membranes stretched between elongated finger bones (Fig. 25), and powerful chest muscles to flap their wings.

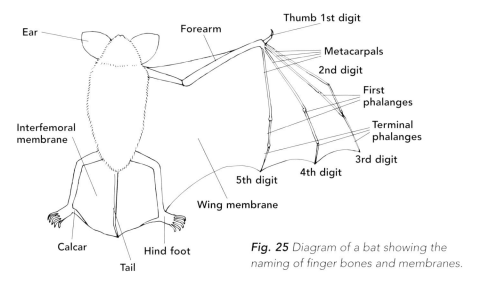

Fig. 25 *Diagram of a bat showing the naming of finger bones and membranes.*

Bats flying at dusk could potentially be confused with birds. Flying-foxes are similar in size to some raptors, while small insectivorous bats are similar in size to small swifts that are often flying in similar habitats. However, they can be distinguished by the shape of their wings and bodies, and by their pattern of flight.

With the exception of a few distinctive species, most bats are difficult to identify unless they can be captured and examined closely. In the hand, most species, or at least groups of species, can be distinguished based on easily visible characteristics and measurements. Fur colour and wing patterns are useful for identifying some species, though in other groups colour is highly variable and not reliable for identification. For some species it may be necessary to examine the skull or dentition for confirmation. With care, the teeth can be examined in a live bat by gently opening the mouth with a toothpick or similar tool. A small magnifying glass is helpful to see details. The skull itself can only be examined in a museum specimen, but many features of skull shape are reflected in the outward appearance of the head and, with practice, most species can be identified in life.

For many of the insectivorous bats, echolocation calls can be another useful aid to identification. These calls are most readily described for the horseshoe and roundleaf bats, in which a constant-frequency component to the call is highly distinctive for each population and differs among species. When calls are known, they are provided in the species accounts, although these must be considered cautiously outside the region where they were recorded, as substantial geographic variation has been observed in some species.

Juvenile bats are capable of flight before they are fully grown. They tend to be smaller and coloured differently from adults. Young are generally much duller in colour, grey or grey-brown. If held against a bright light, the wing joints of immatures appear banded where the cartilage has not yet turned to bone (the adult joint looks like a solid lump). By the time the joints are fully ossified and solid, bats are fully grown, although they may take a bit longer to gain full adult colours.

Bat research has a long history in South-East Asia, but nevertheless much remains to be learned. Many of the more effective survey techniques, such as harp traps, mist nets and bat detectors, have come into use only recently. Relatively few areas have been subject to intensive surveys, and most new surveys turn up new distributional records or even previously unknown species. Furthermore, genetic studies are revealing that many taxa formerly considered to be one species actually represent a complex of species. Much research remains to be done to resolve these species complexes, not only to determine reliable ways to distinguish the species based on morphology, but also to determine the appropriate name for each species in the complex.

The species descriptions in this book thus represent the current state of knowledge of bats in the region, as published at the time of writing, but many changes are anticipated. If there are known taxonomic issues for a species, these are usually mentioned in the accounts.

South-East Asian bats are classified into nine families, which can be distinguished by ear shape, muzzle shape, the presence or absence of a noseleaf and the tail pattern. Within each family, genera can be distinguished by a variety of characters, such as noseleaf shape, dentition, or even colour. In many cases, identification can be greatly facilitated by first determining the genus characters. To assist with sorting out the very large number of bats in the region, general accounts of each family and genus are given in addition to the species accounts.

Family *PTEROPODIDAE* FRUIT BATS

Fruit bats have large, conspicuous eyes which reflect a dull red eyeshine when a light is shone on them at night. The ears are relatively small and simple, with a complete unbroken margin. The muzzle appears rather dog-like, without modifications or leaflets, although the nostrils are well developed and sometimes slightly tubular. The tail is short or lacking, and the interfemoral membrane is narrow. The second finger is well developed, independent of the third finger and usually with a claw at the tip (except *Eonycteris*). The teeth have simple cusps, quite unlike the sharp W-shaped cusps of other bats.

Many of these features are reflections of their behaviour. Fruit bats lack echolocation (except *Rousettus*), and rely instead on eyesight and smell to find their way. Thus they need large, reflective eyes to see well at night. They feed mainly on nectar and fruits, and often climb through trees using the claws on their wings as well as their feet to grip branches.

Twelve genera of fruit bats are currently recognized from mainland South-East Asia. For identification, these can be divided into groups based on morphology and feeding behaviour. The largest group includes *Cynopterus*, *Dyacopterus*, *Megaerops*, *Chironax*, *Sphaerius*, *Balionycteris*, *Penthetor* and *Aethalops*, which have short, relatively powerful jaws with reduced numbers of large, heavily cusped teeth for feeding on fruit (Fig. 26b,c,d). The macroglossine bats, which include *Macroglossus* and *Eonycteris*, have a long narrow muzzle, weak jaws, small teeth and a relatively long tongue for nectar feeding (Fig. 26f,g). *Rousettus* (Fig. 26e) and *Pteropus* (Fig. 26a) are somewhat intermediate in shape, with an elongate muzzle and moderately well-developed teeth, and may be closer to the ancestral form from which the others evolved. Dental characters are important for distinguishing genera but must be examined carefully, as some teeth, particularly the smaller cheek teeth, are sometimes missing or shed in older individuals. This may be due to deterioration of the teeth associated with the high sugar content of their diets. Thus, it is important to consider the shapes and sizes of teeth and not just the number.

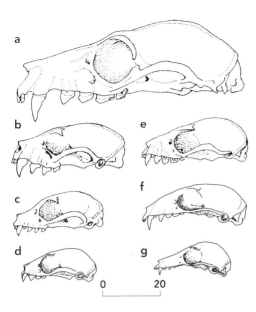

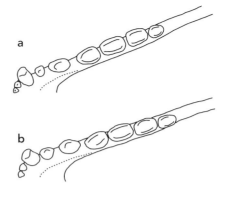

Fig. 26 *Profiles of selected fruit bat skulls:*
Pteropus vampyrus *(a),* Dyacopterus
spadiceus *(b),* Cynopterus brachyotis *(c),*
Aethalops alecto *(d),* Rousettus
amplexicaudatus *(e),* Eonycteris spelaea *(f)*
and Macroglossus minimus *(g).*

Genus *Rousettus* Moderately large bats
with a fairly long muzzle, a claw on the second digit and a well-developed tail. Produce
a distinctive clicking call with the tongue,
which is used for echolocation, presumably
mainly to navigate in dark caves. Skull moderately long with slightly decurved rostrum
(Fig. 26e). Cheek teeth unspecialized with
poorly developed cusps. Dental formula 2/2
1/1 3/3 2/3.

GEOFFROY'S ROUSETTE
Rousettus amplexicaudatus PLATE 7
Measurements FA 78–87, T 15–21,
E 16.5–19.5. Wt 55–80; males average
slightly larger than females
Identification Upperparts grey-brown to
brown, darker on top of head; underparts
paler grey-brown. Fur short and sparse
except for long pale hairs on chin and neck.
Adults, especially males, sometimes have
pale yellow tufts of hair on the sides of the
neck. Third lower molar nearly circular, only

Fig. 27 *Right lower toothrows of* Rousettus
amplexicaudatus *(a) and* R. leschenaultii *(b).*

slightly longer than wide (Fig. 27a). **Similar
species** Leschenault's Rousette, *R. leschenaultii*, has a more elongate third lower
molar and smaller incisors; nectar bats,
Eonycteris spp., lack a claw on the second
digit; Dayak Fruit Bat, *Dyacopterus
spadiceus*, is similar in size, but has a much
thicker, shorter muzzle and fewer, larger
cheek teeth (Fig. 28d). Bare-backed Rousette, *R. spinalatus*, known from Borneo and
Sumatra, might be expected in Peninsular
Malaysia; it is distinguished by having the
wings joined together over the middle of the
back, unlike other *Rousettus*, which have
wings attached to sides of back, separated
by a broad band of fur.
Ecology and habitat Roosts in caves, sometimes in complete darkness, often in association with Cave Nectar Bat, *Eonycteris
spelaea*. Feeds on fruit as well as nectar and
pollen.
Distribution and status SE Asia: S Myanmar,
Thailand, Vietnam, Laos, Cambodia and
Peninsular Malaysia. Also Borneo and most
Indonesian islands through New Guinea,
Solomon Islands and the Philippines. Not
currently at risk, but has declined in some
areas due to excessive hunting.

LESCHENAULT'S ROUSETTE
Rousettus leschenaultii PLATE 7
Measurements FA 75–85, T 10–18, E 18–24.
Wt 60–100; males heavier than females

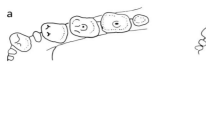

Fig. 28 *Right lower toothrows of* Cynopterus horsfieldi *(a,b)*, C. sphinx *(c) and* Dyacopterus spadiceus *(d).*

Identification Upperparts grey-brown to buffy-brown, paler underneath. Fur short and sparse except for long pale hairs on chin and neck. Third lower molar elongate, about twice as long as wide (Fig. 27b). **Similar species** Geoffroy's Rousette, *R. amplexicaudatus*, is similar in size, but averages slightly darker in colour with a slightly shorter toothrow, and has a more rounded third lower molar.
Ecology and habitat Like other *Rousettus*, produces an audible clicking call when flying that is used for echolocation. Roosts in caves, including wells, mines and artificial caves. Diet mainly flower nectar, pollen and fruit.
Distribution and status SE Asia: Myanmar, Thailand, Laos, Vietnam, Cambodia and Peninsular Malaysia. Also Pakistan, India, Nepal, S China, Sumatra and Java. Not currently at risk.

Genus *Pteropus* Very large bats, considerably larger than any other South-East Asian bats, including the largest bats in the world. First finger very long; second finger has a well-developed claw. Skull large and elongate with an almost tubular braincase (Fig. 26a). Three upper premolars, but anterior very small and often missing in older individuals. Remaining teeth relatively simple and unspecialized. Dental formula 2/2 1/1 3/3 2/3. Four or five species in the region, depending upon whether *P. intermedius* is recognized as a distinct species.

LARGE FLYING-FOX
Pteropus vampyrus PLATE 5
Measurements FA 185–200, T none.
Wt 645–1,100
Identification Very large bat, with a wingspread up to 1.5m. Colour somewhat variable, but back usually black with grey streaking, sharply separated from orange-brown mantle and back of head. Sides of head and front of neck mixed reddish-brown and black, blending into blackish-brown underparts. Immatures uniform dull grey-brown.
Similar species Indian Flying-fox, *P. giganteus*, tends to be slightly smaller, with paler head and pale brown underparts; Lyle's Flying-fox, *P. lylei*, and Island Flying-fox, *P. hypomelanus*, are both substantially smaller.
Ecology and habitat Roosts in large, established colonies on open branches of trees, often in mangrove or nipah palm. Sometimes flies long distances to feed in flowering or fruiting trees. May migrate seasonally to follow fruiting and flowering cycles. Eats both nectar and fruit, including some orchard species such as rambutans and mangoes. Pollinates the flowers of many forest trees, including durian.
Distribution and status SE Asia: lowland areas of S Myanmar, S Thailand, Cambodia, S Vietnam and Peninsular Malaysia. Possibly Laos. Also Sumatra, Borneo, Java, Lesser Sundas and the Philippines. Vulnerable.

Populations in many areas declining due to overhunting and loss of habitat.

INDIAN FLYING-FOX
Pteropus giganteus   PLATE 5
Measurements FA 140–180, T none
Identification Very large bat. Back black, lightly streaked grey; mantle pale yellow-brown; head brown; underparts buffy-brown. Some individuals are darker. **Taxonomic notes** Some authorities recognize Intermediate Flying-fox, *P. intermedius*, from central Myanmar as a distinct species; it resembles *P. giganteus*, but has browner underparts. Further specimens are required to determine whether it is, in fact, a distinct form. **Similar species** Lyle's Flying-fox, *P. lylei*, can be similar in colour but averages smaller and does not overlap in range; Large Flying-fox, *P. vampyrus*, usually has darker underparts, different distribution.
Ecology and habitat Roosts in large, established colonies on open branches of trees, including in grounds of temples and in urban areas. May fly many kilometres in search of food. Eats both nectar and fruit including some orchard species. Pollinates the flowers of many forest trees.
Distribution and status SE Asia: known only from W Myanmar. Also Pakistan, Nepal, India and Sri Lanka. Not currently at risk, but probably some decline due to excessive hunting; need to protect roosts from disturbance.

LYLE'S FLYING-FOX
Pteropus lylei   PLATE 5
Measurements FA 145–160, T none.
Wt 390–480
Identification Medium-large flying-fox with back and wings dark brown or black; mantle and head buffy to orange-brown, sharply separated from back colour; muzzle dark, with dark pattern sometimes extending to whole front of head. Underparts vary from buffy-brown to black. **Similar species** Large Flying-fox, *P. vampyrus*, is much larger and nearly always has dark underparts; Island Flying-fox, *P. hypomelanus*, is smaller, with rounded ears.

Ecology and habitat Roosts in large, established colonies on open branches of large trees. Most known colonies are in temples or in the middle of towns or cities. Feeds on fruits and may raid fruit orchards.
Distribution and status SE Asia: known only from S Thailand, Cambodia and Vietnam. Vulnerable: limited range and population with evidence of substantial recent declines, including loss of some colonies, probably due to hunting or persecution.

ISLAND FLYING-FOX
Pteropus hypomelanus   PLATE 5
Measurements FA 120–145, T none, E 2. Wt 210
Identification Smallest flying-fox in the region (but still much larger than other fruit bats). Lower back dark blackish-brown, sometimes heavily frosted with pale tips such that back appears grey; upper back, neck and back of head pale golden-brown to dark reddish-brown; underside varies from dark blackish-brown to buffy-brown. Ears relatively broad and rounded. **Similar species** Lyle's Flying-fox, *P. lylei*, is only slightly larger, but its ears are more pointed.
Ecology and habitat Roosts mainly on islands, in the fronds of coconut palms or amongst the branches of trees. Sometimes flies to the mainland to feed.
Distribution and status SE Asia: small islands off coastal Myanmar, Thailand, Vietnam, Cambodia, Malaysia and sometimes adjacent mainland. Also Andamans, Indonesia, the Philippines, New Guinea and the Solomons. Not currently at risk, but subject to hunting in some areas, and has probably declined somewhat.

Genus *Cynopterus* Medium to large bats with short, stout muzzle. Fur is typically yellowish-brown with a reddish or orange collar, best developed in males. Wing bones and rims to ears are usually contrastingly white. Most individuals have brown fur with a yellowish or reddish tinge and contrasting whitish wing bones and rims to the ears, although some old individuals have darker rims to the ears, and young bats can be very grey. Skull compact with a short rostrum (Fig. 26c). Anterior upper premolar very small. Upper canines have a slight posterior secondary cusp; cheek teeth fairly stout, generally unspecialized. Dental formula 2/2 1/1 3/3 1/2.

FOREST SHORT-NOSED FRUIT BAT
Cynopterus cf. *brachyotis* *"Forest"* PLATE 6
Measurements FA 56–63, T 9–10, E 13–16. Wt 24–35. Skull: gl 26.4–28.8
Identification Generally brown to yellowish-brown with a brighter collar, dark orange-brown in adult males, more yellowish in females. Immatures greyer with indistinct collar. Ears and wing bones edged in white. Muzzle relatively short. Two pairs of lower incisors (Fig. 29a). **Taxonomic notes** Recent genetic analyses indicate that bats formerly referred to *C. brachyotis* belong to several different species, of which at least two species co-occur in mainland South-East Asia. These are here called "Forest" and "Sunda" *C.* cf. *brachyotis* as it is not yet clear which one is actually *C. brachyotis*. A specimen from Myanmar was genetically distinct and may represent a third species in the region, but further study is required to determine its distinguishing characteristics. **Similar species** Sunda Short-nosed Fruit Bat, *C.* cf. *brachyotis* "Sunda", is difficult to distinguish, but has longer forearm (on average), proportionately longer muzzle, and more yellowish-orange collar.
Ecology and habitat Largely restricted to more mature forests, from lowlands to hills, where it has been found in both the forest understorey and the canopy. Roosts under large leaves of trees, especially palms or large-leaved trees such as *Macaranga*. Sometimes modifies leaves into a "tent" by biting the mid-rib. Feeds mainly on fruits, especially figs.
Distribution and status SE Asia: Peninsular Malaysia. Also Borneo. Not currently at risk, though apparently much less common than Sunda species.

SUNDA SHORT-NOSED FRUIT BAT
Cynopterus cf. *brachyotis* *"Sunda"* PLATE 6
Measurements FA 59–70, T 8–10, E 14–17. Wt 32–42. Skull: gl 27.2–29.6
Identification Generally brown to yellowish-brown with an orange collar in adult males, more yellowish collar in females. Ears and wing bones edged in white. Two pairs of lower incisors (Fig. 29a). **Taxonomic notes** Recent genetic analyses indicate that this species is distinct from the Forest Short-nosed Fruit Bat, *C.* cf. *brachyotis* "Forest", which co-occurs with it in Peninsular Malaysia and Borneo. **Similar species** Forest Short-nosed Fruit Bat, *C.* cf. *brachyotis* "Forest", averages smaller with a darker orange collar and shorter muzzle; Greater Short-nosed Fruit Bat, *C. sphinx*, has longer forearm, longer ears and longer skull; Horsfield's Fruit Bat, *C. horsfieldi*, is larger and has more rectangular, heavily cusped molars (Fig. 28a,b); Dusky Fruit Bat, *Penthetor lucasi*, has only one pair of lower incisors (Fig. 29b), lacks white edges to the ears and is greyer; Hill Fruit Bat, *Sphaerius blandfordi*, has pale rims to the ears and pale wing bones but differs in colour, lacks a tail and has a thickly furred interfemoral membrane.
Ecology and habitat Occurs in a wide variety of disturbed habitats, including orchards, plantations and second growth, where it can be very common. Not usually found in the interior of mature forests. Roosts singly or in small groups, usually under the leaves of trees, including coconut palms. Feeds on small fruits, sucking out the juices and soft pulp, as well as bananas, nectar and pollen.
Distribution and status SE Asia: S Myanmar, S Thailand, S Laos, Cambodia, S Vietnam

Fig. 29 *Front views of lower canines and incisors of* Cynopterus brachyotis *(a) and* Penthetor lucasi *(b).*

and Peninsular Malaysia. Also Java and Borneo. Not currently at risk.

GREATER SHORT-NOSED FRUIT BAT

Cynopterus sphinx PLATE 6
Measurements FA 65–76, E 18–24. Wt. 40–57. Skull: gl 29–33

Identification Upperparts brown to grey-brown; underparts paler. Collar orange-brown in males, yellowish in females. Ears and wing bones edged in white. Lower cheek teeth rounded without accessory cusps (Fig. 28c). **Similar species** Short-nosed fruit bats, *Cynopterus* spp., are smaller, with shorter ears; Horsfield's Fruit Bat, *C. horsfieldi*, has squarer cheek teeth with extra cusps or ridges; Hill Fruit Bat, *Sphaerius blandfordi*, has pale rims to ears, but differs in colour, lacks a tail and has a thickly furred interfemoral membrane.

Ecology and habitat Found in disturbed habitats and open forests, where it is relatively common. Roosts in trees, under palm fronds, under the leaves of large epiphytic ferns and occasionally near the entrances of caves, in rock crevices or under roofs. Feeds on nectar and fruit.

Distribution and status SE Asia: Myanmar, Laos, Vietnam, Cambodia, S Thailand to northern part of Peninsular Malaysia. Also Sri Lanka, India through S China, Sumatra, Java, Timor and adjacent islands. Not currently at risk.

HORSFIELD'S FRUIT BAT

Cynopterus horsfieldi PLATE 6
Measurements FA 68–76, T 14, E 17–20. Wt 50–70. Skull: gl 31–34

Identification Upperparts grey-brown; underparts slightly yellowish-brown; collar dark reddish-brown in adult males, paler in females. Ears and wing bones edged in white. Cheek teeth broader and squarer than those of other *Cynopterus*, with distinct cusps or ridges on the last lower premolar and first lower molar (Fig. 28a,b). **Similar species** Greater Short-nosed Fruit Bat, *C. sphinx*, has smaller, more rounded cheek

teeth; Dayak Fruit Bat, *Dyacopterus spadiceus*, is larger, lacks the small anterior upper premolar, has more massive teeth (Fig. 28d) and differs in colour.

Ecology and habitat. Roosts in trees or under banana leaves, which may be modified into a tent by biting the mid-rib. Also roosts in solution cavities in limestone cliffs or caves. Feeds mainly on fruit, tending to eat larger fruit than other *Cynopterus*.

Distribution and status SE Asia: S Vietnam, Laos, Cambodia, Thailand and Peninsular Malaysia. Also Borneo, Sumatra, Java and adjacent islands. Not currently at risk.

Genus *Penthetor* Medium-sized bats, very similar to *Cynopterus*, but coloration generally dark grey-brown; cheek teeth slightly wider and flatter; only one pair of lower incisors (Fig. 29b); outer upper incisors about half the length of the inner pair. Dental formula 2/1 1/1 3/3 1/2.

DUSKY FRUIT BAT

Penthetor lucasi PLATE 6
Measurements FA 57–62, T 8–13, E 14–16.5. Wt 30–44

Identification Upperparts dark grey-brown; underparts pale buffy-grey. Top of head often distinctly darker down the centre and paler near the eyes. Ears have dark edges. Only one pair of lower incisors (Fig. 29b); outer upper incisors shorter than inner pair. **Similar species** Short-nosed fruit bats, *Cynopterus* spp., are brighter-coloured with two pairs of lower incisors; tailless fruit bats, *Megaerops* spp., lack a tail, have broader, higher nostrils, light brown fur with pale grey bases, and small, even upper incisors.

Ecology and habitat Roosts in colonies in rock shelters or caves, sometimes in near-total darkness. Eats fruit, which it sometimes carries back to the cave to eat.

Distribution and status SE Asia: Peninsular Malaysia and extreme S Thailand. Also Borneo, Sumatra and Riau archipelago. Not currently at risk, though uncommon in most areas.

Genus *Megaerops* Small to medium-sized bats, similar to *Cynopterus* but with a slightly shorter nose; usually no visible tail; only one pair of lower incisors. Skull similar to *Cynopterus*, but with a shorter, higher rostrum (Fig. 30). Canines lack secondary cusps. Upper incisors small and roughly equal, evenly spaced between the canines. Dental formula 2/1 1/1 3/3 1/2.

SUNDA TAILLESS FRUIT BAT
Megaerops ecaudatus PLATE 5
Measurements FA 51–58, T none. Wt 20–38. Skull: cbl 24.0–26.2
Identification Upperparts yellowish-brown to reddish-brown with pale grey bases to fur; underparts paler and greyer. Ears with dark edges. Muzzle short with broad and slightly tubular nostrils. One pair of lower incisors. Interfemoral membrane narrow and thinly haired, with no visible tail. Skull with short, high rostrum (Fig. 30b). **Similar species** Northern Tailless Fruit Bat, *M. niphanae*, is very similar, distinguished by more pointed muzzle and smaller nostrils; White-collared Fruit Bat, *M. wetmorei*, is smaller with more pointed muzzle and (in males) white shoulder tufts; short-nosed fruit bats, *Cynopterus* spp., have white or pale edges to ears, a short tail and two pairs of lower incisors; Dusky Fruit Bat, *Penthetor lucasi*, has a short tail and darker fur; Grey Fruit Bat, *Aethalops alecto*, has a more pointed muzzle and a thickly furred interfemoral membrane.
Ecology and habitat Has been found mainly in tall forest, but sometimes also in disturbed forest.
Distribution and status SE Asia: S Thailand and Peninsular Malaysia, overlapping range of *M. niphanae* in Thailand; northern limits of range poorly known because of past confusion with *M. niphanae*. Also Sumatra, Borneo. Not currently at risk.

NORTHERN TAILLESS FRUIT BAT
Megaerops niphanae PLATE 5
Measurements FA 53–61, T none. Wt 22–39. Skull: cbl 24.4–26.8

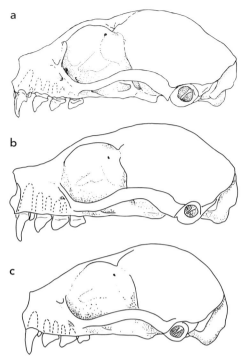

Fig. 30 *Skulls of* Megaerops niphanae *(a),* M. ecaudatus *(b) and* M. wetmorei *(c) showing differences in rostrum shape.*

Identification Upperparts brownish with pale grey bases to fur; underparts paler and greyer. Ears with dark edges. Muzzle sloped in profile with slightly tubular nostrils (Fig. 30a). One pair of lower incisors. Interfemoral membrane narrow and thinly haired, with no visible tail. **Similar species** Sunda Tailless Fruit Bat, *M. ecaudatus*, is very similar, differing mainly in the shape of the head, with more upturned rostrum (Fig. 30b) and protruding nostrils.
Ecology and habitat Found in a wide variety of forests, including partially disturbed areas.
Distribution and status SE Asia: throughout much of Laos, Vietnam, Cambodia and Thailand except in south. Most likely in Myanmar, though not yet reported. Also NE India. Not currently at risk.

WHITE-COLLARED FRUIT BAT
Megaerops wetmorei PLATE 5
Measurements FA 45–51, T 0–4, E 12. Wt 14–18. Skull: cbl 21.2–22.0

Identification Body fur pale grey-brown, lower back slightly darker. Adult males have large white tufts on sides of neck that extend onto back to form a broken collar. Interfemoral membrane narrow and sparsely covered with hairs. Tail very short or lacking. Muzzle short and thick. One pair of lower incisors. Rostrum of skull less upturned than in Sunda Tailless Fruit Bat, *M. ecaudatus* (Fig. 30c). **Similar species** Sunda Tailless Fruit Bat, *M. ecaudatus*, is larger, lacks white neck tufts and has a thicker muzzle; Black-capped Fruit Bat, *Chironax melanocephalus*, has two pairs of lower incisors and dark head; Grey Fruit Bat, *Aethalops alecto*, has a more pointed muzzle and thickly furred interfemoral membrane.

Ecology and habitat Mainly in mature lowland forest, where most common in canopy.

Distribution and status SE Asia: Peninsular Malaysia. Also Sumatra, Borneo and the Philippines. Vulnerable, due to loss of lowland rainforest in all parts of range.

Genus *Dyacopterus* Similar to *Cynopterus*, with a distinct tail, short muzzle and thick jaws (Fig. 26b), but cheek teeth greatly enlarged, with squared corners, large cusps and ridges (Fig. 28d). Only 3 upper cheek teeth. Dental formula 2/2 1/1 2/3 1/2.

DAYAK FRUIT BAT
Dyacopterus spadiceus PLATE 7
Measurements FA 77–81, T 19–24, E 17.5–21. Wt 75–100

Identification Upperparts dark grey-brown; underparts paler. Fur short. Some adults have dull orange tufts on each side of the neck. Very thick jaw, stout muzzle with massive rectangular cheek teeth (Fig. 28d). **Similar species** Rousettes, *Rousettus* spp., have narrow muzzles and smaller teeth; short-nosed fruit bats, *Cynopterus* spp., differ in colour, and have smaller muzzles and teeth.

Ecology and habitat Reported roosts include hollow trees and vicinity of limestone caves. Feeds mainly in canopy of mature lowland rainforests; has been caught feeding in fig trees. Adult males have been reported lactating, but it is not known whether they can suckle young.

Distribution and status SE Asia: peninsular Thailand and Malaysia. Also Borneo and the Philippines. Near Threatened, owing to loss of lowland rainforest.

Genus *Chironax* Small bat, very similar to *Cynopterus*, but lacking a tail; canines lack an inner cusp; premaxillaries fused (in contact but not fused in *Cynopterus*). Dental formula 2/2 1/1 3/3 1/2.

BLACK-CAPPED FRUIT BAT
Chironax melanocephalus PLATE 6
Measurements FA 43–46, T none, E 13. Wt 15.7

Identification Upperparts dark grey or brown; head darker, sometimes black; underparts pale brownish-grey; chin yellowish. Most adults have yellow-orange tufts on sides of neck. Two pairs of lower incisors. **Similar species** Other small tailless fruit bats have only one pair of lower incisors (as in Fig. 29b), and differ in colour.

Ecology and habitat Has been netted in the understorey of tall dipterocarp forest, but more common in canopy. Reported roosts including small groups in tree ferns, and shallow caves. Found in lowlands and hills.

Distribution and status SE Asia: S Thailand and Peninsular Malaysia. Also Sumatra, Java, Borneo and Sulawesi. Not currently at risk, but declining due to loss of forest.

Genus *Balionycteris* A small, dark fruit bat, easily recognized by pale spots on wings. Skull similar to *Cynopterus*, but slightly more elongate with an extra, very small upper molar and only one pair of lower incisors. Upper incisors close together and angled inwards. Canine lacks a supplementary cusp. Dental formula 2/1 1/1 3/3 2/2.

SPOTTED-WINGED FRUIT BAT
Balionycteris maculata PLATE 6
Measurements FA 40–45, T none, E 10–12. Wt 10–15

Identification Smallest fruit bat in region. Upperparts dark blackish-brown, darkest on the head; underparts pale grey-brown. Wing membranes dark brown, sparsely spotted with buff, especially on joints. Pale spots on edge of ear and in front of eye. One pair of lower incisors. **Similar species** Other fruit bats lack spots on wings; Black-capped Fruit Bat, *Chironax melanocephalus*, has two pairs of lower incisors.

Ecology and habitat Lowland dipterocarp forest where active in understorey. In Peninsular Malaysia has been found roosting in small groups in crowns of palms, clumps of epiphytic ferns, hollowed termite nests, rarely in caves.

Distribution and status SE Asia: peninsular Thailand and Malaysia. Also Borneo, Riau archipelago. Near Threatened, owing to loss of lowland rainforest.

Genus *Aethalops* Small, tailless bat similar to *Balionycteris*, but without the second upper molar. Rostrum slightly lower and more sloping than that of *Cynopterus* (Fig. 26d). Upper incisors about equal in length. Interfemoral membrane narrow but thickly furred. Dental formula 2/1 1/1 3/3 1/2.

GREY FRUIT BAT

Aethalops alecto   PLATE 6
Measurements FA 42–46, T none, E 10–13. Wt 14–18

Identification Upperparts dark grey-brown to reddish-brown, underparts slightly paler. Fur thick and long. Interfemoral membrane covered in thick, fluffy fur. Muzzle narrow and pointed. One pair of lower incisors. **Similar species** Tailless fruit bats, *Megaerops* spp., have thicker, shorter muzzles; Black-capped Fruit Bat, *Chironax melanocephalus*, has two pairs of lower incisors; Spotted-winged Fruit Bat, *Balionycteris maculata*, has distinct pale spots all over the wings; Hill Fruit Bat, *Sphaerius blanfordi*, is larger, with white rims to ears and two pairs of lower incisors.

Ecology and habitat. Apparently confined to montane forest above 1,000m.

Distribution and status SE Asia: known only

from hill forest in Peninsular Malaysia. Also Sumatra, Java, Bali and Lombok (form in Borneo is now considered a separate species, *A. aequalis*). Not currently at risk, but some declines due to loss of forest.

Genus *Sphaerius* Medium-small fruit bat with no tail; interfemoral membrane narrow and thickly covered with hairs. Long, low rostrum. Dental formula 2/2 1/1 3/3 1/2.

HILL FRUIT BAT

Sphaerius blanfordi   PLATE 6
Measurements FA 52–60, T none, E 16–19.5. Wt 27–30

Identification Dull grey fur with brown tips, slightly paler below. Interfemoral membrane very narrow, thickly covered with dense fur; no tail. Ears dark and hairless, rimmed with white. Wing bones conspicuously pale, contrasting with darker membranes. Two pairs of upper and lower incisors; incisors relatively well developed, positioned anterior to a line joining front of canines. **Similar species** Short-nosed fruit bats, *Cynopterus* spp., also have white rims to ears, but are brighter in colour (orange or yellow collars in adults), and have broad interfemoral membrane without thick fur, a short tail, larger cheek teeth but smaller incisors; tailless fruit bats, *Megaerops* spp., have light brown fur with pale grey bases, only one pair of lower incisors; Grey Fruit Bat, *Aethalops alecto*, is smaller, with only one pair of lower incisors.

Ecology and habitat Found only in hill forest at altitudes of 300–2,700m.

Distribution and status SE Asia: N Myanmar, N Thailand and N Vietnam. Also NE India, E Nepal, Tibet and SW China.

Genus *Eonycteris* Medium to large fruit bat with a long, narrow muzzle and a very long, sticky tongue. Distinguished from all other fruit bats in the region by the absence of a claw on the second finger. Tail well developed. Skull similar to that of *Rousettus*, but rostrum longer and lower; braincase more heavily deflected downwards (Fig. 26f). Cheek teeth narrow and elongate with reduced cusps.

Lower canines small and simple, heavily curved outwards. Dental formula 2/2 1/1 3/3 2/3.

CAVE NECTAR BAT
Eonycteris spelaea PLATE 7
Measurements FA 62–70, T 15–18, E 17–20. Wt 45–60

Identification Upperparts grey-brown; underparts slightly paler, sometimes tinged with yellow or orange around the neck. Fur short. Muzzle elongate, teeth rather small. Lacks a claw on the second digit. **Similar species** Rousettes, *Rousettus* spp., are larger, with a claw on the second digit; nectar bats, *Macroglossus* spp., are much smaller.
Ecology and habitat Roosts in large, noisy colonies in caves, often in virtual darkness. Flies far daily in search of flowering trees, to feed on pollen and nectar. Important pollinator of many forest trees, including commercially important species like durian, *Durio* spp., mangroves and *Parkia*. Forages in canopy of primary forest, as well as in gardens, mangroves and disturbed areas.
Distribution and status SE Asia: Myanmar, Thailand, Laos, Vietnam, Cambodia and Peninsular Malaysia. Also N India to S China, Sumatra, Java, Borneo, Sulawesi and other Indonesian islands and the Philippines. Not currently at risk, but has declined in some areas owing to disturbance of cave roosts.

Genus *Macroglossus* Small bats with long, narrow muzzle and a very long tongue. Tail minute or lacking. Skull has a very narrow rostrum with the braincase strongly deflected downwards (Fig. 26g). Lower jaw thin and weak. Cheek teeth small with a large diastema between the first two upper premolars. Canines long and needle-like, strongly curved outwards on lower jaw. Upper incisors tiny, projecting slightly forwards and separated from each other and canines by small gaps. Dental formula 2/2 1/1 3/3 2/3.

LESSER LONG-TONGUED NECTAR BAT
Macroglossus minimus PLATE 7
Measurements FA 39–44, T none, E 12–15.5. Wt 11–18

Identification Upperparts buffy-brown with pale bases; underparts paler and greyer. Wing membranes light brown. Long, narrow muzzle with very small teeth except for needle-like canines. Nostrils rounded and facing forwards, with a distinct median groove between them running down to upper lip, and two smaller grooves under nostrils in front. **Similar species** Greater Long-tongued Nectar Bat, *M. sobrinus*, is slightly larger, with longer head, jutting chin, more lateral-pointing nostrils and no grooves on upper lip.
Ecology and habitat In SE Asia, found principally in coastal habitats, particularly in mangroves, but ranges more widely in areas such as Borneo, where *M. sobrinus* is absent. Feeds on nectar and pollen from many sources, including mangrove and banana flowers. Often uses disturbed areas.
Distribution and status SE Asia: S Vietnam, Cambodia, S Thailand and Peninsular Malaysia, mainly in coastal areas. Also the Philippines, Java, Borneo and Indonesian Islands through to New Guinea, the Solomon islands and N Australia. Not currently at risk.

GREATER LONG-TONGUED NECTAR BAT
Macroglossus sobrinus PLATE 7
Measurements FA 44–50, T none, E 15–17. Wt 19–29

Identification Upperparts clay-brown with soft, fine fur; underparts paler. Long, narrow muzzle with angular, slightly jutting chin. Nostrils lacking any distinct grooves between them on the muzzle. **Similar species** Lesser Long-tongued Nectar Bat, *M. minimus*, is smaller with a shorter head, more pointed chin, more forward-pointing nostrils, and distinct median grooves on upper lip.
Ecology and habitat Found primarily in inland habitats, including dipterocarp forest and montane forest up to 2,000m as well as disturbed areas. Feeds on nectar and pollen, especially from banana flowers, both wild and cultivated. Has been found roosting in young rolled banana leaves.
Distribution and status SE Asia: Myanmar,

Thailand, Laos, Vietnam, Cambodia and Peninsular Malaysia. Also E India, Sumatra, Java and some small adjacent islands. Not currently at risk.

Family *RHINOPOMATIDAE* MOUSE-TAILED BATS

Medium-sized bats with a very long tail, most of which protrudes beyond the interfemoral membrane. A thickened band of skin joins the ears across the top of the forehead. There is a thickened pad on the muzzle, which may have a slight ridge. The ears have a distinct tragus. Three species are currently recognized in the family, of which one or two have been reported from mainland South-East Asia – there are no recent records, and there is still some uncertainty about the identity of the specimens that have been recorded from Myanmar and Thailand. To aid identification of any further specimens, the accounts below include both species, although only one is illustrated on the plates.

Genus *Rhinopoma* The only genus in the family. Only one pair of upper incisors and one upper premolar. Skull has a very short rostrum with swollen nasal cavities. Dental formula 1/2 1/1 1/2 3/3.

GREATER MOUSE-TAILED BAT
Rhinopoma microphyllum
NOT ILLUSTRATED
Measurements FA 60–75, T 50–77, E 18–22. Skull: ccl 17.2–22.7
Identification Large mouse-tailed bat (FA averages 68). Fur is short and fine, grey-brown above, paler below, restricted to head and front half of body. Membranes, lower back and lower belly naked, with brown skin. Tail long and protruding, usually shorter than forearm. Dermal ridge on muzzle very small and indistinct. **Similar species** Lesser Mouse-tailed Bat, *R. hardwickii*, is smaller, with proportionately longer tail and larger dermal ridge on muzzle.
Ecology and habitat Found mainly in arid areas, roosting in small caves, tunnels and buildings, often in relatively bright areas. In some parts of India undertakes seasonal migrations of up to 900km. When foraging, appears to be a relatively weak flier, with rapid wing beats interspersed with steady glides. Feeds on insects.
Distribution and status SE Asia: individual specimens of *Rhinopoma* have been recorded from peninsular Thailand and Myanmar, but it is uncertain which species they represent; possibly these were vagrant, migrating bats. Also Africa, through Middle East to Afghanistan, Pakistan and India, as well as N Sumatra. Not currently at risk.

LESSER MOUSE-TAILED BAT
Rhinopoma hardwickii PLATE 8
Measurements FA 53–64, T 56–78, E 17–21. Skull: ccl 15.5–17.5
Identification Medium-sized mouse-tailed bat (FA averages 59). Fur is grey-brown above with paler bases, greyer below. Extensive areas of bare skin on lower back and belly. Tail very long, usually longer than forearm. Tip of nose forms a thickened pad with a distinct ridge of skin (dermal ridge) that forms a rudimentary noseleaf. **Similar species** Greater Mouse-tailed Bat, *R. microphyllum*, is larger and has a proportionately shorter tail and smaller noseleaf.
Ecology and habitat Primarily found in relatively dry habitats. Roosts in caves, between large boulders, in deserted houses or temples, often using relatively bright areas. In northern climates builds up fat reserves during periods of insect abundance, then moves to more sheltered roosts to live off reserves in winter. Roosts range from a few to several hundred individuals and are sexually segregated.
Distribution and status SE Asia: see notes under Greater Mouse-tailed Bat, *R. microphyllum*. Also Africa through Middle East to India. Not currently at tisk.

Family *EMBALLONURIDAE* SHEATH-TAILED AND TOMB BATS

Small to medium-sized bats with a distinctive short tail that emerges from the middle of the interfemoral membrane (Plate 8). When legs are stretched out, membrane largely encloses tail. Muzzle is simple with no noseleaf. Ears are short to moderate, with a short rounded tragus. Eyes are relatively large and these bats often roost in fairly bright areas, suggesting vision may be important, perhaps for detecting potential predators. Echolocation usually involves multiple harmonics, and lower frequencies of echolocation calls of some species are audible to humans. The wings are long and narrow. The skull has a high, full braincase and a moderately short rostrum (Fig. 31d). The postorbital processes are long and slender and the premaxillary bones (where the upper incisors attach) are small and delicate.

Genus *Emballonura* Small and dark brown. Two distinct pairs of upper incisors; anterior upper premolar very small. Skull with narrow rostrum, very shallow depression between the eyes. Dental formula 2/3 1/1 2/2 3/3.

LESSER SHEATH-TAILED BAT
Emballonura monticola   PLATE 8
Measurements FA 43–45, T 11–14, E 12–13. Wt 4.5–5.5. Skull: ccl 11.8–12.8

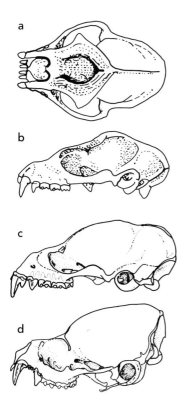

a

b

c

d

Fig. 31 *Skulls of* Nycteris tragata *(a – top, b – side),* Megaderma spasma *(c) and* Taphozous melanopogon *(d).*

Identification Body fur uniform dark brown, sometimes with a strong reddish tinge. Short tail protruding from the middle of the interfemoral membrane. Distinctive posture, supported by the wrists, and distinct, sharp, audible alarm call when disturbed enables easy recognition of this genus at roost. **Similar species** This is the only small, dark, sheath-tailed bat known from mainland SE Asia; tomb bats, *Taphozous* spp., are much larger.
Ecology and habitat Lives in forests, roosting in shallow caves or rock crevices, or under fallen tree trunks.
Distribution and status SE Asia: peninsular Myanmar, Thailand and Malaysia. Also Sumatra, Java, Borneo, Sulawesi and other Indonesian islands. Not currently at risk; widespread, but has declined substantially in many areas due to loss of lowland rainforest.

Genus *Taphozous* Medium-large bats, variably coloured. Most species have a flap of skin forming a pocket in the wing, at the wrist (metacarpal pouch); some species have a glandular pouch on the throat. Tomb bats (including *Saccolaimus*) can be recognized in flight by long, narrow wings, strong, high flight and often audible clicks of echolocation calls; species can sometimes be identified by size or colour (such as the very white wings of *Saccolaimus saccolaimus*). Only one pair of upper incisors, which are very small and sometimes fall out. Skull with broad rostrum, deep hollow between eyes (Fig. 31d). Dental formula 1/3 1/1 2/2 3/3.

THEOBALD'S TOMB BAT
Taphozous theobaldi PLATE 8
Measurements FA 70–76, T 25–30, E 22–28
Identification Upperparts usually dark brown to grey-brown with paler bases to hair, underparts paler. Well-developed metacarpal pouch (see colour plate). Chin well haired without a throat pouch. Some adult males may have a patch of dark hairs forming a beard. Legs, feet and interfemoral membrane lack hair. Wings attach to tibia, above ankle. **Similar species** Pouched Tomb Bat, *Saccolaimus saccolaimus*, differs in colour and has a well-developed throat, pouch but lacks a metacarpal pouch and has shorter ears; Black-bearded Tomb Bat, *T. melanopogon*, is similarly coloured but smaller, with fur on interfemoral membrane and base of wing membranes.
Ecology and habitat Most known roosts are in caves, sometimes forming colonies of over 1,000 individuals. Feeds on insects flying high over the forest.
Distribution and status SE Asia: S Myanmar, C Thailand, Laos, Cambodia and Vietnam. Also India, Java, Sumatra, Borneo and Sulawesi. Not currently at risk, but is known from relatively few colonies, and vulnerable to disturbance of cave roosts and quarrying.

BLACK-BEARDED TOMB BAT
Taphozous melanopogon PLATE 8
Measurements FA 60–63, T 25-28, E 19–22. Wt 23–26
Identification Upperparts vary from grey-brown to buff-brown; underparts usually paler, sometimes almost white. Chin covered with fur, lacking a throat pouch; most adult males have a black "beard". Fur on upper surface of wing membrane limited to about one-third length of upper arm (humerus). Well-developed metacarpal pouch. Tail slightly swollen at tip. Wing membrane attaches to tibia, above ankle. Wings pale, appearing whitish in flight. **Similar species** Pouched Tomb Bat, *Saccolaimus saccolaimus*, has a reduced wing pouch and a distinct throat pouch; Theobald's Tomb Bat, *T. theobaldi*, is larger and lacks hair on the legs; Long-winged Tomb Bat, *T. longimanus*, is slightly smaller, has a naked chin with a throat pouch in males, longer metacarpals, tail tapering evenly to the tip and wing membrane attached at the ankle.
Ecology and habitat Roosts in caves, large crevices in rocks and temples, often in fairly well-lit areas such as near cave entrance. Colonies range from a few individuals to several thousand. Like other tomb bats, flies rapidly and high, foraging for insects over forests or other habitats, including highly disturbed areas.
Distribution and status SE Asia: Myanmar, Thailand, Laos, Vietnam, Cambodia and Peninsular Malaysia. Also Sri Lanka, India to southern China, Sumatra, Java, Borneo and smaller islands. Not currently at risk.

LONG-WINGED TOMB BAT
Taphozous longimanus PLATE 8
Measurements FA 54–63, T 20–30, E 16–19
Identification Colour dark brown to blackish, occasionally speckled with white. Chin naked; males have a throat pouch while females have only a rudimentary fold. Wings long and narrow, dark brown and attached at ankle. Longest wing bone on third finger (metacarpal 3) longer than forearm. Moderately developed metacarpal pouch. Tail tapers narrowly to tip. Short fur on legs, interfemoral membrane, and upper surface of wing membrane to about half length of humerus and femur. **Similar species** Pouched Tomb Bat, *Saccolaimus saccolaimus*, is larger, lacks a metacarpal pouch and has bare legs; Black-bearded Tomb Bat, *T. melanopogon*, has a furred chin in both sexes with no throat pouch, wing membrane attached to side of leg above ankle, tail thickened near tip, third metacarpal shorter, about 90% of forearm length, less extensive fur on flight membranes.
Ecology and habitat Has been found roosting under eaves of houses, in hollow trees, under rocks, in crowns of palm trees and in caves, often in relatively bright areas.
Distribution and status SE Asia: Myanmar, Thailand, Cambodia and Peninsular Malay-

sia. Also Sri Lanka, India, Sumatra, Java, Borneo, Flores and Bali. Not currently at risk.

NAKED-RUMPED TOMB BAT
Taphozous nudiventris PLATE 8
Measurements FA 71–80, T 22–46, E 18–25
Identification Fur dark brown above with pale grey bases; paler below. Dorsal surfaces of wing and tail membranes, legs and arms lack fur. Lower back and lower abdomen naked. Ears long and relatively narrow. Wing has a moderately developed metacarpal pouch, with fur on underside of wing. Chin and throat naked; males have a large gular sac and chest gland, which are lacking in females. **Similar species** All other tomb bats usually have fur extending over all of body; Pouched Tomb Bat, *Saccolaimus saccolaimus*, lacks metacarpal pouch; Black-bearded Tomb Bat, *T. melanopogon*, has a furred chin in both sexes with no throat pouch, wing membrane attached above ankle, tail thickened near tip.
Ecology and habitat Roosts in caves, crevices in rocks, temples and other buildings. Has been found roosting under the eaves of houses, in hollow trees and under rocks. Most colonies are small, with only a few individuals, although a colony of several hundred individuals has been reported. May develop large fat reserves when insects are abundant at end of monsoon period, which are visible under skin on rump. In some areas may undertake seasonal migrations, and spends winter in a state of torpor. Forages on insects with rapid, strong flight high in sky.
Distribution and status SE Asia: NW Myanmar. Also Africa, India and Pakistan. Not currently at risk; only a few records from region, but common elsewhere.

Genus *Saccolaimus* Medium-large bats, similar in size, shape and behaviour to *Taphozous*, but differing in lack of a pouch on the wing, presence of a groove on the lower lip, completely ossified auditory bullae and a relatively large anterior upper premolar. Dental formula 1/3 1/1 2/2 3/3.

POUCHED TOMB BAT
Saccolaimus saccolaimus PLATE 8
Measurements FA 71–78, T 33–34, E 19–21. Wt 40–50
Identification Upperparts blackish-brown variably marked with white; underparts usually pure white, but sometimes all dark brown. No metacarpal pouch. Has a distinct glandular pouch under the chin in both sexes, though slightly smaller in females. Legs and feet hairless. **Similar species** Other species of tomb bat, *Taphozous* spp., have well-developed metacarpal pouches; Black-bearded and Long-winged Tomb Bats, *T. melanopogon* and *T. longimanus*, are smaller, with fur on the legs; Theobald's Tomb Bat, *T. theobaldi*, lacks pouch under chin and has longer ears.
Ecology and habitat Sometimes found in houses, in colonies varying from a few individuals to a few hundred. Also roosts in hollow trees and rock crevices. Forages high above the ground with a strong, rapid flight.
Distribution and status SE Asia: S Myanmar, S Thailand, S Vietnam, Cambodia, and Peninsular Malaysia. Also India, Sri Lanka, Sumatra, Java and Borneo through to New Guinea and Australia. Not currently at risk.

Family *CRASEONYCTERIDAE* HOG-NOSED BATS
This family, with only one known species, was not discovered to science until 1974. These bats are very small, with no visible tail and no calcar, but a well-developed interfemoral membrane. Muzzle is thickened around the nostrils and chin, with crescent-shaped nostrils opening to the front of the face, giving a pig-like appearance. Ears are relatively large, separated on the head, with a well-developed tragus. Males have a glandular swelling on the throat. Dentition resembles *Rhinopoma*, but upper incisors proportionately larger. Dental formula 1/2 1/1 1/2 3/3.

KITTI'S HOG-NOSED BAT

Craseonycteris thonglongyai PLATE 8

Measurements FA 22–26, T none, E 9–12. Wt 2–3.2

Identification Fur brown to reddish-brown in adults; juveniles greyer. Distinguished from all other bats by very small size, pig-like muzzle with a slight ridge on the front and lack of a tail.

Ecology and habitat Roosts in limestone caves in small colonies. Tolerant of limited disturbance within cave roosts. Leaves the caves just before dusk to forage for insects around trees. Can manage in areas with extensive agriculture and disturbance, provided some areas of trees remain.

Distribution and status SE Asia: Found only in a limited area of W Thailand and adjacent areas of Myanmar. Vulnerable, owing to limited range, small population size and evidence of recent declines.

Family *NYCTERIDAE* HOLLOW-FACED BATS

Medium to large bats with very long ears separated at the base, and a short, rounded tragus. The tail is long with a T-shaped tip and fully enclosed in the interfemoral membrane. The face has a deep groove in the middle, bordered by leaf-like flaps of skin. The skull is distinguished by a deep frontal depression with broad ridges on either side (Fig. 31a,b). The premaxillae are broadly attached to the palate. Dental formula 2/3 1/1 1/2 3/3. The family contains only the genus *Nycteris*.

MALAYAN SLIT-FACED BAT

Nycteris tragata PLATE 9

Measurements FA 46–55, T 65–72, E 29–31. Wt 12–22

Identification Fur long and fluffy, greyish-brown to pale red-brown. Noseleaf and ears grey-brown with irregular pale patches. Deep hollow groove in middle of face, fringed with large flaps which form a type of noseleaf. Ears long and rounded, not joined at bases. Tragus short and bent. Very long tail with T-shaped tip, totally enclosed in interfemoral membrane. **Taxonomic notes** Sometimes considered same species as form occurring in Java, *N. javanica*. **Similar species** All other bats in region have very differently shaped noseleaf; false-vampires, *Megaderma* spp., also have ears joined at base, long forked tragus and no tail.

Ecology and habitat Roosts in small groups in hollow trees or caves, largely in mature rainforest. Feeds on large insects which it gleans from the surface; may hunt by passive listening for prey.

Distribution and status SE Asia: S Myanmar, Thailand and Peninsular Malaysia. Also Sumatra and Borneo. Near Threatened by loss of lowland rainforest.

Family *MEGADERMATIDAE* FALSE-VAMPIRES

Medium to large bats with a large, erect noseleaf and large ears joined across the top of the head. The tragus is long and forked. The tail is very short, not visible externally, although the interfemoral membrane is well developed. Despite the name, these bats do not drink blood and are unrelated to South American vampire bats (which do drink blood). Several genera occur throughout the world, but only one, with two species, is recognized from South-East Asia.

Genus *Megaderma* Interorbital region of skull not especially concave (Fig. 31c). Premaxillaries minute with no upper incisors; canines project well forwards with a distinct secondary cusp; anterior upper premolars minute and displaced inwards. Dental formula 0/2 1/1 2/2 3/3.

GREATER FALSE-VAMPIRE

Megaderma lyra PLATE 9

Measurements FA 65–72, T none, E 35–45. Wt 37–52

Identification Fur long, greyish-brown above, paler below. Posterior lobe of noseleaf elongate with stiffened central ridge, approximately parallel-sided flaps on sides and squared off at the top; base of lobe (intermediate noseleaf) narrower than anterior noseleaf, not heart-shaped; anterior noseleaf relatively small, not covering muzzle. Muzzle protruding, relatively short of hairs. Ears very large, joined at bases. Tragus long and forked in two. No visible tail, although interfemoral membrane is well developed. **Similar species** Lesser False-vampire, *M. spasma*, is smaller, and has shorter noseleaf with convex sides and heart-shaped intermediate noseleaf.

Ecology and habitat Roosts in caves, temples, disused buildings and tunnels. Eats mainly vertebrates, including lizards, small mammals and birds, as well as large insects. In India, proportion of insects in diet varies seasonally from 30 to 50%. Can hunt by listening for prey-generated sounds, such as rustling in the leaves. May use echolocation calls of other bats to detect them as potential prey.

Distribution and status SE Asia: Myanmar, Thailand, Laos, Vietnam, Cambodia and Peninsular Malaysia. Also Afghanistan to S China, Pakistan, India and Sri Lanka. Not currently at risk.

LESSER FALSE-VAMPIRE
Megaderma spasma PLATE 9
Measurements FA 56–63, T none, E 30–42. Wt 18–28

Identification Fur pale grey to grey-brown. Noseleaf has long dorsal lobe with stiffened central ridge and broad convex flaps on the sides. Base of lobe (intermediate noseleaf) heart-shaped, nearly as broad as anterior noseleaf. Anterior noseleaf also broad, largely covering muzzle, which is not lacking fur. Ears very large, joined at bases. Tragus long, forked into two branches. No visible tail, although interfemoral membrane is well developed. **Similar species** Greater False-vampire, *M. lyra*, is larger with posterior noseleaf longer, more parallel-sided and squared at top, with median noseleaf narrower and not heart-shaped; Hollow-faced Bat, *Nycteris javanica*, has very different-shaped noseleaf, short tragus and very long tail with a T-shaped tip.

Ecology and habitat Roosts in small groups in caves, tunnels and hollow trees. Diet consists mainly of large insects, which it probably picks up from vegetation rather than on the wing. Has been known to kill other bats in traps and to eat lizards in captivity, and hence may sometimes eat small vertebrates in the wild.

Distribution and status SE Asia: Myanmar, Thailand, Laos, Vietnam, Cambodia and Peninsular Malaysia. Also Sri Lanka, India, the Philippines, Sumatra, Java, Borneo, Sulawesi, Maluku and other Indonesian islands. Not currently at risk.

Family *RHINOLOPHIDAE* HORSESHOE BATS

Horseshoe bats are small to medium-sized bats with an elaborate noseleaf (Fig. 32). The anterior section is rounded and roughly horseshoe-shaped. In the middle, behind the nostrils, is a raised portion called the sella. Behind this is the posterior noseleaf, which usually rises to a long point, called the lancet. The shape of the sella (Fig. 33) and the connecting process which joins it to the posterior leaf (see colour plates) varies between species and is a useful diagnostic character. The ears are large, with a prominent fold on the outside edge, the antitragus. The eyes are small and may be partially hidden from the front by the noseleaf. The tail is moderately long and almost completely enclosed within the interfemoral membrane.

The family contains only one genus: *Rhinolophus*. Most of the species can be distinguished by a combination of size and the shape of the noseleaf, but a few species are very similar in external appearance, sometimes differing only in skull characters, particularly the shape and size of the nasal chambers. In the field, these species can often be distinguished by the frequency of the echolocation calls. In the *Rhinolophus* genus these calls consist of a

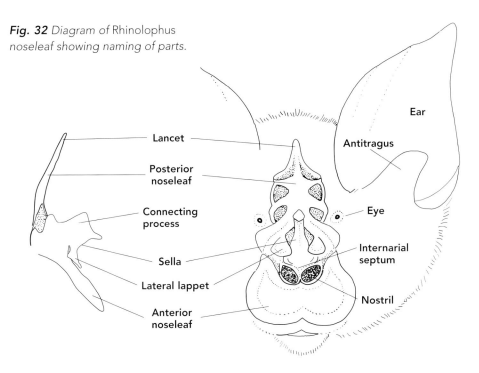

Fig. 32 *Diagram of* Rhinolophus *noseleaf showing naming of parts.*

relatively long, constant-frequency component, with a short frequency-modulated sweep at the end. This constant-frequency component is usually characteristic of the species, at least in a given region, and can be determined using a bat detector (see Introduction for more information on bat detectors). If known, this frequency is given in the text, together with the location where it was recorded, as it may vary geographically. In some cases, the taxonomy is still not fully understood, and some groups currently recognized as one species may, after additional research, prove to represent multiple species.

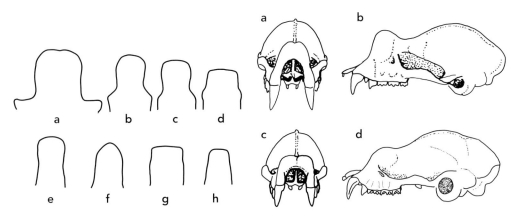

Fig. 33 *Front views of sella of selected species of* Rhinolophus: R. marshalli *(a),* R. yunanensis *(b),* R. pearsonii *(c),* R. robinsoni *(d),* R. affinis *(e),* R. stheno *(f),* R. malayanus *(g) and* R. lepidus *(h).*

Fig. 34 *Front and side views of typical* Rhinolophus *(a,b) and* Hipposideros *(c,d) skulls showing differences in shape of inflated nasal area.*

The skull is long with an inflated bump on the rostrum (Fig. 34a) that contains a series of nasal chambers, which vary in size and shape and are presumably involved in echolocation. Upper incisors are small and located on prolonged premaxillaries, which are attached only to the palate and not to the maxillaries. Anterior upper premolar and middle lower premolar are often very small and displaced inwards. The canines are heavy but simple, without conspicuous secondary cusps. Dental formula 1/2 1/1 2/3 3/3.

To help identification of the large number of species, they are here divided into groups with similar morphological characters – these do not necessarily represent taxonomic groups. The first three species have well-developed lateral lappets at the base of the sella (Fig. 32), with long woolly hair. They can be distinguished by colour and size.

TREFOIL HORSESHOE BAT
Rhinolophus trifoliatus PLATE 10
Measurements FA 45–56, T 27–37, E 23–27. Wt 10–20
Identification Fur long and woolly, pale buffy-brown to brownish-grey. Noseleaf pale yellow; ears and wing membranes yellowish-brown with yellow elbows and knees. Noseleaf has lateral lappets at base of sella.
Echolocation 50–54kHz (Sabah and Peninsular Malaysia). **Similar species** Greater and Lesser Woolly Horseshoe Bats, *R. luctus* and *R. sedulus*, also have lateral lappets but have dark brown fur and blackish noseleaf, and are much larger and smaller respectively.
Ecology and habitat Occurs in understorey of forests from lowlands to hills, including secondary forests. Roosts alone in foliage of forest understorey, including under palm and rattan leaves. Hunts by hanging from an open branch, echolocating and waiting for insects to fly by.
Distribution and status SE Asia: S and W Thailand, S Myanmar and Peninsular Malaysia. Also NE India, Sumatra, Java, Borneo and some small adjacent islands. Not currently at risk, but has probably declined due to loss of forest habitat.

LESSER WOOLLY HORSESHOE BAT
Rhinolophus sedulus PLATE 10
Measurements FA 38–45, T 22–25, E 21–24. Wt 7–11
Identification Fur long and fluffy, uniformly dark brown to dark grey. Noseleaf and ears dark grey. Noseleaf has lateral lappets at base of sella. **Echolocation** 67kHz (Peninsular Malaysia), 62kHz and 76kHz (two individuals in Sabah). **Similar species** Great Woolly Horseshoe Bat, *R. luctus*, is similarly coloured but much larger; Trefoil Horseshoe Bat, *R. trifoliatus*, is larger and has pale grey fur and a yellowish noseleaf.
Ecology and habitat Roosts in bushes or hollow trees. Forages in the understorey of tall forest up to 1,500m. Occurs at relatively low densities.
Distribution and status SE Asia: Peninsular Malaysia. Also Borneo. Near Threatened, owing to loss of lowland rainforest.

GREAT WOOLLY HORSESHOE BAT
Rhinolophus luctus PLATE 8
Measurements FA 62–76, T 50–58, E 31–42. Wt 30–45
Identification Largest horseshoe bat in the region. Fur long and woolly. Upperparts brownish-black; underparts slightly greyer. Noseleaf and ears dark grey-brown. Noseleaf has lateral lappets at base of sella. This species shows geographic variation in both size and echolocation (e.g. individuals in Laos have a mean FA of 73 compared with a mean of 63 in Peninsular Malaysia), and may prove to include more than one species.
Echolocation 40–42kHz (Sabah and Peninsular Malaysia), 32–34kHz (peninsular Thailand and Laos). **Similar species** Lesser Woolly Horseshoe Bat, *R. sedulus*, and Trefoil Horseshoe Bat, *R. trifoliatus*, have a similar noseleaf but are smaller; latter has paler fur and a yellowish noseleaf.
Ecology and habitat Roosts in small groups in caves and rock crevices, in hollow trees and among roots of trees. Sometimes forages by hanging from a branch, flying out

periodically to grab food, then returning to its branch. Found in both primary and disturbed forests.

Distribution and status SE Asia: Myanmar, Thailand, Laos, Vietnam, Cambodia and Peninsular Malaysia. Also N India through S China, Taiwan, Sumatra, Java, Borneo and Bali. Not currently at risk.

The following four species have an elongate sella (e.g., Fig. 33a), greatly enlarged ears and an expanded internarial cup at the base of the sella. Despite the similarities, genetic analyses suggest that the first two are not closely related to the other two. They can be distinguished from one another by size, and the shape of the sella and the internarial cup at the base of the sella.

BIG-EARED HORSESHOE BAT
Rhinolophus macrotis PLATE 9
Measurements FA 42–47, T 17–25, E 22–28. Wt 6–9.5

Identification Very large ears with well-developed, rounded antitragus. Sella broad and tall, broadest at base and narrowing gradually to rounded tip; base expanded into an internarial cup in front of sella. Connecting process tall, parallel to sella at base, rounded at top and forming a distinct notch where it meets sella, which is angled forwards at tip. Lancet well developed, rounded at top. Horseshoe broad, covering muzzle, with well-developed secondary noseleaf beneath it. Upperparts mid-brown, underparts paler. **Echolocation** 48kHz (Peninsular Malaysia), 51–52kHz (Laos). **Similar species** Siamese Horseshoe Bat, *R. siamensis*, is smaller, with higher frequency echolocation calls; Marshall's Horseshoe Bat, *R. marshalli*, has low, arched connecting process, internarial cup continuing behind sella, shorter lancet and broader noseleaf.
Ecology and habitat Has been seen in a variety of forest types, including primary forest and disturbed forests, from lowlands to 1,000m. No information on roosting sites.
Distribution and status SE Asia: scattered records from throughout Thailand, Myanmar,

N Laos, N Vietnam and Peninsular Malaysia. Also Pakistan, N India, Nepal and S China. (Note: specimens from the Philippines formerly referred to this species are not closely related, and represent a distinct species, *R. hirsutus*.) Not currently at risk.

SIAMESE HORSESHOE BAT
Rhinolophus siamensis PLATE 9
Measurements FA 38–42, T 16–22, E 19–22. Wt 4.5–5.7

Identification Very similar in shape and general appearance to Big-eared Horseshoe Bat, *R. macrotis*, with a similarly shaped noseleaf. Differs mainly in smaller size and higher echolocation frequency. **Taxonomic notes** Formerly considered a subspecies of *R. macrotis*, but occurs in the same areas as larger bats with different frequency echolocation calls suggesting they are not the same species. **Echolocation** 68–74kHz (Laos). **Similar species** Other small *Rhinolophus* have shorter sella and smaller ears, and do not have expanded internarial cup.
Ecology and habitat Has been found in disturbed forest near limestone caves.
Distribution and status SE Asia: individuals apparently referable to this species have been found in N Thailand, Laos and Vietnam. Status poorly known, but probably not currently at risk.

BOURRET'S HORSESHOE BAT
Rhinolophus paradoxolophus PLATE 9
Measurements FA 53–57, T 21–33, E 32–35. Wt 8–14

Identification Enormous ears, about 60% of forearm length, with long, narrow antitragus. Sella very broad and tall, with a broad, rounded cup-like structure at the base that continues behind the sella to join the connecting process. Connecting process low, extending in a long arch to the tip of the sella. Lancet low and rounded. Horseshoe very broad, and completely covering the muzzle with a deep notch in the front. Fur of upperparts brown with paler bases, underparts paler. **Echolocation** 24–25kHz (Laos). **Similar species** Marshall's Horseshoe Bat,

R. marshalli, has similarly shaped noseleaf but is substantially smaller, with proportionately shorter and narrower sella, longer lancet, and more laterally extended internarial cup.

Ecology and habitat Known roosts all in limestone caves. Found in a variety of forest types, including dry deciduous, pine, moist evergreen and disturbed riverine forests.

Distribution and status SE Asia: N Thailand, Laos, N Vietnam. Also S China. Not currently at risk, but probably declining somewhat due to loss of forests.

MARSHALL'S HORSESHOE BAT

Rhinolophus marshalli PLATE 9

Measurements FA 41–48, T 16–26, E 25–30. Wt 6.5–7.5

Identification Enormous ears, with long narrow antitragus. Sella broad and tall, with a cup-like structure at base that continues behind sella to join connecting process (Fig. 33a). Basal cup extends laterally to sides. Connecting process low, extending in a long smooth arch to tip of sella. Lancet rounded and relatively short. Horseshoe very broad, covering muzzle, with a deep anterior notch. **Echolocation** 40–41kHz (Laos). **Similar species** Bourret's Horseshoe Bat, *R. paradoxolophus*, is larger, with a proportionately longer sella and shorter lancet; Big-eared Horseshoe Bat, *R. macrotis*, has a tall, rounded connecting process, and internarial cup not extending behind sella.

Ecology and habitat Has been found roosting in limestone caves, and in a variety of forest types from lowlands to hill forest at 800m.

Distribution and status SE Asia: known from scattered localities in C and N Thailand, N Laos, N Vietnam and extreme N Peninsular Malaysia. Not currently at risk, though relatively uncommon.

The following two species have a distinctive short lancet, thickened at top and sides to enclose base of strongly arched connecting process. Both are very similar, distinguished primarily by size and echolocation frequency.

CROSLET HORSESHOE BAT

Rhinolophus coelophyllus PLATE 10

Measurements FA 41–45, T 16–24, E 18–19. Wt 6.2–8.6. Skull: gl 18.4–19.8, mt 7.0–7.7

Identification Noseleaf has relatively short lancet, thickened at sides and top to form lobes that protrude forwards and enclose base of connecting process. Lancet, including pocket in lobes, covered with long hairs. Connecting process tall and broadly arched from lancet to tip of sella. Sella is roughly parallel-sided with a triangular tip. Noseleaf broad, nearly covering muzzle, with rudimentary secondary noseleaf beneath it. Fur typically mid-brown above, buffy-white below, but some individuals are dull orange or reddish. **Echolocation** males 83–84kHz, females 86kHz (Laos). **Similar species** Shamel's Horseshoe Bat, *R. shameli*, is very similar, differing in slightly larger size, broader noseleaf and lower echolocation call frequencies.

Ecology and habitat Has been found roosting in limestone caves, in colonies of up to several hundred individuals. Forages in a range of forest types from lowlands to hills.

Distribution and status SE Asia: C Myanmar, Thailand, Laos and N Peninsular Malaysia. Not currently at risk.

SHAMEL'S HORSESHOE BAT

Rhinolophus shameli PLATE 10

Measurements FA 44–49, T 15–25, E 16–22. Wt 7.5–12.5. Skull: gl 19.3–21.6, mt 7.6–8.5

Identification Very similar to *R. coelophyllus* with same shape noseleaf, but somewhat larger with lower echolocation frequency. Noseleaf typically broader than muzzle. **Echolocation** Males 65–67kHz, females 69–72kHz (Laos). **Similar species** Croslet Horseshoe Bat, *R. coelophyllus*, is slightly smaller, with higher echolocation frequency.

Ecology and habitat Has been found in vicinity of limestone caves. Forages in deciduous and evergreen forests, including heavily disturbed areas, up to 1,000m.

Distribution and status SE Asia: C Myanmar, Thailand, Laos, Vietnam and Cambodia. Not currently at risk.

The next group of species is distinguished by having a triangular or pointed connecting process. It includes some of the smallest horseshoe bats in the region, as well as the medium-sized R. acuminatus. Within species, the shape of the connecting process may vary from triangular to horn-shaped, and thus does not appear to be reliable for identification. Some species are known only from dried skins, and details of their noseleaf shape are not well known. Further research, using genetics and echolocation recordings, may help to clarify species limits and identification in this group.

ACUMINATE HORSESHOE BAT
Rhinolophus acuminatus PLATE 10
Measurements FA 44–50, T 22–31, E 18–21. Wt 11–16
Identification Noseleaf simple without lateral lappets on sella; connecting process triangular, with blunt or sharp point at tip. Sella approximately parallel-sided, but in some populations may be narrow in middle. Lancet has concave sides and narrow pointed tip. Two colour phases. In some, upperparts are dark greyish-brown with pale frosting on tips of fur, underparts only slightly paler. In others, fur is bright orange all over, slightly paler below. Noseleaf and ears dark greyish-brown in both colour phases. Ears moderately large. Has a distinctive, strong musky smell. **Echolocation** Females 88–90kHz (Sabah); males 86–90kHz, females 93–95kHz (Laos). **Similar species** Intermediate Horseshoe Bat, *R. affinis*, has rounded connecting process; other species with pointed connecting process are much smaller.
Ecology and habitat Recorded roosting in caves and hollow trees. Has been found in understorey of dry evergreen and dry dipterocarp forest in Laos and lowland rainforest in Malaysia.
Distribution and status SE Asia: Myanmar, Thailand, Laos, Cambodia, Vietnam and Peninsular Malaysia. Also the Philippines, Sumatra, Java, Borneo and many smaller Indonesian islands. Not currently at risk.

LEAST HORSESHOE BAT
Rhinolophus pusillus PLATE 10
Measurements FA 33–40, T 13–26, E 13–20. Skull: gl 14.8–16.5, mt 5.4–6.3, c–c 3.4–3.9
Identification Very small horseshoe bat with simple noseleaf and triangular, pointed connecting process. Noseleaf small, not covering muzzle. Lancet broadly pointed, slightly concave on sides. Sella parallel-sided. Upperparts vary from dark brown to smoky-grey or cinnamon-red brown, underparts paler. **Taxonomic notes** Genetic and size variation across range suggest it may represent more than one species. **Echolocation** 108–110kHz (Laos). **Similar species** Blyth's Horseshoe Bat, *R. lepidus*, averages larger.
Ecology and habitat Has been found roosting in caves, clumps of bamboo and even houses. Forages in a wide range of forest habitats including mature forest and disturbed areas.
Distribution and status SE Asia: Myanmar, Thailand, Laos, Vietnam, Cambodia and Peninsular Malaysia. Also India, S China, Borneo, Java and small adjacent islands. Not currently at risk.

BLYTH'S HORSESHOE BAT
Rhinolophus lepidus PLATE 10
Measurements FA 39–43, T 18–24, E 17–18.5. Wt 4.5–8.0. Skull: gl 15.8–17.4, mt 5.7-6.7, c–c 3.7–4.2
Identification Small horseshoe bat with connecting process triangular and pointed, sometimes hooked slightly forwards. Lancet bluntly pointed, usually with concave sides. Noseleaf narrower than muzzle. Three grooves on lower lip. In Peninsular Malaysia, has two colour phases: dark blackish-grey or reddish-brown, in both cases with long pale tips to fur giving a frosted appearance. **Taxonomic notes** Populations in peninsular Thailand and Malaysia are sometimes considered a separate species, *R. refulgens*. **Echolocation** 98–100kHz (Peninsular Malaysia). **Similar species** Least Horseshoe Bat, *R. pusillus*, averages smaller, with more sharply pointed connecting process; Convex Horseshoe Bat, *R. convexus*, has rounded

lancet; long, pointed connecting process.

Ecology and habitat In south, largely restricted to mature lowland rainforest. Elsewhere, found in dry deciduous and semi-deciduous forests.

Distribution and status SE Asia: Myanmar, Thailand, Cambodia, Vietnam and Peninsular Malaysia. Also Afghanistan, N India, Pakistan, S China and Sumatra. Not currently at risk.

CONVEX HORSESHOE BAT
Rhinolophus convexus PLATE 10
Measurements FA 42–43, T 18–22, E 15–16. Wt 7.2–8.2. Skull: gl 16.9–17.4, mt 6.4–6.6, c–c 4.1–4.2
Identification Small horseshoe bat with tall, pointed connecting process, low rounded lancet. Sella with straight sides that converge towards tip. **Echolocation** 92kHz (Laos). **Similar species** Other small *Rhinolophus* have more pointed lancet.
Ecology and habitat Has been found in upper montane rainforest in Malaysia (1,600m). Similar-looking individuals have been found in hill forest in Laos, but identity is uncertain.
Distribution and status SE Asia: known only from Peninsular Malaysia and possibly Laos. Status uncertain; apparently rare.

LITTLE NEPALESE HORSESHOE BAT
Rhinolophus subbadius NOT ILLUSTRATED
Measurements FA 33–38, T 16–19, E 14–18. Skull: gl 14.4–15.0, mt 5.2–5.6, c–c 2.7–3.2
Identification Very small horseshoe bat with pointed connecting process that is slightly constricted in the middle and angled forwards. Lancet triangular with concave sides. Upperparts light brown with greyish bases to fur; shoulders and underparts slightly paler. Rostrum narrow, as reflected in width across upper canines. Upper canines slender and moderately long. **Echolocation** Not recorded. **Similar species** Least Horseshoe Bat, *R. pusillus*, is very similar in external appearance but tends to be slightly larger, with a broader rostrum.
Ecology and habitat Recorded from 1,200m in N Myanmar.

Distribution and status SE Asia: N Myanmar. Also Nepal, India. Status unknown.

SHORTRIDGE'S HORSESHOE BAT
Rhinolophus shortridgei NOT ILLUSTRATED
Measurements FA 39–42, T 20–25, E 16–19. Skull: gl 17.2–18.0, mt 6.5–7.2
Identification Small horseshoe bat closely resembling *R. lepidus*, with triangular connecting process, but with slightly larger skull and larger canines more than twice height of posterior premolar. Upperparts light brown, hairs with grey bases and brown tips; underparts paler. **Echolocation** Not recorded. **Similar species** Separated from other small *Rhinolophus* with triangular connecting process by heavier canines.
Ecology and habitat Unknown.
Distribution and status SE Asia: C Myanmar. Also NE India. Status poorly known; recorded from only a few specimens in C Myanmar and one from India.

The remaining species have an unmodified noseleaf structure and a rounded connecting process. These resemble what is thought to be the ancestral form of Rhinolophus, without any additional flaps or special elongation of the connecting process. Despite morphological similarities, these are probably not all closely related to one another; they are distinguished from one another by a combination of size, shape of the sella (Fig. 33) and shape of the lancet. In some cases, echolocation calls are the easiest way to distinguish species.

INTERMEDIATE HORSESHOE BAT
Rhinolophus affinis PLATE 11
Measurements FA 48–54, T 20–32, E 19–24. Wt 12–20. Skull: gl 21.1–23.7, mt 8.4–9.7
Identification Upperparts dark brown to reddish-brown; underparts only slightly paler. Ears moderately large. Noseleaf relatively large, covering muzzle, simple without extra lappets on sella; connecting process broadly rounded, originating from below tip of sella, forming a slight notch. Lancet tall, triangular, with straight sides. Sella is narrow

with concave sides (Fig. 33e). Second phalanx of third digit (longest finger) is long, 66–80% of the length of the metacarpal. **Echolocation** 77–78kHz (Peninsular Malaysia), 73–78kHz (Laos). **Similar species** Lesser Brown Horseshoe Bat, *R. stheno*, is smaller, with a parallel-sided sella, and usually relatively paler underparts; Acuminate Horseshoe Bat, *R. acuminatus*, has a pointed connecting process; Pearson's Horseshoe Bat, *R. pearsoni*, has long woolly fur, sella broad at base, constricting abruptly in middle; Rufous Horseshoe Bat, *R. rouxii*, has shorter lancet with strongly convex sides, and second phalanx of third digit less than 66% of metacarpal length.

Ecology and habitat Has been found roosting in caves. Forages in understorey of forest, including mature lowland rainforest, dry forest and disturbed areas.

Distribution and status SE Asia: Myanmar, Thailand, Laos, Vietnam, Cambodia and Peninsular Malaysia. Also India through China, Sumatra, Java and Borneo. Not currently at risk; this species is widespread and common.

LESSER BROWN HORSESHOE BAT
Rhinolophus stheno PLATE 11
Measurements FA 42–48, T 15–21, E 15–22. Wt 6–10.5. Skull: gl 18.0–20.5, mt 6.7–8.1
Identification Medium-sized horseshoe bat with moderately large horseshoe. Connecting process rounded, joining sella just below tip to form a slight notch. Sella is narrow, parallel-sided and slightly pointed at the top (Fig. 33f). Upperparts vary from dark brown to reddish-brown; underparts contrastingly paler. Noseleaf usually dark at edges, contrasting paler in middle. **Taxonomic notes** Subspecies *R. s. microglobosus* from Vietnam and Laos averages slightly smaller (mean FA 44 vs 46 in Malaysia) with higher frequency echolocation and may prove to be specifically distinct. **Echolocation** 85–86kHz (Peninsular Malaysia), 94.5–96.5kHz (Laos). **Similar species** Malayan Horseshoe Bat, *R. malayanus*, is slightly smaller, has broader sella with square top (Fig. 33g), lower fre-

quency echolocation calls; Peninsular Horseshoe Bat, *R. robinsoni*, has dark fur above and below, with sella abruptly constricted in middle (Fig. 33d); Intermediate Horseshoe bat, *R. affinis*, is larger, on average, with underparts only slightly paler than upperparts, sella constricted in the middle (Fig. 33e); Thomas's Horseshoe Bat, *R. thomasi*, has darker fur, short lancet with abrupt point in middle; Indochinese Horseshoe Bat, *R. chaseni*, has more uniform-coloured fur, darker noseleaf.

Ecology and habitat Roosts in crevices of rock boulders, limestone caves and hollow trees. Forages in primary lowland rainforest, dry forest and disturbed areas with some tree cover.

Distribution and status SE Asia: Myanmar, Thailand, Laos, Vietnam and Peninsular Malaysia. Not currently at risk.

MALAYAN HORSESHOE BAT
Rhinolophus malayanus PLATE 11
Measurements FA 38–44, T 18–27, E 17–20. Wt 5–9. Skull: gl 17.0–18.2, mt 6.5–7.2
Identification Medium-small horseshoe bat with moderately large horseshoe. Connecting process rounded, joining sella just below tip to form a slight notch. Sella is moderately broad, parallel-sided and squared off at top (Fig. 33g). Lancet tall and triangular. Upperparts usually brown with contrasting pale buff or whitish underparts; sometimes overall colour is more orange-brown. Noseleaf dark grey with pinkish middle. **Echolocation** 75kHz (Thailand), 77–80kHz (Laos). **Similar species** Lesser Brown Horseshoe Bat, *R. stheno*, has narrower sella that is slightly pointed at top (Fig. 33f), and higher frequency echolocation calls; Least Horseshoe Bat, *R. pusillus*, has proportionately much smaller noseleaf with pointed connecting process; Thomas's Horseshoe Bat, *R. thomasi*, has darker fur, short lancet with abrupt point in middle.

Ecology and habitat Roosts in limestone caves, sometimes in colonies of several hundred; has been found in a variety of dry forest types, including heavily degraded forest.

Distribution and status SE Asia: S Myanmar, Thailand, Laos, N Vietnam and N of Peninsular Malaysia. Not currently at risk; locally common in many areas.

INDOCHINESE HORSESHOE BAT
Rhinolophus chaseni PLATE 11
Measurements FA 43–46, T 20–27, E 17–22. Wt 8–14.5

Identification Medium-sized horseshoe bat with moderate-sized noseleaf that does not completely cover muzzle; connecting process rounded; lancet tall and triangular. Sella slightly broader at base, narrowing very slightly in middle, broadly rounded at top. Upperparts dark brown, hairs with slightly paler tips; underparts only slightly paler. Noseleaf dark. **Taxonomic notes** Formerly considered conspecific with *R. borneensis*, but genetically and morphologically distinct. Specimens referred to *R. borneensis* have been reported from Peninsular Malaysia, but their identification has not been confirmed. **Echolocation** 77.5–78.5kHz (Laos). **Similar species** Peninsular Horseshoe Bat, *R. robinsoni*, has broader sella with more marked constriction in middle, lower echolocation frequency; Thomas's Horseshoe Bat, *R. thomasi*, has short lancet with abrupt point in middle; Lesser Brown and Malayan Horseshoe Bats, *R. stheno* and *R. malayanus*, have underparts markedly paler than upperparts, paler centre of noseleaf, different-shaped sella.

Ecology and habitat Has been found in dry dipterocarp forest, including in disturbed areas.

Distribution and status SE Asia: Laos, Cambodia and Vietnam. Not currently at risk.

THOMAS'S HORSESHOE BAT
Rhinolophus thomasi PLATE 11
Measurements FA 42–46, T 18–25, E 17–24. Wt 7–11. Skull: gl 17.9–20.0, mt 6.8–7.7

Identification Fur uniformly medium to dark brown, only slightly paler below; noseleaf dark grey, slightly pinkish in middle. Noseleaf moderately broad, not quite covering muzzle; small notch in anterior leaf, sella parallel-sided or slightly broader at base; connecting process rounded; lancet short, stubby with a narrow point in the middle. Upper canines relatively small, only slightly longer than premolars. **Echolocation** Males 76–77kHz, females 83–85.5kHz (Laos). **Similar species** Indochinese Horseshoe Bat, *R. chaseni*, has tall, well-developed lancet; Chinese and Rufous Horseshoe Bats, *R. sinicus* and *R. rouxii*, very similar, distinguished by larger size (on average), and more massive canines.

Ecology and habitat Roosts in limestone caves. Has been found in dry forests, including disturbed forests, around cave areas.

Distribution and status SE Asia: Myanmar, Thailand, Laos and Vietnam. Also S China (Yunnan). Not currently at risk.

CHINESE HORSESHOE BAT
Rhinolophus sinicus PLATE 11
Measurements FA 44–55, T 19–30, E 16–21. Skull: gl 18.4–21.0, mt 7.0–8.4

Identification Medium to moderately large horseshoe bat with moderate-size noseleaf that does not cover muzzle. Lancet strongly concave at sides (hastate), with tip usually short and stubby, but sometimes longer; sella approximately parallel-sided, rounded at top; connecting process rounded. Wing is relatively long: on third digit (longest finger), second phalanx (last finger bone) is 66–80 per cent of length of the metacarpal (first bone). Upperparts dark brown, underside slightly paler; noseleaf dark. Upper canine is large, nearly twice as long as largest premolar. **Similar species** Rufous Horseshoe Bat, *R. rouxii*, has more rounded wing; Thomas Horseshoe Bat, *R. thomasi*, has smaller upper canine, only slightly longer than largest premolar.

Ecology and habitat In India, found mainly in areas of higher elevations.

Distribution and status SE Asia: N Myanmar and N Vietnam. Also N India, Nepal and S China. Not currently at risk.

RUFOUS HORSESHOE BAT
Rhinolophus rouxii PLATE 11

Measurements FA 44–52, T 20–33, E 15–22. Skull: gl 20.0–22.8, mt 7.9–9.2

Identification Medium-sized horseshoe bat with noseleaf that does not cover muzzle. Two colour phases, which may vary within individuals: upperparts dark brown, bases slightly paler, underside slightly paler; or uniformly orange-rufous above and below. Wing is relatively shorter and more rounded: on third digit (longest finger), second phalanx (last finger bone) is 53–67% of length of metacarpal (first bone). Upper canine large, more than 30% longer than largest premolar. **Echolocation** 73–79kHz (Sri Lanka), 84kHz (India). **Similar species** Chinese Horseshoe Bat, *R. sinicus*, is similar, but with differently shaped wing; Thomas Horseshoe Bat, *R. thomasi*, is smaller, with upper canine only slightly longer than largest premolar.

Ecology and habitat In India, found mainly in wet forested areas, roosting in caves, tunnels, hollow trees, wells and temples. Forages on insects within forest canopy, either on the wing or by hanging from a perch and sallying out to catch passing prey.

Distribution and status SE Asia: C Myanmar. Also India and Sri Lanka. Not currently at risk, though poorly known in region.

PENINSULAR HORSESHOE BAT
Rhinolophus robinsoni PLATE 11

Measurements FA 43–46, T 19–25, E 19–23. Wt 7.2–8.9. Skull: gl 19–20, mt 6.7–7.5

Identification Medium-small horseshoe bat with rounded connecting process. Sella broad at base, getting slightly wider towards middle, then narrowing abruptly just above middle, with squared-off top (Fig. 33d). Noseleaf moderately large, connecting process rounded, lancet broadly triangular. Well-developed supplementary leaflet below horseshoe. Upperparts brown to reddish-brown, underparts only slightly paler. Noseleaf dark grey, slightly paler in middle. Three grooves in lower lip. **Taxonomic notes** A separate subspecies, *R. robinsoni tha-*

ianus, has been described from N Thailand, but it is not clear whether it represents this species. **Echolocation** 64–68kHz (Peninsular Malaysia). **Similar species** Other similar-sized *Rhinolophus* do not have stepwise constriction in middle of sella; Pearson's Horseshoe Bat, *R. pearsoni*, is larger with longer noseleaf, long woolly hair, and a single groove in the lower lip.

Ecology and habitat Lowland and hill forest, mainly in tall forest. Roosts in crevices in rock boulders, or in palm leaves in forest understorey.

Distribution and status SE Asia: Peninsular Malaysia and peninsular Thailand. Near Threatened; relatively uncommon, and declining due to loss of lowland rainforest.

PEARSON'S HORSESHOE BAT
Rhinolophus pearsonii PLATE 11

Measurements FA 49–55, T 16–29, E 23–29. Wt 10–16. Skull: gl 21.6–24.3, mt 8.3–10.0

Identification Relatively large horseshoe bat with long woolly hair; hair is dark brown to greyish-brown with pale tips, slightly paler on underparts. Connecting process broadly rounded, joining sella at tip without any notch. Sella tall, broad at base, narrowing abruptly in middle (Fig. 33c). Noseleaf broad, covering muzzle, dark, with tall triangular lancet. A single deep groove on lower lip. **Echolocation** 65kHz (Thailand), 56–59kHz (Laos). **Similar species** Dobson's Horseshoe Bat, *R. yunanensis*, is larger; Intermediate Horseshoe Bat, *R. affinis*, has narrow sella, slightly constricted in middle, shorter fur, and connecting process joining slightly below tip of sella, forming a notch.

Ecology and habitat Roosts in limestone caves. Has been found in a variety of forest types at altitudes ranging from 160m in Laos to 3,400m in Nepal. Appears to use torpor regularly and may hibernate in northern parts of range during cold seasons.

Distribution and status SE Asia: Myanmar, Thailand, Laos and N Vietnam. Also N India, Nepal and S China. Not currently at risk.

DOBSON'S HORSESHOE BAT
Rhinolophus yunanensis PLATE 11
Measurements FA 51.5–64, T 18–26, E 23.5–32. Wt 20–22. Skull: gl 24.6–27.2, mt 10.1–11.2
Identification Large horseshoe bat with long woolly hair; fur either light sandy-brown or dark greyish, only slightly paler below. Noseleaf broad, covering muzzle, with tall triangular lancet. Connecting process broadly rounded, joining sella at tip without any notch. Sella tall, broad at base, narrowing abruptly in middle (Fig. 33b). A single deep groove on lower lip. **Echolocation** 49kHz (Thailand). **Similar species** Pearson's Horseshoe Bat, *R. pearsonii*, very similar, but smaller, with higher frequency echolocation calls; Great Woolly Horseshoe Bat, *R. luctus*, has lateral lappets on sella.
Ecology and habitat Roosts in limestone caves. Forages in a variety of forest habitats.
Distribution and status SE Asia: Myanmar and Thailand. Also E India. Not currently at risk, but apparently much less common than *R. pearsonii*.

Family *HIPPOSIDERIDAE* ROUNDLEAF BATS
The roundleaf bats (sometimes called roundleaf horseshoe bats or leafnose bats) vary in size from very small species with a forearm of 34mm, weighing only 4g, to moderately large species with a forearm over 100mm, and weights of 60–70g. Like horseshoe bats (Rhinolophidae) they have an elaborate noseleaf (Fig. 35). The anterior noseleaf is rounded and somewhat horseshoe-shaped (except in *Coelops*). The median leaf is a low cushion-like structure expanded laterally, without a sella, while the posterior leaf is low and rounded, usually divided by vertical septa into several pockets. The internarial septum varies from very narrow to broadly expanded. Some species have additional lateral leaflets below the anterior noseleaf. The number of lateral leaflets can be important for species identification. The ears vary from moderately small to large with a low antitragus. The eyes are small.

Recent genetic and morphological studies indicate that several of the currently recognized species, including *Hipposideros bicolor*, *H. cineraceus*, *H. pomona* and *H. larvatus*, are actually a complex of two or more species. However, the species limits and diagnostic characters have been only partially determined, and the appropriate names for each form have not yet been worked out, so most of these species complexes are here treated as single species, though in some cases more than one is illustrated. Echolocation calls similar to, but generally much shorter than, those of *Rhinolophus* bats, also with a characteristic constant-frequency component that can help with species identification.

Genus *Hipposideros* Typical horseshoe-shaped anterior noseleaf (Fig. 35). Tail short to moderate, largely enclosed in interfemoral membrane. Skull generally similar to *Rhinolophus*, but rostrum with paired swellings on top (Fig. 34c,d), although these are sometimes low. Anterior upper premolar variably reduced; upper canines heavy but simple, without prominent supplementary cusps. Dental formula 1/2 1/1 2/2 3/3.

BICOLOURED ROUNDLEAF BAT
Hipposideros bicolor PLATE 14
Measurements FA 41–48, T 29–34, E 17.5–21. Wt 7–10

Identification Upperparts brown to grey-brown, individual hairs with brown tips, white bases; underparts paler, usually buffy-white. Some individuals bright orange. Ears moderately large and rounded. Noseleaf pale pinkish-brown to greyish, simple and small, lacking lateral leaflets; internarial septum straight and only slightly widened at base. **Taxonomic notes** Recent genetic and echolocation studies indicate this includes two species, one with a mean echolocation frequency of 131kHz, and one with a mean of 142kHz, but it is not yet known which belongs to the name *H. bicolor*. The 131-kHz species tends to be slightly

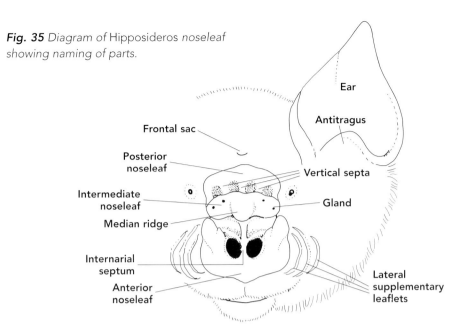

Fig. 35 *Diagram of* Hipposideros *noseleaf showing naming of parts.*

- Frontal sac
- Posterior noseleaf
- Intermediate noseleaf
- Median ridge
- Internarial septum
- Anterior noseleaf
- Ear
- Antitragus
- Vertical septa
- Gland
- Lateral supplementary leaflets

larger (mean FA 46), with a slightly flatter, pinker noseleaf, while the 142-kHz species tends to be smaller (mean FA 44), with the noseleaf greyer and slightly curved up at the edges; the most reliable way to separate them is by echolocation. **Echolocation** 127–134kHz (131-kHz species), 138–144kHz (142-kHz species) (Peninsular Malaysia). **Similar species** Ashy Roundleaf Bat, *H. cineraceus*, is smaller with shorter ears, internarial septum distinctly swollen in the middle; Large-eared Roundleaf Bat, *H. pomona*, has larger ears (about 20% longer, on average).

Ecology and habitat Roosts mainly in caves or tunnels, often in large colonies, but also in crevices between large boulders and probably hollow trees. Forages in understorey of lowland rainforest.

Distribution and status SE Asia: peninsular Thailand and Malaysia. Also Sumatra, Java, Borneo, Philippines, Sulawesi and smaller islands. Not currently at risk, but has probably declined somewhat due to loss of mature forest.

LARGE-EARED ROUNDLEAF BAT

Hipposideros pomona PLATE 14
Measurements FA 38–43, T 29–36, E 20–26. Wt 6–9

Identification Fur dark brown with pale bases, underparts only slightly paler. Some individuals are dark orange, with slightly paler orange underparts. Noseleaf small and simple. Ears very large and rounded. **Taxonomic notes** Genetic analyses suggest this may be a complex of species, but distinguishing characters have not yet been determined. **Echolocation** 120–126kHz (Laos). **Similar species** Bicoloured Roundleaf Bat, *H. bicolor*, has shorter ears and slightly longer forearm; Ashy Roundleaf Bat, *H. cineraceus*, is smaller with smaller ears and noseleaf.

Ecology and habitat Roosts mainly in caves. Has been found in a variety of forest types, including disturbed areas.

Distribution and status SE Asia: Myanmar, Thailand, Laos, Vietnam, Cambodia and N Peninsular Malaysia. Also India and S China. Not currently at risk.

MALAY ROUNDLEAF BAT

Hipposideros nequam NOT ILLUSTRATED
Measurements FA 46, E 19. Skull: mt 6.3
Identification Medium-small roundleaf bat, known only from a single damaged specimen, so its characteristics are not well known. Generally similar to Bicoloured Roundleaf Bat, *H. bicolor*, with large round-

ed ears, but with larger noseleaf (6 wide x 8 tall). Skull differs in having a thinner vomer (bone on top of the palate), and in having a small anterior upper premolar inserted in toothrow (displaced to the side in *H. bicolor*). May eventually prove to be the same as one of the other related taxa.

Ecology and habitat Unknown.

Distribution and status SE Asia: known only from a single specimen from Selangor, Peninsular Malaysia. Status unknown.

ASHY ROUNDLEAF BAT
Hipposideros cineraceus PLATE 14

Measurements FA 33–42, T 24–30, E 18.5–21. Wt 4–5.5. Skull: ccl 13.2–13.9

Identification Upperparts buffy-brown to greyish-brown; underparts pale brown to buffy-white. Ears large and rounded. Noseleaf simple, lacking lateral leaflets; anterior noseleaf with only a slight notch. **Taxonomic notes** Recent genetic and morphological analyses indicate this name is being used for at least two species that are not closely related. A larger form (mean FA 37.5), known only from Sabah and Peninsular Malaysia, has internarial septum with a small, slightly raised, flattened oval disc in the middle; a smaller form (mean FA 35.2) found throughout region has internarial septum straight-sided but slightly swollen vertically. It is not yet known which names are appropriate for each. **Echolocation** Sabah and Peninsular Malaysian form 137–138kHz (Sabah), 144kHz (Peninsular Malaysia); widespread form ~155kHz (Peninsular Malaysia and Laos). **Similar species** Thai Roundleaf Bat, *H. halophyllus*, has kidney-shaped lobes on internarial septum, notched anterior noseleaf; Least Roundleaf Bat, *H. doriae*, lacks supporting septa on posterior noseleaf; Bicoloured Roundleaf Bat, *H. bicolor*, is larger with straight internarial septum.

Ecology and habitat Roosts in caves, usually in small to moderate-size colonies. Has also been found roosting in culverts. Forages in forest of many types, where usually found in small numbers.

Distribution and status SE Asia: Myanmar,

Thailand, Laos, Vietnam, Cambodia and Peninsular Malaysia. Also Pakistan, N India, Sumatra, Borneo and various small islands. Not currently at risk, but may be declining somewhat due to loss of forest.

THAI ROUNDLEAF BAT
Hipposideros halophyllus PLATE 14

Measurements FA 35–38, T 25–28, E 16. Skull: ccl 12.7–13.1, mt 4.7–4.8

Identification Noseleaf small, simple with no lateral leaflets; internarial septum with swollen kidney-shaped lobes on each side; anterior noseleaf with a deep notch. Fur of upperparts mid-brown with pale bases; underside whitish. Noseleaf mostly pink, with darker internarial septum and sometimes posterior noseleaf. **Echolocation** 180–185kHz (Malaysia and Thailand). **Similar species** Ashy Roundleaf Bat, *H. cineraceus*, has different-shaped internarial septum, shallow notch on anterior noseleaf.

Ecology and habitat Roosts in limestone caves.

Distribution and status SE Asia: Central and S Thailand, and N Peninsular Malaysia.

DAYAK ROUNDLEAF BAT
Hipposideros dyacorum PLATE 14

Measurements FA 38–43, T 19–24, E 15–18. Wt 5–8

Identification Fur uniformly dark brown, often with slightly paler tips. Noseleaf small and simple without lateral leaflets, usually strongly pigmented dark grey-brown. Internarial septum slightly swollen at base, narrow in middle. Ears broadly triangular and pointed. **Echolocation** 167–170kHz (Sabah). **Similar species** Bicoloured Roundleaf Bat, *H. bicolor*, tends to have more pinkish noseleaf, fur with brown tips and white bases, and larger rounded ears; Fawn Roundleaf Bat, *H. cervinus*, is larger, with a wider noseleaf and 2 lateral leaflets.

Ecology and habitat Has been found roosting in caves, under rocks and in hollow trees. Forages in the understorey of tall forest.

Distribution and status SE Asia: S peninsular Thailand and Peninsular Malaysia. Also

Borneo. Near Threatened, owing to loss of lowland rainforest.

LEAST ROUNDLEAF BAT
Hipposideros doriae PLATE 14
Measurements FA 34–37. Wt 4–6g. Skull: ccl 12.9, mt 4.4–5.1
Identification Upperparts dark greyish-brown to brown, underparts paler. Noseleaf very small and simple with no lateral leaflets; anterior horseshoe with small central notch; posterior noseleaf lacks supporting septa; internarial septum slightly swollen. Ears and noseleaf pigmented grey. Ears broad, rounded, bluntly pointed at top. **Taxonomic notes** Formerly called *H. sabanus*. **Echolocation** 195–200kHz (Peninsular Malaysia). **Similar species** Ashy Roundleaf Bat, *H. cineraceus*, and other similar species have posterior noseleaf divided into four compartments by 3 supporting septa.
Ecology and habitat Found in lowland and hill forest up to 1,500m elevation, usually at low densities. Roosting sites unknown.
Distribution and status SE Asia: Peninsular Malaysia. Also Borneo and Sumatra. Near Threatened, due to loss of mature rainforest.

RIDLEY'S ROUNDLEAF BAT
Hipposideros ridleyi PLATE 13
Measurements FA 47–51, T 25–29, E 25–30. Wt 7–12. Skull: ccl 17.0–17.5, mt 6.6–6.8
Identification Fur uniformly dark brown. Ears, noseleaf and wing membranes dark grey. Ears very large and rounded. Noseleaf large, covering whole muzzle; no lateral leaflets; internarial septum expanded into large flat disc (2.8–3.1 across), which largely obscures nostrils. **Echolocation** 65–67kHz (Sabah), 61–62kHz (Peninsular Malaysia). **Similar species** Small-disc Roundleaf Bat, *H. orbiculus*, has slightly smaller noseleaf, shorter ears, smaller internarial disc that does not completely cover nostrils; Annamite Roundleaf Bat, *H. rotalis*, has one pair of lateral leaflets,
Ecology and habitat Roosts in fallen hollow trees; also found in culverts and drainage pipes. Occurs in lowland dipterocarp forest.

Distribution and status SE Asia: peninsular Thailand and Malaysia. Also Borneo. Vulnerable, owing to loss of lowland rainforest.

SMALL-DISC ROUNDLEAF BAT
Hipposideros orbiculus PLATE 13
Measurements FA 46–49, T 26–34, E 20–23.5. Wt 9.3–10.3. Skull: ccl 16.1–16.9, mt 6.4–6.6
Identification Fur dark chocolate-brown; ears, noseleaf and wing membranes dark. Ears large, rounded. Noseleaf large, covering muzzle; no lateral leaflets; internarial septum expanded into a medium-size disc (1.9–2.2mm across). **Echolocation** 80kHz (Peninsular Malaysia). **Similar species** Ridley's Roundleaf Bat, *H. ridleyi*, has larger internarial disc, larger ears, lower frequency echolocation; Thai Roundleaf Bat, *H. halophyllus*, is much smaller with small noseleaf.
Ecology and habitat Has been found roosting in drainage pipes. Recorded from a rubber plantation in primary forest (Sumatra), peatswamp forest (Peninsular Malaysia).
Distribution and status SE Asia: Peninsular Malaysia. Also Sumatra. Vulnerable, owing to low densities and loss of forest habitats.

ANNAMITE ROUNDLEAF BAT
Hipposideros rotalis PLATE 13
Measurements FA 45–49, T 32–39, E 24–27, Wt 7.5–11. Skull: ccl 16.8–17.0, mt 6.4–6.6
Identification Upperparts brown, individual hairs with white bases, brown middles and pale tips; underparts paler. Noseleaf broad, covering muzzle; enlarged internarial disc (width 2.3–2.6mm); anterior noseleaf angular with deep indentation in the middle. **Echolocation** 68.5–71.5kHz (Laos). **Similar species** Ridley's Roundleaf Bat, *H. ridleyi* is darker, lacks lateral leaflets and has less indented anterior noseleaf; Khaokhouay Roundleaf Bat, *H. khaokhouayensis*, has smaller internarial disc.
Ecology and habitat Has been found near limestone caves in disturbed evergreen forest, and mixed dry dipterocarp and evergreen forest.

Distribution and status SE Asia: known only from C Laos. Not currently at risk, though some loss of habitat within its limited range.

KHAOKHOUAY ROUNDLEAF BAT
Hipposideros khaokhouayensis PLATE 13
Measurements FA 46–49, T 35–37.5, E 24–26. Wt 7.7–9.6. Skull: ccl 16.0–17.6, mt 6.4–6.7
Identification Upperparts mid-brown, individual hairs with white bases, brown middles and pale tips; underparts paler. Noseleaf broad, covering muzzle; moderate-sized internarial disc (width 1.5–1.8mm); narrow notch in anterior noseleaf; no lateral leaflets. **Echolocation** 87–91kHz (Laos).
Similar species Annamite Roundleaf Bat, *H. rotalis*, has larger inter-narial disc, well-developed lateral leaflets, lower frequency echolocation calls; Small-disc Roundleaf Bat, *H. orbiculus*, has dark noseleaf with more rounded anterior noseleaf, shorter tail, lower frequency echolocation.
Ecology and habitat Has been found in patches of intact and disturbed evergreen forest, both near limestone caves and far from known caves.
Distribution and status SE Asia: known only from C Laos. Not currently at risk, though some loss of habitat within its limited range.

FAWN ROUNDLEAF BAT
Hipposideros cervinus PLATE 13
Measurements FA 44–52, T 21–28, E 14–17. Wt 8–12
Identification Fur colour varies from grey-brown or yellowish-brown to bright red-brown or orange; underparts somewhat paler. Noseleaf greyish-pink. Ears broadly triangular. Noseleaf simple with 2 lateral leaflets; median noseleaf narrower than posterior noseleaf. **Echolocation** 118–124kHz (Sabah), 122–127kHz (Peninsular Malaysia).
Similar species Cantor's Roundleaf Bat, *H. galeritus*, has median noseleaf broader than posterior noseleaf, ears broader and more rounded, tail longer; Intermediate Roundleaf Bat, *H. larvatus*, is larger, with 3 lateral leaflets; Dayak Roundleaf Bat, *H. dyacorum*, and other species with a small noseleaf do not have lateral leaflets.
Ecology and habitat Usually roosts in caves, sometimes in very large colonies (up to 300,000 in Sabah). Feeds in the forest understorey.
Distribution and status SE Asia: Peninsular Malaysia. Also Sumatra, Java, Borneo, the Philippines and E Indonesia through New Guinea to Australia. Not currently at risk.

CANTOR'S ROUNDLEAF BAT
Hipposideros galeritus PLATE 13
Measurements FA 45–50, T 32–42, E 14–17. Wt 6.3–10.0
Identification Fur usually dark grey-brown, occasionally with a reddish tinge. Noseleaf pinkish-grey. Ears broad, rounded at base, triangular at tip. Noseleaf with 2 lateral leaflets; median noseleaf broader than posterior noseleaf. **Taxonomic notes** Consists of several disjunct populations which may prove to represent distinct species.
Echolocation 109–117kHz (Sabah), 85–93kHz (Peninsular Malaysia), 107–110kHz (Laos).
Similar species Fawn Roundleaf Bat, *H. cervinus*, has median noseleaf narrower than posterior noseleaf, more triangular ears, shorter tail.
Ecology and habitat Roosts in caves, often in small groups with the Fawn Roundleaf Bat, *H. cervinus*, but sometimes in colonies of several hundred. Also found near large boulders. Forages in a variety of forest types from lowland rainforest to dry disturbed areas.
Distribution and status SE Asia: S Laos, S Vietnam, Cambodia, S Thailand and Peninsular Malaysia. Also India, Sri Lanka, Borneo and Java. Not currently at risk.

INTERMEDIATE ROUNDLEAF BAT
Hipposideros larvatus PLATE 12
Measurements FA 51–67, T 32–35, E 21–25. Wt 15–23
Identification Medium-sized roundleaf bat that has 3 lateral leaflets on noseleaf. Upperparts dark grey-brown to reddish-brown; underparts slightly paler. Noseleaf,

ears and wing membranes brown. **Taxonomic notes** Recent studies indicate that this is a complex of several species with considerable geographic variation in size, echolocation frequency and genetics; multiple forms differing in size and echolocation frequencies occur sympatrically in Laos. *H. grandis* may be the correct name for one of these species. However, because diagnostic characters and correct names for each form have not yet been worked out, they are treated together here. **Echolocation** 97–100kHz (Peninsular Malaysia); large form 93–97kHz, medium form 86–89kHz, small form 99–102kHz (Laos). **Similar species** Diadem Roundleaf Bat, *H. diadema*, is larger, and has buff or white shoulder marks; Pendlebury's Roundleaf Bat, *H. turpis*, is larger, with narrow posterior noseleaf.

Ecology and habitat Roosts in caves, rock crevices, temples and old mines. Cave colonies may be very large.

Distribution and status SE Asia: throughout Myanmar, Thailand, Laos, Vietnam, Cambodia and Peninsular Malaysia. Also Bangladesh to S China, Sumatra, Java, Borneo, Sumba and adjacent small islands. Not currently at risk.

DIADEM ROUNDLEAF BAT
Hipposideros diadema　PLATE 13
Measurements FA 76–87, T 53, E 27–18.5. Wt 30–47
Identification Fur of upperparts dark brown with pale bases, white patches on the shoulders and sides; underparts greyish-white. Adult females often with orange or orange-buff replacing the white. Juveniles dark grey and white. Moulting individuals can be a mixture of brown, grey, orange and white. Noseleaf with 3 or 4 lateral leaflets; posterior noseleaf large and rounded. **Echolocation** 59–62kHz (Peninsular Malaysia), 64–66kHz (Sabah). **Similar species** No other Asian *Hipposideros* has pale shoulder patches; Great Roundleaf Bat, *H. armiger*, and Pendlebury's Roundleaf Bat, *H. turpis*, have posterior noseleaf narrower than anterior;

Boonsong's Roundleaf Bat, *H. lekaguli*, has thickened posterior noseleaf with deep inverted pockets; triangular protuberance on median leaf.

Ecology and habitat Usually roosts in large colonies in caves, often mixed with other species; has been recorded in hollows in trees, or roosting alone under palms. Feeds by hanging from a perch and waiting for prey to pass by. May select several perches over one square kilometre during a night. Forms large maternity colonies of females and young. Forages in various forested habitats, including highly disturbed areas.

Distribution and status SE Asia: Myanmar, Thailand, S Laos, S Vietnam, Cambodia and Peninsular Malaysia. Also Sumatra, Java, Borneo and the Philippines through to the Solomon Islands and Australia. Not currently at risk.

BOONSONG'S ROUNDLEAF BAT
Hipposideros lekaguli　PLATE 13
Measurements FA 71–79, T 44–54, E 26–33
Identification Upperparts pale greyish or brownish-white; underparts and throat dull creamy-white. Ears triangular, large and broad. Anterior noseleaf large, almost covering muzzle with no notch in middle, and 3 well-developed lateral leaflets. Internarial septum slightly swollen; raised flaps on either side of nostrils. Intermediate leaf thickened with triangular wedge protruding in middle. Posterior leaf formed into 3 backward-facing pockets, median pocket smaller than lateral pockets. **Echolocation** 45–46kHz (Thailand). **Similar species** No other similar size roundleaf bat has enlarged, backward-facing pockets in posterior leaf, with triangular lappet in intermediate noseleaf.

Ecology and habitat Roosts in caves. Forages in forested habitats, including very disturbed areas.

Distribution and status SE Asia: S Thailand and Peninsular Malaysia. Vulnerable due to limited range and population declines as a result of roost disturbance as well as loss of habitat.

GREAT ROUNDLEAF BAT

Hipposideros armiger PLATE 12

Measurements FA 85–103, T 54–69, E 25–35. Wt 44–67 (males much larger than females)

Identification Largest roundleaf bat in SE Asia. Fur generally dark brown all over, sometimes paler beneath. Anterior horseshoe relatively small, not covering muzzle, fairly straight across; 4 lateral leaflets, outer ones often very small; median noseleaf swollen; posterior noseleaf thick, but narrower than anterior noseleaf. In males, face behind and around noseleaf may be greatly thickened and swollen. **Echolocation** 69–71kHz (Laos). **Similar species** Pendlebury's Roundleaf Bat, *H. turpis*, is similar, but smaller and with less swelling behind noseleaf.

Ecology and habitat Roosts in caves; may fly low around trees to hunt, but also flies very high in open sky, possibly commuting to foraging sites.

Distribution and status SE Asia: Myanmar, Thailand, Vietnam, Laos, Cambodia and Peninsular Malaysia. Also N India, Nepal, S China and Taiwan. Not currently at risk.

PENDLEBURY'S ROUNDLEAF BAT

Hipposideros turpis PLATE 12

Measurements FA 75–81. Wt 27–34

Identification Large roundleaf bat with dark brown fur. Anterior noseleaf does not cover muzzle; 3 lateral leaflets; posterior noseleaf narrower than anterior, with weakly developed swellings on each side behind it. **Taxonomic notes** Includes *alongensis* (from Vietnam), *turpis* (from Taiwan) and *pendleburyi* (from Thailand), but some uncertainty as to whether all are the same species. **Echolocation** 85kHz (Thailand). **Similar species** Great Roundleaf Bat, *H. armiger*, is larger, with more developed swellings behind posterior noseleaf, 4 lateral leaflets; Diadem Roundleaf Bat, *H. diadema*, has white or buff shoulder patches, posterior noseleaf broadly rounded and wider than anterior leaf; Shield-faced Roundleaf Bat, *H. lylei*, has posterior noseleaf as wide as anterior, with enlarged lobes behind it.

Ecology and habitat Found in areas near limestone karst, so likely roosts in caves. Forages in dry forest, both intact and disturbed.

Distribution and status SE Asia: peninsular Thailand and N. Vietnam. Also Taiwan. Vulnerable; populations in both Vietnam and Thailand small and fragmented, and at risk from forest loss and cave disturbance.

SHIELD-FACED ROUNDLEAF BAT

Hipposideros lylei PLATE 12

Measurements FA 73–84, T 48–55, E 30. Wt 35–52. Skull: ccl 24.1–26.5, mt 10.4–11.9

Identification Large roundleaf bat with prominent enlarged lobes behind posterior noseleaf. Anterior noseleaf moderately broad (width 8.8–9.2), rounded, with a deep notch in the middle; 2 lateral leaflets; posterior noseleaf similar in width to anterior leaf, joined on sides to anterior leaf; posterior lobes of male greatly enlarged, pointed at tip, joined at base and extending around sides of noseleaf; lobes of female small, partly hidden in fur. Ears large and triangular. Fur of upperparts pale grey to light brown; underparts similar or paler. **Echolocation** 70–75kHz (Thailand). **Similar species** Shield-nosed Roundleaf Bat, *H. scutinares*, has broader noseleaf with less-developed posterior lobes, lower frequency echolocation; Pratt's Roundleaf Bat, *H. pratti*, has larger skull, anterior noseleaf not connected to posterior leaf.

Ecology and habitat Roosts in limestone caves; has been found in both understorey and canopy of lowland primary forest in Malaysia. In Thailand reported from both disturbed and fragmented forests.

Distribution and status SE Asia: Myanmar, Thailand, Peninsular Malaysia and N Vietnam; probably N Laos. Also S China. Not currently at risk, but colonies are small and affected by cave disturbance and hunting.

SHIELD-NOSED ROUNDLEAF BAT

Hipposideros scutinares PLATE 12

Measurements FA 78–83, T 50–59, E 28–30. Wt 38–42. Skull: ccl 26.5–27.9, mt 11.5–12.3

Identification Large roundleaf bat, with

enlarged lobes behind posterior leaf. Anterior noseleaf broad (width 9.5–10.5), rounded, with a conspicuous notch in the middle; 2 lateral leaflets; posterior leaf similar in width to anterior, and joined on sides to anterior leaf; posterior lobes enlarged in males (7–14 tall), smaller in females (3–4), separated by deep notch. **Echolocation** 61–64kHz (Laos). **Similar species** Shield-faced Roundleaf Bat, *H. lylei*, has narrower noseleaf with (in males) larger posterior lobes, smaller skull, higher frequency echolocation; Pratt's Roundleaf Bat, *H. pratti*, has longer forearm, larger skull, narrower noseleaf and posterior leaf not joined to anterior noseleaf.

Ecology and habitat Roosts in limestone caves; has been found in disturbed evergreen forest near limestone.

Distribution and status SE Asia: Laos and C Vietnam. Vulnerable, owing to limited range, small population size and loss of forest.

PRATT'S ROUNDLEAF BAT
Hipposideros pratti PLATE 12
Measurements FA 81–89. Skull: ccl 27.8–30.0, mt 12.1–12.8
Identification Large roundleaf bat, with enlarged lobes behind posterior leaf. Anterior leaf moderately broad (width 8.3–9.7), rounded, with shallow notch in front margin; 2 lateral leaflets; posterior leaf similar in width to anterior leaf, not connected on sides; posterior lobes larger in males than females. **Echolocation** 61–62kHz (China). **Similar species** Shield-faced and Shield-nosed Roundleaf Bats, *H. lylei* and *H. scutinares*, have shorter forearm and smaller skull, posterior noseleaf joined on sides to anterior leaf.

Ecology and habitat Roosts in limestone caves.

Distribution and status SE Asia: N Vietnam. Also S China. Not currently at risk, though status poorly known in region.

Genus *Coelops* Very small bats. Anterior noseleaf divided in middle, and expanded to sides. Lateral leaflets large and expanded

forwards. No visible tail, although interfemoral membrane is well developed. Skull and dentition as *Hipposideros*, but rostral swellings generally low; upper canines have well-developed secondary cusp; lower incisors separated from canines by a distinct gap. Dental formula 1/2 1/1 2/2 3/3.

MALAYSIAN TAILLESS ROUNDLEAF BAT
Coelops robinsoni PLATE 14
Measurements FA 34–37, T none, E 12–14. Wt 3.5–5.0. Skull: ccl 12.7, mt 4.7
Identification Fur long and soft, brown to dark brown with paler tips; underparts brownish to slightly grey. Ears rounded, lacking supporting ridges. Narrow interfemoral membrane with no visible tail. Anterior margin of noseleaf deeply notched, forming 2 separate lobes; one pair of lateral leaflets expanded forwards to form wide, rounded lobes under the anterior noseleaf; posterior noseleaf low with a small median lobe. **Similar species** Asian Tailless Roundleaf Bat, *C. frithii*, has lower lobes of noseleaf elongated and narrow, and is usually larger.

Ecology and habitat Known roost sites include one in a cave, and one in hollow buttress of a large tree. Has been found in understorey of mature lowland rainforest, but relatively rarely recorded.

Distribution and status SE Asia: peninsular Thailand and Malaysia. Also Borneo and possibly the Philippines if *hirsutus* is conspecific. Poorly known; has probably experienced considerable population declines as a result of loss of lowland rainforest.

ASIAN TAILLESS ROUNDLEAF BAT
Coelops frithii PLATE 14
Measurements FA 34–44, T none, E 14–16. Wt 3.0–7.0. Skull: mt 5.7
Identification Fur long and soft, brown to blackish with paler tips; underparts slightly greyer. Ears rounded and lacking supporting ridges. Narrow interfemoral membrane with no visible tail. Anterior margin of noseleaf deeply notched, forming 2 lobes; one pair of lateral leaflets extending from underneath

them to form narrow, elongated lobes; posterior noseleaf low with a small median lobe.
Taxonomic notes Specimens referred to this species exhibit a very large size range, and may represent more than one species.
Similar species Malaysian Tailless Roundleaf Bat, *C. robinsoni*, has broad, rounded lobes on lateral leaflets.
Ecology and habitat Roosts in caves or hollow trees, sometimes in small groups. Forages in forests.
Distribution and status SE Asia: Myanmar, Thailand, Laos, Vietnam, Cambodia and Peninsular Malaysia. Also E India, S China, Taiwan, Sumatra, Java and Bali. Not currently at risk, though apparently occurs at very low density throughout its range.

Genus *Paracoelops* This genus is known only from the damaged holotype; hence its appearance is poorly known. Like *Coelops*, it lacks a tail, but has a well-developed interfemoral membrane. However, ears are greatly enlarged. Dental formula 1/2 1/1 2/2 3/3.

LARGE-EARED TAILLESS ROUNDLEAF BAT

Paracoelops megalotis NOT ILLUSTRATED
Measurements FA 42, T none, E 30. Wt 7
Identification Known only from one dried skin: upperparts are brownish, with golden-yellow patch on top of head; underparts beige. Ears very large, apparently funnel-shaped. Lacks a tail, but interfemoral membrane well developed, supported by long calcar. Noseleaf apparently horseshoe-shaped, but damaged and not well described. **Similar species** Other tailless roundleaf bats, *Coelops* spp., have short rounded ears, and noseleaf divided into

flaps; *Hipposideros* spp. have tails that are well developed.
Ecology and habitat Unknown.
Distribution and status SE Asia: known only from Vinh, S Vietnam. Status unknown.

Genus *Aselliscus* Posterior noseleaf raised into 3 points; anterior noseleaf with 2 lateral leaflets, upper ones joining in the middle; median noseleaf contiguous with internarial septum. Tail relatively short, protruding slightly beyond interfemoral membrane. Skull and dentition similar to *Hipposideros*, but braincase low, rostral swellings relatively low, canines small and weak. Dental formula 1/2 1/1 2/2 3/3.

TRIDENT ROUNDLEAF BAT

Aselliscus stoliczkanus PLATE 14
Measurements FA 39–45, T 33–44, E 10–13. Wt 4.5–6.5
Identification Small roundleaf bat with posterior noseleaf raised into 3 points; median noseleaf merges with internarial septum to form nearly triangular pad in middle of nose; 2 lateral leaflets, upper ones joined in front of face. Ears short, broad with point at top. Upperparts brown, fur with white bases, underparts whitish. Adult males may have tuft of longer, yellowish fur on either side of chest. **Echolocation** 124–129kHz (Laos).
Similar species Similar-sized small *Hipposideros* lack points on posterior noseleaf, have larger ears.
Ecology and habitat Roosts in limestone caves. Forages in forest, including disturbed areas.
Distribution and status Myanmar, Thailand, Laos, Vietnam and N Malaysia. Also S China. Not currently at risk, though susceptible to disturbance of caves.

Family *VESPERTILIONIDAE* COMMON BATS

The largest, most diverse and most widespread family of bats, occurring on every continent except Antarctica. The nose is simple, without any noseleaf, at least in all South-East Asian species. The ears vary from relatively small to very large, but always with a well-developed tragus. The shape of the ear and tragus can be very helpful for identification, especially for distinguishing the different genera. The tail is long, and completely or nearly completely enclosed in the interfemoral membrane, although the terminal vertebra sometimes pro-

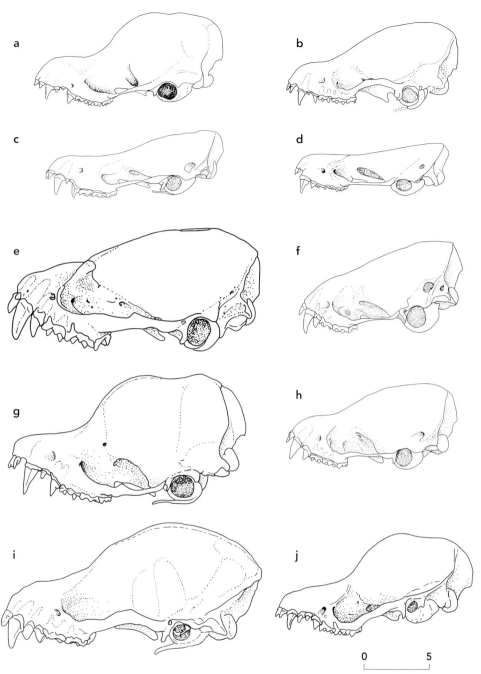

Fig. 36 *Skull profiles of selected vespertilionid bats:* Myotis annamiticus *(a),* Myotis rosseti *(b),* Eudiscopus denticulus *(c),* Tylonycteris pachypus *(d),* Thainycteris aureocollaris *(e),* Hesperoptenus blanfordi *(f),* Miniopterus magnater *(g),* Glischropus tylopus *(h),* Murina cyclotis *(i) and* Kerivoula picta *(j).*

trudes. The skull and dentition vary among genera and species, and are often important for identification (Figs 36–38). The ancestral condition for these bats is believed to have had 2 upper and 3 lower incisors, and 3 upper and lower premolars, a condition still found in

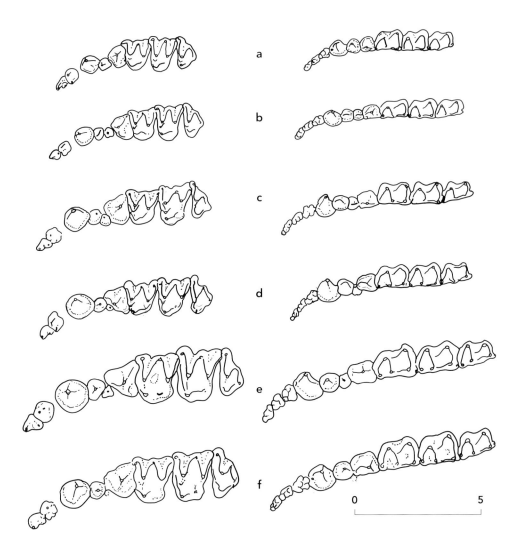

Fig. 37 *Upper (on left) and lower (on right) toothrows of selected* Myotis *showing variation in number, size and position of* premolars: M. rosseti (a), M. siligorensis (b), M. horsfieldi (c), M. hasseltii (d), M. montivagus (e) and M. annectans (f).

Kerivoula and most *Myotis*, although the middle premolar is often reduced and sometimes missing in *Myotis*. In most other genera, there has been a trend towards shortening of the jaws and reduction in the number of teeth.

South-East Asian species are grouped into 4 subfamilies containing 22 genera. When trying to identify vespertilionid bats, it is very helpful first to determine to which genus the species belongs, by comparing it with the colour plates as well as the genus descriptions. In most cases, the genus can be determined by a combination of external features, such as ear and wing shape, as well as dental characters. With care, it is possible to examine the teeth in a live bat by gently opening the mouth with a toothpick or the edge of a glove, though a magnifying glass is often necessary to see the teeth clearly. Overall skull shape can usually also be determined in a live bat, because it is reflected in the head shape – in some cases it may be necessary to smooth the fur with a finger to determine the shape of the head.

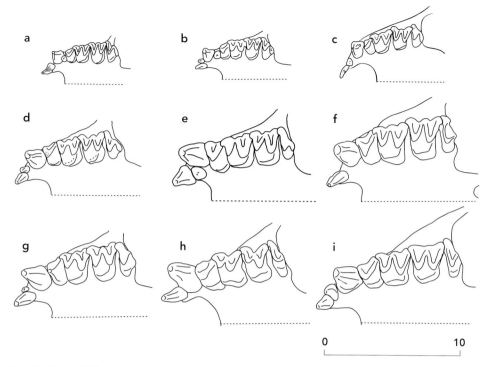

a

b

c

d

e

f

g

h

i

0   10

Fig. 38 *Upper left toothrows of selected pipistrelle-like bats:* Pipistrellus abramus *(a),* Glischropus tylopus *(b),* Philetor brachypterus *(c),* Arielulus circumdatus *(d),* Hesperoptenus tomesi *(e),* Scotomanes ornatus *(f),* Thainycteris aureocollaris *(g),* Scotophilus heathi *(h) and* Eptesicus serotinus *(i).*

Once the genus has been determined, species can be identified by a combination of size, fur colour, dental characters and other characters as described in each account. In a few groups, especially the *Pipistrellus*, reliable external identification characters are poorly known, and it may not be possible to identify some species except through detailed examination of museum specimens. In these cases, for the benefit of museum workers, the text also gives some information on selected skull and baculum identification characters for these bats.

Subfamily *VESPERTILIONINAE*

Genus *Myotis* Ears moderately long and triangular at the tip; tragus tapered, bluntly pointed and bent slightly forwards (see colour plates). The species are divided into subgenera that differ in a number of characters, including the size and shape of the feet. Skull relatively unspecialized with variably elevated braincase, narrow rostrum (Fig. 36a,b). Usually 3 upper and 3 lower premolars; middle premolar small and displaced inwards in many species, lacking in three species (Fig. 37); anterior premolar always well developed and not displaced inwards, unlike *Pipistrellus*. Dental formula: 2/3 1/1 2–3/2–3 3/3.

The genus has been divided into several subgenera. Although recent genetic analyses suggest these may need to be revised, the species are grouped by subgenera here to facilitate identification. Recent genetic analyses indicate that several additional species may occur in some groups, but species limits and diagnostic characters have not yet been worked out.

Subgenus *Myotis* Feet slightly enlarged; ears relatively long; braincase low, skull profile gradually sloping from rostrum to back of skull; middle upper and lower premolars somewhat reduced, but usually still within toothrow; anterior 2 pairs of lower incisors with 4 small lobes.

CHINESE MYOTIS
Myotis chinensis PLATE 16
Measurements FA 65–69, T 53–58, HF 16–18, E 20–23. Wt 25–30. Skull: ccl 20.5–22.2, mt 9.5–9.9
Identification Largest *Myotis* in region. Upperparts dark greyish-brown, hairs with blackish bases; underparts paler, with grey tips to hairs. Ears long and slender, tragus tapered and angled slightly forwards. Middle premolars slightly more than half size of anterior premolars and in toothrow.
Similar species All other *Myotis* in region are smaller; other large vespertilionids have different-shaped ears and fewer teeth.
Ecology and habitat Has been recorded in or near limestone caves with rivers nearby. Altitudes from 50m to 1,000m. Moderately common in some areas.
Distribution and status SE Asia: Myanmar, Thailand and Vietnam. Also China. Not currently at risk.

SZECHUAN MYOTIS
Myotis altarium PLATE 16
Measurements FA 43–46, HF 11–12, E 22–24. Skull: gl 15.5–16.0
Identification Upperparts light brown with long hairs, underparts paler, individual hairs with dark bases and whitish tips. Ears long and narrow, extending 5mm beyond muzzle when folded forwards; tragus long, thin and bluntly pointed. Hind foot moderately long, over 60% of tibia length; wing membrane attached on side of foot at base of toes; calcar weakly lobed at midpoint. Middle upper and lower premolars small. **Similar species** Large Brown Myotis, *M. montivagus*, has smaller feet, shorter ears, middle upper premolar greatly reduced and intruded in toothrow; Hairy-faced Myotis, *M. annectans*,

lacks middle upper and lower premolars.
Ecology and habitat Only specimen from region was found in a limestone cave near a stream.
Distribution and status SE Asia: N Thailand. Also S China. Status unknown.

Subgenus *Chrysopteron* Ears moderate-sized, typical *Myotis* shape, broadened in middle and tapering bluntly to top with moderate antitragal fold extending halfway up ear; tragus relatively long, bluntly pointed and straight, not bent forwards; feet not especially enlarged; wing membrane attached at base of toes; wings with conspicuous black and orange pattern. Anterior 2 pairs of lower incisors with 4 small lobes, like subgenus *Myotis*.

BLACK-AND-ORANGE MYOTIS
Myotis formosus PLATE 15
Measurements FA 45–52, T 52, HF 11, E 19. Wt 12. Skull: cbl 16.3–17.8, mt 6.8–7.3
Identification Moderately large *Myotis* with orange to orange-brown body and head, black rims to ears; black and orange pattern on wing membranes. **Taxonomic notes** Known from a very wide geographic range, with many populations apparently not geographically connected; may prove to represent a complex of species. **Similar species** Herman's Myotis, *M. hermani*, is larger; Painted Bat, *Kerivoula picta*, is smaller with more funnel-shaped ears, more pointed tragus, no black on head, different dentition.
Ecology and habitat Has been found over a river in evergreen forest.
Distribution and status SE Asia: Laos. Also Pakistan, Afghanistan, India, China, Korea, Taiwan, Japan, Java, Bali, Sulawesi and the Philippines. Status uncertain in region, as known from only one record, but not apparently at risk elsewhere, as relatively common in some areas.

HERMAN'S MYOTIS
Myotis hermani NOT ILLUSTRATED
Measurements FA 56–60, T 58, HF 12, E 20. Wt 16. Skull: cbl 19.5–20.0, mt 8.6

Identification Similar in colour and pattern to *M. formosus*, but larger. Body fur orange to orange-brown, black rims to ears; black and orange pattern on wing membranes.
Similar species Black-and-orange Myotis, *M. formosus*, is smaller; Painted Bat, *Kerivoula picta*, is much smaller with more funnel-shaped ears, more pointed tragus, no black on head.
Ecology and habitat Recorded over rivers in lowland rainforest.
Distribution and status SE Asia: peninsular Thailand and Malaysia. Also Sumatra. Status uncertain: apparently rare and if dependent on mature forest, probably declining.

Subgenus *Selysius* Relatively small feet with wing membrane attached at base of toes. Ears not especially long. Tragus narrow and tapered, typically angled slightly forwards. Middle lower incisors with only 3 lobes. Note that *Myotis siligorensis* has usually been included in *Selysius*, but is here grouped with *Leuconoe* because of its similarity to *M. laniger*.

ASIAN WHISKERED MYOTIS
Myotis muricola PLATE 15
Measurements FA 33–37, T 35–41, E 12.5–14.5, HF 6–7. Wt 4–7. Skull: cbl 12.7–13.1, ccl 11.5–11.8, mt 4.8–5.4
Identification Upperparts brown to grey with dark bases; underparts with dark bases, light brown tips. Ears moderately long, tragus slender, bent forwards and bluntly pointed. Feet small with wing membrane attached at base of toes. Middle upper premolar small and often slightly intruded from the toothrow (as in Fig. 37c). Upper canine much longer than posterior upper premolar.
Taxonomic notes Genetic studies indicate that bats currently referred to *M. muricola* represent a complex of species, but diagnostic characters and appropriate names have not yet been worked out. **Similar species** Eurasian Whiskered Myotis, *M. mystacinus*, is paler with white underparts; Peters's Myotis, *M. ater*, is larger, with a larger skull and smaller second premolars; Small-

toothed Myotis, *M. siligorensis*, is smaller with a domed braincase, lower canines small; Ridley's Myotis, *M. ridleyi*, has shorter forearm, darker fur and lacks the small second premolar; Horsfield's Myotis, *M. horsfieldii*, has larger feet with wing membrane attached at side of the foot; pipistrelles, *Pipistrellus* spp, have different shape tragus and only 2 upper premolars, the anterior displaced inwards; woolly bats, *Kerivoula* spp., have more funnel-shaped ears with long, straight, pointed tragus and longer, fluffier hair.
Ecology and habitat Forages in relatively open areas, including over streams and rivers near forests, and agricultural areas and fields. Roost sites include furled central leaves of banana plants and vegetated areas near cave entrances.
Distribution and status SE Asia: throughout region. Also E India, S China, Indonesia from Sumatra through to New Guinea and the Philippines. Not currently at risk.

EURASIAN WHISKERED MYOTIS
Myotis mystacinus PLATE 15
Measurements FA 34–37, T 32–40, E 12–14, HF 7–8. Wt 4–5.5. Skull: ccl 12.3, mt 5.4
Identification Upperparts greyish buff-brown, hairs with dark brown bases; underparts with broad white to creamy-white tips with dark bases. Ears moderately long, tragus slender, bent forwards and bluntly pointed. Feet small with wing membrane attached at bases of toes. Middle upper premolar small and slightly intruded from toothrow. Upper canine much longer than posterior upper premolar. **Similar species** Asian Whiskered Myotis, *M. muricola*, is darker with buffy-brown underparts, slightly shorter toothrow.
Ecology and habitat Has been found near a cave in disturbed habitats at 1,400m.
Distribution and status Myanmar. Also through much of Palaearctic, from Europe through Nepal and India. Poorly known in region, with only one confirmed record; may have been overlooked owing to confusion with *M. muricola*. Not currently at risk.

PETERS'S MYOTIS

Myotis ater PLATE 15

Measurements FA 34–39, T 43–48, E 13.5, HF 6.5–7.5. Wt 5.0–7.0. Skull: cbl 14.4–14.5, mt 5.8–5.9

Identification Upperparts dark brown, hairs with slightly paler brown tips; underparts with long, dark brown bases and buffy-brown tips; second upper and lower premolars usually very small and displaced inwards, so that the first and third premolars are touching, or nearly so. **Taxonomic notes** It is unclear whether bats referred to this species from mainland SE Asia are actually the same species as those in Maluku, which is the type locality of the name. **Similar species** Asian Whiskered Myotis, *M. muricola*, is very similar, but has smaller skull and teeth, tends to have paler fur, usually shorter forearm; Large Brown Myotis, *M. montivagus*, has slightly longer forearm, substantially larger skull.

Ecology and habitat Has been found over streams in lowland rainforest in Malaysia. Probably uses a variety of habitats.

Distribution and status SE Asia: Vietnam, peninsular Thailand and Malaysia. Also Sumatra, Borneo, the Philippines, Sulawesi and Indonesian islands through to New Guinea. Not currently at risk.

LARGE BROWN MYOTIS

Myotis montivagus PLATE 15

Measurements FA 41–45, T 44–50, E 15–16, HF 8.5–9.5. Wt 13–16. Skull: cbl 16.4–16.9, mt 6.7–7.0

Identification Upperparts with short velvety fur, very dark brown with blackish bases to hairs; underparts similar with paler tips to the hairs, sometimes with orange tinge. Feet relatively small with wing membrane attached at base of toes. Middle upper premolar very small and completely intruded in toothrow; lower middle premolar small (Fig. 37e), varies among populations from completely within toothrow (*M. m. montivagus*) to completely intruded (*M. m. federatus*). **Similar species** Hairy-faced Myotis, *M. annectans*, is similar in size, but lacks middle upper and lower premolars (Fig. 37f), has longer, paler

fur with whitish underparts; Szechuan Myotis, *M. altarium*, has relatively large middle premolars within toothrow, larger feet; Hasselt's Large-footed Myotis, *M. hasseltii*, has larger feet with wing membrane attached at ankle.

Ecology and habitat Recorded from understorey of mature and disturbed forests, at altitudes from lowlands up to 1,000m.

Distribution and status SE Asia: Myanmar, Thailand, Peninsular Malaysia, Laos and Vietnam. Also India, Nepal, Sumatra, and Borneo. Not currently at risk, though relatively uncommon in most areas.

HAIRY-FACED MYOTIS

Myotis annectans PLATE 15

Measurements FA 45–49, T 44–49, E 15.5–17.5, HF 8.5–10.5. Wt 8.5–13

Identification Upperparts with long fur, bases dark brown with short, shiny pale tips, giving frosted effect; underparts with dark brown bases and silvery-white tips, except middle of belly where tips are orange-brown. Middle upper and lower premolars usually lacking (Fig. 37f); sometimes present asymmetrically, but very small. Ears moderately large; tragus long and slender, bent forwards and rounded at tip; wing membrane inserts on side of foot just above base of toe; calcar with little or no keel. **Similar species** Large Brown Myotis, *M. montivagus*, has shorter, darker fur, middle upper and lower premolars small but present; Szechuan Myotis, *M. altarium*, is darker, with well-developed middle premolars.

Ecology and habitat Recorded from hill forest in Laos.

Distribution and status SE Asia: N Thailand, Laos, Cambodia and Vietnam. Also NE India. Not currently at risk.

THICK-THUMBED MYOTIS

Myotis rosseti PLATE 15

Measurements FA 29–31, T 35, E 13–14, HF 7. Wt 4.5–6.0

Identification Small *Myotis* with relatively short fur, greyish-brown above, paler underneath, the individual hairs with dark brown bases and pale tips. Enlarged, thickened, rounded pad on base of thumb, slightly pinker than rest of wing, which is very dark grey; small triangular pad on foot. Ears relatively long, extend 2–3mm past muzzle when bent forwards. Tragus thickened at base, angled forwards and tapering to tip. Feet relatively small with wing membrane attached at side of base of toes. Only 2 upper and lower premolars (Fig. 37a). **Similar species** Ridley's Myotis, *M. ridleyi*, is more blackish and lacks thumb pad; Thick-thumbed Pipistrelle, *Glischropus tylopus*, has shorter, broader ears, smaller and more rounded tragus, smaller and pinker thumb and footpads, distinctive upper incisors.

Ecology and habitat Poorly known. Known to forage over disturbed areas including fields; has been found over a small stream. Roost sites include houses, hollow trees and bamboo.

Distribution and status SE Asia: Thailand, Laos, Vietnam and Cambodia. Probably not currently at risk, though known only from small number of records.

RIDLEY'S MYOTIS
Myotis ridleyi PLATE 15
Measurements FA 27–32, T 30–36, E 10–12, HF 6.0–7.5. Wt 4–6

Identification A small, dark bat with short wings but a relatively heavy body and a typical *Myotis* ear and tragus shape. Upperparts dark grey-brown; underparts paler and greyer. Feet small with wing membrane attached to side of foot. Has only 2 upper and lower premolars (as in Fig. 37a). **Similar species** Most other *Myotis* have 3 upper and lower premolars, though middle one can be small and hard to see; Small-toothed Myotis, *M. siligorensis*, is paler, with a lighter body, short canines and a conspicuous middle premolar; Thick-thumbed Myotis, *M. rosseti*, has thickened thumb pad, longer ears; pipistrelles also have only 2 premolars, but anterior upper premolar is small and usually displaced inwards, ears and tragus are a different shape.

Ecology and habitat Known only from lowland rainforest. Forages in understorey, especially over small streams. Roost sites includes caves, fallen logs and under rocks.
Distribution and status SE Asia: peninsular Thailand and Malaysia. Also Borneo. Near Threatened. Population has declined due to extensive forest loss in its range.

SINGAPORE MYOTIS
Myotis oreias NOT ILLUSTRATED
Measurements FA ~38–39, E ~14. Skull: mt 5.9

Identification. This species is known only from the type, which is in very bad condition, such that it is hard to determine its affinities. Dry skin currently has fur of upperparts with dark brown bases and yellowish-brown tips, belly slightly paler; however, original description said it was greyish-brown, suggesting possible discoloration. Ears moderately long. Only part of the skull remains, with the right upper toothrow; this indicates that middle upper premolar is relatively large, about half the size of the anterior premolar and completely within the toothrow. Although this does not appear to match any species of *Myotis* currently known from the region, the condition makes it hard to be sure of this, and it is possible that it was actually collected elsewhere, and is mislabelled.

Ecology and habitat Unknown.

Distribution and status SE Asia: type was in a collection assembled in Singapore, but it is not clear whether it originated there or elsewhere.

Subgenus *Leuconoe* Bats in this subgenus have the characteristic ear and tragus shape of other *Myotis* but have enlarged hind feet, with the wing attached at the ankle or side of the foot. These large feet are used for scooping insects off water and, in some species, for catching small fish. Middle lower incisors with only 3 lobes.

HORSFIELD'S MYOTIS
Myotis horsfieldii PLATE 16
Measurements FA 35–38, T 37–39, HF 10–11, E 13.5–17. Wt 5–7.5. Skull: cbl 14.3–14.7, mt 5.8–6.0

Identification Upperparts grey-brown; underparts greyer. Ears large. Feet moderately large with wing membrane attached to side of foot 1–2mm from base of toes. Second upper and lower premolars only slightly displaced inwards (Fig. 37c). **Similar species** Hasselt's Myotis, *M. hasseltii*, has wing membrane attached at ankle, middle premolar tiny and protruded inwards (Fig. 37d); Asian Whiskered Myotis, *M. muricola*, and its relatives have smaller feet with wings attached at bases of toes.

Ecology and habitat Roosts in crevices or bell-holes in caves, usually not far from large streams or rivers. Feeds low over open surfaces of water such as wide streams.

Distribution and status SE Asia: Laos, Vietnam, Cambodia, Thailand and Peninsular Malaysia. Also known from India, S China, Borneo, Java, Bali, Sulawesi and the Philippines. Not currently at risk.

HASSELT'S MYOTIS
Myotis hasseltii PLATE 16
Measurements FA 38–43, HF 10–11. Wt 7.5–12.5. Skull: cbl 14.1–14.6, mt 5.6–5.8

Identification Upperparts dark brown to dark grey with pale grey tips to hairs; underparts greyish-white with dark bases. Fur short and velvety. Flight membranes pale grey-brown. Fur appears silvery when spotlit in flight at night. Feet large, with wing membrane attached at ankle. Second upper premolar very small and displaced inwards so that first and third premolars are in contact or nearly so (Fig. 37d). **Similar species** Horsfield's Myotis, *M. horsfieldii*, is smaller, with wing membrane attached at side of foot; Rickett's Myotis, *M. ricketti*, is much larger, with very large hind feet; Australasian Large-footed Myotis, *M. adversus*, has no confirmed records in region, but occurs nearby and may yet be found. It is similar, but distinguished by denser, woolly fur, relatively larger middle upper and lower premolars that are within toothrow or only slightly intruded.

Ecology and habitat Forages for food low over larger areas of open water, such as large rivers, lakes and sea, including coastal areas near mangrove. Catches food by dipping its large feet into the water. Has been found roosting in caves.

Distribution and status SE Asia: Myanmar, Thailand, Vietnam, Cambodia and Peninsular Malaysia, especially in coastal areas and along large rivers and lakes. Also Sumatra, Java, Borneo and smaller intervening islands. Not currently at risk.

RICKETT'S MYOTIS
Myotis ricketti PLATE 16
Measurements FA 53–56, T 51–55, HF 15.5–17.5, E 18–20. Wt 14–22

Identification Large *Myotis* with enormous feet, about 80% of tibia length, with long, curved claws; wing membrane attached at ankles. Upperparts are buffy grey-brown, hairs with darker bases; underparts greyish-white with darker bases. **Similar species** Hasselt's Myotis, *M. hasseltii*, is smaller, and has smaller feet.

Ecology and habitat Roosting sites not reported, but has been found along rocky streams near limestone outcrops and likely roosts in caves. Extremely large feet used for catching prey off water, including small fish.

Distribution and status SE Asia: Laos and N Vietnam. Also China. Not currently at risk.

SMALL-TOOTHED MYOTIS
Myotis siligorensis PLATE 16
Measurements FA 30–35, T 28–38, E 11–12.5, HF 6.5–7.0. Wt 2.3–4.0. Skull: ccl 10.4, mt 4.4

Identification Upperparts light reddish-brown to sandy-brown, the fur with dark brown bases; underparts paler with buffy or white tips to fur. Relatively long forearm, but otherwise very small and light-bodied. Feet medium-sized with wing membrane attached on side of foot about 1mm from base of toes. Ears reach just past tip of nose when folded forwards. Second upper and lower premolars only slightly smaller than corresponding first premolar and in line in toothrow. Skull has distinctly domed braincase (as in Fig. 36a), which is reflected in live animal by forehead rising abruptly from rostrum. Canines small, upper canine similar in height to posterior upper premolar, lower canine about same height as anterior lower premolar. **Similar species** Asian Whiskered Myotis, *M. muricola*, is larger, with longer canines and a flatter skull; Ridley's Myotis, *M. ridleyi*, has a shorter forearm but is otherwise darker and heavier, with only 2 premolars; Indochinese Myotis, *M. laniger*, is similar but slightly larger, with longer ears and slightly larger canines.

Ecology and habitat Has been found roosting in rock fissures in caves. Occurs in lowlands up to 1,600m in both primary forest and disturbed areas. Usually associated with water, including small streams.

Distribution and status SE Asia: Myanmar, Thailand, Laos, Vietnam, Cambodia and Peninsular Malaysia. Also found from Nepal through S China and in Borneo. Not currently at risk.

ANNAMITE MYOTIS
Myotis annamiticus NOT ILLUSTRATED

Measurements FA 31–34, T 33–36, E 13–15, HF 7.0–8.2. Wt 3.3–4.0. Skull: ccl 11.3–11.6

Identification Upperparts brown, fur with dark bases, underparts greyish-brown. Feet somewhat enlarged; wing membrane inserted on side of foot 1–2mm from bases of toes. Ears long and narrow. Skull with domed braincase that rises abruptly from rostrum (Fig. 36a); shape is reflected in steep forehead in live bat. Canines small, upper canine similar in height to posterior premolar; lower canine shorter than posterior premolar. **Similar species** Small-toothed Myotis, *M. siligorensis*, has smaller canines, shorter ears; Indochinese Myotis, *M. laniger*, is slightly larger, especially in skull measurements.

Ecology and habitat Forages over water surface on small streams in forested and disturbed areas. Probably roosts in rock crevices and limestone caves.

Distribution and status SE Asia: Laos and Vietnam. Also S China. Status poorly known, but probably not currently at risk.

INDOCHINESE MYOTIS
Myotis laniger PLATE 16

Measurements FA 31–36, T 33-36, E 13–15, HF 7.2-8.2. Wt 3.3–4.0. Skull: ccl 12.8–13.1

Identification Upperparts brown, fur with dark bases, underparts greyish-brown. Feet somewhat enlarged; wing membrane inserted on side of foot 1–2mm from base of toes. Ears very long and narrow, extending 4–5mm beyond nostrils when folded forwards. Skull with domed braincase that rises abruptly from rostrum (as in Fig. 36a), reflected in steep forehead in live bat. Canines small, upper canine similar in height to posterior premolar; lower canine shorter than posterior premolar. **Taxonomic notes** Formerly included in *M. daubentoni*. Still some uncertainty about relationships between this species and *M. annamiticus*. **Similar species** Small-toothed Myotis, *M. siligorensis*, is smaller, with shorter canines, shorter ears; Annamite Myotis, *M. annamiticus*, is very similar but slightly smaller; Horsfield's Myotis, *M. horsfieldii*, has larger canines, longer than the premolars, and larger, more flattened skull.

Ecology and habitat Forages low over water, especially small streams. Probably roosts in caves.

Distribution and status SE Asia: Laos and Vietnam. Also S China. Poorly known, but probably not currently at risk.

Genus *Eudiscopus* Ear shape somewhat similar to *Myotis*, with narrow tragus bent forwards, but characterized by large pads on feet and very flattened skull (Fig. 36c). Only 2 upper premolars, both within toothrow; 3 lower premolars, middle ones very small and completely intruded within toothrow. Dental formula 2/3 1/1 2/3 3/3.

DISC-FOOTED BAT
Eudiscopus denticulus PLATE 18

Measurements FA 35–38, T 36–40, E 13–14. Wt 5.0. Skull: ccl 12.8–13.4

Identification Upperparts medium sandy-brown; underparts paler buffy-brown. Ears shaped somewhat like *Myotis*, with narrow tragus that bends forwards in middle. Sole of foot modified into an enlarged pink pad like a suction cup, with short toes; wing membrane inserted at end of pad at base of outer toe; calcar extends base of pad to support tail membrane with well-developed keel. Thumb short, thickened at base, but not forming a pad. Skull very flat. **Similar species** Bamboo bats, *Tylonycteris* spp., also have enlarged footpads, but are much smaller, wing membrane inserts at ankle opposite calcar, head is much thinner, ear is a different shape; *Myotis* spp. have similar-shaped ears, but braincase is more elevated, feet do not have enlarged pads.

Ecology and habitat Roosts inside bamboo internodes; footpad provides enough suction to hang from a smooth surface. Apparently forages near thickets, bamboo and forests, with slow, manoeuvrable flight, including hovering.

Distribution and status SE Asia: Myanmar, Thailand, Laos and Vietnam. Status poorly known; relatively rare compared with other bamboo specialists.

Genus *Barbastella* Broad, forward-facing ears joined across forehead. Skull with enlarged braincase, sloping steeply to narrow front of shortened rostrum. Anterior upper premolar tiny, completely displaced inwards. Dental formula 2/3 1/1 2/2 3/3.

EASTERN BARBASTELLE

Barbastella leucomelas PLATE 19
Measurements FA 38–43, T 40–47, E 15–17. Skull: ccl 13.4–14.2

Identification Upperparts black, slightly glossy on the lower back; underparts dark blackish-brown. Ears relatively broad, facing forwards, joined at bases across forehead. Membranes and ears blackish-brown. Muzzle broad, with prominent swellings.

Similar species No other vespertilionids in region have ears joined on forehead.

Ecology and habitat Recorded mainly from montane forest, including coniferous forest, at altitudes above 1,200m. Roosts singly or in small groups, under bark and in tree hollows.

Distribution and status SE Asia: possibly N Vietnam. Also S China, India and Nepal through to N Africa. Reported from Vietnam, but without a precise locality record, so cannot be confirmed. However, confirmed in S China near border of region, and likely to occur in N parts of Myanmar, Laos and Vietnam. Status unknown.

Genus *Pipistrellus* This genus was formerly considered to comprise a broad range of species characterized by having only 2 upper and lower premolars (Fig. 38). More recent analyses indicate that many of these species are not closely related and should be separated into several different genera, including, within our region, *Hypsugo*, *Arielulus* and *Falsistrellus*, as well as *Pipistrellus* itself. All of them are distinguished from *Myotis* by shape of ears and tragus (Fig. 40).

In *Pipistrellus* the anterior premolars, although much smaller than the posterior premolar, are usually reasonably well developed, the upper ones similar in size to the second incisor and only partially intruded within the toothrow. Ears simple, usually somewhat rounded. Tragus usually somewhat club-shaped, rounded at the tip. Calcar has well-developed, rounded lobe on the outside. Incisors relatively small. Males usually have relatively long penis, with elongate baculum, sometimes extremely long. Skull variable, but with braincase generally low; rostrum only slightly shortened. Lower molars typically with nyctalodont cusp pattern (Fig. 39). Dental formula 2/3 1/1 2/2 3/3.

Although some species are very common, others are known from only a few specimens, possibly because their behaviour makes them hard to catch, rather than because they are rare. Recent surveys and genetic studies suggest a number of additional species occur in the region, but the identification characters and their names have not yet been sorted out.

Some species appear extremely similar to one another and appropriate methods for distinguishing them in the field have not yet been worked out. In particular, for a few

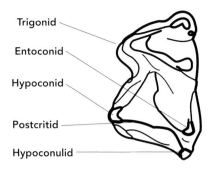
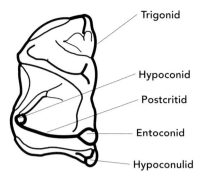

Fig. 39 *First lower left molars showing cusp patterns of a nyctalodont (left:* Pipistrellus javanicus*) and myotodont (right:* Hypsugo pulveratus*) tooth. In the nyctalodont, the postcristid ridge connects the hypoconid to the hypoconulid, while in the myotodont it is further forwards and connects to the entoconid.*

species, the main known identification characters are the size and shape of the penis and the baculum, the bone inside the penis. These differences in reproductive organs indicate that the species are reproductively isolated from one another and hence valid species, but are of limited value in the field and not helpful in identifying females. Nevertheless, they are mentioned here for the benefit of museum workers, and because close examination of these characters may help with discovering additional differences that are more useful for distinguishing these species in life.

JAVAN PIPISTRELLE
Pipistrellus javanicus PLATE 17
Measurements FA 30–36, T 34–40, E 10.5–11.5. Wt 4.0–7.0. Skull: ccl 11.9–13.1, mt 4.6–5.2, m–m 5.6–6.7
Identification Upperparts dark brown with dark bases; underparts slightly paler, tips mid-brown, bases dark brown. Ear moderate length, narrow, with distinct fold at posterior edge; tragus narrow, relatively straight, with rounded tip (Fig. 40a). Anterior upper premolar slightly displaced inwards (as in Fig. 38a). Braincase somewhat elevated, giving a distinct rostral depression. Upper canine

usually has secondary cusp. Male has moderately long penis (more than 6mm); with medium-length baculum. **Similar species** Japanese Pipistrelle, *P. abramus*, and Mount Popa Pipistrelle, *P. paterculus*, have slightly different fur colours, longer penis and baculum; Least Pipistrelle, *P. tenuis*, is smaller with shorter, more sloping skull, shorter baculum; *Myotis* spp. have distinctively shaped ear with tapered tragus, usually 3 upper and lower premolars.
Ecology and habitat Known from a wide variety of habitats, from primary hill forest up to 2,000m to heavily disturbed areas such as rubber plantations and towns. Has been found roosting in treeferns, fallen logs, caves and urban areas.
Distribution and status SE Asia: throughout

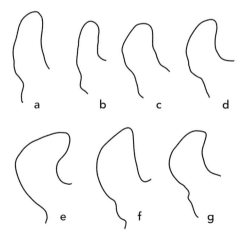

Fig. 40 *Right tragus of selected pipistrelles:* Pipistrellus javanicus *(a),* P. tenuis *(b),* P. ceylonicus *(c),* Arielulus societatis *(d),* P. stenopterus *(e),* Falsistrellus affinis *(f) and* Hypsugo macrotis *(g).*

the region. Also Afghanistan, Pakistan, India, China (Tibet), Sumatra, Java, Borneo and elsewhere in Indonesia, Philippines. Not currently at risk.

JAPANESE PIPISTRELLE
Pipistrellus abramus PLATE 17
Measurements FA 29–33, T 27–31, E 9.5–10.5. Wt 3.8–5.8. Skull: ccl 10.9–11.1, mt 4.2–4.4, m–m 5.2–5.4
Identification Fur of upperparts with greyish-brown tips, darker bases; underparts with pale brown tips and contrasting dark brown bases. Ear with rounded tip, tragus narrow, rounded, angled slightly forwards (as in Fig. 40a). Upper canine with a small secondary cusp on posterior cutting edge. Penis long, baculum ~9mm with strong double curve. **Similar species** Javan Pipistrelle, *P. javanicus*, very similar except for smaller penis in male, slightly larger skull, generally darker brown fur; Mount Popa Pipistrelle, *P. paterculus*, lacks secondary cusp on canine, male has longer penis, long straight baculum.
Ecology and habitat In N Vietnam, common around human settlements and heavily disturbed areas.
Distribution and status SE Asia: Myanmar, and Vietnam. Also E Russia, China, Korea, and Japan. Not currently at risk.

MOUNT POPA PIPISTRELLE
Pipistrellus paterculus PLATE 17
Measurements FA 27–34, T 29–34, E 7.5–12.0. Wt 4.5–6.0. Skull: ccl 10.6–11.6, mt 4.1–4.8, m–m 5.3–5.9
Identification Fur colour uniformly dark brown above, bases essentially same colour as tips; underparts with sandy-brown tips, dark brown bases. Upper canine usually without a secondary cusp. Ear subtriangular with rounded tip, short blunt tragus angled slightly forwards. Male has extremely long penis which is bent at right angles, about 4.5mm from body to bend, then 12.5mm on straight part to tip; narrow, straight baculum, 9–12mm. **Similar species** Japanese Pipistrelle, *P. abramus*, also has long penis, but

baculum has distinctive curve; females are difficult to distinguish, though fur colour may be helpful, at least within local populations.
Ecology and habitat Has been found in disturbed habitats and around villages. Roost sites include holes in tree stumps, thatched roof of a hut.
Distribution and status SE Asia: Myanmar, Laos and Vietnam. Also India and SW China. It is relatively common and is not currently at risk.

COROMANDEL PIPISTRELLE
Pipistrellus coromandra PLATE 17
Measurements FA 26–34. T 28–35, E 9. Wt 3.4. Skull: ccl 10.6–11.9, mt 3.9–4.6, m–m 5.0–6.0
Identification Upperparts generally dark brown, sometimes with reddish-brown cast; underparts noticeably paler with pale brown tips, dark bases to fur. Skull similar to *P. javanicus* but slightly smaller, braincase somewhat flattened with relatively straight rostral profile. Upper canine has distinct secondary cusp. Penis moderate size, baculum thin and straight, 3–4mm long. **Similar species** Javan Pipistrelle, *P. javanicus*, averages slightly larger with more domed braincase, moderately long penis; Japanese and Mount Popa Pipistrelles, *P. abramus* and *P. paterculus*, have much longer penis, latter tends to have more domed skull; Least Pipistrelle, *P. tenuis*, has smaller skull that usually does not overlap in size in areas where both species occur.
Ecology and habitat A wide variety of habitats from forest to agricultural fields and urban areas. Roost sites include under bark or among leaves of trees and in buildings.
Distribution and status SE Asia: Myanmar, Thailand, Laos, Vietnam and Cambodia. Also Afghanistan, India, Nepal, Pakistan and S China. Not currently at risk.

LEAST PIPISTRELLE
Pipistrellus tenuis PLATE 17
Measurements FA 25–31, T 29–35, E 9–11.5. Wt 3–4. Skull: ccl 9.3–10.7, mt 3.5–4.1, m–m 4.5–5.2

Identification Upperparts mid- to dark brown; underparts similar or slightly paler. Ear relatively short, oval, with weak folds on posterior edge; tragus short and rounded, angled slightly forwards (Fig. 40b). Second upper premolar slightly displaced inwards. Upper canine with distinct secondary cusp. Rostrum of skull short, narrow, with evenly sloping profile from nose to top of skull. Penis of moderate size; baculum thin and straight, ~4mm long. **Taxonomic notes** Probably includes more than one species across its very wide geographic range. **Similar species** Coromandel Pipistrelle, *P. coromandra*, averages larger, especially in skull dimensions, but can be hard to distinguish in life; other similar pipistrelles are larger, with much longer penis; Ridley's Myotis, *Myotis ridleyi*, has a typical *Myotis* ear shape, first upper premolar in line in toothrow and not displaced inwards (as in Fig. 37a).

Ecology and habitat Found in a wide range of habitats from forest to highly disturbed open areas. Roosts include hollow branches, among dead leaves and in buildings.

Distribution and status SE Asia: Myanmar, Thailand, Laos, Vietnam, Cambodia and Peninsular Malaysia. Also Afghanistan through India, S China, Java, Sumatra, Borneo, the Philippines and Sulawesi. Not currently at risk.

KELAART'S PIPISTRELLE

Pipistrellus ceylonicus PLATE 17
Measurements FA 33–42, T 30–35, E 13. Wt 7–8. Skull: ccl 13.1–14.3, mt 5.2–5.9, m–m 6.2–7.2

Identification Relatively large *Pipistrellus*; fur of upperparts varies from grey-brown to reddish-brown with dark bases; underparts paler, hairs with dark bases and pale grey tips. Tragus broadly rounded (Fig. 40c). Skull large and broad. Anterior upper premolar relatively large, similar in size to anterior incisor, displaced inwards, but canine and second premolar do not touch; lower anterior premolar about 80% crown area of second. Canine has secondary cusp in Indian examples, but not in only known specimen from Myanmar. Baculum slender, about 4mm long. **Similar species** Narrow-winged Pipistrelle, *P. stenopterus*, has short fifth finger; other *Pipistrellus* spp. are smaller; *Hypsugo* spp. have larger, broader ears, with no keel on calcar, very small anterior upper premolar; Doria's False-serotine, *Hesperoptenus doriae*, lacks small anterior premolar and has large inner incisors.

Ecology and habitat Poorly known in region.

Distribution and status SE Asia: N Myanmar, S Laos and N Vietnam. Also Sri Lanka, Pakistan, India, S China and Borneo. Poorly known in region; not at risk elsewhere.

NARROW-WINGED PIPISTRELLE

Pipistrellus stenopterus PLATE 17
Measurements FA 37–42, T 55–57, E 14–16. Wt 14–22. Skull: ccl 15.1–15.5, mt 5.7–5.8, m–m 7.6–7.9

Identification Fur short; upperparts uniform reddish-brown to dark brown; underparts slightly paler and greyer. Muzzle broad and heavy. Ears moderate, broadly rounded. Tragus broad, hatchet shaped, strongly angled forwards (Fig. 40e). Wing narrow – fifth finger short, not much longer than metacarpal of fourth finger. Anterior upper premolar well developed, similar in size to outer upper incisor, displaced inwards; anterior lower premolar slightly larger in crown areas than posterior premolar. Skull large and robust, forehead sloping or slightly domed in profile. **Similar species** Kelaart's Pipistrelle, *P. ceylonicus*, is smaller, with longer fifth finger; Doria's False-serotine, *Hesperoptenus doriae*, has enlarged conical inner upper incisors, only one upper premolar; *Hypsugo* spp. have greatly reduced anterior upper premolars, longer fifth finger.

Ecology and habitat Forages in open areas, over fields and rivers and most likely over houses. Roosts in hollow trees in forests and rubber plantations, as well as in roofs of houses, sometimes with *Scotophilus kuhlii*.

Distribution and status SE Asia: S peninsular Thailand and Peninsular Malaysia. Also

Sumatra, Borneo and the Philippines. Not currently at risk.

Genus *Nyctalus* Medium-sized to large vespertilionid bats with relatively narrow, elongate wings; fifth finger short, only slightly longer than fourth metacarpal. Wing membrane attached at side of foot. Ears relatively short and broad, triangular; tragus short, broadened at tip, angled forwards and bluntly pointed. Anterior upper premolar very small, usually completely intruded within toothrow, hidden in lateral view by canine. Outer upper incisor similar in crown area to inner incisor, but about half its height. Dental formula 2/3 1/1 2/2 3/3.

EURASIAN NOCTULE
Nyctalus noctula PLATE 19
Measurements FA 49–58. Wt 23. Skull: ccl 17.1–18.6, mt 7.1–7.7, m–m 8.5–9.5
Identification Fur of upperparts uniformly coloured from base to tip, varying among individuals from dark brown to mid-brown; underparts similar but slightly paler. Ear broadly triangular, posterior edge broadened from halfway down ear around below tragus to near side of mouth; tragus short and rounded, broader at tip than base. Wing with fifth finger substantially shorter than fourth finger, third finger elongate. Long calcar with well-developed lobe. **Similar species** House bats, *Scotophilus* spp., have elongate narrow tragus, only 1 upper incisor and 1 upper premolar; Eurasian Serotine, *Eptesicus serotinus*, has narrower ear and tragus with narrow outer ear edge, broader wing, only 1 upper premolar.
Ecology and habitat Feeds high over canopy.
Distribution and status SE Asia: N Myanmar, N Vietnam and possibly Laos. Also widespread from Europe, N Africa through much of Asia to Siberia and S to N India, Himalayas and China. Poorly known in region, with only a few records; relatively common and not currently at risk elsewhere.

Genus *Glischropus* Similar to *Pipistrellus*, but sole of foot and base of thumb with thickened, unpigmented pads; second (outer) upper incisor displaced outwards from toothrow (Fig. 38b). Dental formula 2/3 1/1 2/2 3/3.

THICK-THUMBED PIPISTRELLE
Glischropus tylopus PLATE 18
Measurements FA 29–35, T 28–38, E 9–11. Wt 3.5–5.5
Identification Upperparts dark brown; underparts paler buffy-brown. Fur rather long and shaggy. Short, broad face with rounded head. Base of thumb and sole of foot have thickened, unpigmented, whitish or pink pads; wing membrane inserted at base of toes; calcar with well-developed keel. Second upper incisor displaced outwards; anterior upper premolar small but in line in toothrow (Fig. 38b). **Similar species** Least False-serotine, *Hesperoptenus blanfordi*, has dark thumb pads, short smooth fur, and the second upper incisor displaced inwards (as in Fig. 38e); bamboo bats, *Tylonycteris* spp., have very flat skulls and large, rounded, dark thumb pads; other pipistrelles have second upper incisor in line in toothrow, lack pads on feet.
Ecology and habitat Roosts in dead or damaged bamboo stems, as well as rock crevices or new banana leaves.
Distribution and status SE Asia: Myanmar, Thailand, Laos, Vietnam, Cambodia and Peninsular Malaysia. Also Sumatra, Borneo and the Philippines.

Genus *Philetor* Externally similar to *Pipistrellus* but with short fifth finger (as in *P. stenopterus*). External genitalia quite elaborate: male has elongate penis with bristly pad near end of main shaft, followed by a narrow shaft supporting a broadened triangular structure; female has five separate pads around vulva. Skull slopes evenly in profile; rostrum thickened. Only 1 upper premolar; inner upper incisors long and narrow with 2 cusps (Fig. 38c). Dental formula 2/3 1/1 1/2 3/3.

NARROW-WINGED BROWN BAT

Philetor brachypterus   PLATE 17

Measurements FA 30–36, T 30–38, E 13–16. Wt 8–13. Skull: cbl 14.5, mt 4.7

Identification Upperparts dark brown; underparts paler and greyer. Fur short and dense. Head somewhat flattened, ears broadly triangular, rounded at tip and prominent. Wings narrow with fifth digit shortened, tip reaching only to halfway along first phalanx of fourth finger. Only 1, shortened, upper premolar (Fig. 38c). First upper incisor long and narrow with 2 cusps, second incisor small and conical. Canine with large secondary cusp. **Similar species** Narrow-winged Pipistrelle, *Pipistrellus stenopterus*, also has a narrow wing, but is larger and has an extra upper premolar; Surat Serotine, *Eptesicus dimissus*, has short, broad upper incisors, fifth digit not shortened and less elaborate genitalia.

Ecology and habitat Roosts include hollow trees. Has been found in both pristine forest and disturbed areas, but usually near intact forest.

Distribution and status SE Asia: Peninsular Malaysia. Also Nepal, Sumatra, Java, Borneo, the Philippines, Sulawesi and New Guinea. Probably not immediately at risk, but population has likely declined due to loss of forest.

Genus *Hypsugo* Until recently, included within *Pipistrellus*; the affinities of some species currently placed in this genus are unclear. Ear similar to *Pipistrellus*, but often broader and wider; tragus short, broad, curved slightly forwards (e.g., Fig. 40g). Anterior upper premolar usually small, completely intruded inside toothrow, so that canine and posterior premolar are touching; sometimes missing. Rostrum short, skull usually sloping evenly in profile from front to back. Outer upper incisor usually only slightly smaller than inner one, with very small supplementary cusps; inner upper incisor usually with a small secondary cusp; canine often without a small second cusp. Lower molars typically with myotodont pattern (Fig. 39).

Calcar with only very narrow keel. Baculum short, relatively broad. Dental formula 2/3 1/1 2/2 3/3.

CHINESE PIPISTRELLE

Hypsugo pulveratus   PLATE 17

Measurements FA 32–37, T 32–38, E 10.2–13.8. Skull: ccl 12.4–12.9, mt 4.7–5.3, m–m 5.6–6.2

Identification Upperparts with long, thick fur, dark brownish-black for much of the length, with narrow golden-brown tips; underparts similar, but more broadly tipped with paler buff-brown. Ears and wings dark blackish-grey, ears sometimes with paler edge; ears broadly rounded; tragus short, narrow, rounded at tip, curved slightly forwards. Wings moderately broad, fifth metacarpal similar in length to fourth. Both upper incisors similar in crown area; anterior premolar not especially reduced, and only slightly smaller than crown area of incisors, but completely intruded; upper canine without a secondary cusp; anterior lower premolar about half height of posterior premolar. Skull has moderately long, narrow rostrum with distinctly elevated braincase and rostral depression in profile; zygomata robust, with slight dorsal process. Baculum short (2.4mm). **Similar species** Similar-sized *Pipistrellus* have narrower ears, different fur colour, longer penis and baculum; Cadorna's Pipistrelle, *H. cadornae*, has greatly reduced anterior premolar.

Ecology and habitat Has been found roosting in caves in limestone areas; forages within relatively open, dry dipterocarp forest, as well as highly disturbed areas of mixed scrub and open areas.

Distribution and status SE Asia: Myanmar, Thailand, Laos and Vietnam. Also China. Not currently at risk.

BIG-EARED PIPISTRELLE

Hypsugo macrotis   PLATE 17

Measurements FA 33–34. Skull: ccl 11.7–12.1, mt 4.0–4.3, m–m 5.3–5.4

Identification Fur of upperparts reddish-brown with very dark brown bases; under-

parts similar but paler. Ears large, broad and triangular, extending well above head; tragus short, broad and hatchet-shaped (Fig. 40g). Wing membranes translucent white with a brown tinge. Rostrum short, skull with evenly sloping profile. Anterior upper premolar tiny, completely displaced inwards, so canine and second premolar are touching. **Similar species** No other pipistrelle in its range has similarly large ears and white wings; White-winged Pipistrelle, *Pipistrellus vordermanni*, known from Borneo and Billiton Island off SE Sumatra, also has white wings and large ears, but is smaller (FA ~30, ccl 10.8).
Ecology and habitat Has been seen feeding low over coastal lagoons near mangroves.
Distribution and status SE Asia: Peninsular Malaysia. Also Sumatra, Bali and adjacent islands. Status uncertain; very few records.

MYANMAR PIPISTRELLE
Hypsugo lophurus NOT ILLUSTRATED
Measurements FA 35, T 39. Skull: ccl 13.1, mt 4.8, m–m 6.2
Identification A medium-sized pipistrelle, known only from one male specimen. Upperparts with long, silky hair, dark brown with blackish bases; underparts paler also with black bases. Large tuft of gland-like hairs at base of tail on upper surface of interfemoral membrane, about 12mm in diameter, with hairs 5–6mm in length (not known whether this is also present in female). Upper incisors both well developed with secondary cusps; anterior upper premolar moderately reduced, about two-thirds crown area of inner incisor; anterior lower premolar half to two-thirds crown area of second. Skull has moderately shortened rostrum, profile almost straight but with slight rostral depression; zygomatic arches have well-developed post-orbital process. **Similar species** No other pipistrelle is known to have glandular tuft at base of tail.
Ecology and habitat Only known specimen was found in a cleared area near a village.
Distribution and status SE Asia: known only

from one specimen in S Myanmar. Status unknown.

CADORNA'S PIPISTRELLE
Hypsugo cadornae PLATE 17
Measurements FA 33–37, T 32–34, E 12.5–14. Skull: ccl 12.7–13.1, mt 4.6–4.7, m–m 5.8–5.9
Identification Upperparts reddish-brown with slightly darker bases; underparts similar but tips much paler. Ears moderately large, broadly rounded; tragus relatively short, broad, angled slightly forwards. Wings not especially narrow, fifth metacarpal about equal in length to fourth or third. Both upper incisors similar in crown areas; first upper premolar greatly reduced, a quarter to a half the crown area of incisors. Skull with straight profile from side, zygoma robust with dorsal projection in middle. Penis relatively small. **Similar species** Similar-sized *Pipistrellus* and Chinese Pipistrelle, *H. pulveratus*, have larger anterior upper premolar.
Ecology and habitat Has been found over rivers and pools in dry dipterocarp forest as well as disturbed areas and secondary forest.
Distribution and status SE Asia: N Myanmar, N Thailand, Laos and N Vietnam. Also NE India. Not currently at risk; probably more widespread than current known distribution.

JOFFRE'S PIPISTRELLE
Hypsugo joffrei NOT ILLUSTRATED
Measurements FA 39, T 39, E 14. Skull: ccl 13.9–14.2, mt 5.0–5.1, m–m 7.0–7.2
Identification A medium-sized pipistrelle with a very short fifth finger, tip reaching only halfway along first phalanx of fourth digit. Fur has been described as uniform pale brown, or as having upperparts reddish-brown, underparts pale brown. Dorsal surface of penis has bristly pad near tip. Baculum tiny or rudimentary. Skull has shortened rostrum, broad rounded braincase; zygomatic arches with slight descending process near third molar; incisors small and weak, outer incisor about half crown area of inner; upper canine with distinct posterior

secondary cusp; anterior upper premolar tiny, completely displaced inwards; anterior lower premolar similar in height and crown area to posterior lower premolar. **Similar species** Anthony's Pipistrelle, *H. anthonyi*, is apparently very similar but with darker fur; among other species with shortened fifth finger, Eurasian Noctule, *Nyctalus noctula*, is substantially larger; Narrow-winged Pipistrelle, *Pipistrellus stenopterus*, has well-developed anterior premolar.

Ecology and habitat No information.

Distribution and status SE Asia: known only from a few specimens from Kachin Hills in N Myanmar. Status unknown.

ANTHONY'S PIPISTRELLE

Hypsugo anthonyi   NOT ILLUSTRATED

Measurements FA 39, T 41. Skull: mt 5.3, m–m 7.2

Identification A medium-sized pipistrelle, known only from a single specimen. Fur short, dark brown and velvety. Skull broad with narrow muzzle; zygomatic arches have small (0.5mm) descending process near posterior molar. Canine with well-defined secondary cusp; anterior upper premolar tiny, about one-quarter area of inner incisor; lower premolars slightly reduced and compressed, similar in size to each other. **Similar species** Joffre's Pipistrelle, *H. joffrei*, is apparently very similar, though with lighter fur.

Ecology and habitat Type specimen came from an open valley at 2,100m, with mixed deciduous forest and open, cleared areas.

Distribution and status SE Asia: known only from one specimen from Changyinku, Kachin State, N Myanmar. Status unknown.

Genus *Falsistrellus* This genus was, until recently, included within *Pipistrellus*. Fur is long and woolly. Skull has elongate braincase; relatively long, narrow rostrum; distinct rostral depression in profile. Baculum broad, proximally widened, with deep groove on ventral surface, not swollen at tip. Dental formula 2/3 1/1 2/2 3/3.

CHOCOLATE PIPISTRELLE

Falsistrellus affinis   PLATE 17

Measurements FA 36–38, T 31–34, E 12.0–13.5. Skull: ccl 12.9–13.4, mt 5.3, m–m 6.1–6.3

Identification Fur long and soft, dark blackish-brown with narrow pale grey-brown tips, giving a frosted appearance; underparts with greyish-white bases, dark tips, sometimes all white near base of tail. Ears broad and rounded; tragus broad, pointed at anterior end (Fig. 40f). Muzzle moderately long and narrow. First upper premolar similar in crown area to incisors, only slightly displaced inwards; first lower premolar in toothrow about half size of posterior premolar.

Taxonomic notes Description is based on specimens from C Myanmar. Specimens referred to this species from India have darker underparts, are larger (FA 38.5–41.5, ccl 13.7–14.5) and have a slightly different-shaped baculum; the type locality is in N Myanmar in between these two locations; it is not clear whether all are the same species or, if not, which one is actually *F. affinis*.

Similar species Other similar-sized pipistrelles generally have shorter fur, shorter, broader muzzles, with dark bases to fur on underparts.

Ecology and habitat In Myanmar, has been found roosting in a cave.

Distribution and status SE Asia: Myanmar. Also India. Status poorly known in region, but not currently at risk elsewhere.

Genus *Arielulus* Bats with distinctive pale edges to ears, black fur with reddish tips on upperparts and yellowish tips on belly. Ear moderate, oval-shaped with rounded top, distinct lobe on side of face below tragus; tragus relatively short, angled sharply forwards with blunt tip (Fig. 40d). Outer upper incisor very small, short and about one-quarter crown area of inner incisor; anterior premolar tiny, completely displaced inwards, sometimes missing (Fig. 38d). Anterior lower premolar about one-third to one-quarter crown area of second in toothrow. Baculum Y-shaped. Dental formula 2/3 1/1 2–1/2 3/3.

BLACK GILDED PIPISTRELLE
Arielulus circumdatus PLATE 19

Measurements FA 40–44, T 36. Skull: ccl 14.7–15.4, mt 6.0–7.2, m–m 7.1–7.5

Identification Fur of upperparts long and thick with black bases and red-orange tips; fur of underparts with dark brown bases and pale yellow or greyish-white tips; pale patch on side of neck behind ear. Ear moderately sized with distinct lobe at base near eye; ears and tragus dark brown with buff rims. Anterior upper premolar very tiny and displaced inwards (sometimes lacking); canine and second premolar touching. **Similar species** Benom Gilded Pipistrelle, *A. societatis*, is similar but smaller, with reduced posterior upper molar.

Ecology and habitat Most records in region are from hill forest, 1,300–2,000m.

Distribution and status SE Asia: Myanmar, Thailand, Vietnam and Peninsular Malaysia. Also India, Nepal, S China and Java. Not currently at risk.

BENOM GILDED PIPISTRELLE
Arielulus societatis PLATE 19

Measurements FA 35–38, T 33–37, E 8.5–9.0. Wt 4.3–5.5. Skull: ccl 14.1, mt 5.2, m–m 6.7

Identification Very similar to Black Gilded Pipistrelle, *A. circumdatus*, with similar fur and head colour, but shorter forearm, smaller skull and teeth. Skull has shorter, narrower rostrum, more inflated braincase; teeth less massive, with third upper molar reduced, posterior cusp virtually absent.

Ecology and habitat All records from lowland rainforest. Has been found roosting in a hole in a tree.

Distribution and status SE Asia: Peninsular Malaysia. Near Threatened, owing to loss of primary lowland rainforest.

Genus *Thainycteris* Similar to *Arielulus* and sometimes included in that genus. Differs in larger size, broader, heavier skull and distinctive fur coloration. Skull is heavy and very broad; inner upper incisor large, about half height of canine; second upper incisor tiny

and hard to see; canine without posterior cusp on cutting edge; anterior upper premolar very small and completely displaced inwards, sometimes missing (Fig. 38g); anterior lower premolar about half height and two-thirds surface area of posterior lower premolar. Dental formula 2/3 1/1 2–1/2 3/3.

GOLDEN-COLLARED BAT
Thainycteris aureocollaris PLATE 19

Measurements FA 47–51, T 43–58, E 15–18. Wt 12.5–17

Identification Medium-large bat with very distinctive coloration: upperparts with long fur (10mm), bases black, tips buff to coppery-gold, giving a frosted appearance; underparts similar with white to gold tips; broad band of bright buff to orange under chin and across throat, forming a collar; irregular streak of buff hair across top of head. Ears, nose and wing membranes dark grey. Ears fleshy, broadly triangular with rounded tip; tragus moderately short, broadened at top half and angled forwards. **Similar species** Gilded pipistrelles, *Arielulus* spp., are smaller, without buff collar and with pale rims to ears; Harlequin Bat, *Scotomanes ornatus*, has white streak down reddish back, white patches on shoulder and head.

Ecology and habitat Known from forested areas at 200–1,500m; has been found at forest edges and over ponds and streams, but regular foraging areas not known.

Distribution and status SE Asia: Thailand, Laos and Vietnam. Probably not currently at risk.

Genus *Eptesicus* Similar to *Pipistrellus*, but with only one upper premolar (Figs 38i, 41). Outer upper incisor usually small, inner incisor large; upper canine usually without extra cusps. Ear broadly triangular with rounded top; tragus short, rounded, angled forwards. Skull robust, forehead sloping to tip. Calcar with keel, but sometimes fairly narrow. Baculum very short, less than 2mm, usually triangular or slightly Y-shaped. Dental formula 2/3 1/1 1/2 3/3.

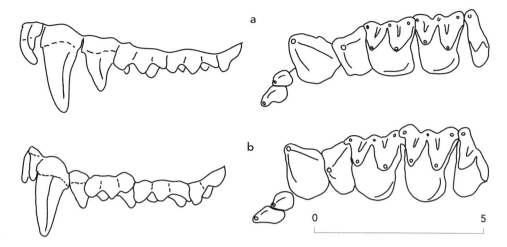

Fig. 41 *Left upper toothrows from side and below of* Eptesicus pachyotis *(a) and* E. dimissus *(b).*

EURASIAN SEROTINE
Eptesicus serotinus PLATE 19
Measurements FA 53–57, T 53–60, E 18–20. Wt 20–24. Skull: ccl 18.5–19.5
Identification A large vespertilionid bat; upperparts dark brown with tips pale, giving a frosted appearance; underparts similar but with contrasting whitish hair tips. Ear narrow, triangular at top with rounded tip, thickened rims; tragus narrow, angled slightly forwards, rounded tip; front part of ear and posterior lobes covered with short, orangish hair. Ears, muzzle and wing membranes dark brownish-grey. Muzzle broad, forehead sloping evenly. Posterior upper molar narrow with only one V-shaped cusp. **Similar species** Other *Eptesicus* are smaller; Eurasian Noctule, *Nyctalus noctula*, has broader ear, short mushroom-shaped tragus, shortened fifth finger; Tomes's False-serotine, *Hesperoptenus tomesi*, has more rounded ears, broad rounded facial profile, second upper incisor displaced inwards.
Ecology and habitat Has been found in wet forest as well as dry dipterocarp forest.
Distribution and status SE Asia: N Myanmar, N Thailand, N Laos and N Vietnam. Also widespread through Palaearctic from Europe and N Africa through Asia, although recent studies suggest SE Asian form is a

different species from European form. Not currently at risk, though poorly known in region.

THICK-EARED SEROTINE
Eptesicus pachyotis NOT ILLUSTRATED
Measurements gl 21.2
Identification Upperparts dark brown, underparts slightly paler. Ears triangular, posterior edge of ear thick and fleshy from just below middle down to lobes at base of ear. Tragus short, expanded at top, curved inwards. Wing membrane inserts at base of toes. Head flat, muzzle short and broad. Second upper incisor small, about half height of bicuspid first incisor; upper premolar large, about two-thirds height of canine; anterior lower premolar about half size of posterior premolar and compressed into toothrow; posterior upper molar moderately narrow with only trace of second cusp (Fig. 41a). **Similar species** Similar-sized pipistrelles have an extra upper premolar (though it can be small and hard to see, especially in *Hypsugo* spp.), and a broader, unthickened ear; Surat Serotine, *E. dimissus*, has wing membrane inserted on side of foot, different dentition.
Ecology and habitat Unknown.
Distribution and status SE Asia: N Thailand and possibly N Myanmar. Also NE India and China (Tibet). Status uncertain; known from only a few specimens.

SURAT SEROTINE

Eptesicus dimissus NOT ILLUSTRATED

Measurements FA. 38–42, T 36–41, E 14–15. Skull: gl 17.4, cbl 15.4, mt 5.9, c–c 5.9

Identification Medium-sized bat, upperparts with short reddish-brown fur, individual hairs with pale bases and brown tips; underparts with hairs uniform pale brown in colour; fur extends in a triangle onto base of tail. Ear relatively short and rounded; tragus short and broad, angled slightly forwards, slightly thickened. Muzzle very broad, skin on top of head loose, sometimes forming fold of skin between ears. Wing membrane attached on side of foot near ankle; calcar with well-developed keel. Incisors relatively short, outer upper incisor about three-quarters height of first incisor; canine with small cusp on posterior edge. Posterior upper molar with relatively well-developed posterior cusp about half size of anterior cusp (Fig. 41b). **Similar species** Thick-eared Serotine, *E. pachyotis*, and similar-sized pipistrelles have wing membranes inserted at base of toes, different dentition.

Ecology and habitat Unknown.

Distribution and status SE Asia: peninsular Thailand. Also Nepal. Status unknown. Only one specimen known from Thailand, but several from Nepal.

Genus *Ia* Very large vespertilionid bat with only one recognized species; sometimes included in *Pipistrellus*. Outer incisor tiny, barely reaching height of cingulum of enlarged inner incisor; anterior premolar very small, completely intruded into toothrow so that canine and posterior premolar are touching; anterior lower premolar about half height and crown area of posterior premolar. Calcar with little or no lobe.

GREAT EVENING BAT

Ia io PLATE 18

Measurements FA 71–79, T 68–70, E 27–28. Wt 48–54. Skull: ccl 25–26, mt 10.5–11.0, m–m 11.0–11.6

Identification Largest vespertilionid bat in

region. Upperparts dark grey-brown with pale tips, producing a slightly glossy effect; underparts paler dull greyish-brown. Ears broadly triangular, rounded at top, with thickened posterior edge; tragus short, broadened at top, bluntly pointed to front; muzzle relatively bare of fur. **Similar species** All other vespertilionid bats in region are substantially smaller.

Ecology and habitat Known roosts all in limestone caves. Recorded from a variety of mature forest types including wet rainforest, mixed forest and deciduous forest.

Distribution and status SE Asia: N Myanmar, N Thailand, Laos and N Vietnam. Also NE India, Nepal and China. Not currently at risk.

Genus *Hesperoptenus* Ears fairly short and rounded, tragus slightly hatchet-shaped, pointed forwards. One species has a small, thickened thumb pad. Only one upper premolar; distinctive upper incisors: first (inner) incisor very large and conical, about half height of canine; second incisor small, in subgenus *Milithronycteris* it is displaced inwards so that the canine and first incisor are in contact (Fig. 38e); in subgenus *Hesperoptenus* it separates canine and first incisor. Dental formula 2/3 1/1 1/2 3/3.

DORIA'S FALSE-SEROTINE

Hesperoptenus doriae PLATE 18

Measurements FA 38–41. Skull: cbl 13.3–13.6, mt 4.9–5.0

Identification Fur uniformly blackish-brown, slightly glossy and fluffy. Head profile rounded. Ear moderately broad, tragus short, bluntly pointed, angled nearly horizontally forwards. Only one upper premolar; first upper incisor large and conical; second incisor slightly displaced inwards, but still separating first incisor from canine. **Similar species** Tomes's False-serotine, *H. tomesi*, is substantially larger, with second upper incisor displaced inwards (Fig. 38e); Narrow-winged Pipistrelle, *Pipistrellus stenopterus*, has small upper incisors and an extra upper premolar.

Ecology and habitat Recorded from lowland forest. Has been found roosting in a palm tree.

Distribution and status SE Asia: Peninsular Malaysia. Also Borneo. Status uncertain, as known from only a few specimens, but probably Vulnerable, owing to loss of lowland rainforest.

LEAST FALSE-SEROTINE
Hesperoptenus blanfordi PLATE 18
Measurements FA 24–29, T 27–32, E 10–12. Wt 5.0–8.5
Identification Very small, with short wings but relatively heavy body. Upperparts dark brown, sometimes with a reddish tone; underparts similar; fur sleek and slightly glossy. Base of thumb and sole of foot have small, thickened, dark brown pads; thumb pad slightly triangular. Second upper incisor small and displaced inwards (as in Fig. 38e). Head slightly pointed with smoothly sloping profile (Fig. 36f). **Similar species** Bamboo bats, *Tylonycteris* spp., have much flatter heads with larger round thumb pads, inner incisors small and separated from canine by second incisor; Thick-thumbed Pipistrelle, *Glischropus tylopus*, has longer fur, more rounded head, white or pink thumb pads and second upper incisor displaced outwards (Fig. 38b); Thick-thumbed Myotis, *Myotis rossetti*, has typical *Myotis*-shaped ears, fluffier fur.
Ecology and habitat Has been found roosting in entrances of caves in small groups; also known from forest away from caves. Forages in open areas above forests, in gaps and above streams and rivers within forests.
Distribution and status SE Asia: S Myanmar, Laos, Cambodia, S Vietnam, Thailand and Peninsular Malaysia. Also Borneo. Not currently at risk.

TOMES'S FALSE-SEROTINE
Hesperoptenus tomesi PLATE 18
Measurements FA 50–53, T 49–53, E 17–18. Wt 30–32. Skull: cbl 20.4, mt 8.5
Identification Upperparts uniform dark blackish-brown; underparts similar. Head

rounded, with fur smoothly curved from forehead to tip of nose; ears broad, somewhat rounded; tragus relatively short, angled horizontally forwards and bluntly pointed. Teeth large with well-developed cusps; first upper incisor large and conical, touching canine; second incisor small and displaced inwards (Fig. 38e); only one upper premolar. **Similar species** Doria's False-serotine, *H. doriae*, is smaller, with second upper incisor not displaced inwards; house bats, *Scotophilus* spp., have paler brown fur with only one pair of upper incisors.
Ecology and habitat Has been found over streams in primary lowland rainforest.
Distribution and status SE Asia: S Thailand and Peninsular Malaysia. Also Borneo. Vulnerable; has probably declined considerably in recent years, owing to loss of lowland rainforest.

TICKELL'S FALSE-SEROTINE
Hesperoptenus tickelli PLATE 18
Measurements FA 49–56, T 47–57, E 16–18. Wt 15–21
Identification Upperparts light yellowish-brown to orange; underparts slightly paler; ears, face and wing bones light orange-brown; wing membranes contrasting dark grey to black; base of tail membrane and wing membrane near body covered with short, orange hairs. Ears oval, moderate in length, broadly rounded at top; tragus short, pointed horizontally forwards. First upper incisor large and conical, touching canine; second incisor small and displaced inwards (as in Fig. 38e); only one upper premolar. **Similar species** Tome's False-serotine, *H. tomesi*, has thick, dark brown fur; house bats, *Scotophilus* spp., have much longer, pointed tragus, dark wing bones, only one pair of upper incisors.
Ecology and habitat Occurs in and around deciduous and semi-deciduous forest. Forages high, above forest canopy, coming low to drink over streams and ponds. Probably roosts in hollow trees.
Distribution and status SE Asia: Myanmar, Thailand, Laos, Vietnam and Cambodia. Also

India, Sri Lanka, Nepal and Bhutan. Not currently at risk.

Genus *Scotomanes* Moderately large vespertilionid bat, similar to *Eptesicus* but with only one pair of upper incisors, and with distinctive coloration. Dental formula 1/3 1/1 1/2 3/3.

HARLEQUIN BAT

Scotomanes ornatus PLATE 19
Measurements FA 54–61, T 50–60, E 20–22. Wt 20–30. Skull: ccl 19.4–19.9
Identification Distinctively coloured large bat; upperparts orange-brown with white patches on top of head, shoulders and sides, and white line down middle of back; underside mixed pattern of black, orange and white with black and white collar. Wing bones orange-brown, wing membranes dark grey-brown, tail membrane brown. Ear moderate, bluntly triangular; tragus relatively short, narrow, curved forwards with rounded tip. **Similar species** Golden-collared Bat, *Thainycteris aureocollaris*, has upperparts black frosted with pale tips, without white patches, second upper incisor small but usually present.
Ecology and habitat Has been found roosting on tree branches, among leaves, but also occurs around limestone caves. Flies in open areas well above ground.
Distribution and status SE Asia: N Myanmar, N Thailand, Laos and N Vietnam. Also NE India and S China. Not currently at risk.

Genus *Scotophilus* Ears moderate; tragus very long, tapering slightly and curved forwards. Skull thick and heavy with only one pair of upper incisors, which are large and well developed (Fig. 38h). Dental formula 1/3 1/1 1/2 3/3.

LESSER ASIAN HOUSE BAT

Scotophilus kuhlii PLATE 19
Measurements FA 45–52, T 39–53, E 13–15. Wt 17–26. Skull: ccl 18.0–18.7
Identification Upperparts brown; underparts paler yellowish-brown; sometimes with

a strong orange tinge. Fur soft and short. Ear with long narrow tragus bent forwards. Only one pair of upper premolars and one pair of large conical upper incisors (as in Fig. 38h).
Similar species Greater Asian House Bat, *S. heathii*, has forearm longer than 55mm; Harlequin Bat, *Scotomanes ornatus*, also has only one pair of upper incisors, but has distinctive pattern of white patches on back and neck; Tickell's False-serotine, *Hesperoptenus tickelli*, is similar in colour, but has short, broad, hatchet-shaped tragus, second upper incisor displaced inwards.
Ecology and habitat Roosts under house roofs, in palm tree leaves and in hollow trees. Forages for aerial insects in open areas, including around towns and over forests.
Distribution and status SE Asia: throughout region. Also Pakistan, India, Sri Lanka, Bangladesh, S China, Taiwan, Sumatra, Borneo, Java, Bali and the Philippines. Not currently at risk.

GREATER ASIAN HOUSE BAT

Scotophilus heathii PLATE 19
Measurements FA 57–69, T 57–72, E 15–19. Wt 29–53. Skull: ccl 19.3–20.9
Identification Upperparts dark orange to reddish-brown, hairs with yellowish bases; fur smooth and shiny; underparts paler yellow-brown to orange. Ears and wing membranes contrasting dark brown, hairless. Ear medium-large with well-developed lobe at base; tragus long, narrow, bent forwards. One upper premolar. Only one pair of large, conical upper incisors (Fig. 38h). **Taxonomic notes** Shows considerable size variation across range, and may represent more than one species. **Similar species** Lesser Asian House Bat, *S. kuhlii*, is smaller, forearm less than 55mm; Tickell's False-serotine, *Hesperoptenus tickelli*, has short, broad, hatchet-shaped tragus and two upper incisors.
Ecology and habitat Often roosts under roofs of houses. Forages for aerial insects around towns, in open areas and over forests.
Distribution and status SE Asia: Myanmar, Thailand, Laos, Vietnam and Cambodia. Also Sri Lanka, Pakistan, India, S China and Taiwan. Not currently at risk.

Genus *Tylonycteris* Body and skull extremely flattened (Fig. 36d); large brown disc-shaped pad on foot, toes short, wing membrane inserted on side of foot; smaller round pad on base of thumb; ears short, bluntly triangular, thickened and fleshy on front and rear edge; tragus short, narrow at base, broader and rounded at top. Dental formula 2/3 1/1 1/2 3/3.

GREATER BAMBOO BAT
Tylonycteris robustula PLATE 18
Measurements FA 26–30, T 29–36, E 11. Wt 6.5–8.5. Skull: ccl 12.3–12.7, mt 4.3–4.5
Identification Upperparts dark brown, hairs with pale tips giving glossy effect – looks pale in some light; underparts paler greyish-brown to sandy-brown. Fur very smooth and sleek. Flattened disc-like pads at base of thumb and on sole of foot, usually grey, but sometimes fairly pinkish. Lower part of posterior margin of ear thickened. Head (skull) and body extremely flattened – can squeeze through a slot less than 5mm wide. **Similar species** Lesser Bamboo Bat, *T. pachypus*, overlaps in forearm length but has smaller body and skull; more reddish, fluffy fur, thinner ear; Thick-thumbed Pipistrelle, *Glischropus tylopus*, has more rounded head; smaller pink thumb and footpads, longer toes, wing membrane inserted at base of toes; Disc-footed Bat, *Eudiscopus denticulus*, has large, sucker-like disc on feet, but only small thumb pads, longer forearm, ears similar to *Myotis*; Least False-serotine, *Hesperoptenus blanfordi*, is less flattened, has thumb pad much smaller and triangular,

distinctive upper incisors.
Ecology and habitat Roosts in the internodes of bamboos, entering through narrow slits created by beetles.
Distribution and status SE Asia: Myanmar, Thailand, Laos, Vietnam, Cambodia and Peninsular Malaysia. Also S China, Sumatra, Java, Borneo, Sulawesi and smaller islands, and the Philippines. Not currently at risk.

LESSER BAMBOO BAT
Tylonycteris pachypus PLATE 18
Measurements FA 24–28, T 27–29, E 8–9. Wt 3.5–5. Skull: ccl 10.4–10.6, mt 3.1–3.5
Identification Upperparts brown to reddish brown; underparts slightly paler usually strongly tinged orange. Fur rather short and fluffy. Body and skull extremely flattened with enlarged disc-shaped pads on thumb and feet. **Similar species** Greater Bamboo Bat, *T. robustula*, overlaps in forearm length, but is otherwise much larger with sleeker fur, thickened lower third of posterior margin of ear.
Ecology and habitat Roosts in small groups in the internodes of bamboos, entering through small slits created by beetles. Frequently chooses small live bamboo stems, while Greater Bamboo Bat, *T. robustula*, prefers larger, often dead stems, although both species may sometimes use same roost holes.
Distribution and status SE Asia: Myanmar, Thailand, Laos, Vietnam, Cambodia and Peninsular Malaysia. Also NE India, S China, Sumatra, Java, Borneo and smaller Indonesian islands, and the Philippines. Not currently at risk.

Subfamily *MURININAE*

Genus *Murina* Nostrils expanded into short tubes, which protrude on either side of the muzzle. Ears rounded, not funnel-shaped; tragus long and pointed. Skull has a long palate and large rostrum. Two upper and lower premolars, both large, well developed and in line in the toothrow. In one group of species (*M. leucogaster*, *M. tubinaris*, *M. suil-*

la and *M. aurata*), the anterior upper premolar is about half the height of the posterior premolar; in the remaining species both premolars are essentially the same size (Fig. 42). The pattern of cusps on the molars is important in differentiating some species (Figs 42, 43). Dental formula 2/3 1/1 2/2 3/3.

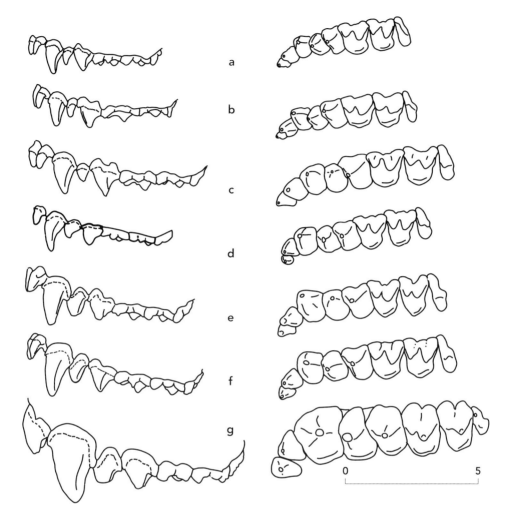

Fig. 42 *Left upper toothrows from side and below of:* Murina aurata *(a),* M. tubinaris *(b),* M. leucogaster *(c),* M. rozendaali *(d),* M. cyclotis *(e),* M. huttoni *(f) and* Harpiocephalus harpia *(g).*

ROUND-EARED TUBE-NOSED BAT
Murina cyclotis PLATE 20

Measurements *M. c. cyclotis*: FA 29–34, T 32–40, E 13–16. Wt 4.5–7.5. Skull: cbl 14.7–15.8, mt 5.0–5.7
M. c. peninsularis: FA 34–41, T 38–50, E 14–17. Wt 7.0–10.5. Skull: cbl 15.4–16.9, mt 5.5–6.2, c–c 4.5–5.3

Identification Upperparts pale orange mixed with grey or grey-brown; underparts paler and greyer. Tail membrane thinly cov-ered in long reddish hairs. Ear rounded, tra-gus long, pointed and white. Nostrils large and tubular. Both upper premolars large. First 2 lower molars have greatly reduced posterior section (talonid), less than one-third surface area of anterior section (trigo-nid) (Fig. 43a); first 2 upper molars with V-shaped notch on outer edge (Fig. 42e).

Taxonomic notes Recent genetic analyses suggest much larger Malaysian form, *M. c. peninsularis*, may be a separate species from that found elsewhere in region, but further study is required to determine range limits and whether there are any intermediate forms. **Similar species** Hutton's Tube-nosed Bat, *M. huttoni*, is similar but with larger median outer cusp on upper molars (Fig.

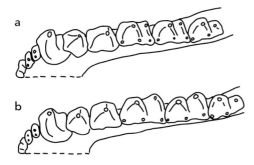

Fig. 43 *Lower right toothrows of* Murina cyclotis *(a) and* M. huttoni *(b), showing difference in relative size of talonid on molars.*

42f), relatively larger talonid on lower molars (Fig. 43b); Hairy-winged Bat, *Harpiocephalus harpia*, is larger, with heavier teeth and greatly reduced third upper molar (Fig. 42g).

Ecology and habitat Found in a wide variety of forest types including wet evergreen forest and semi-deciduous forest.

Distribution and status SE Asia: throughout region. Also Sri Lanka, India, S China, and Borneo. Not currently at risk.

HUTTON'S TUBE-NOSED BAT
Murina huttoni PLATE 20
Measurements FA 35–37, T 37–39, E 16–17.5. Wt 7–11

Identification Upperparts greyish-brown to reddish-brown, the hairs with dark grey-brown bases, the middle slightly paler than the tips; underparts paler, the hairs with buffy-brown or white tips, dark grey-brown bases. Ears long, reaching 3–4mm past nostrils if folded forwards; tragus long and white. Both upper premolars similar in size, about twice as tall as molars, but about half height of canine; anterior lower premolar about 20% smaller than posterior premolar. Posterior section of lower molars (talonid) nearly as large as anterior section (trigonid) (Fig. 43b); first 2 upper molars have moderately well-developed outer median cusp, so there is only a shallow notch on outside edge (Fig. 42f). **Similar species** Round-eared Tube-nosed Bat, *M. cyclotis*, has shorter ears, paler bases to fur and different-shaped

molars; Greater Tube-nosed Bat, *M. leucogaster*, is larger, with anterior upper premolar about half height of posterior premolar.

Ecology and habitat Poorly known. Most records from hill forest at altitudes of 400–1,500m.

Distribution and status SE Asia: N Myanmar, N Thailand, Laos, Vietnam and Peninsular Malaysia. Also Pakistan, N India, Tibet and S China. Status poorly known, but probably not currently at risk.

HARRISON'S TUBE-NOSED BAT
Murina harrisoni NOT ILLUSTRATED
Measurements FA 35.9. Skull: gl 18.4, mt 6.5

Identification Upperparts uniform reddish-brown, hairs only slightly darker at tips; underparts white, individual hairs pale to bases. Upper surface of tail membrane uniformly covered in reddish-brown hairs. Wing membrane attaches to foot at base of toe instead of tip of toes at base of claw. Anterior upper premolar similar in height to posterior molar, canine about twice height of premolars; second incisor about half height of anterior incisor; lower molars with well-developed talonid (as in Fig. 43b). **Similar species** Other *Murina* known from region have wing membrane inserted at base of claw; Greater Tube-nosed Bat, *M. leucogaster*, has small anterior upper premolar, relatively shorter canine.

Ecology and habitat Has been found flying over a stream in disturbed semi-deciduous lowland forest.

Distribution and status SE Asia: Cambodia. Status unknown; only one recorded specimen.

BRONZED TUBE-NOSED BAT
Murina aenea PLATE 20
Measurements FA 34–38, T 35–45, E 13.5–15.5. Wt 6–8.5. Skull: cbl 15.3–16.1, mt 5.7–6.0, c–c 4.7–4.8.

Identification Fur of upperparts brown mixed with shiny gold-orange; short hairs with bands of buff and dark brown, long hairs dark brown with shiny golden or bronze tips; underparts buffy, individual hairs with dark brown bases and pale buff-brown or orange-brown tips. Nostrils long and tubular. Lower molars with reduced talonid, similar to *M. cyclotis* (as in Fig. 43a), but less extreme. **Similar species** Rozendaal's Tube-nosed Bat, *M. rozendaali*, is smaller and paler, back fur with yellow tips, underparts white with pale bases; Golden Tube-nosed Bat, *M. aurata*, is smaller with whitish underparts, smaller teeth, especially anterior premolars; Round-eared Tube-nosed Bat, *M. cyclotis*, has similar dentition, but fur is reddish-brown without gilded tips; groove-toothed bats, *Phoniscus* spp., have similar colour but less tubular nostrils, very different dentition.

Ecology and habitat Has been found in lowland dipterocarp forest and hill forest.

Distribution and status SE Asia: Peninsular Malaysia and adjacent S Thailand. Also Borneo. Vulnerable due to loss of lowland rainforest.

ROZENDAAL'S TUBE-NOSED BAT
Murina rozendaali PLATE 20
Measurements FA 28–32, T 30–35, E 13–14. Wt 3.8–4.8. Skull: cbl 13.7–13.8, mt 5.2–5.3, c–c 3.8–4.1

Identification Fur of upperparts with dark brown bases and shining yellow or golden-brown tips; underparts white to the bases with a buffy or yellowish tinge. Nostrils tubular. Both upper premolars similar in size; canine long, about twice height of premolars (Fig. 42d); lower molars with well-developed talonids (as in Fig. 43b). **Similar species** Bronzed Tube-nosed Bat, *M. aenea*, is larger and darker, with dark bases to belly fur; Golden Tube-nosed Bat, *M. aurata*, has dark bases to fur of underparts, anterior upper premolar small, half size of posterior premolar (Fig. 42a); Lesser Tube-nosed Bat, *M. suilla*, has small anterior upper premolar, and short canine (as in Fig. 42b).

Ecology and habitat Found flying low over streams in disturbed lowland dipterocarp forest.

Distribution and status SE Asia: Peninsular

Malaysia. Also Borneo. Vulnerable, owing to low densities and loss of lowland rainforest.

GREATER TUBE-NOSED BAT
Murina leucogaster PLATE 20
Measurements FA 42, T 40, E 14. Wt 9. Skull: gl 18.4–19.6, ccl 16.5, mt 6.2, m–m 6.5, c–c 4.5

Identification Largest *Murina* in region; upperparts reddish-brown, hairs with dark bases; underparts pale yellowish-white, hairs with dark bases only on sides. Anterior upper and lower premolars small, about half height and surface area of corresponding posterior premolars; canine relatively low, no more than 30% taller than posterior premolar (Fig. 42c). **Similar species** Other large *Murina* have anterior premolar nearly same size as posterior premolar, less contrasting colours of upper and underparts.

Ecology and habitat Has been found over a stream in disturbed secondary forest.

Distribution and status SE Asia: N Vietnam. Also NE India, Nepal and S China. Probably not at risk elsewhere, but status uncertain in region. There is only one confirmed record from the region – previously published records from Thailand were based on misidentified specimens.

LESSER TUBE-NOSED BAT
Murina suilla PLATE 20
Measurements FA 27–32, T 26–35, E 12.5–13.5. Wt 3–5. Skull: cbl 12.6–13.3, mt 4.7–4.9, c–c 3.6–3.7

Identification Upperparts brown, sometimes with orange or greyish tone; individual hairs with grey bases, paler sub-terminal band, then darker tips; underparts greyish-white, the hairs with grey bases, especially on flanks. Some individuals may have shiny tips to fur. Tubular nostrils. Anterior upper premolar half height of posterior premolar (as in Fig. 42b). **Similar species** Rozendaal's Tube-nosed Bat, *M. rozendaali*, has pale yellowish tips to back fur, is slightly larger and has relatively large anterior premolar and canine (Fig. 42d); Whitehead's Woolly Bat, *Kerivoula whiteheadi*, has small nostrils, funnel-shaped ears; dentition different (Fig. 45). **Ecology and habitat** Lowland rain forest, apparently tolerant of moderate disturbance.

Distribution and status SE Asia: peninsular Thailand and Malaysia. Also Sumatra, Java and Borneo. Not immediately at risk, but has probably declined due to loss of lowland rainforest.

SCULLY'S TUBE-NOSED BAT
Murina tubinaris PLATE 20
Measurements FA 28–32.5, T 35–40, E 13.5–15.0. Wt 4.0–5.5. Skull: cbl 13.9–14.7, mt 5.1–5.3, c–c 3.7–3.9
Identification Upperparts appear dark brown mottled with buff; hairs banded with long, dark grey-brown to blackish bases (two-thirds of length), then buffy-grey, then dark grey-brown, then whitish tips; underparts greyish-white, fur with long blackish-brown bases and white tips. Anterior premolar small, about half height of posterior premolar (Fig. 42b). Interfemoral membrane sparsely haired. **Similar species** Lesser Tube-nosed Bat, *M. suilla*, is browner, with fewer bands of colour on fur.
Ecology and habitat Most records from hill evergreen forest.
Distribution and status SE Asia: Myanmar, N Thailand, Laos and Vietnam. Also Pakistan and N India. Not immediately at risk, but has probably declined owing to loss of evergreen forest.

GOLDEN TUBE-NOSED BAT
Murina aurata PLATE 20
Measurements FA 28–30, T 30–32, E 13–13.5. Wt 3.5–7.0. Skull: cbl 12.8–14.0, mt 4.5–5.0, c–c 3.5–3.7
Identification Upperparts yellowish-brown, individual hairs banded with blackish bases, then buff-white middle, then orange-brown to dark brown, with pale golden tips; underparts extensive black bases with white tips. Tail membrane, feet and legs with scattered yellow-brown hairs. Ears small and rounded, tragus long, straight, pointed white. Braincase very tall and rounded, anterior

upper premolar small, half height of posterior premolar; upper canine similar length to posterior premolar; lower canine shorter than posterior premolar (Fig. 42a). **Similar species** Rozendaal's Tube-nosed Bat, *M. rozendaali*, has white underparts, anterior premolar same height as posterior premolar, long canines (Fig. 42d); Scully's Tube-nosed Bat, *M. tubinaris*, is greyer with less domed braincase.
Ecology and habitat Evergreen hill forest.
Distribution and status SE Asia: N Myanmar, N Thailand, Laos and Vietnam. Also Nepal, NE India and S China. Not currently at risk.

Genus *Harpiocephalus* Similar to *Murina*, with tubular nostrils and the same dental formula, but posterior upper molar very small, sometimes lacking (Fig. 42g); anterior upper molars with reduced cusps except the central one, thus resembling the premolars; canines low and massive; rostrum slightly shortened. Dental formula 2/3 1/1 2/2 3/3.

HAIRY-WINGED BAT
Harpiocephalus harpia PLATE 21
Measurements FA 45–51, T 45–55, E 16–19. Wt 12–23. Skull: cbl 18.5–21.1, mt 6.6–7.4, c–c 6.0–7.8, m–m 6.9–7.7
Identification Colour of upperparts varies from bright orange with dark bases (individuals from Malaysian rainforests) to dull orange-brown with grey bases. Underparts similar but slightly greyer. Nostrils elongate and tubular. Ear rounded with long, pointed tragus. Forearm, much of wing membrane and interfemoral membrane covered in short orange hairs. Two upper premolars similar in size; third upper molar tiny, sometimes lacking (Fig. 42g). **Taxonomic notes** This is sometimes treated as two species, with the form *H. mordax* differing in larger skull and more massive teeth, but recent analyses suggest there is only one species in the region, with females much larger than males. **Similar species** Tube-nosed bats, *Murina* spp., are smaller with a relatively larger third upper molar (Fig. 42a–f).

Ecology and habitat Understorey of low-land dipterocarp forest, as well as disturbed areas.
Distribution and status SE Asia: Myanmar, Thailand, Peninsular Malaysia, Laos and Vietnam. Also India, Nepal, S China, Taiwan, Sumatra, Java, Borneo and Maluku. Not currently at risk, but has probably declined due to loss of lowland forest.

Subfamily *KERIVOULINAE*

Genus *Kerivoula* Ears funnel-like, with a fold at the back, and a large flap on the outside; tragus long, narrow and pointed. Fur long and woolly, often covering much of the face. Nostrils small. Skull usually has a high domed braincase (except *K. kachinensis*) and a long rostrum (Figs 36j, 44). Teeth relatively unspecialized, with no reduction in any of the cheek teeth (Figs 44, 45). Dental formula 2/3 1/1 3/3 3/3. *Myotis* spp., have same dental formula, but different-shaped ears with a shorter, bluntly pointed tragus, shorter rostrum and reduced second premolar (Fig. 37). Recent genetic analyses suggest that some taxa, such as *Kerivoula hardwickii* and the *Kerivoula papillosa/lenis* complex, include more species than are currently recognized.

PAPILLOSE WOOLLY BAT
Kerivoula papillosa   PLATE 22
Measurements FA 39–49, T 49–56, E 14–17, Wt 6–13. Skull: ccl 15.4–17.1, mt 7.1–7.8, m–m 6.7–7.1

Identification Fur long and woolly. Upperparts brown to buffy-brown; underparts paler. Ears funnel-shaped with a long pointed tragus. Three upper and lower premolars, all of which are well developed. Braincase is high, with domed forehead (Fig. 44a).
Similar species Indian Woolly Bat, *K. lenis*, overlaps in forearm length, but has shorter skull and toothrow; Kachin Woolly Bat, *K. kachinensis*, has flatter skull.
Ecology and habitat Forages in understorey of lowland rainforest. Roosts in small holes within live trees. Has also been found inside bamboo stems.
Distribution and status SE Asia: Thailand, Laos, N Vietnam, Cambodia and Peninsular Malaysia. Also Sumatra, Java, Borneo and Sulawesi. Not currently at risk.

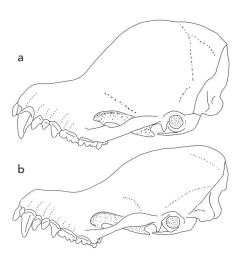

Fig. 44 *Skull profiles of* Kerivoula papillosa *(a) and* K. kachinensis *(b).*

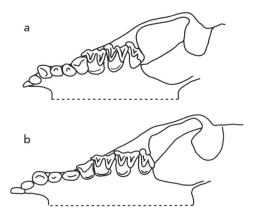

Fig. 45 *Upper left toothrows of* Kerivoula minuta *(a) and* K. whiteheadi *(b).*

INDIAN WOOLLY BAT

Kerivoula lenis NOT ILLUSTRATED

Measurements FA 37–41. Skull: ccl 14.5–15.1, mt 6.6–6.8, m–m 6.0–6.6

Identification Upperparts brown to buffy-brown, underparts paler. Ears funnel-shaped with a long pointed tragus. Braincase high and domed (as in Fig. 44a). **Similar species** Papillose Woolly Bat, *K. papillosa,* has larger skull, longer toothrow; Titania's Woolly Bat, *K. titania*, is smaller, with a shorter, flatter skull; Kachin Woolly Bat, *K. kachinensis*, has flatter skull.

Ecology and habitat Understorey of forest, including both wet and dry forest.

Distribution and status SE Asia: Peninsular Malaysia. Also India and Borneo. Status poorly known; probably not currently at risk.

KACHIN WOOLLY BAT

Kerivoula kachinensis NOT ILLUSTRATED

Measurements FA 41–43, T 56–61, E 14–16. Wt 6.5–9.1. Skull: ccl 15.5, mt 6.8, m–m 6.4

Identification Fur long and woolly; upperparts grey-brown with dark grey bases to fur; underparts slightly paler. Ears funnel-shaped with a long pointed tragus. Three upper and lower premolars, all well developed. Braincase relatively flat in profile (Fig. 44b). **Similar species** Other large *Kerivoula* have high domed braincase (Fig. 44a), producing an abruptly rising forehead, which can be felt in the live bat if the fur is gently pressed down.

Ecology and habitat Has been found in evergreen and mixed deciduous forest.

Distribution and status SE Asia: Myanmar, Thailand, Laos and N Vietnam. Status poorly known, but probably not currently at risk.

HARDWICKE'S WOOLLY BAT

Kerivoula hardwickii PLATE 22

Measurements FA 29–34, T 40–50, E 12–14. Wt 3.5–6.0. Skull: ccl 12.4–13.6, mt 5.2–5.9

Identification Fur long and woolly; upperparts grey-brown with dark grey bases to fur; underparts paler and greyer. Ears moderately large. **Taxonomic notes** Genetic analyses suggest that bats currently referred to *K. hardwickii*

include several different species with similar morphology, but further study is required to determine distinguishing characters and appropriate names for each. **Similar species** Titania's Woolly Bat, *K. titania*, is greyer and slightly larger; Clear-winged Woolly Bat, *K. pellucida*, has pale orange fur with pale bases, long narrow ears; Small Woolly Bat, *K. intermedia*, has orange-brown fur with short ears.

Ecology and habitat Understorey of various forest types, including evergreen and deciduous. Has been found roosting in hollow trees and among clumps of dead leaves.

Distribution and status SE Asia: Myanmar, Thailand, Laos, Vietnam, Cambodia and Peninsular Malaysia. Also Sri Lanka, India, S China, Sumatra, Java, Sulawesi, the Philippines and smaller Indonesian islands. Not currently at risk.

TITANIA'S WOOLLY BAT

Kerivoula titania NOT ILLUSTRATED

Measurements FA 34–36, T 48–53, E 14–15. Wt 4.4–4.8. Skull: ccl 14.0–14.4, mt 6.4

Identification Upperparts grey, individual hairs with blackish bases, paler middles, dark grey tips; underparts paler. Skull moderately flattened, but not as much as in *K. kachinensis*. **Taxonomic notes** Formerly confused with *K. flora*, which does not occur in region. **Similar species** Hardwicke's Woolly Bat, *K. hardwickii*, has shorter forearm, smaller skull; Kachin Woolly Bat, *K. kachinensis*, is larger, with relatively flatter skull.

Ecology and habitat Found mainly in evergreen forest, often near limestone or rivers.

Distribution and status SE Asia: Myanmar, Laos, Vietnam, Thailand and Cambodia. Status uncertain, but probably not currently at risk.

KRAU WOOLLY BAT

Kerivoula krauensis PLATE 22

Measurements FA 29–33, T 35–37, E 11–12. Wt 2.5–3.5. Skull: ccl 11.3–11.5, mt 4.9–5.0

Identification Hair of upperparts largely dark brown to black (90% of length) with shiny golden tips; underparts blackish bases with broad (20%) buff to white tips. **Similar**

species Hardwicke's Woolly Bat, *K. hardwickii* is similar in size but fur is grey-brown with only base of hair dark; Small Woolly Bat, *K. intermedia*, is generally orange-brown in colour with shorter ears; Whitehead's Woolly Bat, *K. whiteheadi*, has pale underparts, elongated premolars.

Ecology and habitat Occurs in understorey of mature lowland dipterocarp forest.

Distribution and status SE Asia: known only from Krau Wildlife Reserve in Peninsular Malaysia. Vulnerable, owing to loss of lowland rainforest.

PAINTED WOOLLY BAT
Kerivoula picta PLATE 22
Measurements FA 32–39, T 37–47, E 13–15. Wt 4.5–5.5. Skull: ccl 12.2–13.3, mt 5.5–5.8

Identification Upperparts with soft, fluffy light orange fur; underparts similar but slightly paler. Ears, wing bones, tail membrane and feet bright orange; wing membranes between fingers with large patches of contrasting black. **Similar species** No other *Kerivoula* has contrasting orange and black wings; Black and Orange Myotis, *Myotis formosus*, has similar colour pattern but is considerably larger, with different-shaped ears and teeth, black edges to ears and feet.

Ecology and habitat Recorded from dry forest and scrubby areas; roosts among dead leaves in trees and bananas. Flight slow and manoeuvrable.

Distribution and status SE Asia: Myanmar, Thailand, Laos, Vietnam, Cambodia and Peninsular Malaysia (Penang Island). Also India, Sri Lanka, Bangladesh, S China, Sumatra, Java and smaller Indonesian islands. Not currently at risk.

CLEAR-WINGED WOOLLY BAT
Kerivoula pellucida PLATE 22
Measurements FA 29–32, T 40–50, E 14.5–17. Wt 3.5–5.0. Skull: ccl 12.0–12.5, mt 5.3–5.6

Identification Upperparts pale orange-brown, individual hairs with paler greyish-white bases; underparts greyish-white. Wing membranes and ears pale orange-brown, almost translucent. Ears long and narrow. **Similar species** Hardwicke's Woolly Bat, *K. hardwickii*, has grey-brown fur with dark bases, shorter ears; Painted Woolly Bat, *K. picta*, has black patches on wing membranes; Small Woolly Bat, *K. intermedia*, has darker orange fur with dark bases, small ears.

Ecology and habitat Roosts in clumps of dried leaves, including dead, curled banana leaves. Forages in understorey of tall forest.

Distribution and status SE Asia: peninsular Thailand and Malaysia. Also Sumatra, Java, Borneo and the Philippines. Near Threatened, owing to loss of lowland rainforest.

SMALL WOOLLY BAT
Kerivoula intermedia PLATE 22
Measurements FA 26.5–31, T 37–41, E 9–11.5. Wt 2.9–4.2. Skull: cbl 11.1–11.8, mt 4.6–5.0

Identification Upperparts orange-brown with dark bases; underparts paler. Ears relatively small. Premolars small and rounded (Fig. 45a). **Similar species** Least Woolly Bat, *K. minuta*, is very similar and overlaps in forearm length, but has smaller skull, lighter body weight; Whitehead's Woolly Bat, *K. whiteheadi*, has different coloration – pale brown above, white below, longer ears and very narrow premolars (Fig. 45b); Hardwicke's Woolly Bat, *K. hardwickii*, is slightly larger, with larger ears and greyer fur with dark grey bases; Clear-winged Woolly Bat, *K. pellucida*, has pale fur with whitish bases and very long ears; Krau Woolly Bat, *K. krauensis*, has gold-tipped dark fur.

Ecology and habitat Understorey of tall lowland forest. Roost sites unknown.

Distribution and status SE Asia: Peninsular Malaysia. Also Borneo. Near Threatened, owing to loss of lowland rainforest, although still relatively common in some forest reserves.

LEAST WOOLLY BAT
Kerivoula minuta PLATE 22
Measurements FA 25–29.5, E 8–10. Wt 1.9–2.3. Skull: cbl 10.0–11.1, mt 4.1–4.6

Identification Very small, light bat. Upperparts orange-brown with brown bases to fur; underparts slightly paler. Ear relatively small. Premolars small and rounded. **Similar species** Small Woolly Bat, *K. intermedia*, is very similar in appearance but is generally heavier with larger skull; Whitehead's Woolly Bat, *K. whiteheadi*, has whitish belly, brown upperparts, narrow premolars (Fig. 45b).
Ecology and habitat Understorey of lowland rainforest, including some disturbed areas. Flight slow and fluttering.
Distribution and status SE Asia: peninsular Thailand and Malaysia. Also Borneo. Near Threatened, due to lowland rainforest loss.

WHITEHEAD'S WOOLLY BAT
Kerivoula whiteheadi PLATE 22
Measurements FA 28–29. Skull: cbl 11.8–11.9, mt 5.0
Identification Upperparts brown, fur with dark grey bases; underparts greyish-white. Ears moderately long. Wing membranes apparently with white tips in mainland form, *K. w. bicolor*, but type and only known specimen has faded and it is no longer possible to check the colours. Anterior 2 upper and lower premolars elongate and oval in cross-section with knife-like cusps (Fig. 45b); inner upper incisors tall, about two-thirds length of canine, with well-developed secondary cusps. **Similar species** Other woolly bats, *Kerivoula* spp., have premolars with nearly circular cross-section (Fig. 45a), and less contrasting colour of underparts.
Ecology and habitat In Sabah, has been found roosting in a group of 20–30 in a hanging cluster of large dead leaves by a river. In the Philippines, has been found in secondary forest, scrub and open grasslands.
Distribution and status SE Asia: peninsular Thailand. Also Borneo and the Philippines. Status uncertain, as only one record from region; elsewhere not apparently at risk, as relatively common in some disturbed areas.

Genus *Phoniscus* Similar to *Kerivoula*, with long woolly fur, but tragus white with distinct notch in posterior margin near base; fur banded with four bands of colour including pale tips; upper canines large with longitudinal grooves on outer faces; outer upper incisor very small, about one-quarter height of anterior incisor; anterior lower premolars elongate, more than 50% longer than wide. Dental formula 2/3 1/1 3/3 3/3.

GREATER GROOVE-TOOTHED BAT
Phoniscus jagorii PLATE 22
Measurements FA 35–42, T 38–45, E 14–17. Wt 7–11. Skull: cbl 15.3–15.9, mt 6.7–7.1
Identification Upperparts overall golden-brown and black – hairs banded with four colours: dark grey-brown bases, then a buff band, then dark brown, then golden tips; underparts paler with slightly greyer tips; short shiny yellow hairs along forearm and fingers. Tragus white with deep notch on posterior edge. Canines long and grooved. Middle upper premolar elongate, projecting beside anterior premolar on inside. **Similar species** Lesser Groove-toothed Bat, *P. atrox*, is smaller, with more rounded second upper premolar; tube-nosed bats, *Murina* spp. have enlarged nostrils, only 2 upper and lower premolars (Fig. 42).
Ecology and habitat Lowland rainforest, as well as dry dipterocarp and semi-evergreen forest.
Distribution and status SE Asia: Thailand, Laos, Vietnam and Peninsular Malaysia. Also S China, Java, Borneo, Bali, Sulawesi, and the Philippines. Probably not immediately at risk, though there are relatively few records from most areas.

LESSER GROOVE-TOOTHED BAT
Phoniscus atrox PLATE 22
Measurements FA 31–35, T 35–40, E 12.5–14. Wt 4.0–5.5. Skull: cbl 12.9–14.1, mt 5.6–6.2
Identification Upperparts overall golden-brown and black – hairs banded with grey and brown bases, black centres and orange-brown or buff tips; underparts paler and greyer. Tragus white with deep notch in posterior edge. Upper canines long with groove on outside; middle upper premolar rounded,

similar in shape to anterior premolar. **Similar species** Greater Groove-toothed Bat, *P. jagorii*, is larger with more elongate upper premolar; woolly bats, *Kerivoula* spp., have shorter canines without any groove, no more than two bands of colour on hairs; tube-nosed bats, *Murina* spp., have long, tubular nostrils and only 2 upper premolars (Fig 42).

Subfamily *MINIOPTERINAE*

Genus *Miniopterus* Bent-winged bats have a distinctive wing shape: third finger has a very short first phalanx and very long terminal phalanx (see colour plates). Ear is short, slightly rounded, with a moderate posterior fold and a short blunt tragus curved slightly forwards. Fur is generally black or dark brown, occasionally with reddish patches or even completely reddish. All species are very similar in appearance, and difficult to distinguish except by size. Forearm length and weight separate most specimens, but since there is some overlap, skull measurements are sometimes necessary for confirmation. Owing to similarities in appearance, the taxonomy is somewhat uncertain – it is difficult to determine which forms in different areas belong to the same species. Genetic studies may help to solve this problem in the future. Skull with large high braincase, slender rostrum (Fig. 36g). Dental formula 2/3 1/1 2/2 3/3.

The conservation status of most *Miniopterus* is poorly known, owing to the uncertain taxonomic situation; some of the most widely distributed species are likely to prove to be a complex of many species; many of the component species may have more restricted ranges. Cave colonies are vulnerable to disturbance or exploitation, and some large colonies have been lost.

LARGE BENT-WINGED BAT
Miniopterus magnater PLATE 21
Measurements FA 47–53. Wt 13–20. Skull: cbl 15.8–16.8, mt 6.4–7.3, m–m 7.4–8.0
Identification See general description of bent-winged bats (above). Largest of the

Ecology and habitat Found in understorey of lowland dipterocarp forest and disturbed areas near primary forest. Has been found roosting in old hanging birds' nests.
Distribution and status SE Asia: S Thailand and Peninsular Malaysia. Also Sumatra and Borneo. Near Threatened, owing to loss of lowland rainforest.

Miniopterus, with an especially wide palate, as measured by width across outer molars.
Ecology and habitat Roosts in caves, but has also been found away from known caves. Flies above canopy catching insects; can be seen flying low over streams and small bodies of water.
Distribution and status SE Asia: Myanmar, Thailand, Laos, Vietnam, Cambodia and Peninsular Malaysia. Also NE India, SE China, Sumatra, Java, Borneo and other Indonesian Islands through to New Guinea. Not currently at risk.

COMMON BENT-WINGED BAT
Miniopterus schreibersii PLATE 21
Measurements FA 42–46. Wt 10–12.5. Skull: cbl 14.5–16.0, mt 5.8–6.7, m–m 6.3–7.3
Identification See general description of bent-winged bats (above). Forearm length overlaps range of Large Bent-winged Bat, *M. magnater*, but averages shorter; body and skull are smaller and narrower.
Ecology and habitat Roosts in caves, sometimes mixed with other species of bent-winged bat.
Distribution and status SE Asia: Myanmar, Thailand, Laos, Vietnam, Cambodia and Peninsular Malaysia. Also throughout much of Europe and Africa to Australia, although it is likely these will prove to be a complex of species. Not currently at risk.

MEDIUM BENT-WINGED BAT
Miniopterus medius PLATE 21
Measurements FA 38–44. Wt. 8.0–10.0. Skull: cbl 13.8–14.5, mt 5.5–6.0, m–m 5.8–6.5
Identification See general description of

bent-winged bats (opposite). Intermediate in size between Common and Small Bent-winged Bats, *M. schreibersii* and *M. pusillus*. Skull larger than that of Small Bent-winged Bat, *M. pusillus*.

Ecology and habitat Roosts in caves. Forages over low rivers in forest.

Distribution and status SE Asia: S Thailand, and Peninsular Malaysia. Also Java, Borneo, Sulawesi, the Philippines and New Guinea. Not currently at risk.

SMALL BENT-WINGED BAT
Miniopterus pusillus PLATE 21
Measurements FA 40–43. Wt 7.0–10.0.

Skull: cbl 12.7–13.4, mt 5.0–5.4, m–m 5.4–5.7

Identification See general description of bent-winged bats (opposite). Similar to Medium Bent-winged Bat, *M. medius*, but slightly shorter and narrower skull and dentition.

Ecology and habitat Roosts in caves and possibly other habitats as well. Forages in open areas, including over small streams and rivers.

Distribution and status SE Asia: Myanmar, Thailand, Laos, Vietnam and Cambodia. Also S India, Nicobar Islands and Hong Kong. Not currently at risk.

Family *MOLOSSIDAE* FREE-TAILED BATS

Medium-small to large bats distinguished by their thick, relatively short tail, which protrudes for well over half its length from the interfemoral membrane. The muzzle lacks a noseleaf and projects well beyond the lower jaw. Lips often with a series of folds in the skin, appearing wrinkled. Ears thick, sometimes joined over the top of the head by a band of skin. Wings long and narrow. Premaxillary bones of skull well developed and attached to the palate and the maxillaries.

Genus *Tadarida* Fur thick and short. Upper incisors long and well developed, evenly spaced between the canines. Skull somewhat flattened without a sagittal crest. Premaxillae in skull not fused. Dental formula 1/2–3 1/1 2/2 3/3.

LA TOUCHE'S FREE-TAILED BAT
Tadarida latouchei PLATE 23
Measurements FA 53–55, T 47–49, E 26–27. Wt 18–26

Identification Relatively large, with long, narrow, naked wings. Relatively large ears, separated except for a narrow skin fold at base. Fur short, dense and velvety; upperparts uniformly dark brown or greyish-brown; underparts greyer. **Taxonomic notes** Formerly included in *Tadarida teniotis*. **Similar species** Wroughton's Free-tailed Bat, *Otomops wroughtoni*, has ears joined for much of length, pale patches on shoulders; other free-tailed bats (*Mops* and *Chaerephon*) are smaller.

Ecology and habitat Known to roost in caves. Recorded in dry evergreen hill forest.

Distribution and status SE Asia: Laos and Thailand. Also China and Japan. Vulnerable, owing to excessive hunting; captured for food in Laos, where tendency to roost in large cave colonies makes it susceptible to over-harvesting.

Genus *Chaerephon* Formerly included in *Tadarida*. Short, thick fur. Premaxillae in skull fused, forming small foramina. Braincase slightly inflated with low sagittal crest. Dental formula 1/2 1/1 2/2 3/3.

ASIAN WRINKLE-LIPPED BAT
Chaerephon plicatus PLATE 23
Measurements FA 40–50, T 30–40, E 21–24, HF 8–9. Wt 17–31

Identification Fur short, dense and soft; upperparts dark brown; underparts paler with grey tips to hairs. Upper lip heavily wrinkled, nostrils protruding slightly in front; ears moderate, thick and rounded, joined across front of head by flap of skin. Two upper premolars, the anterior quite small; posterior upper molar well developed, about half the area of the second molar (Fig. 46a). **Similar species** Johore Wrinkle-lipped Bat, *C. johorensis*, has enlarged "pocket" in membrane joining ears; Sunda Free-tailed Bat, *M. mops*, has darker fur, more massive skull, with only 1 upper premolar and reduced posterior upper molar (Fig. 46b).

Ecology and habitat Roosts in caves in large densely packed colonies, sometimes containing hundreds of thousands or millions of individuals. Often flies out before darkness in dense flocks to forage high above ground.

Distribution and status SE Asia: Myanmar, Thailand, Laos, Vietnam, Cambodia and Peninsular Malaysia. Also Sri Lanka, India, S China, Hainan, Sumatra, Java, Borneo, Lesser Sunda Islands and the Philippines. Although still abundant in many areas, with some large colonies well protected, its tendency to roost in large colonies makes it vulnerable to hunting or disturbance; all large colonies have disappeared in the Philippines, and some large colonies have been lost in Cambodia and Laos.

JOHORE WRINKLE-LIPPED BAT
Chaerephon johorensis PLATE 23
Measurements FA 44–49, T 36–43. Wt 15–25

Identification Upperparts covered in short, dark brown fur; underparts paler with grey tips to fur. Upper lip heavily wrinkled; ears moderate, joined across top of head by flap of skin that is raised at centre and extended backwards to form a "pocket" between ears; under pocket, long tuft of hairs that can be everted and erected. Small anterior upper premolars (as in Fig. 46a). **Similar species** Asian Wrinkle-lipped Bat, *C. plicatus*, has narrower band of skin joining ears, without "pocket"; Sunda Free-tailed Bat, *M. mops*, also lacks pocket, has darker fur, more massive skull, with only 1 upper premolar and reduced posterior upper molar (Fig. 46b).

Ecology and habitat Mainly associated with forest, foraging high over canopy, but also flies lower in large gaps and over rivers.

Distribution and status SE Asia: Peninsular

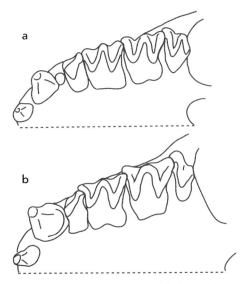

Fig. 46 *Upper left toothrows of* Chaerephon plicatus *(a) and* Mops mops *(b).*

Malaysia. Also Sumatra. Near Threatened, owing to loss of intact forest.

Genus *Mops* Fur thick and short. Upper incisors long and well developed, evenly spaced between the canines. Only 1 upper premolar. Dental formula 1/2 1/1 1/2 3/3.

SUNDA FREE-TAILED BAT
Mops mops PLATE 23
Measurements FA 41–46, T 35–42, E 18–22. Wt 23–35. Skull: cbl 19.1–19.4, mt 7.0–7.4, c–c 5.2–5.7

Identification Fur thick; upperparts and underparts uniform dark brown to reddish-brown; crown of head nearly naked. Ears large and rounded, joined at front across top of head by narrow flap of skin. Upper lip heavily wrinkled. Only 1 upper premolar; posterior molar reduced (Fig. 46b). **Similar species** Asian Wrinkle-lipped Bat, *C. plicatus*, has shorter fur, paler underparts, smaller skull with extra small anterior upper premolars and well-developed posterior molar (Fig. 46a).

Ecology and habitat Forages high above forest or large clearings, and sometimes flies low over rivers. Has been found roosting in hollows in trees, sometimes in association with Naked Hairless Bat, *Cheiromeles torquatus*.

Distribution and status SE Asia: peninsular Thailand and Malaysia. Also Sumatra and Borneo. Near Threatened, owing to loss of intact forest.

Genus *Otomops* Ears long, pointing forwards over head, and joined for much of length by fold of skin; virtually no tragus or anti-tragus; anterior upper premolar well developed, within toothrow. Dental formula 1/2 1/1 2/2 3/3.

WROUGHTON'S FREE-TAILED BAT
Otomops wroughtoni PLATE 23
Measurements FA 63–67, T 36, HF 10–14, E 35. Skull: gl 24–25, mt 8.9–9.3
Identification Upperparts dark brown apart from contrasting pale greyish white collar across back and around under neck and throat; lower belly greyish brown; small tuft of white hairs at base of ears and on skin joining ears; thin line of white hairs down side beside wings. Ears long, pointing forwards over head, joined near front by band of skin. **Similar species** La Touche's Free-tailed Bat, *Tadarida latouchei*, is slightly smaller, with less elongate, separated ears, uniform dark upperparts.
Ecology and habitat One individual was found in open, semi-deciduous dipterocarp forest. Audible component to echolocation call. In India, only known colony roosts in a cave.
Distribution and status SE Asia: Cambodia. Also S India. Status uncertain; appears to be very rare, but too little information available to assess threats.

Genus *Cheiromeles* Large and naked with only scattered hairs on the skin. Ears separate. Skull very robust with a prolonged sagittal crest. Anterior lower premolar minute. Dental formula 1/2 1/1 1/2 3/3.

NAKED BAT
Cheiromeles torquatus PLATE 23
Measurements FA 74–86, T 60–75, E 25–32. Wt 150–185
Identification Heaviest insectivorous bat in the world. Body almost completely naked except for scattered short hairs on the feet and a cluster of long hairs around a scent gland in its neck. Bare skin of body dark grey. Feet large with long sharp claws. Ears well developed, separate. In flight can be recognized by large size, strong flight and audible clicking of echolocation call. Exposed tail and large separate ears can sometimes be seen in flight as well.
Ecology and habitat Roosts in large caves or hollow trees, sometimes associated with Sunda Free-tailed Bat, *Mops mops*. Feeds in open areas over streams or clearings or high over forest canopy.
Distribution and status SE Asia: peninsular Thailand and Malaysia. Also Sumatra, Java, Borneo, Palawan and some nearby small islands. Near Threatened. Populations have declined due to loss of forest as well as trapping for food; formerly large colonies in some caves have been virtually wiped out by hunting.

Order PRIMATES
Prosimians, monkeys and apes

Primates are represented in mainland South-East Asia by the lorises (family Lorisidae), the true monkeys, including macaques and leaf monkeys (family Cercopithecidae), and the gibbons (family Hylobatidae), as well as by the Hominidae, the family that includes humans. All primates have hands and feet that can grasp, digits generally with nails rather than claws and both eyes on the front of the face. The Lorisidae are strictly nocturnal, while the other species are mainly active during the day. Although all species are protected to varying degrees in the region, many primates are threatened due to clearing and conversion of forest, as well as illegal hunting and trapping both for food and for the pet trade. In some cases, accurate survey information is not available, but population declines are inferred from extensive loss of suitable habitat. A few species are now Critically Endangered, with very small remaining populations and a high probability of extinction in the near future.

Family *LORISIDAE* SLOW LORIS

Lorises are small, stocky primates with very short tails, and they are largely nocturnal and arboreal. Unlike most other primates they climb slowly and deliberately, almost never jumping and rarely moving quickly except when threatened or when striking at prey. All the digits have nails, with the exception of the second digit of the foot, which has a short claw. The thumb and big toe are both opposing, allowing the animal to grip branches very strongly.

SUNDA SLOW LORIS
Nycticebus coucang PLATE 24
Measurements HB 260–300, T 15–25, HF 48–63. Wt 375–900g. Skull: gl 55–62
Identification General coloration varies from pale grey-brown to reddish-brown, with broad, dark brown to black stripe from lower back to top of head, where it branches into four lines connecting to the eyes and the ears. Usually has a dark-coloured ring around each eye. Fur soft and dense. Eyes reflect lights clearly at night with a reddish colour.
Similar species Asian Slow Loris, *N. bengalensis*, averages larger, with paler head, narrower dorsal stripe that usually ends on neck with, at most, indistinct forks to eyes and ears; hybrids may occur in area of overlap in peninsular Thailand.
Ecology and habitat Nocturnal and usually arboreal, mostly in small to medium-sized trees. Feeds mainly on fruits, flower nectar, gum and sap, but also eats some small animals, mostly insects. Occurs in tall and secondary forests as well as gardens and cocoa plantations. Mainly solitary.
Distribution and status SE Asia: peninsular Thailand and Malaysia south of the Isthmus of Kra. Also Sumatra, Java and Borneo (Philippine populations are considered a separate species). Endangered. Populations throughout area have suffered from severe loss of habitat due to clearing of forests, as well as illegal hunting and trapping for pet trade, especially in Sumatra and Java.

ASIAN SLOW LORIS
Nycticebus bengalensis PLATE 24
Measurements HB 300–380, T 10–20, E 20–25, HF 55–70. Wt 1–2kg. Skull: gl 62–67
Identification Overall colour orange-buff to light brown, with extensive greyish frosting on neck, head and forelimbs, making head and neck distinctly paler than back; thin, brown dorsal stripe that ends on neck with, at most, indistinct fork on head; dark rings around eyes. **Taxonomic note** Sometimes considered a subspecies of *N. coucang*.
Similar species Sunda Slow Loris, *N. coucang*, averages smaller and has dark stripe continuing to top of head and forking towards eyes and ears; hybrids may occur in area of overlap in peninsular Thailand, Pygmy Loris, *N. pygmaeus*, is smaller, with larger ears.

Ecology and habitat Nocturnal and arboreal. Occurs in both evergreen and deciduous forests, as well as degraded areas such as bamboo groves. Feeds mainly on fruits, tree gums and nectar, but also on some animal matter, including large insects, nestling birds and lizards.

Distribution and status SE Asia: Myanmar, Thailand, Laos, Vietnam and Cambodia. Also NE India, Bangladesh and S China. Vulnerable; populations declining due to loss of forest habitat as well as hunting and trapping for pet trade.

PYGMY LORIS
Nycticebus pygmaeus PLATE 24
Measurements HB 210–290. Skull: gl 48–55
Identification Small loris with finely textured reddish-buff fur, though some animals may be dull brown. Dorsal stripe varies from faint or absent to broad and dark, with indistinct forks on head. Ears long and relatively conspicuous. Some researchers suggest that this may comprise a mixture of two species, while others believe differences are mainly age related, young animals being more orange-coloured and lacking dorsal stripe. Genetic studies may be required to resolve this uncertainty. **Similar species** Asian Slow Loris, *N. bengalensis*, is larger with less conspicuous ears and thin dorsal stripe that does not continue onto top of head.

Ecology and habitat Nocturnal and arboreal. Occurs in a wide variety of forest habitats, including semi-evergreen and evergreen forest as well as degraded forests and bamboo, mainly below 500m altitude. Feeds heavily on animal material, especially insects, as well as plant sap and flowers. Also takes some small vertebrates such as lizards, eggs and nestlings of birds.

Distribution and status SE Asia: Laos, E Cambodia and Vietnam. Also extreme S China. Vulnerable. Declining due to hunting and trapping for food and pet trade.

Family *CERCOPITHECIDAE* MONKEYS

Monkeys in South-East Asia are represented by two distinct groups: the langurs or leaf monkeys (subfamily Colobinae) and the macaques (subfamily Cercopithecinae). The colobines are mainly arboreal, have a long tail, lack cheek pouches and have a large, sacculated stomach with many chambers, which permits breakdown of leafy material into digestible substances and helps detoxify poisonous leaves. The macaques are partly terrestrial, with a short or long tail, cheek pouches for temporary storage of food and a simple stomach capable of breaking down only a limited amount of leafy material. The skull has a large, domed braincase with forward-pointing orbits for the eyes (Fig. 47).

Footprints can be recognized by the five distinct fingers/toes, with an opposable first digit separated from the rest (Fig. 48). Only the macaques regularly forage on the ground, but footprints for other species may be found near water, where they come down to drink or to search for minerals. Tracks of langurs have a relatively longer, narrower foot and shorter first digit compared with those of macaques, but the species of langurs probably cannot be readily distinguished from tracks.

BANDED LANGUR
Presbytis femoralis PLATE 25
Measurements HB 460–590, T 695–765, HF 170–185
Identification Dorsally dark brown or blackish, underside medium to light grey, with conspicuous pale patches, especially on inside of thighs. Head with a distinct central crest, pale grey bare skin around eyes, but rings much darker and less conspicuous than in Dusky Langur, *Trachypithecus obscurus*. Newborn infants have "cruciger" pattern – white or beige, with dark lines down the back and across the shoulders. Separate populations in N and S Peninsular Malaysia/Thailand differ somewhat in appearance: *P. f. femoralis*: blackish above, sometimes with red-brown tone; sharply demarcated mid-

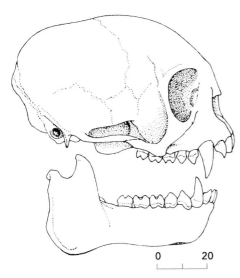

Fig. 47 *Skull of typical leaf monkey,*
Presbytis *sp.*

grey below with white mid-ventral line and
pale patches on inside of legs; *P. f. robinsoni*:
upperparts dark brown to black, with tail and
feet black; underside mid-grey with slightly
paler areas on inside of thighs. Some individuals are all blonde or beige. **Voice** Adult
male loud call is a staccato "ke-ke-ke".
Similar species Sundaic Silvered Langur,
Trachypithecus cristatus, has more uniform

Fig. 48 *Left hind (H) and front (F) footprints
of* Macaca fasciculata *(a),* M. nemestrina *(b)
and a langur,* Presbytis *sp. (c). Within each
species, print size varies considerably with
age and sex.*

fur colour, with no white markings (although
parts of the body may appear whitish in
bright sunlight) and orange-coloured infants;
Dusky Langur, *Trachypithecus obscurus*, has
much more conspicuous white rings around
eyes, and a very different voice.
Ecology and habitat Diurnal and arboreal.
Travels in groups, typically of 3 to 6 individuals. Occurs in dipterocarp forest. Feeds on
leaves and fruits.
Distribution and status SE Asia: *P. f.
femoralis*: S Peninsular Malaysia (Johore) and
Singapore. Reduced to only a few groups in
Singapore, but status on adjacent mainland
is unknown. *P. f. robinsoni*: peninsular Myanmar and peninsular Thailand from about
13°N, south to N Peninsular Malaysia (Perak).
Also occurs in Sumatra. No reliable information on population status.

WHITE-THIGHED LANGUR
Presbytis siamensis PLATE 25
Measurements HB 430–690, T 680–840
(130–160% of HB)
Identification Upperparts, including top of
head and top of arms, brown to greyish-
brown; hands, feet and distal half of tail
black; underside, including underside of
arms and legs, as well as a large patch on
outside of legs, pale grey to whitish. Bare
face skin dark grey to nearly black, but sometimes skin around eye may be paler, forming
indistinct rings. **Similar species** Banded
Langur, *P. femoralis*, is generally darker
above, without contrasting pale outer thighs.
Dusky Langur, *Trachypithecus obscurus*, has

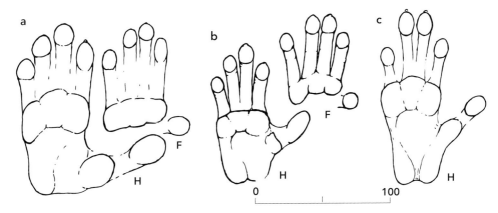

conspicuous pale rings around the eyes.

Ecology and habitat Found in a wide variety of forest types from lowlands to hills, including disturbed forests, orchards and plantations.

Distribution and status SE Asia: Peninsular Malaysia, in between range of *P. f. femoralis* and *P. f. robinsoni*. Also in Sumatra. Status uncertain; population has probably declined due to loss of forest.

SUNDAIC SILVERED LANGUR
Trachypithecus cristatus PLATE 25
Measurements HB 415–540, T 600–760, HF 145–174. Wt 4.0–6.5kg
Identification Entirely dark grey, the individual hairs frosted with pale grey tips. Face dark grey. May appear totally black in poor light. Infants are bright orange. **Voice** Relatively quiet; calls include rattling grunt, as well as shrill squeals and screams, mainly from young. **Similar species** Banded Langur, *Presbytis femoralis*, has contrastingly paler underparts; infants are not orange; Dusky Langur, *T. obscurus*, has large pale rings around eyes, pale lips and less of a crest on the head.
Ecology and habitat Diurnal and generally arboreal. Found in coastal, riverine and swamp forests, as well as some adjacent plantations, rarely more than 40km inland, Diet includes leaves, shoots and fruits, including many mangrove species. Usually found in moderate to large groups of 10 to 50 individuals.
Distribution and status SE Asia: W coast of Peninsular Malaysia. Also Sumatra, Borneo and some adjacent islands. Status uncertain; probably declining as a result of extensive loss of coastal forests including mangroves.

INDOCHINESE SILVERED LANGUR
Trachypithecus germaini PLATE 25
Measurements HB 490–570, T 720–840
Identification Dark black upperparts; slightly paler underparts with paler grey patches on arms and legs, though hands and feet are dark. Tail dark grey. Long, straight whitish hairs on head around face, including crest.

Infants orange. **Similar species** Annamese Silvered Langur, *T. margarita*, has much paler upperparts with contrasting dark hands and feet, pink ring around each eye; Phayre's Langur, *T. phayrei*, has pale marks around eye, lacks contrasting pale hairs around face.
Ecology and habitat Occurs in evergreen, semi-evergreen and mixed forest, especially in riverine areas, mainly at low elevations.
Distribution and status SE Asia: SE Thailand, Cambodia and S Vietnam W of Mekong River. Endangered. Much of forest habitat has been destroyed; occurs at very low densities in most remaining areas, probably due to excessive hunting and trapping.

ANNAMESE SILVERED LANGUR
Trachypithecus margarita PLATE 25
Measurements HB 500–600, T 700–800
Identification Upperparts medium to dark grey with paler frosting; underparts paler, almost whitish with very dark, nearly black lower arms and feet. Head with distinct crest, long pale grey "whiskers" on side of face. Face dark grey except for well-marked pale pink ring around each eye. Infants orange.
Similar species Indochinese Silvered Langur, *T. germaini*, is more uniformly dark grey except for pale hairs around face, lacks pink rings around eye. Phayre's Langur, *T. phayrei*, has generally paler body colour, pale whitish patch around mouth.
Ecology and habitat Found in tall primary forest and coastal forest.
Distribution and status SE Asia: Cambodia, Laos, and C and S Vietnam, largely or exclusively E of Mekong River. Endangered. Much of the coastal forest has been lost, and the species has further declined in some parts of its range due to hunting and trapping.

DUSKY LANGUR
Trachypithecus obscurus PLATE 26
Measurements HB 500–700, T 700–800. Wt 6.5–7.5kg
Identification Upperparts greyish-brown to dark grey; underparts, outside of hind legs, tail and crest on top of head contrasting paler grey; face skin dark grey with strongly

contrasting incomplete white rings around eye, which are narrow on top, broad on the outside, but usually incomplete and dark grey near the nose; contrasting bare pink patches on upper and lower lips. Newborn young pale orange. **Voice** Loud double honking call "ceng-kong". **Similar species** White-thighed Langur, *Presbytis siamensis*, lacks pale eye-rings, has contrasting dark tail and feet, different voice; Tenasserim Langur, *T. barbei*, has dark body without contrasting paler areas; Phayre's Langur, *T. phayrei*, is generally more uniformly coloured and paler.

Ecology and habitat Mainly arboreal, living in a variety of forest types from lowlands to hills; lives in groups of 5 to 20, with one or more adult males, occupying a home range of 5–20 hectares. Feeds mainly on leaves and shoots but also eats some fruits, especially unripe ones.

Distribution and status SE Asia: peninsular Myanmar, Thailand and Malaysia. Also some small offshore islands. Populations have probably declined due to loss of forest, but it is not immediately at risk. Threats include hunting in some areas.

TENASSERIM LANGUR
Trachypithecus barbei PLATE 26
Measurements HB 500–700, T 700–800
Identification Body dark greyish-black without any frosting, only slightly paler underneath; long tail dark grey, slightly paler than body with a pale patch at the base; face grey with large white rings around eye and whitish area of bare skin around mouth. **Similar species** Dusky Langur, *T. obscurus*, has legs and crown paler than body; Phayre's Langur, *T. phayrei*, has browner body colour with paler underparts; Indochinese Silvered Langur, *T. germaini*, has dark face with contrasting pale hairs around head.
Ecology and habitat Forest.
Distribution and status SE Asia: known only from a small area in SE Myanmar and SW Thailand. Status uncertain, but probably at risk because of limited range, loss of forest habitat and apparently low densities.

PHAYRE'S LANGUR
Trachypithecus phayrei PLATE 26
Measurements HB 520–620, T 600–850, HF 170–180. Wt 6–9kg
Identification Fur colour of back and head varies from dark brown to reddish-brown to buff or grey; hind legs and tail similar in colour to back; underparts vary from contrastingly paler, almost white, to only slightly paler than underparts. Bare facial skin dark grey except for pale greyish-white patch around mouth and around eyes; rings around eyes vary in conspicuousness from very broad all around eye (especially in *T. p. crepusculus*, the race found in most of Thailand), to incomplete and noticeable only on the inner side of the eye (in N populations, *T. p. shanicus*). **Similar species** Dusky Langur, *T. obscurus*, has thighs paler than back; Tenasserim Langur, *T. barbei*, is much darker, nearly black, on the back.
Ecology and habitat Primary or secondary evergreen and semi-evergreen forest, but also in some more disturbed habitats, including bamboo-dominated areas. Also in forest on limestone outcrops.
Distribution and status SE Asia: Myanmar, Thailand, Laos and N Vietnam. Also E India, Bangladesh and S China. Endangered. In many parts of range populations have declined severely, owing to loss of habitat and to hunting, including for medicinal values, especially for "bezoar stones" – mineral deposits that form inside the animals when they drink from springs rich in minerals, and that are thought to have magical powers. Still found in moderate numbers in some protected areas.

FRANCOIS'S LANGUR
Trachypithecus francoisi PLATE 27
Measurements HB 470–630, T 740–960
Identification Fur nearly all black, except for a band of elongated white hairs from corner of mouth to above ears like an extended moustache. Tall pointed crest on top of head. Newborn babies are largely orange, turning black with a pale orange head, **Similar species** Hatinh Langur, *T. hatinhen-*

sis, has white facial stripes continuing around to back of head.

Ecology and habitat Found only in subtropical and tropical rainforests and monsoon forest on limestone karst outcrops. Often shelters in limestone caves. Feeds mainly on leaves as well as some shoots, flowers and fruit.

Distribution and status SE Asia: N Vietnam. Also extreme S China. Endangered. Total population in Vietnam probably fewer than 500 animals, fragmented into many relatively small sub-populations due to loss of intervening forests. Major threat is from hunting, especially for traditional medicine.

CAT BA LANGUR
Trachypithecus poliocephalus PLATE 27
Measurements HB 490–590, T 800–900
Identification Body dark chocolate-brown; head and neck vary from pale yellowish to dark orange; patch of paler grey on rump and upper thigh. Tail long and black. **Similar species** No other langur with pale head occurs within its range.
Ecology and habitat Occurs in forests on limestone karst hills. Arboreal and terrestrial. Shelters in caves. Feeds mainly on leaves, as well as some shoots, fruit, flowers and bark.
Distribution and status SE Asia: found only on Cat Ba Island, N Vietnam. Critically Endangered. Fewer than 100 individuals remain, fragmented into several populations. Ongoing threats include disturbance of remaining habitat, illegal hunting and trapping.

HATINH LANGUR
Trachypithecus hatinhensis PLATE 27
Measurements HB 500–660, T 810–870
Identification Overall body largely glossy black except for white moustache that extends from sides of mouth over behind ears to nearly touch on back of neck. Forehead has white band in young animals, but is glossy black in adults. Has distinct black crest. **Similar species** Francois's Langur, *T. francoisi*, has moustache that does not continue behind ears; Lao Langur, *T. lao-*

tum, has white forehead even in adults.
Ecology and habitat Forested habitat in limestone karst and rocky outcrops in mountainous areas. Arboreal and terrestrial. Eats mainly leaves.
Distribution and status SE Asia: E Laos and NC Vietnam. Endangered. Populations have declined owing to loss of habitat, though moderate populations remain in some protected areas. Major threats are illegal hunting and trapping.

LAO LANGUR
Trachypithecus laotum PLATE 27
Measurements HB 460–530, T 800–900
Identification Overall colour of body glossy black above and below; head with long white whiskers that extend from sides of mouth, above ears and around back of head nearly to nape; broad white band on forehead; black crest joined by narrow black stripe down back of neck to black colour on back. **Similar species** Francois's Langur, *T. francoisi*, lacks white forehead band; Hatinh Langur, *T. hatinhensis*, has pale forehead only in juveniles; Indochinese Black Langur, *T. ebenus*, has all-black head.
Ecology and habitat Found only in forest on limestone karst. Arboreal and terrestrial. Feeds mainly on leaves.
Distribution and status SE Asia: known only from C Laos. Vulnerable. Has declined owing to loss of habitat. Threatened by hunting and trapping.

DELACOUR'S LANGUR
Trachypithecus delacouri PLATE 27
Measurements HB 570–730, T 730–970
Identification Most of body and head glossy black above and below; large white patch on rump and outside of thighs; cheeks with long pale grey hairs, topped by "moustache" from sides of mouth to above ears. Tail very long, glossy black. **Similar species** No other monkey has such contrasting white rump and legs.
Ecology and habitat Found only in forest on limestone karst hills, though can tolerate degraded forest. Shelters in limestone

caves. Feeds mainly on leaves, but also some shoots, flowers, fruit and bark.

Distribution and status SE Asia: found only in a limited area of Vietnam S of the Red River. Critically Endangered. Fewer than 250 individuals remain, fragmented into many small sub-populations owing to loss of habitat. Most populations too small for long-term viability – several have been lost in recent years. Major current threat is illegal hunting.

INDOCHINESE BLACK LANGUR
Trachypithecus ebenus PLATE 27
Measurements HB 600–700, T 800–900
Identification Glossy black all over, including head, except for a few scattered pale hairs on chin, hands and feet. Hairs on head raised in a distinct crest. **Similar species** No other langurs are completely glossy black without white on the head or body.
Ecology and habitat Lives in forests on limestone karst, as well as other rock outcrops in steep hills or mountainous areas. Feeds mainly on leaves. Arboreal and terrestrial.
Distribution and status SE Asia: C Laos and Vietnam. Vulnerable. It occurs in a limited range, where it is threatened by hunting and trapping.

CAPPED LANGUR
Trachypithecus pileatus PLATE 26
Measurements HB 500–700, T 800–1,000
Identification Grey to pale brown on back, contrasting with paler buff to yellowish-orange on face, sides of body and underparts; crown of head with distinct black cap, hairs short, sticking straight up; tail coloured as back, with black tip. Colour of underside varies from whitish to dark orange, sides of face usually more orange than rest. **Similar species** No other species has such a distinct dark cap contrasting with yellowish face.
Ecology and habitat Found in evergreen, semi-evergreen and moist deciduous forests, as well as bamboo forests and relatively open woodlands. Mainly arboreal, feeding on leaves, but sometimes descends to ground.

Distribution and status SE Asia: NW Myanmar, W of Chindwin River. Also NE India and Bangladesh. Vulnerable. Populations have declined owing to loss of habitat, hunting and trapping for food and the pet trade.

SHORTRIDGE'S LANGUR
Trachypithecus shortridgei PLATE 26
Measurements HB 600–750, T 900–1,050
Identification Uniformly silver grey on head and body, including underside; slightly paler on legs except for nearly black hands and feet and distal half of tail. Hairs on top of head stick up vertically. Bare face skin dark grey. Eyes pale orange-yellow. **Similar species** Phayre's Langur, *T. phayrei*, has underparts paler than upperparts, white patches on lips and around eyes.
Ecology and habitat Evergreen and semi-evergreen forest. Largely arboreal, feeding on leaves, but sometimes comes down to ground.
Distribution and status SE Asia: NE Myanmar. Also, adjacent NE India and S China. Vulnerable. Populations believed to have declined at least 30% in recent years, but only limited information available on current status. Threats include habitat loss and hunting.

RED-SHANKED DOUC
Pygathrix nemaeus PLATE 28
Measurements HB 610–760, T 560–760
Identification A strikingly coloured primate with back, belly and tops of upper arms speckled-grey; shoulders, inside of upper arms, upper legs and rump, hands and feet black; lower arms and scrotal region white; lower legs (shanks) dark reddish-chestnut. Face skin yellow-brown except around mouth and chin, which is white; broad black frontal band above face; long white cheek whiskers. Tail very long, white, with thick tassel at tip. Eyes slanting, forming an angle of >20° from horizontal. **Similar species** Black-shanked Douc, *P. nigripes*, has black lower arms and legs, bluish-grey facial skin with black streak on sides of face.
Ecology and habitat Largely arboreal, living

in tall evergreen and semi-evergreen forests, from lowlands up to about 2,000m, including on some limestone outcrops. Feeds mainly on leaves and buds, as well as some seeds, flowers and fruit. Moves noisily through branches when relaxed, but disappears quietly when disturbed. Usually found in small groups of three or more individuals.

Distribution and status SE Asia: N and C Vietnam and Laos between about 14°N and 20°N. Endangered. Has suffered extensive habitat loss, especially in Vietnam; biggest current threat is hunting and trapping, both for food and for the pet trade.

BLACK-SHANKED DOUC
Pygathrix nigripes PLATE 28
Measurements HB 610–760, T 560–760
Identification Upperparts and crown dark speckled-grey, underparts paler grey; chin and throat white; arms and legs largely black with some paler frosting on arms. Bare skin on face blue-grey except for yellow-orange rings around eyes; eyes relatively straight, forming an angle of <10° from horizontal; white whiskers on cheeks relatively short; black frontal band above face extends down side of face to connect with black of shoulders, and also forms a wedge on side of face like a sideburn. Tail very long, white, with thin tassel. Sometimes hybridizes with Red-shanked Douc, *P. nemaeus*, in zone of overlap (~13°N to 14°N). **Similar species** Red-shanked Douc, *P. nemaeus*, has white lower arms, red lower legs, orange facial skin, white on sides of face; Grey-shanked Douc, *P. cinerea*, has pale grey legs, yellow-brown facial skin.
Ecology and habitat Largely arboreal, but will travel on ground. Found in evergreen, semi-evergreen and mixed deciduous primary and disturbed forest. Feeds mainly on leaves and seeds, but also eats buds, flowers and fruits.
Distribution and status SE Asia: S Vietnam and adjacent Cambodia from about 10°30'N to 14°30'N. Endangered owing to habitat loss and hunting.

GREY-SHANKED DOUC
Pygathrix cinerea PLATE 28
Measurements HB 610–760, T 560–760
Identification Body, crown, most of arms speckled light grey, paler on underside and lower arms; shoulders, upper legs and part of rump, feet and hands black; lower legs dark speckled-grey. Bare skin on face yellow-brown, except around mouth and chin, which is white; long white whiskers on sides of face; eye slant intermediate, forming an angle ~15° from horizontal; narrow black band on forehead not connected to shoulders; throat white with a broad orange collar bordered by a black line that joins black patches on shoulders and inner surfaces of upper arms. Tail long and white with thin tassel; white patch on rump at base of tail.
Similar species Other doucs have darker bodies; Red-shanked Douc, *P. namaeus*, has red lower-legs, contrasting white forearms; Black-shanked Douc, *P. nigripes*, has uniformly blackish arms and legs, dark sideburns, blue facial skin; hybrids between *P. namaeus* and *P. nigripes* may be found in same area as *P. cinerea*, but do not have grey shanks or white underparts, instead resembling one or the other parent.
Ecology and habitat Evergreen and semi-evergreen primary rainforest, though also in some degraded forests. Largely arboreal, feeding mainly on leaves, but also some buds, fruits and flowers.
Distribution and status SE Asia: recorded only from C Vietnam, between 14°N and 14°46'N. Critically Endangered. Rarest of the doucs, threatened by forest clearing, hunting and trapping.

TONKIN SNUB-NOSED MONKEY
Rhinopithecus avunculus PLATE 28
Measurements HB 510–620, T 660–920
Identification Back, including back of neck, tops of arms and legs, largely black; top and front of head white to brownish-white; underparts including insides of arms and legs white; bare skin on face pale bluish to bluish-grey, with white rings around eyes; face flattened with very short nose and

enlarged pinkish lips. Tail very long, about 50% longer than head and body, largely black, frosted with pale hairs along top and a pale tip. **Similar species** No other primate in region has similar face pattern; Cat Ba Langur, *Trachypitheus poliocephalus*, has pale head, but dark brown body, different head shape, does not overlap in range.

Ecology and habitat Occurs only in forests on limestone karst mountains. Largely arboreal, rarely descending to ground. Feeds on leaves and fruits. Sleeps on lower branches of trees.

Distribution and status SE Asia: known only from a limited area in N Vietnam. Critically Endangered. Remaining world population estimated at fewer than 300 individuals, restricted to a few reserves, where threatened by illegal logging and hunting.

Genus _Macaca_ (Macaques) Six species of macaque are currently recognized in the region. The most distinctive is the Stumptailed Macaque, *M. arctoides*, which has a short, stump-like tail and bare skin on its face. The Southern and Northern Pig-tailed Macaques, *M. nemestrina* and *M. leonina*, are easily distinguished from other macaques by their short tail and distinctive facial pattern, but differences from each other are more subtle. The remaining three species have well-developed tails and differ in shape, average tail length, fur colour, range and habitat. Footprints (Fig. 48) are readily distinguished from those of other animals by the opposable first digit, but difficult to distinguish from one another. The more terrestrial Pig-tailed and Stump-tailed Macaques tend to have larger, broader feet than the other, more arboreal species.

SOUTHERN PIG-TAILED MACAQUE
Macaca nemestrina PLATE 29
Measurements HB 470–585, T 140–230, HF 140–170. Wt adult males 7–9kg, adult females 4–6kg
Identification Upperparts vary from greyish-brown to reddish-brown, with paler, often whitish underparts. Top of head, neck and middle of back distinctly dark brown or blackish. Tail is short and sparsely haired; often held curled above the back, especially in adult males. **Similar species** Northern Pig-tailed Macaque, *M. leonina*, which has minimal overlap in range, is on average slightly smaller with shorter face and shorter limbs; distinct diagonal stripes from corner of eye; crown not as dark; back without distinct black colour; tail with slight tuft of hair near tip.

Ecology and habitat Diurnal. Group size usually 15–40 animals, but solitary males are also encountered. Found in lowland and hill forests. Natural diet includes fruits and small vertebrate and invertebrate animals, but sometimes enters plantations and gardens where can cause damage to grain and fruit crops. If disturbed, tends to run off on ground to escape.

Distribution and status SE Asia: peninsular Thailand (S of about 7°30′N) and Peninsular Malaysia. Also Sumatra, Bangka Island and Borneo. Vulnerable. Declining owing to habitat loss and degradation, as well as hunting.

NORTHERN PIG-TAILED MACAQUE
Macaca leonina PLATE 29
Measurements HB 470–585, T 140–230, HF 140–170. Wt adult males 7–9kg, adult females 4–6kg
Identification Similar to Southern Pig-tailed Macaque, *M. nemestrina*, but lighter build, shorter muzzle; tail slightly hairier, especially at tip, tends to be carried over back arched towards rear, with tip pointing down. Body fur generally brown to golden-brown; whiter on face. Less black on back than *M. nemestrina*, with distinctive red streaks on face pointing diagonally upwards from eyes. Possible hybrids with *N. nemestrina* have been reported from peninsular Thailand around the Isthmus of Kra (around 7°N to 8°N). Identification of animals in some areas is complicated by feral animals that have escaped or been released from captivity.

Ecology and habitat Diurnal. Forages mainly on ground but also climbs trees; inclined to escape into trees if disturbed. Rarely found around temples or gardens, unlike some other macaques. Found in a wide variety of forest habitats, including disturbed forests.

Distribution and status SE Asia: Myanmar, Thailand (S to about 8°N), Laos, Vietnam and Cambodia. Also N India, Bangladesh and S China (Yunnan). Vulnerable. Declining due to degradation of habitat, hunting and trapping for pets or for use in climbing coconut trees.

STUMP-TAILED MACAQUE
Macaca arctoides PLATE 29
Measurements HB 485–635, T 37–78, HF 145–177. Wt 8–12kg
Identification Stout, heavily built macaque with tail reduced to a short, barely visible stump about 10% of head and body length that is usually kept down except when the animal is alarmed. Upperparts vary from dark brown to reddish-brown or blackish, paler underneath. Juveniles tend to be much paler. Hairs on back and sides of head can be very long and shaggy, and may form a beard on adult males. Prominent eyebrows. Bald forehead and largely bare skin on face. Facial skin pink to reddish, becoming darker with age, but also turning bright red when animal is excited. **Similar species** Other macaques have a more prominent tail and a different head shape.
Ecology and habitat Found mainly in upland areas, in primary or secondary forest as high as 2,000m. Feeds mainly on ground, on seeds, fruits, buds, insects and small animals. Typically in relatively large groups, sometimes of up to 50 individuals. If disturbed, usually runs off through undergrowth, but may climb trees.
Distribution and status SE Asia: Myanmar, Thailand, Vietnam, Laos, Cambodia, and extreme N Peninsular Malaysia. Also NE India (Assam) and southern China (Yunnan, Guangxi, Guandong). Vulnerable. Declining owing to loss or degradation of habitat, and hunting and trapping for food, medicinal purposes and pet trade.

ASSAMESE MACAQUE
Macaca assamensis PLATE 29
Measurements HB 510–735, T 150–300 (30–40% of HB), HF 155–175. Wt 5–10kg
Identification Heavy-set macaque with well-haired, relatively short tail. Fur varies from yellowish-grey to dark brown; shoulders, head and arms tend to be paler than hindquarters; hair on underparts relatively pale and sparse, often with bluish skin showing through. Hindquarters greyish and haired to edge of callosities (thickened bare skin on rump). Head has fringe of dark hair on cheeks directed backwards to ear; hair on crown typically parted in middle; facial skin dark brownish to purplish. Calls include a musical "pio". Subspecies in NE India has a longer tail, about 50–60% of head and body.
Similar species Rhesus Macaque, *M. mulatta*, is lighter in build, with reddish hindquarters, hairs on crown directed backwards and not parted in middle; Long-tailed Macaque, *M. fascicularis*, and leaf monkeys have much longer tails.
Ecology and habitat Found mainly in upland areas, as high as 3,500m in the hills, generally in forested areas. Omnivorous, feeding on fruit, insects and small animals. Spends much of time in trees, but will descend to ground to run from predators, and sometimes raids crops.
Distribution and status SE Asia: N Myanmar, Thailand, Laos and N Vietnam. Also NE India, Nepal, Pakistan and S China. Near Threatened. Declining in most parts of range owing to habitat loss and illegal hunting.

LONG-TAILED MACAQUE
Macaca fascicularis PLATE 29
Measurements HB 450–550, T 440–540 (90–120% of HB), HF 120–145. Wt 3.5–6.5kg
Identification Grey-brown to reddish-brown, paler on the underparts. Cheek-whiskers prominent. Infants blackish. Groups often detected by their calls, the most common being "krra!". Individuals tend to be less noisy than langurs when travelling through the tree canopy, but groups are noisier. Tail typically about 10–20% longer than head

and body in southern populations, slightly shorter than head and body in populations from Bangladesh through Myanmar to W Thailand. **Similar species** Other macaques have shorter tails; Rhesus Macaque, *M. mulatta*, has reddish hindquarters; Silvered Leaf Monkey, *Presbytis cristatus* (often in same habitat), is entirely dark blackish-grey with frosted fur (infants orange) and has distinct crest of hairs on top of head.

Ecology and habitat Active periodically from dawn until dusk. Often travels in groups of 20 to 30 individuals, sometimes more, with 2 to 4 adult males, 6 to 11 adult females and the remainder immatures. Usually only part of the group can be seen at one time. Males sometimes solitary or in small groups. A group occupies an area of up to several tens of hectares, travelling from 150 to 1,500m daily. Unlike other monkeys, spends a large proportion of the time active in low trees and thick scrub. Common in coastal forests including mangrove and beach, and along rivers. Also around gardens, villages and plantations. Diet mostly ripe fruits and a wide array of animal material including insects, frogs' eggs, crabs and other coastal invertebrates. Sometimes a pest in commercial crops.

Distribution and status SE Asia: Myanmar, S Thailand, Peninsular Malaysia, S Laos, Cambodia and S Vietnam. Also S Bangladesh, Sumatra, Java, Bali, Borneo and many smaller offshore islands. Not currently at risk.

RHESUS MACAQUE
Macaca mulatta PLATE 29
Measurements HB 470–585, T 205–280 (40–70% of HB), HF 140–170. Wt 3–6kg
Identification Upperparts brownish, with reddish-brown hindquarters, greyer-colour foreparts; paler underneath. Tail is well haired, about half length of head and body. Face is relatively hairy, with bare areas pinkish. Hairs on crown directed backwards. Voice similar to that of Long-tailed Macaque, *M. fascicularis*, but more squealing and less harsh. **Similar species** Assamese Macaque, *M. assamensis*, has similar length tail, but has heavier build and greyish hindquarters; Long-tailed Macaque, *M. fascicularis*, has relatively longer tail, hindquarters same colour as back.

Ecology and habitat Typically gregarious, forming large troops that vary from 10 to over 50 individuals. Frequents secondary forests and disturbed areas, often in close proximity to human settlements. May become a pest in agricultural areas. Reported to be declining in some areas as a result of loss of habitat and persecution, including trapping for use in medical and other research.

Distribution and status SE Asia: N and C Myanmar, Thailand, Laos, Cambodia and Vietnam. Also Nepal, Pakistan, India and China. Minimal overlap in range with *M. fascicularis*, but some hybridization occurs where ranges meet. Not currently at risk.

Family *HYLOBATIDAE* GIBBONS

Gibbons are slender, totally arboreal primates that rarely descend to the ground. They are distinguished from other primates by their long, slender arms and lack of a tail. They can travel very rapidly in the forest canopy, swinging by their arms. Many authors place these all in the same genus, *Hylobates*, but recent research suggests they should be grouped into four separate genera, all of which have representatives in the region, with a total of ten different species.

Most species are separated from each other geographically, often by major rivers, with the exception of the Siamang, *Symphalangus syndactylus*, which overlaps the range of *H. lar* and *H. agilis*. In areas where two species meet, there is sometimes limited hybridization. Species can usually be distinguished by colour patterns as well as the calls, especially the great calls of the females.

The distributional and species limits of crested gibbons, *Nomascus* spp., in Indochina are not well understood. Many areas have, until recently, been difficult to access owing to war.

Recent taxonomic and genetic studies have been largely based on captive animals, for which the precise origin is not always known. Although increased field work is now underway, many areas of the original habitat have been heavily disturbed by logging or hunting, with loss of animals from parts of their former range. Furthermore, in areas where they remain, gibbons become very shy and difficult to observe. Analysis of recordings of their songs appears to be a useful tool, but many areas have not yet been thoroughly surveyed.

All gibbons are protected under Appendix I of CITES (Convention on International Trade in Endangered Species), meaning that no international commercial trade in them is permitted. Many species have experienced severe population declines, and some populations are now threatened with extinction. The major threats are habitat loss (since gibbons are largely dependent on tall forest), as well as illegal hunting for food, medicine and the pet trade.

SIAMANG

Symphalangus syndactylus PLATE 30

Measurements HB 750–900. Wt adult males 10.4–15kg, females 8–11kg

Identification Largest of the gibbons, all black with long shaggy hairs, especially on legs and arms, giving thickset appearance. Both sexes have throat pouch that enlarges during calls. **Voice** Calls consist of a loud boom, followed by series of loud whoops. Female utters some whoops, as well as a series of short barks that gradually accelerate, at the climax of which male gives an extremely loud yell. Calls can be heard several kilometres away. **Similar species** Dark-phase animals of other gibbons within range have pale brows, hands or cheeks, and are smaller and more slender.

Ecology and habitat Diurnal and fully arboreal, dependent on tall forest. Can survive in partially logged forests only if sufficient large trees remain. Generally in small family groups of a pair with up to three immature offspring; unmated adults are solitary. Usually starts calling later in morning than other gibbons, often more than two hours after sunrise. Diet consists of fruits, flowers, leaves and shoots, with some animal food such as insects or birds' eggs. Moves less and eats proportionately more leaves than smaller gibbons.

Distribution and status SE Asia: mountains and hills of extreme S peninsular Thailand and Malaysia. Also Barisan Mountains of Sumatra and Indonesia. Endangered. Siamang populations are declining severely due to loss of forest, selective logging and illegal hunting, as well as trapping for the pet trade.

WHITE-HANDED GIBBON

Hylobates lar PLATE 30

Measurements HB 450–600, HF 133–155. Wt 4–7kg

Identification Body colour varies from dark brown or nearly black to buff or cream. Both pale and dark forms may occur in same family, but colour is not related to sex. Tops of hands and feet, brow band and sides of face contrastingly pale or white. **Voice** Loud call of female a series of slow, high-pitched rising and falling whoops; typically about 7–10 notes in a series over 15–25 seconds. Both sexes give single "hoo" calls. **Similar species** Agile Gibbon, *H. agilis*, has hands and feet same colour as body, less white on face; Pileated Gibbon, *H. pileatus*, females are pale brown, with black patches on underparts and crown; males are similar to dark phase *H. lar*, but have incomplete white facial ring and pale patch extending above ears. Limited hybridization with *H. pileatus* and *H. agilis* has been reported in areas of overlap.

Ecology and habitat Arboreal, rarely descending to ground. Normally in family group with adult male and female and up to three offspring. Sleeps in tops of tall trees, either crouched in fork of tree, or with arms outspread grasping smaller branches. Peak calling activity one to two hours after dawn. Diet mostly fruits, leaves, new shoots and flowers with some animal food including insects; may travel several kilometres a day around territory to visit scattered fruiting trees.

Distribution and status SE Asia: Myanmar, Thailand, NW Laos and Peninsular Malaysia. Also China (S Yunnan) and N Sumatra. Endangered. Populations have declined severely owing to loss of forest habitat and to hunting. Although significant numbers remain in some protected areas, major threat is now illegal hunting for food and trapping for the pet trade.

AGILE GIBBON

Hylobates agilis PLATE 30

Measurements HB 450–650. Wt adult males 4.9–7.3kg, females 4.5–6.8kg

Identification Adults of species have two colour phases, which are not related to sex. Dark phase is black or very dark brown, sometimes with a reddish hue; pale phase is buff to blonde. Both sexes have white brow band (which may be separated); males also have pale cheeks and sometimes a whitish "beard", usually lacking in females. Hands and feet same colour as rest of body or slightly darker. Dark phase most common in mainland SE Asia, but in Sumatra about half of animals are pale. **Voice** Loud call of female a series of high-pitched rising and falling notes, similar to that of White-handed Gibbon, *H. lar*, but shorter in duration. Both sexes give a distinctive "whoo-aa" call, quite distinct from "hoo" calls given by *H. lar*. **Similar species** White-handed Gibbon, *H. lar*, has pale hands and feet, complete white facial ring. Limited hybridization with *H. lar* has been reported from S Thailand, where the ranges meet for the two species.

Ecology and habitat Arboreal. Usually found in small groups of one adult male, one adult female and one to three young. Each group defends a territory of 20–30 hectares. Diet consists of ripe fleshy fruits, young leaves and small insects. Normally found only in tall dipterocarp forests. Peak calling activity is soon after dawn.

Distribution and status SE Asia: extreme S Thailand and N Peninsular Malaysia; range

separates Peninsular Malaysian *H. lar* from *H. lar* in Thailand. Also S Sumatra. *H. albibarbis* in S Borneo is sometimes considered part of this species. Vulnerable. Substantial habitat has been lost recently, especially in Sumatra. Status of remaining populations uncertain.

PILEATED GIBBON

Hylobates pileatus PLATE 30

Measurements HB 470–600. Wt 4–7kg

Identification Sexually dimorphic in adults. Adult males (age 3–4 years or older) are all black except white feet and hands; thick white eyebrow band that continues in a partial ring around the eyes; crown hair flattened towards back of head, with whitish hairs over ears; white genital area. Females are grey or greyish-buff, with dark patch on belly and dark crown, white eyebrows and partial rings around eyes. Young are greyish-white, acquiring black patches on chest and top of head as they mature. **Voice** Loud call involves series of "hoo-ha" notes from male, and series of rising hoots from female that accelerates into a long bubbling trill; female great call averages 60–80 notes over 15–25 seconds. **Similar species** White-handed Gibbon, *H. lar*, dark phase has complete white facial ring and lacks pale tufts over ears; pale phase does not have dark patches on underparts and head; great call of female lacks accelerating trill. Limited hybridization between *H. lar* and *H. pileatus* has been reported in areas of overlap in SE Thailand.

Ecology and habitat Arboreal, found principally in tall forests. Occurs in small family groups. Calling typically starts soon after daybreak, but may continue to late morning. Diet consists mainly of fruits, especially figs, and also young leaves and shoots, with some insects.

Distribution and status SE Asia: SE Thailand, SW Laos and Cambodia W of Mekong. Vulnerable. Although population appears to be stable in Thailand, range is very restricted and population is declining in Cambodia.

HOOLOCK GIBBON
Hoolock hoolock PLATE 31

Measurements HB 450–650. Wt 6–9kg

Identification Adult male largely black with bushy white eyebrows, sometimes with a tuft of white on chin; adult female buffy-brown to brown, middle of underparts and cheeks darker, often blackish; white face-ring and white streak from cheeks up under eyes and across top of nose. Newborn young are white, but turn all black by end of first year. In populations W of Chindwin River in Myanmar (*H. h. hoolock*) males have eyebrows joined together and black underparts; E of Chindwin River (*H. h. leucomedys*, sometimes considered a separate species) eyebrows are separated, male tends to have pale brownish on underparts; intermediates occur in headwaters of Chindwin. Small laryngeal sac is present in both sexes. **Voice** Male and female vocalizations similar, consisting of mixture of two-part notes ("ow-wa"), simple hoots and growls; these are interspersed in an accelerating duet during the great call. **Taxonomic note** Genus formerly called *Bunopithecus*. **Similar species** White-handed Gibbon, *Hylobates lar*, has white hands, call lacks "ow-wa".

Ecology and habitat Arboreal and diurnal, being most active from dawn until middle of afternoon. Found mainly in primary evergreen and some semi-evergreen forests. Occurs in small family groups of 3 to 6 individuals. Feeds mainly on fruits as well as leaves and buds, with a very small amount of animal matter such as insects. Male song may begin before dawn, with male-female duets mainly one to three hours after dawn.

Distribution and status SE Asia: N Myanmar. Also NE India (Assam) and SW China (SW Yunnan). Endangered. Major population declines due to ongoing loss of habitat, especially in India, as well as hunting.

Genus *Nomascus*, Crested Gibbons These gibbons have tufts of hair on the top of their heads, forming a crest, and patches of bushy hair on their cheeks that are contrastingly pale in some species. Juveniles of most species go through a range of colour changes, starting all buffy with a dark face, then progressing to dark body with pale head that eventually turns black. Although some species can be difficult to tell apart, there is limited overlap in range among the species.

BLACK CRESTED GIBBON
Nomascus concolor PLATE 31

Measurements HB ~500. Wt 6–9kg

Identification Male completely black, with small throat sac visible only during loud vocalizations. Female greyish-brown with extensive black on underside, as well as dark streak on crown and inside of limbs. Juvenile completely black. Both sexes have hairs on crown of head raised in a tuft. **Voice** Males produce a low boom (during inflation of throat sac), short staccato single notes, and "whoops" that rise, or fall then rise rapidly in frequency; females produce only the last of these in their great call. **Similar species** Hainan Crested Gibbon, *N. hainanus*, male is very similar, but female lacks black on underparts; other *Nomascus* gibbons have pale cheeks in males; Hoolock Gibbon, *Hoolock hoolock*, male has white eyebrows.

Ecology and habitat Arboreal and diurnal. Largely restricted to tall forests in subtropical and montane forests. Feeds on fruits, leaf-buds and shoots.

Distribution and status SE Asia: restricted areas in parts of N Laos and N Vietnam, N of about 20°N. Also S Yunnan (China). Critically Endangered. Formerly widespread in much of S China and N Indochina, but global population now estimated at fewer than 2,000 animals, restricted to a few isolated areas with no more than a few hundred in each of Laos and Vietnam. Several known populations have disappeared recently. Threats include loss of habitat, illegal hunting and trapping.

BUFF-CHEEKED GIBBON
Nomascus gabriellae PLATE 31

Measurements HB ~500. Wt 6–10kg

Identification Male black with pale reddish

or reddish-yellow patches on cheeks rounded at top, reaching less than halfway up ears; hairs on top of head raised into a crest; chest brownish, contrasting with rest of body. Female orange-brown, rarely with any white on face, dark triangular patch on crown, no dark on belly. Hairs on cheeks appear brushed sideways in both sexes. **Voice** Male produces short hoots as well as descending long hoots that each end in a sharp upwards note; female produces long, upwardly modulated calls that increase in pitch and frequency during the great call. **Similar species** Southern White-cheeked Gibbon, *N. siki*, has paler cheeks and darker chest in males; more distinct white face-ring in females. **Ecology and habitat** Arboreal and diurnal. Found in tall evergreen and semi-evergreen forest. Feeds mainly on fruits. Group size typically 3–5 individuals. **Distribution and status** SE Asia: E Cambodia, S Laos, S Vietnam from Mekong delta N to about 15°30'N. Endangered. Although more common than other crested gibbons (*Nomascus* spp.), it has disappeared from many suitable areas, and habitat has been greatly reduced in parts of range, especially in Vietnam. Threats include loss of habitat, illegal hunting and trapping for food and pet trade.

NORTHERN WHITE-CHEEKED GIBBON
Nomascus leucogenys PLATE 31
Measurements HB ~500. Wt 6–10kg
Identification Male largely black, with some silvery hairs, except for white or very pale yellow cheek-tufts that are pointed at top, reaching level of top of ears but not touching corners of mouth; female creamy-orange or buffy with no dark hairs on underparts; dark brown elongate patch on crown, white hairs around face, forming a distinct face-ring. **Voice** Similar to that of Black-crested Gibbon, *N. concolor*: the male has a mixture of low boom, short hoots and strongly frequency-modulated whoops, while the female has a series of rising whoops that

increase in pitch and frequency during the great call, typically with more notes than *N. concolor*. **Similar species** Buff-cheeked Gibbon, *N. gabriellae*, male has more reddish cheeks with hairs that stick out to side, brownish patch on chest; female has indistinct buff face-ring. **Ecology and habitat** Arboreal and diurnal. Largely restricted to tall forests. **Distribution and status** SE Asia: Laos and Vietnam, E to Black River, N of about 19°N. Also adjacent extreme S China (SW Yunnan), although Chinese population may now be extinct. Critically Endangered. Remaining populations highly fragmented and greatly reduced due to loss of habitat, illegal hunting and trapping.

SOUTHERN WHITE-CHEEKED GIBBON
Nomascus siki PLATE 31
Measurements HB ~500. Wt 6–10kg
Identification Males and juveniles black except for white cheek whiskers; cheek patches reach only halfway up ears with a pointed upper end, but extend at bottom to margin of upper lips and onto sides of chin. Female creamy-orange with dark triangular patch on crown, white ring around face. **Voice** Similar to that of Northern White-cheeked Gibbon, *N. leuocogenys*, but typically with fewer notes in great call. **Similar species** Northern White-cheeked Gibbon, *N. leucogenys*, is very similar, but with longer hair, and male has white cheek patches higher on face; Buff-cheeked Gibbon, *N. gabriellae*, male has orange or yellow cheeks with pale patch on chest, female lacks white ring around face. **Ecology and habitat** Arboreal and diurnal. Largely restricted to tall forests. **Distribution and status** SE Asia: C Vietnam and Laos between 15°45' and 20°N. Endangered. Although moderate populations continue to persist, many families occur in forest patches too small to ensure long-term persistence, and species is still threatened by ongoing loss of forest, illegal hunting and trapping.

HAINAN CRESTED GIBBON
Nomascus hainanus NOT ILLUSTRATED
Measurements HB ~500. Wt 6–10kg
Identification Adult male all black with relatively long hair; adult female light brownish-grey to brownish-yellow, with no black on underparts, indistinct elongate oval dark patch on crown. **Voice** Male produces short staccato notes, and sharply rising whoops; female great call is strongly vibrato, like a trill, increasing in pitch and accelerating to end. **Taxonomic note** Sometimes known as *N. nasutus*. **Similar species** Black-crested Gibbon, *N. concolor*, is very similar, but female has dark patches on underparts; other *Nomascus* gibbons have pale cheeks on males.
Ecology and habitat Arboreal and diurnal. Largely restricted to tall, tropical valley and montane rainforests.
Distribution and status SE Asia: Cao Bang province in Vietnam, NE of Red River. Also Hainan Island in China. Critically Endangered. Population on Hainan estimated at ~2,000 individuals in 1950s had declined to fewer than 20 animals by 1993, and has not recovered despite habitat protection. Status of Vietnam population, which may or may not be same species, uncertain, but numbers are very low.

Order CARNIVORA
Dogs, bears, weasels, martens, otters, civets, mongooses and cats

The carnivores are a diverse group of mammals that have largely evolved, as their name implies, with adaptations for hunting and killing vertebrate prey, ranging from fish in the case of otters, to large mammals in the case of tigers and leopards. However, many species also eat plant food, especially fruits, and some of the civets are largely frugivorous. There is considerable variation among families in the skull and form of dentition, as might be expected given this variety of diets.

Family *CANIDAE* DOGS
The skull of a dog has a relatively elongate muzzle (Fig. 49), with dentition adapted for eating meat. The dental formula is 3/3 1/1 4/4 2/2. The canine is relatively large and pointed; there are usually 3 upper and lower incisors, with a gap (diastema) between the incisors and the upper canine, into which the lower canine fits when the mouth is closed. The last upper premolar and first lower molar are formed into carnassials – elongated sharpened teeth used for tearing flesh. There are only 2 upper molars, the last relatively small.

Apart from the Domestic Dog, *Canis familiaris*, which occurs throughout the region, there are four species of wild dog currently known to occur in South-East Asia. Each of these has a distinctive shape and coloration, and is fairly easily separated from others if seen well. However, care must be taken not to confuse them with free-ranging Domestic Dogs, which can show a wide variety of shapes and colour patterns.

The footprints of dogs have a small pad on the sole and four large pads on the toes with broad, blunt nails (Fig. 50); those of wild dogs are difficult to distinguish from those of Domestic Dogs.

GOLDEN JACKAL
Canis aureus PLATE 32
Measurements HB 600–800, T 200–250. Wt 7–10kg
Identification Generally greyish-brown to golden-brown, with black-tipped hairs on shoulders and back tending to form a saddle-like pattern. Ears broadly pointed, tail moderately bushy and dark at tip. **Voice** A series of ascending whines, followed by several quick yelps. **Similar species** Dhole, *Cuon alpinus*, is larger and heavier, more reddish-brown without back pattern, all dark tail; free-ranging Domestic Dogs, *Canis*

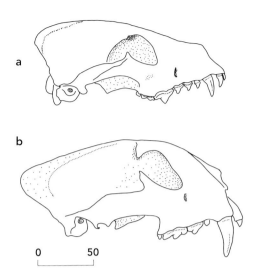

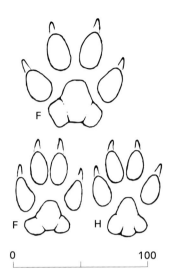

Fig. 49 *Skulls of two large carnivores, a dog and a cat:* Cuon alpinus *(a) and* Panthera pardus *(b).*

Fig. 50 *Footprints of* Cuon alpinus *in soft soil (top) and on firm soil (bottom).*

familiaris rarely have black saddle pattern.

Ecology and habitat Largely found in drier, open areas. Forms large groups in India, but in Thailand usually seen singly or in pairs. Groups may call at night, especially just after dusk and before dawn.

Distribution and status SE Asia: Myanmar, Thailand, Laos, Vietnam and Cambodia. Also from N Africa, S Europe through to India. Not currently at risk. Generally tolerant of human disturbance, but has declined in some areas owing to excessive trapping.

RED FOX
Vulpes vulpes PLATE 32
Measurements HB 550–700, T 350–450. Wt 3.5–5.5kg

Identification Relatively slender canid with long tail, pointed face and pointed ears. Usual colour, upperparts uniformly reddish-brown; paler underneath; bushy, reddish tail, sometimes with white tip, though usually all dark in Asian populations; black behind ears. Some animals are all dark brown. **Voice** A high-pitched bark and various other calls. **Similar species** Dhole, *Cuon alpinus*, is considerably heavier, with a thicker muzzle, dark tail and rounded ears with white centres; Golden Jackal, *Canis aureus*, is greyish-

brown and has a shorter tail.

Ecology and habitat No information from region, but elsewhere found in a wide variety of habitats from forests to open areas that have been heavily disturbed by humans. Feeds on small mammals, birds, frogs, insects and sometimes fruits.

Distribution and status SE Asia: N Vietnam. Also throughout much of northern hemisphere, including Europe through Asia to Himalayas, N India and parts of China, as well as North America. Globally not at risk. In region, poorly known; may only be an irregular visitor from China.

RACCOON DOG
Nyctereutes procyonoides PLATE 32
Measurements HB 500–680, T 130–250. Wt 4–6kg

Identification Generally yellowish-brown, with black tips on shoulders, back and tail. Black "mask" on face that goes around eyes and under chin. **Similar species** Some civets also have dark patterns on face, but are a different shape with a much longer tail.

Ecology and habitat Mainly in forested areas. Largely solitary, most active at night. In northern parts of range, species hibernates after increasing weight nearly 50 per cent, but presumably not farther south, although

278

little is known of the species in SE Asia. Feeds on small animals, including rodents, frogs, fish, crabs and insects, as well as fruits. **Distribution and status** SE Asia: N Vietnam. Also S Siberia through E China and Japan, and widely introduced in western Russia and eastern Europe. Globally not at risk, but has become very rare in region, probably owing to loss of forest and excessive trapping.

DHOLE
Cuon alpinus PLATE 32
Measurements HB 800–1,050, T 300–450, SH 420–550. Wt male 15–21kg, female 10–17kg
Identification Largest and heaviest wild dog in region. Body reddish-brown, often paler underneath. Tail long and bushy, largely black or very dark. Ears rounded with conspicuous long, white hairs inside. **Voice** Relatively quiet, but occasional yaps or whistling sounds. **Similar species** Domestic Dogs, *Canis familiaris*, are sometimes a similar reddish colour, but if so they lack the long, bushy black tail and rounded ears with white centres. Golden Jackal, *Canis aureus*, is smaller, more greyish-brown, with dark saddle-like pattern on back.
Ecology and habitat Found in a wide variety of forested areas, including evergreen forest, montane forests, and semi-open forest. Avoids contact with humans. Hunts in packs,

usually at night. Preys on a variety of animals, including pigs and deer.
Distribution and status SE Asia: Myanmar, Thailand, Laos, Vietnam, Cambodia and Peninsular Malaysia. Also S Siberia to India, Sumatra and Java. Near Threatened. In many areas has declined owing to hunting and trapping, as well as to loss of habitat.

DOMESTIC DOG
Canis familiaris NOT ILLUSTRATED
Measurements HB about 800–1,000, T about 300–350
Identification Domestic dogs have been bred into a tremendous diversity of shapes and sizes, ranging from miniature "toy" forms to extremely large forms. Free-ranging dogs may be encountered in wild areas in almost any part of the region. Some of these are similar in shape to some of the wild dogs; many are dull orange-brown although black or pied forms are often encountered. Nevertheless, they rarely have the exact coloration and shape of the wild forms, and are usually less shy.
Ecology and habitat Usually associated with humans. Feral (free-ranging) dogs occasionally encountered far from human settlements, often in poor condition.
Distribution and status SE Asia: may be found throughout region, especially in areas where there are human settlements.

Family *URSIDAE* BEARS
Bears are large, powerfully built, omnivorous mammals with a short tail and good sense of smell, but poor sight and hearing. Two species of bear occur in the region, both of them mainly black apart from pale markings on the chest. The species can be distinguished by fur texture and length, head and ear shapes, and size. Bears, although mainly feeding on fruit and plant material, insects or smaller animals, are potentially dangerous to humans, owing to the unpredictability of their behaviour. The Red Panda, *Ailurus fulgens*, has sometimes been placed in the bear family, but is here considered to be in its own family, the Ailuridae.

Bear footprints have an elongate sole, slightly triangular with five toe prints all similar in size, and very long claw marks, longest on the front feet (Fig. 51). The prints of the Asian Black Bear, *Ursus thibetanus*, are larger than those of the Sun Bear, *Helarctos malayanus*.

SUN BEAR
Helarctos malayanus PLATE 33
Measurements HB 1.1–1.4m, T 30–70. Wt 27–63kg

Identification Body entirely black, except for grey muzzle and a white or yellowish V- or C-shaped mark on the upper chest. Chest mark normally prominent but occasionally

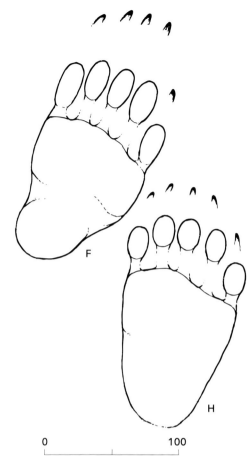

Fig. 51 *Prints of left front (F) and hind (H) feet of Helarctos malayanus.*

very faint. Ears short and rounded. Fur short and smooth. Has distinct posture when walking, with head held very low. Signs are more often seen than the bear itself: prominent claw marks gouged into a tree trunk where it has climbed the tree, or remains of bee or termite nests ripped open in standing or fallen trees. The claw marks are much more conspicuous than the faint marks of other carnivores or monitor lizards. **Voice** Occasionally utters hoarse grunts or loud roars; rarely short barks like that of a muntjac, *Muntiacus* spp. **Similar species** Asian Black Bear, *Ursus thibetanus*, is much heavier, with long shaggy fur, large ears; Binturong, *Arctictis binturong*, is much smaller, with a prominent long bushy tail.

Ecology and habitat Active periodically during day and night, on the ground and in tall trees. Builds nests of small branches in tall trees for sleeping. Diet includes bees' nests, termites, small animals, fruits and the hearts of coconut palms. Occurs in extensive areas of forest, but sometimes enters gardens or oil-palm plantations.

Distribution and status SE Asia: Myanmar, Thailand, Laos, Cambodia, Vietnam and Peninsular Malaysia. Also Sumatra and Borneo. Endangered due to illegal hunting and trapping, and to loss of natural habitat.

ASIAN BLACK BEAR
Ursus thibetanus PLATE 33
Measurements HB 1.2–1.5m, T 65–100, HF 175–195, E 120–180. Wt up to 100kg or more
Identification A large bear, mainly black apart from a white 'V' on the chest and a pale muzzle. Pale marks on muzzle rarely extend as far back as eyes. Has large erect ears and long shaggy hair. Signs include deep claw marks on trees. **Similar species** Sun Bear, *Helarctos malayanus*, is about half the body weight, has short fur, short rounded ears that barely extend above head in profile, more stooped posture and more extensive pale area on muzzle.

Ecology and habitat Generally solitary, except in breeding season. Mainly in forested areas, both evergreen and deciduous. Sometimes enters cultivated areas near forest. In southern part of range, found only in hill forest. Usually rests during day in hollow trees, caves or rock crevices, emerging in the evening to feed, but sometimes active during day. Feeds mainly on fruits, berries, beehives, invertebrates and small vertebrates such as amphibians and rodents, but sometimes hunts larger mammals as well.

Distribution and status SE Asia: Myanmar, Thailand, Laos, Cambodia and Vietnam. Also Pakistan, India, Nepal, China, Siberia and Japan. Vulnerable; declining due to illegal hunting and trapping, especially for alleged medicinal values.

Family *AILURIDAE* RED PANDAS

Red Pandas have sometimes been placed in the same family as bears, along with the Giant Panda. Other researchers have considered them part of the Procyonidae or Raccoon family. They are currently considered to belong in their own family. They are readily distinguished by colour and shape from all other animals in the region.

RED PANDA

Ailurus fulgens PLATE 33

Measurements HB 510–630, T 280–480. Wt 3–6kg

Identification Body fur long and soft, upperparts reddish, darkest in middle of back; underparts paler. Tail long and bushy, inconspicuously ringed. Head pale, with white rims to ears, dark marks under eyes. **Voice** Includes short whistles and squeaking notes. **Similar species** No other mammal in region has this combination of colour and shape, with long bushy tail and black marks under the eyes.

Ecology and habitat Found mainly in montane forests at 1,800–4,000m, often in bamboo thickets. Mainly nocturnal, sleeping curled on a branch during the day. Climbs well, but also feeds on the ground on bamboo shoots, grasses, roots, fruits, acorns and sometimes insects, eggs and small vertebrates. In winter is largely dependent on bamboo leaves for food. May be solitary, in pairs or in small family groups.

Distribution and status SE Asia: N Myanmar. Also Nepal, India, Bhutan and S China. Vulnerable. Major threats include loss of habitat, fragmentation of remaining habitat leading to isolation of populations, and illegal hunting and trapping.

Family *MUSTELIDAE* MARTENS, WEASELS, BADGERS AND OTTERS

The mustelids are a rather diverse group and are usually divided into subfamilies. The subfamily Mustelinae includes martens and weasels, both slender, agile mammals adapted to hunting small vertebrate animals, as well as invertebrates. Martens tend to be more arboreal than weasels. The subfamily Melinae (which is sometimes combined with the Mustelinae) includes the ferret-badgers and Hog Badger. The ferret-badgers are much smaller than the Hog Badger with distinctive patterns as a genus, but the species are hard to tell apart unless the animal is captured and the teeth can be examined. The subfamily Lutrinae includes the otters, which can be distinguished by their semi-aquatic existence, webbed or partially webbed feet, and broad muzzle. The different species of large otter are difficult to distinguish in the field unless seen well.

Mustelids appear to be closely related to the Viverridae, or civet family, but can usually be distinguished by having 34 to 38 teeth, whereas all viverrids (except the linsangs, *Prionodon* spp.) have a total of 40 teeth. Mustelids also tend to have stockier limbs and broader feet, and are generally more strictly carnivorous.

Footprints vary considerably within the family, though all species show five toe prints, unlike dogs or cats, which show only four. The sole pad has a relatively complex pattern of lobes (Fig. 52). Hog Badger prints have distinctive long claw marks (Fig. 52d), while otter prints usually show distinct webbing between the toes (Figs 52f,g,h) and sometimes do not show claw marks.

STONE MARTEN

Martes foina PLATE 34

Measurements HB 400–540, T 220–300 (about 55–60% of HB). Wt 1.1–2.3kg

Identification Colour mostly brown, frequently with reddish, yellowish or grey tinge; underside slightly paler than upperparts. Throat white or yellowish with variable brown patches, sometimes largely brown. During moult, fur can have pale creamy-white patches. **Similar species** Yellow-throated Marten, *M. flavigula*, has longer tail, yellow throat

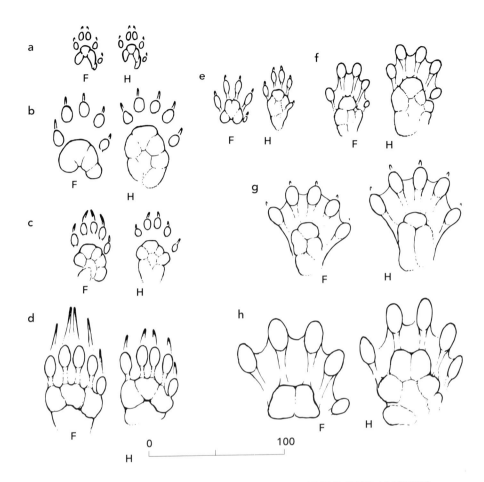

a

F   H

b

F

H

c

F   H

d

F

H

e

F   H

f

F   H

g

F   H

h

F

H

0   100

Fig. 52 *Prints of left front (F) and hind (H) feet of selected* Mustelidae *and* Herpestidae: Mustela nudipes *(a),* Martes flavigula *(b),* Melogale *sp. (c),* Arctonyx collaris *(d),* Herpestes javanicus *(e),* Aonyx cinerea *(f),* Lutra lutra *(g) and* Lutrogale perspicillata.

with dark head and/or sides of throat; weasels, *Mustela* spp. are much smaller with more slender body.

Ecology and habitat In region, usually at high altitudes, 1,300m up to over 3,000m. Inhabits conifer forests or open rocky areas.

Distribution and status SE Asia: N Myanmar. Also Europe through to China, Himalayas. Not currently at risk. Only marginally occurs in region where status uncertain, but populations apparently stable elsewhere.

YELLOW-THROATED MARTEN

Martes flavigula PLATE 34

Measurements HB 450–650, T 370–450, HF 90–110, E 28–40. Wt 1.3–3.0kg

Identification Colour pattern varies geographically. Back colour varies from medium brown to pale yellowish-brown; lower back, hind legs, lower half of front legs and tail contrastingly darker, varying from dark brown to black; conspicuous black stripe on side of neck behind ear; top of head varies from black, continuous with neck stripe, to dark brown. Chin, throat and chest yellowish, whitish or buff, contrasting with slightly darker lower belly. In the field, the long, slender body, long tail and lithe, bounding motion are distinctive. Tail may be held down, up with the tip drooping or almost horizontal (if moving quickly). **Voice** A series of soft, rapid "chuk"s. **Similar species** Stone Marten, *M.*

foina, lacks dark border to throat and has shorter tail; weasels, *Mustela* spp. with white throats have shorter tails and lack the contrasting black or dark brown pattern on the neck, lower legs and tail; mongooses have a more pointed muzzle, tend to hold head and tail down while walking, and walk quickly but rarely bound; civets are normally active only at night and have different colour patterns.

Ecology and habitat Active mainly during the day, but sometimes at night. Agile, moving fairly quickly on the ground or in the tree canopy. Diet includes a wide range of small vertebrates and invertebrates, bees' nests and nectar. Rests in tree holes and on large branches. Usually alone or in pairs, but sometimes in family groups. Occurs in a wide variety of forest types, both natural and disturbed. Often enters plantations and gardens in search of food.

Distribution and status SE Asia: Myanmar, Thailand, Laos, Vietnam, Cambodia and Peninsular Malaysia. Also Pakistan, Nepal, India, China, Russia, Sumatra, Java and Borneo. Not currently at risk.

MALAY WEASEL
Mustela nudipes PLATE 35
Measurements HB 300–360, T 220–260, HF 49–55, E 23–25. Wt 1kg
Identification Body colour typically orange to golden-brown, but sometimes more greyish-brown. Basal half of tail same colour as back, but distal half is typically all white, though sometimes only the extreme tip. Head white to behind ears. Tail bushy. **Similar species** Siberian Weasel, *M. sibirica*, has white limited to front of muzzle, usually has dark mask around eyes, and does not overlap in range; some large squirrels are similar in size and proportions, but have differently shaped heads, and none has same colour pattern of pale head and tail tip with orange or reddish body.
Ecology and habitat Mainly terrestrial. Apparently active both day and night. Sleeps in holes in ground. Diet includes small animals. Recorded in lowland and hill rainforests as well as disturbed areas. Poorly

known, but appears to be tolerant of a range of habitats.
Distribution and status SE Asia: peninsular Thailand and Malaysia. Also Sumatra and Borneo. It is rarely encountered, but apparently not currently at risk. Probably adversely affected by clearing and conversion of forests.

SIBERIAN WEASEL
Mustela sibirica PLATE 35
Measurements Male: HB 280–390, T 150–210, HF 40–50, Wt 650–820g. Female: HB 250–305, T 130–165, HF 35–45. Wt 350–450g
Identification Colour of body varies from golden-brown and dark chocolate to reddish, only slightly paler underneath. Has pale patch on front of muzzle and often upper throat, usually with dark mask around and in front of eyes. Tail medium-long and bushy, same colour as back. **Similar species** Yellow-bellied Weasel, *M. kathiah*, is pale yellow underneath and lacks mask; Malay Weasel, *M. nudipes*, has white head extending to behind ears.
Ecology and habitat Found in a variety of habitats from dense forest to dry areas and villages, mainly at 1,500–5,000m. Eats small animals including rats, and has been known to attack domestic fowl.
Distribution and status SE Asia: N Myanmar, N Thailand, Laos; probably N Vietnam. Also Himalayas, China, Siberia, Taiwan and Japan. Status poorly known, but has declined recently in parts of China.

LEAST WEASEL
Mustela nivalis PLATE 35
Measurements HB 200, T 90 (45% of HB)
Identification Smallest weasel in region, with brown upperparts, white underparts, relatively short tail. **Taxonomic notes** SE Asian form, *M. n. tonkinensis*, is larger, with longer tail than most populations of *M. nivalis*, and may represent a distinct species, but is poorly known. **Similar species** Other weasels in region are larger, with longer tails.
Ecology and habitat Unknown in region.

Elsewhere, found in a variety of open and disturbed habitats.

Distribution and status SE Asia: N Vietnam. Also throughout N parts of Europe, Asia and North America, with isolated populations at high altitudes in SW China (Sichuan), if they are the same species. Status in region uncertain: *M. n. tonkinensis*, is known from only one specimen from Chapa, Tonkin, Vietnam.

YELLOW-BELLIED WEASEL
Mustela kathiah PLATE 35
Measurements HB 200–290, T 130–180 (60–70% of HB)

Identification Upperparts dark chocolate-brown sometimes with reddish tinge; underparts yellow or light orange-brown with whitish on chin and upper lip; tail moderately long and bushy, same colour as upperparts. **Similar species** Siberian Weasel, *M. sibirica*, has dark underparts nearly same colour as upperparts, except for pale throat and muzzle.

Ecology and habitat Has been reported from forested areas 1,000m or higher including above tree line. May be tolerant of disturbed habitats. Feeds on birds, rodents and other small mammals.

Distribution and status SE Asia: N. Myanmar, Laos and Vietnam. Also Nepal, N India (Assam) and S China. Status poorly known, with relatively few species records in region.

STRIPE-BACKED WEASEL
Mustela strigidorsa PLATE 35
Measurements HB 275–325, T 145–205 (~60% of HB), HF 47–54, E 20–23

Identification Dark chocolate-brown to reddish-brown above and below, including tail, except for a thin white or buff stripe down the back, from the top of the head to the base of the tail, and a yellowish-white patch on the lower cheeks, chin and upper throat, extending into a buff or cream stripe down the centre of the belly. Tail medium-long and bushy. **Similar species** No other species of similar size and shape has a single pale

stripe down the middle of the back; Javan Mongoose, *Herpestes javanica*, lacks stripe and differs in shape.

Ecology and habitat Primarily recorded from evergreen forest in hills and mountains, but also some records in disturbed areas and scrub. Has been observed foraging on ground, where it presumably catches a range of small animals

Distribution and status SE Asia: Myanmar, Thailand, Laos and Vietnam. Also Nepal, NE India (Assam) and S China. Status poorly known, with relatively few species records in region.

LARGE-TOOTHED FERRET-BADGER
Melogale personata PLATE 34
Measurements HB 330–390, T 145–210, HF 55–70. Wt 1–3kg

Identification Head has distinct pattern of black (or dark brown) and white; pattern varies among individuals. Body brownish to greyish, paler underneath, sometimes with orange tinge. Sides of body heavily frosted white, contrasting slightly with darker back. White stripe on back of neck extending at least to middle of back, and often as far as rump or tail; bushy tail pale, usually white on distal half. Large, massive teeth, especially fourth premolar, which is over one-third length of all cheek teeth (Fig. 53b). **Similar species** Small-toothed Ferret-badger, *M. moschata*, tends to have shorter, interrupted white back streak, white on tail restricted to tip, more black on face; reliably identified only by much smaller teeth (Fig. 53a).

Ecology and habitat Nocturnal and largely terrestrial, digging burrows with its strong claws, but also sometimes climbs trees. Diet mainly invertebrate prey such as large insects, snails, earthworms. Found in forested areas as well as grasslands and rice fields.

Distribution and status SE Asia: Myanmar, Thailand, Laos, Cambodia and Vietnam. Also Nepal and India (Assam). Status uncertain, Poorly known, especially as many field records have not been distinguished from *M. moschata*.

SMALL-TOOTHED FERRET-BADGER
Melogale moschata PLATE 34
Measurements HB 330–380, T 140–160
(40–45% of HB)

Identification Distinct black-and-white head pattern, generally with more black than *M. personata* but quite variable. Body colour greyish to light brown, with flanks similar colour to back, belly whitish. White stripe on top of head narrow and incomplete, rarely extending much past shoulders. Tail proportionately shorter than that of Large-toothed Ferret-badger, *M. personata*, darker with only tip white. Teeth relatively small with distinct gaps between premolars (Fig. 53a).
Similar species Large-toothed Ferret-badger, *M. personata*, has longer white stripe on back, more white on tail, large teeth; Masked Palm Civet, *Paguma larvata*, also has black-and-white face pattern, but is much larger, more slender, with much longer tail.
Ecology and habitat Nocturnal and largely terrestrial, though can climb trees. Ecological differences from *M. personata* not well understood.
Distribution and status SE Asia: N Myanmar, Laos and Vietnam. Also E India (Assam), C and SE China, Hainan and Taiwan. Status uncertain, but apparently not currently at risk.

HOG BADGER
Arctonyx collaris PLATE 34
Measurements HB 550–700, T 120–170, HF 115–135. Wt 7–14kg

Identification A large badger with a long, pig-like snout, short tail, dark stripes on head. Overall body colour varies from greyish to brown. Stripes on head vary from dark brown to black, and vary in extent, with lower dark stripe sometimes reduced. **Similar species** Ferret-badgers, *Melogale* spp., are much smaller, with longer tails.
Ecology and habitat Nocturnal and terrestrial, sleeping during day in burrows. A powerful digger, feeding on tubers and roots as well as invertebrates such as worms, insects and other small animals. Usually in forests as well as plantations near forests. Mainly in

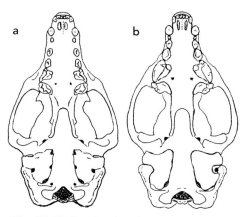

Fig. 53 *Skulls of* Melogale moschata *(a) and* M. personata *(b) showing difference in relative and absolute size of teeth.*

hills, but also in lowlands in Cambodia.
Distribution and status SE Asia: Myanmar, Thailand, Laos, Vietnam and Cambodia. Also NE India, China and Sumatra. Near Threatened. Populations have declined due to hunting and loss of habitat.

EURASIAN OTTER
Lutra lutra PLATE 36
Measurements HB 550–720, T 375–480, HF 100–130

Identification Upperparts rather dark brown, with paler chin and upper throat. Underparts markedly paler. Fur dense, consisting of short hairs and longer paler guard hairs, producing a somewhat grizzled appearance. Rhinarium (tip of nose) hairless; edge of fur and nose forms 'W'-shape. End of tail circular in cross-section. SE Asian form, *L. lutra barang*, is smaller than races found in Europe. **Similar species** Hairy-nosed Otter, *L. sumatrana*, and Smooth Otter, *Lutrogale perspicillata*, generally paler, without frosted appearance, and live primarily in coastal and flatland habitats; Oriental Small-clawed Otter, *Aonyx cinerea*, is substantially smaller.
Ecology and habitat Diet includes fish, other small vertebrates and crustaceans. Most SE Asian records are from hill or mountainous areas in streams and lakes.
Distribution and status SE Asia: Myanmar, Thailand, Laos and Vietnam. Also Europe,

North Africa, through much of N Asia, India, Sri Lanka, China, Taiwan, Japan, Sumatra, and possibly Borneo. Poorly known in region; although stable in other parts of range, has probably declined considerably in region owing to loss of habitat, including damming of rivers, as well as hunting.

HAIRY-NOSED OTTER
Lutra sumatrana PLATE 36
Measurements HB 500–800, T 370–500, HF 105–130
Identification Entirely brown, except lips, chin and upper throat, which are whitish. Fur rather rough but short. Rhinarium covered in hair. Tail flattened, oval in cross section. Feet fully webbed between the digits. Claws prominent. Penis of adult male not visible externally. Skull flatter than that of Smooth Otter, *Lutrogale perspicillata*, (Fig. 54c).
Voice Contact call between otters a single-syllabic chirp; adult females call to cubs with a staccato chatter. **Similar species** Eurasian Otter, *L. lutra*, has long, pale guard hairs on a dark coat, underparts paler than upperparts; Smooth Otter, *Lutrogale perspicillata*, can be hard to distinguish in field, but has smoother coat, paler underparts, and hairless rhinarium.
Ecology and habitat Occurs in coastal areas and on larger inland rivers, solitary or in groups of up to four. Diet includes fish. Pairing of male and female may be limited to the breeding period.
Distribution and status SE Asia: Myanmar, S Thailand, Cambodia, S Vietnam and Peninsular Malaysia. Also Sumatra and Borneo. Critically Endangered: only a few remaining viable populations, widely scattered in region. Species is threatened by loss of lowland wetland habitats, hunting for fur and meat, and accidental killing during fishing.

SMOOTH OTTER
Lutrogale perspicillata PLATE 36
Measurements HB 650–750, T 400–450, HF 100–140
Identification Upperparts are mid-brown, underparts distinctly paler, buffy. Throat and

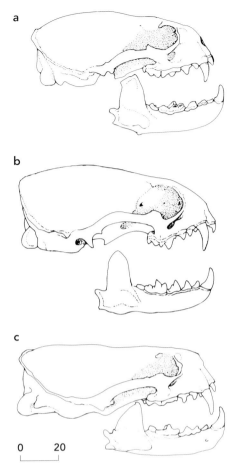

Fig. 54 *Skulls of* Aonyx cinerea *(a),* Lutrogale perspicillata *(b) and* Lutra sumatrana *(c).*

sides of neck cream-coloured. Fur short, smooth and sleek. Rhinarium hairless; edge of fur and nose forms straight line. Tail flattened on underside, rounded on top. Feet webbed only up to last joint on digits. Claws prominent. Penis of adult male protrudes beyond body wall. Dorsal edge of skull slightly rounded in profile (Fig. 54b). **Voice** Contact call "wiuk". **Similar species** Hairy-nosed Otter, *Lutra sumatrana*, has belly same colour as back, rhinarium covered with hair, more fully webbed feet; Eurasian Otter, *Lutra lutra*, has long, pale guard hairs on a dark coat, tail rounded in cross section.
Ecology and habitat Lives on coast or inland in extensive flatlands, including lakes,

rivers and streams. Several individuals may cooperate in fishing. Sometimes forages on dry land.

Distribution and status SE Asia: Myanmar, Thailand, Laos, Vietnam, Cambodia and Peninsular Malaysia. Also Afghanistan, Bangladesh, India, S China, Sumatra, Java and Borneo. Vulnerable. Population declining owing to loss and degradation of lowland wetland habitats, as well as hunting.

ORIENTAL SMALL-CLAWED OTTER

Aonyx cinerea PLATE 36
Measurements HB 360–550, T 225–350, HF 85–110
Identification Upperparts dark brown or greyish-brown; underparts slightly paler. Chin, throat, cheeks and sides of neck buffy. Digits only partially webbed. Claws short, not extending beyond the end of the digits. **Voice** Contact call is "wiuk"; various other calls are also made. **Similar species** Other otters in region are substantially larger and have prominent claws.

Ecology and habitat Diurnal. Diet includes crabs, other crustaceans and molluscs, as well as some fish. Occurs in many habitats where there is permanent water and some tree cover, from the coast to inland hill forest, including seacoast, large rivers, small hill streams, ponds and lakes. Solitary individuals sometimes encountered, but often in large groups.

Distribution and status SE Asia: Myanmar, Thailand, Laos, Vietnam, Cambodia and Peninsular Malaysia. Also India, S China, Sumatra, Java, Borneo and Palawan. Endangered. Formerly common and widespread, but has declined dramatically in much of region, due largely to hunting and trapping for fur, meat and traditional medicine.

Family *VIVERRIDAE* CIVETS

Civets are a diverse group of carnivores, mostly active at night. Some species are largely terrestrial, while others spend nearly their whole lives in trees. Most species have a relatively pointed muzzle and long tail (except the Otter Civet, *Cynogale bennetti*, which has a broad muzzle and short tail); a total of 40 teeth (the linsangs, *Prionodon* spp., have 38). Most civets (except linsangs and male Small-toothed Palm Civet, *Arctogalidia trivirgata*) have perineal scent glands.

Viverrids share many features with the mustelids, but the latter have fewer teeth and lack perineal scent glands. Most species can be fairly readily identified by colour patterns.

Footprints of most civets have five distinct toe impressions, except those of the *Viverra* and *Viverricula*, which have only four toes visible and closely resemble the prints of dogs (Fig. 55).

LARGE INDIAN CIVET

Viverra zibetha PLATE 37
Measurements HB 750–850, T 380–460, HF 110–140. Wt 8–9kg
Identification Large civet with bold black-and-white throat pattern consisting of three black collars separated by white collars. General colour grey or tawny-brown with dark pattern on flanks consisting of wavy lines, often with some spotting on legs; pattern is sometimes very indistinct. Erectile crest of hairs from back of neck to base of tail. Tail banded to tip, with five or six broad black bands separated by narrow but complete white rings. Bottoms of feet heavily haired between pads, with skin sheath over nail on third and fourth toes. **Taxonomic notes** Taynguyen Civet, *Viverra tainguensis*, was recently described from Vietnam, but recent analyses of specimens suggest it is the same thing as *V. zibetha*. **Similar species** Malay Civet, *V. tangalunga*, is smaller, with many more black bands on tail, and black dorsal crest continues along top of tail. Large-spotted Civet, *V. megaspila*, has larger head with longer, more swollen muzzle; body with distinct dark spots or bands on flanks; black crest continuing along top of tail so that white bands are broken; distal half of tail usually dark.

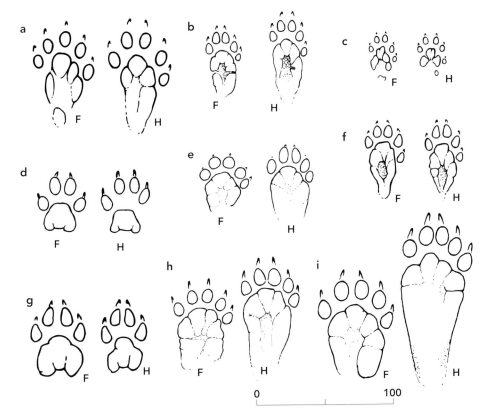

Fig. 55 *Left footprints of front (F) and hind (H) feet of civets:* Cynogale bennetti *(a),* Arctogalidia trivirgata *(b),* Prionodon linsang *(c),* Viverricula indica *(d),* Paradoxurus hermaphroditus *(e),* Hemigalus derbyanus *(f),* Viverra tangalunga *(g),* Paguma larvata *(h);* Arctictis binturong *(i).*

Ecology and habitat Nocturnal and largely terrestrial, though can also climb trees. Found mainly in forested habitats, but also uses secondary forests and some plantations. Eats any animal it can catch, including lizards, small mammals, birds and fish, as well as fruits and other plant materials.

Distribution and status SE Asia: Myanmar, Thailand, Laos, Vietnam, Cambodia and Peninsular Malaysia. Also Nepal, NE India and S China. Not currently at risk.

LARGE-SPOTTED CIVET

Viverra megaspila PLATE 37
Measurements HB 720–850, T 300–370, HF 130–138. Wt 8–9kg

Identification Large civet with bold black-and-white throat pattern; body colour varies from greyish to brown, with pattern of dark brown or black spots on flanks. Pattern very variable, but usually spots are distinct, or fused into vertical or horizontal bars. Tail with black crest along top, usually dark on distal half, incomplete white bands at base.
Similar species Large Indian Civet, *V. zibetha*, has proportionately slightly smaller head, (usually) wavy bands rather than spots on flanks, tail with complete white bands; skin sheath on toenails and hairy soles of feet (visible only if animal has been captured); Malay Civet, *V. tangalunga*, is smaller, with many more bands on tail.
Ecology and habitat Poorly known; recent records are largely from evergreen forest, but it is also found in disturbed forests. Forages largely at night and on ground, hunting for prey in leaf litter. Appears to be located mainly in lowland forests, below 300m, although there are some records from higher plateaux. Less tolerant of habitat

fragmentation than other *Viverra* civets.

Distribution and status SE Asia: Myanmar, Cambodia, Thailand, Vietnam, Laos and Peninsular Malaysia. Also S China. Vulnerable. In most of range occurs in low densities; threatened by forest loss, hunting and trapping.

MALAY CIVET
Viverra tangalunga PLATE 37
Measurements HB 610–670, T 285–355, HF 94–105. Wt 4–5kg

Identification Upperparts greyish with numerous black spots; a black stripe along the midline extends to tip of tail; underparts white with bold black markings on the throat; legs blackish; tail with about 15 black bands.
Similar species Large Indian and Large-spotted civets, *V. indica* and *V. megaspila*, are larger, with fewer bands on tail.
Ecology and habitat Nocturnal and usually terrestrial, but occasionally climbs into trees. Diet includes a wide variety of invertebrates and small vertebrates taken mainly from the forest floor. May visit forest camps to feed on food scraps. Occurs in forests and cultivated land adjacent to forest. Tolerant of moderate forest disturbance.
Distribution and status SE Asia: Peninsular Malaysia. Also Sumatra and adjacent small islands, Borneo, Sulawesi and the Philippines. Apparently introduced on several islands. Not currently at risk.

SMALL INDIAN CIVET
Viverricula indica PLATE 37
Measurements HB 530–640, T 300–430, HF 85–100. Wt 2–4kg

Identification General body colour grey, light grey or buff, with numerous dark spots that form longitudinal rows along back and sides. Throat white with dark lines. Tail with 6–9 black and white rings and long pale tip.
Similar species *Viverra* civets are larger, with longer legs, larger, broader muzzle, a dark crest down back, less distinct rows of spots, bolder black-and-white markings on throat, generally dark tip to tail.
Ecology and habitat Primarily nocturnal and terrestrial, but sometimes active during day.

Frequents relatively open areas, including long grass and scrub; may enter villages or rural buildings. Diet includes birds, small mammals, frogs, reptiles, insects and fruits.
Distribution and status SE Asia: Myanmar, Thailand, Laos, Vietnam, Cambodia and Peninsular Malaysia. Also Pakistan, India, Nepal, Bangladesh, S China, N Sumatra, Java and Bali. Not currently at risk.

BANDED LINSANG
Prionodon linsang PLATE 38
Measurements HB 350–450, T 300–420, HF 50–70. Wt 600–800g

Identification Whitish to golden or buff, with a pattern of large, dark brown spots that merge into about 5 dark, transverse bands on upperparts, and longitudinal bands on sides of neck. Tail has black and pale bands along full length, typically about 7 dark bands. Small, slender and cat-like. Claws retractile, like a cat's. **Similar species** Spotted Linsang, *P. pardicolor*, has smaller spots on body that do not blend into large splotches or bars, tail with more, narrower bands; Banded Civet, *Hemigalus derbyanus*, has broad bars on upperparts, but no spots, and a mainly black tail; Leopard Cat, *Prionailurus bengalensis*, has a differently shaped head, lacks broad barring along length of tail.
Ecology and habitat Nocturnal. Largely arboreal but also active on ground. Sleeps during day in a nest made in a hole, either in the ground or in a tree. Diet includes small mammals, birds, reptiles and arthropods. Occurs in tall and secondary forests, plantations and gardens.
Distribution and status SE Asia: peninsular Myanmar, Thailand and Malaysia. Also Sumatra and adjacent islands, Java and Borneo. Poorly known, but arboreal habits make it hard to survey; not currently at risk.

SPOTTED LINSANG
Prionodon pardicolor PLATE 38
Measurements HB 350–370, T 313–340, HF 60–70. Wt 600g

Identification Whitish to light brown to

orange-buff, with many irregular black spots on back and sides of body. Spots tend to remain separate, not to blend into blotches, except for dark lines on either side of neck. Tail with black and buff bands, typically about 8 or 9 complete dark bands. **Similar species** Banded Linsang, *P. linsang*, has larger splotches that tend to blend into dark bands on back, fewer bands on tail; Owston's Civet, *Chrotogale owstoni*, has distinct dark bands on back, and largely dark tail; Small Indian Civet, *Viverricula indica*, has many more spots that form into narrow rows with lines on throat, and different posture.

Ecology and habitat Largely nocturnal and arboreal, but also hunts on ground. Most records from mountain and hill forest to at least 2,000m altitude, but also occurs in secondary forest. Believed to prey largely on small mammals and birds, but probably eats arthropods and other animals as well.

Distribution and status SE Asia: N Myanmar, N Thailand, Laos, Cambodia and N Vietnam. Also E India, Nepal and SE China. Not currently at risk, but apparently rare in most of region, and suffering some habitat loss.

COMMON PALM CIVET
Paradoxurus hermaphroditus PLATE 38
Measurements HB 420–500, T 330–420

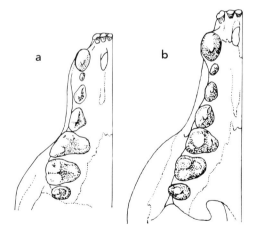

Fig. 56 *Right upper toothrow of* Paradoxurus hermaphroditus *(a) and* Arctogalidia trivirgata *(b).*

(usually 70–90% of HB), HF 70–76. Wt 2–3kg
Identification Upperparts vary from olive-brown or occasionally reddish-brown to dark grey-brown; underparts paler. Limbs and tail dark brownish or black. Cheeks and front of face black, forming a dark mask; often with pale spots on sides of head which sometimes extend over forehead in a large white area; pattern varies among individuals. Three indistinct, broken dark lines along midline of back, with irregular rows of spots on flanks, sometimes forming extra lines. In northern part of range, spot pattern can be indistinct and obscured in thick winter coat. Adult females have 3 pairs of mammae.
Similar species Small-toothed Palm Civet, *Arctogalidia trivirgata*, has tail longer than head and body; three stripes on back but without additional spots on sides of body; dark head usually with narrow white stripe on forehead; larger skull with relatively straight toothrow, narrow molars and widely spaced teeth (Fig. 56b); and two pairs of mammae in females. Masked Palm Civet, *Paguma larvata*, is larger, lacks spots or stripes on back or sides, has pale stripe on forehead.

Ecology and habitat Nocturnal; sleeps during day in trees or sometimes in buildings. Arboreal and terrestrial, but more often active on ground than Small-toothed Palm Civet. Diet includes fruits, leaves, arthropods, worms and molluscs. Occurs in tall and secondary forests, plantations and gardens. Often seen near human settlements.

Distribution and status SE Asia: Myanmar, Thailand, Laos, Vietnam, Cambodia and Peninsular Malaysia. Also Sri Lanka, India, Nepal, Bangladesh, S China, Sumatra, Java, Borneo, Sulawesi and smaller Indonesian islands and the Philippines. Not currently at risk.

MASKED PALM CIVET
Paguma larvata PLATE 38
Measurements HB 510–760, T 510–640, HF 95 -104. Wt 3–5kg
Identification Body colour highly variable, from very light brown, almost blonde, to dark brown or reddish, darker on legs and

top of head. Tail may be dark throughout or only on distal half, sometimes with white tip. Dark "mask" around eyes and on muzzle, with white on cheeks or sometimes most of head. White stripe on top of head from nose to back of neck, shorter and less conspicuous in Peninsular Malaysia. Northern forms (near Himalayas) may have head largely dark with only narrow white stripe on forehead. **Similar species** Common Palm Civet, *Paradoxurus hermaphroditus*, has dark face mask, but lacks white stripe on forehead and has dark stripes and spots on back and sides; Small-toothed Palm Civet, *Arctogalidia trivirgata*, has only small white stripe on forehead, no conspicuous "mask", smaller, more slender build, three stripes on back, relatively longer tail.

Ecology and habitat Mainly nocturnal, generally arboreal, but also travels and hunts on ground. Sleeps in tree holes or forks in large trees. Diet includes fruits and small animals. Occurs in tall and secondary forests; may enter plantations and gardens to feed.

Distribution and status SE Asia: Myanmar, Thailand, Laos, Vietnam, Cambodia and Peninsular Malaysia. Also Himalayas, including Nepal, N India, China, Taiwan, Hainan, Sumatra and Borneo. Not currently at risk, but populations have declined in some parts of Vietnam and Laos, owing to excessive hunting.

BINTURONG
Arctictis binturong PLATE 39
Measurements HB 650–950, T 500–800, HF 120–180. Wt 6–9kg
Identification Long, coarse black fur frosted with whitish or reddish grizzling. Grizzling heaviest around head, making head paler than body. Ears round, edged in white, with long tufts of hair at ends. Tail long, thickly haired, especially near base, and prehensile. **Similar species** Sun Bear, *Helarctos malayanus*, is larger, has a short tail and no ear tufts, and very different shape; melanistic (dark) wild cats have shorter hair, a slender, non-prehensile tail and no ear tufts; other civets have shorter fur and are rarely all dark.

Ecology and habitat Mainly arboreal, but also seen on ground. Mainly active at night, but sometimes also during the day. Moves slowly in trees, using tail for balance and to cling to branches while feeding. Diet includes ripe fruits, especially figs, and small animals. Occurs in tall and secondary forests; sometimes in cultivated areas near to forest.

Distribution and status SE Asia: Myanmar, Thailand, Laos, Vietnam, Cambodia and Peninsular Malaysia. Also NE India, S China (Yunnan), Sumatra, Java, Borneo and Palawan. Vulnerable. Appears to be relatively rare in much of range and declining due to loss of forest as well as hunting and trapping for the pet trade.

SMALL-TOOTHED PALM CIVET
Arctogalidia trivirgata PLATE 38
Measurements HB 440–530, T 480–660 (about 110–120% of HB), HF 75–95. Wt 2–2.5kg
Identification Fur colour varies from olive-brown to greyish, rarely reddish-brown. Underfur reddish-brown. Face, ears, feet and much of tail blackish. Usually has three fine, dark stripes or series of close, dark spots extending along midline from neck to base of tail. Usually has narrow pale stripe from forehead to tip of nose. Females have two pairs of mammae. **Similar species** Common Palm Civet, *Paradoxurus hermaphroditus*, has shorter tail, distinct "mask" on face without white on forehead, additional rows of spots on flanks, smaller skull but with relatively large, broad teeth, curved toothrow (Fig. 56a); Masked Palm Civet, *Paguma larvata*, is larger and heavier, with usually broader white stripe on forehead, pale cheeks, no black stripes on back.

Ecology and habitat Usually nocturnal and arboreal, rarely descending to ground. Very agile. Diet includes fruits and small animals. Occurs in tall and secondary forests.

Distribution and status SE Asia: Myanmar, Thailand, Laos, Vietnam, Cambodia, and Peninsular Malaysia. Also NE India, S China (Yunnan), Sumatra, Java, Bali, Borneo and some smaller islands. Not currently at risk.

BANDED CIVET

Hemigalus derbyanus PLATE 39

Measurements HB 450–560, T 250–360, HF 72–88. Wt 1–3kg

Identification Body colour usually pale buff to golden-brown, paler underneath, with distinct dark brown or black bars across back, dark longitudinal stripes on neck and face. Some individuals are light grey, while others can be very reddish. Tail mostly dark brown, banded only at base. Feet have strongly curved claws that are retractile, like those of cats. **Similar species** Owston's Civet, *C. owstoni*, has similar pattern, but has dark spots on sides and legs, more elongate muzzle and does not overlap in range; Banded Linsang, *Prionodon linsang*, is smaller with shorter legs and an entirely banded tail.

Ecology and habitat Nocturnal. Travels and feeds mainly on the ground, but sleeps in holes either in the ground or in trees. Diet includes earthworms, insects and other small animals, both invertebrate and vertebrate. Largely restricted to lowland forest, but also found in some secondary forests.

Distribution and status SE Asia: peninsular Myamar, Thailand and Malaysia. Also Sumatra and Borneo. Vulnerable. Populations declining due to loss of lowland forest and some hunting.

OWSTON'S CIVET

Chrotogale owstoni PLATE 39

Measurements HB: 510–630, T 380–480

Identification Body colour varies from greyish-white to buffy-brown, paler underneath; distinct broad black bands across back, and stripes on neck and face; dark spots on sides of neck and legs. Pattern of spots and bands individually variable. Tail banded at base, dark on distal two-thirds. Underparts are strongly washed with bright orange-red in adult males, yellowish in adult females. Skull has elongate rostrum with relatively narrow, widely spaced teeth. **Similar species** Banded Civet, *Hemigalus derbyanus*, lacks spots on sides of legs and neck, has larger teeth, does not overlap in range.

Ecology and habitat Nocturnal, largely terrestrial. Feeds on invertebrates such as earthworms. Found largely in wet evergreen broadleaf forest, but sometimes in disturbed areas.

Distribution and status SE Asia: N and C Laos, and N Vietnam. Also S China (Yunnan). Vulnerable. Low population densities in limited range, threatened by illegal hunting and trapping.

OTTER CIVET

Cynogale bennettii PLATE 39

Measurements HB 575–680, T 120–205, HF 102–110

Identification Entirely dark brown, with faint grey grizzling and pale underfur; lips prominent, broad and white, with very long white whiskers; a faint pale spot above each eye. Ears small. Feet with partial webbing between digits. Tail short. **Similar species** Otters have longer, tapering tails, pale chin and throat, and no white on muzzle or above eyes; Flat-headed Cat, *Prionailurus planiceps*, is paler with white on chin and chest, and short, slender muzzle.

Ecology and habitat Little known. Terrestrial and aquatic. Diet includes aquatic animals. Largely restricted to lowland forest near rivers, though has been recorded at altitudes of up to 1,000m in Borneo. Has limited tolerance of disturbed forest.

Distribution and status SE Asia: S Thailand and Peninsular Malaysia. Also Sumatra and Borneo. Endangered. Appears to occur naturally in low numbers, and is threatened by loss of lowland forest and wetland areas.

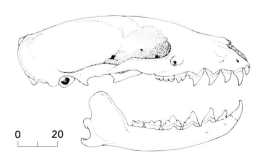

0   20

Fig. 57 *Skull of Otter Civet,* Cynogale bennetti.

Family *HERPESTIDAE* MONGOOSES

Mongooses can be distinguished in the field from civets by their sharply pointed muzzle, tapering tail with hair longer near the base than at the tip, and rather slender legs with long claws. They are largely active during the day, unlike civets. Distinctive posture while walking, with hindquarters arched above the level of the forequarters and tail. The footprints have relatively narrow toe pads (Fig. 52e).

SHORT-TAILED MONGOOSE
Herpestes brachyurus PLATE 40

Measurements HB 380–445, T 205–250 (less than 55% of HB), HF 75–90

Identification Entirely blackish-brown with fine sandy-brown or orange speckling (speckling visible only from close range); chin and throat pale brown. Head and tail somewhat paler than body. Tail relatively short. **Similar species** Other mongooses are paler in colour, with longer tails, and usually found in more open habitats.

Ecology and habitat Mainly diurnal and terrestrial. Diet includes arthropods and small vertebrate animals. Mainly restricted to lowland forest, but sometimes enters secondary forest, plantations and gardens.

Distribution and status SE Asia: Peninsular Malaysia. Also Sumatra, Borneo and Palawan. Poorly known. Likely to have declined as result of loss of lowland forest.

SMALL ASIAN MONGOOSE
Herpestes javanicus PLATE 40

Measurements Males HB 360–420, T 275–315 (70–75% of HB), HF 60–70. Wt 875–1,800g. Females HB 320–360, T 250–265 (70–75% of HB), HF 55–65. Wt 530–840g

Identification Individual hairs of fur finely banded dark brown and pale buff, giving overall impression of grizzled yellowish to olive-brown; animals in much of region have strong reddish-orange tinge, especially around head, but form in S and W Myanmar (and India) lacks reddish colour. Tail moderately long. **Similar species** Short-tailed Mongoose, *H. brachyurus*, is much darker, without orange tinge, has shorter tail and is largely restricted to forest; Crab-eating Mongoose, *H. urva*, is substantially larger, pale grey with pale stripe on neck.

Ecology and habitat Active both day and night. Primarily in grasslands and scrubby areas; avoids dense evergreen forest. Feeds on rodents and many other small vertebrates, including birds, reptiles and frogs, as well as crabs and large insects.

Distribution and status SE Asia: Myanmar, Thailand, Laos, Vietnam, Cambodia and Peninsular Malaysia. Also Pakistan, N India, Nepal, S China, N Sumatra and Java, and introduced to many islands in Caribbean and elsewhere. Not currently at risk.

INDIAN GREY MONGOOSE
Herpestes edwardsii PLATE 40

Measurements Males HB 400–480, T 370–420 (80–95% of HB). Wt 1.4–2.0kg. Females HB 370–410, T 330–390 (80–95% of HB). Wt 0.9–1.3

Identification Individual hairs banded black and white, giving grizzled grey appearance overall; worn fur acquires a brownish tinge. No pale shoulder stripe. Tail long with pale tip. **Similar species** Small Asian Mongoose, *H. javanicus*, is smaller with yellow or orange tinge; Crab-eating Mongoose, *H. urva*, has long white patch on each side of neck.

Ecology and habitat Active by day or night. In India, occurs largely in open areas, including scrub and cultivated lands. In some areas enters villages, where often seen during day. Feeds on rodents and a wide variety of vertebrate and invertebrate prey, sometimes including domestic chickens.

Distribution and status SE Asia: Peninsular Malaysia. Also Iran, Arabia, Pakistan, India and Sri Lanka. Formerly occurred between Penang and Malacca in Peninsular Malaysia, where believed to have been introduced, possibly from shipping. No recent records, and may now be extirpated from Malaysia.

CRAB-EATING MONGOOSE

Herpestes urva   PLATE 40

Measurements HB 440–480, T 260–310 (~60–65% of HB), HF 90–110. Wt 3–4kg

Identification Large mongoose with comparatively short tail. Overall colour is brown to grey, with individual guard hairs banded black and white, giving grizzled appearance. Conspicuous white stripe on side of neck and white chin. Rest of underparts dark. Long guard hairs make animal appear very shaggy. **Similar species** Small Asian Mongoose, *H. javanicus*, is smaller, lacks white neck stripe and has shorter coat hairs; Indian Grey Mongoose, *H. edwardsii*, lacks shoulder stripe and has longer tail.

Ecology and habitat Active both day and night. Found in a variety of forest and scrub habitats, often near streams. Feeds on aquatic animals such as crabs, frogs, fish and molluscs, but probably takes other prey as well. Can squirt a strong-smelling fluid from anal glands near base of tail, presumably for defence.

Distribution and status SE Asia: Myanmar, Thailand, Laos, Vietnam, Cambodia and Peninsular Malaysia. Also Nepal, Bangladesh, NE India and S and E China. Not currently at risk.

Family *FELIDAE* CATS

Members of the cat family range in size from very large species, such as the Tiger and the Leopard, which prey upon large mammals like deer or pigs, down to several smaller species, similar in size to a domestic cat, which feed mainly on small animals such as rodents or fish. All species have basically similar structure and body form. The skull has a relatively short rostrum, with teeth highly specialized for carnivory. The dental formula is 3/3 1/1 2–3/2 1/1 (Fig. 49b). The canines are very long, and the posterior premolar is greatly enlarged in the form of a carnassial for tearing meat. The anterior small premolar is sometimes missing, and the upper molar is very small.

The footprints show only four toes on both the front and hind feet (Fig. 58); the front feet have a fifth toe, but it is small and does not touch the ground. The claws are retractile, and do not usually appear in footprints. The main variation among species in footprints is in size, although there is some variation in the shape of the footpads (Fig. 58).

There is considerable uncertainty in the generic relationships of cats, owing to the limited number of differentiating characters. Some authorities place most species in the genus *Felis*, while others split them into several genera, the approach followed here.

TIGER

Panthera tigris   PLATE 41

Measurements HB 1,700–2,300, T 950–1,150. Wt 180–245kg

Identification Easily recognized by very large size and pattern of vertical black and pale orange stripes along the body. Pattern of striping varies considerably, and can be used to recognize individuals in photographs. Tail is proportionately shorter than that of other large cats. Footprints can be distinguished by their large size and by the absence of claw marks (front feet 90mm or longer – Fig. 58g,h).

Ecology and habitat Tigers are found in a wide range of forested and partially open habitats, provided suitable prey is available. Main prey items are deer and pigs, though many other animals may be taken, ranging from fish to rodents and birds. Occasionally, tigers may hunt humans or take domestic animals, but most remaining tigers in region are very shy of humans, after years of persecution.

Distribution and status SE Asia: Myanmar, Thailand, Laos, Vietnam, Cambodia and Peninsular Malaysia. Also India, Nepal, China, Siberia and Sumatra. Presumed Extinct on Java and Bali. Endangered. Still found in most countries of region, but in greatly reduced numbers. Major threats are illegal hunting and trapping, but also suffering from loss of habitat and prey base.

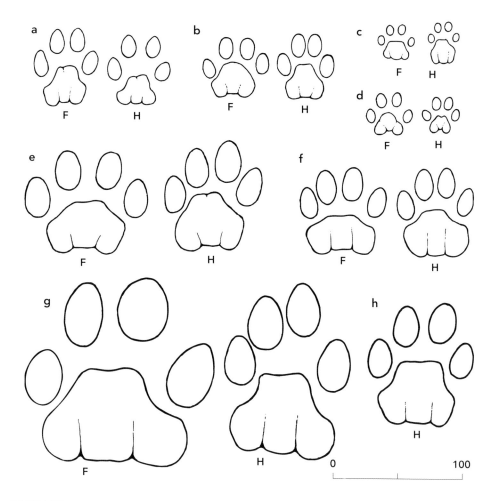

a

b

c

F   H

d

F   H

e

F

H

f

F

H

g

F

h

H

H   0   100

Fig. 58 *Left footprints of front (F) and hind (H) feet of various cats:* Felis temminckii *(a),* Prionailurus viverrinus *(b),* P. planiceps *(c),* P. bengalensis *(d),* Panthera pardus *(e),* Neofelis nebulosa *(f) and* Panthera tigris, *showing a relatively large (g) and relatively small individual (h).*

LEOPARD

Panthera pardus PLATE 41

Measurements HB 1,050–1,300, T 800–1,000. Wt 45–65kg

Identification Large cat with two colour phases. Spotted form has pale yellowish or yellowish-brown base colour, with black spots clustered in rosettes on back and singly on sides. Dark form also has rosettes, but base colour is also black, so rosettes can be seen only in good light. Dark phase is most common in S Thailand and Peninsular Malaysia. Footprints (Fig. 58e) are similar to Tiger, *P. tigris*, but generally shorter (length less than 80mm). **Similar species** Clouded Leopard, *Neofelis nebulosa*, is smaller, with irregular pattern of "clouds" on coat; Binturong, *Arctictis binturong*, is sometimes mistaken for a black Leopard, but has long shaggy hair, ear tufts, no coat pattern, prehensile tail and very different shape.

Ecology and habitat Found in a wide range of habitats, though mainly in wooded areas.

Distribution and status SE Asia: Myanmar, Thailand, Laos, Vietnam, Cambodia and Peninsular Malaysia. Also throughout much of Africa, Asia as far north as N China and Java. Vulnerable. Populations have declined owing to loss of habitat, declines in prey base and illegal hunting.

CLOUDED LEOPARD

Neofelis nebulosa PLATE 41

Measurements HB 650–950, T 550–800. Wt 15–23kg

Identification Usually pale sandy-brown to orange, with "cloud" patterns on sides and neck consisting of darker brown splotches with incomplete dark borders. Rarely, base colour is very dark and animals appear almost black. Footprints shorter with narrower pads than those of Leopard (Fig. 58f). Upper canines very large relative to skull, with clear diastema between them and cheek teeth. **Similar species** Marbled Cat, *Pardofelis marmorata*, is smaller, with more irregular pattern of lines and dark areas that do not form discrete clouds, more extensive small spots on legs; Leopard, *Panthera pardus*, has rosettes of spots, not clouds, longer legs with more erect posture, thinner tail.

Ecology and habitat Mainly nocturnal and arboreal, but sometimes active during the day. In logged forest, often travels on the ground. Diet includes pigs, deer, primates and smaller mammals. Occurs mainly in tall forests, but also secondary forests and other disturbed habitats.

Distribution and status SE Asia: Myanmar, Thailand, Laos, Vietnam, Cambodia and Peninsular Malaysia. Also Nepal, NE India, S China, Taiwan, Sumatra and Borneo. Vulnerable. Threatened by loss of habitat and illegal hunting.

MARBLED CAT

Pardofelis marmorata PLATE 42

Measurements HB 450–530, T 470–550, HF 115–120, E 35–40. Wt 2–4kg

Identification Sides and back brownish with dark splotches and black lines, reminiscent of Clouded Leopard, *Neofelis nebulosa*, but black-edged blotches on sides of body less distinct, tending to blend together in a marbled pattern, rather than forming discrete "clouds"; black spots on legs smaller and more numerous. Fur soft and thick. **Similar species** Clouded Leopard, *N. nebulosa*, is larger, with patterns forming discrete "clouds".

Ecology and habitat Mainly nocturnal and arboreal, though also forages on ground. Diet probably includes a broad range of small animals, including rodents. Occurs mainly in tall forests, including regenerating forest.

Distribution and status SE Asia: Myanmar, Thailand, Laos, Vietnam, Cambodia and Peninsular Malaysia. Also Nepal, NE India, S China (Yunnan), Sumatra and Borneo. Vulnerable. Overall rare, potentially threatened by habitat loss and hunting.

ASIAN GOLDEN CAT

Catopuma temminckii PLATE 42

Measurements HB 760–840, T 430–500 (about 60% of HB). Wt 12–15kg

Identification A large cat with relatively plain coat, usually lacking distinct markings except for black and white stripes on sides and front of head. Coat colour quite variable, ranging from golden-brown to light tawny-brown to greyish. Some individuals are very dark brown or reddish. Generally darker along spine and paler underneath. Tail moderately long, darker above, pale below, often with dark tip. Has indistinct spots or blotches on belly, as well as sometimes on legs and shoulder. Race *C. t. tristis*, which may occur in N Myanmar, has extensive dark spots, stripes and splotches on upperparts (somewhat similar to Marbled Cat, *Pardofelis marmorata*), but can be recognized by distinctive face pattern and white underside to tail. Rarely, some individuals are all dark brown. **Similar species** Jungle Cat, *Felis chaus*, has taller, pointed ears, bands on tail, lacks white stripes on face; Flat-headed Cat, *Prionailurus planiceps*, is smaller with very short tail.

Ecology and habitat Reported from both dry forests and tropical rainforests. Occurs in disturbed areas but only near forest. Mainly terrestrial but can climb trees. Diet includes various medium and large animals including hares, small deer and large birds.

Distribution and status SE Asia: Myanmar, Thailand, Laos, Vietnam, Cambodia and Peninsular Malaysia. Also Nepal, NE India, S China and Sumatra. Near Threatened. Still occurs in much of region, but in reduced numbers. Threats include loss of habitat and illegal hunting.

FLAT-HEADED CAT
Prionailurus planiceps PLATE 42
Measurements HB 445–505, T 130–170 (27–34% of HB), HF 95–107, E 36–39. Wt 1.5–2.2kg

Identification Appears brownish at a distance, but hair of upperparts brown with fine grey and pale buff speckling. Chin and chest white. Indistinct dark and pale stripes on sides of face and forehead. Ears small, top of head long and flattened. **Similar species** Asian Golden Cat, *Catopuma temminckii*, is substantially larger with longer tail; Otter Civet, *Cynogale bennetti*, is darker with very broad muzzle.

Ecology and habitat Nocturnal and terrestrial. Probably feeds mostly on fish. Found mainly in tall lowland forests near streams, but tolerant of some forest disturbance.

Distribution and status SE Asia: peninsular Thailand and Malaysia. Also Sumatra, and Borneo. Vulnerable. Relatively rare, population declining owing to loss of lowland forest.

LEOPARD CAT
Prionailurus bengalensis PLATE 42
Measurements HB 400–550, T 230–290 (more than 50% of HB), HF 110–125, E 40–45. Wt 3–5kg

Identification Reddish-orange or yellowish-buff, with black spots over entire upperparts including tail; underparts contrasting white with black spots. Pattern and size of spots varies considerably among individuals, ranging from large, round black spots to numerous small spots to large irregular splotches with browner centres. Spots may be rounded or elongate in shape; often form into lines on back; top of head and back of neck with several distinct black stripes. **Similar species** Fishing Cat, *P. viverrinus*, is larger and greyer, with shorter tail, buffy underparts, black spots usually fairly small, forming distinct rows; Marbled Cat, *Pardofelis marmorata*, has more complex pattern of lines, dark and

pale areas, not just spots; Banded Linsang, *Prionodon linsang*, is smaller, with different shape, relatively thick tail with bands, not spots, along entire length.

Ecology and habitat Most widespread and common small cat in region, occupying a wide range of habitats, including forests, plantations and gardens. Usually nocturnal, mainly terrestrial but can climb trees; swims well. Diet includes small mammals, lizards, amphibians and large insects.

Distribution and status SE Asia: Myanmar, Thailand, Laos, Vietnam, Cambodia and Peninsular Malaysia. Also Pakistan, India, Nepal, China, Siberia, Taiwan, Sumatra, Java, Bali, Borneo and the Philippines. Not currently at risk.

FISHING CAT
Prionailurus viverrinus PLATE 42
Measurements HB 720–780, T 250–290 (~40% of HB), E 44–50, HF 150–170. Wt 7–11kg

Identification Medium-large, greyish or olive-brown in base colour with black stripes on top of head and rows of small black spots on back and sides. Spots vary from rounded to elongate. Underside paler, buffy to greyish, but not white. Tail relatively short. **Similar species** Leopard Cat, *P. bengalensis*, is substantially smaller, more yellowish or orange with contrasting white underside, black spots often larger, tail longer (more than 50% of head and body).

Ecology and habitat Mainly found in drier, scrubby habitat, usually near water, including swamps and marshes. Feeds on fish, crabs, rodents, birds, molluscs and other animals.

Distribution and status SE Asia: Myanmar, Thailand, Laos, Vietnam and Cambodia. Also Pakistan, Sri Lanka, S China (Yunnan), India, Nepal, Java and Sumatra. Vulnerable. Rare and declining in many parts of region due partly to loss of wetland habitats.

JUNGLE CAT
Felis chaus PLATE 42
Measurements HB 500–650, T 260–310 (about 50% of HB), HF 145–154, E 70–80. Wt 4–6kg

Identification Fur light ashy-grey to yellowish-brown, paler underneath; no stripes or spots on body. Tail with 4 or 5 dark rings on distal half. Ears tall and pointed, with black tuft on tip; legs relatively long. **Similar species** Asian Golden Cat, *Catopuma temminckii*, has shorter, more rounded ears, stripes on forehead and cheeks, bicoloured tail without rings.

Ecology and habitat Found in relatively open, drier habitats with suitable natural cover, such as tall grass, open deciduous forest or scrub, usually near wetlands, including streams or rivers. Mainly terrestrial, rarely climbing trees. Mostly nocturnal, though sometimes active during day. Feeds on rodents, lizards, birds and other animals, as well as carrion.

Distribution and status SE Asia: Myanmar, Thailand, Laos, Vietnam and Cambodia. Also Middle East, Afghanistan, Pakistan, India and S China (Yunnan). Endangered in region, though less at risk elsewhere. Population has declined considerably, with very few recent records. Threats include loss of natural habitat and illegal trapping.

DOMESTIC CAT
Felis catus NOT ILLUSTRATED
Measurements HB about 450–550, T variable, often short and bent
Identification Coloration variable, often white with irregular orange patches. Unlike wild cats, free-ranging Domestic Cats rarely flee from people and are often seen during the day. **Similar species** Wild cats usually have a more symmetrical coat pattern and are very shy of people.
Ecology and habitat Always associated with humans. Domestic Cats abandoned in disused temporary settlements fare much better than Domestic Dogs, *Canis familiaris*, in the same situation, and tend to stay near the old buildings, feeding on a variety of small animals.
Distribution and status Found worldwide. Found near most human settlements.

Order CETACEA
Whales, dolphins and porpoises

The cetaceans include the largest animals that have ever lived in the world – the largest Blue Whales are larger than the largest known dinosaurs. Because they live completely in the water they are often thought to be fish, but they are true warm-blooded mammals that have lost their legs and most of their hair, and acquired fins and other modifications for living in the sea. They still breathe air, and give birth to live young and feed them on milk.

If not seen well, some dolphins and small whales could be mistaken for sharks, as the dorsal fin sometimes appears similar. However, among other differences, dolphins have a blowhole on top of the head, visible when the animal breathes, and horizontal tail flukes instead of a vertical tail. They also swim quite differently, rising up and down, and sometimes even jumping out of the water.

Whales and dolphins are often difficult to identify, as they are usually hard to see well in the water. Even experienced observers familiar with the behaviour of the animals cannot identify every cetacean seen, and it can be especially difficult for a beginner. However, some species are quite tame, allowing good views, while others show themselves several times, eventually allowing enough to be seen for identification.

Until recently, relatively little was known about cetaceans in South-East Asia. Most confirmed records related to specimens that became stranded, or that had died and were then washed up on a beach. In the past decade there has been substantially increased boat-based survey work in the region, prompted by concern about declining populations. These have provided increased information on the status of many of the smaller porpoises and dolphins that are regularly found in the offshore waters, including the Irrawaddy Dolphin that regular occurs in some of the largest freshwater rivers. Several other species, including species of large whales, are likely to pass through South-East Asian waters at least occasionally. Because so little is known about them, all of the species known to occur in the tropical Pacific or Indian Ocean are included here, even if they have not definitely been recorded from the region, in the expectation that they are likely to show up.

Unfortunately, many cetaceans are now of significant conservation concern. Most species breed slowly, not starting to breed until they are many years old, and then producing only one young every few years. As a result, most populations cannot sustain hunting of more than 1 or 2 per cent of the total population per year without starting to decline. Historically, large whales were hunted very heavily, with the result that nearly all species declined dramatically, some almost to extinction. Although commercial whaling has been largely stopped, most populations have not yet recovered, and are still threatened by entanglement in nets, collisions with ships, and pollution. Smaller cetaceans such as dolphins were rarely hunted commercially on a large scale, but in many areas, including South-East Asia, they are threatened by accidental entanglement in fishing nets, which leads to drowning, injury from illegal dynamite fishing, collisions with boats and some targeted hunting by local fishermen despite legal protection in most areas. More than half the species that occur in South-East Asia are thought to have experienced major population declines and to be locally at risk. Cetacean numbers are exceptionally low off the coast of Vietnam, probably due to excessive mortality from fishing and other operations.

Family *DELPHINIDAE* OCEANIC DOLPHINS

This family includes all of the well-known dolphins, as well as the larger Orca or Killer Whale. All species have rows of peg-like teeth in both jaws, well-developed dorsal fins and often a distinct beak.

MELON-HEADED WHALE

Peponocephala electra PLATE 43

Measurements TL 2.2–2.7m

Identification No prominent beak; forehead smoothly curved downwards in profile; head conical or triangular from above. Dorsal fin tall and curved. Flippers long, slim and pointed. Colour generally black, sometimes paler on the belly. Teeth 20–25 in each row.

Similar species False Killer Whale, *Pseudorca crassidens*, is substantially larger, has a slightly more rounded profile and bent flippers; Pygmy Killer Whale, *Feresa attenuata*, has rounded flippers and a dark cape contrasting with paler sides, a pattern rarely present in Melon-headed Whale.

Ecology and habitat Usually occurs in large herds of up to several hundred animals, which can travel very quickly. Primarily in deeper, offshore waters. Feeds on squid and small fish.

Distribution and status Found in tropical and sub-tropical oceans, mainly in deep water. SE Asia: frequently reported around the Philippines, with records in Peninsular Malaysia, the Gulf of Thailand and Vietnam; also occurs near India and thus likely to occur throughout Bay of Bengal. Globally not currently at risk.

PYGMY KILLER WHALE

Feresa attenuata PLATE 43

Measurements TL 2.2–2.6m

Identification General colour dark grey-brown to black with paler sides, giving an indistinct caped look; there are irregular patches of white on the belly, chin and lips. Head rounded with no beak. Dorsal fin tall and curved back in centre of back; flippers rounded at the tips. Upper jaw has 8–11 teeth on each side, lower jaw has 11–13.

Similar species Melon-headed Whale, *Peponocephala electra*, can be hard to separate but head shape is more triangular (from above), flippers are more pointed; False Killer Whale, *Pseudorca crassidens*, is longer and more slender, more uniformly dark, with hump on flippers and proportionately smaller dorsal fin.

Ecology and habitat Often forms large groups, but less active than many dolphins. May sometimes attack other cetaceans.

Distribution and status Worldwide, in tropical and sub-tropical seas. SE Asia: occurs off east coast of India, Indonesia and in South China Sea; records from Thailand and Vietnam. Globally not currently at risk, but occurs in low numbers, and potentially threatened by overhunting.

FALSE KILLER WHALE
Pseudorca crassidens PLATE 43

Measurements TL 3.2–4m; males up to 6.1m; females up to 4.9m

Identification Mainly black, sometimes slightly paler around the head and on the chest. Long, slender body with relatively small, rounded head. Conspicuous dorsal fin, curved backwards; flippers with hump on leading edge, unlike other black whales. Large conspicuous teeth, 8–11 in each row.

Similar species Killer Whale, *Orcinus orca*, is much larger, with a tall, triangular fin, broad rounded head and large white patches; pilot whales, *Globicephala* spp., have a more rounded, bulbous head, broader lower dorsal fin and long, pointed flippers; Pygmy Killer and Melon-headed Whales, *Feresa attenuata* and *Peponocephala electra*, are smaller and have paler markings, often with white on the lips.

Ecology and habitat Gregarious, usually in groups, often forming large herds; very active, frequently playing near boats. Eats mainly squid and larger fish, but has been reported attacking other cetaceans.

Distribution and status Throughout tropical seas and into warmer temperate areas. SE Asia: recorded from coastal waters off Pakistan and India, through Sumatra, Borneo and eastern Indonesia. In region, recorded from Singapore, Cambodia, Thailand and Vietnam. Globally not currently at risk, but some local populations are threatened by overhunting.

KILLER WHALE
Orcinus orca PLATE 43

Measurements TL adult males up to 9.5m; females up to 7m, but usually smaller

Identification Tall, triangular dorsal fin, lower and more curved in females. Black with large, well-marked white areas behind the eye, on the throat and belly, and behind the dorsal fin – pattern varies with individuals. Eye patch often visible when swimming. Flippers broad and rounded. Adult males easily recognized; females smaller, with a more dolphin-like dorsal fin, but often in company of adult male.

Similar species False Killer Whale, *Pseudorca crassidens*, is more slender, with no white markings and more rounded head; Risso's Dolphin, *Grampus griseus*, is much smaller, usually paler and greyer, with rounded, beakless head; pilot whales, *Globicephala* spp., have bulbous forehead and low, broad-based dorsal fin.

Ecology and habitat Diet varies among populations, some eating mainly fish and others specializing in marine mammals such as seals and other cetaceans. Very social, with group size varying from a few individuals to 30 or more; larger groups may represent several pods coming together.

Distribution and status Worldwide, but less often seen in tropical waters. SE Asia: recorded from Bay of Bengal and around Indonesian islands, including Borneo, with regional records from Thailand and Vietnam. Globally not currently at risk; probably only migrates through local waters.

SHORT-FINNED PILOT WHALE
Globicephala macrorhynchus PLATE 43

Measurements TL males 4.2–5.4m; females 3–4m

Identification Generally black with greyish-white marks under the throat and usually large pale patch behind dorsal fin. Dorsal fin long and low. Thick, bulbous forehead with no visible beak in adults. Flippers sickle-shaped. Teeth 7 to 9 in each row. **Similar species** False Killer Whale, *Pseudorca crassidens*, has a more tapered head and a more slender, erect dorsal fin; Killer Whale,

Orcinus orca, is larger, with tall, erect dorsal fin; Long-finned Pilot Whale, *Globicephala melas*, is extremely similar, but not known to occur in the tropics: it is slightly larger, has 8–12 teeth in each row and longer flippers, but can rarely be distinguished at sea.

Ecology and habitat Found in small groups, often in the company of dolphins. Feeds mainly in deep waters, but often comes close to shore. Believed to feed mainly on squid.

Distribution and status Worldwide in tropical and sub-tropical waters. SE Asia: has been recorded off coasts of Borneo and Java, and in the Bay of Bengal; regional records from Peninsular Malaysia, Cambodia and Thailand. Globally not currently at risk.

RISSO'S DOLPHIN
Grampus griseus PLATE 43
Measurements TL 3.6–4m
Identification High, domed forehead, bisected in the middle by a deep, longitudinal crease; no conspicuous beak. Body generally dark grey when young, turning pale grey to whitish with age, especially around the head; extensively covered with long scars; tall, erect dorsal fin, slightly curved back. No upper teeth and usually fewer than 7 pairs of peglike lower teeth. **Similar species** False Killer Whale, *Pseudorca crassidens*, is darker and generally unscarred, forehead not grooved; Common Bottlenose and Indo-Pacific Humpbacked Dolphins, *Tursiops truncatus* and *Sousa chinensis*, have a long beak; beaked whales, *Mesoplodon* spp., have a smaller dorsal fin and tapered head, and grow to be much larger.

Ecology and habitat Feeds mainly on squid, but also some fish; usually in groups, but sometimes in singles or pairs. Prefers deep water.

Distribution and status Worldwide, in tropical to sub-tropical seas. SE Asia: recorded from South China Sea, with records from Sarawak and off coast of Vietnam; also known from Sri Lanka and likely to occur in Bay of Bengal. Globally not currently at risk, but possibly declining in region due to mortality in fishing nets.

LONG-BEAKED COMMON DOLPHIN
Delphinus capensis PLATE 44
Measurements TL up to 2.5m, but usually less than 2.3m
Identification Back brownish-black to black, belly white; dark V-shaped saddle below dorsal fin, with large buff or white patch in front, and large grey patch behind that appear to form criss-crossing stripes. Dorsal fin tall and triangular, all dark, or with pale patch in middle. Beak long and narrow.
Taxonomic notes Form found around Asia may represent a distinct species, *D. tropicalis*. **Similar species** Striped Dolphin, *Stenella coeruleoalba*, has thin dark stripes from the eye to the anus and from the eye to the flippers, and has a different side pattern.
Ecology and habitat Feeds mainly on small, schooling fish and squid. Very active during the day, often jumping and "playing" in the water. Most frequently seen near shore.
Distribution and status Tropical and sub-tropical seas. SE Asia: reported from Bay of Bengal, Borneo, Straits of Malacca off Malaysia, Gulf of Thailand, Cambodia and Vietnam. Globally not currently at risk, but relatively uncommon in region.

FRASER'S DOLPHIN
Lagenodelphis hosei PLATE 44
Measurements TL 2.3–2.7m
Identification Short beak; relatively small, pointed flippers and triangular dorsal fin. Generally dark blue-grey above, with paler sides, a distinct black stripe on each side from the eye to the anus and a white belly. Fin, flippers and flukes are dark. **Similar species** Striped Dolphin, *Stenella coeruleoalba*, has a narrower dark side-stripe, distinct pattern of white stripes on sides, longer beak and larger fin; Common Dolphin, *Delphinus delphis*, has larger fin, V-shaped dark dorsal saddle and distinct pale patches on sides.
Ecology and habitat Eats fish, shrimp and squid, often at depths of 250–500m. Usually in large groups, sometimes mixed with other species. Mainly offshore in deep waters.
Distribution and status Tropical seas in

most parts of the world. SE Asia: occurs off Sri Lanka, Borneo (type specimen was found stranded in Sarawak), Taiwan and the Philippines, with regional records in Thailand and Vietnam. Globally not currently at risk, but populations declining from excessive hunting in some areas.

PANTROPICAL SPOTTED DOLPHIN

Stenella attenuata PLATE 44

Measurements TL up to 2.5m

Identification Dark grey to brownish-grey cape that is very broad below dorsal fin, narrow on forehead; underside whitish except dark flippers and a thin stripe from beak to flippers; pale grey stripe from side to lower back; can be heavily spotted with pale spots above, dark spots below, but some animals are relatively unspotted. Beak long and narrow, often with white tip and lips. **Similar species** Bottlenose dolphins, *Tursiops* spp., similar to unspotted individuals, but more robust with thicker, shorter beak, plainer coloration; Indo-Pacific Humpbacked Dolphin, *Sousa chinensis*, sometimes heavily spotted, but usually has low dorsal fin with thickened base and more uniform mantle pattern; Spinner, Striped and Common Dolphins differ in shape of mantle.

Ecology and habitat Feeds on fish and squid; often congregates in large herds, sometimes mixed with other species; both coastal and offshore waters. Very active, often leaping high or "playing" in the water.

Distribution and status Throughout tropical waters and sometimes into warm temperate seas. SE Asia: likely in waters throughout region including Borneo, the Philippines and Taiwan, with confirmed records from Thailand, Cambodia and Vietnam. Globally still relatively common, but some populations have declined substantially due to fishing operations; regionally affected by mortality in fishing nets.

STRIPED DOLPHIN

Stenella coeruleoalba PLATE 44

Measurements TL 1.8–2.7m

Identification Long, narrow black stripes from eye to flipper and eye to anus; broad, pale grey streak above eye to below dorsal fin. Back dark grey to bluish-grey; sides light grey; belly white. Fin moderate and slightly curved; beak long and distinct. **Similar species** Spinner Dolphin, *S. longirostris*, has a more even grey stripe on the side without black stripes, and less curved back fin; Common Dolphin, *Delphinus delphis*, has a different pattern of stripes; bottlenose and Pantropical Spotted dolphins, *Tursiops* spp. and *Stenella attenuata*, sometimes have an indistinct pale blaze on the shoulder, but lack the black stripes on the sides; Fraser's Dolphin, *Lagenodelphis hosei*, has broader black side-stripes, shorter snout and small dorsal fin.

Ecology and habitat Eats mainly small fish, shrimp and squid. Usually in large groups well offshore, but sometimes enters nearshore waters. Very active, often jumping clear of the water.

Distribution and status Worldwide in warm-temperate to tropical seas. SE Asia: occurs around Indonesia and the Philippines, with confirmed records off Thailand and Vietnam; potentially occurs anywhere in region. Globally not currently at risk, but SE Asian population now very small, affected not only by fishing mortality in region, but also by over-hunting in Japan, where they are believed to migrate seasonally.

SPINNER DOLPHIN

Stenella longirostris PLATE 44

Measurements TL 1.3–2.3m

Identification Long, narrow beak with relatively low forehead; dorsal fin nearly triangular and sometimes even curved forwards in adult males; tail base often with a strong keel or ridge. Upperparts dark grey, paler grey stripe along sides forming a relatively straight border from dark mantle; underparts white with a dark line from eye to flipper. Dwarf form, *S. l. roseiventris*, which is most frequently seen in region, is substantially smaller than the typical deepwater forms. **Similar species** Bottlenose dolphins, *Tursiops* spp., are larger, with a more curved fin and a shorter beak with a pale tip and lips; Common Dolphin, *Delphinus delphis*, has V-shaped dark saddle on back; Striped Dolphin, *S. coeruleoalba*, has distinct black stripe on sides.

Ecology and habitat Forms very large, active groups, often jumping and twisting (from which they get their name); sometimes mixed with other species. Dwarf form occurs in relatively shallow waters and feeds mainly on bottom-dwelling and coral reef organisms; larger form in deep offshore waters, feeds mainly on fish and squid.

Distribution and status Tropical and subtropical regions of the world's oceans. SE Asia: dwarf form, *S. l. roseiventris*, which may prove to be a distinct species, recorded from Myanmar, Peninsular Malaysia, Gulf of Thailand, Cambodia, Vietnam and probably in coastal waters throughout region; typical larger form, *S. l. longirostris*, regularly seen around the Philippines and probably occurs in deeper waters throughout South China Sea. Globally not currently at risk, but populations in SE Asia threatened by excessive mortality in fishing operations.

ROUGH-TOOTHED DOLPHIN
Steno bredanensis PLATE 45
Measurements TL 1.8–2.8m
Identification Forehead and sides of head slope evenly into long, slender beak. Prominent, tall dorsal fin and large flippers. Generally dark grey to blackish, with pale lips and underparts; pale streaks along sides set off dark back in an indistinct narrow saddle; often has pale splotches on sides. **Similar species** Other beaked dolphins have a distinct crease where the bulbous forehead meets the beak; bottlenose dolphins, *Tursiops* spp., have shorter beaks and more uniform grey coloration; Indo-Pacific Humpbacked Dolphin, *Sousa chinensis*, can sometimes be similar in colour, and may lack hump, but has smaller fin and differently shaped head; Pantropical Spotted Dolphin, *Stenella attenuata*, and Spinner Dolphin, *Stenella longirostris*, have more distinct colour patterns.

Ecology and habitat Eats mainly fish and squid. Typically in groups of 10 to 20 individuals, mainly in deeper offshore waters.
Distribution and status Widely distributed in tropical and warm-temperate seas. SE Asia: recorded from Bay of Bengal through Java and Borneo, with reports from Thailand and Vietnam. Global status uncertain.

INDO-PACIFIC HUMPBACKED DOLPHIN
Sousa chinensis PLATE 45
Measurements TL 2.4–2.8m
Identification Adults usually have a long, low hump on the back with a small triangular fin on top, but some forms lack the hump and have a larger fin. Quite variable in coloration, from uniform dull grey to pure white or pink, with some speckled individuals. Colour variation is partly related to age, with younger animals dark grey, becoming mottled grey then whitish or pink, but there may be genetic variation in colour as well. **Taxonomic notes** May comprise more than one species, but further genetic and morphological study is required; names that have been used in the past include *S. plumbea*, *S. lentiginosa* and *S. borneensis*. **Similar species** Bottlenose dolphins, *Tursiops* spp., can be very similar to forms without a hump, but tend to be more uniform grey with shorter beak and taller dorsal fin and usually form larger, more active groups.

Ecology and habitat Eats mainly fish. Usually in sheltered coastal waters; sometimes in mangrove swamps and estuaries.
Distribution and status Throughout Indian and western Pacific Oceans, in warm temperate to tropical waters; a closely related species occurs in the eastern Atlantic. SE Asia: coastal waters throughout region including Myanmar, Peninsular Malaysia, Thailand, Cambodia and Vietnam. Global status uncertain, but probably declining; regionally threatened by entanglement in fishing gear, as well as chemical contamination from pollution.

INDO-PACIFIC BOTTLENOSE DOLPHIN

Tursiops aduncus PLATE 45

Measurements TL up to about 2.6m; males slightly larger than females

Identification Fairly uniform grey body, slightly darker on back and paler on sides, forming an indistinct cape; whitish on the belly, often with dark spots. Beak moderately short and thick; large flippers; dorsal fin tall and curved back. **Similar species** Common Bottlenose Dolphin, *T. truncatus*, is very similar but averages slightly larger; Indo-Pacific Humpbacked Dolphin, *Sousa chinensis*, if it lacks hump, is usually whiter and has smaller, more triangular dorsal fin; Rough-toothed Dolphin, *Steno bredanensis*, has a more conical head with no crease separating the beak, and a very narrow cape; Risso's Dolphin, *Grampus griseus*, has no beak; adults are paler with white around the head and no distinct cape; Pantropical Spotted Dolphin, *Stenella attenuata*, has a more complex pattern, usually with spots, and a longer, slimmer beak.

Ecology and habitat Found mainly in shallow coastal waters, usually in small groups.

Distribution and status Coastal waters around Indian Ocean and South Pacific to northern Australia. SE Asia: probably occurs in coastal waters throughout region, with records off Myanmar, Peninsular Malaysia, Cambodia, Thailand and Vietnam. Global status uncertain; regionally threatened by entanglement in fishing nets and deliberate hunting.

COMMON BOTTLENOSE DOLPHIN

Tursiops truncatus NOT ILLUSTRATED

Measurements TL 2.4–3.8m; males average slightly larger than females

Identification Very similar to Indo-Pacific Bottlenose Dolphin, *T. aduncus*, and difficult to distinguish in the field, but tends to be rather larger, with more robust body, stouter beak, more convex melon and proportionately smaller dorsal fin, and is generally slightly darker and lacking speckling.

Ecology and habitat Eats a wide variety of food including fish and invertebrates. Found in shallow to oceanic waters, usually in small groups. Frequently quite tame, approaching ships or swimmers.

Distribution and status Worldwide except in very cold waters. SE Asia: poorly known, as most records were not distinguished from *T. aduncus*. Most frequently seen near shore, but probably regular in deeper waters with confirmed records off Borneo and Vietnam. Globally not currently at risk, but threatened by fishing activities in region.

IRRAWADDY DOLPHIN

Orcaella brevirostris PLATE 45

Measurements TL 2–2.5m

Identification Varies from mid-grey to dark slate-blue, paler underneath, with no distinctive pattern. Small dorsal fin behind middle of back, rounded or slightly falcate. Forehead high and rounded; no beak. Broad, rounded flippers. **Taxonomic notes** Populations around Australia are morphologically distinct and they may represent a different species. **Similar species** Finless Porpoise, *Neophocaena phocaenoides*, is smaller and has no back fin; Indo-Pacific Humpbacked Dolphin, *Sousa chinensis*, is larger, has a longer beak and larger dorsal fin and is generally more active.

Ecology and habitat Prefers inshore waters and estuaries, including very muddy and murky waters; also occurs quite far inland on large rivers. Quiet and inconspicuous, rarely leaping or jumping.

Distribution and status India through Indonesia to Australia. SE Asia: coastal waters from Myanmar, around Malay Peninsula, through Gulf of Thailand to Cambodia and S Vietnam. Seen most often in estuaries and bays; also in inland rivers, including Irrawaddy, up to 1,400km inland in Myanmar, and Mekong inland to S Laos. Globally at risk, with several local populations, especially in rivers, having experienced dramatic declines; some river populations now Critically Endangered. Threats include accidental mortality during fishing activities, degradation of water quality from logging and deliberate hunting.

Family *PHOCOENIDAE* PORPOISES

Similar to dolphins, but with no beak. The only species found in the region has no dorsal fin.

FINLESS PORPOISE
Neophocaena phocaenoides PLATE 45
Measurements TL 1.5–2.0m
Identification Uniform grey, sometimes very pale, but usually slate. Rounded head; no dorsal fin. **Similar species** Irrawaddy Dolphin, *Orcaella brevirostris*, occurs in similar areas and also has a rounded head, but is larger, with a small but distinct dorsal fin; other dolphins are larger with large dorsal fins.
Ecology and habitat Eats small squid, prawns and small fish. Found in shallow coastal waters and river estuaries, in small groups or singles.
Distribution and status Coastal waters from India through to Japan. SE Asia: confirmed records include coastal waters and estuaries off Thailand, Peninsular Malaysia, Cambodia and Vietnam; may also occur off Myanmar. Globally at risk; local populations have experienced dramatic declines, and it is now relatively rare.

Family *PHYSETERIDAE* SPERM WHALES

This family includes one of the largest whales as well as some of the smallest, but they appear to be related. They all have a huge, bulbous forehead containing a large cavity full of oil and spermaceti, a wax-like substance highly valued by whalers. The lower jaw is relatively small and underslung, with a row of well-developed teeth that fit into sockets in the upper jaw.

GREAT SPERM WHALE
Physeter macrocephalus PLATE 47
Measurements TL males 10–12m, max 18m; females 8–9m, max 12m
Identification Huge head, with large square forehead. Overall colour dark brownish-grey to brown; "wrinkled" skin on back. Distinct dorsal hump with a series of low bumps leading to the tail – clearly visible when tail is thrown high before a deep dive. Tail flukes straight across the end, all dark below. Teeth on lower jaw only. Distinctive blow, angled forwards and to the left. **Taxonomic notes** Formerly called *P. catadon*. **Similar species** Humpback Whale, *Megaptera novaeangliae*, could appear similar when diving at a distance, but tail flukes differ in shape and colour; beaked whales, *Mesoplodon* spp., have a high forehead, but long beak and prominent dorsal fin; blowhole well back on head.
Ecology and habitat Feeds primarily on large squid. Usually in deep water; sometimes dives to over 1,000m. Remains near surface for 10 minutes or more to breathe after a deep dive.
Distribution and status Worldwide. SE Asia: occurs in both Indian Ocean and South China Sea, but only a few confirmed records from SE Asian waters. Globally Vulnerable due to very large declines caused by historic over-hunting; currently still threatened by entanglement in fishing nets and collisions with boats.

PYGMY SPERM WHALE
Kogia breviceps PLATE 46
Measurements TL 2.7–3.4m (males and females similar)
Identification Head appears shark-like, with underslung lower jaw. General colour dark bluish-grey fading to whitish on belly, with a gill-shaped light and dark mark at the side of the head. Dorsal fin low, behind centre of back. Teeth thin, curved inwards and sharp; 12 to 16 pairs in lower jaw, none in upper; up to 30mm long, 4.5mm in diameter. Usually swims slowly and sluggishly when on the surface, sometimes resting. **Similar species** Dwarf Sperm Whale, *K. sima*, is smaller, has a taller, dolphin-like fin and fewer, smaller teeth; some beaked whales, *Mesoplodon* spp., may appear similar at a distance, but have a quite different head shape.

Ecology and habitat Feeds mainly on squid and octopus, but also some fish and crabs. Usually alone or in small groups. Often in shallow water, frequently stranded.

Distribution and status Most parts of the world, in temperate to tropical waters. SE Asia: records from all around region (east of India, South China Sea and Sarawak) but no confirmed records within region. Globally not currently at risk, but potential threats include entanglement in fishing nets and ingestion of plastic.

DWARF SPERM WHALE
Kogia sima PLATE 46
Measurements TL 2.1–2.7m
Identification Coloration and shape very similar to that of Pygmy Sperm Whale, *K. breviceps* – dark grey above, whitish below – but slightly smaller, dorsal fin larger and further forwards (as in Common Bottlenose Dolphin, *Tursiops truncatus*), sometimes a few creases or grooves on throat, and fewer, smaller teeth (7 to 12 pairs on lower jaw – Pygmy usually has 12 to 16). Similar species Dolphins with similar fins have beaked heads; Pygmy Killer Whale, *Feresa attenuata*, and Melon-headed Whale, *Peponocephala electra*, have different head shapes, but could appear similar at a distance; both are much more active and usually in groups.

Ecology and habitat Feeds mainly on squid, but also fish and crustaceans. Can dive up to 300m, but often in inshore waters. Sometimes lies motionless on surface of water.

Distribution and status Worldwide, in tropical to temperate seas, but until recently confused with Pygmy Sperm Whale and many records have not been separated. SE Asia: confirmed records from all around region (E India, Lesser Sundas and Taiwan), but none from within region. Globally not currently at risk, but potential threats include entanglement in fishing nets and ingestion of plastic.

Family *ZIPHIIDAE* BEAKED WHALES
A poorly known group of medium to small whales, with an indistinct beak. The lower jaw has a few large teeth in males, only vestigial teeth in females. Bodies often covered with long, pale scars.

CUVIER'S BEAKED WHALE
Ziphius cavirostris PLATE 46
Measurements TL 5.5–7.5m; males typically about 0.5m shorter than females
Identification Sloping forehead; poorly defined beak, lower jaw longer than upper. Colour extremely variable, from dark rust-brown to slate-grey or fawn; belly usually paler; head sometimes whitish in older adults; back and sides usually covered with linear scars. Males have two conical teeth at front of jaw. Similar species Blainville's Beaked Whale, *Mesoplodon densirostris*, has a longer beak, teeth at side of jaw; Tropical Bottlenose Whale, *Indopacetus pacificus*, is of a similar size with a large bulbous forehead and long beak like a dolphin.
Ecology and habitat Feeds mainly on squid and deepwater fish. Can probably dive very deeply; submerges for up to 30 minutes. Often raises flukes before diving. Apparently wary of boats and hard to observe.

Distribution and status Worldwide except in Arctic waters, though less common in the tropics. SE Asia: recorded from Indian Ocean, from Java to Maluku in Indonesia, off Sabah and off coast of Thailand. Global status uncertain, but apparently one of the more common beaked whales; threatened by entanglement in fishing nets, especially drift nets.

BLAINVILLE'S BEAKED WHALE
Mesoplodon densirostris PLATE 46
Measurements TL up to about 4.7m
Identification Generally black or dark grey, paler below, often with extensive pale blotches and white scars (presumably from fighting). Forehead low with a distinct beak; lower jaw highly arched, especially in males, which have a single large tooth in the middle of the arch. Similar species Cuvier's Beaked

Whale, *Ziphius cavirostris*, has a less prominent beak, less arched jaw and often a pale forehead. Male Ginkgo-toothed Beaked Whale, *M. ginkgodens*, has less arched jaw with smaller, bilobed tooth. Females and young probably indistinguishable in field from other *Mesoplodon*.

Ecology and habitat Seen most often in slope waters, 500–1,000m deep. Feeds on small fish and squid.

Distribution and status Reported from tropical and sub-tropical waters in most parts of the world. SE Asia: recorded from Nicobar Islands in Indian Ocean and the Philippines, China and Taiwan, with one record from Thailand. Global status uncertain.

GINKGO-TOOTHED BEAKED WHALE
Mesoplodon ginkgodens PLATE 46
Measurements TL up to about 4.9m

Identification Generally black or dark grey, paler below. Tends not to have linear scars, unlike other *Mesoplodon*. Forehead low with a distinct beak; lower jaw moderately arched, especially in males, which have a bilobed tooth in the middle of the arch.
Similar species Cuvier's Beaked Whale, *Ziphius cavirostris*, has a less prominent beak, a more sloped forehead in profile and an unarched jaw; male Blainville's Beaked Whale, *M. densirostris*, often has more scarring, and has a more strongly arched jaw with conspicuous single large tooth.

Ecology and habitat Little known; presumed to feed mainly on squid.

Distribution and status Indian Ocean and tropical to temperate N Pacific. SE Asia: not yet recorded, but there are nearby confirmed records from Sri Lanka, E Sumatra and Taiwan. Global status uncertain.

Family *BALAENOPTERIDAE* RORQUALS OR BALEEN WHALES

The rorquals, or baleen whales, include some of the largest whales, and can be recognized by their huge size and small dorsal fins near the back of the body. They feed by filtering food and water through huge baleen plates in their mouths. At a long distance they can often be distinguished from the Sperm Whale by the shape of the spout when they breathe – tall and conical or low and bushy, as opposed to the Sperm Whale's spout, which is angled forwards and to the left. This, however, is less conspicuous in warm, tropical air.

Several of the rorquals can be separated only when seen well. Key features include size, the shape and position of the dorsal fin, the shape of the head and the coloration. The size and colour of the baleen can be helpful for distinguishing dead whales found stranded on beaches.

BLUE WHALE
Balaenoptera musculus PLATE 47
Measurements TL 22–24m, formerly up to 30.5m, but excessive hunting has led to the extermination of most of the larger, older individuals. Females slightly larger than males.
Identification Largest of the whales. General colour light bluish-grey mottled with greyish-white; belly sometimes yellowish. Head flat from the side; broad and U-shaped from above. Dorsal fin tiny, in last quarter of back – rarely visible until whale dives. Flukes lifted only slightly out of the water or not at all when diving. Baleen relatively short, stiff and all black. **Similar species** Fin Whale, *B.* *physalus*, is closest to this species in size but has a plain grey back and asymmetrical white on the underparts, a more V-shaped head and a larger dorsal fin.

Ecology and habitat Feeds mainly on krill (small crustaceans) within 100m of the surface. Migrates long distances between tropical seas and cold waters.

Distribution and status Worldwide, with seasonal migrations between polar and tropical areas. SE Asia: southern animals migrate regularly to the Indian Ocean, and are likely to occur occasionally in the Andaman Sea, while northern animals migrate regularly as far south as Taiwan and may be expected in the South China Sea. A specimen in a museum in Myanmar was apparently stranded on the coast there. Globally Endangered due to very large historic declines caused by excessive whaling; population recovery potentially threatened by climate change impacts on Antarctic krill.

FIN WHALE

Balaenoptera physalus PLATE 47

Measurements TL 18–20m, maximum 24–27m; males about 2m shorter than females

Identification Dark grey to brownish-black above with little or no mottling; whitish below. Often paler patch behind blowhole. Asymmetrical head colour – lower lip and palate white on right side, dark on left. Right front baleen white, remainder striped dark grey and whitish; up to 720mm long and 300mm wide. Dorsal fin somewhat variable in shape, shallowly angled; usually conspicuous shortly after blow. Head broadly V-shaped from above, with a central ridge. Tail flukes rarely raised before diving. Tall, cone-shaped blow. **Similar species** Blue Whale, *B. musculus*, averages larger, and is mottled blue-grey with U-shaped head and tiny dorsal fin; Bryde's Whale, *B. edeni*, and Sei Whale, *B. borealis*, can be difficult to distinguish, but lower jaw and baleen are grey on both sides, dorsal fin is steeper (over 45° angle) and visible at same time as blow.

Ecology and habitat Eats a wide variety of food including crustaceans, squid and small fish. Can dive up to 200m, but also feeds near surface. Winters in tropical areas and migrates to colder, richer feeding areas in summer.

Distribution and status Worldwide. SE Asia: no confirmed records from region, but individuals of northern population reach the Philippines and are likely to occur in South China Sea. Globally Endangered due to historic declines caused by whaling; ongoing threats include boat strikes.

SEI WHALE

Balaenoptera borealis PLATE 47

Measurements TL 12–14m, maximum

17–21m; females larger than males

Identification Body uniform dark grey with ovoid white scars; belly whitish. Conspicuous dorsal fin about one-third of way forwards from tail; angle of front of fin usually more than 40°. Single prominent ridge from blowholes to front of rostrum (rostral ridge); tip of snout slightly down-turned in profile. Dorsal fin usually visible at same time as blow. Baleen uniform grey-black with white fringes; sometimes a few half-white plates near front of mouth. **Similar species** Fin Whale, *B. physalus*, has shallower dorsal fin, visible just after the blow, and asymmetric white lower lips; Bryde's Whale, *B. edeni*, is very similar, distinguished reliably only by having three ridges on top of head.

Ecology and habitat Rarely dives very deeply, often feeding near the surface, breathing smoothly at regular intervals. Eats krill, squid and small fish. Often in small groups. Migrates annually from high-latitude feeding grounds to low-latitude wintering grounds.

Distribution and status Worldwide, mainly in temperate and sub-tropical waters. SE Asia: uncommon in region, but confirmed from Gulf of Thailand, where an individual was found on a beach in the peninsula. Globally Endangered as a result of historic declines caused by whaling.

BRYDE'S WHALE

Balaenoptera edeni PLATE 47

Measurements TL usually less than 12m in SE Asia (can be up to 14m elsewhere)

Identification Dark grey above; whitish below. Three prominent ridges on top of head. Baleen slate-grey, up to 420mm long by 240mm wide. Rolls sharply to expose fin and base of tail before diving. **Taxonomic note** Sittang Whale, *B. e. edeni*, is substantially smaller and genetically distinct from populations elsewhere (*B. e. brydei*), and the two are sometimes considered different species. **Similar species** Other large whales have only one ridge on the head; Fin Whale, *B. physalus*, is larger, with white right lower lip; Sei Whale, *B. borealis*, is larger than typical Asian forms, with different feeding patterns.

Ecology and habitat Primarily feeds on schooling fish; best studied populations usually dive deeply, returning irregularly to surface to breathe; not known whether SE Asian form has similar habits.

Distribution and status Throughout tropical and sub-tropical seas. SE Asia: Sittang Whale, *B. e. edeni*, occurs in shallow waters in eastern Indian Ocean and west Pacific; confirmed records from Myanmar, Malaysia and Thailand, as well as around the Philippines and South China Sea. Status uncertain, in part due to taxonomic uncertainty, but probably at risk.

MINKE WHALE
Balaenoptera acutorostrata PLATE 47
Measurements TL 7–8m, males max 9.8m; females max 10.7m

Identification Smallest of the rorquals, with narrow, pointed V-shaped rostrum and a single ridge on top of the head. Black to dark grey above, white below, usually with pale grey areas on the sides or back; usually has conspicuous white bands on flippers. Baleen about 200mm long, by 120mm wide, mainly cream-coloured or white. **Similar species** Fin, Sei and Bryde's Whales, *B. physalus*, *B. borealis* and *B. edeni*, are much larger with more rounded heads and more conspicuous blows; beaked whales have similar dorsal fins, but distinctive head shapes. The very similar Antarctic Minke Whale, *B. boaerensis*, is found primarily in the southern hemisphere, but may occasionally cross the equator and could show up in SE Asia. It is distinguished by pale flippers that usually lack a banding pattern, and asymmetrically-coloured baleen – white at the front of the mouth, dark grey at the back, with more white on the right side than the left side.

Ecology and habitat Feeds mainly on krill in the south, but also on small shoaling fish in the north. Populations in colder seas migrate seasonally to warmer waters.

Distribution and status Found from Arctic waters to tropical waters, including Indian Ocean, though largely north of the equator. SE Asia: potentially in any of the coastal waters; recorded off coasts of Malacca and Penang in Peninsular Malaysia as well as peninsular Thailand. Globally not currently at risk, but some populations are threatened by fisheries by catch and hunting.

HUMPBACK WHALE
Megaptera novaeangliae PLATE 47
Measurements TL 11.4–12.4m, males max 15m; females max 16m

Identification Generally black or dark grey, with varying amount of white on belly. Dorsal fin usually relatively small, sometimes similar to Blue or Fin Whales, *Balaenoptera musculus* or *B. physalus*, but often stepped. Very long flippers, white below and usually partially white above. Tail raised high out of the water on deep dives, with distinctive deep notch in middle, and individually variable amounts of white and dark grey on the underside. Baleen generally all black, 700mm x 300mm. Blow bushy and rounded.

Similar species Other rorquals have ridges instead of knobs on the head and smaller flippers, and do not raise their tails very high or at all before diving; Sperm Whale, *Physeter macrocephalus*, can also appear hump-backed when diving, but its tail is all dark, without a deep notch, the head shape is quite different when seen well, and the blow is forward.

Ecology and habitat Feeds on krill and schooling fish. Migratory.

Distribution and status Worldwide, migrating between temperate and polar feeding areas and tropical breeding areas. SE Asia: only a few records in region, though could potentially occur anywhere; nearest known breeding areas to the west of India, and north of Taiwan. Globally Vulnerable; experienced very large population declines due to historic over-hunting, and has only partially recovered.

Order SIRENIA

Sea cows

Family *DUGONGIDAE* DUGONG

The order Sirenia contains two families: the Trichechidae, found in the Americas, and the Dugongidae, found in Africa, Asia and Australasia. Like the cetaceans, the sirenians are adapted to a life completely in the water, but they appear to have evolved separately. Sirenians live in shallow coastal seas, feeding only on plant material. The forelimbs are flippers and there is a tail flipper, or fluke, but no dorsal fin. In adult Dugongs there is one pair of tusk-like incisors in the upper jaw and none in the lower jaw. There are no canines or premolars, but a total of 10 to 12 molars, only some of which are visible at one time; the deeper ones replace the top ones as they wear out.

DUGONG

Dugong dugon   PLATE 45

Measurements TL 2.5–3.5m. Wt 150–250kg

Identification Broad, rounded head with two nostrils at front of face and mouth on the underside; thick, paddle-like flippers; fluked tail. Colour generally dull, brownish-grey. Has a few sparsely scattered hairs on body and stiff bristles on upper lip. **Similar species** Distinguished from small cetaceans by very different head shape, nostrils in front of face (not on top of head) and no dorsal fin. Less active than most small cetaceans.

Ecology and habitat Usually rests during the day in deep water and feeds on sea grasses and other vegetation in shallow waters at night. Usually found in small groups, which are believed to travel long distances between feeding areas.

Distribution and status Seas off E Africa through India, Sri Lanka, Indonesia, the Philippines, New Guinea and N Australia. SE Asia: still occurs off coasts of peninsular Myanmar, Malaysia, Thailand, Cambodia and Vietnam, but numbers have declined dramatically in recent years, due to hunting, entanglement in fishing gear and changes in coastal habitats resulting from the clearing of mangroves and from trawling. Globally Vulnerable, but locally Endangered; it is probably the most threatened marine mammal in region.

Order PROBOSCIDEA

Family *ELEPHANTIDAE* ELEPHANTS

Elephants are the largest land animals still alive today, and include two genera, *Loxodonta* and *Elephas*. The former includes the African elephants, which differ from the Asian Elephant in several respects, of which the most conspicuous is their much larger ears. The Asian Elephant has two sorts of teeth: tusks and cheek teeth. It possesses only four cheek teeth at a time (one on each jaw), which are shed periodically when they are worn and no longer functional; a sixth and final set emerges at an age of about 40 years.

Elephants have been domesticated for a long time in Asia, being used particularly for moving heavily loads, including hauling logs in forestry operations, as well as for transport and even in warfare. In many areas where there has been extensive loss of forest, wild elephants may come into conflict with people by feeding on agricultural crops, particularly palms. They are also subject to poaching, especially for their ivory. Elephants can be dangerous to humans, especially if disturbed accidentally.

ASIAN ELEPHANT
Elephas maximus PLATE 48

Measurements SH 1,500–3,000, HB 3,000–6,000, T 1,000–1,500. Wt 3,000– 5,000kg

Identification Very large mammal with distinctive long trunk. Generally grey-brown, but paler when dry and blackish when wet. Infants covered in black bristly hair. Adult males may have tusks up to 2m long, although only about half is usually visible from outside; tusks are usually not visible externally in females and younger males. Footprints very large

Fig. 59 Prints of left feet of Elephas maximus *(a),* Rhinoceros sondaicus *(b),* Dicerorhinus sumatraensis *(c) and* Tapirus indicus *(d). H = hind foot, F = front foot. Print of fourth front toe on tapir may not be visible on firm ground.*

(about 450mm across in adult), oval, with three toe prints at front and one at side, all within the oval (Fig. 59a). **Voice** Has a broad vocal range including very low frequency booms for long-distance communication; loud trumpeting when alarmed; softer snorts within herd, often silent.

Ecology and habitat Mostly active from about two hours before dusk, through the night until two hours after dawn. Diet consists mainly of tender parts of various plants, including soft grasses, the growing parts of palms and banana stems. Fruits and the bark of latex-producing trees are also eaten, but only in relatively small quantities. Water and minerals are important to elephants, and may influence their distribution. Usually found in groups of typically between 3 and 40 individuals, although larger groups have sometimes

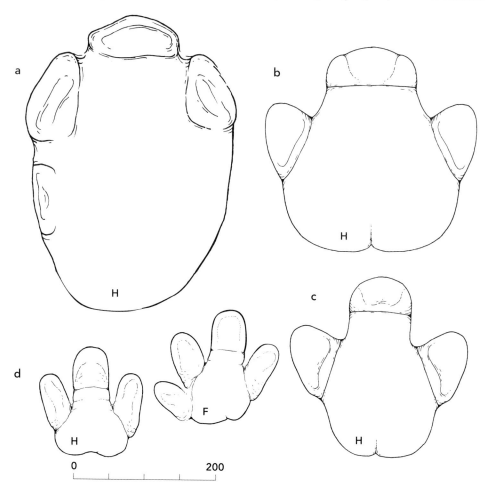

0   200

311

been reported. Groups split and merge, but normally contain one or more adult females with young of both sexes and various ages. Adult males occur loosely attached to herds, or as solitary individuals, or in groups of two or three. They can swim across rivers.

Distribution and status SE Asia: Myanmar, Thailand, Laos, Vietnam, Cambodia and Peninsular Malaysia. Also India, Sri Lanka, Sumatra and Borneo. Endangered. Populations have declined dramatically in much of range, owing to illegal hunting as well as to conflicts between humans and elephants in agricultural areas.

Order PERISSODACTYLA
Odd-toed ungulates

Members of this order are large, herbivorous mammals with one or three toes on each foot (except tapirs, which have four toes on each front foot). They include horses, rhinoceroses and tapirs. The stomach is rather small and simple, while the caecum (large intestine) is large. Three species occur in the region, though the rhinoceroses are now extremely rare.

Family *TAPIRIDAE* TAPIRS

Four species of tapir are currently recognized, all in the same genus, of which three occur in South America, and only one species in Asia. All are very similar in shape, with an elongate nose, curved back and short tail.

ASIAN TAPIR
Tapirus indicus PLATE 49
Measurements SH 900–1,050, HB 2,000–2,400, T 50–100. Wt 250–350kg
Identification Adult has front part of body black, including head and front legs, as well as lower part of hind legs, the remainder being white. Newborn young dark grey, completely covered with horizontal white stripes and rows of spots; gradually starts to acquire adult pattern at about four months of age. Tracks similar to those of rhinoceros, but smaller (150–170mm across), front foot with fourth toe, though this is usually visible only on soft ground (Fig. 59d). **Similar species** Asian Two-horned Rhinoceros, *Dicerorhinus sumatrensis*, is larger, with dif-ferent colour pattern; pigs, *Sus* spp., are smaller, with longer, more pointed head, thinner legs, different footprints.

Ecology and habitat Found mainly in intact rainforest, from lowlands up to about 2,000m in northern part of range where most lowland forest has been lost. Most active at night. Often found near streams, but does not wallow in mud baths.

Distribution and status SE Asia: S Myanmar, S Thailand and Peninsular Malaysia. Also Sumatra. Vulnerable. Still moderately common in some protected areas in Malaysia, but overall the population has declined substantially because of loss of habitat as well as hunting.

Family *RHINOCEROTIDAE* RHINOCEROSES

Rhinoceroses are characterized by a large, stocky body; short, stout legs with three toes on each foot; and either one or two horns, made of compacted hairs on top of the muzzle. There are five living species of rhinoceros (two in Africa and three in Asia) of which two occur in our region. However, rhinoceroses have a long fossil history, and millions of years ago there were also forms occurring in Europe and the Americas. All of the rhinos are legally protected throughout their range, but are still illegally persecuted for their horns and other parts of the body, which are falsely believed to have medicinal properties. The two species in the region are both Critically Endangered, with very small remaining populations that are very much at risk of extinction unless this illegal trade can be stopped.

ASIAN TWO-HORNED RHINOCEROS

Dicerorhinus sumatrensis PLATE 48

Measurements SH 1,200–1,300, HB 2,400–2,600, T 650. Wt 900–1,000kg

Identification General coloration usually dark brown, but appearance may vary after bathing in water or mud. Skin thick with extensive sparse hairs, especially when young, but hairs may be hard to see in field. Only one fold of skin crosses back, behind shoulder; folds of skin on neck and lower belly do not cross over back; no folds of skin on hind legs. Two horns, front one relatively narrow, typically 250–300mm in males and smaller in females; rear horn short, rarely more than 100mm, and often not visible in field. More often detected by tracks than seen: footprints of adults on firm soil 185–235mm at widest point, showing three clear toe marks (Fig. 59c). Mud wallows can be distinguished from those of pigs by clear, deep horn marks in sides of wallow. Dung consists of balls of coarsely chopped woody material about 90mm in diameter, usually found in small piles, sometimes in mounds frequently used over long periods. When disturbed unexpectedly, this rhinoceros usually flees rapidly, sometimes giving a series of short, hoarse barks. **Similar species** Lesser One-horned Rhinoceros, *Rhinoceros sondaicus*, is larger, with three folds of skin crossing back; footprints of similar shape but larger; Asian Tapir, *Tapirus indicus*, has similar, but smaller footprints, conspicuous black-and-white body colour; large pigs, *Sus* spp., have much lighter bodies with slender legs, relatively large head and two-hoofed footprints.

Ecology and habitat Mainly active from late afternoon to mid-morning. Usually rests during hot hours of day in a mud wallow, shaded spot or ridge top. Feeds on mature leaves and twigs from a wide range of woody plants, including saplings, lianas and small trees, which may be pushed over to obtain the leaves. Occasionally eats fallen fruits. Usually found within 10–15km of natural mineral sources. Formerly occurred in a variety of forest types, but now largely in lowland rainforest, although sometimes in fairly hilly areas. Uses regenerating forests, but rarely enters open areas.

Distribution and status SE Asia: Peninsular Malaysia. Also Sumatra and Borneo. Critically Endangered. Formerly widespread throughout mainland SE Asia, but illegal hunting has reduced the numbers to fewer than 300 individuals in a few scattered populations in Sumatra, N Borneo and Peninsular Malaysia.

LESSER ONE-HORNED RHINOCEROS

Rhinoceros sondaicus PLATE 48

Measurements SH 1,600–1,800, HB 3,000–3,200, T 700. Wt 1.5–2kg

Identification Large, distinctly shaped heavy animal; thick, dark grey skin; three folds of skin across back, one on neck, one behind shoulders and one over lower back; an additional horizontal fold on rump just below tail, and on hind leg. There is a single, relatively thick horn on the tip of the nose, rarely longer than 150mm in male (maximum ~250mm); smaller and inconspicuous in female. Footprints of adults large, about 280–300mm across, with three conspicuous toe prints (Fig. 59b). **Similar species** Asian Two-horned Rhinoceros, *Dicerorhinus sumatrensis*, is smaller, with only one fold of skin across back; often has a second horn.

Ecology and habitat Currently restricted to dense lowland rainforest with extensive wet areas, including streams and mud wallows. Formerly occurred in a greater variety of habitats, including mixed forest and grasslands.

Distribution and status SE Asia: S Vietnam. Also W Java. Critically Endangered. Formerly occurred throughout region. Now fewer than 10 individuals left in region, with perhaps 50 more in Java.

Order ARTIODACTYLA
Even-toed ungulates

The even-toed ungulates are terrestrial mammals with two functional hoofed toes and two small dew toes on each foot. The dew toes are situated well above the main toes and, except in pigs, rarely appear in footprints except in very soft soil or mud. Most species, other than pigs, feed mainly on plant material. The stomach is rather large and complex, with 2 or 3 chambers in pigs, 3 in mousedeer and 4 in other species. The caecum is small. For all species other than pigs, food is partially digested in the stomach and then brought back up into the mouth one or more times for further chewing, to increase the amount of nutrition that can be obtained from grasses and leaves, which contain a high percentage of cellulose that is difficult to digest. This also permits ruminants to ingest large amounts of food quickly before moving to sheltered places, better protected against predators, for chewing.

Family *SUIDAE* PIGS
Unlike other artiodactyls, pigs have incisors in the upper jaw and an omnivorous diet, including animal material (Fig. 61). Pigs can be distinguished by their elongate snout with a flattened tip and nostrils in the middle. Canines of males are greatly enlarged, forming tusks that protrude sideways.

EURASIAN WILD PIG
Sus scrofa   PLATE 49
Measurements SH 600–800, HB 1,350–1,500, T 200–300. Wt of large male 75–200kg

Identification Colour varies from blackish to reddish; muzzle elongate without a beard; long black hairs on upper back and neck, forming a mane. Young are born dark brown with elongate white stripes along body. Footprints more rounded and symmetric than those of deer, with imprints of the dew toes apparent except on very hard ground (Fig. 60). **Voice** Pigs in herds relatively noisy, making many grunting and squealing noises; also often sounds of breaking vegetation. **Taxonomic notes** "Banded Pig", *S. scrofa vittatus*, from Peninsular Malaysia and Indonesia, is distinctly smaller with sparser hair, and sometimes considered a separate species. **Similar species** Bearded Pig, *S. barbatus*, averages taller, has longer legs, longer muzzle with beard and bristly warts; domestic pigs, which are descended from *S. scrofa*, are sometimes very similar, but generally tamer, and usually lack a black mane.

Ecology and habitat Found in a wide variety of habitats, including mature forests, disturbed areas, secondary forest, gardens and plantations. Feeds on roots, seeds and a wide variety of other vegetable and animal matter, such as invertebrates, worms and small vertebrates including birds' eggs and nestlings, if encountered on the ground. In gardens and plantations can cause extensive damage to growing crops.

Distribution and status SE Asia: Myanmar, Thailand, Laos, Vietnam, Cambodia and Peninsular Malaysia. Also much of Europe, N Africa and mainland Asia, with introduced populations elsewhere. Not currently at risk.

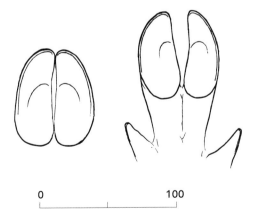

0   100

Fig. 60 *Left hind footprints of* Sus scrofa *on hard ground (left) and soft ground (right).*

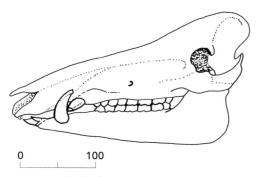

0   100

Fig. 61 Skull of Sus barbatus.

BEARDED PIG
Sus barbatus PLATE 49
Measurements SH 900, HB 1,200–1,500,
T 170–250. Wt 50–120kg (sometimes
considerably heavier when storing fat)
Identification Colour varies from blackish (in
young animals) to reddish-brown or yellow-
grey; may also be affected by colour of mud
wallow. Head long; fleshy protuberance
("wart") above each side of mouth with
upwards-pointing bristles, larger in males
than females; large beard of long wiry hairs on
snout. Lower canines of males relatively
straight, protruding to sides. Body size varies
greatly with food supply. Females have five
pairs of mammae. Mud wallows are a distinctive feature of pig activity. Footprints similar
to those of other wild pigs (Fig. 60). **Voice**
Various squeals and grunting, as well as loud
snorts or crunching sounds of pigs feeding on
hard plant material. **Similar species** Eurasian
Wild Pig, *S. scrofa*, is smaller, with shorter
legs, lacks facial protuberances and beard.
Ecology and habitat Active day and night;
tends to be more nocturnal where heavily
disturbed. Diet includes fallen fruits and
seeds, roots, herbs and other plant material,
earthworms and other small animals which it
finds by grubbing on the ground. Can cause
damage to plantations, feeding on the growing parts of young palms and on cocoa fruits.
In regions of extensive forest, periodically
forms very large herds which travel great distances in search of food, swimming across
rivers and climbing into mountain ranges.
Adult females make nests of saplings and
shrubs, which are bitten or torn off and piled
up on the ground, where they give birth to
young (from 3 to 11 at one time). Nests are
made on dry ground not liable to flooding.
Distribution and status SE Asia: Peninsular
Malaysia. Also Sumatra, Borneo and some
adjacent islands. Near Threatened globally.
In Peninsular Malaysia population has
declined dramatically due to loss and fragmentation of habitat, and appears to be
Endangered; it has disappeared even from
large protected areas, possibly due to dis-
ruption of traditional migration routes. In
Borneo, still relatively common in many
areas, but has declined substantially due to
loss of habitat and over-hunting.

VIETNAMESE WARTY PIG
Sus bucculentus NOT ILLUSTRATED
Measurements Skull: gl 350–390
Identification Uncertain whether this represents a legitimate species. Known only from
two skulls from Vietnam, and an additional
skull of a juvenile from Laos. Supposedly differs from Eurasian Wild Pig, *S. scrofa*, in having a more elongate skull, straighter dorsal
margin of the braincase, higher occipital
crest and relatively larger premolars.
However, recent genetic analyses of the Lao
specimen found that it fitted within genetic
sequences of typical *S. scrofa*, suggesting it
may not be a distinct species.

Family *TRAGULIDAE* MOUSEDEER
Mousedeer are small, forest-dwelling ungulates with slender legs and without antlers. The
back is strongly arched. The lower canines are long, and may protrude out of the mouth from
the upper jaw of males. Three or four species are currently recognized from the region.

LESSER MOUSEDEER
Tragulus kanchil PLATE 50
Measurements SH 200–230, HB 400–550,
T 60–90. Wt 1.4–2.5kg
Identification Upperparts with relatively fine
fur, reddish-brown mixed with fine black,

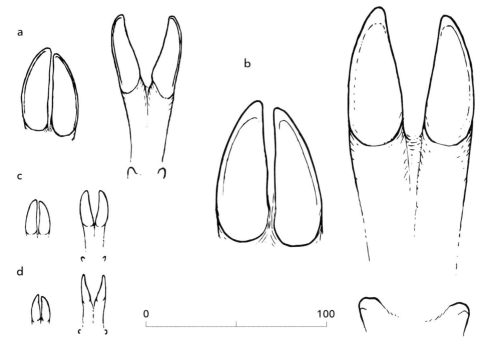

a

b

c

d

0   100

appearing fairly uniform coloured overall; centre of nape usually blacker than rest of back, often forming a distinct stripe. Underparts white, with variable brown stripes up middle or along sides of belly; distinctive dark brown and white markings on throat and upper chest, typically with triangular white stripe up middle, bordered by dark brown triangle, then one diagonal stripe on each side, which usually join on chin; in profile white appears as a single line from chin to side of chest. Some geographic variation in colour, with populations in peninsular Thailand and Malaysia darker and more reddish; those on rest of mainland duller, often lacking nape stripe; additional colour variations occur on islands. Footprints similar in shape to other deer, but much smaller (Fig. 62). **Taxonomic note** Formerly considered part of species *T. javanicus*, which is now considered to be restricted to Java; population in N Thailand is larger and sometimes considered a separate species, *T. williamsoni*, but only the type specimen is known, and its distinctiveness is uncertain. **Similar species** Greater Mousedeer, *T. napu*, is larger, with more flecked coloration on upperparts and different throat markings; Silver-backed Mousedeer, *T. versicolor*, has

Fig. 62 Left hind footprints on hard ground (left) and soft ground (right) of Muntiacus muntjak *(a),* Rusa unicolor *(b),* Tragulus napu *(c) and* T. kanchil *(d).*

orange-brown on sides of neck and shoulders contrasting with finely speckled silver lower back and rump.

Ecology and habitat Active periodically both night and day. Diet includes fallen fruits, leaf shoots and fungi. Usually solitary. Both adults and young rest in any sheltered spot under forest cover. Occurs in tall and secondary forests, sometimes entering gardens and mixed scrub.

Distribution and status SE Asia: Myanmar, Thailand, Laos, Vietnam, Cambodia and Peninsular Malaysia. Also SW China, Sumatra, Borneo and many adjacent islands. Not currently at risk, but populations in many areas are declining as a result of forest loss and excessive hunting.

GREATER MOUSEDEER
Tragulus napu PLATE 50
Measurements SH 300–350, HB 520–572, T 60–100, HF 140–157. Wt 3.5–4.5kg
Identification Upperparts appear coarsely

mottled orange-buff, grey-buff and blackish; hairs on upperparts grey-buff to orange-buff with blackish tips; darker in midline and paler on sides of body; often with a darker nape patch. Intensity of coloration varies between individuals. Underparts white, usually without brown stripes on belly; pattern of brown and white markings on upper chest and underside of neck, typically with triangular white stripe in centre, bordered by dark brown stripes, then two separate diagonal white stripes on each side, one originating near front of chin, and one in middle of throat, though sometimes these join; in profile, usually appears as two separate white bars on side of neck. Footprints similar in shape to those of Lesser Mousedeer, but distinctly larger (Fig. 62c). **Similar species** Lesser Mousedeer, *T. kanchil*, is substantially smaller, with more finely patterned reddish fur, usually only a single white stripe on side of throat; Silver-backed Mousedeer, *T. versicolor*, is smaller, with silver-grey speckling on back.

Ecology and habitat Occurs in tall and secondary forests, sometimes entering gardens. Mainly nocturnal, but sometimes also active during day. Diet includes fallen fruits, leaf shoots and other vegetation.

Distribution and status SE Asia: S Myanmar, S Thailand and Peninsular Malaysia. Also Sumatra, Borneo and adjacent islands, and Palawan (the Philippines). Near Threatened. Populations have declined throughout range, owing to loss of forest habitat and excessive hunting.

SILVER-BACKED MOUSEDEER
Tragulus versicolor PLATE 50
Measurements SH 250, HB 400–450. Wt 1.7kg
Identification Head, sides of neck and shoulders reddish-orange mottled with black, especially on back of neck, which typically shows a distinct darker stripe; rest of back, flanks and hindquarters silver-grey finely speckled with dark grey-brown. Underparts white in middle; upper chest and throat with pattern of reddish-brown and white stripes, usually with one continuous white stripe on side of neck. **Similar species** Lesser Mousedeer, *T. kancil*, is slightly smaller, with upperparts all mottled reddish-brown and black.
Ecology and habitat Believed to inhabit understorey of tall lowland forest.
Distribution and status SE Asia: S Vietnam. Uncertain, with very few known records; probably Endangered or Critically Endangered, owing to limited range, extensive loss of lowland forest and excessive hunting.

Family *MOSCHIDAE* MUSK-DEER
Medium-sized ungulates closely related to deer with relatively small head and enlarged ears. Both sexes lack antlers, but males have long, narrow upper canines that protrude from upper jaw as backwards-curving tusks. Hind legs are longer than forelegs, so that shoulder is slightly lower than rump; this allows it to jump very strongly. All four toes on feet relatively well developed, and can be used to support animal when climbing in lower branches of trees. Several species of musk-deer occur in China, the Himalayas and Siberia, with two species in the region, one in N Myanmar and one in N Vietnam. Adult males have a gland on the underside of the belly which produces a strong-smelling musk that is highly sought-after for perfumes; illegal hunting to obtain this musk has caused declines in all species, and some are now Endangered. A few species are now farmed in China.

FOREST MUSK-DEER
Moschus berezovskii PLATE 51
Measurements SH 500–600, HB 700–800, T 40. Wt 6–9kg
Identification Upperparts are dark brown, finely speckled with olive-brown or orange-brown spots, darker on lower back and rump as well as top of head; underparts including legs reddish-brown to yellowish-orange; throat and neck with long, pale

orange or white stripes on underside, one in the middle and one on each side, sometimes broken into separate spots; ears orange-brown at base, black at tip, white inside. Newborn young blackish-brown above with rows of buff spots on back. **Similar species** Black Musk-deer, *M. fuscus*, is darker with dark underparts, black ears, reduced markings on neck.

Ecology and habitat Largely forested areas on limestone karst outcrops in Vietnam. In China, occurs in a variety of forested habitats, mostly at higher elevations.

Distribution and status SE Asia: N Vietnam. Also S and C China. Vulnerable. In Vietnam, population has declined from several hundred individuals to only a few, largely due to illegal hunting. In China, still moderate numbers remaining, but declining dramatically due to loss of habitat and illegal hunting.

BLACK MUSK-DEER

Moschus fuscus PLATE 51

Measurements SH ~600, HB ~700. Wt 8kg

Identification Upperparts dark brown to blackish; head, neck, ears, black; underparts dark, similar to back; throat dark, often with two incomplete yellowish collars. Juveniles dark brown with buff spots. **Similar species** Forest Musk-deer, *M. berezovskii*, has pale underparts, long yellow stripes on neck.

Ecology and habitat Forest, at higher altitudes near tree line, in pine forests and rhododendron.

Distribution and status SE Asia: N Myanmar. Also S China (Yunnan, Tibet), NE India (Assam) and Nepal. Status poorly known, but apparently rare and probably at risk. Threats include hunting and the illegal trade in musk.

Family *CERVIDAE* DEER

Males have distinctive antlers, which are usually shed and regrown at regular intervals (probably annually), unlike the horns of Bovids, which are permanent. Antlers are a form of bone and grow from permanent projections, called pedicels, on the skull. The larger deer have traditionally all been placed in the genus *Cervus*, but recent taxonomic studies suggest the SE Asian species should be placed in four separate genera: *Cervus, Rusa, Rucervus* and *Axis*. They tend to walk with the head held high and the back fairly straight. Muntjacs, *Muntiacus* spp., walk with the head carried low, the back slightly arched and the hindquarters high, lifting the feet high off the ground at every step. Adult male muntjacs have long upper canines which protrude beyond the lip and are loose in their sockets. A rattling noise, probably produced by these loose teeth, is sometimes heard from muntjac observed at close range.

SAMBAR

Rusa unicolor PLATE 52

Measurements SH 1,400–1,600, HB 1,500–2,000, T 210–280. Wt 180–260kg Length of antlers along greatest curve typically 300–550

Identification Large deer with dark brown skin and hair; upperparts generally grey-brown, sometimes slightly reddish, usually darker along midline; underparts same colour as back or darker. Tail bushy, mainly blackish except for white on base of underside. Middle of rump sometimes paler than rest of back. Adult males with long, coarse hair on neck. Young usually without spots. Adult males typically have 3 tines to each antler, 1 in front, and 2 at the tip of the main beam; inner branch of terminal fork of antler normally somewhat smaller than the outer, which appears to be a continuation of the main beam of the antler. Two-year-old males have antlers with only 1 point; three-year-old males have antlers with 2 points. Footprints relatively large, pointed at front (Fig. 62b). **Voice** Call is a distinctive yelp or shrill bark. **Similar species** Eld's Deer, *Rucervus eldii*, is more reddish, underside pale, tail not black, brow tine of antler forming continuous curve with main branch.

Ecology and habitat Active mainly at night, also early morning and late afternoon. Diet includes grasses, herbs, shrubs, young leaves of woody plants and fallen fruits.

Often visits natural mineral sources. Usually solitary, but groups of two are sometimes seen, consisting of adult male and female, female and young, or adult females. Nocturnal activity and solitary nature possibly a consequence of heavy hunting pressure. Most common in secondary forests on gently sloping terrain, but also in tall dipterocarp forests on steep terrain and in swamp forests. Enters gardens and plantations to feed.

Distribution and status SE Asia: Myanmar, Thailand, Laos, Vietnam, Cambodia and Peninsular Malaysia. Also Sri Lanka, India, S China, Sumatra, Borneo and many larger adjacent islands and the Philippines. Near Threatened: has declined dramatically in many parts of range, especially Indochina, as result of excessive hunting.

SIKA

Cervus nippon PLATE 52
Measurements SH 650–1100, HB 950-1800, T 75–150. Wt 80kg
Identification Moderately large deer with dark brown to reddish-brown upperparts, usually with rows of large white spots; underparts paler. In winter, coat is darker and longer, with fewer white spots. Rump has small white patch around base of tail. Tail small. Young with extensive spots. Ears relatively small. Adult males typically have 5 tines on each antler. Footprints similar to those of other large deer. **Voice** During mating season, male gives loud bugling call. **Taxonomic notes** Mainland forms may be a different species from those in Japan, in which case name may change. **Similar species** Sambar, *Rusa unicolor*, is larger, without spots in adults, antlers usually have fewer tines; Eld's Deer, *Rucervus eldii*, has brow tine of antler forming continuous curve with main branch.
Ecology and habitat Poorly known in region. Probably largely nocturnal and solitary.
Distribution and status SE Asia: Vietnam. Also E China, Japan and Taiwan. Endangered in wild, with most wild populations greatly reduced. Vietnam population

believed extinct in wild, but persists in captivity, as well as semi-captive populations in some reserves.

ELD'S DEER

Rucervus eldii PLATE 52
Measurements SH 1,200–1,300, HB 1,500–1,700, T 220–250. Wt 95–150kg
Identification Upperparts reddish-brown, males darker than females; underparts whitish. Adult males have thick long hair on neck, forming a mane. Brow tine of antler angled strongly forwards, forming continuous curve with main branch, in a bow shape; many small tines at tip of antler. Fawns have many pale spots, which sometimes persist in adults. Footprints similar to those of Sambar, *Rusa unicolor* (Fig. 62b). **Similar species** Sambar, *Rusa unicolor*, is more greyish-brown with a black tail, antlers with front tine angled backwards.
Ecology and habitat Lowland swampy areas, as well as open, dry dipterocarp forest and grasslands. Feeds mainly on grasses; sometimes enters rice fields.
Distribution and status SE Asia: Myanmar, Laos, Vietnam, Cambodia. Formerly occurred in Thailand. Vulnerable. Populations have declined in most areas, owing to hunting and habitat loss.

SCHOMBURGK'S DEER

Rucervus schomburgki PLATE 52
Measurements SH 1,050
Identification Upperparts uniform brown, slightly darker on top of tail, white under tail, forehead and legs reddish; underparts pale. Antlers with short main beam and numerous branches with a total of 10–30 tines on both antlers. Fawns with pale spots. **Similar species** Other deer have many fewer tines on antlers.
Ecology and habitat Formerly found mainly in swampy plains and river floodplains, in areas of long grasses, canes and shrubs.
Distribution and status SE Asia: Formerly C Thailand. Possibly also S China (Yunnan). Probably Extinct – died out in China (from where last reliable reports were in 1930s)

from conversion of habitat to rice farms, and from excessive hunting.

HOG DEER

Axis porcinus   PLATE 51

Measurements SH 650–720, HB 1,400–1,500, T 170–210. Wt 70–110kg

Identification Upperparts brown to dark brown in winter, greyer in summer; underparts paler. Tail coloured as back, with white underside; centre of back darker; fawns with rows of small white spots that may persist in adults. Antlers of males slender, forked at tip of main beam, with small third prong at base pointing upwards. Footprints similar in shape to those of Sambar (Fig. 62b), but smaller. **Similar species** Sambar, *Rusa unicolor*, is much larger, with longer legs, larger antlers, dark tail; Large-antlered Muntjac, *Muntiacus vuquangensis*, is similar in size, but has much larger pedicel, antlers not forked at tip, short triangular tail, not spotted, different habitat.

Ecology and habitat Natural habitat mainly wet or moist tall grasslands in lowland floodplains, feeding mainly on grasses.

Distribution and status SE Asia: Myanmar and Cambodia, formerly Thailand, Laos and Vietnam. Also Pakistan, N India, Nepal, Bangladesh and S China, with some introduced populations elsewhere. Vulnerable. Probably extirpated from Thailand, Laos and Vietnam, with small remaining populations in Myanmar and Cambodia. Threats include hunting and conversion of wet grasslands to agriculture. Reintroduced into Thailand.

TUFTED DEER

Elaphodus cephalophus   PLATE 51

Measurements SH 500–700, HB 1,000–1,200, T 70–150. Wt 17–30kg

Identification Upperparts dark chocolate brown, blacker on legs, slightly greyer on head and neck; underparts paler; hair coarse and slightly shaggy. Top of head pointed in profile with distinct tuft of black hair; pedicel very short with small antlers, often hidden by tuft of hair. Ears with conspicuous white marks; tail dark with white underside. Upper

canines elongate, visible outside mouth in males. **Voice** A sharp bark. **Similar species** Muntjacs, *Muntiacus* spp., tend to be somewhat smaller, without tuft on top of head and with longer antlers.

Ecology and habitat Upper montane areas in damp forest near snowline.

Distribution and status SE Asia: N Myanmar. Also China. Status uncertain. Appears to be very rare in Myanmar, where no recent records, but more common in China.

Genus *Muntiacus* Muntjacs can be distinguished from other deer by their relatively small size, and by their distinctive posture with curved back and head held low. Males have large bony pedicels, and generally small antlers. Several species are currently recognized from the region, many of which have been confirmed from genetic studies, but there is moderate confusion about their identifications, as some have been reported only from trophies found in villages, and the field characters are not described. In particular, there is uncertainty over the number of species of small dark muntjacs found in Indochina, and no information is available on how to tell them apart in the field.

RED MUNTJAC

Muntiacus muntjak   PLATE 50

Measurements SH 500–550, HB 900–1,100, T 170–190. Wt 20–28kg. Antler length 70–130, pedicel length 70–150

Identification Small, reddish deer, males with very large pedicels and relatively small antlers. Upperparts vary from deep reddish-brown or rufous to paler reddish-yellow, generally darker along midline; underparts pale whitish or greyish; tail coloured as back above, white below. Antlers rough with small spike near base, sharp curve near tip. Pedicel thick and straight, with a burr where antler joins; continues as bony ridge down forehead, usually with conspicuous black lines. Female has tuft of stiff hair in place of pedicel or antlers. Young normally with white spots. Footprints with relatively elongate toes, pointed at front (Fig. 62a), probably indistinguishable from those of other muntjacs except by size. **Voice** Adults of both sexes give short, loud, barking calls. **Similar species** Fea's Muntjac, *M. feae*, is browner, with dark legs, pale top of head; Gongshan Muntjac, *M. gongshanensis*, has black belly and legs; Leaf Muntjac, *M. putaoensis*, is smaller, with short pedicels; Large-antlered Muntjac, *M. vuquangensis*, is substantially larger, with long antlers and relatively short pedicels.

Ecology and habitat Found in a wide variety of forest habitats, from tropical rainforest to dry dipterocarp forest, lowlands to hills. Browses on leaves and twigs more often than grazing on grass; also eats fallen fruits. Mainly nocturnal, although also active during day in areas where not hunted. Largely solitary except during breeding season.

Distribution and status SE Asia: Myanmar, Thailand, Laos, Vietnam, Cambodia and Peninsular Malaysia. Also Sri Lanka, India, S China, Taiwan, Sumatra, Java, Borneo and some adjacent islands. Not currently at risk, though declining, owing to excessive hunting in some areas. This is the most widespread muntjac in the region, and the only species in many areas.

ROOSEVELT'S MUNTJAC

Muntiacus rooseveltorum   NOT ILLUSTRATED
Measurements Estimated SH ~400
Identification Small muntjac with dark

brown coat, white throat, short brown tail; large glands on chin, dark legs; moderate antlers. **Similar species** Apparently very similar to Annamite Muntjac, *M. truongsonensis*. Latter may be darker with shorter antlers, but field identification characters poorly known because species descriptions based on incomplete skulls and trophies.

Ecology and habitat Apparently found mainly in evergreen wet hill forest.

Distribution and status SE Asia: N Laos, possibly N Myanmar and probably N Vietnam. Status uncertain owing to confusion with *M. truongsonensis*.

ANNAMITE MUNTJAC

Muntiacus truongsonensis   PLATE 50
Measurements Estimated SH ~400.
Wt ~15kg

Identification Small, blackish muntjac, with short pedicels (about 40mm) and very short antlers, about 20mm long. Canines relatively large in both males and females. A muntjac described in life from Laos, which may have been this species, had dark brown to black fur on most of the body and legs, with orange-brown crown and light brownish neck, very short antlers. **Similar species** Roosevelt's Muntjac, *M. rooseveltorum*, is genetically distinct and may have longer antlers, but field characters to identify species uncertain; Gongshan Muntjac, *M. gongshanensis*, is similar in colour, but substantially larger, with a heavier build and proportionately larger head.

Ecology and habitat Evergreen wet hill forest above 1,000m in Annamite Mountains.

Distribution and status SE Asia: mountains of Vietnam, Laos and possibly Myanmar. Status uncertain; camera trap and hunter surveys suggest small dark muntjacs are relatively common in hill forest over 1,000m, but species identifications uncertain. Probably threatened by excessive hunting.

PUHOAT MUNTJAC

Muntiacus puhoatensis   NOT ILLUSTRATED
Identification Small dark muntjac that apparently differs from Annamite Muntjac,

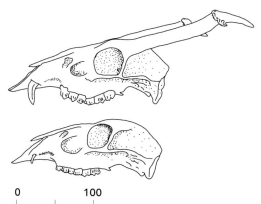

Fig. 63 *Skull of male (top) and female (bottom) Muntiacus muntjak.*

0   100

M. truongsonensis, in genetic characters, but differences in appearance of live animals not presently known.

Ecology and habitat Evergreen wet hill forest above 1,000m in Annamite Mountains.

Distribution and status SE Asia: Vietnam. Status uncertain, owing to confusion with *M. truongsonensis* and *M. rooseveltorum.*

LEAF MUNTJAC

Muntiacus putaoensis PLATE 50

Measurements Estimated SH ~400. Wt 15kg

Identification Small muntjac, similar in size to Annamite Muntjac, *M. truongsonensis,* also with short pedicels (less than 40mm in length) and short, unbranched antlers 10–35mm long, but differing genetically and in colour. Fur generally reddish-brown with slightly darker legs and face; some individuals may be darker. **Similar species** Annamite Muntjac, *M. truongsonensis,* is believed to be darker on body, paler on head; Red Muntjac, *M. muntjak,* is much larger, with longer pedicels and larger antlers.

Ecology and habitat Temperate and subtropical hill forest.

Distribution and status SE Asia: N Myanmar. Status uncertain, but camera trapping suggests it may be reasonably common in some areas. Probably threatened by excessive hunting and trapping.

GONGSHAN MUNTJAC

Muntiacus gongshanensis PLATE 50

Measurements SH ~ 500–550, HB 900–1,100, T 200. Wt 21–28kg

Identification Body mid- to dark brown, with belly, outsides of legs and top of tail black; insides of legs, underside of tail contrasting white. Head pale brown with dark lines on pedicels. Antlers relatively short. **Taxonomic note** Some recent genetic studies suggest this may be a form of Black Muntjac, *M. crinifrons,* a species otherwise known from China, but further analyses are required. **Similar species** Red Muntjac, *M. muntjak,* is uniformly reddish, with larger pedicels and antlers; Leaf Muntjac, *M. putaoensis,* is sub-

stantially smaller; Fea's Muntjac, *M. feae,* has underparts same colour as back, rather than black, with brown rather than black upper legs.

Ecology and habitat Subtropical and temperate forest in montane areas, up to alpine scrub.

Distribution and status SE Asia: N Myanmar. Also S China (Tibet, Yunnan). Status poorly known, but probably threatened by excessive hunting and trapping.

FEA'S MUNTJAC

Muntiacus feae PLATE 50

Measurements SH ~ 500–550, HB 880, T 100. Wt 22kg

Identification Upperparts dark brown, finely speckled with yellow; underparts brown, sometimes with pale areas; legs darken to black near hoof, white stripe on front of hind leg; face dark brown on sides, yellowish-brown on crown, pedicels and bases of ears, except for black stripe from just above eyes on inside of pedicel; tail short with black upperside, white underside. Pedicels well developed, antlers relatively short. Well-developed lachrymal gland (in front of eye). **Similar species** Red Muntjac, *M. muntjak,* is reddish-orange in colour without contrasting paler top of head; Gongshan Muntjac, *M. gongshanensis,* has black belly, legs all black.

Ecology and habitat Evergreen forest in hilly or mountainous areas.

Distribution and status SE Asia: S Myanmar and peninsular Thailand. Near Threatened. Restricted range, with much habitat lost historically, some ongoing habitat loss and some threats due to hunting.

LARGE-ANTLERED MUNTJAC

Muntiacus vuquangensis PLATE 51

Measurements SH 650–700. Wt 34kg

Identification Relatively large muntjac, with distinctive large antlers in male; antlers up to 280mm long on moderately long, stout pedicels; fork at base well developed, up to 100mm long. Fur colour yellowish-brown or tan to grey-brown, with grizzled effect caused by banding on individual hairs; black lines on forehead; white spot on knee of male; tail short and triangular, coloured as back above, white below. **Similar species** Red Muntjac, *M. muntjak*, is smaller, with reddish coat, longer tail, shorter antlers and longer pedicel; Hog Deer, *Axis porcinus*, has darker, greyer fur, short pedicel, with thinner, more forked antlers.

Ecology and habitat Main habitat is mature evergreen forest, mostly in hills, but somewhat tolerant of disturbed forest.

Distribution and status SE Asia: Annamite Mountains of Laos and Vietnam. Vulnerable. Appears to be rare compared to other muntjacs in range, with populations declining due to excessive hunting.

Family *BOVIDAE* CATTLE, BUFFALO, ANTELOPES, GOATS AND SHEEP

This family is characterized by cattle, buffalo, antelope, goats and sheep. All of them have horns that are never shed and that continue to grow as the animal gets older. Both males and females have horns in all species in the region, though males are usually larger, with larger horns.

Most species in this group have suffered substantial population declines resulting from loss of habitat and from hunting. At least one form, the Kouprey, *Bos sauveli*, is probably extinct, although there is some controversy as to whether it was a distinct species or a hybrid between Banteng, *Bos javanicus*, and domestic cattle. An additional species, Spiral-horned Ox, *Pseudonovibos spiralis*, has been described based on horns from Vietnam. However, genetic analysis and closer study of the horns indicate that this was based on artificially altered horns of domestic cattle, and no such animal has ever existed. A number of strains of domestic cattle may resemble some of the wild cattle, in some cases having been interbred with Banteng, but can usually be distinguished by their relatively tame behaviour, and by being near human settlements.

BANTENG

Bos javanicus   PLATE 53

Measurements SH 1,500–1,700, HB 1,900–2,250, T 650–700. Wt 600–800kg

Identification Adult males dark chestnut-brown in most parts of mainland; adult females and young males pale brown to bright rufous-brown. In S Thailand (as well as Java and Borneo) males are darker, often jet-black, both sexes with distinctive white band around muzzle, white buttocks and white "stockings" on lower part of the legs. Adult females smaller and more slender than adult males, with smaller horns. Horns of male narrow, curving outwards and forwards, then inwards at tips; female horns closer together and more upright. Horny patch of thick skin between horns. Footprints relatively large, with curved hoof (Fig. 64b). **Similar species** Gaur, *B. frontalis*, is larger and more muscular, without white on rump or muzzle. Most domestic cattle lack white on the buttocks, but some can be very hard to distinguish, in particular those descended from wild Banteng, except by less muscular backs in males and tamer behaviour.

Ecology and habitat Mainly nocturnal, probably partly as a result of hunting pressure. Found in a variety of forest types, including dry semi-open forest, lowland forest and swamp forest. Often along banks of major rivers. Feeds mainly in clearings and open areas, where diet is mainly grasses, with some herbaceous and low woody vegetation. Visits natural mineral sources. Now found mainly in fairly small groups, but formerly herds were much larger. Domestic forms are kept in some areas.

Distribution and status SE Asia: Myanmar, Thailand, Laos, Vietnam and Cambodia. Formerly Peninsular Malaysia. Also S China (Yunnan), Java and Borneo. Endangered. Wild populations have declined throughout range, due to loss of habitat and hunting. Also some risk from hybridization with domestic cattle, and from disease.

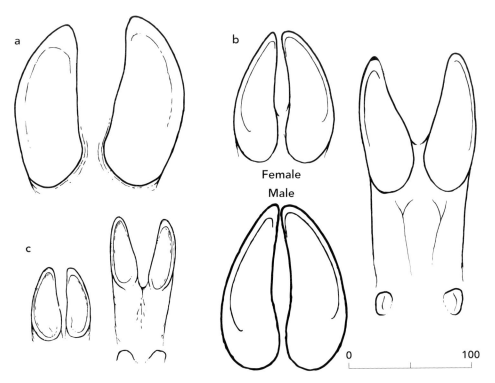

a

b

Female

Male

c

0   100

Fig. 64 *Footprints of* Bubalus bubalis
(a), Bos javanicus *(b) and* Capricornis
sumatrensis *(c). In soft ground, for all
species, the toes are more spread out, and
the hind toes may be visible.*

GAUR

Bos frontalis PLATE 53

Measurements SH 1,700–1,850, HB
2,500–3,000, T 700–1,050. Wt 650–900kg

Identification Large and muscular, adult
male with high ridge of muscles on back; relatively short neck; variably developed flap of
skin under neck (dewlap). Body largely black;
legs, from knees down, greyish-white or
golden-yellow. Newborn young brown with
black stripe on back, turns to black by 4–5
months. In Indian populations, and possibly
some in region, young are golden-brown,
turning to reddish-brown in young males
and adult females. Forehead of male raised
up in pale yellowish-brown ridge that is concave in profile. Horns relatively short, rounded in cross section, relatively far apart on
head, curved outwards and upwards.
Domestic descendents of Gaur, called

Mithan or Gayal, are sometimes kept in
region, but are generally much less muscular.
Footprints similar to Banteng, *B. javanicus*
(Fig. 64b) but average somewhat larger.
Taxonomic notes Sometimes called *Bos
gaurus*. **Similar species** Banteng, *B. javanicus*, has white rump patch, usually much
browner, especially in females, smaller horns,
less muscular.

Ecology and habitat Found principally in
forested areas; may enter grasslands to feed,
but returns to forest for shelter. Feeds on various grasses, including bamboo, as well as
leaves. Mainly nocturnal in most of region,
but also active during day in areas where
protected from disturbance by humans.
Regularly visits natural mineral sources and
salt licks.

Distribution and status SE Asia: Myanmar,
Thailand, Laos, Vietnam, Cambodia and
Peninsular Malaysia. Also India, Nepal,
Bangladesh and extreme S China. Vulnerable. Populations throughout region greatly
reduced, due to loss of habitat and excessive hunting. Also at risk from diseases of
domestic cattle.

KOUPREY

Bos sauveli PLATE 53

Measurements SH 1,700–1,900, HB 2,100–2,200, T 1,000–1,100. Wt 700–900kg

Identification Adult males largely dark brown to black; lower legs white or greyish; area on forehead between horns black, rump dark, same colour as rest of back; females and young greyish, with paler underparts. Male with very large flap of skin (dewlap) under neck, sometimes nearly reaching ground. Horns of male curve outwards and forwards, with a tendency for tips to split; horns of female smaller, lyre shaped, with a corkscrew-like twist. **Similar species** Banteng, *B. javanicus*, has white rump, differently shaped horns; Gaur, *B. frontalis*, has pale-coloured hollow forehead shield, smaller dewlap, larger back muscles, horns curved backwards and upwards.

Ecology and habitat Was found in mixed savannah, open grasslands and patches of dense forest. Foraged mainly in grasslands, but sheltered in forests.

Distribution and Status SE Asia: formerly found in SE Thailand, S Laos, Cambodia and S Vietnam. Critically Endangered or Extinct. Apparently hunted to extinction.

WATER BUFFALO

Bubalus bubalis PLATE 53

Measurements SH 1,600–1,900, HB 2,400–2,800, T 600–850. Wt 800–1,200kg

Identification Entirely greyish, except for a pale V-shape usually present on the underside of the neck. Horns long, swept out to sides and curved; somewhat triangular in cross section. Footprints very large and broad, often rather splayed in soft ground (Fig. 64a). **Similar species** Domestic Water Buffalo looks similar but is generally smaller, less muscular, relatively tame. Gaur, *Bos frontalis*, has white lower legs, horns shorter and rounded in cross section.

Ecology and habitat Wild Water Buffalo is associated with grassland on alluvial soil; domestic forms occur in many areas of the region.

Distribution and status SE Asia: Myanmar, Thailand, Cambodia and possibly Vietnam. Also NE India, Nepal and Bangladesh. Formerly much more widespread in region. Domestic animals found in many parts of world, with escaped wild populations in several areas. Endangered in wild. Wild populations severely reduced by conversion of habitat to rice farming and by illegal hunting. Also at risk from hybridization with domestic forms, and diseases from domestic cattle.

TAKIN

Budorcas taxicolor PLATE 54

Measurements SH 700–1,400, HB 1,000–2,400, T 70–120. Wt 150–400kg

Identification Thick-bodied animal with short thick legs, arched back, thick neck, face with distinctive outward-curved profile. Horns rise near middle of forehead, turn outwards, then curve abruptly backwards. Females and young have straighter horns than males. Colour varies from dark greyish-black with white patches through dark brown to golden-yellow brown. Females and young usually greyer than males, and often with dark line down back. Hair long and shaggy. **Similar species** Gorals, *Naemorhedus* spp., and serows, *Capricornis* spp., have thinner legs, different shaped head, straighter horns.

Ecology and habitat Found in hill forests and thickets in montane areas at altitudes of 1,000–4,000m. In summer may be near tree line, but comes lower in winter. Feeds by browsing on bushes and grazing on grass. May travel long distances to reach salt licks. Often in medium-sized herds of 20–30 animals, but sometimes seen in herds of up to 300 animals. Old bulls may be solitary.

Distribution and status SE Asia: N Myanmar. Also NE India (Assam), S China including Tibet. Vulnerable. Rare in Myanmar, where threatened by illegal hunting and trapping.

SAOLA

Pseudoryx nghetinhensis PLATE 54

Measurements SH 800–900, HB 1,500. Wt 85–100kg

Identification Slender, antelope-like animal

with long, smooth horns slightly curved backwards. Fur dark grey-brown to reddish-brown. Distinctive face pattern, with white stripe above eye and several white spots and stripes on chin and muzzle. Legs generally darker than body, with white marks on ankle. Horns of young animals short and goat-like. **Similar species** Serow, *Capricornis* spp., have shorter, more curved horns and lack white markings on head.

Ecology and habitat Wet, evergreen hill forests, apparently restricted to large contiguous blocks of forest.

Distribution and status SE Asia: Laos and Vietnam. Critically Endangered. Occurs at low numbers in limited range in Annamite Mountains, where threatened by illegal hunting and trapping as well as forest loss.

BLUE SHEEP

Pseudois nayaur PLATE 54

Measurements SH 800–900, HB 1,200–1,650, T 100–200. Wt 55–70kg

Identification Adult male light greyish-brown to blue-grey, with black line along flanks and along front edge of both back and front legs; black chest; white belly; white on back sides of all legs with white marks on ankles; white rump and tail. Males have long, smooth horns. Females similar but without black markings and with shorter horns. **Similar species** Serows, *Capricornis* spp. have shorter, narrower horns, longer legs, thick mane, occur in more forested habitats.

Ecology and habitat Montane habitats, often above tree line, in bare rocky areas and open grasslands at 2,500–6,500m altitude.

Distribution and status SE Asia: extreme N Myanmar. Also China, Himalayas (N India, Nepal, Bhutan and N Pakistan). Not currently at risk in main part of range, but very rare and probably threatened by hunting in Myanmar.

SOUTHERN SEROW

Capricornis sumatraensis PLATE 55

Measurements SH 850–940, HB 1,400–1,550, T 110–160. Wt 85–140kg

Identification Long-legged, relatively short-bodied, goat-like animal with short, nearly straight horns with marked striations (circular ridges). Colour generally black, greyer in younger animals, with black legs. Black crest of hairs on back, adults with well-developed mane of long hairs on back of neck, varying from dirty-white to buff or reddish, sometimes black mixed with a few white hairs. Has large, open gland in front of eye. Footprints more rounded than those of deer, but narrower than those of pigs (Fig. 64c). **Similar species** Chinese Serow, *C. milneedwardsi*, has extensive white bases to fur on flanks, with pale lower legs; Chinese Goral, *Naemorhedus griseus*, is much smaller, with smaller head, thinner neck, paler body colour.

Ecology and habitat Thick forests, usually on fairly steep terrain, including limestone outcrops and hill forest. Usually solitary, except female with young.

Distribution and status SE Asia: S Thailand and Peninsular Malaysia. Also Sumatra. Vulnerable. Main threats are loss of forest habitat, but also illegal hunting and trapping.

CHINESE SEROW

Capricornis milneedwardsi PLATE 55

Measurements SH 850–940, HB 1,400–1,550, T 110–160kg

Identification Similar to Southern Serow, differing mainly in colour. Hairs on most of body black with extensive white bases showing through, giving overall greyish colour; black stripe on back; head browner; underside often paler; white or pale brown hairs on throat, often forming pale patch; legs black on upper half, contrasting reddish or whitish on lower half; long mane with long white hairs, sometimes extensively mixed with black. **Similar species** Southern Serow, *C. sumatraensis*, is blacker, without white hair bases on most of body, black legs; could possibly hybridize in areas of overlap in peninsular Thailand.

Ecology and habitat Occurs mainly in hill forest and rugged terrain such as limestone karst, though sometimes in lowland forest. Tolerant of some forest degradation, but not clearing for agriculture.

Distribution and status SE Asia: Myanmar, Thailand, Laos, Vietnam and Cambodia. Also S China. Near Threatened. Populations fragmented in many areas, owing to loss of habitat and intervening forest clearance, with excessive hunting in many areas.

RED SEROW

Capricornis rubidus PLATE 55
Measurements SH 850–950,
HB 1,400–1,550, T 110–160kg

Identification Shape and size similar to other serows, but overall fur colour red-brown, hairs with black bases; usually with dark stripe down back; mane relatively short, dark reddish, blending with back. Often with white patch on throat and white belly. Some individuals are darker, black with reddish tone, and may sometimes hybridize with Chinese Serow, *C. milneedwardsi.* **Similar species** Red Goral, *Naemorhedus baileyi*, is smaller, without distinct mane, fur smoother and shorter, shorter legs, horns smaller and more slender.

Ecology and habitat Tropical and subtropical forest, mainly in hills.

Distribution and status SE Asia: N Myanmar. Also NE India. Vulnerable. Population declining throughout range, due to loss of habitat and excessive hunting.

CHINESE GORAL

Naemorhedus griseus PLATE 55
Measurements SH 500–700, HB 800–1,200, T 80–200. Wt 20–30kg

Identification Relatively small, goat-like animal with short fur and short, slender horns. Fur light greyish-brown to brown with darker brown stripe down middle of back and darker brown forehead and ridge of nose; legs paler, golden-brown with dark wedge on front; underside pale greyish-brown; throat white to orange-white; tail mostly dark brown. **Similar species** Serows, *Capricornis* spp., are much larger, with darker fur with long coarse hairs, thicker neck and larger head.

Ecology and habitat Generally in steep, hilly terrain at 1,000–4,000m altitude, often near cliffs. Feeds on leaves, grasses and twigs. Usually in small groups of 5–10 animals.

Distribution and status SE Asia: N Myanmar and N Thailand. Not confirmed in Laos. Also S China. Vulnerable. Populations have declined substantially, due to hunting and habitat loss.

RED GORAL

Naemorhedus baileyi PLATE 55
Measurements SH 550–600, HB 900–1,050, T 100–150. Wt 20–30kg

Identification Upperparts fairly uniform reddish-brown, without white or black flecking; narrow dark stripe down middle of back; legs coloured as back; underparts paler, chin and throat with pale patch. **Similar species** Red Serow, *Capricornis rubidus*, is substantially larger with longer legs, bigger head and neck, longer, coarser fur and distinct mane; Chinese Goral, *N. griseus*, is greyer.

Ecology and habitat Mainly in coniferous hill forests with rocky outcrops.

Distribution and status SE Asia: N. Myanmar. Also S China and NE India (Assam). Vulnerable. Population is declining, owing to illegal hunting.

Order RODENTIA
Squirrels, rats and porcupines

Rodents can be recognized by their dentition, with large, curved, chiselling incisors in both the upper and lower jaws; no canines and a wide diastema (toothless gap) before the cheek teeth (Fig. 65). All rodents in South-East Asia have five well-developed toes on the hind foot, but unlike insectivores and treeshrews, only four long, clawed digits on each front foot. The thumb is short, with a nail instead of a claw, and does not show in the footprint. Footprints of porcupines can be distinguished by size; those of squirrels differ from those of rats in having the front toes closer together and relatively larger footpads (Fig. 67). Although many species of rat have distinctive patterns of footpads, these can rarely be distinguished clearly enough to separate species based on prints.

Family *SCIURIDAE* SQUIRRELS

The squirrel family includes both regular squirrels and flying or gliding squirrels. Formerly, the flying squirrels were thought to belong in their own family because of their distinctive shape and morphology, but recent genetic research indicates that they evolved as an offshoot of one branch of tree squirrels. The remaining squirrels in the region are allocated to two separate sub-families. Ratufinae includes the two species of giant squirrel, while Callosciurinae includes several genera that are mainly arboreal, although a few species spend much of their time on the ground. Squirrel skulls can be distinguished from those of murid rodents by being generally broader, with well-developed supraorbital processes (Fig. 66), and 4 or 5 cheek teeth (Fig. 65).

Subfamilies *RATUFINAE, CALLOSCIURINAE* GIANT, TREE AND GROUND SQUIRRELS

Squirrels are among the small mammals most frequently seen by people, as they are active during the day, and some species regularly occur in gardens, orchards and other disturbed areas, although others are restricted to more natural forests. Most squirrels have distinctive coloration, but identification is complicated by extensive variation in colour within some species, particularly in *Callosciurus*. Much of this variation is geographical, such that populations of the same species in different areas can be very different colours. In addition, some species, particularly the Variable Squirrel, *Callosciurus finlaysoni*, may have different colour morphs occurring together in the same area. In some cases, these are thought to represent seasonal changes in colour pattern of the same individuals, while others may be due to small genetic differences within interbreeding populations – further research is needed to determine which type of variation is occurring in each area. This variation complicates understanding of speciation in these squirrels, and in several groups the currently recognized species limits are still very provisional. Genetic analyses of samples are required from a wide geographic area to resolve these uncertainties.

Identifying squirrels in the field is usually easiest if they can be observed with binoculars, so that the colours and shape can be seen more clearly. Some of the key patterns to look for include the presence or absence of stripes on the belly, sides or back, and the colour of the belly and back. Conditions are rarely ideal, however, and many ground squirrels are glimpsed only briefly in dim light, while tree squirrels are often obscured by leaves or silhouetted against the sky. Some species can be trapped fairly easily in cage traps for closer study, though traps may need to be placed in trees to catch the more arboreal species.

Treeshrews, *Tupaia* spp., could be mistaken for squirrels but they generally have more pointed muzzles (although some squirrels also have pointed muzzles), a pale mark on their shoulder and very different dentition, without the enlarged yellowish incisors typical of rodents (Fig. 23).

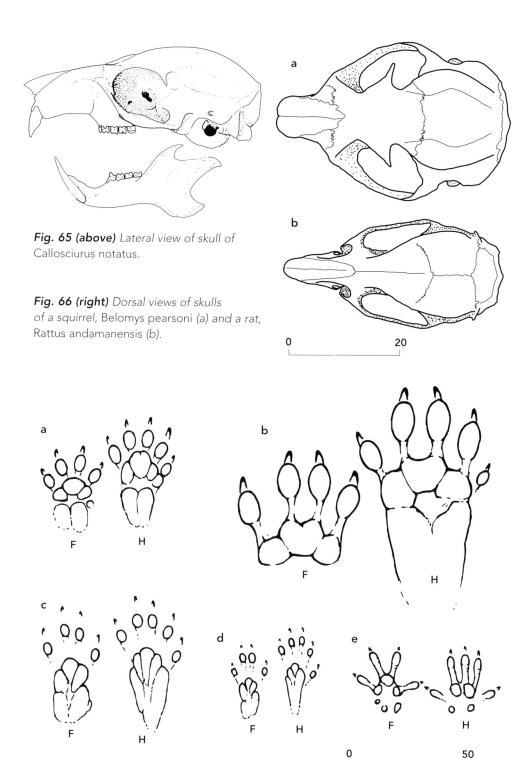

Fig. 65 (above) *Lateral view of skull of* Callosciurus notatus.

Fig. 66 (right) *Dorsal views of skulls of a squirrel,* Belomys pearsoni *(a) and a rat,* Rattus andamanensis *(b).*

0   20

a

b

a

b

c

d

e

F   H

F   H

F   H

F   H   F   H

0   50

Fig. 67 *Footprints of selected rodents:* Trichys fasciculata *(a),* Hystrix brachyura *(b),* Ratufa affinis *(c),* Lariscus insignis *(d) and* a typical rat, Rattus *sp. (e).* F = front foot; H = hind foot.

Genus *Ratufa* These are among the largest squirrels in the world, with large bodies and long, bushy tails. They are largely confined to tall forest, where they remain mainly in the canopy. They have a distinctive posture when sitting or feeding, the tail often hanging down vertically. Two species occur in the region, one of them widespread, the other mostly confined to peninsular Thailand and Malaysia.

BLACK GIANT SQUIRREL
Ratufa bicolor PLATE 56
Measurements HB 370–405, T 425–500, HF 84–91, E 30–38
Identification Largest tree squirrel in the region. Upperparts typically black in fresh pelage, but some individuals may be dark brown or reddish-tinged black; underparts vary from pale buff to orange. Cheeks white with dark mark like a moustache. Some geographic variation in extent of white on forelegs and presence or absence of ear tufts. **Similar species** Cream-coloured Giant Squirrel, *R. affinis*, is much paler, with little contrast between upper and underparts; Prevost's Squirrel, *Callosciurus prevostii*, is smaller, with distinct white stripe on flank separating black back from orange belly. Some Variable Squirrels, *C. finalysonii*, may have similar colour patterns, but are substantially smaller and usually have more extensive white on head, tail or feet.
Ecology and habitat Primarily in canopy of tall forest, rarely descending to the ground. Feeds mainly on fruits and nuts, but also some insects and animal matter.
Distribution and status SE Asia: Myanmar, Thailand, Laos, Vietnam, Cambodia and Peninsular Malaysia. Also E Nepal, Assam, S China, Sumatra, Java and Bali. Near Threatened; although widespread, has declined considerably in many areas due to loss and fragmentation of tall forest, as well as to hunting.

CREAM-COLOURED GIANT SQUIRREL
Ratufa affinis PLATE 56
Measurements HB 310–380, T 370–440, HF 66–86. Wt 875–1,500

Identification A very large tree squirrel with orange-brown to pale buff upperparts, buffy to white underparts. Animals in the northern peninsula are generally darker orange, while those in the southern peninsula are paler. Outside the region, in Borneo, individuals may be much darker, closely resembling the Black Giant Squirrel, *R. bicolor*. When moving quickly through the tree canopy, the tail is held out horizontally, but when sitting on a branch it hangs vertically. **Voice** Loud call is a short, harsh chatter, often audible for several hundred metres. It also has a distinctive soft call, a series of "hgip ... hgip …", audible only when close to the animal. **Similar species** Pale forms of Variable Squirrel, *Callosciurus finlaysonii*, are smaller and not found in the same geographic areas.
Ecology and habitat Diurnal, usually emerging from the nest well after dawn and retiring for the night before dusk. Nest is a neat, globular array of twigs, usually built in the crown of a tall tree. Mostly active in tall trees, descending to the ground only to cross gaps in the tree canopy. Diet mainly seeds with some leaves and bark. Occurs in lowland and hill forests with tall trees, including some selectively logged forests, but rarely enters plantations.
Distribution and status SE Asia: peninsular Thailand, Malaysia and Singapore. Also Sumatra, Borneo and some smaller Indonesian islands. Near Threatened, due mainly to destruction of tall forests, as well as hunting.

Genus *Callosciurus* Moderately large tree squirrels; many species are very colourful with distinctive patterns. There is extensive geographic variation in the colour patterns of many species, with some exhibiting very different patterns across their range. The taxonomic limits for some of these species are not well known and may not be fully resolved until genetic studies have been done. From the perspective of field identification it can be very helpful to check the species distribution maps, because there is only limited overlap among the more variable species.

PREVOST'S SQUIRREL

Callosciurus prevostii PLATE 56

Measurements HB 200–270, T 200–270, HF 45–60. Wt 250–500

Identification Upperparts largely black with grey on side of face; belly dark reddish-orange; broad white stripe on flanks. Outside region, for example in Borneo, colour varies considerably, with white stripe thin or lacking in some forms, and grey or brown upperparts in others. **Voice** A loud, harsh chatter. **Similar species** Black Giant Squirrel, *Ratufa bicolor*, is larger, with paler underparts and no distinct flank stripe; no other *Callosciurus* in its range has similar colour patterns.

Ecology and habitat Diurnal, most active in the early morning and late afternoon. Usually arboreal, descending to the ground only to cross gaps in the tree canopy. Diet includes fruits, especially those with a sweet or oily flesh, and insects, notably ants, termites and beetle larvae, which are gnawed out of dying wood. Occurs in tall and secondary forests. Enters gardens and plantations from adjacent forest to feed on fruits.

Distribution and status SE Asia: peninsular Thailand and Malaysia. Also Sumatra, Borneo, Sulawesi and smaller Indonesian islands. Not currently at risk.

PLANTAIN SQUIRREL

Callosciurus notatus PLATE 56

Measurements HB 175–223, T 160–210, HF 42–52. Wt 150–280

Identification Upperparts brownish agouti. Underparts reddish-orange, varying from very pale to fairly dark, sometimes with a greyish wash. Distinctive stripes on flanks, with black stripe next to belly, buff stripe above it. Tail tip usually orange, though orange restricted to a few hairs in some individuals. **Voice** A shrill, scolding chatter as well as sharp, bird-like chirp, repeated continuously for long periods. **Similar species** Sunda Black-banded Squirrel, *C. nigrovittatus*, also has black and buff stripes on sides, but has grey underparts and no reddish on tip of tail; Pallas's Squirrel, *C. erythraeus*,

lacks black and buff stripes on sides.

Ecology and habitat Diurnal, most active early morning and late afternoon. Travels and feeds mainly in small trees. Diet includes a wide variety of fruits and insects, mostly ants. Commonly found in gardens, plantations and secondary forests, and can live and breed entirely in monoculture plantations. Less frequently found in the interior of undisturbed tall forests, but usually common in coastal and swamp forests.

Distribution and status SE Asia: peninsular Thailand and Malaysia, and Singapore. Also Sumatra, Java, Borneo and many smaller offshore islands around them. Not currently at risk. One of the most common squirrels of disturbed areas in its range.

SUNDA BLACK-BANDED SQUIRREL

Callosciurus nigrovittatus PLATE 56

Measurements HB 170–240, T 145–230, HF 40–50

Identification Upperparts speckled brownish agouti; buff stripe above black stripe on sides of body; underparts uniform grey. Tail as back colour, without reddish tip. Sides of head and upper chin reddish brown. **Voice** A rattling chatter or chuckle; also a sharp, repeated bird-like chirp. **Similar species** Plantain Squirrel, *C. notatus*, has sides of head same colour as back, reddish belly and reddish tip to tail.

Ecology and habitat Diurnal and arboreal, mainly in canopy and middle storey of both primary and secondary lowland forest.

Distribution and status SE Asia: peninsular Thailand and Malaysia. Also Sumatra, Java, Borneo and many smaller offshore islands around them. Not currently at risk.

IRRAWADDY SQUIRREL

Callosciurus pygerythrus PLATE 56

Measurements HB 170–200, T 170–200, HF 41–45

Identification Upperparts agouti, with overall colour varying from slightly reddish to olive-brown to grey. Underparts vary geographically from pale buff to grey to orange. Within populations, fur colour varies sea-

sonally, being brighter in wet season than dry season. In wet season, has pale patches on hips, but these are often lacking in dry season. Major racial variation within Myanmar is as follows: *C. p. pygerythrus* (W of Sittang, E of lower Irrawaddy): underparts reddish, more buff near front, hip patch buff or lacking; *C. p. janetta* (W of Irrawaddy, E of lower Chindwin): underparts light buff, hip patch white; *C. p. owensi* (W of Irrawaddy, E of upper Chindwin): more reddish upperparts and underparts, hip patch buff; *C. p. mearsi* (W of lower Chindwin): underparts buff, hip patch white, buff eye-ring; *C. p. stevensi* (W of upper Chindwin): underparts grey, upperparts reddish, hip-patch buff. **Similar species** Inornate Squirrel, *C. inornatus*, never has pale patches on hips and does not overlap in range; Phayre's Squirrel, *C. phayrei*, has black stripe on flank and usually darker orange underparts; Pallas's Squirrel, *C. erythraeus*, tends to be slightly larger, lacks pale patch on hips, has dark reddish underparts with (usually) agouti stripe in middle of belly; Grey-bellied Squirrel, *C. caniceps*, is similar to *C. p. stevensi* but lacks pale hip patch and does not overlap in range.
Ecology and habitat Diurnal and arboreal. Broadleaved and coniferous evergreen forest, including disturbed areas and secondary growth.
Distribution and status SE Asia: NW and C Myanmar. Also Nepal, Bangladesh and E India. Not currently at risk.

PHAYRE'S SQUIRREL
Callosciurus phayrei PLATE 56
Measurements HB 210–250, T 230–270
Identification Upperparts mottled grey and brown agouti; underparts pale buff to orange-brown, usually separated from back colour by a distinct, wide black stripe. However, stripe may be indistinct or missing in some individuals. Tail agouti with distinct black tip. **Similar species** Some colour forms of Pallas's Squirrel, *C. erythraeus*, may look similar, but lack a black stripe on the flank (or have at most a very thin stripe).

Ecology and habitat Diurnal and arboreal. Primary and secondary broadleaved forest.
Distribution and status SE Asia: Myanmar, between lower Sittang and Salween Rivers. Also adjacent parts of China (SW Yunnan). Not currently at risk.

PALLAS'S SQUIRREL
Calosciurus erythraeus PLATE 57
Measurements HB 200–260, T 190–250, HF 44–55, E 18–23
Identification Considerable geographic variation in colour pattern; may include more than one species, but appropriate species limits uncertain. In most forms, upperparts are speckled olive-brown (agouti), sometimes with a black stripe down the back, and underparts are reddish, though this varies from dark maroon to red-brown. In many populations there is a stripe of agouti down the middle of the belly, separating the reddish belly into 2 bands. The major variations within the region are as follows: *C. e. erythraeus* group (Peninsular Malaysia, W Thailand, S and NW Myanmar, NE India, N Vietnam and N Laos): upperparts agouti, feet and tail as back, underparts reddish, with an agouti stripe up the middle – in some parts of S Myanmar underparts may be all agouti without any red; in W Thailand and S Myanmar, lower back has a distinct, broad black stripe (sometimes considered a separate subspecies, *C. e. atrodorsalis*). *C. e. flavimanus* group (S Vietnam, S Laos and Cambodia): upperparts agouti, feet pale, often yellowish-orange, underparts vary from cream to rich reddish-brown. *C. e. sladeni* group (Myanmar between Chindwin and Irrawaddy Rivers): a highly variable form with some populations similar to typical *C. erythraeus*, but others may be greyish-white above, pale orange below and on the feet; medium grey mixed with agouti above, cream below and on the feet; or even completely dark rufous-red all over and only slightly paler on the underparts. **Taxomonic notes** *C. flavimanus* is sometimes considered a separate species. **Similar species**

Variable Squirrel, *C. finlaysonii*, never has the combination of agouti upperparts and tail with reddish underparts; however, some populations can resemble some of the variations of the *C. e. sladeni* group, though typically not those in the same geographic areas; Phayre's Squirrel, *C. phayrei*, has a black band on the sides; Plaintain Squirrel, *C. notatus*, has a black and buff band on the flanks.

Ecology and habitat Diurnal and arboreal. In southern part of range mainly confined to hill forests, but elsewhere occurs in a variety of habitats including primary and secondary forests, as well as disturbed areas and plantations.

Distribution and status SE Asia: Myanmar, Thailand, Laos, Vietnam, Cambodia and Peninsular Malaysia (where confined to central mountain range above 1,000m elevation). Also E Nepal, Assam, and S and E China. Not currently at risk.

VARIABLE SQUIRREL
Callosciurus finlaysonii PLATE 58
Measurements HB 210–220, T 220–240, HF 45–50, E 19–23

Identification A highly variable squirrel with no single combination of features that can diagnose the species. There is extensive variation both among geographic areas and within populations. Some of this variation appears to be seasonal, but this has been little studied; it appears that some squirrels may change from maroon-red to white at different times of year. Further field study, following individuals through the year, is required to clarify these patterns. Plate shows some of the major colour variations, but many other combinations occur. The major population variations are described here as subspecies, but there is intergradation among these, especially where ranges overlap, and genetic studies have not yet been done to determine how distinct these populations really are. The mainland variations are: *C. f. sinistralis* (NW Thailand): upperparts agouti, often with strong reddish cast, underparts reddish-orange, tail deep red-brown with white ring around base. *C. f. menamicus* (E part of N Thailand and N Laos): varies from largely reddish-brown with agouti flanks to reddish-brown upperparts with white belly, feet and head, and many intermediates in between; tail varies from red to grey with a buff tip or white with grey on top. *C. f. bocourti* (E C Thailand, from S to N): varies from completely creamy white, to having black back, with white head, underparts, legs and tail; tail sometimes black above, white below. *C. f. boonsongi* (NE Thailand): usually very dark grey to black all over, sometimes with white or red edges to ears; some individuals have extensive white on underside, feet and face. *C. f. annellatus* (SE Thailand, C and E Cambodia, and S Laos W of Mekong): uniform deep reddish-brown except for pale ring around base of tail. *C. f. williamsoni* (E part of Mekong plain in Laos and N Cambodia): red to orange above, clearly separated from dark chestnut below; red tail. *C. f. cinnamomeus* (SE Thailand and SW Cambodia): all red, or largely red with some agouti on head and limbs. *C. f. floweri* (SC Thailand, near Bangkok): olive-brown upperparts including head with white marks around eye, sometimes forming a complete ring; white underparts. *C. f. nox* (SE Thailand): all black. *C. f. ferrugineus* (E Myanmar): typically all reddish-brown. In addition, there are distinctive populations on several of the small islands off the coasts of Thailand and S Vietnam. *C. f. finlaysonii* (Si Chang Is, Thailand): all yellowish-white. *C. f. folletti* (Phai Is, Thailand): greyish-white to beige upperparts; creamy underparts often with an orange wash; light, buffy tail. *C. f. trotteri* (Lan Is, Thailand): mid-grey upperparts with lower back darker; pale grey belly; white tail. *C. f. frandseni* (Chaing Is, Thailand): dark reddish-brown above mixed with brownish-olive (agouti) on head, neck, flanks and upper parts of legs; underparts buffy-orange. *C. f. albivexilli* (Kut Is, Thailand): all black except for a white tip to the tail. *C. f. harmandi* (Phu Quoc, Vietnam): upperparts dark reddish-brown to grey-brown, underparts orange-red; tail greyish-white. *C. f. germaini* (Condor Is, Vietnam): all black. **Similar species** Some populations of Pallas's Squirrel, *C. erythraeus*, may be similar to some populations of *C. finlaysonii*, but can usually be separated by details of the colour pattern, especially an agouti banded tail.

Ecology and habitat Diurnal and arboreal, found in a variety of habitats including dense forest, open woods and coconut plantations. **Distribution and status** SE Asia: S Vietnam, Thailand, Cambodia, Laos and part of E Myanmar. Introduced in Singapore. Not currently at risk; still common in many areas.

STRIPE-BELLIED SQUIRREL
Callosciurus quinquestriatus   PLATE 57
Measurements HB 210–240, T 160, HF 40
Identification Upperparts speckled brown (agouti), often with a strong reddish tinge. Underparts white, with a black stripe on each flank, and a black stripe up the middle of the belly. Tail lightly banded with a black tip. **Similar species** No other species has a white belly with black stripes on each flank and in middle of belly.
Ecology and habitat Diurnal and arboreal. Hill and montane evergreen forest.
Distribution and status SE Asia: NE Myanmar, E of upper Irrawaddy River. Also adjacent parts of China (Yunnan). Not currently at risk.

GREY-BELLIED SQUIRREL
Callosciurus caniceps   PLATE 57
Measurements HB 210–240, T 185–245, HF 49–54, E 19–23
Identification Upperparts vary from grey-agouti to golden-brown; underparts usually silvery-grey, but may have reddish wash on part of underparts; tip of tail black in most parts of Thailand, but grey in Peninsular Malaysia. In northern parts of range, back is a very bright orange in the dry season, but greyish-agouti in the wet season. In Peninsular Malaysia, back is mottled orange-brown year round. Some populations have patches of rufous on underparts. **Voice** A

loud, harsh chuckle; also a bird-like cheep repeated for long periods. **Similar species** Sunda Black-banded Squirrel, *C. nigrovittatus*, has black and buff bands on flanks without orange on upperparts; Pallas's Squirrel, *C. erythraeus*, has underparts all reddish, or reddish with agouti in the middle, lacks golden-orange tinge on back, and has a pale tail tip; Inornate Squirrel, *C. inornatus*, is very similar but lacks black tail tip and does not overlap in range.
Ecology and habitat Diurnal and primarily arboreal. Found in a wide range of forest types, including plantations, cultivated areas, second growth and gardens, as well as intact forest. May range up to 1,500m in hills, but mainly in lowlands.
Distribution and status SE Asia: Laos W of Mekong River, SE Myanmar, C and W Thailand, and Peninsular Malaysia. Not currently at risk.

INORNATE SQUIRREL
Callosciurus inornatus   PLATE 57
Measurements HB 220–230, T 200–240
Identification Upperparts mottled brown (agouti), sometimes with a reddish tinge, underparts uniform grey. **Similar species** Grey-bellied Squirrel, *C. caniceps*, has black tail tip, and does not overlap in range, occurring only to west of Mekong River.
Ecology and habitat Diurnal and arboreal. Evergreen forests including hill conifer forest, as well as degraded forest and scrub.
Distribution and status SE Asia: N and C Laos, and N Vietnam, E of Mekong River. Also S China. Not currently at risk.

Genus *Tamiops* A group of small, striped squirrels, distinguished from most other squirrels by their arboreal habits and pattern of dark and pale stripes on the back. Currently, four species are recognized, differing in size, in the brightness and width of the stripes and in belly colour. However, there is also moderate variation within each species, and further study, preferably involving genetic analysis, is required to determine whether these are actually appropriate species limits. Field identification is aided by the fact that there appears to be relatively little overlap in distribution among the species, although parts of Vietnam and Laos may have more than one species.

WESTERN STRIPED SQUIRREL
Tamiops mcclellandii PLATE 59
Measurements HB 110–125, T 110–140, HF 27–32, E 15–22
Identification Upperparts mottled grey and brown, with 5 dark stripes and 4 pale stripes down middle of back. Central back stripe usually blackest, with others varying from nearly black to only slightly darker than rest of body. Pale stripes vary from white to buff with outer pair typically much wider, paler and brighter than inner pair. Outer stripe contiguous with white stripe on cheeks. Underparts usually buff to dull orange, with grey bases to fur. Conspicuous white tufts on ears. There is some geographic variation, with pale stripes narrower and less conspicuous in some northern populations. **Voice** A bird-like chirp repeated for long periods at intervals of about one second; also a descending trill of shrill chirps. **Similar species** Cambodian Striped Squirrel, *T. rodolphii*, has central stripes similar in width and brightness to outer stripes, underparts often more orange; other *Tamiops* usually have cheek stripes separate from side stripe.
Ecology and habitat Diurnal and arboreal. Uses a variety of forest types, from primary hill forest to gardens and fruit trees. Diet consists of fruits, vegetable matter and some insects. Uses holes in trees for shelter. Primarily found above 700m altitude in Thailand and Malaysia, but also in lowlands farther north.
Distribution and status SE Asia: N Myanmar, N and W Thailand, N Laos (W of Mekong River) south through Peninsular Malaysia. Not currently at risk.

CAMBODIAN STRIPED SQUIRREL
Tamiops rodolphii PLATE 59
Measurements HB 105–125, T 115–130, HF 25–30

Identification Upperparts mottled grey-brown, with 5 dark stripes and 4 pale stripes down middle of back. Pale stripes all similar in width and brightness, but inner stripes tend to be more buff-orange than outer ones. Central black stripe usually has a thin, indistinct brown stripe in middle. Back of neck and top of head with strong reddish tinge in parts of Thailand, dull brown further S in Cambodia and Vietnam. Outer pale stripe continuous with pale stripe on side of head. Underparts dull orange. **Similar species** Western Striped Squirrel, *T. mcclellandii*, has outer pale stripes wider and more conspicuous than inner pair; Eastern Striped Squirrel, *T. maritimus*, is larger, has greyish-white underparts, outer stripes brighter than inner and not connected to cheek stripe.
Ecology and habitat Diurnal and arboreal. Found in a variety of habitats with trees, from forest to scrub, plantations, and gardens.
Distribution and status SE Asia: SE Thailand, S Laos, Cambodia and S Vietnam. Not currently at risk; common in many areas.

SWINHOE'S STRIPED SQUIRREL
Tamiops swinhoei PLATE 59
Measurements HB 120–155, T 100–120, HF 30–38
Identification Upperparts brownish, with 5 dark stripes separated by 4 pale stripes on back. Dark stripes very black in fresh pelage; outer stripes become browner in winter. Inner pale stripes relatively dull, only slightly paler than nape and head; outer pale stripes much brighter, varying from orange-buff to white. Outer pale stripes do not connect with cheek stripes. Pelage relatively thick and bushy. **Similar species** Eastern Striped Squirrel, *T. maritimus*, is very similar, but dark stripes away from centre tend to be browner and less distinct, pelage is thinner – note only limited overlap in distribution.
Ecology and habitat Diurnal and arboreal. Forest, including disturbed areas with trees, primarily in montane and hill areas.
Distribution and status SE Asia: NE Myanmar and NW Vietnam. Also SW China. Not currently at risk.

EASTERN STRIPED SQUIRREL

Tamiops maritimus PLATE 59

Measurements HB 100–145, T 95–120, HF 30–35

Identification Upperparts brownish with 5 dark stripes and 4 pale stripes in middle of back. Median dark stripe black, but outer dark stripes tend to be mixed with reddish-brown. Outer pale stripes brighter and more conspicuous than inner stripes, but not connecting with cheek stripes. Pelage relatively thin. Underparts greyish-white, fur having grey bases and white tips. **Similar species** Swinhoe's Striped Squirrel, *T. swinhoei*, is very similar and most reliably distinguished by range; Cambodian Striped Squirrel, *T. rodolphii*, has all 4 pale stripes relatively bright, underparts mixed orange and grey.

Ecology and habitat Diurnal and arboreal, but may be found in low shrubs and sometimes on ground. Occurs in a wide variety of forest types, including disturbed areas.

Distribution and status SE Asia: Laos, Vietnam. Also SE China, Hainan and Taiwan. Not currently at risk.

Genus *Sundasciurus* A group of small to medium-sized squirrels with many species in the Sunda Islands and Philippines, but only three species in the region, restricted to S peninsular Thailand and Malaysia. Most species are smaller and plainer-coloured than *Callosciurus*, with the exception of *S. hippurus*, which is relatively large and bright. They are both arboreal and terrestrial, spending more time on the ground than most *Callosciurus*.

HORSE-TAILED SQUIRREL

Sundasciurus hippurus PLATE 59

Measurements HB 210–290, T 240–290, HF 54–64

Identification Upperparts reddish-brown with contrasting grey head, shoulders and thighs; underparts dark reddish-orange; tail thick and bushy, largely black. **Voice** Most commonly heard call is "CHEK! CHEK! chekchekchekchek ...". **Similar species** No

other squirrel has the contrasting greyish and reddish pattern on the upperparts, with rufous underparts.

Ecology and habitat Diurnal. Most often seen in small trees, shrubs or on the ground, but sometimes climbs high into trees. Diet includes seeds, fruits and insects. Occurs in tall and secondary forests, mainly in lowlands and lower hill forest up to 1,000m, but most common in intact forest.

Distribution and status SE Asia: peninsular Thailand and Malaysia. Also Sumatra and Borneo. Near Threatened, owing to loss of forests.

LOW'S SQUIRREL

Sundasciurus lowii PLATE 59

Measurements HB 130–150, T 80–100 (about 60–70% of HB), HF 30–35

Identification Upperparts speckled-brown to reddish-brown and underparts buffy-white, sometimes with a reddish tinge. Indistinct pale, reddish-buff ring around each eye. Tail short and bushy. **Voice** Most commonly heard call consists of a series of bird-like "chik"s. **Similar species** Slender Squirrel, *S. tenuis*, has a longer, thinner tail and greyer underparts; Shrew-faced Ground Squirrel, *Rhinosciurus laticaudatus*, is larger, with more pointed head, more reddish tinge to fur.

Ecology and habitat Diurnal. Most active in the early morning and late afternoon. Diet includes fruits, insects and fungi. Travels and feeds in small standing trees, in fallen trees and on the ground. Occurs in tall and secondary forests, including scrub near forests.

Distribution and status SE Asia: peninsular Thailand and Malaysia. Also Sumatra, Borneo and some smaller Indonesian islands. Not currently at risk.

SLENDER SQUIRREL

Sundasciurus tenuis PLATE 59

Measurements HB 115–155, T 125–132 (85–95% of HB), HF 30–36

Identification Upperparts speckled olive-brown; underparts grey with white or buffy-brown tips. Pale marks around eyes and above facial whiskers. Facial profile slightly turned-up. Tail rather long and slender. **Similar species** Low's Squirrel, *S. lowii*, has a shorter bushy tail and white or buffy underparts without grey bases; Grey-bellied Squirrel, *Callosciurus caniceps*, is larger with reddish or orange tinge to back and bushier tail that often has black tip; Lesser Treeshrew, *Tupaia minor*, has more pointed muzzle and relatively longer tail.

Ecology and habitat Diurnal and primarily arboreal, ranging from bushes near the ground to canopy. Diet includes inner bark and insects from tree trunks, fruits and seeds. Occurs in tall and secondary forests as well as scrub and gardens.

Distribution and status SE Asia: extreme S peninsular Thailand and Peninsular Malaysia, and Singapore. Also Sumatra, Borneo and some smaller Indonesian islands. Not currently at risk; common in many areas.

Genus *Dremomys* Medium-sized squirrels with relatively long noses, found mainly in hill or montane forest, where they are active mostly in relatively low vegetation or on the ground. All species are largely brown, distinguished from one another by the colour of the underparts and the pattern of red (or lack thereof) around the head and tail. There is only limited overlap in the distribution of species in the region, except in N Vietnam and N Myanmar.

RED-CHEEKED SQUIRREL
Dremomys rufigenis PLATE 60
Measurements HB 170–210, T 143–147, HF 50–51, E 22–24
Identification Upperparts, including top of tail, speckled olive-brown mixed with grey; cheeks, side of face and underside of tail contrasting reddish-chestnut; underside white with light grey underfur, sharply demarcated from olive-brown upperparts. Small white or buff patch behind ear. **Similar species** Redthroated Squirrel, *D. gularis*, has darker underparts with red throat; Red-hipped Squirrel, *D. pyrrhomerus*, has less conspicuous red cheeks, large red patch on thigh; no other squirrels have such contrasting red cheeks.

Ecology and habitat Diurnal. Found both in trees and on ground. Occurs in primary and secondary forests, mainly in hills. Eats both insects and plant material. Animals in northern part of range tend to be more arboreal than those in Peninsular Malaysia.

Distribution and status SE Asia: widespread throughout hillier areas of region, from N Myanmar through Thailand, Laos (also in lowlands), Vietnam and Cambodia to hills of Peninsular Malaysia. Also adjacent areas of S China. Not currently at risk.

RED-THROATED SQUIRREL
Dremomys gularis PLATE 60
Measurements HB 220, T 168, HF 52
Identification Upperparts, including top of tail, speckled olive-brown mixed with grey. Dull red on sides of face, throat, underside of legs and under tail. Rest of underparts grey with white tips to fur in middle. **Similar species** Red-cheeked Squirrel, *D. rufigenis*, has whiter underparts, with no red on throat.
Ecology and habitat Diurnal. Found mainly near ground level in forest. Occurs at higher elevations than sympatric populations of Red-cheeked Squirrel, *D. rufigenis*.
Distribution and status SE Asia: N Vietnam. Also adjacent areas of Yunnan in S China. Status poorly known, but probably not currently at risk.

RED-HIPPED SQUIRREL
Dremomys pyrrhomerus PLATE 60
Measurements HB 215, T 120, HF 54
Identification Upperparts, including top of tail, speckled olive-brown mixed with grey; cheeks, sides of face, hips, thighs and underside of tail contrasting reddish-chestnut; underside white with light grey underfur, sharply demarcated from olive-brown upperparts. **Similar species** Red-cheeked Squirrel, *D. rufigenis*, has slightly shorter rostrum, more conspicuous red cheeks, and has hips and outer thighs grey.
Ecology and habitat Diurnal.
Distribution and status SE Asia: extreme N Vietnam. Also S and E China, Hainan. Status poorly known; probably not currently at risk.

ORANGE-BELLIED SQUIRREL

Dremomys lokriah PLATE 60

Measurements HB 170–200, T 120–140, HF 20–23

Identification Upperparts finely speckled olive-brown and grey. Some individuals have dark line down middle of back. Underparts mixture of orange or buff and grey, brightest on throat, but with considerable individual variation. Buff spot behind each ear. **Similar species** *Callosciurus* squirrels have longer, bushier tails, tend to be more arboreal and have different colour patterns (either greyer or redder underparts).

Ecology and habitat Diurnal. Found mainly near ground level in both primary and secondary forest.

Distribution and status SE Asia: E Myanmar. Also from Assam west to C Nepal and nearby parts of China. Not currently at risk.

PERNY'S LONG-NOSED SQUIRREL

Dremomys pernyi PLATE 60

Measurements HB 180–210, T 130–165, HF 42–28

Identification Upperparts finely speckled olive-brown and grey (agouti), as other species in genus. Underparts greyish-white. Orange spots behind ear. Often with some reddish around base of tail. Muzzle relatively elongate. **Similar species** Orange-bellied Squirrel, *D. lokriah*, has less elongate muzzle, orange throat and breast. Other *Dremomys* have orange cheeks.

Ecology and habitat Diurnal. Active mainly near ground level in shrubs and lower parts of trees. Occurs in primary and secondary forests, including highly disturbed areas.

Distribution and status SE Asia: N Myanmar and Vietnam. Also S China. Not currently at risk.

Genus *Lariscus* Medium-sized squirrels, largely terrestrial. Only one species occurs in the region, but additional species occur in Sumatra, Borneo and the Mentawai Islands.

THREE-STRIPED GROUND SQUIRREL

Lariscus insignis PLATE 60

Measurements HB 170–230, T 100–135, HF 33–46, E 14–18

Identification Upperparts brown with 3 black stripes along back; underparts white or buff (turning dark yellow in old skins), sometimes with a faint red tinge. **Similar species** Other species of striped squirrel (*Menetes* and *Tamiops*) have buff as well as black stripes on back; Shrew-faced Ground Squirrel, *Rhinosciurus laticaudatus*, is also terrestrial and similar in colour, but lacks stripes and has a more pointed muzzle.

Ecology and habitat Diurnal and mainly terrestrial. Diet includes fruits and insects. Occurs in tall and secondary forests, sometimes entering disturbed areas.

Distribution and status SE Asia: peninsular Thailand and Malaysia. Also Sumatra, Java, Borneo and some intervening islands. Not currently at risk.

Genus *Menetes* A medium-sized ground squirrel with many similarities to *Lariscus*, but can be distinguished by pattern of dark and pale stripes on the sides instead of black stripes on back. Only one species currently recognized in genus.

INDOCHINESE GROUND SQUIRREL

Menetes berdmorei PLATE 59

Measurements HB 180–210, T 140–175, HF 40–46

Identification Overall colour speckled-brown, sometimes slightly redder on the back, with 2 pale stripes on each side, separated by a darker stripe. Dark stripe also present above top pale stripe in some areas, but inconspicuous or absent in others. Brightness of stripes varies geographically and seasonally; pale stripes vary from buff to rufous. **Similar species** Striped squirrels, *Tamiops* spp., are smaller, more arboreal, and have stripes in the middle of the back; Three-striped Ground Squirrel, *Lariscus insignis*, has 3 dark stripes on back, but no pale stripes.

Ecology and habitat Diurnal and mainly terrestrial, though also forages in low bushes, bamboo and scrub. Found mainly in drier, more open forests and savannah.

Distribution and status SE Asia: Myanmar, Thailand, Laos, Vietnam and Cambodia. Also SW Yunnan in China. Not currently at risk.

Genus _Rhinosciurus_ Medium-sized ground squirrel with elongate nasal bones, making the head profile relatively pointed and superficially resembling _Tupaia_ treeshrews. Only one species currently recognized in genus.

SHREW-FACED GROUND SQUIRREL
Rhinosciurus laticaudatus PLATE 60
Measurements HB 195–233, T 131–170 (usually less than 70% of HB), HF 40–46
Identification Upperparts dark brown without stripes; underparts white or buff, turning to yellow in old skins. Tail short and bushy, often held upwards with fluffed-out hairs when the squirrel is active. Muzzle is pointed. **Similar species** Treeshrews, _Tupaia_ spp., have relatively long tail, even more pointed muzzle, darker underparts and very different dentition.
Ecology and habitat Diurnal and terrestrial. Diet includes insects taken from fallen trees and branches. Occurs in lowland rainforest, including mature forests and selectively logged forests.
Distribution and status SE Asia: Peninsular Malaysia, extreme S Thailand, and Singapore. Also Sumatra, Borneo and adjacent small islands. Not currently at risk, but populations have probably declined due to clearing of forests for agriculture.

Subfamily _SCIURINAE_, Tribe _PTEROMYINI_ FLYING SQUIRRELS

Flying squirrels, although incapable of true flight, unlike bats, have membranes stretched between the fore and hind legs, which enable them to glide long distances between trees. Unlike in the Colugo, which also glides, the tail is not enclosed by a membrane.

Flying squirrels are mainly nocturnal and most active high up in trees, so they are difficult to see, especially the small species. The larger flying squirrels are often active just around dusk. If the light is adequate, or if a powerful headlamp or spotlight is available, the larger species can often be distinguished by colour patterns, especially with binoculars. Several of the small to medium-sized flying squirrels are quite similar in appearance, and may be difficult to identify unless seen at close range. Pygmy flying squirrels have a diagnostic white tip to the tail.

The skulls of flying squirrels have relatively large, well-developed auditory bullae with complex patterns of septa within them. Differences in shape and size of the bullae can be helpful for distinguishing genera of museum specimens, especially some superficially similar groups, such as _Hylopetes_ and _Petinomys_ (Fig. 68).

Small flying squirrels can occasionally be captured by field workers for study in mist nets at night, or in cage traps set in trees, well above the ground, but are more often caught by searching nest holes in tree trunks. Many flying squirrels caught in this way are immature, which can make them more difficult to identify.

Genus _Petaurista_ Very large flying squirrels with long, rounded tails. Currently, five species recognized from region, but with considerable geographic variation in all species; taxonomic limits, both within and among species, are not well understood. For example, some populations currently allocated to _P. petaurista_ were formerly considered part of _P. alborufus_, a species that otherwise occurs only in China. Conversely, some populations now allocated to _P. philip-_ pensis were formerly included within _P. petaurista_. Recent molecular genetic studies from China indicate that _P. yunanensis_, formerly considered a subspecies of _P. philippensis_, is actually a distinct species. Further genetic studies may lead to additional changes in species limits within SE Asia. The text describes characteristics of different populations, and the major different types are illustrated, but in some areas there may be intermediates between these forms.

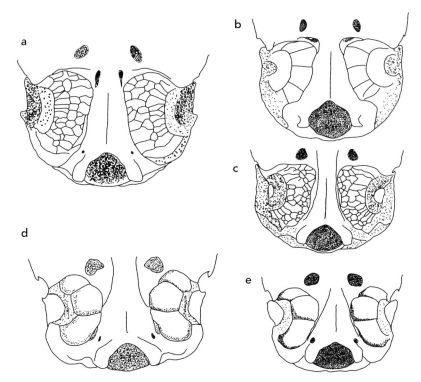

Fig. 68 *Underside of posterior half of skulls of selected small flying squirrels, showing variation in shape of auditory bullae:* Petinomys genibarbis (a), Petinomys setosus (b), Petinomys vordermanni (c), Hylopetes spadiceus (d), Petaurillus kinlochii (e).

RED GIANT FLYING SQUIRREL
Petaurista petaurista PLATE 61

Measurements HB 400–520, T 400–600, HF 70–100. Wt 1.6kg–2.9kg (larger in north than south)

Identification Considerable geographic variation in colour pattern, and possibly more than one species is involved. Peninsular Malaysian form (*P. p. melanotus*) has entire body dark reddish except for black on nose, chin, eye-ring, behind ears, feet and tail tip. In S Myanmar and W Thailand (*P. p. taylori*), colour is similar but with light speckling on head and back. In most of rest of Thailand and Myanmar (*P. p. candidula*), overall colour is pale orange-brown with white speckling, especially on head; tail brownish or greyish with black tip; throat white; rest of underparts off-white, pale line over each shoulder. **Similar species** Lesser Giant Flying Squirrel, *P. elegans*, has conspicuous white spots on back; Indian Giant Flying Squirrel, *P. philippensis*, has either all-dark or all-grey tail, depending on the population.

Ecology and habitat Mostly nocturnal, but becomes active shortly before dusk and may be seen climbing up large trees or gliding between trees just before dark. Occasionally active during day or seen resting on exposed parts of tall trees until mid-morning. Can make continuous glides of up to 100m. Nests in holes in large trees, usually at least 10m above ground. Found alone or in small groups. Diet includes leaves and seeds. Occurs in forests, including highly disturbed areas with some tall trees.

Distribution and status SE Asia: Myanmar, Thailand, possibly N Laos and Peninsular Malaysia. Also Nepal, N India, S China, Java, Sumatra and Borneo. Not currently at risk.

INDIAN GIANT FLYING SQUIRREL

Petaurista philippensis PLATE 61

Measurements HB 400–490, T 400–550, HF 65–90

Identification Moderate geographic variation in colour pattern, and may include more than one species. W Myanmar forms (*P. p. cineraceus*): upperparts, including tail and membranes, medium grey; back heavily frosted with long white tips to hairs; underparts greyish-white. E Myanmar and Thailand (*P. p. lylei*): upperparts very dark grey, heavily frosted with white; dorsal surface of membrane, feet, and tail black; underparts buff. Vietnam (*P. p. annamensis*): upperparts dark brown or dark red, heavily frosted with white, underparts pale orange-brown, tail dark. **Similar species** Red Giant Flying Squirrel, *P. petaurista*, in areas of overlap, is more rufous with paler head, tail with a discrete black tip.

Ecology and habitat Nocturnal. Occurs in hill dipterocarp and lower montane forests.

Distribution and status SE Asia: Myanmar, Thailand, Laos, Cambodia and Vietnam. Also Sri Lanka, India, S China, Taiwan and Hainan. Not currently at risk, but experiencing some declines due to loss of forest and hunting.

YUNNAN GIANT FLYING SQUIRREL

Petaurista yunanensis PLATE 61

Measurements HB 400–500, T 400–550, HF 65–90

Identification Upperparts dark grey, with reddish bases to fur, and white frosting on many hairs; gliding membranes dull red; feet black; tail dark grey. **Taxonomic notes** Formerly considered a form of *P. philippensis*, but recent genetic studies indicate it is distinct and more closely related to *P. petaurista*. **Similar species** Red Giant Flying Squirrel, *P. petaurista*, is more rufous with paler head, tail with a discrete black tip; Indian Giant Flying Squirrel, *P. philippensis*, does not have combination of grey back and red gliding membranes.

Ecology and habitat Nocturnal. Occurs in hill forests. Occurs sympatrically with *P. philippensis* in China, but differences in ecol-

ogy have not been studied as only recently recognized as distinct.

Distribution and status SE Asia: Myanmar, N Laos and N Vietnam. Also SW Yunnan in China. Precise distribution limits not yet determined, as only recently recognized as distinct. Status uncertain, but probably not currently at risk.

CHINDWIN GIANT FLYING SQUIRREL

Petaurista sybilla PLATE 61

Measurements HB 350–400, T 350–370, HF 60

Identification Similar in size and shape to *P. elegans*, but without any white spots. Overall, largely reddish-brown with slightly greyer-brown on back, without distinctive characters. **Taxonomic notes** Sometimes considered a form of *P. elegans*. **Similar species** Red Giant Flying Squirrel, *P. petaurista*, is larger with a black tail tip; Lesser Giant Flying Squirrel, *P. elegans*, has white spots on back.

Ecology and habitat Nocturnal. Hill forest.

Distribution and status SE Asia: mountains of N Myanmar. Also adjacent areas of Yunnan in China. Status uncertain, but probably not currently at risk.

LESSER GIANT FLYING SQUIRREL

Petaurista elegans PLATE 62

Measurements HB 340–365, T 340–365, HF 60–66. Wt 840–1,240

Identification In Peninsular Malaysia and extreme S Thailand, upperparts, including membranes, dark rufous mixed with black, with extensive large white 'spots' of heavy white flecking; tail black; underparts pale rufous. Elsewhere in region: upperparts brown, with fewer white spots mainly on head and centre of back; feet and tail reddish-brown. Outside region, in Java, may lack white spots. May be some intermediate forms in S Thailand. **Similar species** Chindwin Giant Flying Squirrel, *P. sybilla*, lacks spots; Red Giant Flying Squirrel, *P. petaurista*, is either uniform reddish or frosted white, without discrete clumps of white, and tail is reddish or brown with discrete black tip; Indian Giant Flying Squirrel, *P. philippensis*, is greyer without large white spots.

Ecology and habitat Nocturnal. Occurs in hill dipterocarp and lower montane forests. In areas of sympatry with other species of *Petaurista*, more often occurs at higher elevations, though may extend to lowlands.

Distribution and status SE Asia: Myanmar, Thailand, Laos, Vietnam and Peninsular Malaysia. Also S China (Yunnan), Java, Sumatra and Borneo. Not currently at risk. Still common in some areas of hill forest.

Genus *Aeromys* This genus contains two species of large flying squirrels, of which one occurs in the region. Superficially similar to *Petaurista*, with long, rounded tails, they differ in a number of skull characters, including simpler patterns on the molars and pale yellow instead of orange incisors. The one species in the region is readily identified by colour.

BLACK FLYING SQUIRREL

Aeromys tephromelas PLATE 62

Measurements HB 355–426, T 410–470, HF 67–78. Wt ~ 900

Identification Upperparts, tail and cheeks dark grey-brown, almost black, with fine, pale speckling on the back; underparts slightly paler, with sparse, fluffy hair. **Similar species** Other large flying squirrels, *Petaurista* spp., are coloured differently, although they can look black in poor light at night; Smoky Flying Squirrel, *Pteromyscus pulverulentus*, is much smaller and has creamy underparts.

Ecology and habitat Nocturnal. Occurs in tall and secondary forests, including some tree plantations and gardens.

Distribution and status SE Asia: Peninsular Malaysia and S Thailand. Also Sumatra and Borneo. Not currently at risk.

Genus *Belomys* Cheek teeth have an exceptionally complex pattern of ridges, similar to *Trogopterus*, with which it is sometimes combined. The auditory bullae are relatively small, but slightly bulbous with a honeycomb pattern of septa that may be hard to see owing to thick bone.

HAIRY-FOOTED FLYING SQUIRREL

Belomys pearsonii PLATE 62

Measurements HB 190–200, T 150–160, HF 34

Identification Upperparts blackish, with reddish-brown or white tips, giving an overall speckled-reddish or speckled-grey appearance; gliding membrane darker, almost black, with a pale edge; underparts including throat, breast and belly, creamy white. Tail bushy, rounded above, flattened below; reddish-brown with a paler grey base. Feet have long, sensory hairs. Tufts of long hairs behind ears. **Similar species** Particoloured Flying Squirrel, *Hylopetes alboniger*, is more uniformly coloured without a contrasting reddish-brown tail and lacking tuft of hairs behind ears; Smoky Flying Squirrel, *Pteromyscus pulverulentus*, is larger, greyer and does not overlap in range.

Ecology and habitat Nocturnal. Nests in holes in trees. Occurs in broadleaved hill forest.

Distribution and status SE Asia: N Myanmar, Thailand, Laos and Vietnam. Also E Nepal, S China, Hainan and Taiwan. Status uncertain.

Genus *Pteromyscus* Cheek teeth have relatively complex pattern of ridges, but differ in pattern from *Belomys*. Hairs on tail longer on sides than on top or bottom, producing a slightly flattened effect. Auditory bullae relatively large, divided into discrete sections by 5 septa.

SMOKY FLYING SQUIRREL

Pteromyscus pulverulentus PLATE 62

Measurements HB 220–290, T 215–235, HF 41–44. Wt 232–305

Identification Upperparts very dark grey-brown with fine, pale greyish speckling; underparts creamy with some grey. Tail dark grey-brown with grey-buff at base. Cheeks greyish. Tail slightly flattened above, flat below. **Similar species** Black Flying Squirrel,

Aeromys tephromelas, is larger with darker upperparts, greyish, fluffy hair on the underparts.

Ecology and habitat Nocturnal. Nests in tree holes. Occurs in tall lowland rainforest.

Distribution and status SE Asia: Peninsular Malaysia. Also Sumatra and Borneo. Rarely seen and poorly known, but believed Vulnerable, due to clearing of primary forest in its range and apparently low tolerance of disturbed areas.

Genus *Iomys* Only one species in the region, with an additional species in Indonesia. This species can be recognized by its medium-large size and generally dull-orange colour, especially on the tail. The genus is characterized by relatively square cheek teeth with a distinctive cusp in each corner. The auditory bullae are relatively small but bulbous, with 1 or 2 internal septa.

HORSFIELD'S FLYING SQUIRREL
Iomys horsfieldi PLATE 62
Measurements HB 165–230, T 160–207, HF 33–40. Wt 135–215

Identification Upperparts brown to dark grey, hairs with buff or dull-orange tips; underparts orange-buff or white with orange around the edges. Gliding membrane fringed with rusty-brown. Tail relatively round and rusty-brown. Cheeks buffy or rusty, contrasting with darker top of head. **Similar species** Vordermann's Flying Squirrel, *Petinomys vordermanni*, is similar colour but much smaller; *Hylopetes* flying squirrels have a white margin to the gliding membranes and a flatter tail.

Ecology and habitat Nocturnal. Occurs in forests, plantations and gardens with tall trees. Usually sleeps in tree holes, but may sometimes use leafy nests.

Distribution and status SE Asia: Peninsular Malaysia and Singapore. Also Sumatra, Java and Borneo. Not currently at risk.

Genus *Petinomys* Several species in the region, superficially similar to *Hylopetes*, mostly with distichous tails. Auditory bullae broad and relatively flat with multiple septa. In some species septa are both transverse and horizontal, forming a complex honeycomb pattern (Fig. 68a,c); in others septa are in a radial pattern forming discrete chambers (Fig. 68b), but with bullae still relatively flat. Most species can be distinguished by colour patterns.

WHISKERED FLYING SQUIRREL
Petinomys genibarbis PLATE 63
Measurements HB 160–180, T 155–188, HF 31–32

Identification Upperparts reddish-brown with grey underfur, speckled with grey anteriorly, and with reddish posteriorly, giving an unusual pinkish tinge; underparts cream or dull orange-buff. Gliding membrane with a white margin. Tail rusty-coloured with darker brown streaking. Whitish hairs at the base of each ear and a distinct tuft of long whiskers on the cheek behind the eye. Auditory bullae with honeycomb pattern. **Similar species** No other flying squirrels have a pinkish rump or prominent tuft of whiskers behind the eye.

Ecology and habitat Nocturnal. Occurs mainly in primary lowland rainforest, but also in some secondary forests.

Distribution and status SE Asia: Peninsular Malaysia. Also Sumatra, Java and Borneo. Vulnerable, due to loss of lowland rainforest.

TEMMINCK'S FLYING SQUIRREL
Petinomys setosus PLATE 63
Measurements. HB 105–125, T 93–115, HF 21–25. Skull: cbl 27.6–29.6

Identification Upperparts dark brown or black with pale buff tips; underparts white with pale grey underfur. Fur soft and silky. Margin of gliding membrane not distinctly pale. Tail dark brownish-grey, with pale patch of whitish hairs at base. Cheeks greyish. Dark ring around eye that usually connects with a black streak to the nose. Form in N Myanmar and NW Thailand is slightly larger, with a white tip to the tail. **Similar species** Phayre's Flying Squirrel, *Hylopetes phayrei*, is substantially larger, without a white tip to the tail and with a different skull structure; other small flying squirrels have at least some orange on the upperparts, base of tail or cheeks.

Ecology and habitat Nocturnal. One record of a nest hole, 19mm wide, in a tree trunk at 0.5m above the ground. Occurs in lowland rainforest in S part of range, but hill deciduous forest in north.

Distribution and status SE Asia: N Myanmar, NW Thailand and extreme S Thailand and Peninsular Malaysia. Also Sumatra and Borneo. Vulnerable, owing to loss of lowland rainforest.

VORDERMANN'S FLYING SQUIRREL

Petinomys vordermanni PLATE 63
Measurements HB 95–120, T 89–115, HF 21–23. Skull: cbl 28.2–30.0

Identification Hair of upperparts blackish with rusty-coloured tips; underparts buffy-white. Top of head and tail brown to reddish-brown. Gliding membrane with a buff (not white) margin. Tail brown to reddish-brown with paler buffy hairs at base; slightly rounded above, but very flat below. Cheeks orange. Black ring around each eye. Tuft of bristle-like hairs at front of base of ear. Auditory bullae of skull with honeycomb pattern. **Similar species** *Hylopetes* spp. have white margins on the gliding membranes and a different face pattern; Horsfield's Flying Squirrel, *Iomys horsfieldi*, is larger.

Ecology and habitat Nocturnal. Nest holes recorded at 0.3–6.0m above the ground. Mainly reported from lowland rainforest. Occurs in tall and secondary forests.

Distribution and status SE Asia: S Myanmar, S Thailand and Peninsular Malaysia. Also Borneo and small islands off E Sumatra. Vulnerable due to loss of lowland rainforest.

Genus *Hylopetes* A genus of about 10 medium to small species, of which 4 occur in the region. Tail is usually distichous. Superficially similar to many species of *Petinomys*, but skull is very different, with auditory bullae that are bulbous with only 2 or 3 septa (Fig. 68d).

RED-CHEEKED FLYING SQUIRREL

Hylopetes spadiceus PLATE 63
Measurements HB 157–184, T 152–166, HF 29–35. Wt 80–157. Skull: gl 33–39

Identification Upperparts blackish or dark grey-brown with rust-coloured markings, especially along midline; underparts white with orange tinge and grey bases. Gliding membrane blackish with a thin white margin. Tail dark, slightly orange-brown with buffy underfur; distinctly orange at the base. Cheeks orange brown on grey. In skull, auditory bullae are relatively large. **Similar species** Grey-cheeked Flying Squirrel, *H. platyurus*, is somewhat smaller and has principally greyish-white cheeks and base of tail, with only traces of a yellowish tinge; Vordermann's Flying Squirrel, *Petinomys vordermanni*, has buff margin to gliding membrane, distinct face pattern and is smaller; Phayre's Flying Squirrel, *H. phayrei*, has no orange, and has tail rounded above.

Ecology and habitat Nocturnal. Nest holes, about 32mm wide, recorded at 0.3–3.3m above the ground. Occurs in a variety of forest types; generally more abundant in tall forest than disturbed areas.

Distribution and status SE Asia: Myanmar, Thailand, S Laos, S Vietnam, Cambodia, Peninsular Malaysia and Singapore. Also Sumatra, Java and Borneo. Not currently at risk.

GREY-CHEEKED FLYING SQUIRREL

Hylopetes platyurus PLATE 63
Measurements HB 117–135, T 118–120, HF 29–30. Skull: gl 29–38

Identification Upperparts blackish or dark grey-brown with rust-coloured markings, especially in the midline; underparts white or buffy-white with grey underfur. Gliding membrane with a narrow white margin. Tail narrow at base, then broad, then tapers to tip, dark brownish-grey to black. Cheeks and patch on each side of base of tail pale grey, often tinged with yellow but never distinctly orange. In skull, auditory bullae are relatively small. **Taxomomic notes**: formerly considered part of *H. lepidus* from Java and

Borneo. **Similar species** Red-cheeked Flying Squirrel, *H. spadiceus*, has orange cheeks and base of tail; Vordermann's Flying Squirrel, *Petinomys vordermanni*, has buff margin to gliding membrane, yellowish-buff cheeks, reddish tail.

Ecology and habitat Nocturnal. Occurs mainly in lowland rainforests, but apparently tolerant of moderate habitat disturbance.

Distribution and status SE Asia: extreme S Thailand and Peninsular Malaysia. Also Sumatra. Status uncertain.

PARTICOLOURED FLYING SQUIRREL
Hylopetes alboniger   PLATE 63
Measurements HB 175–225, T 180–230, HF 36–45. Skull: gl 46–51

Identification Upperparts with dark greyish bases to fur, paler brown or greyish tips. Underparts white. Tail greyish to greyish-brown, paler at base, darker at tip, flattened below, but somewhat rounded above.

Similar species Phayre's Flying Squirrel, *H. phayre*, is similar but usually smaller, with proportionately larger auditory bullae in skull.

Ecology and habitat Nocturnal. Occurs mainly in hill and montane forest, up to 3,000m in Thailand, especially in oak forest.

Distribution and status SE Asia: N Myanmar, Thailand, Laos, Vietnam and Cambodia. Also Nepal through Assam to S China, Hainan. Status uncertain.

PHAYRE'S FLYING SQUIRREL
Hylopetes phayrei   PLATE 63
Measurements HB 145–195, HF 30–36. Skull: gl 37–43

Identification Overall colour of upperparts greyish-brown to mottled brown and black; individual hairs with dark slaty to blackish bases, and very extensive greyish-buff to brown tips. White mark behind ear. Underparts pale buff. Tail narrow at base, then broad, then tapering gradually to tip; rounded above, flattened below; greyish-brown to slightly cinnamon-brown, with darker tip. **Similar species** Particoloured Flying Squirrel, *H. alboniger*, is very similar but larger, with proportionately smaller auditory bullae; Red-cheeked Flying Squirrel, *H. spadiceus*, has tail flattened above and below, reddish cheeks and base to tail.

Ecology and habitat Nocturnal. Occurs in tall and secondary forests, including disturbed areas and cultivated orchards. Feeds on fruits.

Distribution and status SE Asia: Myanmar, Thailand, Laos and Vietnam. Also Nepal through Assam to S China, Hainan. Not currently at risk.

Genus *Petaurillus* Among the smallest flying squirrels in the world, with two species, only one of which occurs in the region. Tail feather-like (distichous). In skull, auditory bullae relatively swollen and bulbous with 2 septa, similar to *Hylopetes* but smaller (Fig. 68e).

MALAYSIAN PYGMY FLYING SQUIRREL
Petaurillus kinlochii   PLATE 63
Measurements HB 80–90, T 80–98, HF 19–20. Skull: cbl 25.2

Identification Upperparts very dark grey with pale buff streaks, especially in the midline; underparts off-white with grey underfur. Tail buffy at base, becoming blacker near the end, with a white tip. Cheeks buffy-white with a strong grey tinge beneath the eye. A whitish spot behind each ear. **Taxonomic notes** Sometimes considered a form of *P. hosei* from Borneo. **Similar species** Other small flying squirrels in its range are larger and do not have a white tail tip.

Ecology and habitat Nocturnal. Roosts and nests in holes in trees. Reported from both natural forest and rubber plantations.

Distribution and status SE Asia: Peninsular Malaysia. Status uncertain.

Superfamily *MUROIDEA* RATS AND MICE

Rodents of the superfamily Muroidea, commonly called rats and mice, can be found nearly everywhere on Earth, whether native or introduced by humans. Worldwide, this group contains over 1,500 recognized species, of which 70 are presently recognized in mainland South-East Asia.

The selection of English names for this group is particularly challenging. Even the choice of the name "rat" or "mouse" is often rather arbitrary. In Europe, the name "rat" is applied to larger species, of which the best known are in the genus *Rattus*, while the name "mouse" is applied to smaller species, especially in the genus *Mus*. However, these names have since been applied to genera all over the world, largely on the basis of size, with little regard for actual relationships. Many species called "mouse" are much more distantly related to *Mus* than *Mus* is to *Rattus*. Recently, there has been a tendency to develop new English group names, based on the scientific names, to reflect relationships more accurately. For some genera, such as *Maxomys* and *Niviventer*, these new names are used here in the interests of consistency and to avoid long, complicated names. However, whenever practical, the familiar names of "mouse" or "rat" have been retained as part of the English name to make them easier to remember and recognize.

Some rats and mice are confined to human settlements or to vegetation that has been disturbed or modified by man. Others are strictly forest dwellers, either terrestrial or partially or mainly arboreal. All South-East Asian rats and mice are mainly active at night.

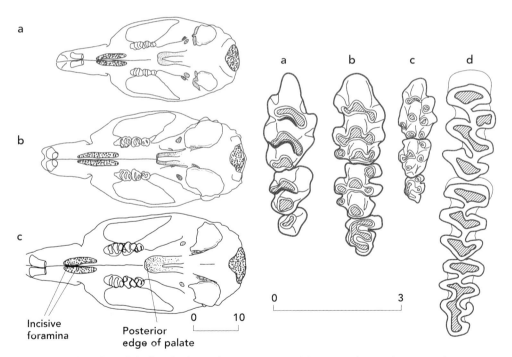

Fig. 69 *Undersides of skulls of selected rats showing differences in size and position of incisive foramina and posterior edge of palate relative to teeth: Niviventer langbianis (a), Rattus argentiventer (b) and Leopoldamys edwardsi (c).*

Fig. 70 *Upper right toothrows, with anterior at top, of selected mice and voles: Mus musculus (a), Apodemus draco (b), Micromys minutus (c) and Eothenomys melanogaster (d).*

346

It is normally necessary to catch rats and mice for positive identification. In some cases, it may be necessary to prepare the animal as a museum specimen and examine the skull to confirm the identity. For the benefit of people who may be working in a museum, or who may find a dead animal, the text sections include some information on skull characters, particularly those that help to diagnose the genus, including the position and relative length of the incisive foramina and the bony palate (e.g., Fig. 69).

The size and shape of the teeth, especially the pattern of cusps on the molars, are also important for identification, especially for separating genera; some genera have many separate cusps on the molars, while in others the cusps are fused to form parallel ridges (Figs 70, 71). In a live animal, teeth can usually be examined only if it has first been anaesthetized. Some care is required in examining cusp patterns, because the teeth become worn with age, and cusps that are separate in a young animal may appear joined in a very old animal.

In most cases there are also external characters that help with identification, and with practice it should be possible to identify most species in life.

The presence and relative density of spines in the fur are important for identifying many rats. The spines are often hard to see but are easily detected by feel – they are stiff, but not sharp, and can be found by running a finger backwards along the fur. Also important are the relative length and colour pattern of the tail (particularly whether it is all dark or bicoloured).

The sizes and shapes of footpads are also useful identification characters (Figs 72, 73). All rats have pads on the bottom of their feet, which vary among species in size, shape and the

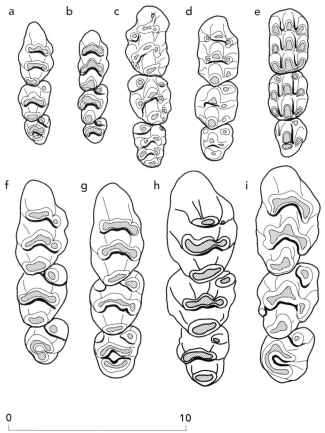

Fig. 71 Upper right toothrows, with anterior at top, of selected medium and large murid rodents: Rattus rattus (a), Niviventer confucianus (b), Lenothrix canus (c), Pithecheir parvus (d), Hapalomys longicaudatus (e), Leopoldomys edwardsi (f), Sundamys muelleri (g), Bandicota indica (h) and Dacnomys millardi (i).

amount of fine striations (like fingerprints) on the bottom. Species that climb well tend to have shorter feet with larger, better developed footpads and more conspicuous striations.

The arrangement of the mammary glands (mammae) is a useful identification character for females and can help to distinguish genera and species (Fig. 74). The number of pairs of mammae is given as the number near the front legs (axillary – typically one pair just in front and one or two pairs just behind the base of the leg) and the number near the back legs (abdominal and inguinal) using a formula such as mammae: 3 + 3. The number of pairs varies among most species from two (0 + 2) to six (3 + 3), but one species (*Bandicota bengalensis*) sometimes has up to 10 or more pairs.

Immature rats are frequently found and can be difficult to identify as they often differ in appearance from adults. Not only are the measurements smaller, but the colour and texture of the fur is different – usually softer and greyer. Any rat or mouse that differs

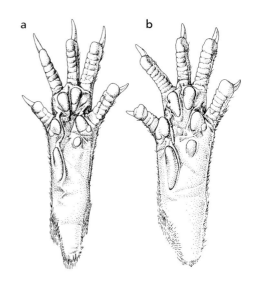

Fig. 72 *Undersides of left hind feet of* Rattus argentiventer *(a) and* R. rattus *(b). In addition to having larger pads,* R. rattus *has much deeper and more conspicuous striations (like fingerprints) on the pads (not shown in sketch).*

from all of the illustrated species and is distinctly smaller than the most similar species described may be an immature. Immatures can be recognized by disproportionately large heads and feet (which grow faster than the rest of the body) and incompletely developed sexual organs. Adult females have several pairs of distinct, readily visible nipples, while adult males have a large scrotum and testes; both are small and inconspicuous in immatures. Immatures moulting into adult pelage can sometimes be recognized by having a patchwork of immature and adult fur colour. In addition, young rats have unworn teeth that may not be fully erupted from the gums; and their skull bones are not solidly fused, tending to fall apart if the animal is prepared as a museum specimen.

Even among sexually mature rats, measurements must be considered somewhat cautiously because most murids continue to grow as adults. It can be useful to examine the teeth – an animal with very worn teeth is likely to be an older individual that may be larger, for a particular species, than a younger adult with less worn teeth.

A rat or mouse that does not seem to fit any description and yet appears to be mature could be an undescribed species. Several new species and even new genera have been described from the region in recent years, and additional species are likely. An animal that is entirely new to specialists working in the field is sometimes collected and preserved as a museum specimen, either as a skin and skull or preserved in formalin or alcohol as described in the introduction. The colours are described as accurately as possible, as they tend to change with time: red sometimes fades, and fur can turn yellowish. Colour photographs help, ideally taken with a colour reference strip in the photo. The specimen is labelled with the date, location and habitat of capture, and sent to a reputable museum for identification.

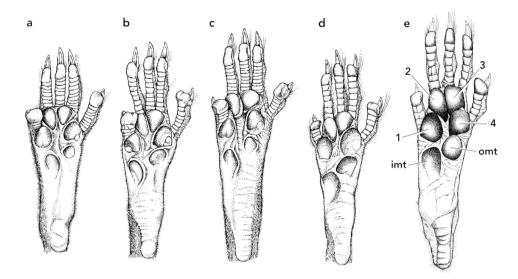

Fig. 73 Undersides of left hind feet of Chiromyscus chiropus (a), Niviventer langbianis (b), Niviventer fulvescens (c), Saxatilomys paulinae (d) and Tonkinomys daovantieni (e), showing differences in size and shape of the 4 interdigital (1–4), inner metatarsal (also called thenar) (imt) and outer metatarsal (also called hypothenar) (omt) pads.

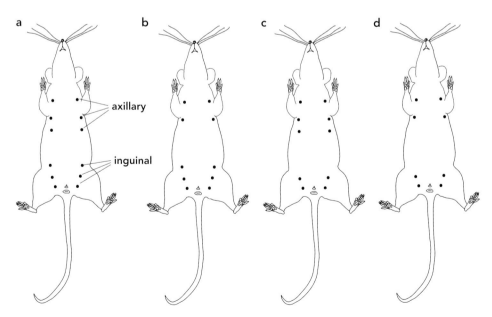

Fig. 74 Undersides of adult female rats showing some of the different patterns of axillary and inguinal mammae (teats): 3 + 3 (a); 2 + 3 (b); 3 + 2 (c); 2 + 2 (d), as described in the species accounts. The pair of mammae in front of the arms are also called pectoral, and those immediately behind them post-axillary.

The order in which families, subfamilies and genera are presented varies considerably among published books. Here, these are arranged based generally on size and morphological similarities, starting with the most widespread family (Muridae) and the genus *Rattus*, followed by other genera of larger species (rats) in this family, followed by the various genera of smaller species (mice).

Family *MURIDAE*

This is one of the largest families of rodents, with more than 560 species currently recognized worldwide in 126 genera. All of the South-East Asian forms are in the subfamily Murinae. These can be distinguished from other families of rodents in the region by having only 3 cheek teeth, with patterns of cusps on the teeth that vary from many separate cusps to parallel ridges (Figs 70a,b,c, 71). The tail is usually moderately long to very long, covered with scales and only sparsely haired.

Genus *Rattus* Small to large rats. Tail is usually entirely dark except in some Norway Rats; spines numerous on upperparts, scarce on underparts, but stiffness varies somewhat among species; generally soft, like stiff hairs. In skull, incisive foramina elongate, extending behind first upper molar, posterior edge of bony palate extending beyond third upper molar (Fig. 69b). Most cusps on teeth fused into curved ridges (Fig. 71a). Differences among species subtle and somewhat variable; it is important to examine several features when identifying species. Small *Rattus*, including juveniles, can be distinguished from *Mus* by elongate instead of rounded inner metatarsal pad on hind foot (Fig. 72). Mammae vary among species from 3 + 3 to as few as 2 + 2 (Fig. 74). Experience is required to identify specimens accurately, especially with dry skins where fur colour may have altered.

HOUSE RAT

Rattus rattus   PLATE 64

Measurements HB 105–215, T 120–230 (95–120% of HB; usually just over 100%), HF 26–40, E 17–25. Wt 100–200. Skull: cbl 33–43, mt 6.2–7.0

Identification Medium-sized rat. Upperparts finely grizzled olive-brown, sometimes with greyish or reddish tone; underparts usually buffy-brown with grey bases but sometimes creamy-white. Dorsal fur moderately spiny, especially on flanks, with long black guard hairs especially on lower back. Ears large and thinly furred. Tail similar length to body, dark above and below, very rarely with a white tip. Hind foot broad with prominent pads with clear striations; hairs on upper surface of foot usually brown with white hairs on toes, sometimes all white. Front foot has dark fur over wrist with white hairs on toes. Indian/European forms of *R. rattus*, which may occur in some towns ("Black Rat") are all dark blackish-grey including underparts. Mammae usually 2 + 3, sometimes 3 + 3, in which case both post-axillary pairs are generally very close together. **Taxonomic notes** This is actually a complex of species, with South-East Asian forms often called *Rattus tanezumi*, differing in chromosome count from true *Rattus rattus*, which is apparently native to India and introduced in much of the rest of the world. However, recent genetic studies suggest that there are more than two similar species, and the most appropriate names for each are uncertain, so they are treated together here.   **Similar species** Malaysian Wood Rat, *R. tiomanicus*, always has whitish underparts and sleeker upperparts with less prominent guard hairs; Ricefield Rat, *R. argentiventer*, has upperparts more speckled with black, often with small tuft of orange fur in front of ear; underparts grey to silvery; feet darker with less developed footpads; White-footed Indochinese Rat, *R. nitidus*, has narrower hind feet, pure white front and hind feet, darker woollier dorsal fur; Indochinese Forest Rat, *R. andamanensis*, has larger pads on hind feet, longer tail, more prominent guard hairs along entire length of back; Pacific Rat, *R. exulans*, is usually much smaller.

Ecology and habitat Nocturnal and sometimes diurnal. Diet includes a wide range of plant and animal matter. In most areas, largely confined to human settlements, plantations and gardens, where it is a major pest in stored crops. In areas where other species, such as *R. argentiventer*, are absent, including parts of Laos, can be abundant in agricultural fields. Climbs well, including inside buildings, but also spends much time on ground.

Distribution and status SE Asia: Myanmar, Thailand, Laos, Vietnam, Cambodia and Peninsular Malaysia. *R.* "*tanezumi*" form also in Nepal, N India, Bangladesh, S and C China, Korea, Japan, Sumatra, Java, Borneo, the Philippines, Sulawesi and many other Indonesian and Philippine Islands (probably introduced in most island areas, including Sunda Shelf). Other forms of *Rattus rattus* group occur in much of the rest of the world. Not currently at risk; considered a pest in most areas.

MALAYSIAN WOOD RAT

Rattus tiomanicus   PLATE 64

Measurements HB 140–190, T 150–200 (95–120% of HB), HF 28–35. Wt 55–150. Skull: cbl 34–45, mt 6.0–8.0

Identification Upperparts finely grizzled olive-brown; underparts usually pure white or slightly off-white. Fur smooth and sleek with short stiff spines; black guard hairs short to moderate length distributed evenly through the pelage. Tail entirely dark brownish. Feet quite broad with well-developed pattern of fine ridges on footpads for climbing (similar to *R. rattus*, Fig. 72b). Ears large and thinly furred. Mammae 2 + 3. **Similar species** House Rat, *R. rattus*, has longer dark guard hairs on lower back giving it a more shaggy appearance, and usually has darker base to fur on underside; Ricefield Rat, *R. argentiventer*, has grey-tinged underparts, orange tuft in front of ear, dark speckling on back, more slender feet with less developed

pads; Annandale's Rat, *R. annandalei*, has softer, shaggy fur, without stiff spines, fewer mammae.

Ecology and habitat Nocturnal. Occurs in secondary and coastal forests, plantations, gardens, scrub and grassland, but rarely in houses or tall dipterocarp forests. Climbs well and spends much of time in trees, but also often found on ground. Diet includes a wide range of plant and animal matter, including oil palm fruits. Shelters in piles of cut palm fronds, stumps, fallen logs and crowns of palms.

Distribution and status SE Asia: peninsular Thailand (S of Isthmus of Kra) and Peninsular Malaysia. Also Sumatra, Java, Borneo, and many smaller adjacent islands. Not currently at risk; very abundant in some areas and considered a pest in some areas in oil palm plantations.

RICEFIELD RAT

Rattus argentiventer   PLATE 64

Measurements HB 140–210, T 130–205 (80–125% of HB, usually just under 100%), HF 30–40, E 16–24. Wt 85–240. Skull: cbl 35–45, mt 6.7–8.2

Identification Upperparts pale brown to orange-brown with black speckling, giving a mottled appearance; underparts wholly silvery-grey, often with a dark streak along the middle. Fur moderately spiny. Ears large, lightly furred. Tail entirely dark brown. Feet rather slender with relatively small footpads (Fig. 72a), with inconspicuous patterns of ridges. Often has an orange-brown tuft of fur in front of each ear, but this may fade in older individuals or dry skins. Mammae 3 + 3.

Taxonomic notes Includes the recently described *R. hoxaensis* from Vietnam, which is now considered a synonym of this species.

Similar species No other *Rattus* has a tuft of orange fur in front of ear, but this may be missing in older animals. House Rat, *R. rattus*, has long guard hairs on lower back, underparts either pure white (not grey) or with grey bases and buff tips; Malaysian Wood Rat, *R. tiomanicus*, has sleeker, more uniform-coloured upperparts with less prominent guard hairs, creamy-white under-parts, broader feet with well-developed ridges; Lesser Ricefield Rat, *R. losea*, averages slightly smaller with smaller furry ears, upperparts softer orange-brown, underparts with grey bases but white or cream tips.

Ecology and habitat Nocturnal. Largely associated with open areas including rice-fields, grassland and plantations. Mainly in lowlands but may extend to higher altitudes in areas of extensive cultivation. Active principally on ground, but can climb some trees. Burrows extensively and nests in holes in ground. Diet includes many types of plant material, such as rice plants, grain, flowers and fruit of oil-palm, as well as insects. Can breed rapidly, producing several large litters per year when food is abundant.

Distribution and status SE Asia: Thailand, Laos, Vietnam, Cambodia and Peninsular Malaysia. Also Sumatra, Java, Borneo, Sulawesi, the Philippines, New Guinea and many intervening islands. Not currently at risk; widespread and abundant, one of the major agricultural pests in region. Probably native to Indochina but introduced into many other areas with the spread of agriculture, especially rice cultivation.

PACIFIC RAT

Rattus exulans   PLATE 64

Measurements HB 90–140, T 105–160 (about 110% of HB), HF 21–26, E 15–18. Wt 25–60. Skull: cbl 27–30, mt 4.5–6.0

Identification Smallest *Rattus*. Upperparts usually greyish-brown on mainland, but may be reddish-brown elsewhere; coarse spiny fur, spines white with dark brown tips. Underparts with cream or white tips and grey bases. Facial whiskers very long, reaching beyond ears when folded back. Tail brown. Hind foot with elongate inner metatarsal pads with well-developed ridges (similar to Fig. 72b). Mammae 2 + 2. **Similar species** House Mouse, *Mus castaneus*, and relatives are smaller, with inner metatarsal pad short and rounded and near front of foot; House Rat, *R. rattus*, is much larger when full-grown, with longer guard hairs, more mammae.

Ecology and habitat Diet includes plant and animal material. In region, mainly found in gardens, secondary areas around houses, and inside houses; raids grain stores. Also sometimes enters rice fields, especially near buildings. In Pacific islands lacking some of the other rat species, occurs in many more habitats and can be a major pest of many crops. Tends to grow larger on smaller islands. Climbs well, often climbing large grasses, small trees and houses. Makes nest of grasses in fields of tall grass or thatched roofs of village houses.

Distribution and status SE Asia: C and S Myanmar, Thailand, Laos, Vietnam, Cambodia, Peninsular Malaysia and Singapore. Also Bangladesh, Taiwan, Sumatra, Java, Borneo, Sulawesi and many smaller Indonesian Islands, the Philippines, New Guinea, New Zealand, Hawaii and other Pacific islands. Probably native to mainland South-East Asia and spread to islands either with humans or through natural rafting on drifting vegetation. Not currently at risk; widespread and common; considered a pest in some areas.

NORWAY RAT

Rattus norvegicus   PLATE 65

Measurements HB 160–265, T 170–250 (80–97% of HB), HF 35–50. Wt 200–500. Skull: cbl 41–56, mt 6.8–8.8

Identification Large, mainly terrestrial rat. Fur without flattened spines, but with moderately long guard hairs, giving shaggy apprearance. Upperparts brown; underparts paler, grey to grey-brown, without a sharp contrast; sometimes with a pale chest patch. Tail dark above, usually slightly paler below, but sometimes mottled with pale patches; thinly covered with sparse hairs. Eyes and ears relatively small. Front and hind feet largely white. Footpads poorly developed with low inconspicuous ridges. All-black, melanistic forms occur in some areas. Mammae 3 + 3. **Similar species** House Rat, *R. rattus*, is smaller, with more mottled upperparts, flattened spines, longer and more uniformly dark tail, less evenly coloured upperparts, larger footpads with fine ridges, larger ears; bandicoot rats, *Bandicota* spp., have larger ears, dark feet, broader incisors.

Ecology and habitat Mostly nocturnal. Largely terrestrial. Builds large and complex burrow systems in some areas. Diet includes plant and animal material. Lives largely in towns and cities, especially ports, where feeds extensively on garbage and waste and is considered an urban pest. Sometimes occurs in agricultural fields, but mostly near cities.

Distribution and status SE Asia: Myanmar, Thailand, Vietnam, Peninsular Malaysia, Singapore, possibly Laos and Cambodia. Also most of the rest of the world, mainly in large cities. Probably native to Japan, Siberia and N China, and spread elsewhere by humans. Not currently at risk; non-native in most of region and usually considered a pest.

INDOCHINESE FOREST RAT
Rattus andamanensis PLATE 65
Measurements HB 155–200, T 185–240 (typically 115–120% of HB), HF 32–37, E 23–25. Wt 100–150. Skull: gl 40–43, mt 6.5–7.5

Identification Upperparts orange-brown with conspicuous long black guard hairs all along back, giving a shaggy appearance. Underparts white or cream, sometimes with red-brown patch on chest. Ears longest of any *Rattus* in region. Face whiskers (vibrissae) long and thick, extending well behind ear when folded back. Hind foot thickly haired with mix of white and dark hairs on top; large, prominent pads on soles of feet. Tail dark, sometimes with short white tip. In skull, auditory bullae relatively small. Mammae 3 + 3. **Taxonomic notes** Formerly *R. sikkimensis*, *R. remotus* or *R. koratensis* but recent research suggests all are the same thing and *R. andamanensis* is the oldest name for the species. **Similar species** House Rat, *R rattus*, has proportionately shorter tail, smaller ears, guard hairs mainly restricted to lower back, smaller footpads.

Ecology and habitat Mostly nocturnal. A highly arboreal species found in a variety of forest and forest edge habitats including native forest and disturbed forest, as well as clumps of large bamboo. Has been found in gardens near forest.

Distribution and status SE Asia: Myanmar, Thailand (N of Isthmus of Kra except for some offshore islands), Laos, Vietnam and Cambodia, including some offshore islands. Also Nepal, NE India, S China, Andaman and Nicobar Islands. Not currently at risk.

WHITE-FOOTED INDOCHINESE RAT
Rattus nitidus PLATE 65
Measurements HB 160–180, T 165–190 (100–105% of HB), HF 34–40, E 20–24. Wt 110–140. Skull: gl 34–44, mt 6.0–7.2

Identification Medium-sized with soft, woolly fur and long, broad snout. Upperparts brown, belly creamy-white with grey bases to hairs. Hind and front feet including lower part of front legs white. Narrow feet, but with large, well-developed, ridged footpads for climbing. Tail dark, slightly paler below. Mammae 3 + 3. **Similar species** House Rat, *R. rattus*, usually has dark tops to feet, paler coarser upperparts with stiffer spines, broader feet; Indochinese Forest Rat, *R. andamanensis*, has white-based fur on underparts, longer tail, long guard hairs, dark tops to feet.

Ecology and habitat Mostly nocturnal. In region, mainly restricted to hills. In Thailand, found mainly on hills, but also in fields. In south China, a major agricultural pest where found in many fields.

Distribution and status SE Asia: Myanmar, N Thailand, Laos and Vietnam. Also Nepal, Bhutan, N India, Bangladesh and much of S China including Hainan, where probably native; Philippines, Sulawesi and New Guinea, where probably introduced. Not currently at risk; considered a pest in some parts of China.

LESSER RICEFIELD RAT
Rattus losea PLATE 64
Measurements HB 120–180, T 110–165 (typically 90–100% of HB), HF 24–32, E 15–20. Wt 40–90. Skull: gl 33–38, mt 6.3–7.1

Identification Medium-small rat. Fur long, slightly shaggy but sometimes sleek, with soft transparent spines, medium-length black guard hairs protruding no more than 10mm from fur. Upperparts vary from dull grey-brown in N Vietnam and China to more reddish-brown in rest of region; underparts with grey bases and white or cream tips, darker with buff tinge in south. Tail shorter than body, slightly paler below in north, all dark in south. Some individuals in peninsular Thailand are very dark brown. Feet narrow, footpads relatively small, smooth, lacking striations (even smaller than in Fig. 72a); fur on feet varies from whitish-grey to grey-brown. Mammae 2 + 3. **Taxonomic notes** Populations in Cambodia, Thailand and S Vietnam differ in colour and genetics from those in N Vietnam and S China and may represent a different species. **Similar species** Most other *Rattus* are larger, with tail longer than body; most species other than larger Ricefield Rat, *R. argentiventer*, have striated pads on soles of feet for climbing; Pacific Rat, *R. exulans*, is smaller with long tail, fewer mammae; Osgood's Rat, *R. osgoodi*, is smaller with darker fur, shorter tail, shorter toothrow, and is found higher in mountains.

Ecology and habitat Mostly nocturnal. Grassy and scrub habitats, mainly terrestrial in lowlands up to about 850m altitude. Has been found in natural grasslands in hill pine forest, and in disturbed areas. Can be a significant pest in rice fields, where it burrows and feeds on plants. Most common where *R. argentiventer* is uncommon or absent.

Distribution and status SE Asia: Thailand (N of Peninsula), Laos, Vietnam and Cambodia. Not currently at risk; common in many areas and sometimes considered a pest.

OSGOOD'S RAT
Rattus osgoodi PLATE 64
Measurements HB 125–170, T 100–140 (85% of HB), HF 26–37. Skull: gl 31–36, mt 5.3–6.0
Identification Fur dense, long and soft. Upperparts rich dark brown, sides slightly paler buffy-brown. Underparts dark grey, with brownish wash in middle. Ears and upper sides of feet dark brown. Tail dark brown. Mammae 2 + 3. **Similar species** Lesser Ricefield Rat, *R. losea*, has thinner, shaggier fur and paler underparts, and is larger with slightly longer tail, longer toothrow; Pacific Rat, *R. exulans*, is smaller with greyer upperparts, spiny fur, pale grey underparts, long tail, fewer mammae; other *Rattus* are larger with longer tails, coarser fur, paler upperparts.

Ecology and habitat Mostly nocturnal. Found in montane areas at 900–2,000m. Believed to be mainly terrestrial in grasslands and low shrubs.

Distribution and status SE Asia: S Vietnam, where known only from the Langbian Plateau. Poorly known, but not currently considered at risk; surveys required to determine whether occurs in other hill areas in region.

ANNANDALE'S RAT
Rattus annandalei PLATE 65
Measurements HB 145–220, T 160–270 (100–150% of HB), HF 35–40, E 18–23
Identification Upperparts greyish-brown, underparts white or pale yellow. Fur soft and shaggy without prominent spines. On skull, incisive foramina short, anterior to first molar, bullae relatively large and inflated. Mammae 2 + 2. **Similar species** Malaysian Wood Rat, *R. tiomanicus*, has smooth fur with short stiff spines, females have more mammae, skull with long incisive foramina; Müller's Rat, *Sundamys muelleri*, has even longer, shaggier fur, averages larger.

Ecology and habitat Nocturnal. Secondary forest, scrub and rubber plantations. Rarely found in primary forest. Found mainly low in trees, but sometimes also on ground. Not known to be a significant pest.

Distribution and status SE Asia: Peninsular Malaysia and Singapore. Also Sumatra. Not currently at risk, although may be adversely affected by conversion of forest cover to agriculture.

Genus _Bandicota_ Medium to large rats having long shaggy fur with very long guard hairs, most conspicuous on lower back. Distinguished externally from _Rattus_ by broad upper incisors (combined width more than 3.5mm), relatively small pads on feet and hence poor climbing ability. Cusps on molars largely fused to form nearly straight parallel ridges (Fig. 71h). Skull has large bullae, long incisive foramina that extend back to level with the front or middle of the first molar, long bony palate that extends posterior to last molar. Mammae 3 + 3, but _B. bengalensis_ varies from 2 + 3 up to 3 + 7. Genus contains three species. An additional species, _B. bangchakensis_, was described in 1989 from Thailand, but is now considered to be a synonym of _B. savilei_.

GREATER BANDICOOT RAT
Bandicota indica   PLATE 65
Measurements HB 190–330, T 190–280, HF 46–60, E 25–33. Wt 400–900. Skull: gl 49–64, mt 10.7–12.4
Identification Very large, dark rat with long, shaggy fur. Upperparts dark blackish-brown, somewhat greyer along sides, with very long black guard hairs. Underparts dark brownish-grey. Tail slightly shorter than head and body, very dark brown with relatively large scales. Feet very large and broad, dark brown to blackish. Upper incisors very broad (more than 4mm across the pair) angled straight down or slightly curved backwards. On skull, nasal bones long, hiding nostrils and incisors from above. Mammae 3 + 3.
Similar species Other _Bandicota_ are substantially smaller and paler in colour and can be distinguished from juvenile _B. indica_ by shorter toothrows and narrower feet; _Rattus_ are generally smaller, with shorter feet; Müller's Rat, _Sundamys muelleri_, is browner with sharply demarcated pale underparts, tail longer than head and body, fewer mammae in females, relatively narrow incisors.
Ecology and habitat Mostly nocturnal. Naturally occurs in wet swampy areas, but now exploits wet rice fields in both upland and lowland areas. Usually near human activity. Swims well. Builds extensive tunnel systems, sometimes in colonies with many adults and young. Feeds on plant materials as well as invertebrates; food selection may vary with population density.
Distribution and status SE Asia: Myanmar, Thailand, Laos, Vietnam and Cambodia. Introduced in parts of Peninsular Malaysia. Also India, Nepal, Sri Lanka, Bangladesh, S China and Taiwan, and introduced in Java. Not currently at risk; very common and considered a pest in some areas; hunted for food.

SAVILE'S BANDICOOT RAT
Bandicota savilei   PLATE 65
Measurements HB 150–240, T 125–230, HF 33–44, E 20-30. Wt 150–320. Skull: 42–52, mt 8.6–10.0
Identification Medium-sized. Moderately shaggy fur with long guard hairs; pelage softer than other _Bandicota_. Upperparts with mixture of black and buff hairs, overall tone varying from brownish-grey to reddish-brown; underparts greyish-buff, the hairs with grey bases and buff tips. Feet grey. Tail slightly shorter than head and body, uniformly grey-brown, sometimes with a short white tip. Upper incisors straight down or slightly curved backwards. On skull, nasal bones long, hiding nostrils and incisors from above. Mammae 3 + 3. **Similar species** Greater Bandicoot Rat, _B. indica_, larger with broader feet, larger teeth, even in juveniles; Lesser Bandicoot Rat, _B. bengalensis_, has more upturned snout, paler forwards-projecting incisors, shorter, broader feet, usually more mammae in females; Norway Rat, _Rattus norvegicus_, has white feet, narrower incisors.
Ecology and habitat Mostly nocturnal. Occurs in open degraded habitats including ricefields and cornfields, as well as edges of natural forest. Mainly in lowland areas.
Distribution and status SE Asia: C Myanmar, Thailand, S Laos, Vietnam and Cambodia. Not currently at risk; locally abundant and considered a pest in some areas; also hunted for food.

LESSER BANDICOOT RAT

Bandicota bengalensis NOT ILLUSTRATED

Measurements HB 160–210, T 110–160, HF 27–38, E 20–24. Wt 200–400. Skull: gl 36–44, mt 6.6–8.3

Identification Medium-sized with moderately shaggy harsh fur, blunt, slightly upturned snout. Upperparts with mixture of buff and dark brown hairs and moderately long black guard hairs, giving overall colour dark brownish-grey grizzled with black; underparts grey sometimes tipped with buff. Tail all dark brown; feet with dark brown or brownish-grey hairs, long narrow claws. Upper incisors broad with pale orange to creamy enamel; protruding forwards. On skull, nasal bones short, not hiding nostrils from above. Mammae vary from 2 + 3 up to 3 + 7 or even more in India; most commonly 7–9 pairs. **Similar species** Savile's Bandicoot Rat, *B. savilei*, has more pointed snout, incisors angled backwards, longer, narrower feet.

Ecology and habitat Mostly nocturnal. Found in villages and towns in rural areas, and associated crop lands. A good swimmer, often found in wet rice fields. Constructs elaborate burrow systems. Feeds on plants and grains as well as animal matter, including crustaceans and molluscs.

Distribution and status SE Asia: Myanmar. Introduced in Penang in Peninsular Malaysia, and Phuket Island in Thailand. Also native to Pakistan, India, Sri Lanka, Nepal and Bangladesh, and introduced in Sumatra, Java and Saudi Arabia. Not currently at risk. Considered a pest in many areas.

Genus *Berylmys* Medium to large rats with smooth, stiff fur; upperparts steely-grey turning slightly browner when worn; underparts pure white, sharply demarcated from upperparts. Incisors relatively wide and stout, usually with very pale enamel, white or cream to pale orange, though sometimes darker orange in *B. bowersii* or *B. mackenziei*; in contrast, most other murid rodents have dark orange enamel on outside of incisors. Upper incisors either stick straight down or protrude slightly forwards, not curved backwards. Molars have some discrete cusps, but cusps tend to appear fused and hard to differentiate when teeth are worn; posterior molars small relative to others. Skull with incisive foramina ending anterior to or level with front molars; palate relatively short, ending anterior to posterior molars. Braincase broadly triangular when viewed from above, rather than the more oval shape of *Rattus*. Long, narrow hind feet with 6 medium-sized pads lacking ridges. Mammae 2 + 2 in *B. bowersii*, 3 + 2 in other species.

BERDMORE'S RAT

Berylmys berdmorei PLATE 66

Measurements HB 190–260, T 150–190, HF 37–46, E 22–29. Wt 180–300. Skull: gl 38–50, mt 6.6–8.0

Identification Upperparts with smooth, stiff fur, steel-grey; underparts pure white, sharply demarcated from underparts. Tail dark brown on top and sides; dark brown or mottled pale greyish-white underneath; lacking a white tip; considerably shorter than head and body. Front and hind feet white or grey above. Upper incisors angled slightly forwards; bullae relatively larger than those of other *Berylmys*. Upper incisors 2.8–3.5mm across. **Similar species** Other *Berylmys* have tail equal to or longer than head and body, often with white tip; Bowers's Rat, *B. bowersi*, is considerably larger, especially feet and skull.

Ecology and habitat Mostly nocturnal. Mainly terrestrial. Digs extensive burrows. Found in forest and scrub, but sometimes enters agricultural areas near forest; reported from swampy forest and marshy areas in Thailand. Found from sea-level to 1,400m. In most areas infrequently found, but can be locally common.

Distribution and status SE Asia: S Myanmar, Thailand, Laos, S Vietnam, Cambodia. Not currently at risk; may occasionally be a pest in some agricultural areas.

BOWERS'S RAT

Berylmys bowersi PLATE 66

Measurements HB 235–300, T 240–310, HF 52–61, E 27–37. Wt 270–650. Skull: gl 51–63, mt 9.0–10.6

Identification Upperparts with smooth, stiff fur, colour varying from dark grey to bright brownish-grey with tan on sides; upperparts pure white, sharply demarcated from underparts. Tail colour varies geographically: uniformly dark brown, sometimes slightly paler below in Laos and Vietnam; dark brown at base with distal one-half to one-third white in Malay Peninsula; dark brown with short white tip in N Myanmar. Feet white on sides and toes, dark brown on top. Mammae 2 + 2. Upper incisors 3.5–4.5 across. **Taxonomic notes** Populations in peninsular Thailand, Malaysia and Sumatra are geographically isolated and differ in some ways from those elsewhere; specimens from N Myanmar and Laos are smaller than those elsewhere; further study is needed to determine whether these populations are specifically distinct. **Similar species** Mackenzie's Rat, *B. mackenziei*, averages smaller and greyer, has more white on tail in areas of overlap in Myanmar; females have additional pair of post-axillary mammae; other *Berylmys* are considerably smaller.

Ecology and habitat Mostly nocturnal. Terrestrial, digging extensive burrow systems. Most specimens from 1,000–1,500m altitude, but has been recorded from as low as 200 to as high as 1,600m. In Malaysia, most common in primary forest, but also found in disturbed forest and secondary scrub. Feeds mainly on plant matter, including fruits; more rarely on insects and snails.

Distribution and status SE Asia: Myanmar, Thailand, Laos, Vietnam and Peninsular Malaysia. Also NE India, S China and NE Sumatra. Not currently at risk.

MACKENZIE'S RAT

Berylmys mackenziei NOT ILLUSTRATED

Measurements HB 155–240, T 150–250, HF 44–51, E 25–35. Skull: gl 40–54, mt 8.1–9.8. Specimens from S Vietnam average about

15% larger than those from Myanmar.

Identification Moderately large. Upperparts with smooth, relatively thick fur, dark grey or steel-grey; underparts pure white, sharply demarcated from upperparts. Tail colour varies geographically: all dark brown, sometimes with a short white tip in Vietnam; dark brown base with distal one-third to two-thirds white in Myanmar. Feet white on sides and toes, dark brown on top. Mammae 3 + 2. Upper incisors 3.0–3.9 across. **Taxonomic notes** Further study is required to ascertain whether these apparently separate populations are really the same species. **Similar species** Bowers's Rat, *B. bowersi*, averages larger, females with fewer mammae, less white on tail in Myanmar population.

Ecology and habitat Mostly nocturnal. Apparently occurs mainly at higher altitudes, 1,000–2,000m, presumably in forest.

Distribution and status SE Asia: C and S Myanmar, and S Vietnam. Also NE India and S China (Sichuan). Previously published records from Thailand have been reidentified as *B. bowersi*. Status uncertain; further surveys required to determine full extent of range.

MANIPUR RAT

Berylmys manipulus PLATE 66

Measurements HB 135–185, T 140–185, HF 33–40, E 23–25. Skull: gl 36–41, mt 6.2–6.7

Identification Smallest of the *Berylmys*. Upperparts with smooth, stiff fur, steel-grey; underparts pure white, sharply demarcated from upperparts. Tail dark brown at base, sometimes paler underneath, with distal one-half to two-thirds white. Front and hind feet white above. Upper incisors 2.3–2.9 across, protrude slightly forwards. **Similar species** Berdmore's Rat, *B. berdmorei*, is not known to overlap in range, has shorter tail without white tip; other *Berylmys* are larger.

Ecology and habitat Mostly nocturnal. Strictly terrestrial, digging extensive burrows. Found in wooded and scrub habitats, as well as moist rainforest; not reported near human settlements. Feeds on plants, including leaves and seeds, as well as on insects and other invertebrates. Altitudinal range 100–1,500m.

Distribution and status SE Asia: N and C Myanmar. Also India and S China (Yunnan). Status uncertain, but has probably declined following extensive loss of forest cover.

Genus _Tonkinomys_ This genus, with only one known species, was first described in 2006. Feet with large bulbous pads lacking fine striations, apparently adapted for climbing on limestone rocks (Fig. 73e); all toes with pointed claws. Incisive foramina short and broad, bony palate long, extending far behind molars. Incisors smooth with pale orange enamel. Mammae 2 + 2.

TONKIN LIMESTONE RAT
Tonkinomys daovantieni PLATE 66
Measurements HB 185–215, T 155–185 (85% of HB), HF 37–41, E 29–31. Wt 140–205. Skull: gl 47–53, mt 8.0–8.8
Identification Upperparts slightly shaggy, shiny dark greyish-black, often with a white blaze on forehead; fur a mixture of soft dark grey underfur, moderate-length flexible spines pale grey with dark tips, and long guard hairs with pale bases and dark brownish-black tips. Underparts uniformly grey except for white patch on chest, colour blending into darker colour of upperparts. Feet whitish-pink except for brown patch in middle on tops of hind feet. Ears moderately long, grey; lips unpigmented pinkish. Tail relatively short with stubby tip, dark grey on top and sides for 60–75% of length, unpigmented pinkish-white on underside and all round at tip. **Similar species** Lao Limestone Rat, _Saxatilomys paulinae_, is smaller with longer tail, dark feet; _Berylmys_ spp. have grey upperparts, sharply contrasting white underparts, much smaller footpads; _Leopoldamys_ spp. have contrasting white underparts, tail longer than head and body; all species of _Niviventer_ are smaller with different fur colour, longer tail.
Ecology and habitat Mostly nocturnal. Known only from limestone outcrops where has been found among vine-covered lime-

stone boulders and inside caves.
Distribution and status SE Asia: N Vietnam. Status uncertain; only known records are from Huu Lien Nature Reserve in Vietnam, but probably occurs in other limestone areas in region.

Genus _Saxatilomys_ A recently discovered genus, with only one known species, first described in 2005. Similar in many respects to _Niviventer_, it differs in colour pattern, narrow incisive foramina that end anterior to the upper molars, long bony palate that extends beyond molars, toothrows diverging posteriorly and other details of skull. Feet with large bulbous pads, lacking fine striations, probably adapted for climbing on rocks (Fig. 73d); all toes with pointed claws. Incisors smooth on surface, dark orange enamel on uppers, pale orange on lowers. Mammae 2 + 2.

LAO LIMESTONE RAT
Saxatilomys paulinae PLATE 66
Measurements HB 145–150, T 165–170 (110–115% of HB), HF ~32, E 24–25. Skull: gl 40–41, mt 7.3
Identification Upperparts shiny greyish-black with soft dark grey underfur, moderate-length flexible spines with pale grey bases and dark tips, and long guard hairs with pale bases and black tips extending 5–10mm beyond underfur. Underparts lightly frosted dark grey, hairs uniformly grey with unpigmented tips giving a slight frosting effect; blends into colour of upperparts. Feet covered with dark brown hairs. Tail long with slender tip, dark brown above and on sides, pale underneath, but not contrasting sharply. Ears moderately long, grey; lips unpigmented pinkish. **Similar species** Tonkin Limestone Rat, _Tonkinomys daovantieni_, has similar colour and footpads but is much larger, has relatively short tail with white tip, usually has white patches on chest or forehead; _Rattus_ spp. have smaller footpads with fine striations in arboreal species; _Niviventer_ have brown or brown-grey upperparts, contrasting white underparts.
Ecology and habitat Mostly nocturnal.

Known only from limestone rocky outcrops. **Distribution and status** SE Asia: C Laos. Status unknown; known only from a few individuals found by villagers or in owl pellets around Khammouane Limestone. Might be expected in similar habitats in Vietnam.

Genus *Sundamys* Very large rats with long dark tail. Shaggy fur with prominent long black guard hairs on upperparts. Skull with moderate-length, narrow incisive foramina ending near anterior molars; bony palate ending slightly posterior to molars; relatively small bullae; large stocky molars with relatively large posterior molar, cusps similar in shape to *Rattus* (Fig. 71g). Feet with relatively small pads. Several species in Greater Sundas, but only one in region. Mammae 2 + 2.

MÜLLER'S RAT
Sundamys muelleri PLATE 65
Measurements HB 210–280, T 250–370 (usually 110–120% of HB), HF 47–55, E 20–27. Wt 200–470. Skull: gl 53–62, mt 9.4–11.5
Identification Very large with long dark tail. Upperparts dark tawny-brown, darkest on top and paler on sides; fur harsh and slightly shaggy but without stiff spines, prominent long black guard hairs 10–15mm beyond overfur; underparts with short dense fur, sharply demarcated from upperparts, usually white or pale grey, sometimes darker grey with buff tinge. Tail longer than head and body, entirely dark brown. Ears round and dark brown. **Similar species** Most other rats are smaller with shorter, sleeker fur; bandicoot rats, *Bandicota* spp., have even longer, shaggier fur, underparts darker, not sharply demarcated from upperparts, tail shorter than head and body, females with more mammae.
Ecology and habitat Mostly nocturnal and terrestrial, but can also climb. Often found near streams. Feeds on plant and animal matter. Occurs in lowland tropical forests, but also in some areas of secondary forest near primary forest.
Distribution and status SE Asia: peninsular Myanmar, Thailand and Malaysia. Also Sumatra, Borneo, Palawan and adjacent islands. Status uncertain, but may be at risk owing to loss of primary lowland rainforest.

Genus *Niviventer* Tail usually at least 125% of head and body length (except in *N. hinpoon*), usually with longer hairs at tip forming a slight tuft, often bicoloured. Fur varies in texture from soft to semi-spiny, sometimes in the same species, and varies in length from short to moderately long; guard hairs moderately long and conspicuous in some species, inconspicuous in others. In most species, upperparts some shade of brown or reddish-brown, underparts pure white, but in preserved animals white may discolour to bright yellow, especially in formalin. Hind feet long and slender in most species (Fig. 73c), but relatively broad in the most arboreal species, *N. cremoriventer* and *N. langbianis* (Fig. 73b). Hind feet with 6 well-developed pads, somewhat larger in arboreal species. Incisors smooth with dark orange enamel, uppers angled straight downwards or slightly backwards. Molars relatively small, anterior molars narrow, third molar much smaller than others (Fig. 71b). Skull long and slender with long, narrow incisive foramina ending just in front of molars; bony palate ending roughly level with back of molars (Fig. 69a). Auditory bullae relatively small. Mammae usually 2 + 2, sometimes 1 + 2. **Taxonomic notes** Taxonomy of group still somewhat uncertain; some species occurring north of peninsular Thailand can be difficult to identify.

DARK-TAILED NIVIVENTER
Niviventer cremoriventer PLATE 67
Measurements HB 130–165, T 150–200 (usually about 125% of HB), HF 20–29, E 15–21. Wt 53–100. Skull: gl 33–38, mt 5.5–6.4
Identification Upperparts reddish-brown to orange-brown, darker on back and rump, sometimes with scattered patches of white hairs. Fur a mixture of four types of hairs: soft grey underfur with dull orange-brown tips; longer overfur with grey base and bright orange-brown tips; similar-length stiff, flattened spines, translucent at base and tipped

with black on back and rump, orange-brown on sides; and long black-tipped guard hairs extending 15–20 mm beyond overfur. Underparts whitish or creamy, also with a mixture of flexible spines and softer hairs, all hair types white to base; sometimes turns yellowish, especially in older skins. Short face with relatively large ears and long facial whiskers. Feet dark brown above, relatively short and broad with large footpads (as in Fig. 73b). Tail usually entirely dark brown, but sometimes paler below (especially in Borneo); covered in short hairs with longer, more prominent hairs on the distal 2 cm forming a slight tuft extending 5–8mm beyond tip. Mammae 2+2. **Similar species** Cameron Highlands Niviventer, *N. cameroni*, is larger (especially hind foot), tail pale underneath without tuft of hairs; Indomalayan Niviventer, *N. fulvescens*, has bicoloured tail and, in areas of overlap in range, is more yellowish-brown.

Ecology and habitat Nocturnal. A good climber, active in small trees, lianas and shrubs to at least 5m above ground; also active on ground. Occurs in tall and secondary forests, forest edge and lightly wooded areas from near sea-level to 1,900m. Feeds on plant matter, including fruits and seeds, as well as insects.

Distribution and status SE Asia: peninsular Thailand and Peninsular Malaysia. Also Sumatra, Java, Borneo and adjacent smaller islands. Not immediately at risk, but population has probably declined substantially owing to loss of lowland forest.

INDOCHINESE ARBOREAL NIVIVENTER

Niviventer langbianis   NOT ILLUSTRATED

Measurements HB 125–170, T 150–200 (125–135% of HB), HF 27–32, E 20v25. Skull: gl 33–40, mt 6.0–6.7

Identification Upperparts brownish-grey mixed with pale yellowish-orange with distinctive olive-grey tone; darker on back and lower rump owing to more long black hairs; paler on sides, with yellow-orange at lower edge of flanks. Underparts white or cream. Fur a mixture of softer hairs, spines and long

guard hairs, as *N. cremoriventer*, but often somewhat softer with fewer spines. Cheeks, sides of neck and upper arms often brighter yellow-orange, contrasting with back. Tail very long, uniformly dark brown with tuft of hairs at tip. Ears relatively large, dark brown. Feet relatively short and broad with large footpads (Fig. 73b). Skull has long incisive foramina and relatively large bullae. Mammae 2 + 2. **Similar species** Dark-tailed Niviventer, *N. cremoriventer*, is similar in shape and size but more reddish-brown with smaller ears, does not overlap in range; Fea's Tree Rat, *Chiromyscus chiropus*, is similar in size and shape but has brighter orange on face with dark eye-ring, nail instead of claw on first toe, bicoloured tail.

Ecology and habitat Mostly nocturnal. Tropical evergreen forest as well as mixed forest, at altitudes from near sea-level to 2,800m. Spends much time in trees and vines, but also sometimes found on ground.

Distribution and status SE Asia: Myanmar, Thailand (N of Isthmus of Kra), Laos, Vietnam and SW Cambodia. Also NE India. Not currently at risk, but probably declining owing to loss of forest.

CAMERON HIGHLANDS NIVIVENTER

Niviventer cameroni   PLATE 67

Measurements HB 130–170, T 205–270 (130–180% of HB), HF 30–38, E 18–25. Wt 58–129. Skull: 40–43, mt 6.3–7.2

Identification Upperparts bright reddish-brown, fur with many flexible spines and long black guard hairs, as in *N. cremoriventer*. Underparts white. Tail very long, dark brown above and all around at base, whitish on remainder of underside and all around at tip. Mammae 2 + 2. **Taxonomic notes** Formerly called *N. rapit*, but that species is now considered to occur only in Borneo. **Similar species** Dark-tailed Niviventer, *N. cremoriventer*, has smaller hind feet, all-dark tail; Indomalayan Niviventer, *N. fulvescens*, is smaller with yellowish-brown upperparts.

Ecology and habitat Mostly nocturnal. Occurs in forests above 1,000m where generally found on ground.

Distribution and status SE Asia: known only from Cameron Highlands, Peninsular Malaysia. Vulnerable owing to very limited range and conversion of montane forest to agriculture and tea plantations.

CONFUCIAN NIVIVENTER
Niviventer confucianus PLATE 67
Measurements HB 125–170, T 150–220 (125–135% of HB), HF 28–32, E 20–23. Skull: gl 34–41, mt 5.6–5.9
Identification Upperparts brown, sometimes with yellowish or greyish tinge; fur long and soft, usually without stiff spines or conspicuous guard hairs. Underparts white, sharply demarcated from upperparts. Tail moderately long, dark brown above, pale below, sometimes pale all around at tip; short tuft of hairs (~5mm) at tip. Mammae 2 + 2. **Taxonomic notes** Formerly considered part of *N. niviventer*. **Similar species** Other *Niviventer* in its range have coarser fur with stiff spines and conspicuous guard hairs, but this is somewhat variable; can be difficult to distinguish from Indomalayan Niviventer, *N. fulvescens*.
Ecology and habitat Mostly nocturnal. In region, found at high elevations in moss forest, but in China occurs in a variety of habitats including disturbed and secondary forest.
Distribution and status SE Asia: N Myanmar, NW Thailand and NW Vietnam. Also China. Not currently at risk.

INDOMALAYAN NIVIVENTER
Niviventer fulvescens PLATE 67
Measurements HB 130–170, T 155–220 (115–130% of HB), HF 25–35, E 18–21. Wt 60–135. Skull: gl 31–42, mt 5.4–6.4
Identification Upperparts vary from yellowish-brown to reddish-brown, hairs with a mixture of yellowish or reddish overfur, dark brown-tipped spines and conspicuous black guard hairs on back. Underparts pure white, sometimes slightly yellow, sharply demarcated on sides; also with extensive short, stiff white spines. Tail very long, dark brown above, white below, sometimes with pale tip, no tuft of hairs at tip. Top of hind foot silvery grey to pale brown, sometimes with dark brown patch in middle. Colour varies geographically, with Malaysian individuals more yellow-brown. Feet relatively long (Fig. 73c). Mammae 2 + 2. **Taxonomic notes** Populations from S Thailand, Peninsular Malaysia and Sunda shelf often separated as *N. bukit*. **Similar species** Dark-tailed Niviventer, *N. cremoriventer*, has all-dark tail; Confucian Niviventer, *N. confucianus*, tends to have less spiny fur, but this is somewhat variable and they can be difficult to distinguish; Indochinese Mountain Niviventer, *N. tenaster*, is more yellowish-brown with longer ears.
Ecology and habitat Mostly nocturnal. Found in a wide variety of forested habitats as well as gardens and disturbed areas with vegetation. Active both on ground and in trees, frequently climbing large lianas and vines.
Distribution and status SE Asia: Myanmar, Thailand, Laos, Vietnam, Cambodia and N Peninsular Malaysia. Also Nepal, N India, Bangladesh, S China (including Hainan, Hong Kong), Sumatra, Java and Bali. Not currently at risk; relatively common in many areas.

INDOCHINESE MOUNTAIN NIVIVENTER
Niviventer tenaster NOT ILLUSTRATED
Measurements HB 120–190, T 175–235 (125–140% of HB), HF 32–35, E 23–26. Wt 50–140. Skull: gl 37–42, mt 5.9–6.5
Identification Upperparts yellowish-brown with conspicuous dark brown guard hairs. Underparts white, sharply demarcated from upperparts. Tail dark brown above, paler below, often with a pale tip. Ears relatively long. Mammae 2 + 2. **Similar species** Indochinese Arboreal Niviventer, *N. langbianis*, has all-dark tail; Indomalayan Niviventer, *N. fulvescens*, in areas of overlap in range, is more reddish-brown.
Ecology and habitat Mostly nocturnal. Hill forest, from 1,000–2,200m. Mainly active on ground, low vines and fallen logs.
Distribution and status SE Asia: C and S

Myanmar, NW Thailand, Laos, Vietnam and SW Cambodia. Also China (Yunnan and Hainan). Not currently at risk.

LIMESTONE NIVIVENTER
Niviventer hinpoon PLATE 67
Measurements HB 120–160, T 120–160 (~100% of HB), HF 25–28, E 17–21. Wt 50–70. Skull: gl 34–37
Identification Upperparts dull buffy-grey, hairs mixed with extensive spines; underparts dull buff, hairs with grey bases and buff tips. Tail similar in length to head and body, sharply bicoloured dark above, pale below for entire length. Mammae 2 + 2. **Similar species** Other *Niviventer* in its range have white underparts; *Rattus* spp. have dark tails.
Ecology and habitat Mostly nocturnal. Forested limestone outcrops, in scrubby forest at base of cliffs, as well as inside caves.
Distribution and status SE Asia: known only from Korat Plateau in C Thailand. Status uncertain; habitat vulnerable to disturbance from forest clearing and limestone quarrying; surveys needed to determine current status and full extent of range.

BRAHMAN NIVIVENTER
Niviventer brahma PLATE 67
Measurements HB 135–145, T 200–225 (150% of HB), HF 28–33, 20–25. Skull: gl 34–36, mt 6.4–7.0
Identification Medium-sized with very long tail. Fur relatively long (15mm above, 10mm on underparts), dense and soft without stiff spines. Upperparts bright orange-brown to yellow-brown; dark brown ring ~2 mm around each eye, connected across top of muzzle by narrow dark brown band. Underparts greyish-white, individual hairs with bases grey and distal half white. Ears dark brown with short hairs. Tail very long, brownish-black above, brownish-grey below, well haired, hairs longer towards tip forming distinct brush 6–8mm long. Hind feet silver-grey on sides, grey-brown on top. Mammae 1 + 2. **Similar species** Smoke-bellied Niviventer, *N. eha*, is paler brown, eye-rings do not connect over muzzle, has tuft of hairs at

base of ear; other *Niviventer* in its range have all-white belly, stiff spines in fur.
Ecology and habitat Mostly nocturnal. Reported from wet montane broadleaf forest at 2,500m altitude. Found on ground and fallen logs.
Distribution and status SE Asia: N Myanmar. Also NE India and NW Yunnan (China). Not currently at risk.

SMOKE-BELLIED NIVIVENTER
Niviventer eha PLATE 67
Measurements HB 110–130, T 165–195 (150% of HB), HF 27–31, E 17–20. Skull: gl 30–33, mt 5.1–5.6
Identification Fur thick and soft. Upperparts pale brownish-orange; dark rings around eye but without a dark mask-like mark joining to other eye. Underparts light grey, individual hairs with grey bases and distal one-third white. Ears dark brown, densely covered with long hairs, and a long brownish-black tuft of hairs at base of each ear. Hind feet silver-grey on sides, grey-brown on top. Tail very long, brownish-black above, grey below, with moderate-length hairs forming short tuft at tip. Mammae 1 + 2. **Similar species** Brahman Niviventer, *N. brahma*, averages larger and darker, lacks ear tuft, has longer tuft of hair on tail; other *Niviventer* in range have white bellies with spines in pelage.
Ecology and habitat Mostly nocturnal. Mainly terrestrial. Recorded from scrub and wet montane temperate forests, around areas of boulders at 2,400–3,300m altitudes.
Distribution and status SE Asia: N Myanmar. Also Nepal, India and S China. Poorly known in region, but probably not at risk.

Genus *Chiromyscus* Similar to *Niviventer* but distinguished by relatively short feet with large pads, and shortened first hind toe with rounded nail instead of a pointed claw (Fig. 73a). Mammae 2 + 2.

FEA'S TREE RAT
Chiromyscus chiropus PLATE 67
Measurements HB 145–160, T 200–225, HF 27–29, E 19–20. Skull: gl 41–43, mt 7.0–8.0

Identification Upperparts orange-brown; face up to behind ears is relatively bright orange with small darker ring around eye; underparts pure white, sharply demarcated from upperparts. Feet and toes largely unpigmented, but with orange hairs on top. Tail bicoloured, dark above and pinkish below. First hind toe shortened with rounded nail instead of pointed claw. **Similar species** Indochinese Arboreal Niviventer, *Niviventer langbianus*, also has reduced first toe with very small claw, but claw is distinctly pointed (Fig. 73b), tail is all dark, back has extensive long black guard hairs, face is not as orange.

Ecology and habitat Nocturnal. Arboreal with feet well adapted for climbing; found in a variety of forest types including moist deciduous and evergreen. May use degraded forest, but not open areas.

Distribution and status SE Asia: E Myanmar, N Thailand, Laos and Vietnam. Also S China. Not currently at risk.

Genus *Dacnomys* Large rats, somewhat similar to *Niviventer* or *Leopoldamys* in skull morphology. Auditory bullae relatively very small; incisive foramina long, extending past anterior face of anterior molar; teeth wide and chunky with very high crowns; toothrow proportionately and absolutely very long (>20% of skull length); cusps on teeth angular and partly fused into V-shaped ridges (Fig. 71i). Upper incisors orange. Mammae 2 + 2.

MILLARD'S GIANT RAT

Dacnomys millardi PLATE 65

Measurements HB 230–290, T 260–360 (115–140% of HB), HF 50–56. Skull: gl 53–61, mt 11–12.5

Identification Very large. Fur thick, short, lacking stiff spines. Upperparts brown flecked with buff; underparts whitish, varying from creamy to light grey with buff tinge. Feet large and brown. Long tail all dark brown. **Similar species** Most other rats are smaller, with much smaller toothrows; Edward's Giant Rat, *Leopoldamys edwardsi*, has more uniform brown upperparts without

pale flecks, extensive short spines in fur, smaller teeth.

Ecology and habitat Mostly nocturnal. Recorded only in upper montane rainforest.

Distribution and status SE Asia: N Laos and NW Vietnam. Also NE India, E Nepal and S China. Might also be expected in N Myanmar. Status unknown; relatively few records.

Genus *Leopoldamys* Large rats with a very long tail; sleek smooth fur, guard hairs only slightly longer than rest of fur, numerous spines that are soft and hair-like; upperparts dark, colour varying with species, sharply demarcated from pale underparts; tail mixed dark and pale. In skull, incisive foramina relatively short, ending in front of molars; bullae relatively small; posterior edge of bony palate level with end of toothrow (Fig. 69c). Large, strong incisors with bright orange enamel. Cusps on molars partly fused into V-shaped ridges (Fig. 71f). Five species in region, only some of which overlap in range. Mammae 2 + 2.

LONG-TAILED GIANT RAT

Leopoldamys sabanus PLATE 68

Measurements HB 200–275, T 270–415 (at least 135% of HB), HF 42–52. Wt 250–500. Skull: cbl 51–60, mt 8.7–10.3

Identification Large, long-tailed rat. Fur sleek and smooth, without protruding guard hairs. Upperparts buffy-brown to orange-brown, darker brown in middle of back, brighter orange-brown on sides; underparts creamy-white. Tail dark all around at base and on top for most of length, pale underneath and at tip; pattern of dark and pale areas irregular and somewhat variable. Juveniles plain light brown above. **Taxonomic notes** Considerable geographic variation in size and pattern, and may represent more than one species. **Similar species** Other *Leopoldamys* have dark brown or grey-brown upperparts, without contrasting orange flanks.

Ecology and habitat Nocturnal. Mainly terrestrial and in lower parts of trees up to at least 3m above ground. Occurs in tall and secondary forests, mainly in lowlands up to 1,200 m in Peninsular Malaysia.

Distribution and status SE Asia: Myanmar, Thailand, Laos, Vietnam, Cambodia and Peninsular Malaysia. Also Sumatra, Java, Borneo and various smaller islands. Not currently at risk; very common in some forested areas.

SUNDAIC MOUNTAIN RAT
Leopoldamys ciliatus NOT ILLUSTRATED
Measurements HB 215–255, T 300–390 (120-165% of HB), HF 45–55, E 25–32. Wt 300–425. Skull: cbl 54–63, mt 9.5–10.8
Identification Large, long-tailed rat. Upperparts and flanks dull dark brown, underparts white, often with dark patch on chest between front legs. Tail usually all dark. **Taxonomic notes** Formerly considered part of *L. edwardsi*. **Similar species** Long-tailed Giant Rat, *L. sabanus*, has contrasting orange flanks, lacks dark patch on chest, usually found at lower altitude; other *Leopoldamys* do not overlap in range.
Ecology and habitat Mostly nocturnal. Montane forest, usually above 1,000m. Probably mainly terrestrial and low in trees and shrubs.
Distribution and status SE Asia: Peninsular Malaysia. Also Sumatra. Probably not immediately at risk, though probably declining from loss of hill forest, especially in Sumatra.

EDWARD'S GIANT RAT
Leopoldamys edwardsi PLATE 68
Measurements HB 210–280, T 290–360, HF 46–54, E 29–33. Wt 340. Skull: cbl 55–65, mt 9.5–10.5
Identification Upperparts uniform, plain brown, slightly darker in front of eye; underparts sharply demarcated white. Tail mainly dark, but with some white hairs on underside near tip. **Taxonomic notes** Genetic and morphological studies suggest population in C Vietnam may represent a distinct species. **Similar species** Long-tailed Giant Rat, *L. sabanus*, is darker in middle of back with contrasting orange sides, Neill's Rat, *L. neilli*,

is distinctly smaller with mottled upperparts; Sundaic Mountain Rat, *L. ciliatus*, does not overlap in range.
Ecology and habitat Mostly nocturnal, primarily montane, separating altitudinally from *L. sabanus*.
Distribution and status SE Asia: N Myanmar, N Thailand (only in Phu Kadeung Plateau), N Laos, and N and C Vietnam. Also NW India, and S and C China.

MILLET'S GIANT RAT
Leopoldamys milleti NOT ILLUSTRATED
Measurements HB 210–280, T 290–360, HF 46–54, E 29–33
Identification Similar to *L. edwardsi*, but with very dark blackish-brown upperparts; skull has relatively large bullae. **Similar species** Edward's Giant Rat, *L. edwardsi*, has paler brown upperparts.
Ecology and habitat Mostly nocturnal. Hill forest above 1,500m.
Distribution and status SE Asia: known only from Langbian highlands in S Vietnam. Status poorly known; further research is needed to understand distribution and identification characters.

NEILL'S RAT
Leopoldamys neilli PLATE 68
Measurements HB 200–235, T 240–300, HF 39–45, E 25–29. Wt 220. Skull: gl 49–54, mt 7.7–8.9
Identification Upperparts mixed black and buffy-brown; underparts plain white. Tail dark basally and along top for two-thirds of length, white at tip and underneath. Feet pale with dusky line on top. Juvenile plain grey above. **Similar species** Edward's Rat, *L. edwardsi*, is substantially larger; Long-tailed Giant Rat, *L. sabanus*, has contrasting orange flanks; Tonkin Limestone Rat, *Tonkinomys daovantieni*, has short tail, dark grey underparts.
Ecology and habitat Mostly nocturnal. Most records from limestone outcrops, where climbs among rocks and caves; also reported from some areas of lowland bamboo scrub.
Distribution and status SE Asia: N and SW

Thailand. Might also be expected in limestone hills in Laos and Vietnam. Status unknown; few records, but relatively few surveys in suitable habitat.

Genus *Diomys* This genus has only one recognized species. Thumb small, reduced to a small pad. Soles of front feet unpigmented, with 3 pads between toes and 2 behind them. Hind feet with greatly reduced pads; 4 moderately small pads between bases of toes and only 1 small metatarsal pad in middle of foot; lacking second elongate inner metatarsal pad found in most other rats (e.g. Fig. 72 or 73). Fifth toe relatively short, similar in length to first toe. Upper incisors relatively pale, slightly protruding forwards, often faintly grooved. In skull, incisive foramina long and thin, extending to level of middle of anterior molars; bony palate extends 0.5–1.0mm posterior of molars. Possibly closely related to *Millardia*.

CRUMP'S SOFT-FURRED RAT
Diomys crumpi   PLATE 66
Measurements HB 100–135, T 110–135 (100–105% of HB), HF 24–28, E 20–26. Skull: gl 29–33, mt 5.2–5.6
Identification Relatively small. Fur soft, silky and short (10mm long on rump). Upperparts dark blackish-grey to brownish-grey; underparts greyish-white, with grey bases and white tips. Tail sharply bicoloured, dark brown to blackish above, greyish-white below. Front and hind feet white, contrasting with dark body. Ears relatively large, dark brown. Incisor breadth 2mm. **Similar species** White-toothed rats, *Berylmys* spp., are generally larger with stiff, spiny fur, tails all dark or with pale tips. Popa Soft-furred Rat, *Millardia kathleenae*, has paler upperparts, averages slightly larger, with tail usually shorter than head and body.
Ecology and habitat Mostly nocturnal. Terrestrial. Burrows in the ground. Has been reported from areas of tall grass in N Myanmar.
Distribution and status SE Asia: N Myanmar. Also NE India and SW Nepal. Status poorly known; only one record from region, though more records elsewhere.

Genus *Millardia* A genus of primarily Indian rats, of which one species is found in region. These rats are mainly terrestrial, found in dry areas. Fur is generally soft. Hind feet have greatly reduced fifth toe, similar to *Dacnomys*. Most species have only 4 or 5 small plantar footpads. In skull, incisive foramina long and thin, extending to level of middle of anterior molars; bony palate relatively long. Mammae 0 + 2 in only species in region (but 1 + 2 or 2 + 2 in other recognized species elsewhere).

POPA SOFT-FURRED RAT
Millardia kathleenae   PLATE 66
Measurements HB 130–165, T 120–155 (90–95% of HB), HF 25–30, E 20–23. Skull: gl 34–36, mt 5.5–6.0
Identification Fur soft but relatively short. Upperparts light brown to greyish; underparts white or pale greyish-white. Hands and feet white. Tail distinctly bicoloured, dark above, whitish below, sometimes with white tip, distinctly shorter than head and body. Upper incisors narrow, yellow and plain; bullae relatively large, about 20% length of skull. Only 4 pads on soles of feet. **Similar species** Crump's Soft-furred Rat, *Diomys crumpi*, is slightly smaller with darker upperparts, longer fur, relatively longer tail; most other rats with bicoloured tails have stiff spines in fur, better developed plantar footpads.
Ecology and habitat Mostly nocturnal. Terrestrial. Found in dry areas of C Myanmar, where has been recorded in scrubby areas with sandy or stony ground. Presumably burrows in ground.
Distribution and status SE Asia: known only from C Myanmar. Status poorly known, but apparently locally abundant in some areas and not currently at risk.

Genus *Maxomys* Tail bicoloured, similar in length to head and body. Fur short and dense, without conspicuous long guard hairs. Most species in region have extensive stiff, prominent spines on upperparts, but one species has soft fur. Hind feet long and narrow, with relatively small footpads, smooth and not well adapted for climbing; only 5 pads, lacking outer metatarsal pad in most species; if pad is present it is small and rounded. Upper incisors orange, not protruding forwards; molars relatively wide. Skull has relatively broad braincase with elongate rostrum; short, wide incisive foramina that end well in front of toothrow, posterior margin of palate slightly in front of level with posterior molars. Mammae 2 + 2 (but some species outside region have 1 + 2).

RAJAH MAXOMYS
Maxomys rajah PLATE 68
Measurements HB 165–225, T 160–210 (90–95% of HB), HF 35–43. Wt 95–220. Skull: gl 41–49, mt 6.9–8.1
Identification Upperparts brown, sometimes tinged reddish or orange, darker in the midline and with numerous stiff grey-brown spines; underparts white, with many short, soft white spines, usually with dark brown streak along middle in adults. White on inner sides of thighs normally extends unbroken to feet. Tail sharply bicoloured, dark brown above, pale below, thinly haired. **Similar species** Red Spiny Maxomys, *M. surifer*, is brighter reddish, lacks dark streak on underparts, usually has orange collar under neck and orange band around leg; immatures of both species are very difficult to distinguish from each other.
Ecology and habitat Nocturnal and predominantly terrestrial. Occurs in tall and secondary lowland forests, possibly in drier areas than *M. surifer*; the two species have rarely been found in the same locations.
Distribution and status SE Asia: peninsular Thailand and Malaysia. Also Sumatra, Borneo and adjacent smaller islands. Has declined considerably owing to extensive loss of lowland forest, but still common in some areas.

RED SPINY MAXOMYS
Maxomys surifer PLATE 68
Measurements HB 160–210, T 155–210 (95–100% of HB), HF 38–47, E 22–28. Wt 125–285. Skull: gl 40–48, mt 6.0–7.5
Identification Upperparts distinctly orange- or reddish-brown, slightly darker along midline, with numerous short, stiff, dark spines; underparts white with soft white spines. Orange-brown usually extends around part or all of underside of neck, forming a collar, and around inner side of front leg above ankle. Tail bicoloured. **Taxonomic notes** Considerable geographic variation in size and genetics, and may represent more than one species. **Similar species** Rajah Maxomys, *M. rajah*, is less brightly coloured, usually has dark brown streak in middle of underparts, lacks orange-brown collar and band around leg; juveniles of both species are grey and difficult to distinguish.
Ecology and habitat Nocturnal and mainly terrestrial. Occurs in primary and secondary forests and adjacent gardens, but not heavily disturbed areas.
Distribution and status SE Asia: Myanmar, Thailand, Laos, Vietnam, Cambodia and Peninsular Malaysia. Also S China (Yunnan), Sumatra, Java, Borneo and adjacent islands. Not currently at risk, but populations in some areas have probably declined substantially as a result of deforestation.

WHITEHEAD'S MAXOMYS
Maxomys whiteheadi PLATE 68
Measurements HB 105–150, T 90–125 (85–90% of HB), HF 22–30. Wt 35–80. Skull: gl 29–34, mt 5.1–6.2
Identification Small and spiny; upperparts reddish-brown to dark brown with grey underfur, brown-tipped overfur and numerous stiff pale grey spines with black tips; underparts grey to orange-grey, the hairs with grey bases and orange-buff tips mixed with numerous soft, pale spines; tail dark above, pale below. Hind feet with only 5 pads. **Similar species** Malayan Mountain Maxomys, *M. inas*, is bigger, with longer tail; *Niviventer* spp. are larger with tail longer than head and body, 6 large

footpads, white belly; Pacific Rat, *Rattus exulans*, has entirely dark tail significantly longer than head and body.

Ecology and habitat Nocturnal. Mainly terrestrial. Diet includes ants and other insects as well as plant matter. Occurs in tall and secondary forests, mainly in lowlands, including plantations and disturbed areas, but only if adjacent to forest.

Distribution and status SE Asia: peninsular Thailand and Malaysia. Also Sumatra, Borneo and adjacent islands. Possibly at risk; population has declined considerably owing to loss of lowland forest in many areas.

MALAYAN MOUNTAIN MAXOMYS

Maxomys inas PLATE 68
Measurements HB 125–160, T 135–165 (95–105% of HB), HF 31–33, E 19–22. Skull: gl 36–40, mt 6.2–6.7
Identification Upperparts reddish-brown with extensive stiff spines in fur; underparts grey with chestnut tips to fur. Tail usually slightly longer than head and body, sharply bicoloured dark above and white below. Hind feet with only 5 pads. **Similar species** Whitehead's Maxomys, *M. whiteheadi*, is smaller with shorter tail.
Ecology and habitat Mostly nocturnal. Montane forests, usually above 900m.
Distribution and status SE Asia: known only from Peninsular Malaysia, though might also be expected in extreme S Thailand. Not currently at risk.

INDOCHINESE MAXOMYS

Maxomys moi PLATE 68
Measurements HB 140–215, T 155–200 (95–105% of HB), HF 37–44, E 22–27. Skull: gl 40–46, mt 5.8–6.6
Identification Upperparts very bright orange, fur dense and soft without spines. Underparts white, sharply demarcated from dorsum. Hind feet usually with only 5 pads. **Similar species** Red Spiny Maxomys, *M. surifer*, in Indochina has duller-coloured fur with extensive spines, averages larger and usually has 6 footpads; *Niviventer* spp. have

tails substantially longer than head and body, usually less bright orange with extensive spines, larger footpads.

Ecology and habitat Mostly nocturnal. Found in primary and secondary hill forest up to 1,500m, but some records as low as 200m. Not found in heavily disturbed areas.

Distribution and status SE Asia: known only from highlands of S Laos (Bolaven Plateau) and adjacent S Vietnam. Not currently at risk, but suffering from some habitat loss owing to deforestation; still relatively common in some areas.

Genus *Lenothrix* Dense, woolly hair without spines; tail dark at the base, white at the distal end. Skull has relatively small bullae; short incisive foramina ending well in front of molars; posterior edge of bony palate ends between molars; teeth with well-developed, discrete cusps not fused into ridges (Fig. 71c). Mammae 3 + 2.

GREY TREE RAT

Lenothrix canus PLATE 66
Measurements HB 165–220, T 190–270, HF 30–37. Wt 80–220. Skull: gl 43–48, mt 8.2–9.3
Identification Fur soft and woolly. Upperparts grey to greyish-brown; underparts white to pale buff. Tail dark near body, white on distal third. Short, broad hind feet, adapted for climbing but with claws on all toes.
Taxonomic notes Formerly called *L. malaisia*, but now considered the same species as *L. canus* from Sumatra. **Similar species** Bowers's Rat, *Berylmys bowersi*, also has white tip to tail, but is substantially larger with coarser fur.
Ecology and habitat Nocturnal. Largely arboreal, in trees and bushes. Recorded from primary forest, disturbed forest and tree plantations, mainly in lowlands.
Distribution and status SE Asia: Peninsular Malaysia. Also Tuangku Island (W of Sumatra), Borneo. Not currently at risk. Reportedly locally common in some areas.

Genus *Pithecheir* Medium-sized rats with naked, prehensile tail; feet adapted for climbing, first toe widely separated from others with enlarged pads at tips; claws instead of nails on all toes. Long soft fur. Molars have cusps distinctly separated (Fig. 71d), instead of fused into ridges like many other rats. Two known species, one from Java and the other from Peninsular Malaysia.

MALAYAN WOOLLY TREE RAT

Pithecheir parvus   PLATE 66
Measurements HB 150–180, T 170–215, HF 26–30, E 15–19. Wt 80–135g. Skull: gl 39–44, mt 7.5–8.2
Identification Fur very long and soft without spines, extending about 18mm along base of tail. Upperparts brownish-red, with slate-grey basal half of hairs; underparts creamy-white with buff tinge on flanks and chin. Ears short and translucent. Face relatively short. Feet pink, hairs on upper side white. Tail hairless beyond base, with smooth tip.
Taxonomic notes Formerly included with *P. melanurus*, which is now considered restricted to Java. **Similar species** Marmoset Rats, *Hapalomys* spp., have nails on first toe instead of claw, different fur colour, distinctive teeth; other arboreal rats such as *Rattus*, *Niviventer* and *Chiromyscus* have shorter hair, usually mixed with soft spines, sparse hairs along tail.
Ecology and habitat Nocturnal. Largely arboreal. Found mainly in primary lowland rainforest up to 1,000m altitude, but has been reported from disturbed forest.
Distribution and status SE Asia: known only from Peninsular Malaysia. Status uncertain; populations may have declined substantially owing to loss of primary lowland forest.

Genus *Hapalomys* Marmoset-Rats are medium-sized, rat-like rodents, well adapted for climbing in bamboo and small branches. Feet adapted for gripping; broad and wide with long, well-spaced digits; underside of digits with extensive ridges; ridged pads on soles of feet, and broadened pads at tips of toes. Hind toe is opposable, with flattened nail instead of pointed claw. Probably most closely related to *Chiropodomys*, which is smaller. Teeth with distinctive U-shaped cusps (Fig. 71e). Two recognized species, both occurring in region. Mammae 2 + 2.

GREATER MARMOSET-RAT

Hapalomys longicaudatus   PLATE 70
Measurements HB 150–170, T 170–200, HF 26–32, E 12–15. Skull: gl 39.5–41.5, mt 7.5–8.5
Identification Medium-sized with short rostrum, soft, dense woolly fur. Upperparts greyish-brown including upper lips and cheeks; underparts white with strip of orange-brown on flanks separating upperparts from underparts; slight orange-brown tinge elsewhere on underparts. Dark brown ears fringed with long, black whisker-like hairs originating inside ear. Feet as described for genus. Tail all dark, sparsely haired at base with longer hairs at tip.
Similar species Lesser Marmoset-Rat, *H. delacouri*, is smaller, with dark reddish-brown upperparts, no orange band on flanks, sparsely haired tip of tail; Fea's Tree Rat, *Chiromyscus chiropus*, has nail on hind toe, but foot is more elongate with relatively shorter toes that lack swollen pads at tip, head is elongate like *Niviventer*, upperparts are orange-brown with flat spines in fur.
Ecology and habitat Nocturnal. In Malaysia, mainly hills above 400m, but possibly in lowlands further north. Associated with limited range of bamboo species, on which it feeds. Nests inside internodes of bamboo, making holes 3.5cm in diameter. Hole surrounded by 1cm band where outer layer is stripped. Lines nest with bamboo leaves.
Distribution and status SE Asia: SE Myanmar, S Thailand and Peninsular Malaysia. Status poorly known, but may be Endangered in parts of range, as no recent records from Myanmar or Thailand, where much of suitable habitat has been destroyed.

LESSER MARMOSET-RAT

Hapalomys delacouri   PLATE 70
Measurements HB 100–135, T 135–170, HF 22–24, E 13–15. Skull: gl 29–34, mt 5.8–6.7

Identification Fur thick and silky. Upperparts dark orange-brown; underparts white, extending to upper lips and edges of cheeks. Relatively long brown ears with long brown hairs inside. Feet as described for genus. Tail relatively long, sparsely haired to tip. Individuals from N Laos have smaller skulls and longer hairs on the tail, compared with Vietnamese individuals. **Similar species** Greater Marmoset-Rat, *H. longicaudatus*, is larger with grey-brown upperparts including face, contrasting orange-brown on flanks; Indomalayan Pencil-tailed Tree-mouse, *Chiropodomys gliroides*, is smaller with grey fur, distinct tuft of hair at tip of tail.

Ecology and habitat Nocturnal. Known individuals in region found in branches and trees in hill deciduous and evergreen forests at 1,200–1,500m. Little else known about habitat, but might be expected in bamboo and branches of low trees. Has not been found in disturbed areas.

Distribution and status SE Asia: Laos and Vietnam. Also S China and Hainan. Status poorly known, but thought to be Vulnerable, as much of hill forest in known range has been damaged or converted to agriculture.

Genus *Mus* A widespread genus of small mice, with several species closely associated with humans, sometimes as pests. Distinguished from other mice by large first molar, more than half length of toothrow, with only two cusps in back row of cusps; third molar very small (Fig. 70a). Hind feet with 6 pads on sole of foot, all small and rounded and towards front of foot. Mammae 3 + 2 in all species in region.

ASIAN HOUSE MOUSE
Mus musculus PLATE 69
Measurements HB 65–90, T 67–92 (~105% of HB), HF 14.5–18.5. Wt 9–17. Skull: gl 18.5–22, mt 2.9–3.5

Identification Upperparts dark brown and grey, often with reddish-brown patches, underfur grey; underparts only slightly paler greyish-brown. Fur soft. Tail entirely dark brownish. Feet same colour as back except

for pale toes. **Taxonomic notes** SE Asian form is often considered a separate species, *Mus castaneus*. **Similar species** Other *Mus* in region have pale underparts; Pacific Rat, *Rattus exulans*, is larger with stiff spines in fur, elongate inner metatarsal pad on sole of foot, similar to *R. rattus* (Fig. 72b).

Ecology and habitat Nocturnal. Diet includes wide range of plant and animal material. Restricted to buildings in towns. Runs very fast.

Distribution and status SE Asia: Myanmar, Thailand, Laos, Vietnam, Cambodia and Peninsular Malaysia. SE Asian form, *M. castaneus*, also found in India and China and introduced into many Pacific islands. Other forms native to Europe and now introduced throughout much of world. Not currently at risk.

RICEFIELD MOUSE
Mus caroli PLATE 69
Measurements HB 65–85, T 65–95 (~100% of HB), HF 16.5–19.2. Wt 8–14. Skull: gl 19–22, mt 3.1–3.5

Identification Upperparts vary from rich brown to brownish-grey; underparts white or white with grey bases to fur. Tail very dark grey above, sharply contrasting whitish below. Feet vary from dark grey to white. Upper incisors with dark orange enamel, curved slightly forwards then angled straight down. In skull, nasal bones short so that incisors are visible from above, incisive foramina short, ending level with front of first molars. **Similar species** Fawn-coloured Mouse, *M. cervicolor*, has shorter tail, paler grey above, pale upper incisors; Asian House Mouse, *M. musculus*, has grey-brown underparts and entirely dark tail.

Ecology and habitat Occurs in rice fields and grassland, often in the same fields as *M. cervicolor*. Also reported from grassy areas in open pine savannah. Digs small holes in mud banks for nests, which can be recognized by round pellets of excavated mud at entrance. Diet includes plant material and animals such as insects.

Distribution and status SE Asia: S Myanmar, Thailand, Laos, Vietnam, Cambodia and Peninsular Malaysia (where possibly introduced). Also S China, Taiwan, Ryukyu Islands, Sumatra, Java and some smaller islands; possibly inadvertently introduced in Indonesian localities. Not currently at risk.

FAWN-COLOURED MOUSE
Mus cervicolor   PLATE 69

Measurements HB 70–95, T 50–70 (~75% of HB), HF 15–18. Wt 10–25. Skull: gl 19.5–23.5, mt 3.2–3.9

Identification Upperparts brownish-grey; underparts pale, varying from almost white to light grey. Tail mid-grey above, paler below, shorter than body. Upper incisors with pale, buff enamel, curved slightly forwards then angled straight down. In skull, nasal bones long, hiding incisors from above, incisive foramina long, ending level with middle of first molars. **Taxonomic notes** In Thailand and Myanmar, forms found in natural forest are larger than those in rice fields and have been considered a distinct subspecies, *M. c. popaeus*, but they appear to interbreed where they meet. **Similar species** Ricefield Mouse, *M. caroli*, has darker tail as long as head and body, dark orange incisors; Fragile-tailed Mouse, *M. fragilicauda*, is very similar in appearance, but has slightly longer tail with loose skin.

Ecology and habitat Mostly nocturnal. Occurs in rice fields as well as natural grasslands in hill forest savannah. Feeds on seeds and insects.

Distribution and status SE Asia: Myanmar, Thailand, Laos, Vietnam and Cambodia. Also N India, S China, Sumatra and Java; probably inadvertently introduced to Indonesian localities. Not currently at risk.

FRAGILE-TAILED MOUSE
Mus fragilicauda   NOT ILLUSTRATED

Measurements HB 66–88, T 55–67 (~80–85% of HB), HF 14–16. Wt 9–15. Skull: gl 9.3–10.1, mt 3.5–4.0

Identification Upperparts brown with a mixture of pale brown and dark brown hairs; underparts paler brownish-grey. Feet white. Tail relatively short, dark brown above, somewhat paler, pinkish below; tail skin tears and comes off easily when handled; this may help the animal to escape from predators. **Similar species** Fawn-coloured Mouse, *M. cervicolor*, is very similar in appearance but differs genetically and tail skin is not especially prone to tear; Shortridge's Mouse, *M. shortridgei*, also sheds tail skin readily but is much larger with spiny fur.

Ecology and habitat Mostly nocturnal. Has been found in dry rice fields and patches of scrub.

Distribution and status SE Asia: SC Thailand. Probably also S Laos. Status uncertain; described as a distinct species as recently as 2003.

COOK'S MOUSE
Mus cookii   PLATE 69

Measurements HB 80–105, T 71–95 (90–100% of HB), HF 17–21. Wt 18–30. Skull: gl 23–26, mt 4.0–4.4

Identification Relatively large, with large teeth. Upperparts brown to greyish-brown with quite stiff fur; underparts pale grey with dark bases. Feet grey or brown. Tail dark grey above, paler below, only slightly shorter in length than head and body. Upper incisors curved slightly backwards, with pale enamel. **Taxonomic notes** Populations from W Myanmar and India are smaller (about 15% shorter head and body and tail), and sometimes considered a separate species, *M. nagarum*. **Similar species** Ricefield Mouse, *M. caroli*, is smaller with shorter toothrow, dark forwards-curved incisors; Fawn-coloured Mouse, *M. cervicolor* has shorter tail, smaller toothrow and forwards-curved incisors.

Ecology and habitat Mostly nocturnal. Mainly in hilly areas, including grassy fields in pine savannah, open dipterocarp forest, and hill rice fields. Also some records in lowlands in riverine grassland.

Distribution and status SE Asia: Myanmar, Thailand, Laos and Vietnam. Also Nepal, India and S China.

LITTLE INDIAN FIELD MOUSE

Mus booduga PLATE 69

Measurements HB 60–75, T 45–55 (80–90% of HB), HF 14.5–17. Wt 9–15. Skull: gl 19–21.5, mt 3.0–3.6

Identification Very small mouse with narrow rostrum, relatively short tail. Upperparts light brown; underparts pure white or white with grey bases, sometimes with brown spot on chest. Tail bicoloured, dark above and paler below. Upper incisors curved backwards. First upper molar broad. **Similar species** Other *Mus* are usually larger, many species with incisors angled forwards; Harvest Mouse, *Micromys minutus*, has relatively longer, thinner tail, small ears.

Ecology and habitat Mostly nocturnal. Dry scrubby areas and agricultural fields. In India occurs in wet rice fields.

Distribution and status SE Asia: C Myanmar. Also Pakistan, Nepal, India, Sri Lanka and Bangladesh. Not currently at risk; may be a pest in some crops.

INDOCHINESE SHREWLIKE MOUSE

Mus pahari PLATE 69

Measurements HB 75–105, T 70–100 (90–100% of HB), HF 19–22. Wt 20–25. Skull: gl 23–26, mt 3.4–4.0

Identification Relatively long, shrew-like nose, ears small, scarcely projecting above nape, eyes small. Fur with extensive spines. Upperparts dark bluish-grey to brownish-grey; underparts white with grey bases to fur. Feet white. Tail grey, moderately long. **Similar species** Shortridge's Mouse, *M. shortridgei*, has shorter tail, pale brown upperparts, large ears and eyes; other *Mus* spp. in region have fur without spines, larger eyes, less pointed head.

Ecology and habitat Mostly nocturnal. Found in grassy areas within montane forest; probably tolerant of disturbed forest.

Distribution and status SE Asia: N Myanmar, Thailand, Laos, Vietnam and Cambodia. Not currently at risk, though not common anywhere.

SHORTRIDGE'S MOUSE

Mus shortridgei PLATE 69

Measurements HB 95–120, T 60–90 (70% of HB), HF 19–22. Skull: gl 26–30, mt 4.4–5.2

Identification Fur with extensive stiff, flattened spines; ears relatively large; eyes not especially small. Upperparts greyish-brown; underparts greyish-white, fur with grey bases and white tips, ears relatively large. Tail dark grey, sometimes weakly bicoloured pink underneath. Skin on body and tail loose; tail skin sheds easily if animal is picked up by tail. **Similar species** Other *Mus* spp. average smaller and lack spines; Pacific Rat, *Rattus exulans*, has relatively longer tail, elongate pads on sole of foot, darker underparts.

Ecology and habitat Mostly nocturnal. Found in dry grass and clumps of small bamboo in open dry dipterocarp and pine forest.

Distribution and status SE Asia: Myanmar, Thailand, Laos, Vietnam and Cambodia. Not currently at risk; distribution fragmented, but can be locally abundant and tolerant of some disturbance.

Genus *Micromys* One of the smallest rodents, with a relatively short tail. Bony palate does not extend much behind teeth. Teeth small with multiple separate cusps (Fig. 70c). First digit (big toe) of hind foot has pointed claw.

HARVEST MOUSE

Micromys minutus PLATE 70

Measurements HB 50–75, T 50–80, HF 13–16, E 8–10. Wt 5–7. Skull: gl 17.5–18.5, mt 2.6–3.3

Identification Very small with short rounded head, small rounded ears, well haired. SE Asian populations have upperparts greyish-brown, underparts silvery grey; in Europe and other parts of range, upperparts are orange-brown and underparts white. Long tail slightly longer than body (same length or shorter in Europe), thin and naked, partly prehensile; dark pinkish-brown above, pink below. Feet relatively broad for gripping on grass stems. **Taxonomic notes** Further study may show

that more than one species is represented across this broad geographic range. **Similar species** Majority of other mice in region are larger with more conspicuous ears, thicker tail; Long-tailed Climbing Mouse, *Vandeleuria oleracea*, has nails instead of claws on outer toes.
Ecology and habitat Mostly nocturnal. Feeds on seeds, fruits, buds and insects. Found in grassy fields, including grain fields, low shrubs and bracken, but not forest; well adapted for climbing on herbaceous vegetation. Builds a globe-shaped nest of grass 60–130mm in diameter, attached to stems of large grasses.
Distribution and status SE Asia: N Myanmar and NW Vietnam. Also throughout most of Europe and N Asia as well as NW India. Not currently at risk.

Genus *Chiropodomys* Medium-small arboreal mice with a short head, small body, large eyes, long whiskers on muzzle and above eye, long tail with a brush-like tip of long hairs and specialized feet for climbing; feet are short and broad, first digit short with a broad pad and a short flat nail instead of a sharp claw; remaining digits with enlarged pads at tips with short, sharp claws. Only one species in region, but additional species occur in Borneo, the Mentawei Islands and Palawan. Mammae 0 + 2.

INDOMALAYAN PENCIL-TAILED TREE-MOUSE
Chiropodomys gliroides   PLATE 70
Measurements HB 70–105, T 95–145 (~135% of HB), HF 15–22, E 13–19. Wt 15–35g. Skull: gl 24–27, mt 3.3–4.2
Identification Fur short, thick and soft. Upperparts bright, varying from pale red-brown to grey-brown colour; underparts white. Sometimes narrow orange-red band on flanks separating white underparts from upperparts. Tail brown, hairy, with brush of hairs 4–5mm long at tip. Long whiskers on muzzle much longer than half of head and body length. Foot with nail on first toe.
Similar species Marmoset-rats, *Hapalomys*

spp., have nail on first toe, but toe is relatively longer, and animals are larger.
Ecology and habitat Nocturnal. Occurs in a wide variety of forest types including heavily disturbed areas, usually associated with extensive bamboo. Nests in tree holes, internodes of bamboo and similar places; in bamboo, makes neat circular hole 2.5cm in diameter.
Distribution and status SE Asia: Myanmar, Thailand, Laos, Vietnam, Cambodia and Peninsular Malaysia. Also NE India, S China, Sumatra, Java and Bali. Not currently at risk.

Genus *Vandeleuria* Small mice with flattened nails instead of pointed claws on first and fifth digits of hands and feet. Mammae 2 + 2. Three species currently recognized, of which only one occurs in region.

LONG-TAILED CLIMBING MOUSE
Vandeleuria oleracea   PLATE 69
Measurements HB 55–85, T 90–130 (150–180% of HB), HF 16–18, E 12–14. Wt 10–20
Identification Small with soft fur, very long tail. Upperparts orange-brown to pinkish-brown, underparts white, sometimes tinged light brown, not sharply demarcated from upperparts. Tail uniformly brown with short hairs along length, no tuft at end. Outer toes on hind feet have nails instead of claws and are opposable, allowing them to grip well around grass stalks and other vegetation.
Taxonomic notes Geographic variation in chromosomes and other features suggests may represent more than one species.
Similar species Harvest Mouse, *Micromys minutus*, has short rounded ears, claws instead of nails on all toes; Vernay's Climbing Mouse, *Vernaya fulva*, has pointed claws on all toes; Indomalayan Pencil-tailed Tree-mouse, *Chiropodomys gliroides*, averages larger, with broad pads at tips of toes, flat nail only on first digit with claw on fifth digit, tuft of hair at tip of tail.
Ecology and habitat Mostly nocturnal. Dense tangles of vines, tall cane and brush. Arboreal, climbing on small branches and

tall grasses. Builds globe-shaped nest of grasses in cane, 1–2m above ground.

Distribution and status SE Asia: Myanmar, Thailand (N of Isthmus of Kra), Vietnam and SW Cambodia. Probably Laos. Also India, Sri Lanka, S Nepal and SE China.

Genus *Vernaya* Small mice, superficially similar to *Vandeleuria* but all digits have pointed claws instead of nails, except vestigial first finger (thumb) on front feet. Mammae 1 + 2. Poorly known with few reported specimens.

VERNAY'S CLIMBING MOUSE
Vernaya fulva PLATE 70
Measurements HB 60–80, T 100–140 (170–200% of HB), HF 16–18. Skull: gl 22, mt 3.3

Identification Small with very long tail. Upperparts brown with yellowish tinge, especially on flanks and cheeks; underparts grey with buff tips to hairs. Fur without spines. All toes on hind feet have claws instead of nails. Tail all dark. **Similar species** Harvest Mouse, *Micromys minutus*, is smaller with shorter tail; Long-tailed Climbing Mouse, *Vandeleuria oleracea*, has flattened nails instead of claws on outer toes; *Mus* spp. have shorter, thicker tails.

Ecology and habitat Mostly nocturnal. Known from mountains above 2,100m; Myanmar specimens found in areas of low shrubs and thick bracken.

Distribution and status SE Asia: N Myanmar. Also S China. Status poorly known, with few records, but probably not at risk.

Genus *Apodemus* Medium to small soft-furred mice, generally similar to typical mice (*Mus*) but first and second molars with 3 well-developed posterior cusps (Fig. 70b), rather than only 2 as in *Mus*. Ears relatively large, tail generally moderately long. Front feet with 4 well-developed toes, all with claws; hind feet with 5 well-developed toes, all with claws. Incisors narrow with yellow enamel. Incisive foramina moderate, ending in front of or level with front of first molar;

bony palate extending posterior to last molar. Mammae vary between the species. Widely distributed throughout Europe and Asia, with at least 20 species. Two species have been reported in the literature from Myanmar, but there is some uncertainty as to whether both actually occur there; published reports of *A. latronum* from Myanmar have toothrow measurements that fit within the range for *A. draco*. Both species are described here, but further research is required to confirm the number of species in Myanmar.

SOUTH CHINA WOOD MOUSE
Apodemus draco PLATE 70
Measurements HB 80–105, T 90–130 (100–125% of HB), HF 20–25. Skull: gl 24–28, mt 3.7–4.4

Identification Upperparts yellowish-brown to dark orange-brown, the hairs with grey bases; underparts sharply contrasting greyish white, the individual hairs with grey bases and silvery tips. Fur short, soft and velvety. Ears relatively large, dark. Tail moderately long, dark above, usually somewhat paler below, sparsely covered with short, whitish hairs. Mammae 2 + 2. **Taxonomic notes** Includes *A. orestes*, which has sometimes been considered a separate species. **Similar species** Large-eared Wood Mouse, *A. latronum*, averages larger with a longer toothrow.

Ecology and habitat Forest heath and scrubby areas in mountains at 1,300–3,800m.

Distribution and status SE Asia: N and EC Myanmar. Also NE India and China. Fairly common in some areas, and not currently at risk.

LARGE-EARED WOOD MOUSE
Apodemus latronum NOT ILLUSTRATED
Measurements HB 95–110, T 100–120 (100–120% of HB), HF 24–27. Skull: gl 28–30, mt 4.5–5.1

Identification Relatively large with long, soft silky fur. Upperparts orange-brown to greyish-brown, the hairs with dark grey bases; underparts contrasting greyish-white, individual hairs with grey bases and silvery white tips. Tail generally somewhat longer than head

373

and body, varying from bicoloured (dark above, whitish below) to all dark; sparsely haired with short hairs. Ears large, blackish, noticeably darker than back. Mammae 1 + 2. **Similar species** South China Wood Mouse, *A. draco*, has smaller skull and toothrow.

Ecology and habitat Hill and lower montane areas in a variety of habitats, including scrub and bracken.
Distribution and status SE Asia: N Myanmar. Also S China. Not currently at risk.

Family *PLATACANTHOMYIDAE*

This family has some resemblance to dormice of the family Gliridae (which do not occur in South-East Asia) and has sometimes been included with them, but differs in having only 3 cheek teeth on each side of each jaw and small auditory bullae without septa.

The family includes two genera, *Platacanthomys* with spiny fur, which is now restricted to India, although fossil species have occurred more widely, and *Typhlomys* from South-East Asia and China.

Genus *Typhlomys* Only one species is currently recognized in the genus, though the only population known from the region, in N Vietnam, has sometimes been considered a separate species from that found in China. Cusps on molars form folded ridges that are angled diagonally inwards, quite unlike the separate cusps or horizontal ridges of mice in the family Muridea (e.g., Fig. 70a,b,c) or the zig-zag patterns of Cricetid voles (Fig. 70d)

SOFT-FURRED PYGMY-DORMOUSE
Typhlomys cinereus   PLATE 70
Measurements HB 70–100, T 95–135
(125–135% of HB), HF 20–23. Skull: gl 25–26
Identification Small and mouse-like with prominent ears, soft dense fur, small eyes, and narrow hind feet. Upperparts uniformly dark brownish-grey, sometimes almost black. Underparts with grey bases and buffy tips in Vietnamese form (greyish-white tips in Chinese populations). Tail long and thin, scaly with sparse hairs near base, longer, denser hairs on distal half forming a distinct brush, often with a white tip. Hands white, hind feet dusky. **Taxonomic notes** Form in N Vietnam has sometimes been considered a separate species, *T. capensis*, which differs in slightly larger size and darker underparts from typical Chinese *cinereus*, but recent research suggests it is within the variation of the species, and should at most be considered a subspecies, *T. c. capensis*. **Similar species** Other rodents have different patterns of cusps on the molars; long-tailed mice, *Vandeleuria* and *Vernaya* spp, are smaller, with even longer tails, broader feet adapted for climbing.
Ecology and habitat High montane forest, at elevations of 1,200–2,100m. Has been recorded from moss forest with undergrowth of bamboo, but poorly known.
Distribution and status SE Asia: NW Vietnam. Also mountains of S China. Species probably not currently at risk, but *T. c. capensis* is very poorly known, with few records.

Family *CRICETIDAE*, Subfamily *ARVICOLINAE* VOLES

The family Cricetidae is currently considered to include several subfamilies, of which only one is represented in the region. This subfamily is widely distributed through the Old and New Worlds, primarily in the northern hemisphere.

Most voles in the region have short, blunt heads with short, rounded ears, rounded bodies and relatively short tails. The molars have a complex zig-zag pattern that is quite unlike those of other rodents in the region, and lack roots (e.g. Fig. 70d).

Genus *Eothenomys* Similar to *Microtus*, but posterior margin of palate in skull straight across. Mammae 0 + 2. Cusps of first lower molar matched up on opposite sides, forming loops (Fig. 70d). Tail moderately covered with short hairs that partly hide scales. Eight species currently recognized, of which only two are known from the region. Two additional species have been reported from SW Yunnan, near the border with Myanmar, and might be expected to occur in Myanmar. These are *E. olitor*, which is similar to *E. melanogaster* but smaller in size, with dark greyish-brown upperparts with pale frosted tips; and *E. miletus*, which is similar in size and colour to *E. cachinus* but with a relatively shorter tail and higher skull profile.

KACHIN VOLE

Eothenomys cachinus PLATE 70
Measurements HB 110–125, T 43–60 (40–50% of HB), HF 18–21, E 12–15. Skull: gl 27–28, mt 6.2–7.0
Identification Upperparts bright tawny-brown, underparts grey with buff tips. Medium-length tail (for a vole). **Taxonomic notes** Formerly sometimes considered a subspecies of *E. miletus* from China. **Similar species** Père David's Vole, *E. melanogaster*, is smaller with darker, less bright underparts, shorter tail; Clarke's Vole, *Microtus clarkei*, has cusps of lower molar more alternating, darker fur, longer tail.
Ecology and habitat Montane forest at 2,300–3,200m.
Distribution and status SE Asia: NE Myanmar, west of Salween River valley. Also adjacent NW Yunnan in China. Not currently at risk.

PÈRE DAVID'S VOLE

Eothenomys melanogaster PLATE 70
Measurements HB 90–100, T 21–42 (20–40% of HB), HF 15–17, E 11–14. Skull: gl 23–26, mt 5.5–6.6
Identification Upperparts dark brown to blackish, underparts slate-grey, sometimes tinted buffy or brown. Medium-short tail.

Similar species Kachin Vole, *E. cachinus*, averages larger, with a longer tail, brighter fur. **Ecology and habitat** In Myanmar, reported from relatively open habitats, including meadows, edges of cultivated fields, at altitudes of 1,200–2,750m. Reported from mossy rhododendron forest in N Thailand. Makes burrows in earth at sides of banks.
Distribution and status SE Asia: N Myanmar, N Thailand and N Vietnam. Also S China. Not currently at risk.

Genus *Microtus* Similar to *Eothenomys*, but in skull, central septum of bone extends backwards from posterior edge of palate. First lower molar with alternating cusps forming 5 closed triangles. Upper incisors broad with reddish enamel, sometimes with a slight groove in Asian species. Mammae 0 + 2.

CLARKE'S VOLE

Microtus clarkei PLATE 70
Measurements HB 105–120, T 60–65 (50–60% of HB), HF 19–20, E 14–16. Skull: gl 27–28.5, mt 6.3–6.6
Identification Relatively large with moderately long hair. Upperparts dark brown; underparts slate-grey with silver tips to fur. Medium-long tail covered with short hairs, thicker at tip forming a slight tuft, not completely covering scales. **Taxonomic notes** Sometimes included in genus *Volemys*, but recent morphological analyses suggest it is closer to *Microtus*. **Similar species** Other voles have tail <50% of head and body; *Eothenomys* spp. have inner and outer cusps of lower molars opposite each other.
Ecology and habitat Coniferous forest and alpine meadows in high mountains at 3,300–4,300m.
Distribution and status SE Asia: N Myanmar. Also S China (SE Tibet, Yunnan and Xizang). Not currently at risk.

Genus *Neodon* Small voles, similar to *Microtus* but with cusps of first lower molar forming only three alternating closed triangles. Taxonomic relationships are still somewhat uncertain and the genus is sometimes considered a subgenus of *Microtus*, *Pitymys* or *Phaiomys*.

FORREST'S MOUNTAIN VOLE
Neodon forresti PLATE 70
Measurements HB 95–115, T 30–45 (40% of HB), HF 17–19, E 14–16. Skull: 25–27, mt 5.5–6.5
Identification Upperparts deep dark brown with blackish-grey bases; underparts pale brown or greyish. Tail bicoloured, dark above, paler below. Upper incisors relatively wide with pale to dark orange enamel, sometimes with faint grooves on outer sur-

face. **Taxonomic notes** Formerly considered a subspecies of *N. irene*, but distinctly larger and with longer darker fur. **Similar species** Clarke's Vole, *Microtus clarkei*, has slightly larger skull and relatively longer tail, fewer closed triangles in first lower molar; Kachin Vole, *Eothenomys cachinus*, has paler upperparts.
Ecology and habitat High mountains at 3,300–3,600m.
Distribution and status SE Asia: N Myanmar. Also NW Yunnan in China. Poorly known, but probably not at risk.

Family *SPALACIDAE*, Subfamily *RHIZOMYINAE* BAMBOO RATS

The bamboo rats are sometimes placed in their own family, but more recently have been considered a subfamily of the family Spalacidae, which includes several different groups from Africa and Asia. Bamboo rats are characterized by short faces and thick, rounded heads; small eyes; thick, tube-like bodies with no obvious necks; short, smooth, sparsely haired tails without scales; short legs and stout claws. All of these are adaptations for burrowing. The zygomatic arches are broad, the skull somewhat flat with a triangular braincase. The incisors are thick and relatively blunt, and used both for digging and eating; like those of most rodents, they continue growing throughout the life of the animal.

Genus *Cannomys* Smaller than other bamboo rats, with prominent incisors that protrude forwards, large gap between incisors and molars (diastema) exceeding 40% of condylobasal length, first upper molar larger than second, and footpads that are smooth, without granular ridges. Currently only one species recognized in genus, but some authorities suggest this may actually be a complex of species.

LESSER BAMBOO RAT
Cannomys badius PLATE 71
Measurements HB 150–265, T 45–75, E 7-11, HF 30–35. Wt 500–800. Skull: cbl 40–45, mt 8–12
Identification Small, stout rat with short, broad head, short legs, strong feet. Fur soft and dense, upperparts dark reddish-brown with dark slate-grey underfur that shows through as fur becomes worn; underparts slightly paler with thinner hair. Sometimes has white patch on forehead. Ears short and largely hidden in fur. Tail short, with soft wrin-

kled skin, sparse short hairs. **Similar species** Other bamboo rats, *Rhizomys* spp., are much larger, with granular pads on soles of feet, different fur colour and visible ears.
Ecology and habitat Bamboo thickets in hilly or mountainous areas. Spends much of time underground in fairly conspicuous burrows that it digs into side of a bank, under bamboo or elsewhere. Emerges at night to feed on bamboo roots and shoots, grass seeds and fallen fruits.
Distribution and status SE Asia: Myanmar, Thailand, Laos, NW Vietnam and N Cambodia. Also Nepal, NE India, Bhutan, Bangladesh and S China. Status uncertain; common in some areas, but heavily trapped for food and may be declining.

Genus *Rhizomys* Large bamboo rats with gap between incisors and molars (diastema) less than 40% of condylobasal length of skull, first upper molar larger than second. Ears short, visible through fur. Three recognized species in genus, all occuring in region.

HOARY BAMBOO RAT

Rhizomys pruinosus PLATE 71

Measurements HB 260–350, T 100–120 (35–40% of HB), E 18–25, HF 45–60. Wt 1,000–3,000. Skull: cbl 56–67, mt 13.5–15.5

Identification Upperparts dark greyish-brown to chocolate-brown with grey bases to hairs; many long guard hairs with long white tips, giving frosted appearance; underparts slightly paler. Some individuals, especially in south, are smaller and paler, making guard hairs less conspicuous. Fur dense and soft, especially in north, but sometimes more sparse and harsh in south. Feet brown with granular pads on soles; two separate posterior pads on hind foot. **Similar species** Chinese Bamboo Rat, *R. sinensis*, averages larger, with pale throat, more uniform colour without white tips to hairs; Indomalayan Bamboo Rat, *R. sumatrensis*, is larger, with coarse hair, contrasting reddish face, only one posterior pad on hind foot.

Ecology and habitat Scrub and hill forest, often with grassy areas and extensive stands of bamboo at altitudes of 1,000–4,000m. Digs extensive burrows, where it stays during day, emerging at night to feed, though also feeds on roots underground.

Distribution and status SE Asia: E Myanmar, Thailand, Laos, Vietnam, Cambodia and N Peninsular Malaysia. Also NE India and S China. Not currently at risk, but exploited for food and does not breed quickly, so may be declining in some areas.

CHINESE BAMBOO RAT

Rhizomys sinensis PLATE 71

Measurements HB 230–450, T 50–90 (15–25% of HB), HF 35–60. Skull: cbl 69–80, mt 14–19

Identification Medium to large, with very short tail; fur thick and soft; overall colour buffy-brown to reddish-brown, mixed with grey; fur has extensive pale to mid-grey bases. Two separate posterior granular pads on hind foot. **Similar species** Hoary Bamboo Rat, *R. pruinosus*, averages smaller, with darker fur and white tips to many hairs, proportionately longer tail

Ecology and habitat Mainly in hill and lower montane forest, especially in areas with extensive bamboo. Digs burrows like other members of genus.

Distribution and status SE Asia: N Myanmar, N Vietnam, and might be expected in Laos. Also S China. Status uncertain; relatively common in some areas, although heavily exploited for food and may be declining.

INDOMALAYAN BAMBOO RAT

Rhizomys sumatrensis PLATE 71

Measurements HB 280–480, T 100–200 (35–50% of HB), E 20–36, HF 46–67. Wt up to 2,000. Skull: cbl 71–78, mt 14–15

Identification Large bamboo rat with sparse coarse hair, relatively long tail. Upperparts pale brownish grey, darker on top of head. Cheeks often contrasting reddish-brown, especially in young animals. Posterior granular footpads on hind foot joined together to form a single large pad. **Similar species** Hoary Bamboo Rat, *R. pruinosus*, is smaller, with dense hair, different colour, 2 separate posterior footpads.

Ecology and habitat Secondary forest with extensive bamboo in lowlands and lower hills. Feeds on bamboo roots and other plant material, often coming above ground to forage at night.

Distribution and status SE Asia: Myanmar, Thailand, Laos, Vietnam, Cambodia and Peninsular Malaysia. Also S China (Yunnan), Sumatra. Status uncertain, but breeds slowly and heavily hunted for food; has declined considerably in many areas where not protected.

Family *DIATOMYIDAE* KHA-NYOU

The sole known living member of this family, the Kha-nyou, *Laonastes aenigmamus*, was first described to science in 2005. At the time, it was thought to represent a new family of mammal, but subsequent research showed that it belonged to a family previously known only from fossils more than 11 million years old. The relationship of this family to other rodents is uncertain – it shows features that are somewhat intermediate between squirrels and rats, but it may be closer to the group that includes porcupines. This species has 4 well-developed cheek teeth on each side, all of similar size (1 premolar and 3 molars; most squirrels have an extra upper small premolar; rats lack premolars), each with 2 broad ridge-like cusps. The feet have large, well-developed pads on the base, lacking fine striations; presumably these help the animals to grip on sharp limestone rocks.

KHA-NYOU

Laonastes aenigmamus PLATE 71

Measurements HB 210–290, T 120–160 (55–60% of HB), HF 37–44, E 21–26. Wt 330–420. Skull: gl 61–71, mt 13.2–14.8

Identification Pointed, rat-like head, but with a bushy, squirrel-like tail. Upperparts dark greyish-black with a mixture of soft grey hairs with pale tips and stiff black guard hairs; amount of grey frosting varies among individuals, with some nearly black and others extensively grey; underparts silvery-grey, individual hairs with grey bases and white tips; extent of pale tips varies among individuals. Tail coloured as back, very bushy. Large hind legs; walks with a waddle-like gait. **Similar species** Squirrels have longer tails, shorter face, more slender body, more bounding gait, moving both feet at the same time; rats and mice have thin hairless tails.

Ecology and habitat Apparently mainly nocturnal. Known only from limestone hills and outcrops in C Laos. Diet is mainly plant material, including leaves and seeds, with some insects.

Distribution and status SE Asia: Laos. Status uncertain; range apparently very restricted, and subject to some local hunting and trapping, but no information on population trends.

Family *HYSTRICIDAE* PORCUPINES

Porcupines are larger and more heavily built than squirrels or rats, with characteristic hard spines or quills over most of the upperparts. The incisors and molars are large and powerful. All three species found in South-East Asia are primarily terrestrial and usually nocturnal, though both the smaller species can climb trees. They sleep during the daytime in underground holes or burrows.

LONG-TAILED PORCUPINE

Trichys fasciculata PLATE 72

Measurements HB 375–435, T 150–240, HF 61–67. Wt 1,500–2,000

Identification Upperparts brown; underparts whitish. Spines short and flattened, dark brown towards ends, whitish towards bases. Tail brown and scaly, with brush of flattened bristles at tip. Like a large rat with coarse fur. Part or all of tail sometimes missing. Cannot bristle or rattle quills. **Similar species** Brush-tailed Porcupine, *Atherurus macrourus*, is larger, has longer spines, and a shorter, thicker tail with a bigger brush; large rats (Muridae) have much smaller softer spines.

Ecology and habitat Often seen feeding on ground, where has been observed feeding on large tree seeds as well as bamboo shoots, but can also climb well. Occurs in forests and cultivated areas.

Distribution and status SE Asia: Peninsular Malaysia. Also Sumatra and Borneo. Not currently at risk.

MALAYAN PORCUPINE

Hystrix brachyura PLATE 77

Measurements HB 590–720, T 60–110, HF 80–95

Identification Generally black; long spines or quills on lower back white with black band in middle; short spines on front parts of body mostly blackish, some with paler bases and tips. Spines along back of neck may form a crest. Tail has hollow, goblet-shaped quills that rattle when shaken. **Similar species** Brush-tailed Porcupine, *Atherurus macrourus*, is smaller, with shorter brown quills, longer scaly tail with brush on tip, beaded tail quills.

Ecology and habitat Mainly terrestrial, digging extensive burrows under forest floor. Feeds on fallen fruits including oil palm, as well as tree bark, roots and tubers. Occurs in forests and cultivated areas.

Distribution and status SE Asia: Myanmar, Thailand, Laos, Vietnam, Cambodia and Peninsular Malaysia. Also India, Nepal, S China, Sumatra and Borneo. Not currently at risk.

BRUSH-TAILED PORCUPINE
Atherurus macrourus   PLATE 72
Measurements HB 380–520, T 140–230, HF 64–75

Identification Upperparts greyish-brown to brown; underparts whitish. Body largely covered with flattened spines, longest in the middle of the back. Tail scaly with tuft of whitish quills at tip, quills shaped like string of beads that rattle when shaken. Tail sometimes broken off. **Similar species** Malayan Porcupine, *Hystrix brachyura*, is larger, black and white in colour, with long conspicuous quills and a short tail; Long-tailed Porcupine, *Trichys fasciculata*, has smaller, inconspicuous quills, small brush on tail with flattened spines that do not rattle.

Ecology and habitat Mainly terrestrial, but can also climb well. Nocturnal, living in burrows during day. Eats roots, tubers, fruits, some cultivated crops and tree bark. Occurs in forests and plantations, rarely cleared areas.

Distribution and status SE Asia: Myanmar, Laos, Thailand, Vietnam, Cambodia and Peninsular Malaysia. Also E India, S China and Sumatra. Not currently at risk.

Order LAGOMORPHA
Hares, rabbits and pikas

Lagomorphs differ from rodents in having two pairs of upper incisors, although the second pair is located directly behind the first pair, and does not have a sharp cutting edge. Both pairs of incisors are completely covered in enamel, which is generally white, not orange as in most rodents. The order includes two families, both of which are very distinctive in shape, and both with representatives in the region.

Family *OCHOTONIDAE* PIKAS

There are about 30 species of pika currently recognized worldwide, more than two-thirds of which have been reported from China, although there is still considerable uncertainty about exact species limits. All are included in the same genus, *Ochotona*, and are generally similar in shape with compact bodies, short faces, small rounded ears that protrude above the head, relatively short legs and no visible tails.

MOUPIN PIKA
Ochotona thibetana   PLATE 72
Measurements HB 140–180, T none, HF 24–32, E 17–23. Wt 75–135. Skull: gl 36–42
Identification Small, with rounded ears and no tail. Fur colour varies seasonally. In summer, upperparts brownish, varying from sandy-brown to reddish-brown to dark brown, sometimes with light speckling; underparts paler varying from light grey to greyish-yellow, except for buffy-brown collar on throat. In winter, upperparts become paler, buffy-brown to dull brown. Ears are rounded, dark brown on outside with white

rim. Pale buffy area behind each ear. **Similar species** Forrest's Pika, *O. forresti*, has darker underparts, with dark grey patch behind ears. **Ecology and habitat** Found at altitudes of 1,800m–4,000m in bamboo and rhododendron forests and subalpine forests, where it digs burrows for shelter. May be seen in openings in forest, near shrubs in more open areas, or around scrub piles in logged areas. **Distribution and status** SE Asia: N Myanmar. Also N India and S China. Status poorly known in region, but not at risk elsewhere.

FORREST'S PIKA
Ochotona forresti NOT ILLUSTRATED
Measurements HB 155–185, T none, HF 27–30, E 18-23. Wt 110–150. Skull: gl 37–41
Identification Small, with rounded ears and no tail. In summer, upperparts blackish-brown to dark reddish-brown, underparts similar; in winter dark grey-brown, underparts only slightly paler. Ears light chestnut with white rim. Patch of dark grey fur behind ears that may form collar on nape. Feet dull white. **Similar species** Moupin Pika, *O. thibetana*, has paler underparts, buffy patches behind ears that do not meet around nape, shorter front claws, narrower skull, especially across zygomatic arches.
Ecology and habitat Forested areas on mountain slopes at elevations of 2,600–4,400m, especially on south-facing slopes. Poorly known; may dig burrows, but also may occur around rock piles.
Distribution and status SE Asia: N Myanmar. Also N India, Bhutan and China (NW Yunnan and SE Tibet). Status poorly known; may be threatened owing to loss of montane forest.

Family *LEPORIDAE* HARES AND RABBITS
This family includes many species worldwide, of which three are found in South-East Asia. The two species of hare are relatively large, with long ears and long, powerful hind legs, readily distinguished from any other mammals in the region, but similar to each other. The Annamite Striped Rabbit, *Nesolagus timminsi*, which was described only as recently as the year 2000, is very similar to the only other member of the genus, *Nesolagus netscheri*, from Sumatra, but very different from all other mammals in the region.

BURMESE HARE
Lepus peguensis PLATE 72
Measurements HB 360–500, T 65–80, HF 90–105, E 65-85. Skull: gl 80–95
Identification Typical hare shape with large hind feet, moderately long ears. Upperparts mottled brown, buff and pale grey with reddish-orange patch on nape; underparts white, mixed with patches of brown including on throat. Ears long with small black tips. Tail with narrow black top, greyish sides, white below. Upper incisors with Y-shaped groove, usually filled with a cement-like substance. **Similar species** Chinese Hare, *L. sinensis*, has brown on top of tail, V-shaped groove on incisors without cement.
Ecology and habitat Found in dry dipterocarp forest and grasslands, mainly in lowlands, often in disturbed areas. Primarily active at night, resting during day in sheltered spot under a bush or in thick grass.

Distribution and status SE Asia: Myanmar, Thailand (N of Malay Peninsula), Cambodia, Laos and S Vietnam. Not currently at risk.

CHINESE HARE
Lepus sinensis PLATE 72
Measurements HB 350–450, T 40–60, HF 80–110, E 65–85. Wt 1,000–1,950. Skull: gl 67–93
Identification Similar shape and size to preceding species. Upperparts overall mottled mixture of dark brown, buff and pale grey, tending to be paler and more yellowish in winter; orange-brown patch on nape; underparts white with areas of pale brown. Ears moderately long, usually with black tip. Tail dark brown on top, buffy on sides, whitish below. Upper incisors with V-shaped groove, lacking cement. **Similar species** Burmese Hare, *L. peguensis*, has black on top of tail, Y-shaped groove on upper incisors.

Ecology and habitat Open grassy areas in hills, up to 4,000m altitude. Mainly nocturnal, but sometimes active during day. Feeds on vegetation. Nests in burrows dug by other animals.

Distribution and status SE Asia: NE Vietnam. Also SE China and Taiwan. Apparently rare in SE Asia, but not considered at risk elsewhere.

ANNAMITE STRIPED RABBIT
Nesolagus timminsi PLATE 72

Measurements HB 350–400, HF 60–70, E 30–40. Skull: gl 70–80

Identification Small with elongate but relatively short ears, short tail, distinctive back pattern. Upperparts pale brownish to brownish-grey with broad black or very dark brown stripes along sides of upper back and across lower back. Orange-brown patch on rump. Underparts paler greyish-white. **Similar species** Hares, *Lepus* spp., are larger, with long ears, lack black stripes; pikas, *Ochotona* spp., are much smaller, with round ears, no stripes.

Ecology and habitat Understorey of wet hill forest in Annamites; altitudes as low as 200m.

Distribution and status SE Asia: Annamite Mountains of C Vietnam and C Laos. Status poorly known, but probably threatened by hunting and trapping.

GLOSSARY

adult sexually mature

agouti a speckled colour pattern found in many rodents, formed from alternating bands of pale and dark colours on the hairs

alveolus socket of a tooth

allopatric occurring in non-overlapping geographic areas

anterior towards the front or head end of an animal

antitragus flap of skin on back of ear of horseshoe bats, which often lack a true tragus (see Figs 32, 35)

arboreal living in trees

arthropod invertebrate animals with hard, jointed exoskeletons, including insects, spiders and crustaceans

auditory bulla (plural **bullae**) thin-walled bony structure on the bottom of the skull that encloses the inner and middle ear

baleen large fibrous plates found in the mouths of some whales, used for filtering food

buff pale yellowish-brown

baculum bone that supports the penis in many mammals

calcar (in bats) long bone protruding from heel that supports posterior edge of interfemoral membrane

canines pointed, usually long, teeth behind the incisors (see Fig. 7)

canine width (c-c) width across the outside of the base of canines (see Fig. 7)

cheek teeth the chewing teeth inside the cheeks, consisting of both molars and premolars

cingulum ridge around the base of a tooth

condylobasal length (cbl) length of the skull from the back of the occipital condyles to the front of the premaxillae (see Figs 5, 7)

condylocanine length (ccl) length of the skull from the back of the occipital condyles to the front of the canines (see Fig. 7)

cusp raised point on a tooth

deciduous teeth first set of "milk" or "baby" teeth, which are shed before the permanent teeth grow in

decurved curved downwards

dental formula shorthand notation for indicating the arrangement and number of teeth (see page 14)

dew toes hind two toes on pigs, deer and other ungulates that only touch the ground on soft soil

digit finger or toe

diastema natural gap between adjacent teeth

distal towards the end (e.g., away from the body)

distichous flattened and feathered (referring to a tail)

diurnal active during daylight

dorsal relating to the back or upper surface

feral domestic animals that have escaped from captivity and breed in the wild state

forearm (FA) part of the arm between the elbow and the wrist on a bat (see Fig. 3)

flukes broadened tail of whales and dolphins

greatest length (gl) the greatest length from the back to the front of a skull excluding the teeth (see Figs 5, 7)

grizzled dark coloration with white or pale speckling at tips of hairs

guard hairs hairs that are longer than the main coat of hairs

incisors front teeth (see Fig. 7)

infant baby animal entirely dependent on its mother

interfemoral membrane (in bats) membrane between the hind legs, often enclosing the tail

internarial in between the nostrils

juvenile young animal, not yet fully grown, but partially or totally independent of its mother

lancet tall, often pointed part of posterior noseleaf of a horseshoe bat (see Fig. 32)

lateral lappets flaps at the base of the sella in some horseshoe bats (see Fig. 32)

mammae mammary glands or nipples. Many mammals have several pairs allowing suckling of several young at the same time.

maxilla bone in the skull that supports all of the upper teeth except the incisors

maxillary toothrow (mt) length of the upper toothrow from the back of the molars to the front of the canines (see Figs 5, 7)

melon large, rounded expanded area on the forehead of some whales and dolphins

metacarpal bone between the wrist and the finger bones (see Fig. 25)

metacarpal pouch (in some bats) extra flap of skin between the forearm and metacarpal at the wrist that forms a pouch

molars relatively large posterior cheek teeth, distinguished from the premolars by not having deciduous precursors or "baby" teeth (see Fig. 7)

molar width (m-m) width across the outside of the upper molars at the bases

muzzle part of an animal's face in front of its eyes, including the nose

nape back of neck

nocturnal active only or mainly at night

noseleaf (in bats) flaps of skin around the nose that are thought to be related to echolocation

olive a greenish-brown colour

orbit area in the skull where the eyes are

palate upper part (roof) of the mouth

perineal around the anus

phalanx (plural **phalanges**) finger bones (see Fig. 25)

pinna (plural **pinnae**) externally visible part of ear

posterior towards the back

prehensile referring to a tail with a tip that can curl and grasp branches

premaxilla (plural **premaxillae**) the small bones at the front of the skull that support the incisors. These vary greatly in size and shape, especially within the bats.

premolars teeth between the molars and canines (see Fig. 7) that are preceded by "baby" teeth, which are shed

rhinarium moist area at the tip of the nose or muzzle

rostrum narrower part of the skull in front of the position of the eyes

sagittal crest ridge of bone in the middle of the skull of many mammals

septum (plural **septa**) thin walls inside a chamber that divide it into compartments

sella elevated part of the centre of the noseleaf of a horseshoe bat (see Fig. 32)

sympatric occurring together in the same geographic area as another species

talonid posterior section of lower molars of bats (see Fig. 43)

terrestrial active on the ground

tines prongs on the antlers of deer

tragus in the ear of most bats, flap of skin supported by cartilage, located immediately in front of the ear canal

trigonid anterior section of lower molars of bats

unicuspids (in shrews) small, single cusped teeth between the incisors and the multi-cusped mollars

underparts throat, chest, belly and insides of the legs

upperparts the back or "top" of a mammal including the outsides of the legs

zygomatic arch a curved arch of bone below the eye socket, found in most mammals (e.g. Fig. 5), but not shrews (see Fig. 6)

SELECTED BIBLIOGRAPHY

A very large number of reference works was consulted in the preparation of this book, including both secondary compilations and original scientific works. The following section lists the major secondary sources, particularly reference books on mammals of the region, as well as a selection of original scientific papers that are either referenced directly in the text, or were published subsequent to some of the major secondary compilations and give important new taxonomic information, particularly species descriptions. More comprehensive lists of literature on mammals in the region are available in the reference lists of some of these other sources, especially Corbet and Hill (1992) and Wilson and Reeder (2006).

Aplin, K.P., P.R. Brown, J. Jacob, C.J. Krebs and G.R. Singleton, 2003, *Field Methods for Rodent Studies in Asia and the Indo-Pacific*, Australian Centre for International Agricultural Research, Canberra.

Bates, P.J.J. and D.L. Harrison, 1997, *Bats of the Indian Subcontinent*, Harrison Zoological Museum, Sevenoaks, Kent, UK.

Bates, P.J.J., M.J. Struebig, S.J. Rossiter, T. Kingston, Sai Sein Lin Oo and Khin Mya Mya, 2004, "A new species of *Kerivoula* (Chiroptera: Vespertilionidae) from Myanmar (Burma)", *Acta Chiropterologica* 6: 219–26.

Borissenko, A.V. and S.V. Kruskop, 2003, *Bats of Vietnam and Adjacent Territories: an Identification Manual*, Zoological Museum of Moscow, Moscow, Russia.

Bumrungsri, S., D.L. Harrison, C. Satasook, A. Prajukjitr, S. Thong-Aree and P.J.J. Bates, 2006, "A review of bat research in Thailand with eight new species records for the country", *Acta Chiropterologica* 8: 325–60.

Corbet, G.B. and J.E. Hill, 1992, *The Mammals of the Indomalayan Region: a Systematic Review*, Natural History Museum, London, UK.

Cranbrook, Earl of, 1987, *Riches of the Wild: Land Mammals of South-East Asia*, Oxford University Press, Singapore.

Csorba, G. and P.J.J. Bates, 2005, "Description of a new species of *Murina* from Cambodia (Chiroptera: Vespertilionidae: Murininae)", *Acta Chiropterologica* 7: 1–7.

Csorba, G., P. Ujhelyi and N. Thomas, 2003, *Horseshoe Bats of the World (Chiroptera: Rhinolophidae)*, Alana Books, Bishop's Castle, Shropshire, UK.

Duckworth, J.W. and R.H. Pine, 2003, "English names for a world list of mammals, exemplified by species of Indochina", *Mammalian Reviews* 33: 151–73.

Duckworth, J.W., R.E. Salter and K. Khounboline, 1999, *Wildlife in Lao PDR: 1999 Status Report*, IUCN/WCS/CPAWM, Vientiane, Lao.

Ellis, R., 1982, *Dolphins and Porpoises*, Knopf, New York, USA.

Ellerman, J.R., 1961, *The Fauna of India Including Pakistan, Burma and Ceylon. Mammalia, Volume 3, Rodentia*, Zoological Survey of India, Calcutta.

Francis, C.M., T. Kingston and A. Zubaid, 2007, "A new species of *Kerivoula* (Chiroptera: Vespertilionidae) from Peninsular Malaysia", *Acta Chiropterologica* 9: 1–12.

Guillén, A. and C.M. Francis, 2006, "A new species of bat of the *Hipposideros bicolor* group (Chiroptera: Hipposideridae) from Central Laos, with evidence of convergent evolution with Sundaic taxa", *Acta Chiropterologica* 8: 39–61.

IUCN, 2001, *IUCN Red List Categories and Criteria: Version 3.1*, IUCN Species Survival Commission, IUCN, Gland, Switzerland and Cambridge, UK.

Jenkins, P.D. and M.F. Robinson, 2002, "Another variation on the gymnure theme: description of a new species of *Hylomys* (Lipotyphla, Erinaceidae, Galericinae)", *Bulletin of the Natural History Museum*, London 68: 1–11.

Jenkins, P.D., C.W. Kilpatrick, M.F. Robinson and R.J. Timmins, 2005, "Morphological and molecular investigations of a new family, genus and species of rodent (Mammalia: Rodentia: Hystricognatha) from Lao PDR", *Systematics and Biodiversity* 2: 419–54.

Kingston, T., B.L. Lim and A. Zubaid, 2006, *Bats of Krau Wildlife Reserve*, Penerbit University Kebangsaan Malaysia, Bangi, Malaysia.

Leatherwood, S. and R.R. Reeves, 1983, *The Sierra Club Handbook of Whales and Dolphins*, Sierra Club, San Francisco, USA.

Lekagul, B. and J.A. McNeely, 1977, *Mammals of Thailand*, Association for the Conservation of Wildlife, Bangkok, Thailand.

Lunde, D.P. and N.T. Son, 2001, *An Identification Guide to the Rodents of Vietnam*, New York: Center for Biodiversity and Conservation, American Museum of Natural History.

Lunde, D.P., G.G. Musser and N.T. Son, 2003, "A survey of small mammals from Mt. Tay Con Linh II, Vietnam, with the description of a new species of *Chodsigoa* (Insectivora: Soricidae)", *Mammal Study* 28: 31–46.

Lunde, D.P., G.G. Musser and T. Ziegler, 2004, "Description of a new species of *Crocidura* (Soricomorpha: Soricidae, Crocidurinae) from Ke Go Nature Reserve, Vietnam", *Mammal Study* 29: 27–36.

Medway, L., 1983, *The Wild Mammals of Malaya (Peninsular Malaysia) and Singapore*, Second edition, Oxford University Press, Kuala Lumpur, Malaysia.

Musser, G.G., 1973, "Zoogeographical significance of the Ricefield Rat, *Rattus argentiventer*, on Celebes and New Guinea and the identity of *Rattus pesticulus*", *American Museum Novitates* 2511: 1–30.

Musser, G.G., 1981, "Results of the Archbold Expeditions. No. 105. Notes on systematics of Indo-Malayan murid rodents, and descriptions of new genera and species from Ceylon, Sulawesi, and the Philippines", *Bulletin of the American Museum of Natural History* 168(3): 225–334.

Musser, G.G. and C. Newcomb, 1983, "Malaysian murids and the giant rat of Sumatra", *Bulletin of the American Museum of Natural History* 174: 327–598.

Musser, G.G., D.P. Lunde and N.T. Son, 2006, "Description of a new genus and species of rodent (Murinae, Muridae, Rodentia) from the Tower Karst Region of Northeastern Vietnam", *American Museum Novitates* 3517: 1–41.

Musser, G.G., A.L. Smith, M.F. Robinson and D.P. Lunde, 2005, "Description of a new genus and species of rodent (Murinae, Muridae, Rodentia) from the Khammouan Limestone National Biodiversity Conservation Area in Lao PDR", *American Museum Novitates* 3497: 1–31.

Nadler, T., 2005, "Molecular evolution, systematics and distribution of the taxa within the silvered langur species group (*Trachypithecus* [*cristatus*]) in Southeast Asia", *Der Zoologische Garten* 75: 238–47.

Nowak, R.M., 1999, *Walker's Mammals of the World*, Sixth edition, Johns Hopkins Press, Baltimore, USA.

Parr, J.W.K., 2003, *A Guide to the Large Mammals of Thailand*, Sarakadee Press, Bangkok, Thailand.

Payne, J. and C.M. Francis, 1985, *A Field Guide to the Mammals of Borneo*, Sabah Society and World Wildlife Fund, Kota Kinabalu, Sabah, Malaysia.

Perrin, W.F., R.R. Reeves, M.L.L. Dolar, T.A. Jefferson, H. Marsh, J.Y. Wang and J. Estacion (eds), 2005, *Report of the Second Workshop on the Biology and Conservation of Small Cetaceans and Dugongs of South-East Asia*, UNEP/CMS Secretariat, Bonn, Germany.

Pocock, R.I., 1939–41, *The Fauna of British India Including Ceylon and Burma. Mammalia, Volumes I and II, Primates and Carnivora*, Taylor and Francis, London, UK.

SAMD, 2006, *Southeast Asian Mammal Databank*, http://www.ieaitaly.org/samd/

Smith, A.T. and Y. Xie (eds), 2008, *A Guide to the Mammals of China*, Princeton University Press, Princeton.

Strien, N.J. van, 1983, *A Guide to the Tracks of Mammals of Western Indonesia*, School of Environmental Conservation Management, Ciawi, Bogor, Indonesia.

Vaughn, T.A., J.M. Ryan and N.J. Czaplewski, 2000, *Mammalogy: Fourth edition*, Saunders College Publishing, Philadelphia, USA.

Watson, L. and T. Ritchie, 1981, *Sea Guide to the Whales of the World*, Dutton, New York, USA.

Wilson, D.E. and D.M. Reeder, 2006, *Mammal Species of the World: a Taxonomic and Geographic Reference*, Third edition, Johns Hopkins University Press, Baltimore, USA.

INDEX

Numbers in **bold** refer to plate numbers. Numbers in roman are page numbers.